Mad Madge

Mad Madge

*The Extraordinary Life of
Margaret Cavendish, Duchess of Newcastle,
the First Woman to Live by Her Pen*

Katie Whitaker

BASIC
BOOKS

A Member of the Perseus Books Group

Designed by Jeff Williams

Library of Congress Cataloging-in-Publication Data
Whitaker, Katie, 1967-
    Mad Madge : the extraordinary life of Margaret Cavendish, Duchess of
Newcastle, the first woman to live by her pen / Katie Whitaker.
        p. cm.
Includes bibliographical references and index.
ISBN 0-465-09161-X
    1. Newcastle, Margaret Cavendish, Duchess of, 1624?-1674. 2. Women and
literature—Great Britain—History—17th century. 3. Authors, English—Early
modern, 1500-1700—Biography. 4. British—Europe—History—17th
century. I. Title.
PR3605.N2Z95 2002
828'.409—dc21

2002008411

02 03 04 05 / 10 9 8 7 6 5 4 3 2 1

For Weem

Contents

List of Illustrations

Acknowledgments

During the course of more than four years' work, I have run up many obligations. In matters financial I am indebted to the British Academy, whose award of a Small Research Grant funded the travels necessary for the preliminary manuscripts research. For permission to quote from manuscript sources, I am very grateful to His Grace the Duke of Sutherland and to the following libraries and archives: the Bodleian Library, Oxford, the British Library, the College of Arms, the House of Lords Record Office, the Huntington Library, Nottinghamshire Archives, and the University of Nottingham's Department of Manuscripts and Special Collections. I would also like to acknowledge the helpful assistance I received from the staff of these institutions, and of the following: the British Library at Boston Spa, the Brotherton Library at the University of Leeds, Cambridge University Library, the Essex Record Office's branches at Colchester and Chelmsford, Hertfordshire Archives and Local Studies, the National Monuments Record, the National Register of Archives, the libraries of North Yorkshire County Council, the Public Record Office at Kew, the library of the University College of Ripon and York St. John, and Westminster Abbey Muniment Room and Library.

The bibliographies and other material produced by the Margaret Cavendish Society have been vital resources for my research, and I have many debts of gratitude to the Society's members: to Professor Anne Shaver, who first put me in touch with the Society; to Dr Emma Rees, President of the Society, for lunch and discussion, for bibliographies and books, and for forwarding my queries to the Society's Discussion List; and to Dr Line Cottegnies, Professor James Fitzmaurice, Dr Paul Salzman, Professor Lisa Sarasohn, and Dr Gweno Williams, who all kindly responded to my queries. I have also benefited greatly from the many studies published by members of the Society.

I would like to offer my thanks to those people who gave me access to various paintings and a large private house of importance to the book: to His Grace The Duke of Buccleuch KT, to Mr Derek Adlam, Mrs Sandra Howat, and the Honourable Mrs George Seymour. I am also grateful to Mr Richard Shackle of Colchester Library and Mr T. Hodgson of Colchester Museum Services for their help during my visit to Colchester, and to the staff who allowed me to look around St. Giles's Church and the site of St. John's Abbey.

For their generous and informative advice on Margaret's dress and its relation to contemporary fashion, I am very grateful to Ms Susan North of the Victoria and Albert Museum and Ms Joanna Marschner of the State Apartments and Royal Ceremonial Dress Collection at Kensington Palace. My warm thanks are also due to Dr Trevor Foulds, Documentary Historian of Nottingham City Museums and Galleries, for dinner and numerous discussions of the Cavendishes and their archives, and especially for his generosity in sharing his typed transcripts of various Cavendish manuscripts with me.

I have benefited greatly from discussions with my literary agents, Peter Robinson and Kathy Anderson, and I would also like to thank my editors, Will Morrison and Marco Pavia, and my copyeditor, Anais Scott, for their many contributions to the book. I am especially grateful for the way in which everyone at Basic Books coped calmly and patiently, even with apparent relish, when late delivery of my typescript made their production schedule very tight. Greatest thanks of all are due to my husband, Weem, who has been unstinting in both help and encouragement.

Prologue

Condemn me not as a dishonour of your sex, for setting forth this work; for it is harmless and free from all dishonesty; I will not say from vanity, for that is so natural to our sex as it were unnatural not to be so.

With these words Margaret Cavendish, marchioness of Newcastle, addressed the female readers of her first published book, a collection of poems that came out in the spring of 1653. For a seventeenth-century woman to print her writing was, Margaret knew, an outrageous rebellion against the norms of her society. Women might circulate their literary work among friends and family, but they did not issue it in print for all the world to see. In the first forty years of the century fewer than eighty books by women had been published in England—making up only one-half of 1 percent of all books printed—and many of these had appeared only posthumously, or else in pirated editions, without their authors' consent. In 1653 the *Poems and Fancies* was the first book of English poetry to be deliberately published by a woman under her own name, and Margaret knew she was heading for trouble. "I imagine I shall be censured by my own sex; and men will cast a smile of scorn upon my book, because they think thereby women encroach too much upon their prerogatives; for they hold books as their crown, and the sword as their sceptre, by which they rule and govern."[1]

Yet in spite of her fears, Margaret was unable to restrain herself. She could not bear to forgo all hopes of public recognition, as most of her female writing contemporaries did. "I have an opinion, which troubles me like a conscience," she explained, "that 'tis a part of honour to aspire towards a fame . . . to love perfection . . . [and] to aim at excellencies." In spite of the social conventions that defined public visibility as the sole preserve of men, Margaret felt that it was her moral duty to put her talents to use and build herself a reputation based on her own achievements. And she was determined not to be put off by disapproval and discouragement. "A smile of neglect cannot dishearten me, no more can a frown of dislike affright me . . . my mind's too big," she asserted boldly, "and I had rather venture an indiscretion than lose the hopes of a fame."[2]

Utterly committed to fulfilling her aspirations in life, Margaret went on from this beginning to become the most prolific and wide-ranging female author that the English language had ever seen. In a literary career of almost twenty years, she produced a total of twenty-three volumes, spanning pretty much every genre of contemporary literature. In an age of polymaths, when philosophers wrote poetry and playwrights studied the sciences, Margaret ranged even more widely than most—two dozen plays, a large collection of short fiction (both realistic and fantastic, in prose and verse), a book of orations, a volume of letters and another of essays, an autobiography and a biography, six philosophical treatises and a utopia.

By the time she reached her forties Margaret had become a literary celebrity. Her work was well known both in the universities and in fashionable London circles. And when she visited the capital in 1667 she played up to her audience, appearing in fanciful costumes she had designed herself, aiming to project her revolutionary identity as a female intellectual. Wherever she went, Margaret drew crowds of a size normally reserved only for royalty. Her charismatic persona enthralled Restoration society at every level, from the hordes of children running through the streets beside her coach, right up to the king himself, who came in person to welcome her to town. The diarist Samuel Pepys pursued her round London over a period of seven weeks in a quest to "understand her." Speculation and comment on her character, at once fascinating and elusive, peppered the letters and diaries of her contemporaries. She was incomparable, heroic, miraculous, "the prince of all wit," some wrote. But to others she seemed merely "fantastical," "extravagant," even mad. And in the course of time a nickname grew up: "Mad Madge of Newcastle."

It was in this rather outlandish manifestation that I first encountered Margaret. I was studying the meetings of the early Royal Society as part of the research for my doctoral thesis in history of science, when I read Pepys's account of her visit to the society in 1667. Pepys, finally succeeding in his ambition to see Margaret close-to, was unimpressed—"her dress so antic and her deportment so unordinary, that I do not like her at all"; "a mad, conceited, ridiculous woman," he wrote angrily in his diary. But I was intrigued. Margaret had, it seemed, been the first woman ever to attend one of the society's meetings, and I turned to the *Dictionary of National Biography* to find out more. There I found the impressive catalog of her publications, unique for a woman of the time, yet all overshadowed by accounts of her eccentricity and folly. But in spite of the dictionary's dismissive tone, I was hooked. How had Margaret come to break so far with social conventions and publish all these books? What sort of person had she been? What had her life been like? And was she really mad?

Chapter One

The Lucases of St. John's

Margaret was the baby of the Lucas family. The last of eight children, she grew up loved and protected by siblings who were all adults before she entered her teens. By the time she reached fourteen, in 1637, she was developing into as great a beauty as her sisters. Sharing the family's rich brown hair, pale complexion, and large, sensitive eyes, she loved to dress finely in costly materials: clothes, for her, were an outlet for imagination and creativity, and an important form of self-expression.

In company, however, Margaret was painfully shy. Visitors to the family home, St. John's near Colchester, might scarcely notice her—a mere child and a girl, of little importance in the wider world, listened silently to the conversation of her elders. Or they might wonder if she would make a wife for one of their male relatives: at fourteen, she was two years over the age of consent, and her large dowry and good family connections made her eminently marriageable. Almost certainly, as she maintained the silence considered proper for unmarried girls—"Maids should be seen and not heard," as the proverb said—they would think her an ordinary, modest, demure, country gentleman's daughter like hundreds of others, well brought up in the conventions of her gender and class. Only the most observant visitors would notice that she was watching them closely, as if taking mental notes for later. And even if something unusual in her dress— a slightly theatrical feel, or some striking detail of decoration that she had designed herself—caught their attention, alerting them to the strain of individuality hidden under her shy and silent exterior, even then they could hardly be expected to guess at her rich private life of imagination and aspiration. For this apparently commonplace girl had been writing passionately and prolifically for two years already, dreaming of achieving some real public success in life, such as would normally be impossible for the daughter of a family like the Lucases.

Margaret was growing up in one of the richest counties in Britain. Seventeenth-century travelers journeying northeast from London on the road to Colchester passed a steady stream of traffic—droves of cattle with the "finest flesh in England,"[1] and wagons laden with grain and flour, fresh vegetables, butter, cheese, beer and spirits, leather, wool and cloth—all heading for the London markets. On either side, fields of wheat and hops and meadows of grazing sheep and cows were scattered with comfortable villages and the grand houses of the local gentry, whose windows looked out over the lands they owned and managed. Essex, the mapmaker John Norden wrote, was "the fattest of the land: comparable to Palestine, that flowed with milk and honey."[2]

Beyond the bustling roadside town of Chelmsford, open uncultivated heaths began to appear, where flocks of sheep roamed among gorse and broom. To modern eyes the scene would seem entirely rural, but this was one of the most industrialized regions of seventeenth-century Britain. Wool from these heaths, which continued northeast into Suffolk and Norfolk, supplied the East Anglian cloth trade, producing high-quality textiles renowned throughout Europe. Spinners, weavers, washers, and fullers worked at home in their cottages; then the cloth was carried to the merchants' warehouses in the towns.

Situated just over fifty miles from London, Colchester was the Essex industry's principal market town. On the brow of a hill, church towers and a massive Norman castle rose above the town walls, which dated from Roman times. In the 1630s Colchester had had little need of military defense for many years and the walls were in poor repair. Houses sprawled far beyond them into the countryside to the south, and eastward as far as the River Colne, where boats docked at the port of the Hythe. This was one of the largest towns in Britain, a full mile across, with a population of around 10,000. Well-built black-and-white timbered houses with bright tiled roofs lined the streets, whose generous raised pavements kept pedestrians out of the mud. Copious fresh water, piped in from springs in the surrounding country, fed the public fountains.

But after this initial impression of prosperity, perceptive travelers might feel uneasy. Colchester's high standard of building derived from its cloth trade, which had flourished some twenty to sixty years before, but by the 1630s the industry was in recession. Weavers' wages had been cut and many were unemployed. In 1637, after a bad harvest the previous autumn, the price of grain was high and the poor were going hungry. The government's determined pursuance of unpopular religious policies had led to further dissatisfaction, and riots were not unimaginable.

Nonetheless for travelers with time to spare there was plenty to do. Parish churches and civic buildings provided architectural attractions, while those interested in textiles and dress went to see Colchester's clothmakers at work. Others gravitated towards the castle, the largest Norman keep in England, dating from the 1080s but believed by seventeenth-century historians to have been built about 800 years earlier by the legendary British king Coelus, grandfather of the Roman emperor Constantine. Roman coins, turned up by ploughmen in the surrounding fields, could be bought for one's antiquarian collection. For those wanting to satisfy more bodily appetites, there were the town's culinary specialties—Colchester's famous oysters and its "eryngos."*

Later in the seventeenth century, travelers like the diarist John Evelyn made their pilgrimage to the north side of the castle to see a shrine from the Civil War—a patch of ground supposed to have miraculous qualities, where the royalist martyrs Sir Charles Lucas and Sir George Lisle were executed without trial in 1648. But in 1637, the war was still five years in the future and the Lucas family were notable mainly as the wealthiest landowners in the neighborhood. Their country house at St. John's was one of the grand sights of the town.

Just a short walk through the southern suburbs brought one to St. John's Green. To the left the parish church of St. Giles contained the Lucas family tombs, dating back to the previous century. Directly ahead stood the imposing great gatehouse of St. John's, with its corner turrets and castellations and strong oak doors below. Proceeding under the huge archway and past the porter's lodge, you entered the ancient precincts of the Benedictine Abbey of St. John the Baptist, founded in 1096 by Eudo, a courtier of King William Rufus. Here the abbey had flourished until the dissolution of the monasteries, now a hundred years in the past, when the Lucases had transformed it into a private mansion. Within the old abbey's perimeter wall thirteen acres of grounds contained all the offices and workrooms needed for the smooth operation of a wealthy gentleman's household. There were stables for the horses, a well, a vast granary, a millhouse, bakehouse and pastryhouse, a vaulted cellar for storing salt-fish, a brewhouse and maltinghouse, and a dairyhouse for processing the family's milk into butter and cheese. The Lucases with their servants made up about thirty people, all living at St. John's and fed from the estate's own resources.[3]

To the left of the gatehouse, a range of old abbey buildings, with dining hall, buttery, and bedchambers, made a considerable dwelling in itself. But the

---

*The roots of sea holly, dug up from the sands near Harwich and candied by a local apothecary to make a tasty after-dinner sweetmeat reputed to have aphrodisiac qualities.

main house lay ahead, towards the southern end of the site—an imposing rank of triangle-topped gable-ends and tall chimneys.

Travelers arriving in winter would find the Lucases away in London for the court and social season, and a housekeeper might give them a tour of the house. But in the summer and autumn the family was sure to be in residence, and visitors of sufficiently high social status—university dons, physicians or clergymen, or relations of the landed gentry or nobility—would have as their guide the owner himself: John Lucas, a serious and scholarly gentleman in his early thirties, soon to be knighted by the king for his enforcement of controversial government policy in Essex.

The house's center was the great hall, where Queen Elizabeth I and her court had dined some sixty years before. Weapons hung on racks along the walls; sideboards were loaded with displays of gold and silver plate on special occasions; from the dais at one end the family and their guests presided at dinner over the rows of trestle tables below. From here visitors might go to John's study or to the house's armory or wine cellars, according to their particular interests.

Outside, the gardens began with formal parterres, bright with flowers in summer; beyond them grassy walks led among avenues of trees. In the middle, the massive twelfth-century tower of the abbey church still stood, a reminder of what the place had been, while to the south, the high garden mount gave views over miles of countryside—cow pastures, orchards, ponds, dovecotes, farms, and houses—much of it owned by the Lucases.

Although now so wealthy and well established, the Colchester Lucases were not an ancient landed family: like most of the Essex gentry, they had gained their riches only in the last few generations.[4] Thomas Lucas, Margaret's great-great-grandfather, was a successful lawyer who, from modest beginnings as secretary to the duke of Bedford, rose to become king's solicitor to Henry VII, before investing his self-made fortune in a grand house and country estate near Bury St. Edmunds in Suffolk, some twenty-five miles north of Colchester. His third son, John, was the first of the family to settle in the town, around a hundred years before Margaret was born.[5]

As a younger son, John inherited little of his father's wealth, but he followed closely in his footsteps, beginning a high-powered legal and political career with an extensive education at Cambridge and one of the London inns of court. In Colchester, he gained the job of Town Clerk and began to establish alliances with the prominent local people who could aid his advancement. His marriages, to Mary Abel and then Elizabeth Christmas, joined him to two of the town's wealthiest families of cloth merchants, bringing him rich dowries and securing his dynastic succession with three sons in addition to several daughters. The local landowning magnate John de Vere, earl of Oxford, became John's patron and ensured his election to Parliament as one of Colchester's two representatives between 1545 and 1553. During these years, John built up connections at court, associating with Lord Protector Somerset, the powerful uncle of the young King Edward VI,[6] and gaining advancement to various responsible and highly lucrative jobs in national government. He sat on the commissions for the confiscation of church goods and the sale of Crown lands, and he was appointed a master of the newly established Court of Requests. This last was a position of great power: the two masters of the court received all the requests and complaints addressed to the king and decided which ones should be seriously considered, while "denying unreasonable and inconvenient suits."[7] No petitioner could reach the king without going through John Lucas or his colleague, and their palms would have been well oiled. Direct reward from the king was also lavish, as Edward VI granted former monastic lands in Essex to John Lucas.[8]

The dissolution of the monasteries in the 1530s had brought vast quantities of new land into private ownership, creating an active land market for the first time since the Norman Conquest. Everywhere rising men with newly made fortunes bought estates and set themselves up as country gentlemen. John Lucas joined the trend, investing his recently acquired wealth in extensive landholdings throughout Essex, and snapping up the site of St. John's Abbey, just outside the Colchester town walls, in 1548. The abbey purchase included over 200 acres of farmland, woods, and marshes, two dovecotes, three orchards, twenty gardens, and some town houses in Colchester, and came to the grand sum of £132.[9]

Much of the old abbey was already falling into ruin, but there was plenty of scope for making a fine gentleman's residence, with offices and workrooms adapted from the abbey buildings, and an imposing house at the south end of the site, probably formed out of the old abbot's lodging. John and his wife, Elizabeth, now furnished their home with the luxury appropriate to their new importance in the world. Walls were covered with brightly covered hangings. Four-poster beds had embroidered curtains of velvet, silk, damask, and satin. Expensive Turkey carpets were draped on tables and sideboards. All these sumptuous textiles, together with the displays of gold and silver plate, formed the main decoration of the house and displayed the family's wealth and importance at a time when art collecting was not yet an aristocratic vogue. John Lucas's exalted position was now affirmed every day at dinner, when he sat at the high table in his great hall with a huge golden saltcellar at his left hand, marking the social distinction between the important people seated with the master of the house above the salt, and the less significant below it. John had created an ancestral home to be handed down to succeeding generations of the Lucas family, and his second wife, Elizabeth, embroidered a set of fine silk hangings for the family's state bed.[10] After John's death in 1556, their eldest son, Margaret's grandfather, Thomas, would continue to consolidate the family's status.

Thomas was twenty-five when his father died, an ambitious young man, eager to make his mark in the world and to build up the Lucas dynasty. Having completed the family's traditional Cambridge and London legal education, Thomas was elected in his father's place as member of Parliament for Colchester, and in the following decades, favored by Queen Elizabeth I, he held a plethora of the government posts by which the wealthy country gentry publicly demonstrated their status and power in their local neighborhood. As a justice of the peace he sat in judgment over local malefactors, and as recorder of Colchester he oversaw the town's legal affairs. He was three times high sheriff of Essex, an annual appointment made by the queen herself that put him in charge of much of the Crown's business in the county. But the job closest to Thomas's heart was his captaincy in the Essex militia. As he donned military dress and mustered and drilled his part-time civilian troops, preparing them to repel foreign invasions or to quell domestic riots, he reenacted the chivalric, military associations of gentility left over from the Middle Ages. Building up a large personal armory of weapons near the great gatehouse at St. John's and assembling flags and campaigning equipment, Thomas created a martial ethos that became a tradition for the men of his family: Margaret's father would be a noted duelist of his day, and her three brothers and a nephew were all to spend part or all of their adult lives as professional soldiers.[11]

Dedicated to the acquisition of wealth and the social status that went with it, Thomas managed his estates energetically to maximize his income, investing his profits in substantial further land purchases. By the time he died in 1611 at the age of eighty, the Lucases were one of the richest families in Essex, with thousands of acres of land bringing in an income of £3,000 or £4,000 per year.[12] But such vigorous estate management also brought Thomas into frequent conflict with his neighbors. Manifold legal disputes over landownership and boundaries, over questions of access and the enclosure of commons, were pursued by Thomas with intransigent insistence on what he considered his rights; by the 1580s he was widely hated in Colchester as a greedy, selfish miser. When local resentment against him finally culminated in a fierce battle between rival bands of the militia, Thomas fled to London, shutting up his home at St. John's for three years.[13]

Though he was unpopular in Colchester, Thomas had successfully established himself at the national level of the royal court. Knighted by the queen in

1571, Sir Thomas Lucas had twice entertained Elizabeth I and her court at St. John's. He was well connected in the best circles of society, with sufficient influence to gain for his eldest daughter, Anne, the coveted appointment of maid of honor, in daily attendance on the queen. But he was soon to lose this court favor by the actions of two of his children.

Sir Thomas Lucas had married well, moving beyond the Colchester mercantile circles his father had joined to wed Mary Fermor, the daughter of a Northamptonshire landed gentleman. The couple had three daughters and two sons. Anne was the first to bring royal displeasure on the family when, while maid of honor at court, she married for love against the queen's wishes.* But the family's eldest son, Margaret's father, Thomas, would anger Elizabeth I much more deeply and irremediably.

Born around 1573, Thomas Lucas Jr. had received the family's traditional training for a high-profile career in law and politics. But unlike his father and grandfather, Thomas was no ambitious, hardworking student. Instead, he was more interested in the fashionable life of the capital, spending his time in acquiring the gentlemanly skills of swordsmanship rather than the penmanship his father had intended.[14] In London society he also met a beautiful and intelligent young woman named Elizabeth Leighton, the daughter of a prosperous city gentleman. She and the twenty-four-year-old Thomas fell in love, and by the summer of 1597 Elizabeth was bearing his child.

As yet the couple had taken no steps towards marriage, and any hopes they had were now to be cruelly prevented after Thomas was insulted by a young courtier, Sir William Brooke. Probably, given the state of Thomas and Elizabeth's relationship, Brooke's insult was some aspersion cast on Elizabeth's reputation. As Margaret related the story almost sixty years later, the injured Thomas Lucas, compelled "by the laws of honour," "could do no less than" challenge his opponent to a duel, "where their swords were to dispute, and one or both of their lives to decide the argument."[15] When the pair met in secret, Thomas, an accomplished fencer, killed his man.

Sir William Brooke had been a man of importance at court and a personal favorite of Queen Elizabeth I. His killer was unlikely to escape lightly, and so, Margaret explained in her autobiography,

> Though my father by honour challenged him, with valour fought him, and in justice killed him, yet he suffered more than any person of quality usually doth in cases of honour; for though the laws be rigorous, yet the present

---

*As her niece Margaret herself would do some fifty or more years later.

princes most commonly are gracious in those misfortunes, especially to the injured: but my father found it not.

The queen could not be appeased and Thomas was declared an outlaw, denied all civil and legal rights, including the inheritance of his father's property. To avoid being convicted and executed for murder, he fled at once into exile abroad, leaving Elizabeth Leighton alone to bear an illegitimate son, a social disgrace that Margaret's account of her family would pass over in silence. Naming her boy Thomas after his father, Elizabeth could only hope that her lover would remain faithful in an absence that stretched out indefinitely into the future.[16]

No record survives of how the exiled Thomas Lucas spent his first four years on the Continent. He may have traveled on the grand tour, which was just emerging as a popular way of finishing a young gentleman's education, or perhaps he served in the English army, fighting alongside the Dutch against the Spanish. However, as an exiled outlaw he could not have held an officer's commission and no certain record survives. The only news linking him to the war—a report that he was killed at the siege of Ostend in September 1601—was without foundation, for Thomas was some 300 miles away at the time, living at Angers in western France. Here he was part of a group of wild young expatriate Englishmen well known to the authorities for the "knightly prowess" they displayed in the expert swordplay of their gambling brawls. By October 1602 Thomas had moved on to Paris, but in spite of all the distractions he could find he was lonely and miserable, and he pleaded desperately to the English court to be allowed to return home.[17]

But Thomas had to wait for his pardon until the following year, when the old queen died and was succeeded by King James I. Then—after Thomas's main enemy at court, Lord Cobham, the brother of the man he had killed, was imprisoned in the Tower for his part in a plot to overthrow the new king—the Lucas family's petitions finally achieved success. In July 1603 the king issued a formal pardon for the killing of Sir William Brooke, and in the following March a bill was prepared in Parliament, restoring Thomas "to his blood and gentry."[18] Almost seven years after his flight abroad, he could now return home and once again be his father's legal heir.

But Thomas did not settle at once in Colchester. Instead he stopped in London, meeting his old love, Elizabeth Leighton, and the six-year-old son he had never seen. His father, Sir Thomas, already angry with the son who had nearly ruined the family, disapproved of Elizabeth: her London family lacked the wealth and social cachet he expected in a match for his heir, and she was tainted with disgrace as an unmarried mother. But the lovers remained devoted to each other and Thomas Jr. defied his father by marrying Elizabeth secretly in August 1604. Told only afterwards, Sir Thomas accepted the fact and offered the couple a home in the range of buildings attached to the great gatehouse at St. John's.

Here Thomas and Elizabeth began to raise a family. In October 1606 a son, John, was born, a legitimate heir for the Lucas family wealth, named after his great-grandfather, who had first settled in Colchester and founded the family's fortunes. Daughters Mary and Elizabeth came next, named for their grandmother and mother. In the summer of 1611 old Sir Thomas died at the age of eighty and was buried in the family vault in St. Giles's Church. Two years later his wife, Mary, followed him, and Thomas and Elizabeth with their growing family moved into the main house at St. John's.[19]

Here they lived happily together, according to Margaret.[20] Thomas, after his years of exile, was no longer concerned with the social and political ambitions that had driven his ancestors. While other landed gentlemen, pressed by a king eager for funds, were paying large sums of money into the royal coffers for the social honors of knighthoods, baronetcies, and peerages, Thomas Lucas resisted all such coercion, though he could easily have afforded the cost. "My father did not esteem titles, unless they were gained by heroic actions," Margaret recorded, and so Thomas remained without even a knighthood though he was one of the wealthiest men in Essex.[21] Apart from a year's service as high sheriff of Essex, appointed by King James I in 1617, he also avoided all public life. He never held local government appointments or sat as MP for Colchester, as his father and grandfather had, and he twice refused the offer of a captaincy in the local militia.

Instead he was content to live privately at St. John's, surrounded by his family and visiting friends. He and Elizabeth kept up a lavish lifestyle—"though my father was not a peer of the realm, yet there were few peers who had much greater estates, or lived more noble therewith," Margaret wrote.[22] The couple used the full limit of their income each year, spending their money freely, especially on their children, believing that if they were brought up in plenty, they would grow up honest and generous, without the mean, sharking qualities that both parents despised. The household at St. John's functioned on a grand scale. In addition to the host of servants employed in all the workrooms that kept the family self-sufficient in its everyday needs, there were nursemaids and private tutors for the children, and an extended family of less well off relatives—including Elizabeth's sister Mrs. Eyres, who acted as housekeeper, and her clergyman husband, William, appointed as vicar in two of

Colchester's parish churches by the patronage of the Lucases. While Thomas Lucas oversaw the estate business, maximizing the family's income by careful land management and the enclosure of common land, Elizabeth took charge of the domestic work, supervising the servants, tending the household's sick, and distributing daily alms to the poor at the gates of St. John's.[23]

Meanwhile their young family continued to grow. Probably there were children who died in infancy, for even among the privileged aristocracy only two-thirds of babies lived to the age of five. But eight of Thomas and Elizabeth's children survived to adulthood. After Thomas, John, Mary, and Elizabeth, there was a third son, Charles, born in 1613, and then two more daughters, Anne and Catherine. Last of all came Margaret, born in 1623 when her father was already fifty and her mother probably in her early forties. Six years in age from her nearest and favorite sister, Catherine, Margaret was a full twenty-five years younger than her eldest, illegitimate brother, Thomas.[24]

By the time of her birth, Thomas had already finished the family's traditional education at Cambridge and was settled on the estate at Lexden, just west of Colchester, which had been bought for him by his father. Two years later, bored with his quiet country life, he left England to become a professional soldier in the Netherlands, fighting for the Dutch in their long-running war of independence against the Spanish. In the following years Thomas returned home only briefly—to be knighted in London by King Charles I in April 1628, and to be married the following winter to Mary Byron, the sister of one of his comrades in the Dutch army. Margaret would hardly have seen her brother until 1632, when she was nine. Then the Dutch made peace with Spain and Thomas returned home to Essex.[25] But even so he remained a distant figure to Margaret—a martial, physically active man who shared an exclusive, masculine ethos with his youngest brother, Charles.

By 1632, Charles had also finished a Cambridge education and was living on estates given him by his father at nearby Fordham. When the two brothers came to visit the family at St. John's, they did not join the peaceful feminine pursuits of their sisters. Courtly arts like dancing and music they disdained as frivolities "too effeminate for masculine spirits."[26] Instead they spent their time with their brother John, in such martial pursuits as fencing, archery, and wrestling. Yet if Margaret was not really close to her eldest and youngest brothers, she still admired them hugely from a distance as military heroes who, though they could have lived safely and idly at home, "rather chose to serve in the wars under the States of Holland."[27] When hostilities recommenced in the Netherlands in 1637, both brothers departed to join the Dutch army besieging Breda, Thomas resuming his command as a cavalry captain while Charles served under him as cornet.[28]

Only her middle brother, John—the Lucases' heir, since Thomas was illegitimate—would Margaret have known well. John was the scholar of the family. Sent abroad to complete his education in France around 1625, he was already being praised as "the most accomplished young gentleman for all good parts that hath gone out of England these many years."[29] By the time he returned, he could read Hebrew fluently as well as the more commonplace Latin and Greek. Skilled in both the disputative arts of Aristotelian logic and the intricacies of modern English law, his ability to argue his own cause to maximum effect was notorious among his contemporaries. He was also an enthusiastic student of philosophy and the sciences, and in 1660 he would become one of the original fellows of the new Royal Society, established to promote the experimental study of nature. Altogether, John had the skills to gain himself the reputation of a leading gentleman scholar of his day—one "who is acknowledg'd (by those that have the honour to know him) so to have master'd all the learned sciences and languages, that it is no easy task to find his equal, not only among those of his own noble order, but [even] among them whose profession hath obliged them to be scholars."[30] Margaret would always admire her brother's learning, and he would be an important resource for her own youthful self-education. Seventeen years her senior, he came to seem to Margaret "as it were the father to take care of us all."[31] For Margaret never knew her real father, who died when she was only two.

Thomas Lucas's death in September 1625, after a sudden and severe illness, brought not just the devastating personal loss of bereavement to Elizabeth Lucas and her family, but also the real threat of financial ruin, because John, the family's heir, was still only nineteen, two years short of legal adulthood when he would be able to inherit his father's estates. In the meantime seventeenth-century law made him a ward of the Crown, which had the right to appoint his guardian as the king and his courtiers chose. Since the guardian was entitled to take all the profits of the estates while his ward grew up, wardships were a valuable commodity at court, often selling for large sums of money. Margaret would herself portray the corruption and abuses of the system graphically in a subplot she created for her play *The Presence*—a satire on court society, which she published in 1668. Here the young gentleman, Underward, is sold in a ruthless business transaction between two courtiers.

SELLER: Will you buy my ward?

BUYER: Yes, if you will take a reasonable sum: but having cut down all his woods, dissolved all the iron-stone, digg'd deep in his coalpits and lead and copper mines, let leases of his lands, ploughed all his mead-

ows, pastures, and parks; to ask twenty thousand pounds is unconscionable!

SELLER: Come, come, you will find enough in the estate to make it worth
your money . . . and when you have made the best of his estate, you
may have a good sum of money for his marriage.

By the time the unfortunate Underward reaches twenty-one, he has been married to a woman he hates and there are no financial assets left except the mere
lands themselves, now so ruined by over-exploitation that "they will produce
nothing but brakes and briars, moss and ling." Because the lands are entailed,
Underward cannot even sell them, and so is unable to provide his younger
brothers with a landed inheritance and his sisters with marriage portions. With
no money and no hopes of marriage, they are forced to abandon their gentry
class and go out to work as servants.[32] In September 1625, Elizabeth Lucas had
to act at once to protect the interests of her children.

In her negotiations with the Crown, Elizabeth had a powerful ally in
Samuel Harsnet, bishop of Norwich, a Colchester baker's son whose first steps
in his church career had been assisted by the patronage of the Lucas family.
Harsnet had been present at the deathbed of Thomas Lucas—"the dearest
friend that ever I did enjoy in this world"—and he now wrote the delicate letter Elizabeth needed. They had one strong bargaining point. Just before he
died, Thomas Lucas had received a proposal of marriage for his eldest daughter, Mary, from the rising young courtier Peter Killigrew. The match was
desired by King Charles I, and Killigrew's suit was preferred to Mary's father
through the highest channels of government. With the tact of the practiced
courtier, Harsnet now replied, sending Elizabeth's humble "consent unto his
Majesty's desires" for the marriage, while at the same time presenting a picture
of the "woeful dissipation" that must come to the Lucas family after Thomas's
death "except his Majesty be pleased to relieve it with his healing hand": Elizabeth's consent to the marriage was being made conditional on her receiving
the wardship of her son herself.[33] Soon the Court of Wards was instructed by
the authorities to show "all possible favour . . . to the ward of Thomas Lucas,
the rather for Mr. Killigrew's sake." Finally, on paying £1,700 into the royal
coffers, with the agreement of £200 more each year of John's minority, Elizabeth was appointed John's guardian, and her daughter Mary was married to
Peter Killigrew, who soon also received a knighthood and state pension from
the king.[34]

In Colchester, Elizabeth now took on the sole management of all the Lucas
family estates. She was in direct control of the lands the Lucases farmed themselves—the grange farms near St. John's that produced their food, and the

commercial sheep-farming that formed the basis of the wealth of so many East Anglian families. Other lands were leased to tenant farmers, involving her in setting the terms of the leases and overseeing the manorial courts in which negotiations between tenants and landlord traditionally took place. Elizabeth found great job satisfaction in exercising so many different skills and she had a real flair for the work. By her energy and business acumen she maintained her family in a high style of living and ensured the inheritance of her children: her daughters would each have a handsome £2,000 dowry on marriage, as their father's will had desired.[35]

In 1627 Margaret's brother John reached twenty-one and took legal possession of his estates. In London the following year he married a granddaughter of Lord Abergavenny, Anne Nevill—"a virtuous and beautiful lady," according to Margaret[36]—and then brought his new wife home to live at St. John's with his mother and four unmarried sisters, Elizabeth, Anne, Catherine, and the five-year-old Margaret. The pattern of family life that Margaret would later recall with nostalgia was now becoming established. While the sisters spent their leisure reading, sewing, and chatting together, John took on the public life and grandeur of the male head of the family. He bought a new family coach; he accepted the command of a troop of heavy cavalry in the Essex militia; and, spending part of the year in London, where he kept a town house in the fashionable area of Blackfriars, he began to build a political career that would make him a court favorite.[37]

Meanwhile Elizabeth continued in charge of much of the estate business. The work was vast and demanding, and Margaret later recalled how her mother with modesty "would often complain that her family was too great for her weak management," urging John to take affairs into his own hands. "Yet," Margaret noted, "I observe[d] she took a pleasure, and some little pride, in the governing thereof."[38] And so, although John was now publicly head of the family in the outside world, Elizabeth remained its de facto head in the private sphere of home life, ruling over the household servants, managing the property, and bringing up the younger children.

Chapter Two

Childhood Ambitions,
1623–1642

$\mathcal{M}$argaret remembered Elizabeth Lucas as an affectionate mother who had raised her children "with a most industrious care and tender love," providing lavishly "not only for necessity, conveniency and decency, but for delight and pleasure." Believing that coercion would corrupt and break their characters, Elizabeth never threatened or beat her children, never even showed open anger to them. "Instead," Margaret recalled, "reason was used to persuade us, . . . the deformities of vice was discovered, and the graces and virtues presented unto us." Elizabeth did not stress the strict obedience and respect that most seventeenth-century parents exacted from their offspring, but rather "did strive to please and delight her children," encouraging them in their "honest pleasures and harmless delights."[1] Growing up in this liberal regime, Margaret never absorbed her culture's ideal of obedience—one of the most important of female virtues, a vital part of any woman's relationships with parents and husband, and a religious duty owed to God. Instead she grew up believing she should be free to follow her own wants in life, so long as they were lawful, honest, and did no harm. In her relations with the family members society placed in authority over her—first her mother and brother, and then her husband—Margaret would be more passionate and persuasive than obedient.

But if Elizabeth Lucas seems surprisingly modern in her liberal, antidisciplinarian ideas, she was very much rooted in her time in other aspects of her educational principles. First there was her concern for maintaining social distinction. Margaret was a gentleman's daughter and was to be brought up in accordance with her high birth. The servants at St. John's were ordered to treat even the youngest of the children with the same respect they showed to Elizabeth herself, and "knowing that youth is apt to take infection by ill examples," Elizabeth allowed her children to mix only with the upper servants of the household, protecting them from the uncouth manners of the "vulgar servingmen." The children each had a personal servant to wait on them, and were themselves taught to treat their social inferiors with politeness while maintaining a sense of social distance. Thus they would grow up only in "noble thoughts and honourable qualities," accustomed to the dignity of their station as well as its duties of civility and noblesse oblige.[2]

But for Margaret this system resulted in much more than just social training. Elizabeth Chaplain—the girl whom Elizabeth Lucas took into St. John's to be her youngest daughter's maid—became not just a servant but a lifelong companion and friend. The two girls grew up together, always in each other's company, and when Margaret finally left home Elizabeth went with her in the capacity of "waiting-maid" or "gentlewoman," helping her mistress to dress in the mornings and accompanying her during the day. The attachment between them was close and affectionate. Elizabeth was enthusiastic in her admiration for her mistress, while Margaret promised she would "always remain your loving friend." Margaret knew that she could rely absolutely on her maid's support, "for being bred with me, your love is twisted to my good, which shall never be undone by any unkind action of mine."[3]

The Lucas girls grew up with all the privileges of their social class— wealth, fine clothes, servants, leisure—but they also suffered under its disadvantages. Though Margaret's great aspiration in life would be to become a writer, as a country gentleman's daughter she received no formal academic or intellectual education to prepare herself for such a calling. A century earlier, educational reformers such as Juan Luis Vives and Sir Thomas More had advocated a full Renaissance education for aristocratic women, and Queen Elizabeth I and many other highborn ladies were trained in classical and modern languages, logic, rhetoric, philosophy, and the sciences. But King James I hated learned ladies. They were ridiculed at his court, and soon the normal Stuart education for girls went little beyond the most basic skills of reading and writing, and the elementary arithmetic they would need in their household management. There were a few exceptions: Bathsua Makin, sister of the mathematician John Pell, was educated with her brothers by her clergyman father; she read and wrote Hebrew as well as Greek, Latin, and modern languages, and was expert in such technical studies as mathematical astronomy. But even she, when she came to open a reforming school for girls near London in the 1670s, only suggested her pupils should pursue academic studies in the time left spare by their more important training in housewifery. In general, educated women were feared. "A learned woman is thought to be a comet, that bodes mischief, whenever it appears," Bathsua Makin admitted.[4] And too much study, it was thought, could damage women's soft, weak minds. In 1645, the governor of the Massachusetts Bay Colony noted in his journal the woeful news that a local woman had lost her reason "by occasion of her giving herself wholly to reading and writing." "If she had attended her household affairs, and such things as belong to women . . . she had kept her wits," he believed.[5]

So Margaret, educated "according to my birth, and the nature of my sex," "never went to school, but only learned to read and write at home, taught by an ancient decayed gentlewoman, whom my mother kept for that purpose."[6] Beginning with a hornbook—a handheld wooden board on which a transparent sheet of horn protected a piece of paper printed with the alphabet, numbers, simple syllables, and the Lord's prayer—she would have learned the basics of literacy, before moving on to the universal child's first reading book: the Bible. Its rhythms and language, events and personalities would often appear in Margaret's adult prose; King Solomon in particular, with the power of his wisdom, caught her imagination and she frequently referred to him in later life. But around this elementary level her formal intellectual training ceased, and she remained without the educational advantages that her brothers, like most young men of their class, received. Margaret never learned the Latin and Greek beaten into boys from an early age—languages that were an essential cultural training at a time when English literature, whether in poetry, philosophy, history, or drama, was strongly influenced by the ancient classics. She never studied the classical arts of logic and rhetoric that trained young men to organize their thoughts, for both speaking and writing. And she learned none of the technically complex mathematics that enabled men of her class to keep up with the latest discoveries in astronomy and mechanics.

For a country gentleman's daughter such as Margaret domestic skills and ladylike accomplishments were more important than literacy, and Elizabeth Lucas provided tutors for all the standard subjects. Ornamental needlework—that universal female occupation normally referred to simply as "work"—was taught to Margaret and her sisters, probably by the same impoverished gentlewoman who taught them to read. There were tutors for singing and music,* for dancing, and probably also for French—a fashionable courtly requirement now that King Charles I had married a French princess. "Yet we were not kept strictly thereto," Margaret remembered, "for my mother cared not so much

---

*The lute and virginals were the most popular instruments for women, while the viol was avoided because of the immodest posture required to play it.

for our dancing and fiddling, singing and prating of several languages, as that we should be bred virtuously, modestly, civilly, honourably, and on honest principles."⁷ Like most mothers, Elizabeth was more concerned that her daughters be virtuous than accomplished, for it was virtue that would maintain their reputations and, with beauty and dowry, would get them married, the goal of a young lady's life.

And in her project to raise virtuous children Elizabeth was a success, or at least Margaret thought so. Looking back on her childhood in her thirties, Margaret contrasted her honorable, serious, and sincere brothers and sisters with the frivolity, dissolution, and bare-faced corruption she was to witness when she left home. Throughout her life she would advocate her mother's principles for the moral education of children "gently, rather with reason than with rods." But she often regretted her own lack of intellectual training, and it was on this subject that she would make her only (and indirect) criticism of her mother. "Women are not educated as they should be," she would write. "Had I children, I would endeavour with all the rational arguments and witty discourses I were capable of to persuade them to delight in poetry and philosophy."⁸ Only with such an intellectual training, Margaret believed, could one achieve happiness in life, for "philosophers and poets are not only the wisest, but the happiest men." Enjoying "all the delights of the mind, and pleasures of thoughts," she thought, "they are happy in any condition, having their happiness always with them and in them," attaining "a Heaven upon Earth, all which silent contemplation brings them unto."⁹

Margaret began her own silent contemplation at an early age: "it pleased God to command His servant Nature to endue me with a poetical and philosophical genius, even from my birth," she would explain to her readers some thirty years later. She was fascinated by the things around her and studied them keenly, "making the world my book, striving by joining every several actions, like several words, to make a discourse to myself."¹⁰ As an adult she would write at length on the natural world, developing her own theories about its structure and operation, but as a child she seems to have been more interested in the realms of humanity and morality. She watched people closely, beginning a lifetime interest in attempting to judge their motivations and "inward dispositions" from their "outward actions," "considering and pondering upon the natures of mankind" as she sought to reach some general understanding of humanity. Moral questions enthralled her and she set up debates in her head about the people she saw, bringing opposing thoughts to accuse and excuse them for their actions. This too was the beginning of a lifetime habit, for she was always fascinated by arguments: broad-minded enough to see both sides of an issue, she was often more interested in understanding how an effective case could be made both pro and con than in actually settling on a fixed opinion. Meanwhile, her more poetical side led Margaret into what she called her "fancies," her rich imaginative life of storytelling and fantasy that would be revealed in the fiction and poems she published in later life.[11]

This life of the mind formed Margaret's greatest pleasure. "Addicted from my childhood to contemplation rather than conversation, to solitariness rather than society," she loved to be alone with her thoughts, and "would walk two or three hours, and never rest, in a musing, considering, contemplating manner," turning over her ideas. "It is as great a grief to leave their society as a joy to be in their company," she found, and before she was twelve she had already begun to write prolifically. By the end of her childhood, the time she lightly called her "baby-years," she would fill sixteen large notebooks—which she later dismissed as her "baby-books"—with observations and reflections, stories and poems.[12]

Margaret never thought it surprising that she had a strong drive to write. Individuality and creativity—spontaneous but at the same time careless, undisciplined, and unschooled—were just what she thought innate to female nature. "Girls," she wrote, "are always busy to no purpose, they will take delight to scratch a coal upon a white wall, or ink with a pen upon paper, whenas they account it a torment to be taught a fair handwriting."[13] This was certainly Margaret's character. She loved to be creative and original, following her own ideas. She hated all formal studies and paid little attention to the tuition provided for her. Her childhood handwriting she later described as mere disjointed "scribbles," irregularly spaced across the page so that "each letter stands so cowardly from th'other, as all the lines of your sight cannot draw, or bring them into words." And though as an adult she grouped her letters closely into words, she would never master the use of a quill pen—an art requiring considerable practice before a writer was able to keep the nib neatly cut and make the ink flow evenly. Margaret's childhood manuscripts were defaced, she noted, by "long hard scratches" and huge, oceanlike ink-blots, and this feature—the dark smudge of a freshly dipped pen gradually fading until the emptying quill left no mark but a scratch—can still be seen in the love letters she wrote when she was twenty-two. Her spelling too was atrocious, her punctuation nonexistent, and she certainly had no interest in the more "feminine" accomplishments. Her voice remained untrained so that, as an adult, she enjoyed singing traditional English ballads but would never attempt the artful, elaborately ornamented songs of contemporary composers. She took no pleasure in dancing, and she found herself unable to acquire foreign languages, even when she lived abroad for fifteen years.[14] Nor did she ever learn the domestic skills of housewifery on which women's lives normally centered. "The truth is, my Lord," she confessed to her husband years later, "I cannot work, I mean such works as ladies use to pass their time withall . . . needle-works, spinning-works, preserving-works, as also baking, and cooking-works, as making cakes, pies, puddings, and the like, all which I am ignorant of."[15]

Instead, left free to pursue her own interests by her mother's lax attitude to formal education, Margaret spent her time in her writing and contemplations and in reading, choosing "rather to read than to employ my time in any other work or practice."[16] In her later writings she would always emphasize her own lack of education and reading, but these statements were intended to pre-empt the criticisms she expected from her better-educated male readers; they do not imply that she was entirely ill read. For though unable, like almost all women, to read the Latin and Greek classics, yet Margaret was well acquainted with the contemporary English works that formed the popular reading matter of her class.

Prominent among these were the fashionable court poets, both those writing when she was in her teens in the 1630s and those of the preceding four decades. Poets like Spenser, Drayton, and Daniel from the Elizabethan period, and Herrick, Marvell, Denham, Jonson, and Suckling in her own day, although never mentioned explicitly by Margaret, had an obvious impact on her own poems, written as she approached the age of thirty.[17] Particularly influential on her was John Donne, whose verse was widely admired not just for its beauty but for its profound religious sentiment. Donne was one of only two poets she loved well enough to quote, and his ideas and imagery can be found in both her verse and prose works.[18]

Margaret also knew the major verse translations of her day. A metrical version of the Psalms and a verse translation of Homer she later criticized, but two other ambitious projects, by the Stuart courtiers Joshua Sylvester and George Sandys, she admired for the translators' sympathy with "the genius of the authors."[19] Both were very popular reading before the Civil War. Sylvester's translation of the French poet Du Bartas's *Divine Weeks and Works* was a Christian epic telling the biblical history of the world. From the first week of Creation and all the wonders of the natural world—the "gaping-fish . . . the subtle smell-strong-many-foot . . . the cramp fish . . . sea fox . . . the many spotted cuttle . . . the phoenix . . . swallow . . . nightingale"—the poem proceeded to the story of Eden and the Fall, Noah's Ark, Babylon, Abraham, and David. Meanwhile, Sandys's translation of Ovid's *Metamorphoses* brought to English readers the riches of classical mythology. The book was especially appealing in its lavish folio edition of 1632, where the tales were illustrated with vivid copperplate engravings crammed full of the monsters, gods and goddesses, battles, fires, shipwrecks, and strange transformations found in the poems. All these poets—

courtiers who moved in the best circles of society and received patronage from the monarch—instilled the good language (the "courtly expressions, and choice, and nice phrases") and the noble ideals (the "high and aspiring thoughts") that Margaret believed essential for "the better sort" of people.[20]

Among prose works, Aesop's Fables, often printed with extra tales written by modern writers, was a universal favorite with children. Margaret still remembered the fables well as an adult, and would apply their morals to her own life.[21] She was doubtless also familiar with the work of the popular Elizabethan author, John Lyly, who wrote plays and a celebrated prose romance, *Euphues*. His characteristic "euphuistic" style—with its repeated use of antitheses, and inclusion of manifold ingenious similes—would influence her later writing.

But, as contemporary educators decried most fiction as immoral, many of the stories children read were factual, including both English works such as Sir Walter Raleigh's *History of the World* and the classical histories of Thucidydes, Plutarch, Livy, and Tacitus, all available in translation. Plutarch's *Lives*, translated in 1579 and reissued in numerous editions throughout the seventeenth century, was a common favorite with children for its vivid, warts-and-all accounts of the great men of Greece and Rome. His stories fired the imaginations of generations of children—both girls and boys—right up to the end of the eighteenth century. That Margaret was familiar at least with his tales of Julius Caesar is clear from her own lifelong admiration of this Roman statesman, general, and orator. As a child, her heroes came from the books she read. While other teenage girls talked to their girlfriends about love and young men, Margaret "confess'd I only was in love with three dead men, which were dead long before my time, the one was Caesar, for his valour, the second Ovid, for his wit, and the third was our countryman Shakespeare." Shakespeare was Margaret's favorite English author for his ability to create vivid, realistic characters of every possible type. His *Midsummer Night's Dream* influenced her poetry, the fools of his plays provided models for her own, and Margaret later became the first woman to write a critical appreciation of his work.[22]

At St. John's, Margaret spent much of her time with her older sisters, joining them as they sat together, reading, sewing, and talking, or when, on fine days, they would walk out into the gardens or the countryside beyond, taking their books and needlework with them, to sit beneath some tree listening to the birds singing, while admiring the beauties of nature all around them.[23] Reading aloud to the family circle was a popular pastime* and Margaret probably got to know many books from her sisters. In particular, romances—popular fiction telling

---

*Margaret would later write her own essays, stories, and plays in the expectation that they would be used in this way.

heroic tales of chivalry, romance, and adventure—were some of her sisters' most preferred books: John's wife, Anne, read the latest French romances before they came out in translation, and Cervantes's *Don Quixote* in particular was a family favorite whose larger-than-life characters provided the sisters with material for jokes and the typecasting of real-life people.[24] Though Margaret would later condemn such books as unrealistic fantasies that could damage people's lives, they had been an important part of her childhood culture, and she would have known them well from her sisters, even if she never read them herself.

From her sisters she also absorbed a wide range of traditional folklore. Women of all classes in the seventeenth century were the main preservers of a rich oral heritage of songs and stories, proverbs and poems, which they told each other over their needlework, or by the fire during the dark winter evenings. Margaret grew up familiar with the old English ballads, which she sometimes sang herself, intoning them in the proper voice "betwixt speaking and singing, . . . and the rumming or humming of a [spinning] wheel should be the music to that tone."[25] She loved old sayings and proverbs: knowing vast numbers of them, she would often quote their folk wisdom in her later writings. And she also re-created this whole oral culture in her book *Nature's Pictures*, where a group assembles around the fire to tell stories.

Her family's talk was a major ingredient in the totally informal self-education that would be Margaret's main preparation for her adult writing career. She listened attentively to the adult conversation of her brothers and sisters as they discussed "the general actions of the world, judging, condemning, approving, commending, as they thought good."[26] And as her family talked of books and ideas, of authors and their rival theories and opinions, Margaret also gained a broad, if rather superficial, acquaintance with the arts and sciences—subjects such as the geography and exploration, astronomy, mechanics, and new medical discoveries that were at once the cutting edge of research and the fashionable conversation topics of the day.[27] Her scholarly brother John was especially important as a resource. To him Margaret came "when I read what I understood not," and he would explain "the sense or meaning thereof."[28]

Intelligent young women with no organized education available to them often relied on a male relative in this way, asking questions, borrowing books, or even persuading a brother home from university to give them a proper course of instruction.* But Margaret had no ambition for scholarship. The idea of being subjected to any intellectual authority was anathema to her, and she

---

*At the end of the seventeenth century, for instance, the orphaned Elizabeth Elstob went to live with her older brother, an Oxford don and antiquarian scholar. Encouraged by him, she learned eight languages and did pioneering work in the new research area of Anglo-Saxon, editing texts and publishing a grammar of the language.

was not a very keen reader. Rather than learning and absorbing the ideas of others—which she feared would threaten her own individuality—she always wanted to create and invent for herself. And this passion for originality and imagination found expression not only in Margaret's childhood writings but also in what she called "attiring, fine dressing, and fashions."[29]

Seventeenth-century clothes could not be bought off the shelf and ready-to-wear: women either designed and made their own dresses or would discuss the choice of material, decoration, and style with the tailors who were to make them up.* Every item was handmade and individual, and with a wide range of rich, exotic materials available—brightly colored silks and satins, velvet, furs, cloth of gold and silver, laces and embroidery—and a huge variety of accessories to choose from at the dressing table each day—muffs, masks, hats, hoods, capes, veils, scarves, gloves, handkerchiefs, and the small trinkets such as fans, purses, combs, looking glasses, jewels, pearls, ribbons, and ostrich feathers that Margaret called "toys"—there was plenty of scope for originality and creativity. Whereas literature and the arts were a male prerogative, beautiful clothes, Margaret thought, were the only outlet her society allowed women for their creativity and imagination—the faculty that Margaret normally called "fancy." "Dressing is the poetry of women, in shewing the fancies," she wrote, and she proudly pointed out how women applied true artistic invention "in their several and various dresses, in their many and singular choice of cloths, and ribbons, and the like."[30] And it was this opportunity for artistic expression that lay at the root of Margaret's own interest in dress. Delighting only in "such fashions as I did invent myself, not taking that pleasure in such fashions as was invented by others," she saw her clothes as a means of projecting her own individual personality. She did not want to set trends for others, only to design original outfits for herself. "I did dislike any should follow my fashions, for I always took delight in a singularity, even in accoutrements of habits."[31] Throughout her life Margaret was to devote considerable time and thought to her appearance: unskilled in the other accomplishments and occupations of women, dress was to be the only conventional female concern that engaged her interest and enthusiasm.

Wrapped up in her life of creativity, Margaret was a serious, intent, thoughtful child, uninterested in childish things. "I never took delight in closets or cabinets of toys, but in the variety of fine clothes and such toys as only were to adorn my person," she reminisced, and "I was never very active, by reason I was given so much to contemplation."[32] And this serious-minded tendency was only intensified by her mother, who would continue to grieve for her dead husband for the rest of her life.

---

*Female dressmakers were an innovation that grew up only during the course of the century.

Elizabeth Lucas had loved her husband deeply and she never remarried. Margaret portrayed her in her autobiography as a solitary recluse who "made her house her cloister, enclosing herself, as it were, therein." "She never forgot my father," Margaret recalled. "Indeed, he remained so lively in her memory, and her grief was so lasting, as she never mentioned his name, though she spoke often of him, but love and grief caused tears to flow, and tender sighs to rise, mourning in sad complaints." As Elizabeth told the legends of a father Margaret had never known—of his honor, courage, and generosity, his unjust exile by Queen Elizabeth I, and the "heroic spirit" that had made him refuse all noble titles out of his high-minded belief that public honors should be won by great deeds and not bought with money[33]—she created an intensely emotional atmosphere, at once mournful, passionately loving, and idealistic, that made a profound impression on her youngest daughter, molding the dominant emotions of her life and firing her ambitions.

Drinking in all these stories of her father's heroic nature and greatness of soul, Margaret was herself inspired with noble ideals. "I have been bred to elevated thoughts, not to a dejected spirit," she wrote proudly. "I am a servant to Truth and not to Flattery," "I do pursue virtue with an entire, and pure love." "Threatened with death to do or act anything against honour," she professed, "I would not do it, nay, I would die first." Faced with the challenge that "this was easy to say so, but hard to do it," she answered that "it was true, but yet there have been examples, that resolution and patience have overcome torment and death, and, said I, I hope well of myself, although the proof doth lie in the trial."[34]

Such heroic aspirations were the high ideals by which the model Renaissance man was supposed to live. Renaissance humanism had revived the ancient ethical and political teachings of Aristotle and Cicero, combining them with the medieval tradition of chivalry, to create a code of honor that guided the lives of sixteenth- and seventeenth-century aristocratic men. Trained in both the martial arts and the learned arts and sciences, they were to apply their gifts for the public good, serving their country as military leaders or politicians. In their public careers, they were to be inspired to do great deeds and be selflessly public spirited by the promise of fame and glory—an eternal memorial in the hearts and minds of men that would provide a kind of temporal immortality to complement the spiritual immortality promised by Christianity. As the idealistic and soon-to-be-murdered young Prince of Wales in Shakespeare's *King Richard III* says of his hero, Julius Caesar,

> Death makes no conquest of this conqueror;
> For now he lives in fame, though not in life.[35]

Fame was the proper goal of a gentleman's life, to be gained by his own merit and abilities, developed during a lifetime of self-improvement and ambition.

Such ideals permeated literature and art, and Margaret would have encountered them everywhere. The Sandys translation of Ovid's *Metamorphoses* that she admired began with a graphic display of the glory won by the great poet: its frontispiece engraving showed the bust of Ovid flanked by Mercury and Apollo, with the figure of Fame blowing her trumpet above the poet's head. "Carmina quam tribuunt, Fama perennis erit [The fame of poets lasts forever]" was the motto above the picture. And Plutarch's *Lives* was an inspiration: presenting the heroes of classical antiquity as examples for his readers' imitation, Plutarch displayed the immortal fame that heroic virtue brought. His account of Julius Caesar and Alexander the Great in particular may have shaped Margaret's childhood, for they, like her, were serious children whose adult ambitions kept them from normal childish play.

But these Renaissance ideals of honor and achievement were essentially masculine, intended to direct the public lives of the aristocratic men who comprised the political and intellectual establishment. For women whose lives were spent at home in the domestic sphere there was a different code of honor, centering on the passive, private, feminine virtues of modesty, chastity, and obedience. By ancient tradition, any aspiration for a public reputation was inappropriate for them. As the great Athenian statesman Pericles said in the fifth century B.C.E., "the greatest glory of a woman is to be least talked about by men."[36]

Yet Margaret could not bear the normal anonymity of women who, as wives, mothers, sisters, and daughters to more publicly active and famous men, gained no reputation for themselves. She wanted to achieve real, important things in the public world, to do some great work in life "wherein I may leave my Idea, or live in an Idea, or my Idea may live in many brains." Her desire for fame was not mere vainglory, the need for empty show and glamour. Fame was to be earned by excellence and worth. "Outward honour should be the mark of inward, worthy a reward," she thought: "fame is seldom gotten with ease, but with pains and labour, danger and trouble, and oftentimes with life itself."[37]

Margaret was building on a commonplace of her day when she wrote that "there is little difference between man and beast, but what ambition and glory makes," for "man is born to produce a fame, by some particular acts to prove himself a man . . . so that those men that die in oblivion, are beasts by nature." As a consequence, she felt that women were being denied a basic human right.[38] "Shall only men sit in honour's chair, and women stand as waiters by? . . . shall only men live by fame, and women die in oblivion?" demands

Lady Victoria, the heroine of Margaret's play *Bell in Campo,* who insists on joining her husband on the battlefield and leading an army of women against the enemy. No, Margaret would answer: women too should be encouraged to undertake "any thing that may bring honour to our sex: for . . . though we be inferior to men, let us shew ourselves a degree above beasts; and not eat, and drink, and sleep away our time as they do . . . and so turn into forgotten dust. But let us strive to build us tombs while we live, of noble, honourable, and good actions."[39]

But how Margaret could hope to fulfil such aspirations in her own life was not at all clear. Her heroes in life, Caesar, Ovid, and Shakespeare, were all men whose public lives she could not seriously hope to imitate. She could not, like her brothers, follow her father's ideals of honor closely and serve as a soldier or politician. The learned professions of medicine, law, and academia were equally closed to her. Even in literature—a possible resort in the nineteenth century for such intelligent and creative women as the Brontës and George Eliot—there were no female role models for her to follow. In the forty years from 1600 until 1640, when Margaret reached the age of seventeen, only forty-two new books by women had been printed, and of these only seven were literary works.[40] There were no prolific or professional women authors. Margaret herself, in the 1650s, would become the first Englishwoman to publish more than a single literary work, while Aphra Behn, who began writing plays for the London stage in the 1670s, is commonly considered the first woman to have supported herself financially by writing.

So in the 1630s, when she was in her teens, Margaret could imagine no real future in which she might follow her ambitions. Only in daydreams and fantasies could she find satisfaction; and the character Lady Contemplation, which she created for one of her plays in the 1650s, gives us some insight into Margaret's own dreams. "I did imagine myself such a beauty as Nature never made the like," Lady Contemplation recounts, "and then that a great powerful monarch, such a one as Alexander or Caesar, fell desperately in love with me." Elegant, witty love letters are exchanged before the young lady travels through many kingdoms, killing millions of men by her beauty, to arrive "only clothed in white satin, and a crown of diamonds on my head, like a bride, for I was to be married as soon as I met the emperor." Again, "I did imagine myself married, my husband being a general of an army, who had fought many battles, and . . . conquer'd many nations." Finally, on "an unfortunate day of battle," her husband's horse falls under him and he is captured by the enemy. Immediately the young wife assembles the army's commanders to tell them "that if they would give me leave, I would take my husband's office, and lead the army." Disposing her troops wisely, she fights at their head dressed in "a masculine suit, and over that a cloth of silver coat, made close to my waist," armed with breastplate, helmet, and sword, mounted on a coal-black horse "only a white star on his forehead, and three white feet."[41] Such fantasies clearly provided an outlet for Margaret's creativity and her obvious fascination with the intricacies of dress and appearance. They also allowed her to imagine herself into the active, public roles she could never hope to fill in reality, becoming a writer admired for her wit and style, a political ruler making wise laws and giving out justice, or a general whose eloquent speeches inspired her soldiers to win battles.

But in real life, away from her imaginings, Margaret was almost a different person—shy, fearful, and totally emotionally absorbed in her close family circle. Surrounded and protected by the family she loved, she would never develop the social skills—the easy chat and detailed knowledge of the proprieties of young ladies' behavior in mixed company—that were normally central to the education of a girl of her class. Afraid of strangers and large groups of people, and aware of her lack of social graces, she was desperately shy in company, hardly able to speak a word. She was comfortable only with her near relations, the people she called her "natural friends," "whose presence used to give me confidence—thinking I could not do amiss whilst any one of them were by." Seeking their approval in everything she did, Margaret found in them a "foundation to stand [on], or guide to direct me."[42] And to them she grew up passionately devoted.

She idolized her three grown-up brothers—John as "a great scholar," and Thomas and Charles as "excellent soldiers" who were inspired by their father's ideals of "heroic actions." She hero-worshipped her mother, who "had such a majestic grandeur, as it were continually hung about her, that it would strike a kind of an awe to the beholders, and command respect from the rudest." "She was of a grave behaviour," Margaret recalled; "her beauty was beyond the ruin of time, for she had a well-favoured loveliness in her face . . . even to her dying hour."[43] Margaret was also devoted to her four beautiful sisters, and especially to the youngest, Catherine, just six years older than Margaret herself. For her Margaret felt a love she described as "infinite": "I thought it was impossible I could love any creature better than you." "Distance of place, nor length of time," she wrote years later, while living in exile on the Continent, "cannot lessen my natural, or rather supernatural affection to you, for certainly my love for you is more than a sister's love."[44]

Yet this passionate love for her family brought Margaret constant torment, "for fear any evil misfortune or accident, or sickness, or death, should come unto them."[45] As her mother endlessly mourned for her dead husband, the experience of sudden bereavement was always vivid in Margaret's mind and she worried incessantly that those she loved might be snatched away from her. She would lie awake at night in the bedroom she shared with Catherine, listening for her breathing. "I remember I have oftentimes waked you out of your sleep, when you did sleep quietly," she reminded Catherine years later, "fearing you had been dead, and oftener have I laid my face over your mouth, to feel if you breath'd, insomuch as I have kept myself waking, to watch your sleeps." At mealtimes, Margaret feared "that that which was to nourish you, should kill you." "Neither could I let you pray in quiet, for I have often knock'd at your closet door, when I thought you were longer at your prayers than usual . . . so as I could not forbear to ask you how you did, and whether you were well, and many the like impertinencies which my extraordinary love troubled you with."[46]

Other fears also preoccupied Margaret. Though she believed she would be prepared to die with courage in a cause of honor, yet in the face of random dangers—"as upon the sea, or any dangerous places, or of thieves, or fire, or the like"—she was, she said, "the veriest coward in nature." Sudden noises startled her. She would jump and stop up her ears at the sound of a gun—"much less have I courage to discharge one"—and she was horrified by violence: "if a sword should be held against me, although but in jest, I am afraid." "According to the constitution of my sex, I am as fearful as a hare," she concluded.[47] And, likening herself to a timid hare, Margaret felt a natural sympathy for hurt or hunted animals. "Though it is a usual custom for ladies and women of quality, after the hunting of a deer, to stand by until they are ripped up, that they might wash their hands in the blood, supposing it will make them white, yet," Margaret wrote in disgust, "I never did it." Appalled by cruelty, she was so tender-hearted that "it troubles my conscience to kill a fly, and the groans of a dying beast strike my soul."[48]

Margaret was a sensitive child—"apt to weep rather than laugh," as she summed up her own character, "more inclining to be melancholy than merry."[49] And this predominant sadness of mood, or "melancholy" as Margaret always called it, would continue through her life, intensifying towards depression at times of grief and loss. Before she married she had already begun to consult Sir Theodore Mayerne, the leading doctor of the day, for her condition.[50] Yet such melancholy would not prevent her from also writing hilarious comedy and viciously witty social satire, for Margaret's character was nothing if not a mass of complexities and contradictions. Dogged by persistent shyness, which could leave her blushing and tongue-tied among strangers even in middle age, she at the same time courted public attention by her individual styles of dress and her publication of her writings, finding the courage to continue her writing career even in the face of considerable criticism and ridicule. Afraid to plead her own case in the parliamentarian court where she came in 1651 to seek an income from her husband's confiscated estates after the Civil War, she would yet be bold enough to reproach the king himself in print in 1667, when she felt that her husband had been wronged. Such contradictions of fear and courage, shyness and self-assertion were among the many enigmas that would make Margaret so gripping an object of curiosity to her contemporaries, puzzling and fascinating them, horrifying some and inspiring others.

BY THE TIME MARGARET reached her teens, most of her sisters had made good marriages into wealthy gentry families. Mary had married the courtier Peter Killigrew in 1625; then, in 1632, Elizabeth wedded an Oxfordshire gentleman, William Walter. And in 1635, when Margaret was twelve, Catherine, her favorite sister, married the wealthy Londoner Edmund Pye. Pye was the grandson of a city butcher, but his father had bought the family's way into the gentry class with the fortune he made in his career as a scrivener—a legal draughtsman and broker of loans. Edmund, the eldest son, was now a leisured landed gentleman with a country mansion and estates in Buckinghamshire and a stylish town house in London's fashionable suburb of Covent Garden.[51]

In spite of their ties to other families, Margaret continued to spend much of her time in her sisters' company. In the summer they commonly all returned to St. John's; then when winter came, the family would reassemble in the capital. Winter was the beginning of the London season, when the rich and fashionable flocked to town, to be near to the political power base of the royal court at Whitehall, and to pursue all the sophisticated pleasures of the metropolis. The Lucases' town house was in the traditionally aristocratic area of Blackfriars, on the western edge of the old walled city. Here Margaret would stay for the season with her mother and her brother John and his wife, Anne, unless, as often happened, she went to live with her sister, Catherine Pye, in Covent Garden.

Even among London's crowds, the Lucases remained a close-knit and exclusive family group. Although the various brothers and sisters lived "dispersed into several houses of their own, yet for the most part they met every day," Margaret remembered.* They "did seldom make [social] visits, nor never went abroad with strangers in their company, but only themselves in a flock together, agreeing so well that there seemed but one mind amongst them."[52]

---

*When Margaret talks of her sisters she would have intended to include her sister-in-law, John's wife, Anne; commonly no distinction was made in the period.

Mornings were normally spent at home: this was the time for ladies' dressing, and Margaret was always exquisitely attired, as "my mother did not only delight to see us neat and cleanly, fine and gay, but rich and costly." Now too Margaret could have time alone writing and reading, before the whole family came together for midday dinner, "feasting each other like Job's children" as each sibling took it in turn to receive all the others at their own home.[53] Then the afternoons were the time for outings and entertainments.

Sometimes the family drove in their coaches through the grand, broad streets of the fashionable West End "to see the concourse and recourse of people," Margaret recalled.[54] Sometimes too they went to the theater, patronizing for the most part not the large, open-air Red Bull and Fortune theaters but the more socially exclusive private playhouses—Salisbury Court and Blackfriars, the Phoenix in Drury Lane, and the Globe in Southwark on the other side of the Thames. Here Margaret would have seen long-popular tragicomedies, pastorals, and romances as well as the racy and often bawdy satirical social comedies that were now being pioneered by court writers like the earl of Newcastle and Sir William Davenant, creating a genre that would flourish as Restoration comedy thirty years later.[55]

With the warmth of spring, the Lucases joined the high society that congregated in the pleasure grounds of Spring Garden, at the northeast corner of St. James's Park, close to the court at Whitehall. Here fashionable ladies walked together among the trees and fountains, chatting and showing off their newest dresses. Lovers courted their mistresses, enticing them into the privacy of the thickets, while gentlemen played and gambled at the archery butts and bowling green. A booth at the garden's center sold refreshments—fancy meats and tarts and Rhenish wine—and parties could be seen picnicking beneath the trees throughout the day. Later in the evening, Margaret's party would sometimes employ a band of musicians to entertain them while they ate supper in a barge out on the Thames, watching the hundreds of boats that passed carrying goods and people up and down or across the river. And in the spring too they would often go to drive in Hyde Park, an old royal hunting ground that King Charles I had recently opened to the public. Here society gathered at the Ring, a circular track about 200 or 300 yards across, where fashionable people drove around in their smartest equipage. May 1st was the big day here, when everyone in London who owned a coach or could afford to rent a hackney carriage came out, dressed in the latest fashion, to see and be seen. But the place was busy throughout the month, and the king and queen drove here regularly in state, closely watched by the eager crowds.[56]

The royal court set the tone for all this polite cultured life, leading and defining the fashions in clothes, in architecture and the arts, and in pastimes and entertainments. By 1638, when Margaret's brother John was knighted and appointed to a prestigious job in the household of the Prince of Wales, the Lucases were people of importance at court. John mixed freely with the greatest and most cultivated patrons of the arts—the king and the queen and wealthy aristocrats such as the earl of Newcastle, who was John's superior in the Prince of Wales's court. He was also friend to some of the leading writers of the day, poets like Sir John Denham, who would later compose a jocular verse poking fun at John's scholarship.[57] With a brother who was part of the favored inner circle among whom the courtier-poets circulated their verses in manuscript copies, Margaret could have kept up with the most current trends in poetry, reading the as yet unpublished works of writers like Milton, Denham, and Herrick. John Lucas and his wife, Anne, themselves became literary patrons and valued customers of London booksellers. Perhaps Margaret joined the parties who drove into the City, to the area around St. Paul's Cathedral where the best booksellers' shops were concentrated. Here polite society met to discuss the latest books and ideas, and the coaches of the nobility and gentry were often so numerous that they filled the narrow medieval streets, leaving no room even for pedestrians to pass.[58]

Although she does not mention it in her autobiography, Margaret would also have accompanied her sisters to court sometimes, joining the fashionable society that gathered in the royal presence chamber to watch the courtiers coming and going, catch up on the latest political news and society gossip, and see the newest fashions—or "to observe humours, hear wit and to see beauties," as Margaret put it.[59] Margaret's sister Mary was married to an established courtier, currently gentleman of the privy chamber to King Charles I, while Elizabeth's and Catherine's husbands, younger men eager to win the king's favor, would achieve distinction in August 1641 when they were both made baronets.[60] Going to court was a standard part of the life of such well connected people. The sisters probably joined the crowds who watched the king and queen dining in state, and they would have been among the polite society who on certain evenings flocked to see the dramatic entertainments laid on by the court in the newly built masquing house at Whitehall.

In her story "The Contract," Margaret describes the fear and wonder experienced by a young woman attending her first masque: fear at the huge crowds all pressing to squeeze in through the doors—"the officers beating the people back, the women squeaking, and the men cursing, the officers threatening, and the enterers praying"—and wonder at the beauties within. Masques were a succession of marvels, from the fantastic views represented in the stage scenery—"the poet's heavens and hells . . . cities, castles, seas, fishes, rocks, mountains, beasts, birds" were some picked out by Margaret—through the grotesquerie of the antimasque where strange figures disported in disorder, until the final resolution of the plot, when king, queen, and courtiers descended in splendor from the clouds as gods, goddesses, and heroes, restoring the world to order.[61] Through such allegorical displays the Stuart court proclaimed its political views of the divinity of monarchy and the king's power to bring peace and wealth to the nation, and Charles I saw these masques as an important defense against rebellion and social disorder. The final wonder for Margaret came when the masque was over, for then the whole audience, dressed in their best finery and jewels, turned to dancing and "the room is made as light with candles, as if the sun shined, and their glittering bravery makes as glorious a show as his gilded beams."[62]

Shy and nervous, Margaret would have been a silent observer rather than an active participant in all these London revels. But she was later glad to have been exposed in her youth to this brilliant social world, feeling that it had been an essential part of her preparation as a writer. Here she could learn the best language—for "in schools and courts," she thought, "are the most significant, choicest, and plentifullest expressions, which make the better sort . . . have finer and sweeter discourse." And, more importantly, she also gained a broad experience of life: as she later acknowledged, "if I had been enclosed from the world, in some obscure place, and had been an anchoret from my infancy, having not the liberty to see the world, nor conversation to hear of it, I should never have writ of so many things; nor had had so many several opinions, for the senses are the gates that lets in knowledge into the understanding, and fancy into the imagination."[63] The habit of close social observation that she now established would provide the basis for the satire and social commentary of the plays, short stories, essays, and letters she wrote in later life.

Finally, in late May or June, the glittering social round came to an end and polite society departed for their country homes where, for a landowning class whose principal business was agriculture, summer and autumn were the busiest times of the year. Margaret, traveling in the family coach, left the streets of London behind her and journeyed out through the rich Essex countryside along the main road to Harwich. The fifty miles to Colchester was too far for a heavy coach to travel comfortably in a day, so she probably broke her journey with an overnight at her brother John's second country house at Shenfield, conveniently placed near to the main road about halfway between London and Colchester. Then her party would proceed on through Chelmsford to cross Lexden Heath late in the day, with the roofs, church towers, and walls of Colchester coming into view ahead. Passing through the outlying streets, they finally entered the great archway of the gatehouse at St. John's.

Margaret's later memories of all this time would be idyllic—of a perfect and peaceful family life, which, as in the biblical story of Job and his children, would be utterly ruined by calamity. In 1642, "this unnatural war came like a whirlwind, which felled down their houses, where some in the wars were crushed to death."[64] For the Lucases were to take an active part in the Civil War, with catastrophic results for many of them.

Chapter Three

The Coming of War, 1642

*A*t the same time as Margaret shared the fashionable leisured life of her sisters, fierce antipathies were growing up in the greater world around them. In Colchester during the 1620s and 1630s, John Lucas and his mother became as unpopular as old Sir Thomas Lucas had been in the 1580s, and for the same reasons. Determined to maximize the income from their estates, they insisted on every right to which they could make any legal claim; John even cut off part of the town's water supply when he did not receive the few shillings in rent due where the pipes ran across the family's estates. He and Elizabeth vigorously contested issues of land boundaries and rights, the enclosure of commons, and liability for local taxes, displaying a ruthless business acumen. And even apparently petty disputes, concerning small sums of money, ran on for years, because to John they were vitally important as matters concerning his rights and honor. Some quarrels he even took as high as the king's Privy Council: "to this necessity enforces me, to vindicate my right and the privileges of my house; they are my inheritance, and as much mine as the house itself, and I must not, will not lose them," he explained angrily.[1] The brother whom Margaret loved and admired as scholar, thinker, and father-figure was to the outside world argumentative, stiff-necked, and litigious. By 1639 he was a hated man in Colchester where, it was reported, "he cannot almost go in quiet up and down the streets, for people calling after him."[2]

During the 1630s these private, local disputes were becoming ever more involved with the national political and religious differences that would bring the country to civil war. In London there had been no Parliament since 1629; King Charles I and his court governed England directly, raising the money they needed through special taxes such as monopolies, customs duties, and ship money, which did not require parliamentary approval. Though technically legal, these measures were widely unpopular, and opposition to the court regime and its policies ran high throughout the country. Especially controversial were the government's religious reforms, overseen by Archbishop of Canterbury William Laud, intended to make the Church of England more ritualistic and anti-puritan. As the influence of the king's French Catholic wife, Henrietta Maria, increased at court, the traditional English fear of Roman Catholicism intensified among puritans into a seething hatred of Archbishop Laud's church reforms as amounting to nothing less than the detested "Popery." Violence erupted in many churches as parishioners destroyed the newly installed altar rails and religious images and tore the elaborate vestments off their pastors' backs.

The Lucases themselves were staunch high Anglicans: John appointed Laudian clergymen to local churches and, in the face of local opposition, he had given his public support to the archbishop's project for repairing St. Paul's Cathedral. Margaret herself, although never especially devout,* would remain a conforming Anglican throughout her life. But around the family at St John's, Essex was the most enthusiastically puritan county in England. Violence against the Laudian church reforms became almost a commonplace during the 1630s, and hostility to the court regime was strong at all social levels, from the poor weavers of Colchester and the other cloth-making towns right up to the county's political and social elite, led by the puritan earl of Warwick and his wealthy gentry friends and relatives. The Lucases, looking to London and the court for their identity and ideology, were in a minority when they came home to Colchester. And by the end of the 1630s, as John emerged as the most loyal and able of the king's political servants in Essex— "one of the best gentlemen of that county, and of the most eminent affection to the King," as the earl of Clarendon put it[3]—the Lucas family would become the prime focus for local discontent with the court regime.

John's meteoric political career, transforming him from a wealthy but obscure country gentleman into a prominent courtier, honored with a knighthood and ultimately a peerage, began during the taxation crisis of 1636. Led by the earl of Warwick's puritan elite, Essex had become the first county to mount large-scale resistance to the payment of ship money, a tax that the king had begun in 1634 to demand annually from each English county. Under Warwick's encouragement and protection, large sectors of the Essex population refused to pay and many local constables were declining to collect the tax. In

---

*While her sister Catherine engaged in long morning prayers in her closet, Margaret would wait impatiently outside.

this impasse, in November 1636, King Charles I appointed John Lucas to his first major political post, as high sheriff of Essex, with overall responsibility for collecting the county's ship money. This task John undertook with energy and success, imprisoning local constables and going out in person, with wagons and servants, to confiscate the possessions of nonpayers. When Warwick and his friends complained to the Privy Council, the king attended the session and had nothing but praise for his sheriff's ability and patriotism. By the time John laid down his commission in November 1637, opposition to the ship money had been successfully crushed and Essex would continue paying regularly, even as resistance grew through the rest of England.

At court, John was soon rewarded for his success and given fresh respon-sibilities. Knighted by the king on May 8, 1638, Sir John was soon after appointed to the prestigious and coveted post of gentleman of the privy chamber in the court of the eight-year-old Prince of Wales, the future King Charles II. Later that year he also took charge of the reception of the French Queen Mother—Marie de' Medici, mother to Charles I's queen, Henrietta Maria—after she arrived with 600 attendants at the port of Harwich, travel-ing to London to visit her daughter and son-in-law. The queen arrived at St. John's on a Saturday, to dine magnificently in the great hall, with her ladies-in-waiting, court officials, and bodyguard. After a night's rest, she spent Sun-day morning with her Roman Catholic priests in prayers, before an afternoon walking in the Lucases' gardens, where the summer flowers of the parterres were now over but the courtiers could still admire the lush, grassy avenues.[4] By the time Marie departed on Monday morning, fifteen-year-old Margaret Lucas had experienced an inspiring re-creation in her own home of all the refined manners and grand ostentation of the royal court that her family admired and emulated.

But such demonstrations of loyalty to king and court could only increase further the local animosity against the Lucases. John had already alienated much of Essex, including the earl of Warwick's powerful faction, during the ship money crisis. Now, entertaining the Catholic Queen Mother and appoint-ing conforming Laudian clergymen to the churches of Colchester, he was also gaining an undesirable reputation as "a favourer of Popery."[5] His success at court also marked him out as part of the ruling regime widely held responsible for the current economic recession, which had decimated the local textile industry, leaving many clothworkers in Colchester and the surrounding towns unemployed and destitute, facing starvation as a series of failed harvests in the late 1630s raised the price of grain. Many people were now eager for revenge, and in the spring of 1640 came the first in a series of reprisals against the hated Lucases.

The Colchester saltpeter men—authorized to enter private property to dig in barns and out-buildings for the dung-impregnated earth from which this essential ingredient of gunpowder was manufactured—arrived at St. John's in March, while the Lucases were away in London. Headed by an alderman of the town, the saltpeter men ignored all the other buildings in Colchester and stayed for four months at St. John's, insulting the servants and taking all possible opportunities to do damage, breaking down doors, and spoiling the family's stores of corn and salt-fish.[6] John was furious and hounded them through the courts, but the incident was only a pale foreshadowing of the violence that was to come two years later as law and order broke down in the months leading up to the Civil War.

Meanwhile King Charles I's religious policies had finally involved him in war with the Scots, who refused to accept Archbishop Laud's Anglican church reforms. The years 1639 and 1640 brought two short wars—short because of the Scots' superior training and the gross inadequacies of the English army: raw conscripts, inadequately fed, badly armed (some had only bows and arrows), and mutinous, commanded for the most part by aristocratic amateur officers without military experience or commitment to the king's cause. Although they achieved worse than nothing for the English as a whole, the wars were important for Margaret because they brought her two brothers back from the Netherlands to fight for their king. Charles Lucas, after just two years' service, had already gained the reputation of a hero for his part in the siege of Breda where, amidst the bloody slaughter of the Dutch army's final assault on the town, he was one of the first two men to fight their way through the breach in the walls. In June 1639, he was knighted by King Charles I for his part in the first Scots war (though this was so short he had seen no actual fighting); then, in the second war of 1640, he served as a captain in the regiment his brother Thomas commanded as colonel. Though raised for service in Ireland, the regiment was first used against the Scots, marching northwest into Lancashire, half unarmed, to face a rumored invasion force. Meanwhile the Scots actually invaded in the east, routing their enemies ignominiously at the Battle of Newburn—"never so many ran from so few," the English lamented[7]—before taking the abandoned Newcastle-upon-Tyne unopposed on August 30. Thomas and Charles were now employed in policing the transport of the £25,000 per month ransom that the Scots had demanded until a permanent peace treaty could be negotiated in London. The two brothers would remain in the North until the summer of 1641, when Parliament, fearing the troops' loyalty to the king in the growing political tension, ordered the army to be disbanded. Thomas finally went to Ireland, where he had already been appointed commissary-general of the horse to the army in January 1640. Here he would soon also take on a leading role in government, as a member of the Irish Privy Council. Meanwhile, Charles moved to London with other unemployed army captains to form the "reformadoes," an informal bodyguard for the king as political unrest increased towards war.

The Scots wars had been expensive and in 1640 Charles I had finally been forced to call Parliament for the first time in eleven years. Two elections took place only months apart in 1640, for the king had dismissed his first Parliament after only three weeks of business for its opposition to his political policies, and then, in desperate need of funds, had been forced to call another. Around the Lucases in Essex, the earl of Warwick's anticourt electioneering was in full swing. Puritan ministers preached from their pulpits in his support, and Warwick used his position as commander of the local militia to put pressure on the voters. All the MPs elected for the county and its boroughs were members of Warwick's party and, once arrived in Westminster, the Essex members spearheaded the anticourt program of the new Parliament—which came to be known as the Long Parliament as it survived undissolved for eighteen years. For like its predecessor, the so-called Short Parliament, this assembly again demanded that the king redress their political and religious grievances suffered during the eleven years when Charles I had ruled without them. Appointing committees to examine a wide range of issues and draw up proposals, Parliament also commenced a determined attack on the king's principal advisers, charging the earl of Strafford and Archbishop Laud with high treason and imprisoning them in the Tower of London. (Laud in particular had been denounced in the House by one of the Essex members as a "sty of pestilent filth that hath infected the state."[8]) In March 1641 the trial of Strafford began, and in May, when Parliament uncovered a court plot to march the northern army to London and seize power for the king, the earl was hurriedly convicted and executed. In Essex on May 12, the crowds of sightseers returned home from the London execution crying jubilantly, "His head is off! His head is off!"[9]

Amidst the political upheavals, normal government and law enforcement were beginning to break down. Crowds rioted against Roman Catholics, Laudian Anglicans and the supporters of the king's court, and the Lucas family again became a target for violence. On May 13, the day after the earl of Strafford's execution, an organized crowd of about a hundred gathered in Colchester at the blowing of a horn, before marching out to the nearby heath of Rovers Tye, where they tore down and burned the fences of the Lucases' new enclosures and destroyed their brick kilns. Twice more that month the horns blew, summoning the mob to local heaths where more of the Lucases' enclosures were destroyed. Witnesses talked of numberless fires that could not be counted, of

Lucas servants attacked, and of rioters who "wished heartily that Sir John Lucas had been there for they would have used him worse and would have burnt him or ended him."[10]

In London, the political conflict was now escalating towards war. Parliament, angered at the king's opposition to its reforms, was becoming more extreme in its demands, and in January 1642, when Charles I attempted to arrest its five most fractious members, the London militia intervened and, under puritan command, formed a guard for Parliament. As armed conflict threatened between this militia and the king's reformadoes, the royal family left the capital and both sides began to recruit armies.

In Essex, the Lucas family was surrounded by their enemies' preparations for war. Where John Lucas, recruiting for the king's wars against Scotland two years before, had found only unwilling conscripts, volunteers now rushed to serve in Parliament's army. Fired by their "zeal to Parliament and love to the Earl of Warwick," they desired to thwart "the hellish designs and actings of a malignant party" that intended to "deprive us both of religion and laws and . . . reduce us to a condition no less miserable than slavish."[11] Throughout the summer of 1642, Warwick's party raised and drilled their troops, collected money and arms, supervised the new fortifications being built around Colchester, and disarmed local Roman Catholics and other enemies of Parliament. Puritan clergy denounced the king's ungodly government, while local Laudians who preached against Parliament were rapidly silenced and imprisoned. By contrast the Essex royalists, lacking the organization and popular support of Warwick's party, achieved nothing of importance, and at St. John's John Lucas began to make his own private arrangements for supporting the king militarily.

By Sunday, August 21, his preparations were complete. A final shipment of arms had arrived at St. John's on the Friday, and there were good horses in the stables, with their saddles and other equipment. John was planning to ride north to Nottingham, where the king was mustering his army, and ten of the Lucas family servants were to go with him as soldiers. A local Laudian vicar named Thomas Newcomen, having administered an oath of loyalty and secrecy to the men, was to accompany them as chaplain. But the preparations had been observed in Colchester. And, as rumors spread through the town putting the people into a ferment of fear and anger, the mayor was alerted. When, around midnight on the Sunday night, John and his men slipped secretly out of a back gate into the fields around St. John's, they found the militia waiting for them. Outnumbered, they retreated back inside while the watch raised the alarm.

What happened next can never be exactly established, for the two rival accounts, royalist and parliamentarian, differ substantially over the facts. Bruno Ryves, author of the royalist pamphlet *Mercurius Rusticus*, published at

Oxford in the summer of 1643, portrayed Colchester's parliamentarian governors as actively stirring up the local population, lighting the warning beacons
and sending horsemen out to neighboring towns (where John Lucas had
enforced the unpopular ship money payments in 1637) to call their followers
to arms. By contrast Colchester's mayor, Thomas Wade, reporting the business
to Parliament immediately after the event, played down any official involvement, emphasized his own efforts to defuse the tension, and distanced his officials from "the rude sort of people" he saw as solely responsible for the
"tumults" that now ensued.*

But however assembled, huge crowds of men, women, and children certainly now gathered in the dark outside the walls of St. John's. The royalist
Ryves estimated there were at least 2,000 (he also mentions two cannon
"brought to make a battery") while the mayor, writing fresh from the heat of
the action, put the number at 5,000, in addition to 400 or 500 soldiers. Fearful
of the wild crowds who "regarded us not, no more than they do a child,"
Mayor Wade now ordered his militia troops, originally called out to oppose the
Lucases, to turn and protect St. John's from the people. But as dawn came the
angry mob broke through.

Mayor Wade passed over the ensuing violence rapidly. "The rude sort of
people broke into Sir John's house and seized upon his horses . . . also they
have found much armour," he reported to Parliament, "and nothing would satisfy these tumultuous people but that Sir John Lucas, his mother and servants
must be committed" to prison. However, according to Bruno Ryves it was a
more horrific story: the mob attacked the parson, Newcomen, tearing the
clothes off his back, beating him with cudgels, and debating whether to kill
him by drowning or stoning. Twenty men rushed into the bedchamber of
John's wife, Anne, and held a sword at her breast, demanding to know where
the arms were hidden. The mob seized the Lucases and carried them off to
prison "attended with swords, guns, and halberds." On the way Elizabeth
Lucas, faint and breathless, was not permitted to rest but was hurried on by
the "rude rabble" while one, mounted on horseback, struck at her head with
his sword and would have killed her if another man's halberd had not crossed
the blow. The Lucases and Newcomen ended up imprisoned in the town's
common jail, only too glad to be safe from the mob, but their home was
unprotected as the wild crowds turned to plunder. The silver and gold plate of

---

*Though written much later than the mayor's account, Ryves's need be regarded as no more unre-
liable: it was based on published newsletters from the time and on the personal testimony of John Lucas's
chaplain Newcomen, and possibly also John himself. Both accounts are strongly biased by their writers'
political interests.

the house, the chests of money, jewels, books, and papers, and all the ordinary household furniture—linen, wool, brass, and pewter—were carried away. "All is prize that comes to hand," wrote Bruno Ryves, "a few hours disrobe the house of that rich furniture that had adorned it many years." The mayor despaired of enforcing any order. "I ver[il]y believe . . . we could not suppress them, unless they be killed, they are so resolute," he wrote to Parliament, begging for help.

Throughout Monday, August 22—the day that, in Nottingham, King Charles I formally raised his standard, declaring war on Parliament—the Colchester crowds raged against the long-hated Lucases. And Bruno Ryves (though not Colchester's mayor, whose report was already written) tells of the destruction wrought by the mob when they finally found nothing left to steal from St. John's. While the town's shops remained shut up, the rioters tore up the Lucases' deeds and legal papers, broke the windows, beat down the doors, spoiled the gardens and walks, and even demolished walls, attempting to pull down the house. At St. Giles's Church, just outside the great gatehouse, they opened the Lucas family vault and stabbed through the coffins with their swords and halberds. Ranging further afield, they drove off the cattle, and tore down the fences and killed the deer in the deer park at Greenstead. Finally the mayor set militia guards upon St. John's and on the jail where the Lucases were shut up. But the militia too were locals with no good will to the family—"as forward as the people to drink their blood" as Ryves put it. And further loot, at first neglected as insignificant, was now carried off from St. John's, most of it to the guards' own houses, according to Ryves.

For the next three days the Lucas family remained in jail while the rioters moved off to attack other hated "malignants," either royalists or Roman Catholics. The spark at St. John's had ignited a train of uncontrolled violence that now spread through East Anglia, terrifying even its parliamentarian rulers. Only on Thursday, when two MPs of Warwick's faction arrived from London, were the beginnings of order restored. A crowd estimated at between 5,000 and 6,000 gathered in the marketplace outside the jail to hear Parliament's orders read out. John Lucas's actions in raising troops for the king were declared high treason: he and parson Newcomen were to be taken to London to stand trial; on the following Monday, John would be called into the House of Commons to be formally charged before being imprisoned in the Tower of London. Meanwhile the assembled multitude were thanked "for the good service they had done" to their country in preventing John from reaching the king. Parliament saw the crowds as honest, peaceable people whose violence had resulted from their fear, and only begged them, now that their service was done, to return to their homes and restore the property they had appropriated. No one was ever to be prosecuted for involvement in the riots.[12]

On Friday, August 26, the day that John Lucas and parson Newcomen departed for London, the women of the Lucas family were finally released from jail to discover the devastation of their old home, described by Colchester's mayor as "much rifled, and more ruinated."[13] Little was left but bare walls—in places even they had been pulled down by the frenzied mob—but the ever-competent Elizabeth Lucas at once set out to repair what damage she could. Finding Parliament's order that the people should restore her goods to be ineffectual, she petitioned the House of Lords, asking that she and her servants be empowered to enter the houses of suspected looters and reclaim her possessions. But Parliament, more sympathetic to the Colchester townspeople than to the Lucases, never replied.[14]

Nineteen-year-old Margaret was profoundly impressed by her mother's energy and resource in the face of adversity, seeing in them evidence of Elizabeth's truly "heroic spirit, in suffering patiently where there is no remedy, or to be industrious where she thought she could help." Margaret also felt deeply shocked by the indignity suffered by the mother she so respected. She had grown up in a courtly family culture, hostile to dissenters and puritans and to the common townspeople who were perpetually infringing her family's rights. Now, in response to the rioters' violence, these feelings intensified into hatred of the rude, uncivilized, "barbarous people" who had treated her mother so cruelly and who, she thought, "would have pulled God out of Heaven, had they had power, as they did royalty out of his throne."[15] Fear of the mob, of the uncontrolled violence of the lower orders, would flavor much of Margaret's later writing, as would a basic belief in the fundamental instability of all political systems. Conflict and war were inevitable, essential properties of all things, always ready to destroy any order that could be created, whether in the man-made political sphere or in the natural world itself, she would write.*

Probably Elizabeth Lucas and her family did not remain long in Colchester, where more violence threatened and many previously royalist gentry,

---

*Whether Margaret herself was actually present during the riot at St. John's is not clear from the surviving sources. The mayor's report mentions only one, unnamed sister of John Lucas, who could have been Margaret or her sister Anne, who also remained unmarried at home. However, the mayor's report may well be unreliable. In the hurry of events and with the Lucases accompanied by their servants, he could easily have failed to notice some of the less significant family members present, and this is suggested by a contemporary newsletter (*Thomason Tracts*, E 114 [34]), which reports that there were "sisters" in the plural present, as well as "children" not mentioned by the mayor—probably John's daughter Mary, and his son John, who died before reaching adulthood.

terrified of the mob, now rushed to demonstrate their loyalty to Parliament by donating money and plate to the war effort.[16] London offered security. Here the Lucases could stay in their own town house or with Margaret's married sisters—Catherine Pye in Covent Garden, or Mary Killigrew, whose courtier husband still had lodgings at Whitehall. As the only close relatives who would become parliamentarians, Mary and Peter Killigrew were to provide useful protection for the Lucases in the coming Civil War, and Elizabeth Lucas was living with them at Whitehall by 1644.[17]

After a month imprisoned in the Tower, John Lucas was released at the end of September 1642 on bail of £40,000, with the conditions that he remain in London and report to Parliament when summoned. From London the reunited Lucas family watched the progress of the war, and of Margaret's two brothers already caught up in it. Thomas Lucas, in Ireland with his wife and children, was still convalescing after having received a dangerous head wound at the Battle of Kilrush, near Ross, in March; back in England Margaret's brother Charles was a lieutenant colonel in the king's cavalry. He had already suffered minor wounds at Powick Bridge, just south of Worcester, and on October 23, 1642, he would fight at Edgehill, the first major pitched battle of the war. Here he exhibited the qualities of command that would make him one of the outstanding cavalry officers of the war: after the royalists' first victorious charge, Charles Lucas was one of only two commanders who kept control of his troops, rallying them to attack the enemy's flank, cutting off four regiments, while the rest of the king's horse, with their general Prince Rupert, rode on unstoppable to the parliamentarian baggage train and took to pillage, only rejoining the battle three hours later. As darkness drew on there was no clear victor, but the next day, when the parliamentarians retreated to Warwick, the king marched on London, to be stopped only six miles short of the city by a force of the London militia and volunteers some 24,000 strong. The two armies faced each other all day before the royalists withdrew. It was mid-November and the king now retreated to winter in Oxford, billeting his troops in the surrounding country. Oxford was to be the royalist headquarters for the remainder of the war.

Meanwhile Queen Henrietta Maria had been in the Netherlands since the spring, gathering money, soldiers, and arms for her husband's cause. In February 1643, she finally returned to England, landing in Yorkshire, where a separate northern army was fighting for the king, commanded by the earl of Newcastle. After a few months' wait while the royalist armies cleared her route of enemy forces, she set out to march south to Oxford at the head of her army of 5,000 infantry and fifty companies of cavalry, with cannons, mortars, and 250 wagons loaded with money, arms, and ammunition. To Margaret, keeping up with the news in London, the queen seemed the sort of heroic figure she herself aspired to be. Stories were told of Henrietta Maria's courage during bombardment by parliamentarian warships in Yorkshire (when she returned under fire to rescue a favorite lapdog). Her role as military leader in the north, consulting with the earl of Newcastle and his generals on strategy, was widely reported in the newsbooks. As she marched through England mounted on horseback at the head of her troops, eating her meals in the fields and mixing affably with her men, feeling like Alexander the Great and calling herself "her she-majesty generalissima over all"[18]—even capturing a parliamentarian town on her way—Henrietta Maria was living through a noble ideal that was close to Margaret's heart. The theme of the heroically spirited woman called from her peacetime occupations to aid her general-husband was one Margaret would later treat in her play *Bell in Campo*. The play includes a humorous version of Henrietta Maria's lapdog story and ends with the lady-general's triumphal entry into her home city, just as Henrietta Maria had entered Oxford in July 1643, greeted by jubilant crowds, peals of church bells, and orators reciting speeches and poems in her praise. In the summer of 1643, hearing that the queen lacked the full complement of ladies-in-waiting to attend on her in Oxford, Margaret was inspired with "a great desire" to become one of her maids of honor.[19]

In her autobiography Margaret would present this ambition to join the court as a loyal desire to serve the royalist cause. But court service was also the only career open to a young woman of her class, and the only way to gain an independent life and identity outside her family home. It was an opportunity to mix with the leading people of the day, to make a good marriage and—especially important for Margaret—"to learn wisdom, and to improve my understanding," as Mistress Bashful, the protagonist of Margaret's autobiographical play *The Presence,* explains. As Margaret admitted, it was her great chance to go "from home to see the world abroad."[20] And she begged her mother to allow her to go to Oxford.

Margaret's brothers and sisters objected to her plan "by reason I had never been from home, nor seldom out of their sight." Their baby sister, they thought, was too "inexperienced in the world": overprotected, she would not know how to behave herself in society and might damage her reputation by imprudence at court. But Margaret was determined and ignored their opinion. Bringing all her considerable powers of persuasion to bear, she recalled later, "I wooed and won my mother to let me go; for my mother, being fond of all her children, was desirous to please them, which made her consent to my request."[21]

In London, Margaret's brother John and her brother-in-law Sir Edmund Pye were also preparing to go to Oxford. Neither of them had much to lose:

for his earlier attempt to join the king, Parliament had declared John a "malignant," and all his property was now liable to confiscation. Pye too, though he had not yet acted publicly against Parliament, was facing substantial financial losses as Parliament introduced new systematic taxes to fund their war effort, previously supported by voluntary contributions alone.[22] Both men left London for Oxford during the summer, and it was probably in their company, with her sister Catherine Pye, her maid, Elizabeth Chaplain, and John's wife, Anne, that Margaret traveled secretly to join the queen.[23] Elizabeth Lucas, however, stayed in London, living with the Killigrews in Whitehall. By conforming to the parliamentary regime and paying the war taxes demanded, she retained possession throughout the war of the estates she had inherited from her husband. While her three sons, as notorious malignants, lost all their lands to the parliamentary sequestrators, Elizabeth continued to receive her normal income and was able to support her family financially—including now the substantial expenses of a daughter living at court.[24] But by remaining in London, Elizabeth was now parting with her youngest daughter for the last time. Margaret, leaving home at the age of twenty, would never see her mother again.

Chapter Four

A Lady at Court, 1643–1645

*B*y the summer of 1643 the university town of Oxford had become a well-fortified military stronghold. The old city walls had been strengthened and new ramparts built to the most modern design, mounted with cannon and sentries, making a line of defenses three miles long, enclosing all the colleges and halls. The rivers had been dammed to flood the low-lying meadows outside the walls, and beyond the defense works buildings and trees were destroyed to create a "free-fire" zone, with no cover for an approaching enemy. While the troops stationed in the town mustered and drilled in New Parks, just behind Wadham College, the king's main field army camped in the countryside beyond.

Few of the university's students and dons remained—parliamentarians had fled to London at the king's approach, while royalists had joined the army as soldiers or chaplains, and many students had decided to stay at home—and the vacated university buildings were taken over and adapted to new purposes. Sword blades were forged in Gloucester Hall and cannon cast in St. Mary's College. The medieval cloisters and tower of New College became the king's magazine, storing guns, bullets, powder, and match; the big guns of the field artillery stood in Magdalen College Grove at the east end of town, with their craftsmen's workshops nearby. Many of the outer college walls formed part of the town's defense works, patrolled by sentries; college rooms were converted into guardhouses and billets for soldiers, while the tallest of the college towers became watch posts constantly manned by lookouts. In the middle of Oxford the recently built Schools Quadrangle, center of the university's formal teaching, was transformed into a complex of workshops and storehouses. Smiths repaired weapons in the tower; the army's boots and clothing were produced in the music and astronomy schools; drawbridges for the fortifications were built in the rhetoric school; and in the law and logic schools grain and cheese were stored in case of siege.

Oxford was not only a military headquarters: it was also the new royal capital of England, home of the court and center of government for the parts of the country still under the king's control. And Christ Church, Oxford's largest and richest college, provided the grandiose settings needed for this official life. Here Charles I had his court in the palatial lodgings of the deanery while government councils met in the audit house and chapter house. Grand formal occasions, such as the king's reception of foreign ambassadors and his inaugural speech to the Oxford Parliament, took place in the college's great hall amidst a wealth of carved and gilded woodwork, fine portraits, and stained glass windows. Here too the king often dined in state, as he had at Whitehall before the war, displaying his majesty to his many subjects who assembled to watch. Soldiers, courtiers, and government ministers all gravitated to this center of military and political power, and the spare rooms in Christ Church and the nearby colleges and town houses were all filled with important officials who worked, ate, and slept in these often cramped conditions.

Further afield, organs of government less dependent on the king's presence found homes in other university settings. At New Inn Hall the royal mint converted silver ore and the colleges' gold and silver tableware into coins to finance the war effort. The London law courts, summoned by the king to Oxford, met in the university schools; the Exchequer managed government finance at Lincoln College. Oxford's university printer was now employed in publishing government proclamations and propaganda, while John Birkenhead, a fellow of All Souls College, had turned journalist and was producing the royalists' weekly news-sheet, *Mercurius Aulicus*.

All the usual trappings of government and court life had been re-created in Oxford and the town was hugely overcrowded, with around half as many people again as its normal peacetime population. In addition to court, government, and military personnel, there was a host of private civilians. Artists, craftsmen, musicians, and London actors whose employment depended on the patronage of court society; royalist parish clergy, bishops, and Cambridge dons dismissed from their jobs in the Parliament-controlled Southeast; the many royalist nobility and gentry who, like the Lucases, could not comfortably remain at home—all, as a royal proclamation put it, "forced hither from their own inhabitation by the insolency and tyranny of the rebels."[1]

Some, wealthy and well-placed, rented luxurious suites of college rooms and consumed fine wines and other delicacies brought up the River Thames from London. But others, who had fled hurriedly, leaving all their possessions behind, lived in poverty. "We, that had till that hour lived in great plenty and great order, found ourselves like fishes out of the water and the scene so changed that we knew not at all how to act," recalled Lady Anne Fanshawe of her own arrival in Oxford, after her father's house had been plundered by Parliament. "For from as good houses as any gentleman of England had we come to a baker's house in an obscure street, and from rooms well furnished to lie in a very bad bed in a garret, to one dish of meat and that not the best ordered; no money, for we were as poor as Job, nor clothes more than a man or two brought in their cloak bags . . . For my own part I began to think we should all like Abraham live in tents all the days of our lives." Margaret was one of the luckier ones, receiving generous funds from her mother in London so "that I was in a condition rather to lend than to borrow, which courtiers usually are not, being always necessitated by reason of [the] great expenses courts put them to."[2]

Civil War Oxford was a place of violent contrasts. In shops and markets business went on as usual, while military parades drilled in front of the king and cavalry bands galloped in and out of town. Amidst the business of war, king and courtiers played tennis or rode out to Woodstock to hunt the deer. In the colleges, society ladies with their children, servants, and lapdogs, rubbed shoulders with the few grave scholars and divines who still remained in these all-male monastic institutions, and there was inevitably friction: "I will not say you are a whore; but get you gone," the elderly president of Trinity College reproached one young lady. Students, however, were fascinated by the society beauties who appeared wearing only loose, informal robes—"half dressed, like angels," as John Aubrey remembered fondly.[3] But as polite society met in the gardens to stroll and chat or sing to the music of a lute, beyond the college walls the unruly troops brawled and dueled, and the full rigors of military discipline were enforced with gibbet and firing squad. Wounded soldiers passed through the streets on their way to treatment, as enemy captives were herded into makeshift prisons in the town's churches and lunatic asylum. Oxford, previously renowned for its health and beauty, was now filthy from overcrowding, its streets turned to quagmires by the constant traffic, or blocked by pigs and their sties. The open streams that supplied the town's fresh water were clogged with rubbish—offal from butchers' slaughterhouses, excrement thrown out of houses, and dead dogs and horses left to lie—and in the heat of summer, epidemics broke out. Smallpox was common, killing rich and poor alike, and typhus, imported from the field army in 1643, was followed the next year by the plague. Yet as corpses were flung into hasty graves on Jews' Mount, the full ceremonial and refined culture of court life were elaborately kept up in the separate households of the king and the queen in Christ Church and Merton College.

At Merton, Queen Henrietta Maria was surrounded by the great aristocratic ladies who had served her in London before the war. Duchesses and
countesses filled the college's best rooms with their fine furnishings brought
from home, while the queen herself took over the lodgings of the warden—a
Parliament man who was now in London. Here the rooms were adapted to recreate the formal hierarchy of physical space and social order that etiquette
demanded for royalty.

Courtiers and visitors first entered the guard chamber, where the
yeomen of the guard controlled admission to the more important rooms
beyond. Servants could go no further, and here Margaret would leave her
maid, Elizabeth Chaplain, while Margaret herself proceeded into the presence chamber. In this room she and the other maids of honor spent much of
their day, sitting on benches against the side walls waiting for orders from
the queen, while courtiers and visitors came and went, wanting to see Henrietta Maria or her ladies. At the upper end of the room was a raised dais
overhung by a cloth of state where the queen, seated on a throne, formally
received important visitors, with her ladies-in-waiting standing in a semicircle behind and around her. On the dais too, a table would be set up in the
middle of the day, where the queen dined in public, watched from the
room's lower end by an assembled audience of visitors. Before the war,
Charles I had made the English court the most formal and ceremonious of all
Europe, and the dining queen was attended with the full rituals of cupbearer,
carver, and sewer, while none but those serving the meal was permitted to
step on the carpet placed under and around the table. At such formal dinners
Margaret and the other maids again stood round in the courtly semicircle,
adding to the queen's grandeur. For Margaret, this was the job's greatest
physical demand, for the hours spent standing still in Henrietta Maria's presence often left her feeling faint and shaky.[4]

Beyond the presence chamber lay the privy chamber, where the maids of
honor could go only when specially called for by the queen. Here Henrietta
Maria sat in semiprivacy during the day, attended by her ladies of the bedchamber, many of them England's greatest noblewomen. Gentlemen ushers
controlled access to the room, admitting only the most socially distinguished
of visitors to the queen's presence—women had to be baronesses or above,
and men at least privy councillors, if they were to enter without the queen's
special permission. Beyond this again was the inner sanctum of the withdrawing chamber, where Henrietta Maria received only her closest advisers and
friends—her Catholic priests, and favorites such as Lord Jermyn and the
countess of Denbigh who, as mistress of the robes, had been Henrietta Maria's
chief lady-in-waiting for over a decade. Beyond this again was the bedchamber,

entered only by the queen's most intimate personal attendants, the ladies and women of the bedchamber.

The daily routine of the court began early, with pages and serving women cleaning the rooms and lighting fires. At nine, the gentleman ushers opened up the presence chamber, where they would supervise all day. Margaret, having been helped at her dressing by Elizabeth Chaplain, would arrive with the other maids of honor some time before eleven in the morning, when they were to join the whole court for morning prayers. The Catholic queen was keen for her ladies to follow her own religion and so, while Margaret and many others attended the Anglican rite, the court's inner circle who had converted to Catholicism joined Henrietta Maria for mass. Then Margaret and the other maids spent the rest of the day until supper in the presence chamber, with only a short break for their midday dinner.

It was only after dinner that the court really came to life, when the king came from Christ Church to spend the afternoons with his wife. Then crowds of courtiers, politicians, soldiers, and royalist gentlemen—drawn like moths to the glamour and power of the royal pair—transformed the warden's lodgings at Merton into a hothouse of political intrigue, military debate, news, rumor, and complex maneuvering for personal power and financial gain.

Oxford society was riven by faction. Headed by Charles I's nephew and general of the cavalry, Prince Rupert, the professional soldiers, trained in the wars in Germany and the Netherlands, resented the influence of the king's civilian advisers in what they saw as a purely military matter. Margaret's brother Charles was a member of this group, disliked by government ministers like the chancellor of the Exchequer, Sir Edward Hyde (the future earl of Clarendon), who favored a peaceful solution and urged the king to negotiate and make concessions.* Hyde and his party were close to Charles I's ear, but their desire to reestablish the king as a constitutional monarch rather than a despot brought them the distrust of the queen. "I fear that there are persons about you, who, at the bottom of their hearts, are not well disposed for royalty," she had already advised her husband. Henrietta Maria had her own favorites—her Catholic coreligionists and the polished, courtly gentlemen like Lord Jermyn whose company delighted her. She was an active politician and military strategist. Keeping up with all the latest news and corresponding reg-

---

*Writing his history of the Civil War, Hyde would leave a hostile portrait of Sir Charles Lucas as a man admittedly "very brave in his person, and in a day of battle a gallant man to look upon and follow; but at all other times and places, of a nature not to be lived with, an ill understanding, a rough and a proud nature." Charles, like Margaret, had a shyness and stiffness with strangers that could put people off, but he was loved by his friends for "the sweet generosity of his nature." A writer of poetry, he was certainly not as uncultured as Hyde asserts. (See Clarendon, *History*, IV, 386; Lloyd, *Memories*, 475.)

ularly with trusted army commanders like the earl of Newcastle, she had strong views and maintained them with vivacity—"I am astonished that you have not made another admiral," and "never consent to an accommodation [with Parliament], without my knowledge, and through me," are samples of how she advised the king.[5] She energetically advanced the interests of her own clique and, as her influence over her husband was well known, many came to her rather than the king with requests for political office, military command, or other favors. Attending on the queen, Margaret frequently observed the "great factions both amongst the courtiers and soldiers," but she later realized that she had been too young fully to understand the complex and devious machinations of all "their intrigues."[6]

Meanwhile, the court continued its prewar artistic life so far as conditions permitted. Poets like Sir John Denham and Abraham Cowley wrote satires against their puritan and parliamentarian enemies, while the poet laureate William Davenant and others, composed verse in praise of the queen. The fashionable painter William Dobson set up his studio in the High Street, producing vigorous portraits of Oxford's courtiers and soldiers—Margaret's brother Charles was among those who sat to him. Actors who had joined the king's army after Parliament closed the London theaters sometimes came into Oxford to perform plays for the court, and at Christmas and New Year they were joined by musicians, as Henrietta Maria kept up the prewar tradition of producing masques for the court's entertainment, where she and her ladies-in-waiting took the principal parts. However, the scale and grandeur of the proceedings were necessarily reduced from their London heyday. Some felt that the elegance of court life had been coarsened by the rough, military men of Prince Rupert's faction, yet the royal household continued to be denounced in the parliamentary newsletters as "a scene of voluptuousness, a stage of luxury and pride," where the queen "cared for nothing but playing with little dogs . . . and masquing, dancing, revelling."[7]

Margaret's duties in this new world were not arduous. The maids of honor were required not so much for any particular work as to dignify the queen by their attendance all day in the presence chamber—"where the state and honour of the Queen ought to be kept," the court's regulations specified.[8] All the more menial work of the court—bedmaking, cleaning, lighting fires, and emptying chamber pots—was done by the page boys and serving women, while the maids of honor performed only such simple tasks as fetching, ordering, passing messages, and accompanying Henrietta Maria when she walked in the college gardens. Sometimes they entertained the queen with their conversation, or with singing, dancing, or acting, but most of their time was spent just sitting on the side benches in the presence chamber. Here they joined the court's visitors in fashionable chitchat, gossip and news, in games of cards, or the delights of romance and flirtation, keeping some needlework or a book in reserve in case there was no company for conversation.

Yet Margaret found this life unbearable. After the freedom of home, her time and behavior were now closely regulated, supervised by the gentleman usher in the presence chamber and by the "mother of the maids," an older woman placed *in loco parentis* over the maids of honor. Her duties kept her always on public view, a torment for someone so shy, and left little time to pursue her childhood interest in writing. In the busy world of the court there was rarely any privacy. As the most junior of the ladies-in-waiting, Margaret probably shared even her bedchamber with another maid of honor, as her autobiographical play *The Presence* suggests. Here, when the new maid of honor Mistress Bashful arrives like Margaret at court, young, shy, and overawed, the other maids are appalled that she might share their bedroom.

"I was so joyed, when I heard you were allotted to be my chamber-fellow," says Mistress Wanton to her old friend Mistress Wagtail, "for I was so afraid of that clod of dull earth, the new-come fellow; for it is reported that she makes conditions not to be with such a chamber-fellow that sits up late, or hath much company."

"She shall not lie with me," says Mistress Quickwit hastily, "let her lie in the chamber of Mistress Self-Conceit."

"With me? By my troth, that shall not be," retorts Self-Conceit, "for shall I that have been here this dozen years, have the rubbish thrown into my chamber?"

"Why, then she must lie with the old Mother, there is no other place," Wanton concludes.[9]

Accustomed to being at the center of a loving, protective family, Margaret had now become just a tiny cog in the large, busy, expensive machine of the court, expected to fit into a culture that was completely alien to her. Around 200 personnel were normally employed in the queen's household, many with Margaret "above stairs," and the rest in more menial positions as cooks, laundresses, dressmakers, and others "below stairs." The establishment had a distinctly exotic character as most of the queen's musicians, priests, and below-stairs staff were French, brought from home by Henrietta Maria when she married Charles I in 1625.[10] The people of the court were strange and new to Margaret. Even the English Protestants were powerful personalities of unaccustomed types—characters such as Lord Jermyn, whose charming courtly surface hid a consuming personal greed and Machiavellian cunning;[11] or Jeffery

Hudson, the queen's dwarf, touchy and irascible under the constant baiting of the courtiers' hostile sense of humor.*

Chief among the personalities and presiding over them all was the queen herself. Henrietta Maria was a notable beauty with delicate features, dark eyes, and a clear complexion, combined with a slender form and graceful movements. Her taste for the French culture of *préciosité* set the tone of her court, with its fashion for pastoral idyll and platonic love.[12] Henrietta Maria was celebrated as the "Queen of Love," a major figure in the court's ideology, whose marriage to the king epitomized an ideal of pure, spiritual love between the sexes that would refine and civilize humanity. Women were placed on a moral and aesthetic pedestal—admired and loved by men for their virtue, intellect, and taste—and romantic courtship was now supposed to assume an esoteric character, as lovers debated the philosophical nature of love itself.**

Vivacious and witty, a lively conversationalist and brilliant raconteur, Henrietta Maria surrounded herself with kindred spirits—sparkling men and women whose rapid repartee entertained the queen but overawed the young Margaret Lucas. The courtiers were pleasure-loving aristocrats who spent their time and money in often reckless gambling. For the women it was cards—"one of the chief pastimes of our sex," Margaret noted—while the men also won and lost large sums on games of dice, tennis, even chess. Margaret, unskilled "in playing at cards, or any other games," could only remain on the edge of such groups.[13] Serious and shy, she felt out of place amidst the frivolity of the court. She had no skill in witty conversation, nor understanding of the complex rules of propriety that governed courtly socializing and love affairs. Alone in a strange new world, Margaret felt confused and afraid. Afraid of the men's flattering courtship, to which she had no idea how to respond— in *The Presence* the newly arrived Mistress Bashful can only stand silent as the men of the court come to greet her with kisses and overblown compliments. Afraid of the women's sharp criticism—"Lord! how simply she looks!"; "What a dull eye she has!"; "She has an unfortunate brow" are the immediate judgments the other maids pass on Bashful.[14] Afraid of the avid gossip of the court, which could ruin a woman's reputation forever—"so full of detraction the world is, that neither maids, wives, nor widows can escape their slandering tongues," Margaret observed, "and it is not only men that slander women, but one woman slanders another, indeed, women are the chief dishonourers of

---

*Though always called the queen's dwarf, Hudson was in fact a midget. He was a little over three feet tall.

**In reality, of course, sexual passion was not so easily vanquished, and platonic love was often a convenient cover for more conventional romance, as Margaret would point out in her later writings.

their own sex . . . by the[ir] reproaches of each other." And she also feared that her social inexperience could easily lead her into grave social blunders that might cost her her reputation, or at least bring her hurtful ridicule—although her autobiography offers no details of her mistakes, her play *The Lady Contemplation* contains the story of a naive new maid of honor who makes herself a laughing stock when she misunderstands the court's cliquish slang and ends up accusing one of the ladies of being a bawd or procuress.[15]

"I was like one that had no foundation to stand [on], or guide to direct me," Margaret recalled in her autobiography, "I durst neither look up with my eyes, nor speak, nor be any way sociable." Especially she "shunned men's company as much as I could." "It is a custom I observe that I never speak to any man before they address themselves to me, nor to look so much in their face as to invite their discourse," she would explain to her future husband.[16] Overcome by her shyness, she sat apart in the presence chamber with her eyes lowered in an attempt to avoid all notice, scarcely even listening to the conversations around her, attending only to the duties required of her by the queen.

But Margaret occupied a prominent position and could not escape attention. Soon the court's gossip reported her to be "a natural fool" and "an idiot" for her silence.

"She did not speak three words; nor can she speak twenty in order," Mistress Ill-favoured scornfully reports of the tongue-tied Bashful in *The Presence*.

"Prithee what is she?" demands Mistress Self-Conceit, "A mere mope; doth she never speak or discourse to you?"

"She hold a discourse!" Mistress Wanton exclaims. "She wants the capacity, she wants the capacity."

"Faith, she is fitter for a nunnery than a court," concludes Self-Conceit.[17]

"I rather chose to be accounted a fool than to be thought rude or wanton," Margaret would defiantly insist afterwards, but at the time the court's ridicule was deeply hurtful. Driven by her ambition and disregarding the advice of her family, she had got into a situation where she was desperately unhappy. "In truth, my bashfulness and fears made me repent my going from home," she confessed, "and much I did desire to return to my mother again, or to my sister Pye." Never too proud to admit her mistakes, she wrote to her mother, asking to be allowed to leave the court. But Elizabeth refused her request, explaining to Margaret that it would be a disgrace for her "to return out of the court so soon after I was placed."[18] Margaret had to remain and endure her unhappiness, and she now developed a lifelong distaste for the falsity of fashionable society, where "there is little to be learned, and worse to be heard," she would later write, "nothing . . . but prodigality, sloth, and falsehood." Her lists of the vices of the court were seemingly endless—"most commonly . . . faction, pride, ambition, luxury, covetousness, hate, envy, slander, treachery, flattery . . . oft-times covered with a veil of smooth professions."[19] And her play *The Presence* would form a biting satire on court life.

Meanwhile, Margaret found some consolation in her family. Her sisters Catherine and Elizabeth, and John's wife, Anne, were all based in or near Oxford with their husbands, and they sometimes came to court to see their youngest sister.* Brothers John and Charles also visited Margaret. Both now colonels in command of cavalry regiments based around Oxford, they told her of the battles they had fought in, explaining the formations and maneuvers, "by which relation," Margaret recalled, she could "see it in my brain as perfectly, as if the battle was pitched, and fought there." This was Margaret's closest experience of actual warfare. Though she saw occasional bodies of troops on the march, "I never saw an army together, nor any encounters in my life," she remembered, "neither have I the courage to look on the cruel assaults that mankind (as I have heard) will make at each other."[20] Her brothers' regular experiences in the cavalry, charging against infantrymen bearing steel-shod pikes up to eighteen feet long, while musketry fire with a range of 200 to 300 yards killed men and horses alike, the shot leaving an exit wound the size of a dinner plate, were left to Margaret's vivid imagination. Yet, she felt, though women rarely endured the horrors of the battlefield, they suffered as much in war as men, "not in their bodies, but in that which is far worse, in their minds." "Worthy men go to wars with joy, hoping to gain honour," she later wrote, "yet women depart from those friends with grief, for fear of their death, and in their absence they never enjoy a minute's rest or quiet." "It is more happy to be dead, than to live in fear," she added, before continuing into an extended metaphor of military dictatorship. "Fear is an absolute conqueror . . . plundering the mind of all content and happiness, banishing all hopes, and then inhabiting it only with the worst of passions, as with grief, sorrow and impatience, making despair governor thereof, [as] I have found myself, praying I may never be the like again." "Those that never had the sweetness of peace, or have not known the misery of war, cannot be truly and rightly sensible of either," she thought.[21]

In September 1643 Margaret's two brothers fought at the Battle of Newbury, where the royalists attempted to cut off the parliamentarian army from London. The battle was indecisive, with huge losses inflicted on both sides before the armies drew apart, but Charles Lucas distinguished himself. Commanding the royalist vanguard, he delayed the entire parliamentarian army

---

*Margaret herself could not leave court at any time without special permission from the queen or her Lord Chamberlain: Societies of Antiquaries, *Collection of Ordinances*, p. 347.

until the king's main force could arrive and join the battle. Though his horse was shot from under him and he received seven separate wounds, he remained on the field until the end of the day. As at Edgehill a year before, he kept control of his troops through the heat of battle, showing himself to be one of the best cavalry commanders of the war, perhaps matched only by Oliver Cromwell. His ability won the respect of his friends and enemies alike, and when the marquess of Newcastle, lord general of the king's army in the North, wrote to Oxford asking for a new lieutenant general of horse to command his cavalry, Charles Lucas was chosen. In November he left Oxford to march into Yorkshire.[22] As with her mother a few months earlier, it was to be a final parting for Margaret.

The Battle of Newbury had begun a change of mood for the royalists. When Margaret first arrived in Oxford in the summer, the war had been going well and the queen, fresh from her triumphant march south at the head of her reinforcements, was in high spirits. But the uncertainty, cruelty, and frequent reverses of war were debilitating. As disappointment grew, Oxford's rival political factions recriminated each other endlessly over military blunders, and soon Henrietta Maria was writing, "I am so weary not of being beaten, but of having heard it spoken of."[23] By the new year of 1644 the prospect was only getting bleaker as the Scots, having made an alliance with Parliament, invaded England. The king's northern army, commanded by the marquess of Newcastle, was outnumbered by around two to one but nonetheless advanced to meet the new enemy, and by the spring Margaret would be reading in Oxford's newspaper *Mercurius Aulicus* of her brother Charles's gallant exploits.[24] However, the real risk of defeat was obvious to all. As the marquess of Newcastle, threatened by a second parliamentarian army marching up from the Midlands, began to retreat south to York, the king dispatched a relief force under Prince Rupert in a desperate bid to save the Midlands and the North.

Oxford no longer felt a safe place to be. The outer walls of Merton formed part of the city's defenses, and Margaret and the queen's court daily saw the sentries on patrol beside their cannon, looking out over the flooded fields to the country beyond, where an enemy army might anytime appear and lay siege to the city. Henrietta Maria was in great personal danger from Parliament, who blamed the war and its political origins largely on her influence over the king and who had already charged her with high treason, offering impunity to anyone who would murder her. By April she was becoming really alarmed. More than six months pregnant, and suffering acute pains in her joints from rheumatic fever, she wanted to leave Oxford to take the waters in Bath and find some safety for the impending birth. The king was unwilling to part from his wife but at last, with the main parliamentarian field army advancing towards Oxford, he allowed her to go. On April 17 Margaret rode out of Oxford as part of the queen's retinue. For five miles the king and the two young princes, Charles and James, accompanied them. Then farewells were said, the king and others shed tears, and the queen's party of coaches departed under cavalry escort.

Four days later in Bath they found the remains of war—rotting corpses in the streets and disease spreading among the survivors. They did not stay, but continued west and south to Exeter. Here, amidst the garrison's preparations for an expected siege, the queen took over the aristocratic mansion of Bedford House and prepared for her lying-in. The French royal midwife came from Paris, and at the end of May the doctors finally arrived from London; Henrietta Maria, still waiting for the birth, was in terrible pain, thinking she was past her nine months. Finally, on June 16, she gave birth to a daughter but, partially blind and with a suffocating pain in her chest, the royal physicians thought she could not live long. Within a fortnight, however, as a parliamentarian army advanced to besiege Exeter, the queen saw that she must flee at once.

Later, stories related how, leaving her newborn baby in Exeter, Henrietta Maria rose from her bed and left the city in disguise, accompanied only by her medical adviser, her father confessor, and one of her ladies. Joined by Lord Jermyn, the dwarf Jeffery Hudson, and a favorite lapdog, they stayed in a hut three miles away for two days without food, hiding under a heap of litter while Parliament's soldiers marched by outside, swearing to carry the queen's head to London to claim the reward offered by the government. Then they walked through the mud to rendezvous with the rest of the court, who had slipped out of Exeter in various disguises to meet at a cabin in the woods in the middle of the night. Together they all fled westwards through Cornwall, the queen borne in a litter, until they reached the harbor of Falmouth. Here, on June 30, they embarked on a ship for France.

The sea voyage brought out the best of Henrietta Maria's great physical courage. Pursued by a parliamentarian warship firing shots that damaged the rigging, she dismayed her ladies by ordering the ship's captain to blow up the powder magazine if they should be overtaken, rather than allow them to be captured. Margaret, down in the ship's hold with the queen and her court for safety, was seasick and terrified with the rest of the ladies. This was just the sort of random danger she most feared, where "my friends, or my honour is not concerned . . . but only my life to be unprofitably lost."[25] Finally, driven on by a storm, they reached the coast of Brittany and were rowed ashore to a wild, rocky cove. Climbing up a dangerous cliff path, they came to a hamlet of poor fishermen's huts where the inhabitants at first took the royal court for pirates. As Henrietta Maria herself admitted afterwards, she must have looked more like a distressed wandering princess out of a romance than a real queen. For Margaret the experience had a lasting impact: fleeing heroic princesses, terrifying voyages, and mariners washed up on barren shores would all feature in the fiction and drama she wrote in later life.

Once Henrietta Maria's identity was known, she was warmly welcomed in France. The best physicians were dispatched from Paris by Anne of Austria— widow of Henrietta Maria's brother Louis XIII, and currently queen regent of France during the minority of her son, Louis XIV. Finding Henrietta still dangerously ill, with a breast abscess causing high fevers and great pain, the doctors unanimously prescribed the spa waters of Bourbon l'Archambault, and the royal party began to travel up the River Loire by gradual stages,[26] grandly entertained by local dignitaries. At Tours on August 18, the diarist John Evelyn watched the queen's state entry to the town, where soldiers, clergy, and populace turned out en masse to greet their fellow countrywoman. After formal speeches of welcome, the archbishop entertained Henrietta Maria at his palace for two days, where Evelyn called and "did my duty to her."[27] Thence, the queen's party continued southeast to Bourbon.

A spa town since Roman times, Bourbon l'Archambault was a quiet country resort, soon to be made fashionable by such courtiers of Louis XIV as the king's mistress Madame de Montespan, the playwright Racine, and the letter-writer Madame de Sévigné. An ancient, ruined château looked down over houses, chapels, and monasteries, at whose center a large square contained the open-air hot medicinal baths, "but nothing so neatly walled and adorned as ours [at Bath] in Somersetshire," thought John Evelyn when he arrived a month later and found the English queen still there.[28] Henrietta Maria, bathing regularly and attended by physicians who lanced her breast abscess, now began a slow recovery. By the end of September, though still too weak to walk unsupported, she was judged fit enough to travel to join the royal court at Paris; however at Nevers, just thirty miles north of Bourbon, she suffered a relapse and had to remain three weeks before continuing her journey.

Finally, on Saturday, November 5, 1644, the English court reached Paris. In the southern outskirts they met a welcome party, led by the queen regent and her six-year-old son, Louis XIV. The royals all descended from their carriages and embraced, Henrietta Maria was invited into the French king's coach, and then the whole procession, with marching soldiers at its head, turned around to make a grand state entry into Paris. At five in the evening as dusk drew in, Margaret, riding amongst the carriages of court and nobility at the column's rear, had her first sight of the city where she would live for most of the next four years.

Paris was Europe's largest city, with a population of more than a quarter of a million, most of it still contained within the medieval walls, although the suburbs were now rapidly spreading along the roads that led out into the country-side beyond. Riding north up the Rue St. Jacques, the royal cavalcade passed under a high gate tower into the walled city, where the grander stone buildings were liberally intermixed with half-timbered houses. Banners and cheering crowds lined the streets as they passed the university at the Sorbonne, surrounded by booksellers' shops, and crossed the Petit Pont onto the Ile de la Cité. On either side narrow medieval streets of craftsmen's shops and houses stretched to Notre Dame cathedral at the east end of the island, and to the center of government administration at the Palais to the west. Then, over the Pont Notre-Dame, they reached the North Bank, where the city's prosperous mercantile district centered on Les Halles, and where fashionable aristocratic society lived on the grand streets and spacious squares created some fifty years before, during the ambitious rebuilding program of King Henri IV. Turning left, the procession headed along the Seine, past Henri's Pont Neuf, towards the royal quarter at the western edge of the city. Here elegant modern noblemen's hotels clustered around the Louvre and the Palais Royal, where Anne of Austria had chosen to bring up her children in the stylish buildings created by Cardinal Richelieu about twenty years before. All the royal accommodation in the Louvre now lay vacant, and Henrietta Maria had been assigned a suite of rooms in the south wing. Crossing the moat on a drawbridge, the royal party passed through a gateway under the palace's east wing and entered a large courtyard. Behind and to the right, the medieval north and east wings were tall gothic buildings, dotted with tiny arched windows beneath gargoyles and conical roofs. Ahead and to the left, the courtyard was completed by more modern wings with regular facades in Renaissance style, lined with classical columns and statues. Here Henrietta Maria entered her magnificent apartments, the city's dignitaries made formal speeches of welcome, and then the French withdrew, leaving the English queen and her court to settle into their new home.[29]

With a generous income settled on her by the French, Henrietta Maria was now restored to the full splendor and ceremony of court life, with her normal complement of ladies-in-waiting, guards, footmen, and carriages. Her apartments, expensively decorated with colored marble, looked out southwards over formal gardens with cypresses, a fountain, and an aviary, all surrounded by a covered cloister. Here, amidst the distant sounds of the city and the bells of Notre Dame, the courtiers could take the air, looking out over the

River Seine towards the Abbey of St.-Germain-des-Prés and its surrounding suburbs on the opposite bank. Running westwards from the queen's apartments, parallel to the riverfront, a vast gallery some 2,000 feet long connected them with the palace of the Tuileries, where Paris's fashionable society met to walk in the gardens every evening.

In these rich surroundings Henrietta Maria's court became the continental headquarters for English royalism. Exiles and émigrés settled in Paris to be near their queen, congregating regularly at the Louvre to share news and plans. Henrietta Maria, though still physically and emotionally depleted after her illness, threw herself into schemes for aiding her husband. Seeking money and arms for the war, she sent ambassadors to the pope, the prince of Orange, and the duke of Lorraine, and herself petitioned the French statesman Cardinal Mazarin—but all without result.

In England the war had reached deadlock. In addition to the indecisive Second Battle of Newbury in October, both sides had suffered major defeats during the year. At Marston Moor near York in July, the combined forces of Parliament and the Scots had routed both the marquess of Newcastle's army and the force under Prince Rupert that had been sent to its relief; at a stroke, the king had lost control of the North. Then in September the royalists had achieved victory at Lostwithiel in Cornwall, cutting off the earl of Essex's entire army and forcing them to surrender. By winter, tired and dispirited troops were deserting from both sides, while their officers began to think the war could not be won militarily. As royalist and parliamentarian negotiators sat down together to discuss possible terms for peace, Henrietta Maria, worrying that the king would concede too much, wrote constantly with her advice and news and affection. She also sent what money she could, taken from her allowance from the French Crown, or raised by pawning her jewels.

As the new year of 1645 began, the winter's peace process ended in failure and the English war recommenced, while Margaret found herself more unhappy than ever. At first there had been relief: after the months of fear and war and travel, she had been glad to be settled in one place with the chance to repair her "totter'd and torn" state.[30] However, as the winter wore on, she became increasingly dispirited. Her brothers were still risking their lives in the war in England: during 1644 John had fought at Lostwithiel and Newbury while Charles had displayed his usual ability and courage at Marston Moor, charging the enemy repeatedly until his horse was killed under him and he was captured by Parliament.* Imprisoned in the Tower of London, he was

---

*A fate Margaret later vividly recreated in the fantasy life of the eponymous protagonist of her play *The Lady Contemplation*.

exchanged in December, and by the spring of 1645 he had returned to the war with an appointment as governor of Berkeley Castle.[31]

Distance of separation could only intensify Margaret's inherent fearfulness for her family, and she now felt even lonelier than she had in Oxford, where she had at least seen her brothers and sisters occasionally. In Paris the queen's court was becoming yet more alien, as Henrietta Maria—at home in the palace where she had been born, and surrounded by friends and family—fell back into her native language and habits. Margaret, unable to speak French and finding herself incapable of learning, became yet more isolated from the world around her, and for a while she was dangerously ill, as a "purging flux"— dysentery—brought her close to death. She was saved, she later acknowledged, only by the skill of Dr. William Davison, a Scotsman who was physician to the French king, as well as treating many of the English community in Paris.[32] Davison prescribed laudanum—a relatively modern drug, invented by the controversial Swiss physician and alchemist Paracelsus, whose original recipe mixed opium with gold and pearls and other luxuries. Davison, a committed Paracelsian, ordered Margaret to take up to four grains of the medicine in a pill of bread on an empty stomach at bedtime every night for a week, and she slept deeply and eventually recovered her strength. But mental well-being was more elusive, for Margaret remained lonely and depressed, not knowing when or how she would ever be able to return home to England.

Chapter Five

The Marquess and
the Queen, 1645

*I*t was one day in April 1645, while she was in attendance at court, that
Margaret first saw the man she would later marry. William Cavendish,
marquess of Newcastle, was newly arrived in Paris and had come to the Louvre to pay his respects to the queen. Court regulations required that marked
respect be shown to Newcastle, one of the lords of the king's Privy Council.
Margaret and the other ladies would all have stood up, as a man of no more
than average height—dressed in the fine silks and laces of fashion, with a neatly
clipped beard and moustache and thick auburn hair falling in curls to his shoulders—passed through the presence chamber, his broad-brimmed hat in his
hand, on his way to the private inner rooms beyond.[1]

Although she had never seen him before, Margaret would have known
Newcastle well by reputation, for he was one of England's wealthiest aristocrats, a prominent London courtier and enthusiastic patron of the arts who,
when the Civil War came, was made lord general in command of the king's
army in the North. However, he had not always been so grand. Born William
Cavendish* without any aristocratic title in 1593,[2] Newcastle was the son of a
Derbyshire knight, Sir Charles Cavendish, who was himself the youngest son of
the Tudor politician Sir William Cavendish and his wife, Elizabeth, best known
by her nickname, Bess of Hardwick. Bess was four times married and widowed
and, inheriting the estates of each successive husband, she amassed huge wealth.
Most of this, together with the grand houses she had built at Chatsworth and
Hardwick in Derbyshire, passed after her death to her favorite son, who later

---

*Often spelled *Candish* by contemporaries, indicating how it was commonly pronounced.

became earl of Devonshire. Meanwhile Bess's youngest son Charles (William's father), served as a soldier in Queen Elizabeth I's army in the Netherlands. Returning to England, he was knighted by the queen in 1582, and in 1591 he married well: Katherine Ogle was a wealthy heiress who would bring into the family vast estates in Northumberland as well as the title baron of Ogle. Now a rich man, Charles substantiated his importance in the Midlands by acquiring the sites for two great country houses: Bolsover Castle in Derbyshire, and Welbeck Abbey just a few miles away in Nottinghamshire. At both he began ambitious building programs, which would be continued after his death by his eldest surviving son and heir, William, the future marquess of Newcastle.[3]

The young William Cavendish had received a broad education, shared with his younger brother, Charles, to whom he would remain very close in adulthood. Together the boys learned the traditional feudal skills of horsemanship and fencing, as well as the modern Renaissance learning of history, politics, languages, literature, music, philosophy, mathematics, and the sciences. In the medieval tradition, they spent some time living with their noble relative, Gilbert, earl of Shrewsbury, as well as at home with their parents at Welbeck. By the age of twelve William was already fluent in French (he would also learn to read Latin and Italian), and in his midteens he went up to St. John's College, Cambridge.[4] A well-born young gentleman's time at university was intended more for social polishing than serious scholarship and so William, as was common, left without taking a degree to continue his education in London.

Here he joined the circle of young aristocrats around King James I's eldest son, Prince Henry, currently the head of a fashionable revival of medieval chivalry. Together the young men trained in horsemanship at the royal tiltyard at Whitehall, learning both jousting and the elaborate dancelike movements of the manège or dressage, which can still be seen today at the Spanish Riding School in Vienna. In 1610, when Henry was installed as Prince of Wales, William took a prominent role in the ceremonies, being knighted by the king, before displaying his jousting skills in the celebratory tournament that followed. The young prince died just two years later, leaving his brother Charles to become king, but the ideals of knightly accomplishment and personal valor that William had imbibed at Henry's court would last his lifetime. Riding and fencing remained his greatest passions, even in his seventies: by his daily practice in both, he developed his own original techniques and became one of the leading masters of his day.*

---

*His innovations in horsemanship he would publish in 1658 and 1667, but his fencing skills were a secret he would teach only to his own sons, and to a son of the duke of Buckingham, who, in medieval fashion, was entrusted to William to be educated with his own children at Welbeck.

Finally, in 1612, William's education was rounded off with a period of foreign travel with the diplomat Sir Henry Wotton. Wotton was going as ambassador to Savoy, taking a party of young aristocrats in his retinue to learn the higher points of official ceremonial and deportment, statecraft and diplomacy. As they traveled out through France, and then back via northern Italy, Switzerland, and Germany, William acquired not only social and political skills but also experience of continental architecture and the wide range of arts and sciences of which Wotton, a future provost of Eton College, was master.

Back in England, William went into politics, the essential and unavoidable—indeed the only—career for a man of his standing. Elected as member of Parliament for his father's local borough of East Retford in 1614, he became one of the "King's Men," the minority party in the House of Commons that sought to defend the privileges of the monarchy. In 1617, when his father died, he inherited the family estates in the Midlands, and soon after he married Elizabeth, the heiress of a wealthy Staffordshire gentleman, William Basset of Blore. Though the match was financially advantageous for both parties, it was also based on love. Elizabeth chose William in preference to a rival suitor and he became an affectionate husband: "dearest heart," his letters to her always began. In a marriage that lasted almost twenty-five years, the couple would have ten children, though only five survived to adulthood: Jane, Charles, Elizabeth, Henry, and Frances.[5]

His marriage had brought William substantial extra wealth and, with the Ogle inheritance from his mother, he became one of the richest men in England, owner of immense estates extending through the Midlands and Northumberland. His new importance had already been marked in 1619, when James I ennobled him as viscount Mansfield. More honors and political powers followed after the accession of Charles I in 1625, as William's continued support for the Crown's privileges against the demands of Parliament made him a popular and trusted man in the royal party. In 1626, court favor brought William the coveted post of lord lieutenant of Nottinghamshire: marking him out as the foremost man of his county, the job gave him supreme command of the local militia, as well as responsibility for the implementation of royal policy, and ultimate authority over the administration of law and justice in the region. In 1628 he was further rewarded with the title of earl of Newcastle, bringing him up to the same rank as his Derbyshire cousins the earls of Devonshire, all of whom were themselves also named William Cavendish.

Unusually among the men who rose to favor under Charles I, William was popular with his neighbors at home in the country as well as with the courtiers in London. He was in fact a hugely likeable man who took delight in pleasing other people—easy and affable in his manners, rarely standing on the ceremony his high social position allowed him. Performing his duties as lord lieutenant with conspicuous integrity (as well as a shrewd eye for public relations), he gained the trust even of his political opponents. His famously lavish hospitality at Welbeck won him the loyalty of the gentry and nobility not only in his home county of Nottinghamshire but through much of the North of England. "No man was a greater prince in all that northern quarter," the parliamentarian Lucy Hutchinson later recalled of these years.[6]

William loved his Midlands home life—his wife and children, his riding and fencing, and his hospitality to his neighbors—and unlike many Caroline courtiers he spent most of his time in the country. Here he enthusiastically continued his father's grandiose building program, employing two generations of the Smithson dynasty of architects, as well as painters, sculptors, and an army of craftsmen, to create two magnificent residences at Welbeck Abbey and Bolsover Castle. His passion for building—inherited from his father and his grandmother, Bess of Hardwick—was visually commemorated in Van Dyck's portrait, where a half-finished column in the picture's background represents William's continually ongoing projects.

Welbeck was the family's main home and here, in the 1630s, William's enthusiasm for the arts and sciences transformed an aristocratic household into a courtly learned academy and center of artistic patronage, which was probably second in the country only to the royal court at Whitehall. From London, composers and musicians—organists, viol-players, and lutenists—came to work at Welbeck, where William's own collection of over forty instruments included fifteen viols in varying states of repair: the bass viol and the elaborate variations or "divisions" improvised on it were his particular love in music. The philosopher Thomas Hobbes came to Welbeck too, explaining his theories of matter, motion, light, and sound to William and his younger brother, Charles, who also lived there. Charles was the family's serious scholar. His specialty was mathematics and the mathematical sciences, and he and the family's chaplain, Dr. Robert Payne, organized an extensive correspondence with the leading philosophers and mathematicians of both England and France—figures including Hobbes, Descartes, Marin Mersenne, William Oughtred, and John Pell. In this way the Welbeck household kept abreast of all the latest discoveries in the emerging sciences of astronomy, optics, and mechanics. Important new books were eagerly sought from booksellers—works such as Galileo's 1632 *Dialogo sopra i due massimi sistemi del mondo*, whose compelling arguments for the Copernican heliocentric system of astronomy would put its author under house arrest by the Catholic church. New mathematical theorems were researched and tested at Welbeck, lenses and telescopes were designed, and in the laboratory at Bolsover William and his chaplain, Robert Payne, performed violently impressive chemical reactions with saltpeter and brimstone.

In 1639 Payne's successor was the poet and playwright Jasper Mayne, an appointment reflecting William's long-standing literary interests more than any religious considerations.[7] William himself wrote both poetry and plays, and he was a generous literary patron, eagerly courted by such fashionable Caroline dramatists as James Shirley, John Ford, and Richard Brome. For almost twenty years he was a close friend of the poet laureate and playwright Ben Jonson, and the two men influenced each other's work. Jonson stayed at Welbeck and in 1631 he acknowledged William as "next to the King, my best patron." In 1634, when the poet, old and ill, was living in poverty, neglected by the court, William's continued generosity brought a more unqualified tribute: simply "my best patron."[8]

Established in such provincial grandeur, William began to desire some role of more national importance, and in 1633, seeking the king's notice, he entertained the court at Welbeck—"in such a wonderful manner and in such an excess of feasting as had never before been known in England," the earl of Clarendon recalled. The occasion included a dramatic entertainment written by Ben Jonson, and the whole cost William some £5,000, significantly more than the Lucas family's entire annual income. The following year he organized an even more magnificent affair. Both king and queen stayed for six days at Welbeck, diverted with feasting, hunting, and jousting displays, before riding out to Bolsover Castle for a daylong entertainment, again composed by Jonson. The bills this time amounted to some £15,000—including not only food, wine, and new household supplies but probably also preparatory building work, especially at Bolsover. Having exceeded any other English subject in his extravagance— "which (God be thanked) . . . no man ever after imitated," Clarendon commented—William had run heavily into debt in his bid for a position at court.

But it was not until four years later that this gamble finally paid off when, in 1638, against considerable competition from other aristocrats, William gained the post of governor of the Prince of Wales, in overall charge of the young royal's independent court at Richmond Palace, ten miles west of London on the River Thames. William would have known Margaret's brother John well during this time, for John too, in reward for collecting the Essex ship money, had won one of the coveted jobs in the eight-year-old prince's newly formed household. As governor, William spent a lot of time with Prince Charles, forming a close bond of affection that would last through their shared lifetime. He taught the young prince to ride, he took him to plays,* and he

---

*When William took the young prince to see one of his own comedies performed at Blackfriars, Charles was an appreciative audience, sending his governor the following short note: "My Lord, I thank

wrote a formal letter advising on the ideal education and character development for a future king.[9] With such guidance and companionship during three
formative years, the future King Charles II would be a very different man from
his serious and reserved father, Charles I. Easygoing and pleasure loving, ready
with an apt joke in any conversation, of bawdy humor and frequent oaths, at
once grand but approachable, doffing his hat to even the lowliest person, an
active participant in masculine sports and exercises, who was also notorious as
a ladies' man—all of these function equally well as descriptions of William and
Charles II. With all this social pleasantry, both men also shared a darker side: a
tendency to appear insincere and unfathomable precisely because of their surface charm, and a capacity to form violent and permanent grudges against
those who offended them.*

William's duties now kept him mostly in London, where he joined the cultivated circle of artists, writers, patrons, and collectors that centered on the
king and the queen. Yet he never fitted fully into court culture, distrusting the
more seasoned courtiers' faction-forming and competitiveness, while preferring a more masculine, martial ideal of nobility than the platonic love and *préciosité* that Henrietta Maria had made popular. His polite manners and
wholehearted loyalty, however, brought him the liking and trust of both monarchs, and when political crisis finally developed into war, his wealth and influence in the Midlands and North made him, as Clarendon recorded, "one of the
most valuable men in the kingdom."[10]

For the Scots War of 1639, William lent £10,000 to the king and raised a
troop of cavalry at his own cost, composed, Clarendon noted, "of the best gentlemen of the North" who had volunteered from their personal allegiance to
William.[11] And when the Civil War began in the summer of 1642, it was this
power to recruit men by his own popularity that brought William his appointment as lord general in supreme command of the royalist army in the North—
an army that he had made into an elite force of some 8,000 prime soldiers by
December. William himself had neither formal training as a soldier nor any
experience of real combat, and so he appointed experienced veterans from the
wars on the Continent as his immediate deputies.**

---

you for the play. I like it so well that I desire to see it again when I come to London. I pray make an end
with your physic, that I may the sooner have your company. Charles" (BL Harleian MS 6988, f. 99).

*Edward Hyde, earl of Clarendon, provoked this response in both men, first offending William in the
1650s, and then being forced to flee from England into exile when Charles II turned against him in 1667.

**James King, Baron Eythin, was general of the foot and William's second-in-command, while
George Goring was his general of the horse. After Goring was captured by Parliament in May 1643, Margaret's brother Charles took over command of the northern cavalry: William was glad to get so able an
officer, and the two men got on well, as Margaret's later account of their conversations reveals.

In spite of his inexperience, William was a popular general. The dignity with which he filled his role, combined with abundant "acts of courtesy, affability, bounty and generosity," made him, as Clarendon observed, "very acceptable to men of all conditions." A humane, even kindhearted leader, William refused to sit among the judges at courts-martial and would often pardon the men his own officers had condemned to death; his army was never guilty of the violent pillage and looting practiced under commanders like Prince Rupert. Meanwhile, in combat William showed "an invincible courage and fearlessness," Clarendon approved. Always present on the field, he sometimes turned the course of a battle by his brave and prompt action, as in June 1643 at Adwalton Moor near Bradford in Yorkshire. Here, when his hard-pressed troops began to retreat, William himself charged at the head of two cavalry companies "into the very rage of the battle," leading to a victory that gave him control of all Yorkshire, at least for a while.[12] A few months later, Charles I rewarded his northern general by raising him from earl to marquess of Newcastle. But William held his new honor and title by himself, for his wife Elizabeth had died that spring. He left the army for her funeral at Bolsover, but the demands of war meant he could not remain there long.

Thus far, William's main field army had suffered no serious defeat, a fact that Margaret would later celebrate proudly in her biography of her husband, and that the earl of Clarendon would also record.[13] However, the following winter William's fortunes (and the king's) turned for the worse, when the Scots invaded to support the English Parliament. William advanced through Northumberland to meet the new enemy but, when two parliamentarian armies also came up from the Midlands, he was forced to retreat inside the city walls of York, outnumbered by perhaps 30,000 enemies to his own 5,000 troops. Besieged, he wrote urgently to the king and Prince Rupert for a relief force, but when Rupert finally arrived in July 1644, with an army of around 14,000 prime troops, disaster ensued at the Battle of Marston Moor, just outside York.

Citing his orders from the king to attack, the twenty-four-year-old general rejected William's advice to delay until reinforcements could come up, and ordered their combined armies out to the field. Amidst the bitter personal rivalry between Rupert and William's deputy, General King, the infantry from York arrived late, and Rupert angrily decided to defer the battle until the next day. However, while he ate dinner and William sat in his coach smoking his pipe, there came "a great noise and thunder of shooting":[14] the Scots and parliamentarians had unexpectedly attacked.

William armed himself and mounted, only to see the royalist right wing already fleeing in panic. Rupert had assigned him no formal command for the battle but, riding now towards the army's center, William found a troop of gentlemen volunteers who chose him their captain. With them, he joined the last cavalry reserve at the royalist center and led their charge, breaking through all three ranks of the enemy army and almost reaching their command headquarters. However, by now, the rest of the royalist cavalry had fled in defeat, carrying Prince Rupert with them off the battlefield. Behind William the infantry were surrounded, and in the end only his own personal infantry regiment, known as the Whitecoats, remained, refusing to surrender. By moonlight now they were slowly slaughtered; they died in their original ranks, without moving from their places; fewer than thirty survived the battle. William, the last royalist commander left on the field, finally returned to York "seeing that all was lost."

Early the next morning he met with Rupert, who proposed to rally the troops. But William had no heart to continue the war. Asking Rupert to give "a just report of him" to the king, "that he had behaved himself like an honest man, a gentleman, and a loyal subject," he decided to leave the country.[15] Riding with seventy of his closest followers to Scarborough, he took ship to Hamburg, while Rupert retreated across the Pennines into Lancashire.

William's despairing flight into exile spoiled his entire reputation as a Civil War general. His personal enemies amongst the royalists had already accused him of being insufficiently ambitious and energetic in his overall campaigning strategy (though no one ever faulted his conduct of actual battles), and after Marston Moor such criticism became both universal and extreme. "Prince Rupert is here mightily condemned for his rashness [in provoking a battle], but the Marquess of Newcastle much more for coming away," was the report from other soldiers who soon followed William's example and fled abroad: "his going lost his army and all those that depended on him."[16] Later, the earl of Clarendon, writing his *History of the Rebellion* with the benefit of hindsight, would argue at length that both generals had been wrong to give up so soon. He and other royalist memoirists would portray William as a lax, pleasure-loving amateur who never seriously undertook "the substantial part, and fatigue of a general," retiring instead "to his delightful company, music, or his softer pleasures." "He had a tincture of a romantic spirit, and had the misfortune to be somewhat of a poet," Sir Philip Warwick commented, "and such sort of witty society (to be modest in the expression of it), diverted many counsels, and lost many fair opportunities." "It was a greater wonder," Clarendon judged of William's military career, "that he sustained the vexation and fatigue of it so long, than that he broke from it with so little circumspection."[17]

William indeed had various of his prewar artistic associates serving in his army—musicians, poets, and playwrights like Christopher Simpson, James

Shirley, and the poet laureate William Davenant. His artistic tastes and love of his pleasures provided an obvious butt for ridicule: after Marston Moor the parliamentarians easily derided him as "one of Apollo's whirligigs; one that when he should be fighting, would be toying with the nine Muses, or the Dean of York's daughters; a very thing; a soul traducted but of perfume and compliment; a silken general that ran away beyond sea in a sailor's canvas."[18] Yet even the (now sharply critical) earl of Clarendon had to admit William's previous courage in battle and his prompt response to many military crises. In July 1644, after the slaughter of Marston Moor, William simply saw no honorable alternative to flight. Believing that the king's ultimate defeat was now inevitable, he was not prepared to betray the trust of his northern friends by recruiting yet more of them as soldiers, only to face death "in a desperate action" with no hope of success.[19] He would later see the royalists' eventual defeat as justifying his decision.

William spent the remainder of 1644 in Hamburg. He had little money with him, and his English estates, now occupied by Parliament, could send no further supplies. He borrowed heavily, however, so that when he moved to join the English queen's court in Paris in April 1645 he traveled in style, with a new coach and nine expensive Holstein horses. Seven of these soon made a magnificent gift to Henrietta Maria, whose trust William was eager to regain after Marston Moor.[20]

Taking lodgings in Paris, William became a regular visitor at the court. At first he would have been a distant figure to Margaret, one of the many important men who came and went, involved in politics and military strategy with the queen. In May he was planning to lead an invasion of England from Ireland; by June there was a ship waiting for him at St. Malo.[21] But the royalists' disastrous defeat at the Battle of Naseby on June 14 interrupted his plans. The king lost all his artillery, ammunition, and baggage; 4,500 of his soldiers surrendered. His correspondence with the queen was captured too, to be published with exultation and derision in the parliamentary news-sheets, incriminating both of them in the eyes of their people. William now remained in Paris, assisting the queen in gathering military supplies for General Goring, who still commanded a substantial army in the West Country.[22]

As he continued coming frequently to court, William began "to take some particular notice of me," Margaret later recalled.[23] At twenty-two, she struck him as a great beauty, with a well-shaped figure ("so straight, so slender and so tall," he wrote), and rich brown hair, exquisitely combed out into individual curls on her forehead—"like pencilled shadows for your lovely face." Her pale complexion ("not falling snow so white") was often suffused with blushes; her skin, "softer than softest silk, beaver or down," appeared as a thin veil "for your

plump flesh."[24] For William, Margaret's youth, shyness, and social inexperience—the very qualities the courtiers so criticized—only added to her allure:

> *A spotless virgin, full of love and truth,*
> *Fresh as is morning's day, or her own youth;*
> *Modest beyond the new-comed buds that's fair,*
> *That dares not look upon the gentle air*
> *For fear of scandal . . .*

And as he drew her out into conversation, he discovered that beneath Margaret's social awkwardness there was an inner strength and peace, "a calm perpetually in your breast, sweet as balm."[25] She was not just beautiful, he now
saw, but kind, intelligent, and witty—a woman whose strong presence could
not but impress itself on those around her:

> *Sweetest of nature, virtue, you are it;*
> *Serenest judgement, fancy for a wit;*
> *So confidently modest, so discreet,*
> *As lust turns love, love homage at your feet . . .*
> *So affable, yet keeps your state, all say;*
> *Strikes such respect as none dares think he may:*
> *Your youth as fresh as morning day we see;*
> *And all this, all is Lucas, that is she.*[26]

Distrusting the glamour and self-confidence of the other court ladies, William
"did approve of those bashful fears which many condemned."[27] Soon he began
to woo Margaret in earnest.

"Sweet, will you entertain me for your servant?" is his first speech of
courtship as recreated in her autobiographical play *The Presence,* where William
appears as Lord Loyalty.*

In the play Mistress Bashful, like Margaret herself in real life, must modestly appear uninterested in love, as etiquette demanded of women. So, "I am
not rich enough in merit to entertain one of your worth," Bashful immediately
responds to Loyalty's opening.

But Lord Loyalty knows the social conventions and is not deterred. As he
offers successively to serve Bashful for her love, for her youth, her beauty, and
her wit, each time she returns a neat refusal, but still he persists. "All your

---

*Lord Loyalty was of course the perfect name for the English aristocrat who perhaps (and in Mar-
garet's view certainly) had done more than any other to support his king in the Civil War.

rhetoric shall not turn me off," he insists, "for I will serve you, although it be against your will."[28]

The play suggests that the courting couple met sometimes in private, away from the hothouse atmosphere of the royal court, in the home of the English diplomatic resident in Paris, Sir Richard Browne, and his kindhearted wife, Elizabeth, who appears as Madam Civility in *The Presence*. Elizabeth Browne often gave assistance to the royalist exiles who, the diarist John Evelyn recalled, "continually frequented her house in Paris, which was not only an hospital, but the asylum to all our persecuted and afflicted countrymen during her 11 years residence."[29] In Margaret's play, Madam Civility is one of the very few people who can see beneath Bashful's shyness and discover that she is in fact no fool, despite the general opinion of the court. She offers her young protégée advice and support as, inevitably in the small, cliquish world of court society, the lovers' initially secret relationship soon becomes a common topic for unkind gossip.

"Tis a wonder to see Bashful alone with a man," is the sarcasm of one of the maids of honor, "for she shuns men as she would do serpents, and locks her chamber-doors against them, and accounts it a crime to be seen undress'd, and a sin not to be forgiven, to be seen in bed."*

"She should not go out to meet such company," comments another, "for all the Kingdom knows, the Lord of Loyalty is none of the chastest men; and he courts her for her youth and beauty; 'tis not likely he will marry her; for he loves variety too well, to tie himself to one."[30]

But William was in fact becoming keen to remarry. During the sea voyage from Scarborough to Hamburg after the Battle of Marston Moor the previous year, his two sons had nearly died of smallpox and measles. Now, anxious to ensure the continuance of his line, he wanted to have more male heirs.[31] His relationship with Margaret was rapidly becoming more serious than the toying of romantic flirtation.

Around the beginning of August, Henrietta Maria's court moved out to St. Germain-en-Laye, where the newer of the two royal châteaux had been assigned to the English queen as her summer residence.[32] Completed some forty years before by Henri IV, the palace far exceeded the Louvre in splendor, extending through grand suites of royal apartments, ornamented with wall and ceiling paintings and stained glass windows, where, forty years later, Henrietta Maria's son, King James II, would also spend his exile. Gardens descended to the River Seine in six massive terraces of formal parterres,

---

*Fashionable ladies often received visitors in their bedchambers while wearing informal "undress."

orchards, canals, fountains, cascades, pavilions, and statues; grottos set back into the hillside contained the most marvelous mechanical automata that money could buy, whole scenes of mythological figures who danced, sang, played music, worked, fought, or swam, all driven by water power. With a tennis court, riding school, pall-mall, and the promise of hunting in the surrounding forests in the autumn, the English courtiers escaped from the heat and smells of the city. But living ten miles from Paris, Margaret could now meet William only occasionally—when she went into the city on the queen's business, or when he joined the parties of English exiles who would share a coach to drive out to visit the court.

Under this enforced separation, William wrote frequently from Paris, sending not only letters and occasional presents but also passionate love poetry. Margaret was deluged in verse as, during their four months of courtship, he composed a total of seventy poems for her—averaging more than one every two days.[33] From his raptures at her beauty and purity, he turned to his longing to see her once again, or to his admiration for her portrait: in the common way of lovers, the couple had exchanged portrait miniatures as keepsakes. He wrote of the agony of separation:

> *If living cannot meet, then let us try*
> *If after death we can; oh, let us die!*

And the ecstasy of reunion:

> *Oh, joy of joys, my love, my sweet,*
> *And do we meet?*
> *Is 't not a mist before mine eyes*
> *That flatters me with lies*
> *And pleasing fancies of my dear,*
> *And you're not here?*

And of the total obsession of being in love:

> *My love, my dear, my joy,*
> *Cupid's a foolish boy*
> *To put such thoughts into my brain,*
> *That I cannot refrain*
> *But still must think of you, you know,*
> *Whether I will or no.*[34]

As the royalists' fortunes in England worsened and Prince Rupert came under siege in Bristol, William told of his own complete abstraction from the world of politics and war:

> *When one doth ask, "What news, I pray you, Sir?"*
> *I answer, "Yet I did not hear from her."*
> *"Zounds, I mean Bristol," says he, "can you tell?"*
> *I answer, "I do hope that she is well."*
> *"The peace is made in Ireland, they say?"*
> *I tell him, "I do think she'll send today."*
> *"Are the Scots turned unto the King? Pray speak."*
> *"If she not love me then my heart will break,"*
> *Say I. Says he, "Your answers mad do make me."*
> *"I swear I love her, else the Devil take me."*
> *"What's this to what I say or do enquire?"*
> *"'Tis true," I tell him, "her I do admire*
> *Of all the world . . . "*

Begging Margaret to return his affections—"As thee I only love, love only me"—William renounced Venus, goddess of love, in favor of Hymen, the god of marriage, promising constancy and an almost religious devotion if Margaret would marry him.[35]

But "I did dread marriage," Margaret remembered later,[36] and such fears were not uncommon. Marriage represented a far greater life change for women than for men. The new bride left the world of her parents and entered her husband's household where, as clergymen preached in wedding sermons, she must become her husband's "servant," obedient to his will in everything, even should he prove unfaithful, drunk, or brutal. "Wives, submit yourselves unto your own husbands, as unto the Lord," they quoted from St. Paul: "it is sinful that the woman should usurp the man's authority."[37] This religious teaching was reinforced by the many etiquette and conduct books that prescribed that the ideal wife should be constantly employed in her husband's housekeeping, which would remove "all opportunities for distractions."[38]

During courtship before marriage the roles were reversed, and it was the chivalrous male lover who professed himself the "servant" of his beloved "mistress," ready to do anything for her. But women often feared what might happen later. William's daughters Jane and Elizabeth, about the same age as Margaret, expressed their own apprehensions in the play they had recently written together at home at Welbeck. *The Concealed Fancies* centers on two sisters, Luceny and Tattiney, who discuss their views on marriage as they are courted by suitors Courtly and Presumption. Luceny hates the idea that "husbands are the rod of authority"; she dreads a husband who will condemn her to be silent, formal, and respectful, "and if it be but the paring of his nails to admire him." Instead the sisters aspire to "an equal marriage" where the couple would "continue the conversation and friendship of lovers without knowing the words of man and wife." "I hate those people that will not understand, matrimony is to join lovers," says Tattiney and, as the two sisters set out to reform their suitors to make them good husbands, the play becomes a reversal of the plot of Shakespeare's *Taming of the Shrew*.[39]

In later life, Margaret too would often write of the perils of marriage. There was great social pressure to marry, she knew—"it is a kind of reproach to live unmarried," "a disgrace to live old maids"[40]—but the risks were huge, since "where one husband proves good, as loving and prudent, a thousand prove bad, as cross and spendthrifts." And the unhappiness that ensued was irremediable, "for if you be once tied with the matrimonial bond, there can be no honourable divorce but by death." "Marriage is a very unhappy life when sympathy joins not the married couple": under such conditions, "it were better to be barred up within the gates of a monastery, than to be bound in the bonds of matrimony." "I cannot advise you to marry," she would write to her sister Anne, who in fact remained single until her death, "unless men's souls, minds and appetites were as visible to your knowledge as their persons to your eyes": defects of character, she explained, could easily "be so obscured, as not to be perceived till you find you are unhappy by them; indeed there is so much danger in marrying, as I wonder how any dare venture."[41]

And yet, in the face of William's courtship, Margaret found "I could not, nor had not the power to refuse him, by reason my affections were fixed on him, and he was the only person I ever was in love with." Unlike the other men she had known at court, William was kind, gentle, considerate, and generous to her, admiring and attentive, affectionate, good-humored, charming, and easy to talk to—"one of the best of men."[42] After all the criticism of the court, he restored Margaret's self-confidence with his outspoken praise:

> Nature, we find,
> Robbed all your kind,
> We know 'tis true,
> To make up you.[43]

He drew Margaret out from her shyness, and listened to her talk. He shared her interest in poetry and philosophy, and like her he loved to write. The two also shared a distinctive outlook on life: both would be described by contemporaries as "romantic,"[44] people with high aspirations for great deeds beyond the normal course of everyday life.*

William was everything Margaret admired. He had fulfilled her ideals, instilled by her mother's stories of her dead father, that honors must be won by one's own heroic actions: William, as she would later record in her biography of him, had gained his noble titles by loyal service to the king in peace and war. The actions of his life—his military command in the war, the love poetry he was now writing for her, and the plays he had written in peacetime—showed him equal to her childhood heroes, with "the valour of Caesar, the fancy and wit of Ovid, and the tragical [and] especially comical art of Shakespeare."[45] Now approaching the age of fifty-two, he was thirty years older than Margaret. But his daily exercise in riding and fencing kept him lean and fit, and his greater life experience as an older man of the world only added to his appeal: Margaret could admire his knowledge and wisdom, his social poise, heroic achievements, and the great reputation he had won himself, all attributes that she felt herself to lack. And the love she felt for him, she judged, was the sort of affection on which it would be safe to build a lifetime of marriage. "It was not amorous love," a purely physical and romantic attraction, "built on fancy, and not on reality," which would soon wane under the strains of married life. Rather, it was a love based on respect and admiration for William's real worth, his character and behavior. Such love would be lasting, she believed: "as amorous love is bred . . . with the appetite" and "dies when beauty is gone," "so virtuous love is created, and shall live with the soul for ever."[46]

Tentatively Margaret acknowledged that she returned William's love. However strongly she felt, she could not speak out openly, for women were supposed to be the recipients of courtship, not active agents in it. And so, "though I love you extremely well," she assured William, "yet I never feared my modesty so small as it would give me leave to court any man."[47] Trying to "be careful in things that may arise to the scandal of my reputation," Margaret could write only infrequently in reply to William's flood of letters and poems. As he complained that she did not love him enough, she was forced to explain her fears: "If I do not send to you, pray excuse me," she begged, "for if I do, they will say I pursue you." "For know, my lord," her next letter continued,

---

*William's own romanticism had been apparent early in the Civil War when, inspired by Homer's *Iliad*, he had challenged the opposing parliamentarian general, Lord Fairfax, to decide the conflict by their single combat, so as to save the lives of their armies. Fairfax declined to fight, as also had the earl of Holland, whom William had challenged to a duel a few years earlier: William's skill as a swordsman was notorious.

"Saint Germain is a place of much censure and thinks I send too often. My lord, I am sorry you should think your love so much transcends mine, but sure it is as uncomely to see a woman too kind as to see a man too negligent."[48]

Yet, sometimes, Margaret's emotion got the better of her judgment and she acknowledged the true extent of her passion. "Though I give you all the love I have, yet it is too little for your merit," she told William. "Could I wish for more love than ever was or shall be, yet my wish could not be so copious but you would be still as far beyond it as your worth is above other men's." But immediately she was ashamed of such strong professions of feeling, "not that my affection can be too large," her next letter explained, "but I fear I discover it too much in that letter, for women must love silently; but I hope you will pardon the style because the intention was good." "My lord," she continued two letters later, in her attempt to rebuild her reputation and self-respect, "I must tell you I am not easily drawn to be in love, for I did never see any man but yourself that I could have married."[49]

But the never-ending gossip of the queen's court rendered the couple's mutually acknowledged love insecure. Despite Margaret's well-known shyness, William heard rumors that she was as profligate as the other court ladies, sitting up and entertaining "much company of men late in her chamber."[50] Slurs were also cast on her mother, Elizabeth, probably alluding to Margaret's illegitimate brother, Thomas. William's old friend, the courtier and art collector Endymion Porter, newly arrived in Paris from England, reported that he had found Margaret rude and unapproachable when he had gone to court, and William was also told that Margaret had been passing unfavorable comments on the miniature portrait that he had given her as a love token. As his letters confronted Margaret with all these accusations, she was forced onto the defensive.

"They that told you of my mother," she responded ironically, "has better intelligence than I." "As for Mr. Porter he was a stranger to me," she explained, "and, my lord, it is a custom I observe that I never speak to any man before they address themselves to me, nor to look so much in their face as to invite their discourse; and I hope I never was uncivil to any person of what degree so ever." She had unfortunately broken the case containing William's portrait, she admitted, but "I never said any such thing as you mentioned in your letter of your picture, nor never so much as shewed it to any creature before yesterday, that I gave it to [be] mended."[51]

William was being strongly advised against marriage, especially by Lord Widdrington, a cousin and close friend who had become one of William's most trusted officers during the Civil War and then accompanied him into exile after Marston Moor. A mere country gentleman's daughter, with a dowry of just £2,000, was too lowly a match for so great a nobleman, Widdrington no doubt argued.* And it was perhaps he who had mentioned Margaret's mother's past to William: Widdrington would have known John Lucas when they served together as gentlemen of the privy chamber to the Prince of Wales. As William told Margaret of the difficulties his friends were raising, she responded with offers of renunciation. "If I shall prejudice you in the affairs of the world, or in your judgement of your bad choice, consider and leave me; for I shall desire to live no longer than to see you happy," she wrote. "Pray, my lord, consider well whether marrying me will not bring a trouble to yourself; for believe me, I love you too well to wish you unhappy, and I had rather lose all happiness myself than you should be unfortunate . . . for hereafter if you should repent, how unfortunate a woman should I be."[52]

For her part, Margaret was also hearing rumors—principally that William was courting another woman, whom she described as "an enemy's daughter." [53] And she, like he, was being warned against getting too seriously involved:

> I must confess [she wrote to William], as you have had good friends to coun-
> sel you, I have had the like to counsel me and tell me they hear of your pro-
> fessions of affection to me, which they bid me take heed of, for you had
> assured yourself to many and was constant to none.[54]

As this letter goes on to report Margaret's sparring with the courtiers on the subject of her relationship with William, it becomes clear that she has by now learned the basic verbal self-defense necessary for survival amidst the court's cutthroat repartee.

"She has found a tongue," exclaims an astonished Mistress Wagtail in *The Presence*, as Bashful too goes through this transformation.

"Nay, the court is the only place to make fools wits," comments Mistress Wanton cynically.[55]

But in spite of all the accusations and counteraccusations, William and Margaret were building a relationship of trust. "My lord, I can believe nothing but what is in honour of you, and I beseech you to believe that I have ever truth of my side," Margaret wrote, and she offered a simple explanation for the many slanders William was hearing against her. "I find such enemies that whatsoever can be for my disadvantage, though it have but a resemblance of truth, shall be declared." "Do not mistrust me," she begged; "I have not power over the imaginations of others. Pray consider I have enemies."[56]

---

*William's daughters, by comparison, were intended to have dowries of £10,000 each (NA MS DDP/29/5).

Gradually a consensus grew up between them—a view of the court as a place of envy and malice, where "witchcraft, sorcery and spell of court devils in their dissembling hell" sought to "untie th' affection of our hearts," as William put it in his poems. Twenty years later, when Margaret came to recreate this episode for *The Presence,* she would portray the court's maids of honor spitefully hatching a formal conspiracy: "how shall we do to break the marriage?" they begin, as they meet to plot the destruction of the play's heroine, rather like the witches in *Macbeth*.[57] For William and Margaret in the autumn of 1645, this shared view of the world served to join them more closely as a couple:

> *In spite of fate we never can be two,*
> *But still united, whate'er they can do,*

William vowed.[58]

By early November, William had come to see himself as a ruined man. With his estates in England sequestered by Parliament, he could only offer Margaret a life of exile and poverty. And as she assured him that this made no difference to her feelings, he wondered at the unworldliness of such "unparalleled love"—especially when he compared their prospects with the latest fashionable wedding in Paris:

> *The Princess Mary marries King of Poland,*
> *And you, my dear, do marry Prince of No-land . . .*
> *She doth embrace all this world's full delight,*
> *And you take me to bid the world good night . . .*
> *Who could do this but you, and only you?*
> *Is't not a dream, a fiction? No, 'tis true . . .*
> *'Tis too much love; for now my thankful heart*
> *Is loath to ruin you, yet will not part.*
> *You over-love; know, pray you, what you do;*
> *You've ruined me with love, and yourself too.*[59]

To such intensity, Margaret responded with the defusing power of humor.

"I wonder not at my love but at yours," she gently joked, "because the object of mine is good. I wish the object of yours were so." "But pray love so as you may love me long," she ended her letter, "for I shall ever be, my lord, your most humble servant, Margaret Lucas."[60]

As their relationship matured, William's poetry ran increasingly on the physical delights of love.

To say we're like one snake, not us disgraces,
That winds, delights itself, with self-embraces,
Lapping, involving, in a thousand rings,
Itself thus tying by love's fancied wings;
And so do we

William wrote, inspired by his own Cavendish family badge—a picture of a serpent, knotted into a figure of eight. Then, likening Margaret's body to a garden, he imagined visiting each part in turn to kiss her lips, her cheeks, her hair, her breasts, until the final culmination when he would

. . . bathe me in love's pool,
My heated love to cool.[61]

He imagined their first night together and how,

Now you're in bed
With trembling maidenhead . . .

he would join Margaret and the two of them would be united as one body:

So all this pleasant night
Be love's hermaphrodite.[62]

But to this overtly sexual passion Margaret responded with reproach. "My lord, there is a customary law that must be signed before I may lawfully call you husband," she reminded William. "If you are so passionate as you say, and as I dare not but believe, yet it may be feared it cannot last long, for no extreme is permanent."[63]

Her great concern was that their marriage be arranged with propriety, and so she wrote to her brother John as head of the family, asking his approval for the match. But as a servant in the royal household Margaret would also need the queen's permission, and queens were often notoriously unwilling to part with their maids: Margaret's aunt Anne, maid of honor to Queen Elizabeth I more than fifty years before, had brought royal displeasure on the Lucas family by her marriage to a courtier. How was Henrietta Maria to be told with delicacy, so she would not be offended at what was really a fait accompli, arranged without her knowledge? William proposed an indirect approach: he could tell Lord Jermyn who, as the queen's closest adviser—doubling up as royal chamberlain, treasurer, and secretary—would be the best person to gain her favor.

But Margaret disapproved: "I think you know yourself too well to seek so low." Instead, "if you please to ask the Queen I think it would be well understood," she suggested.[64]

But William, unsure how to proceed for the best, delayed, and the problem still remained unresolved when John's answer arrived from England—not just permission for the marriage but "so great an injunction as is laid upon me in the name of a brother," Margaret reported.[65] Immediately, she set about making preparations. Lady Elizabeth Browne, the English resident's wife who had already taken Margaret under her wing, now supervised the arrangements for the wedding, which was to be held in the Anglican chapel at the resident's house. But as Margaret sent her maid, Elizabeth Chaplain, into Paris to finalize the details with Lady Browne, she knew that the queen still had to be told. "I fear she will take it ill if she be not made acquainted with our intentions," she advised William: "I think it no policy to displease the Queen, for though she will do us no good she may do us harm."[66]

Finally, in late November or early December, William wrote to Henrietta Maria, and Margaret, confined to her bedchamber for several days with a severe cold, reported on developments from there. "I have not been with the Queen as yet," she informed William, "but I hear she would have me acknowledge myself in a fault, and not she to be in any." "It will be hard for me to accuse myself . . . when I am innocent."[67] When Margaret recovered and visited Henrietta Maria, the situation was at last resolved: "I hope the Queen and I am friends; she saith she will seem so, at least," Margaret told William, "but I find if it had been in her power she would have crossed us." Henrietta Maria refused to make any public acknowledgment of the marriage, informing Margaret that she wanted to know nothing of the wedding arrangements, and Margaret's hope that she and the queen might now "be very good friends again, and maybe the better for the differences we have had" certainly conjures up a stormy interview.[68]

Meanwhile the court's constantly circulating rumors had grown ever more exaggerated, until now it was commonly believed that William and Margaret were already married in secret. The marriage was planned as a quiet affair—"be assured I will bring none to our wedding but those you please," Margaret promised[69]—but some public contradiction of the gossip was necessary to protect her reputation, and so she asked William to allow the court's Anglican chaplain, Dr. John Cosin, to perform the ceremony. A few days later, Margaret accompanied the queen from St. Germain into Paris, and then slipped quietly away to the Brownes' house and chapel in the Faubourg St.-Germain, to be married.

Chapter Six

Parisian Wife, 1646–1648

Marriage brought to Margaret a complete change of life and identity. From Mistress Margaret Lucas, an insignificant minor courtier, she was transformed at a stroke into the Lady Margaret Cavendish, marchioness of Newcastle—a noblewoman ranking above the wives of barons, viscounts, and earls, and below none but duchesses. Accompanied only by her waiting-maid, Elizabeth Chaplain, she left the court for good and moved into her husband's lodgings in Paris, where a new world of people and relationships awaited her.

First there was William's younger brother, Sir Charles Cavendish, now aged about fifty. His only surviving portrait shows a lean figure, clad in black armor and riding boots. The thin, pale face is framed by auburn hair and moustache, features he shared with his brother.[1] But the portrait is at least partly a fiction, for contemporaries' accounts of Sir Charles's appearance concentrate on his physical deformity. "A little, weak, crooked man," notes John Aubrey, while the earl of Clarendon offers a more expansive version.

> He had all the disadvantages imaginable in his person; which was not only of so small a size, that it drew the eyes of men upon him; but with such deformity in his little person, and an aspect in his countenance that was apter to raise contempt than application.

Probably Sir Charles had a twisted spine, but it formed little impediment to a normal life. Educated with his older brother, he was knighted by King James I in 1619, and then served three times as a member of Parliament. From 1642 he accompanied William throughout his Civil War campaigns. Judged too weak for military command, he yet "was present, and charged the enemy in all battles, with as keen a courage as could dwell in the heart of man." Sir

Charles's unpromising exterior, as his friends well knew, concealed "a man of the noblest and largest mind," "a great philosopher . . . and an excellent mathematician," "one of the most extraordinary persons of that age." Everyone who knew him admired Sir Charles for his sweet good nature, his incorruptible moral integrity, and his exceptional knowledge, developed during a lifetime of study.[2] For Margaret he would become a close friend—conversational companion, patron, protector, and intellectual mentor, a man she would look up to and hero-worship.

Other relationships within William's household, however, were not so easy, and especially problematic were William's children from his first marriage. The eldest, Jane, was two years older than her new stepmother, while Charles and Elizabeth were just a few years younger, with Henry and Frances slightly younger again.[3] The two sons had accompanied their father to Paris, but William's daughters were still in England, having remained at home with their mother when the men left for the war in 1642. In the spring of 1643, less than three years before William and Margaret's marriage, the girls were present at their mother's deathbed. Their father, uncle, and brothers returned home briefly for the funeral, but then the sisters were left alone again, in charge of the family servants and Welbeck's royalist garrison.

As William campaigned through the North of England and then fled abroad into exile, the separated family still maintained close emotional ties. To their father's letters and his presents—fans and combs, bracelets, masks, twists of silk for embroidery—Jane and Elizabeth responded with passionate poems of love and praise. Extolling William's courage, wit, and judgment, their verses glorified him as a "great example," "the best of man," a military hero who deserved the name of "William the Conqueror." They thanked God for his safe return from the cavalry charge at Adwalton Moor, but most of all their poems expressed the torment of separation. As theologians taught that Hell was nothing but God's absence so, without their earthly father, his daughters existed in a terrestrial hell. They were dull and dead, buried in the grave; only William's company would transform them back into free, living creatures. Seeing each day the familiar places where they remembered him in the past only increased their grief. Looking into the fire, they thought of the battles where William risked his life. Then, as he fled abroad, their weeping reminded them of the seawater where again he was in peril. Relief at the news of his safe landing on the Continent was soon followed by longing for his return to England. "For God's sake come away and land," they begged.[4]

In addition to their poems, Jane and Elizabeth wrote two longer pieces for their absent father—their play, *The Concealed Fancies,* composed in late 1643 or early 1644 while William was still in England, and a pastoral drama of courting shepherds and shepherdesses, written after William arrived in Paris.[5] Both works told the stories of groups of sisters left alone at home by their father and brothers amidst the battles, sieges, looting, and plunder of civil war. In real life, the three sisters at Welbeck had seen their home garrisoned by the royalist army (while Jane acted as its intelligence agent, sending military information to the king at Oxford), then surrendered to the parliamentarians in August 1644, recaptured by the royalists in a fierce engagement in July 1645 (when they took 200 prisoners and three cannon), visited by the king during his northern campaigns, and finally surrendered once again.[6] As well as these wartime experiences, both dramatic pieces also incorporated the sisters' emotional concerns—their loneliness without their father and their anxiety about courtship and marriage. The pastoral drama in particular centered on the young women's reluctance to form new emotional attachments to lovers or husbands until their family was again reunited. Its theme was doubtless suggested by Elizabeth who at the age of fifteen had been married to John, viscount Brackley, heir to the earl of Bridgewater. Judged too young to live with her nineteen-year-old husband, she had remained at home at Welbeck. But, while the sisters wrote this drama during 1645, she was preparing to move to Ashridge, the Bridgewaters' family home in Buckinghamshire.[7]

William had encouraged his children to write from their earliest years, and he had himself written for their entertainment, producing a masque one Christmas at his daughters' request. Now Jane and Elizabeth modeled their own writing on his, following his inspiration and seeking only his approval. "Upon your stock of wit I feed," Elizabeth wrote, while Jane told of her aspiration "to be your daughter in your pen."[8] For them, their father was not only their physical creator, but also an intellectual liberator who had brought them up "in the creation of good languages," giving them a control of words and thoughts that would enable them to be themselves and direct their own lives without being dominated or deceived by others.[9] The relationship between William and his two eldest daughters was an exceptionally close one. While women commonly wrote for their mothers, husbands, children, and female friends, poems for fathers were very rare. In particular, Jane and Elizabeth's "passion poems" of absence, loss, and longing are probably a unique example of this sort of poetry (normally exchanged only between lovers) being written by daughters for their father.[10]

Such emotional dependence made the sisters anxious about new attachments their father might form. Already, at least a year before William met Margaret, Jane and Elizabeth's play had featured one Lady Tranquility, a caricature of the sort of vain, scheming, social-climbing woman they most feared. Margaret's marriage really was a vast social advancement, and William's new relationship inevitably weakened his bond with his daughters. Margaret and her stepdaughters would never be close. Early contacts could only be by letter; they would not meet until six years later.

Meanwhile, in Paris, Margaret was getting to know her new stepsons. Lord Henry Cavendish, the younger of the two, was now fifteen. His long fair hair, blue eyes, pale face, and smooth unstubbled chin gave him almost feminine good looks, and he was considered the family beauty—"the only piece of Nature's pride," his sisters wrote.[11] But Henry's disposition was not so sweet as his looks: in later life he would be hasty, jealous, hot-tempered, and intractable in dealings with his family. His brother, Charles, viscount Mansfield—now aged eighteen and heir to his father's wealth—was the popular one. Modest and easygoing, he was an affectionate brother to his sisters, and a witty companion whose conversation was prized as a "continual rare banquet."[12] Not physically strong—he described himself as "weak of body and constitution"— he was yet thoroughly groomed for aristocratic life. Privately educated with his brother, Henry, at Welbeck, he had entered public life at the age of thirteen or fourteen, when he was elected as member of Parliament for the Cavendish family's borough of East Retford in 1640. Politics was regarded as the main business of an aristocrat's life and such an early start was not uncommon. Charles lived in London for almost a year. Then, as friction intensified between king and Parliament, he returned home to Welbeck. In 1642 he and Henry accompanied William to the war. Charles was appointed a colonel of horse and foot and lord general of the ordnance in his father's army, while Henry was made a cavalry colonel. However, for boys aged sixteen and twelve, these commands were purely titular. In actuality, they spent their days with their tutor, who was under orders to take them to safety if battle threatened.[13] Having accompanied their father into exile after Marston Moor, they were continuing their studies in Paris.

Moving into her husband's lodgings, Margaret joined not just William's near relations but also the extensive personnel of servants that comprised a nobleman's "family." Etiquette prescribed that William, as a marquess, should have a comptroller or steward to manage his household, a secretary to write his letters, a gentleman of the horse overseeing equestrian affairs, and two gentlemen ushers, who organized admission to his presence and walked bareheaded in front of him when he went out.[14] In exile, William had reduced his staff for the sake of economy, sending many servants back to England, where his long-serving secretary, John Rolleston, remained. But there were still many new faces for Margaret, including three influential middle-aged men who, spending much of their lives in the Cavendish family's service, were as much old friends to William as employees.

Captain John Mazine was his master of the horse, "the best horseman that ever I knew," William judged, perhaps not impartially, since he had himself taught Mazine to ride in the manège. Mazine had trained the horses at Welbeck before the war, and then served as William's equerry. At Marston Moor, he had fought beside his master, before joining his flight into exile where, in William's manège-less Paris establishment, there was little for him to do.[15] Mark Anthony Benoist, on the other hand, was fully occupied as tutor to William's sons. The son of a Protestant pastor in the South of France, he had studied at Montauban and Geneva before moving to England and taking up his position at Welbeck.[16] He would remain with the family for decades, educating William's grandsons while acting as his business agent in London.

Lower in social status than Mazine and Benoist, but closest of all to William, was John Proctor, whose skullcap and plain dark suit marked him out as a lesser servitor among the flamboyant silks and laces and cavalier hats worn by gentlemen-servants like Captain Mazine. Proctor was William's personal servant or "man," dressing his master in the mornings, attending on him through the day, carrying his cloak and hat, riding out with him, sitting in the lobbies of great houses while William visited his friends. He had already served William for twenty years and would continue in his duties for another thirty, until death finally parted the two men. A careful, attentive, and dutiful servant, absolutely trusted by the family, Proctor kept the keys to William's treasury, carried his master's purse, handled his cash payments, acted as witness and trustee in some of William's most confidential legal business, and was known to have influence with his master.[17]

Over all these people the shy, twenty-two-year-old Margaret was placed in authority. "My Lady," everyone called her. But, uninterested in the multifarious skills of feminine domesticity, Margaret could only find her new position difficult, and in this close family group she felt resented as an interloper. "When a second wife comes into a family," she wrote, "all the former children, or old servants, are apt to be factious, and do foment suspicion against her, making ill constructions of all her actions; were they never so well and innocently meant, yet they shall be ill taken." Margaret experienced stubborn opposition from those around her, who thought "themselves enriched not so much by what they get, but by what she loseth."[18]

Her relationship with her new husband was Margaret's great consolation. Admiring and proud of William, she always treated him with a ceremonious respect. "My Lord," she addressed him, and signed her letters "your humble servant." Such expressions marked the obedience that social convention required a wife to show her husband, and Margaret was glad to conform. William was a great nobleman, whose honors were "the mark of merit and his master's royal favor." "It were a baseness for me to neglect the ceremony thereof," she thought.[19]

Such formalities of etiquette in no way precluded a close and loving relationship. William was an attentive, affectionate husband. Affable and approachable, wearing his noble dignity lightly, he was never one to stand on ceremony in his social life, and his relationship with his wife was no exception. Avoiding the formal modes of address that conduct books recommended husbands use to emphasize their authority over their wives, William nicknamed Margaret "Peg," even in front of the servants.[20] For more intimate occasions there were the endearments he used so freely in his love poetry: sweet, dear, my love, my joy. For many years he continued to write love poems for her, as passionate as any of their courtship before marriage.[21] Even in the poverty of exile, he bought her pearls and trinkets.

Especially treasured by Margaret was the time they spent together, talking, reading, joking, sparring gently. She loved to listen to her husband, so much older and wiser than she, telling of his past life and his wide knowledge and experience. As she got to know William better, she admired him all the more. With "his sweet, gentle and obliging nature," he was also true, just, courageous, civil, and modest, "a kind husband, a loving father, a generous master, and a constant friend." "Heroic fortitude, noble generosity, poetical wit, moral honesty, natural love, neighborly kindness, great patience, loyal duty, and celestial piety"—catalogs of virtues fell from her pen when she thought of William. The hero worship Margaret had previously reserved for her childhood family now found a new object, and her love, "fixed like eternity, and . . . as full as infinite,"[22] involved her emotionally in all William's concerns. She became the confidante of his worries and disappointments, the sharer of his joys and enthusiasms, an adviser for decisions in both his private finances and his public political life, and a passionate partisan, proud of her husband's achievements and furiously angry if he suffered injury or injustice.

In return, she too sought support from William, wanting his approval for all she did. William became the sole person who really mattered to Margaret—"he I only desired to please." "Your favour is more than the world to me," she still assured him after twenty years of marriage, "for which all the actions of my life shall be devoted and ready to serve you."[23] With William's encouragement and admiration—"proud of the respects he used to me, and triumphing in the affections he professed for me"—Margaret gained in self-confidence, "esteeming myself the more for being, my lord, your most humble servant." After the depression of lonely exile, her spirits were rising. "My lord, I have not had much experience of the world, yet I have found it such as I could willingly part with it," she wrote, "but since I knew you, I fear I shall love it too well, because you are in it." "I begin to admire Paris because you are in it," she added.[24]

William's love poetry had promised Margaret a happy marriage and, in spite of the stresses of exile, the couple remained close. Their relationship would provoke some of Margaret's most inspirational writing. A successful marriage, she thought, constituted "the happiest and sweetest life" and the most "perfect friendship." Husband and wife were "like one root or body, [so] that whatsoever toucheth the one is truly sensible to the other." "They lessen one another's grief, and increase one another's joy; the very noise of their children is music to their ears; industry and labour is a recreation . . . their house is their heaven." "Love crowns their lives with peace, and enrobes or enclothes them with happiness."[25]

WILLIAM'S PARISIAN LODGINGS lay in one of the suburbs outside the old city walls[26]—probably in the Faubourg St.-Germain, where many royalist émigrés lived, clustered close to the house of their resident, Sir Richard Browne.* Here the English congregated to talk and hear the news and, in many cases, to be mothered, as Margaret was, by Sir Richard's wife, Elizabeth, a woman "obliging upon all occasions" to those who needed help.[27] In the resident's private chapel (one of the last places still celebrating the Anglican rite after the parliamentarians abolished the Church of England), the émigrés assembled regularly for Sunday services and for grander occasions like society weddings and funerals, and the ordination of priests.

New arrivals in Paris gravitated here, and in October 1646 William and Margaret would first have met the young diarist, artist, and intellectual, John Evelyn, fresh from his two-year tour through France and Italy. Evelyn became a regular at the Brownes' house, attaching himself especially to their eleven-year-old daughter Mary. The following June, when he and Mary were married in the resident's chapel, the Newcastles were among the "few select friends" present. Margaret, carried away by her gratitude to Elizabeth Browne for arranging her own marriage, promised Mary a wedding gift of £1,000 when they should all be once again returned home—a promise she would later forget, causing some resentment. Meanwhile William composed verses for the bridegroom, congratulating him on his young wife—a spotless lily or rose unsullied by any other love, a young plant to tend and train, a young horse that Evelyn could school for his own hand only.[28]

From the Faubourg St.-Germain, the English drove into Paris proper, passing under the city walls at a massive gatehouse, whose doors were guarded

---

*In 1647, a good apartment here was costing John Evelyn four pistoles a month—around £3 10s.

and locked at night. On the Pont Neuf—where the passing crowds were harangued by puppet shows, clowns, and mountebanks selling quack medicines—they crossed the Seine, lined along both banks by the huge ships and barges that supplied the city's provisions. Arrived on the North Bank, they were now close to the Louvre, where Henrietta Maria and her court passed the colder seasons before returning to St. Germain-en-Laye to spend the summer in the country.

Margaret's first appearance at the English court after her grand marriage must have caused a sensation, she later thought.

"Come, pray, let us go see how she looks since she is married," suggests one of the excited and envious maids of honor in *The Presence*.

"Proud, I'll warrant you."

"I dare say she will carry state now," the others expect.

"She was proud enough before she was married, she cannot be much prouder than she was," rejoins the first.

"You say right, for what everybody thought was bashfulness and modesty in her, was merely pride."[29]

Margaret knew that her shyness distanced her from other people, making her seem stiff and formal, and her visits to court can only have been full of awkwardness.

The Louvre formed the cultural as well as the political center of English life. The poet laureate Sir William Davenant—William's lieutenant general of ordnance during the Civil War—was now part of the queen's establishment, living in Lord Jermyn's lodgings in the Louvre. The poets Edmund Waller and Abraham Cowley were here too—Cowley employed as Jermyn's secretary, translating the encoded letters that passed between the queen and her husband back in England. In the summer of 1646, William's former pupil Prince Charles arrived to join his mother. For a few months Charles maintained a company of English actors, and William was among those who wrote pieces for them—a feat "which sheweth in him either an admirable temper and settledness of mind," the parliamentarian newsmen conjectured, "or else an infinite and vain affection unto poetry, that in the ruins of his country and himself he can be at the leisure to make prologues and epilogues for players." That Christmas and New Year, masques were put on at court as usual.[30]

From Henrietta Maria's apartments, the English toured the vast palace of the Louvre, with its courtyards and fountains, its paintings and statues, and its Long Gallery running beside the Seine. On the gallery's ground floor they viewed the work of some of Europe's finest artists and craftsmen, pensioned by the French Crown. They visited too the king's printing house, while at the royal Jardin des Plantes they admired the rare and exotic species and the well-equipped laboratory. Such tours ended in the gardens of the neighboring but newer palace, the Tuileries, where French society gathered in the evenings to enjoy the groves of elms and mulberries, the labyrinth of cypress and hedges of pomegranate, the fountains and pools, the orangery of rare shrubs, the aviary, and the menagerie of wild beasts.

On the other side of Rue St. Honoré was yet another grand royal complex, the Palais Royal, where Anne of Austria governed France as queen regent and her young son, Louis XIV, was undergoing an education for kingship. Here, as at the English court, William was well connected with "many persons of the first quality," French aristocrats who still remembered him respectfully thirty years later.[31] The English émigrés visited the Palais Royal frequently, viewing its galleries of paintings and its gardens, gambling at games of pall-mall, watching the royals in the presence chamber, or attending performances in its theater. Here Margaret saw French court ballets—an experience she would later use for the culminating spectacle of her play *The Presence*. She saw French and Italian plays too: though she can have understood little of the dialogue, she disliked their style of acting as too artificial, departing from "the tracts or paths of Nature."[32] With other English exiles, she probably also experienced the new art form of Italian opera, first introduced to France in 1647, when the composer Luigi Rossi and twenty singers were invited to perform Rossi's *Orfeo* at the Palais Royal.[33] The work was performed in Italian, but a plot synopsis in French was distributed to the audience of courtiers.

The émigrés also filled their time by touring the sights of Paris—the bridges and statues, the university and its neighboring bookshops, the grand symmetry of the recently built Place Royale,* the gothic Notre Dame cathedral surrounded by narrow medieval streets of craftsmen's workshops. Paris had several academies for young aristocrats, teaching them the noble arts of riding, fencing, dancing, music, and practical mathematics. Some academies kept nearly a hundred horses, all trained for the manège, and here William would have joined with other exiles, watching the skilled riding he loved and advising his friends on the purchase of good horses.[34]

For those with French friends and introductions, it was also possible to tour the great houses and art collections of the French nobility and royalty. Especially inspiring for Margaret would have been the paintings of heroic women, associated with the fashion for the *femme forte,* now flourishing under Anne of Austria. Aristocratic ladies were being painted in heroic roles, dressed in armor, or as personifications of the more martial classical goddesses—Bellona, or Venus Armata. Galleries of heroic portraits were created, including

---

*Now the Place des Vosges.

both historical figures like Joan of Arc and moderns like Anne of Austria and Marie de' Medici, the previous queen regent.* Marie had herself commissioned such a gallery from the painter Rubens in the 1620s, and visitors to the Palais du Luxembourg still saw these romantic portraits, showing the queen riding into battles that in reality she never saw.** Set out in books like Jacques Du Bosc's *La Femme Heroïque* and Pierre Le Moyne's *Gallerie des Femmes Fortes*, this new movement idealized strong women who possessed all the male virtues of courage, energy, physical and moral strength, generosity, fortitude, patriotism, and liberality, while still retaining their feminine beauty and compassion.[35] Such women, and the possibilities their lives might contain, would be one of the central themes of Margaret's future plays and fiction.

Meanwhile, at home in William's lodgings, Margaret found herself acting as hostess to her husband's plethora of royalist friends and acquaintances. Some, like Bishop John Bramhall, Sir William Carnaby, and Lord Widdrington, had served in William's Civil War army and then fled with him into exile. Widdrington especially "had a very particular and entire friendship" for William. A hot-tempered, handsome, big man—"near the head taller than most tall men"—he was a Northumberland cousin through William's mother; he had served with William in the Prince of Wales's household in the late 1630s and then become president of the Council of War in his Civil War army.[36] Many other acquaintances dated from William's days as a courtier in London—men like the art collector Endymion Porter and the poet laureate Sir William Davenant. Others, like the philosopher Thomas Hobbes, had known William at Welbeck. Yet others were new acquaintances in Paris—younger men like John Evelyn and the scholar and poet John Birkenhead, who had produced *Mercurius Aulicus*, the newspaper of royalist Oxford.

William was a brilliant host, at once "pleasant, witty and instructive." Admired for the quickness of his sparkling repartee and his "smartness of expression," he was also good at opening up whole new areas of conversation "by giving easy and unforced occasions." Interspersing "short pleasant stories and witty sayings" into his talk, he was a good raconteur and he was completely versatile, adapting himself "to men of all circumstances and conditions . . . being able to discourse with every man in his own way."[37]

Margaret, however, found this social life difficult. Her relations with some of William's closest friends were necessarily strained: Lord Widdrington and Endymion Porter, she knew, had advised her husband against marrying her. With everyone, there were the problems caused by her own

---

*The same queen who had visited the Lucases in Colchester in 1638.
**These pictures are now in the Louvre.

diffidence. Eager to please, she did her best to keep up a conversation, knowing that "when I am to entertain my acquaintance . . . though I do not speak so well as I wish I could, yet it is civility to speak." But she was dissatisfied with the results—"the truth is I am neither eloquent by nature, nor art." Feeling inadequate for anything more taxing, she found herself engaged only in trivialities, talking "of the general news of the times and the like discourse." "My company is too dull to entertain, and too barren of wit to afford variety of discourse," she concluded.[38]

William and his brother continued the cultured life they had fostered at Welbeck before the war, and many of those who visited the Newcastles' lodgings were scholars, writers, and intellectuals. The poet Edmund Waller came to dinner, tall and thin, with big popping eyes and a wrinkled brow. His "great mastership of the English language" and his "graceful elocution" brought him admiration as both speaker and writer. In Paris, his unusual access to his landed income at home meant that he kept one of the best-stocked tables of all the exiles. Another poetical guest—when he was not away on diplomatic missions for the queen—was Sir William Davenant, "a man of quick and piercing imagination," who wore a black patch over the place where his dissolute lifestyle had lost him his nose to syphilis.[39]

William's old protégé and friend, Thomas Hobbes, now approaching his sixties, also came to dinner "very often," joining the company's debates on whether man could fly and whether there were witches. Hobbes was a witty conversationalist, widely admired "for his pleasant facetiousness and good nature." In merry humor, his eyes closed up to slits with laughter, but when discussing more serious matters, his manner changed completely. Wide and round, his eyes shone like bright, live coals and every word he spoke in his broad West Country accent was carefully and long considered.[40] Politics and public finance, wars and armies, theories of education, philosophy, religion, and theology—these were the weightier topics of the Cavendish household, where William and Hobbes alike cast off their bonhomie for earnest discussion.[41] William's lodgings were the location of the famed debate between Hobbes and Bishop Bramhall concerning the theology of free will, with the Calvinist Hobbes advocating predestination against Bramhall's Arminian affirmation of man's ability to choose—a disputation that the two antagonists later wrote up at William's request, and that was published in 1655 with the permission of neither the authors nor their patron.

With Hobbes came his young assistant William Petty, glad to be introduced to the company's eminent scholars and aristocratic patrons. Petty was drawing the diagrams and writing up the fair copy of Hobbes's current work on optics, created for presentation to William, and written in English rather than Latin at William's special request. A medical student, Petty was also employed performing dissections, teaching Hobbes the anatomical knowledge he needed to produce his grand scheme of a complete philosophical theory of the world.[42]

Another, older, acquaintance was the gentleman scholar, Sir Kenelm Digby, whom William had come to know and admire during his days as a courtier in London. Naval commander and diplomat, linguist, philosopher, theologian, chemist and alchemist, astronomer and astrologer, book collector and poet, Sir Kenelm was widely recognized as "the most accomplished cavalier of his time," a veritable "magazine of arts."[43] He shared with William an interest in horsemanship and the manège, and a passion for collecting medical prescriptions. But he was also an uncritical repeater of tall tales, who loved to persuade his listeners that his wild stories were utterly true—a characteristic that brought him a reputation as "an arrant mountebank."[44]

Many French savants were also regular visitors, coming to discuss the technicalities of their work with William's brother, Sir Charles Cavendish. As they joined the more general conversation around the dinner table, Margaret found herself acting as hostess to France's leading philosophers and mathematicians—René Descartes, Pierre Gassendi, Giles Roberval, Claude Mydorge, and Marin Mersenne. Mersenne—a friar who held weekly meetings of all these French intellectuals in his cell at the Minim convent near the Place Royale—was a long-standing correspondent of William's brother. With Hobbes and other English scholars, Sir Charles now joined Mersenne's weekly salons. He borrowed the friar's books, heard of the latest French theories and experiments, and in return informed Mersenne of the work of his own philosophical and mathematical friends.[45] He and Mersenne were both "intelligencers," keeping their numerous learned acquaintances informed of each others' work, advising and encouraging them in their researches, reading drafts of their writings, mediating in their disputes. Through their widespread correspondence they connected Parisian intellectuals to the rest of Europe—to Torricelli in Italy, to Constantijn Huygens, Samuel Sorbière, Sir William Boswell and John Pell in the Netherlands, and thence, through Pell, to the English parliamentarian intelligencer, Samuel Hartlib.

Living at the heart of this intellectual activity, Margaret gained acquaintance with the researches that preoccupied this Parisian circle. Central to the work of both English and French was the "new philosophy"—the grand project that had originated late in the sixteenth century, aimed at finding a modern replacement for the old Aristotelian orthodoxy of prime matter, the four causes and the four elements (earth, air, fire, and water) that had dominated intellectual life since the Middle Ages. The new philosophy was based on new research methods, new experiments and instruments, and the new discoveries they brought. Its central icons of success were the telescope and the microscope (with the previously unimaginable worlds they revealed, large and small), the Copernican and Keplerian heliocentric models of astronomy (now widely accepted in place of the old Aristotelian-Ptolemaic system), and William Harvey's empirical demonstration of the circulation of the blood. These new ideas fired people's imaginations. Poets filled their verses with novel philosophical imagery, storytellers imagined voyages to the new world in the moon, and philosophers developed new theories of the physical nature of the universe—theories that, among the Cavendishes' Parisian circle, took their inspiration from the ancient Greek atomists Democritus and Epicurus.

The great aim of this revived atomism was to explain all the observed phenomena of the world, using only the shapes and qualities and interactions of atoms. But within this unified project there was huge diversity of ideas. Were atoms just hard, extended bodies in motion, as Descartes thought? Or did they have other, more complex properties? Were they endowed with the forces, attractions, and repulsions of the alchemical and Neoplatonic philosophies, as English philosophers, raised in a different tradition from the French, tended to think? Was there a vacuum, an empty space through which the atoms moved, as Gassendi believed, or was there a plenum of continuously circulating atoms, as Descartes thought? Or perhaps there was some other sort of matter, different from atoms, a subtle fluid ether that filled the space between the atoms, as Hobbes would come to believe.

Aiming at universal explanation, these philosophers' theories extended to discuss a vast variety of phenomena. Fire, heat, light, sound, colors, magnetism, gravity, the motion of the planets, the causes of the weather, plant and animal anatomy and physiology, the operations of the human body and mind— every philosopher had his own theory of the atomic operations involved. Descartes's purely mechanical system had recently been published (in his *Principia Philosophiae*), as had Sir Kenelm Digby's more Aristotelian theory (Digby's *Of Bodies*, published in 1644, made the traditional four elements into kinds of atoms). Hobbes, a slow, reluctant writer, was still ten years from publishing his own views in the *De Corpore*, while Gassendi's careful reworking of Epicurean theory was now imminently forthcoming, eagerly awaited by Sir Charles Cavendish and others.

As these philosophers descended to specific explanations, their disagreements only grew. What shape, for instance, were fire atoms—circular so they could move quickly, or pyramidal, with sharp biting points to cause pain? Were they the same as the atoms that made light? Or were there no special "fire atoms" and "light atoms" at all? Were fire, heat, and light all "secondary qualities," produced when the atoms of some substance adopted a rapid motion, as both Descartes and Hobbes believed? And might this motion of heat, affecting the invisible atomic parts of bodies, produce all the variety of things in the universe, as William had suggested in expounding his own theory, back in 1636?[46]

The possibilities for debate were endless, and rival camps formed. Kenelm Digby admired Descartes, which distanced him from his old friend Hobbes, who hated Descartes and preferred the ideas of Gassendi. Mersenne and Sir Charles Cavendish stood in the middle, trying to maintain good relations, but passions ran high. Originality obsessed these intensely competitive intellectuals: to be the first discoverer of a new idea was critically important. Hobbes and Descartes had already quarreled over which of them first thought of the theory of light they largely shared; now they refused to speak to each other; when finally reconciled by Mersenne, they met once, only to quarrel again and part finally and forever.

Margaret, with her ideals of "singularity," eagerly approved of this cult of originality. The idea that a writer must be entirely individual would inspire her adult writing. For a brief while, she would also become a proponent of atomism. But it was from William and his brother, rather than their philosophical guests, that she really learned, overcoming her shyness and talking freely. With others Margaret was always more reserved. "I never spake to Master Hobbes twenty words in my life," she noted.[47] Only with a few of the more assiduously courtly visitors to the family's lodgings did she establish a relationship. John Birkenhead was one of these, a successful social climber whose witty company was loved by the aristocrats he flattered. As he sought and received Margaret's favor, she in turn gained her first experience as a literary patron, with all the recognition and gratitude that impecunious writers so eagerly offered.[48]

Over all this rich cultural life hung constant financial worry. Most of the exiles were ill clothed and poorly housed; some were even hungry. Endymion Porter, living "so retired into the skirts of a suburb that I scarce know what they do at the Louvre," had just one set of clothes, "that poor riding suit I came out of England in"; "were it not for an Irish barber that was once my servant, I might have starved for want of bread." William Petty, "driven to a great straight for money," managed to survive for a week on two pennyworth of walnuts,[49] but in May 1646 he returned to England, seeking the parliamentarians' more lucrative patronage. In November, Prince Charles's theatrical company was disbanded—"the English audience being there so poor and few that they were not able to maintain the charges of the stage: it is wonder sufficient to me, how they can maintain themselves," a parliamentarian journalist gloated.[50] Henrietta Maria, sending what money she could to her husband in England, reduced her own establishment until "at last nothing could be more mean than her train and appearance."[51]

The Newcastles, though better off than some, still lived poorly by aristocratic standards, occupying lodgings in part of a building rather than renting a complete house. On the couple's marriage, William had written to Elizabeth Lucas, asking for his wife's dowry of £2,000. But with the three Lucas brothers' estates still under parliamentary sequestration, there was no money for Margaret. Although Elizabeth's own possessions were never sequestered, the family's ready cash had all been spent in January 1645, when John was made Lord Lucas of Shenfield.* Like other royalists, John sought his title as a reward for his loyal service to the king, but it still cost him dear, with the large customary payments to the Crown and to the courtiers involved in the transaction.[52] And so William was forced to "live upon the courtesy of those that were pleased to trust him," as Margaret put it.[53]

Borrowing brought its own troubles—the tradesmen's visits demanding payment, the need to inspire confidence in creditors who could not be repaid, the debts and interest spiraling ever upwards. By March 1647 William felt desperately insecure. "He saith that what he hath, he hath it all upon trust, and knows not how long his creditors will continue it, nor how soon they will call upon him to give them satisfaction," the parliamentarian news reported. "He professeth that the poorest of all are not in a worse condition for want of money than himself."[54]

It all preyed on Margaret. She dreaded that William would be imprisoned for debt, "where sadness of mind, and want of exercise and air, would have wrought his destruction." Although "extreme love did consume my body and torment my mind," she did her best to conceal her feelings from William, remembering how her childhood fears had irritated her sister Catherine. "I have some more discretion now than I had then," she wrote to Catherine, "and though extraordinary love will hardly allow or admit discretion, yet reason doth persuade love, and brings many arguments not to be impertinently troublesome."[55] Margaret's spirits suffered, however, and the news from England only increased her depression.

After their defeat at the Battle of Naseby in the summer of 1645, the royalists never recovered. As the war grew more bitter, Margaret's brother Charles joined the cycle of atrocities and reprisals, killing prisoners of war with the words, "Why should they have any more quarter than we had?"[56] (Although regarded as cruel, such behavior was permitted by the rules of war

---

*Shenfield was the Lucases' second house in Essex, which lacked the recent unhappy associations of St. John's.

when a garrison had refused to surrender.) In the autumn, the king's army in the West Country was defeated, and General Goring fled to Paris. The parliamentarians captured Bristol and Charles Lucas was forced to surrender nearby Berkeley Castle. Rejoining the king's much diminished forces in Oxford, Charles was appointed lieutenant general of the horse and then spent the winter recruiting around Worcester. Three thousand troops were raised, but as they marched back to Oxford in March 1646, they were intercepted at Stow-on-the-Wold. In the ensuing battle the last royalist field army was defeated; Charles Lucas was captured by the parliamentarians, rescued by his men, and then recaptured. In June, the royalist headquarters in Oxford finally surrendered and Margaret's brother John marched out with the others to begin a new life in parliamentarian England.

In London, John and Charles joined the many other royalists now petitioning to compound for their estates. Swearing an oath of loyalty to Parliament, the royalists paid fines calculated as proportions of their total wealth—proportions that ranged from one-tenth to two-thirds, depending on the extent of their "delinquency." Then they regained their possessions from parliamentary sequestration. In October, Thomas Lucas in Ireland also made his peace with the English Parliament. The three brothers would pay a total of some £3,800 in fines, Charles paying at the rate of one-sixth, while the others paid a tenth.[57] With the king in parliamentarian hands, the war was over. The royalists in Paris could foresee no return home; their plots for invasions had become mere chimeras.

Personal loss also came to Margaret when her sister Mary died, of the same consumption that had recently killed Mary's much beloved daughter. Soon afterwards Elizabeth Lucas also died, peacefully, in her sleep—as if Death himself "was enamoured with her," Margaret thought, "for he embraced her in a sleep, and so gently, as if he were afraid to hurt her." Yet Margaret felt bitter at her family's sufferings—at how "my mother lived to see the ruin of her children, in which was her ruin, and then died."[58] By the summer of 1647 her own health was suffering. Sir Thomas Cademan, physician to Queen Henrietta Maria, recommended crocus metallorum (a poisonous compound of antimony) to purge the dangerous ill humors from her body. "My Lady Marquess of Newcastle is one of those that is so hardly moved to cast, that her Ladyship must have a double dose at least."[59]

William himself was still healthy. "The joy you have in my sweet Lady, and happy tranquility at home in your blessed family is the best preservative of your health," Cademan thought. But illness was becoming an increasing preoccupation, and about this time William began to collect a huge range of medical prescriptions. From physicians and apothecaries, both French and

English, came medicines for sore eyes and diarrhea, poultices for swellings and infected cuts, balsams for wounds and ulcers. Dr. Davison, who had saved Margaret's life with laudanum, provided recipes for curing coughs and cooling fevers. Cademan described the "steel liquor" with which he had treated Prince Charles. Margaret's own "receipt to cure a flux or dysentery" was included. "Take a pretty quantity of milk and boil it well three times over, and scum it every time and then drink it as hot as you can endure it. Probatum est"—a remedy that, at worst, would do less harm than the many toxic chemicals used by professional doctors. Kenelm Digby, now on an embassy from Henrietta Maria to the pope, sent the latest medical discoveries from Rome, and forwarded the medicines of the duke of Northumberland, a noted chemist and a Roman Catholic like Digby. The duke's "great cordial, invented by himself . . . the surest remedy against all poisons and the plague," his method for preparing "great oil of sulphur, a great and safe remedy," his "tincture of gold . . . an admirable remedy" were all to be prepared with elaborate chemical equipment.[60]

In the autumn of 1647 William and Margaret's debt problems came to a crisis. One day the family's steward approached William "to tell him that he was not able to provide a dinner for him, for his creditors were resolved to trust him no longer." William, "being always a great master of his passions, was—at least showed himself—not in any manner troubled at it," Margaret told the story, "but in a pleasant humour told me that I must of necessity pawn my clothes to make so much money as would procure a dinner." Margaret pointed out "that my clothes would be of small value" and so passed the problem on to Elizabeth Chaplain, asking her "to pawn some small toys* which I had formerly given her, which she willingly did." The family ate their meal, and then that afternoon William spoke to his creditors "and by his civil deportment and persuasive arguments, obtained so much that they did not only trust him for more necessaries, but lent him money besides to redeem those toys that were pawned."[61]

Soon Margaret sent Elizabeth Chaplain to England, to ask her brother John for her still unpaid dowry, while William sent his sons' tutor, Mr. Benoist, to seek loans from his friends and relatives. There is no record of when, or even whether, Margaret's dowry was paid. Perhaps she received at least part of it now, since John, restored to his estates, was again able to borrow money. Benoist, however, was certainly unsuccessful, writing back to William that "everybody was so afraid of the Parliament that they durst not relieve him, who was counted a traitor for his honest and loyal service to his King and

---

*Jewelry or other trinkets of little value.

country." In this impasse, William began to consider rich marriages for his sons, "hoping by that means to provide both for them and himself." In December Charles and Henry were sent back to England, but they rebelled against their arranged marriages. Instead they remained in London, "living as well as they could," while attempting to compound for their estates.[62]

It was Henrietta Maria who finally brought financial salvation to the Cavendish household, paying £2,000 to William in partial return for the money he had given her five years before in Yorkshire. "So great and generous was the bounty and favour of her Majesty to my Lord," exclaimed Margaret, "even at the time when her Majesty stood most in need of it [money]." Thus enriched, William inspired yet more confidence in his creditors and, early in 1648, he rented a grand house "and furnished it as well as his new-gotten credit would permit."[63] He bought a new coach, so that Margaret could go out in style to the tree-lined avenues of the Course, an area like London's Hyde Park, where fashionable society drove in their carriages before returning to walk in the gardens of the Tuileries in the evening. For himself, William bought two expensive Barbary horses, so he could once again practice his beloved manège.

This carefree spending, always living better than he could afford, was an essential part of William's success as a borrower. His grandeur, style, and obvious belief in his financial worth inspired creditors to lend him money that they denied to others. (Endymion Porter had already been forced to leave Paris, unable to find credit.) Margaret was hugely proud of William's ability to negotiate loans. She would later tell many stories of their parlous finances, admiring the charm and eloquence by which William achieved his never-ending triumphs over incredible odds.

The Cavendishes spent their money on intellectual as well as material riches, indulging the family's longstanding passion for telescopes. First used to study the night sky by Galileo in 1609, the telescope had revealed exciting discoveries—the moons of Jupiter, sunspots, the mountains and craters of the moon, new stars invisible to the naked eye—discoveries that Galileo had used to support the Copernican system of astronomy, removing mankind and the Earth from the center of the universe and denying the heavens their immutable Aristotelian perfection. All over Europe the excitement spread, and telescopes were built and turned skywards. Researchers like Hobbes and Sir Charles Cavendish built their own; professional scholars like Galileo and Torricelli had a lucrative sideline in constructing them for clients; and the first professional workshops emerged, with specialized craftsmen manufacturing some of the largest and finest lenses.

In the 1640s the instrument was still in its infancy, unstandardized in design, each one individually produced. The shapes of the lenses (whether convex or concave on either side), the techniques for grinding their surfaces, the composition of the glass—every maker had his own methods, often kept as closely guarded secrets. The merits of rival telescopes were eagerly debated, and the best were much sought after. For years Sir Charles Cavendish's correspondence had been full of such matters, and early in 1648 he and William invested heavily.

In February they possessed two telescopes, newly arrived from "the famous Torricelli," court mathematician to the grand duke of Tuscany, the larger of the two being nearly sixteen feet long. Another still larger glass, built by Fontanus, was a gift from Sir Kenelm Digby, still on his embassy in Rome. Eighteen feet long, it was reputed to be the maker's best instrument, "but we have not yet looked in it, the tube* for it being not yet come, but we daily expect it." There were also four telescopes from the Roman workshop of Eustachio Divini, famous for grinding especially large lenses. These were the first of Divini's instruments ever imported into France: most exciting was a monster machine, twenty-nine feet long, that the Cavendishes had not yet tried, but that "if it be well wrought will doubtless excel all the rest, being of so great a length." In addition, there was Sir Charles's own older telescope, and another was still expected from the German Capuchin friar and astronomer, Schyrlaeus de Rheita, whose main innovation was to use four convex lenses to produce an erect and very large image: in its long journey this telescope had now arrived in the Netherlands "and hath been there, as I remember they writ, tried and said to be very rare."[64]

The collection was outstanding, and by the summer news "that the Marquess of Newcastle hath gathered together all the exquisite masterpieces for optical glasses" was circulating round the intellectual networks of Europe. With William and Sir Charles as her mentors, Margaret could now observe the latest astronomical discoveries through the very best instruments. She also had her own microscope—"my Lady's multiplying glass," eighteen inches long, focused with a screw of ten threads—for observing the many newly discovered phenomena at the opposite end of the spectrum of scale.[65]

But despite their greater material comfort, both Margaret and William were now oppressed by ill health. Early in 1648 they began years of consultation with England's most famous doctor, Sir Theodore Mayerne. Physician to king, queen, and court before the Civil War, Mayerne was still living in London, where he conducted his aristocratic medical practice by post, rarely leaving his house. In response to William's letter, Mayerne diagnosed both his patients as "melancholic hypochondriac," suffering from a serious imbalance in the four

---

*The outer casing, which would contain the lenses.

humors—blood, phlegm, black bile, and yellow bile—which governed the operation of the human body. In both patients, he judged, too much black bile, or "melancholy," was being produced by disorders in the "hypochondria"—the abdominal organs of stomach, liver, and spleen. In William this was producing wind in the stomach, cloudy vision, and ringing in his ears. In Margaret the symptoms were probably nothing more than unhappiness and constipation—a condition to which she was very prone, and which seventeenth-century doctors thought terribly serious because it concentrated noxious humors in the body that should have been evacuated.

On her own initiative, Margaret was already taking vomits—a standard means for removing excess humors and restoring the proper bodily balance. But Mayerne did not approve of her practice: "let her remember," he advised, "that the stomach is a very precious part, to which she must have a special regard; for if the kitchen* fail, farewell to all the rest." Instead, he recommended gentler remedies—especially the drinking of spa water. Diet too was vital: foods with hot and dry qualities were to be avoided, as producing melancholy, while cooling, moistening foods would tend to remedy the condition. So William was to avoid wine and ale "which do easily turn into vinegar" in the stomach; nor was he to eat salads "which cannot be without lemon or vinegar." Lettuce was especially pernicious "being hurtful to the brain"; but apples, strawberries, cherries, and melons should be eaten in season. Small beer was permissible, and would become positively medicinal if oatmeal and "iron scales"—flakes of oxidized metal—were added to the barrel kept in the cellar. But best of all was to drink pure water "whereof there is no want at Paris and St. Germain." Then there was tea, "an herb which comes from China and Japan." "I think it is not amiss that you try it," Mayerne advised William. Though he knew little of it himself, "some merchants who have lived a long while in the Indies have assured me that the decoction of it drunk warm doth marvels, especially to abate fumes, [and] to keep a man awake when he hath business . . . I understand that this drug is very well known in France; you may inform yourself of those that use it, and do as others do."[66]

Mayerne also offered advice on another problem that was causing the couple great distress: after more than two years of marriage, Margaret was still not pregnant. William was desperate for children. In England, his son Henry was suffering from convulsive fits and might not live—the doctors were prescribing a poisonous brew of vomits and enemas, mercury and gold to kill the worms they thought caused the disease and, at mealtimes, "the powder of frogs dried in an oven, and putten upon his meat as if it were nutmeg."[67] In spite of

---

*The stomach was thought to "concoct" or cook food, preparing it for the body.

all their attentions, Henry would recover a year later, but Margaret felt under huge pressure, finding her husband "so desirous of male issue that I have heard him say he cared not (so God would be pleased to give him many sons) although they came to be persons of the meanest fortunes."[68]

Mayerne was cautious. "There are many particulars whereof I should be informed before I can give solid counsel for generation," he wrote,

> and I know not if in the estate she's in, you ought earnestly to desire it. It is hard to get children with good courage when one is melancholy, and after they are got and come into the world . . . very often one loses them, as I have tried to my great grief, and am sorry to have had them. Be in good health and then you may till your ground.

Nonetheless, wishing Margaret "the accomplishment of her good desire," he recommended that she drink spa water and then bathe at Bourbon-l'Archambault.[69]

However, it is not at all clear that the couple's childlessness was Margaret's fault. William, now in his midfifties, was suffering from impotence. His greatest hope for a cure came from Sir Kenelm Digby, who sent news from Rome of a new miracle cure—powder of vipers, made by a "rare apothecary," Antonio Manfredi, who killed 3,000 adders each year to produce his medicine, as well as buying expensive drugs from Egypt, Arabia, and India. "By a long use of such flesh of vipers, old men grow young," Digby promised, "and men grown eunuchs by age become Priapus again; indeed they [the vipers] restore nature strangely if they be constantly used every day for a long time, as for a year or more." "If your lordship will have any," Digby advised, "you must bespeak in time for the viper season": Manfredi had "done such miracles" with the powder that his stock was sold out within three months of making it each year, except only "such store as his concubine . . . maketh him keep for himself, for by means of it . . . , she findeth him a cavalier of 25 years old, though indeed he be 70." William was to take half a dram each day dissolved in wine or broth. When he complained that the powder was full of hairs, Digby replied that these were parts of the snakes' backbone. "Some are of opinion it is the most effective part of the viper, and therefore by no means put it away," he advised. In return, William told Digby his own secret recipe against syphilis.[70]

William also consulted the Parisian doctor Nodin, who recommended a diet of heating foods: wine, spices, and eggs, with young rabbits, larks, quails, pigeons, partridges, and other small birds—all meats that were thought to provoke lust and procreation because the animals themselves were lustful. If this diet was not sufficient, William was to take Nodin's "strengthening electuary" morning and evening for "two or three days before he will come to his end." Then, on the great day itself, he was to eat "mutton dressed with new-laid eggs, with a little nutmeg and amber" at four in the afternoon, followed at nine by a double dose of the electuary: "afterwards let him expect with patience." If even this failed and "nature is lazy and slow," then "with the other helps that very prentices in this trade knoweth as well as the master, he shall receive relief and comfort by anointing the great toe of the left foot with an oil in which cantharides* hath been dissolved," Nodin added.[71]

His advice certainly conjures up a stressful, precarious sex life, but in the spring of 1648 renewed political hopes provided Margaret and William with some distraction, at least. Following a winter of widespread unrest in England, civil war had again broken out. Part of the parliamentarian fleet had mutinied and there were royalist forces in Northumberland, Essex, and Kent. In Essex, Margaret's brother John, doubtless despairing of the uprising's success, "did do some good offices . . . to the Parliament's party"; he then fled from any further involvement, bringing his wife and children up from Colchester to London, which was still safely under Parliament's control.[72]

Charles Lucas also thought the cause hopeless. But, after the news falsely reported him to be already involved in the risings, he was forced to flee from London (where he had been living in private retirement, writing both a military treatise and royalist poems expressing his grief at the state of his country). In Essex, the rebels chose him as their leader and—in spite of his oath of loyalty to Parliament, and another more personal oath to Lord General Fairfax that he would not bear arms for the king again—he accepted the command. Charles's royalism was irrepressible: on the subject of honors and rewards he was often heard to say "that he preferred the style of loyalty before any dignity Earth could confer upon him."[73] Early in June, he joined up with the Kentish rebels, and then they marched north, planning to continue through East Anglia recruiting. But at Colchester they were overtaken by Lord Fairfax's pursuing parliamentarian army and besieged.

In Paris, the émigrés' hopes were high. Prince Charles and his cousin Prince Rupert left the city late in June, to take command of the mutinous parliamentarian warships now in Holland. Soon afterwards the queen, distrusting the eighteen-year-old Prince of Wales and his rash young cousin, asked William, older and wiser, to follow them. To enable him to leave, she arranged for her courtiers to stand as security for his now sizeable debts. Just one of the ensuing legal bonds was for £1,300, owed to a single merchant.[74] Still needing funds for his traveling expenses, William managed to borrow a further £300 or

---

*The dried beetle Cantharis vesicatoria or Spanish Fly, a common aphrodisiac.

£400, nearly a hundred of it coming from Thomas Hobbes, who at the same time took back a telescope for which William had not yet paid him.[75]

After little more than six months in their grand new house, Margaret and the rest of the family packed up their possessions. In the third week of July they set off, William and Margaret riding in a little chariot that held just the two of them, while Sir Charles Cavendish, Elizabeth Chaplain, Lord Widdrington, and others occupied the family coach. Three wagons full of possessions and various servants riding on horseback completed the cavalcade.[76]

Chapter Seven

Dutch Scholar, 1648–1651

*F*rom Paris they journeyed north into the Spanish Netherlands, where William was everywhere treated with great respect. At Cambrai they arrived after dark and the city's governor—"a right noble Spaniard," Margaret wrote—sent torchbearers to meet them. He offered William the keys of the city, asked him to choose the password for the guard that night, and sent rich provisions to his lodgings.[1] Thence the travelers continued through Brussels to Antwerp, where they took ship to Rotterdam, one of the busiest ports of the Dutch United Provinces. Here they heard that Prince Charles and the English fleet had already set sail.

William at once "resolved to follow him, and for that purpose hired a boat, and victualled it," Margaret recalled. "But since nobody knew whither his Highness was gone, and I being unwilling that my Lord should venture upon so uncertain a voyage, and (as the proverb is) seek a needle in a bottle of hay, he desisted from that design." Margaret's fears had predominated, but Lord Widdrington and others, lacking such wifely persuasions, set out to seek their prince. They returned unsuccessful, however, "having by a storm been driven towards the coast of Scotland, and endangered their lives," Margaret noted in justification of her own foresight.[2]

In Rotterdam William now kept "an open and noble table for all comers," and especially for military men, hoping to lead them back to England. But the royalist rebellion there was going badly. Charles Lucas had now been besieged in Colchester for two months. Lord Fairfax's earthworks surrounded the town, his artillery bombarded the royalist positions, and within the walls soldiers and townspeople starved together. The Lucases' house at St. John's had already been captured by Fairfax, after heavy artillery bombardment. Half the house was destroyed when the royalists' powder magazine there exploded. The

104

remainder fell victim to the parliamentarian soldiers who, finding only stools and bedsteads to plunder, "exercised their brutal rage upon the bare walls." Thence they proceeded to St. Giles's Church next door. Entering the Lucases' burial vault, they broke open the tombs and "scattered the bones about with profane jests." Margaret's mother and her sister Mary were so recently buried that their hair remained undecayed and this the soldiers "cut off . . . and wore it in their hats."[3]

By now the royalists' only hope lay with an invading Scots army—this time fighting in support of the king. But on August 28 news reached Colchester of the Scots' defeat by Cromwell in Lancashire, and Charles Lucas and the other commanders were forced to agree to Lord Fairfax's uncompromising conditions of surrender: while the ordinary soldiers were guaranteed their lives, their officers must "deliver themselves up prisoners at mercy."[4] They were herded into the town's common jail in the Moot Hall, whence Fairfax chose three for summary execution, to set an example to other rebels.

Sir Charles Lucas, Sir George Lisle, and Sir Bernard Gascoigne were summoned by Fairfax and his council of war and told they were to be shot without trial. When Lucas asked that the execution be delayed until the next day so they could "make some addresses to God above, and settle some things below, that I might not be hurried out of this world with all my sins about me," he was refused. Then "do your worst," he responded, "I shall soon be ready for execution." After receiving communion from one of the royalists' chaplains, the three men were taken out to the north wall of the town's castle to face the firing squad.

At the last moment Gascoigne was reprieved, when the parliamentarians realized he was a foreigner. Then Margaret's brother spoke his last words. "Remember me to all my friends, and tell them that I have died in a good cause" and, to his executioners, "I pray God forgive you all, I pray God forgive you, gentlemen. Farewell, I pray God's vengeance may not fall on you for it." And then: "I have often looked death in the face on the field of battle, and you shall now see I dare die." He prayed briefly and then tore open his shirt and pulled down his hat over his eyes: "See, I am ready for you; and now, rebels, do your worst!"[5]

Lisle was shot next. Then Fairfax fined the townspeople £12,000 to pay off his troops and prevent them from pillage. Marching away to London with his prisoners, he left Colchester in ruins, with thousands of people homeless. The houses were gradually rebuilt, but the town never recovered its prosperity and most of the churches were still derelict when Daniel Defoe passed through in the 1700s.

Charles Lucas and George Lisle had become royalist martyrs, their heroic deaths commemorated by poets and pamphleteers. The frontispiece of one news-sheet, *The Loyall Sacrifice*, shows Lisle standing fearless beside his dead comrade. "Shoot rebels," he says,

> *Your shot, your shame;*
> *Our fall, our fame.*

The site of the execution became a place of pilgrimage, where visitors like John Evelyn were shown "a kind of miracle"—an area "bare of grass for a large space, all the rest of it abounding with herbage."[6]

The loss of "my dear brother . . . most inhumanly murdered" lay heavy on Margaret—especially as Charles's death was followed next year by that of his brother Thomas, who had never fully recovered from his head wound of 1642. "They loved virtue, endeavoured merit, practised justice, and spoke truth," Margaret passionately commemorated her brothers, "they were constantly loyal, and truly valiant." In the space of three years, she had lost four of her closest family, and she was torn with grief. "I shall lament the loss so long as I live."[7] Thoughts of mortality obsessed her. "Death seems terrible, I am sure it doth to me, there is nothing I dread more than death," she wrote. "Nature hath made our bodily lives so short that if we should live the full period, it were but like a flash of lightning that continues not and for the most part leaves black oblivion behind it."[8]

During the next few years these morbid ideas would become the driving motivation behind Margaret's ambition to write. The fate of her mother and sister had persuaded her of the vanity of earthly memorials: it was "but a folly" to plan costly tombs "since not only time, but wars will ruin them." Instead she would seek the Horatian construction of a *monumentum aere perennius*—a monument more lasting than bronze:

> *I care not where my dust or bones remain,*
> *So my works live, the labour of my brain.*[9]

By the end of August 1648 the new civil war was over. Prince Charles's fleet, facing strong coastal defenses, had failed either to relieve Colchester or to release King Charles I, now imprisoned on the Isle of Wight. Early in September, they returned to the Netherlands for reprovisioning, and Charles went to live at the Hague, where his sister Mary was the wife of the Dutch stadtholder, William II of Orange. From Rotterdam, William visited the prince regularly during September "expecting some opportunity where he might be able to show his readiness to serve his King and country." But nothing arose. With new debts mounting steadily from his expensive public entertainments, William decided that he must "retire to some place where he might live privately" (and cheaply). "His choice for the most pleasantest and quietest place to retire himself and [his] ruined fortunes" was Antwerp, some seventy miles south of the Hague, in the Spanish Netherlands.[10]

Antwerp was bounded on its western edge by the broad River Scheldt where, in the city's sixteenth-century heyday, as many as 2,500 ships were regularly seen at anchor, waiting up to three weeks for a mooring. Since the Dutch revolt against their Spanish rulers, Antwerp's position as the Netherlands's foremost trading center had been taken by Amsterdam in the United Provinces, but the city still retained a flourishing mercantile community. Its glassworks rivaled those of Venice, producing rich colored vessels, decorated with gold and silver. Its tapestry and furniture industry supplied items all over Europe; when seeking something of extra luxury—perhaps an ebony or tortoiseshell cabinet bound in silver or gold—the English exiles knew that "the best choice is at Antwerp."[11] Here in profusion were goldsmiths, tailors, and sweetmeat manufacturers—marshmallows were a specialty. There were twenty-six marketplaces, each vending its individual goods: the fish market in particular was known for the quality and variety of its local produce, both from salt and fresh water. Wealthy guild-houses lined the city's spacious squares. Shops in its colonnaded exchange sold a wide variety of commodities while, a few streets further north, the London Merchant Adventurers' Company had their own English exchange. With such a thriving mercantile community, the rush hour was a scene of wonder to visitors. "Imagine," one commentator exclaimed, "twice a day, at noon and in the evening, more than 5,000 men all heading for their place of business!"

In this cosmopolitan city, the inhabitants—including the women—commonly spoke three or four languages, some as many as seven. Antwerp was well known for the warm welcome it extended to foreigners. It was known too for its beauty, in which many people thought it exceeded even such great Italian cities as Florence. Its public buildings were magnificent, its sumptuous churches and monasteries overflowed with polished marble, carvings, statues, stained glass, and the paintings of the city's recent masters (especially Rubens, who had died just eight years before). Visitors remarked on Antwerp's broad streets, so clean that it was a pleasure to walk in them, and on its open, airy squares, lined with trees. They climbed the 400-foot cathedral bell tower—from which elaborate chimes rang out over the city every hour—to see the view extending over the countryside to Brussels in the south and to the distant sea in the north. In the grand brick houses below, visitors found expensive private art collections and gardens of rare plants, fountains, and orange and lemon trees. Antwerp's inhabitants were mad on gardening; it was said that there was no herb in the whole world not cultivated here.

As a place for civilized, aristocratic retirement the city was ideal, offering not only material magnificence but also a great historic tradition in both art and scholarship. Here three long-established literary societies were dedicated to promoting Dutch culture, bringing together historians, poets, classicists, mathematicians, and art-lovers for regular meetings and dinners, poetry readings and theatrical performances. Here the painters Van Dyck and Rubens had both spent significant portions of their working lives, and a vast art trade was still conducted in painters' studios and dealers' galleries. In the world of books, Antwerp's Plantin press was the foremost publishing house in Europe. With twelve printing presses and an exceptional collection of over a hundred typefaces—including Hebrew, Syriac, and musical notations—the Plantin house turned out books renowned for their neatness and accuracy, and attracted an international community of authors and book buyers to the city.

Late in September 1648, William visited the Hague for the last time to take his leave of Prince Charles; then the family departed from Rotterdam, where they had spent some £3,000. In Antwerp they put up at an inn while William sought a suitable house to rent. As time drew on, his old friend Endymion Porter, "not willing that a person of such quality as my Lord should lie in a public house," offered William part of his own lodgings "and would not be at quiet until he had accepted of them." But at last William found what he was seeking—the house that the artist Peter Paul Rubens had designed and built for himself some thirty years before, and that the painter's widow now wanted to let.[12]

To the street, it presented a long, regular facade of plain windows; simple, even austere. But entry through the oak double doors past the porter's lodge revealed a courtyard of Renaissance splendor. The house was arranged around three sides of the court. On the right as you entered was the painter's huge studio, its walls exquisitely decorated with classical figures. Ancient gods lined the top story above a frieze of scenes from mythology—Perseus rescuing Andromeda, Bacchus in triumph in his chariot drawn by bears, and many others. On the next story below, arched windows alternated with the busts of classical philosophers, and at ground level were grotesque busts of the more comic figures of antiquity. Large windows lit the two-story space inside, where Rubens and his assistants had worked.

Then there were two lower wings of living quarters. To the left of the entrance gateway, by the porter's lodge, a low doorway led through towards service rooms and the kitchen. Beyond them was a series of more important rooms—dining room and bedrooms and, at the end of the wing, Rubens's gallery, where he had displayed much of his huge art collection. This was the largest room in the house after the painter's studio, with a semicircular museum at one end, a rich confection of pink, yellow, and white marble columns and niches, lit by a cupola in the roof, inspired by the Pantheon in Rome. The room was suitable for receiving grand visitors and perhaps became William's bedchamber, while the bedroom directly above it—the second largest in house, with views out over the garden—was perhaps used by Margaret.

Important visitors could also enter the house by turning right at the great gateway, where a spacious oak staircase with Triton banisters led up to a first floor balcony overlooking the courtyard. Beyond was the great chamber—the room where Rubens and his family had spent their evenings. It had the grandest fireplace of all the living quarters, flanked by marble columns, and windows looking out over the courtyard on one side and the street on the other. Above all this, a top floor of garrets provided lodgings for servants. Back outside, the fourth side of the courtyard was finished with a stone screen in classical style, topped by bronze statues of Hermes and Athena, symbolizing Antwerp's culture of commerce conjoined with art. Through the screen's three arches could be seen the garden beyond—a parterre of flowers surrounded by low hedges—where Margaret and others could walk in peace, secluded from the bustling life of the city. A columned pavilion at the end of the view provided a place to sit in shelter from sun or rain.

The whole formed an intimate space—decidedly small for such social occasions as the ball for the English court, which the Newcastles would later hold here. The entire house would have fitted into a single wing of William's residences at Welbeck and Bolsover. But with its exterior friezes and its interior decor of inlaid marble fireplaces and elaborately carved wooden door surrounds and mantelpieces, the house was a gem of art and taste. Here William had indeed found something "which might fit him and his small family . . . and also be for his own content."[13]

But once again the family found themselves "much necessitated for money." William sought anxiously for loans—a difficult undertaking when he was "not only a stranger in that nation, but, to all appearance, a ruined man." Finally he managed to borrow £200 from the duke of Buckingham's English agent in Antwerp and, by skillful use of this small sum, he established his creditworthiness among the local tradesmen. Needing furniture for his new house, he "was credited by the citizens for as many goods as he was pleased to have," Margaret recalled, "as also for meat and drink, and all kind of necessaries and provisions, which certainly was a special blessing of God."[14]

And so the Cavendish family, with the help of Divine Providence, settled into their new home, resolving "to remain here till it shall please God to reduce the sufferings of England to such a condition of peace or war as may become honest men to return home."[15] As autumn turned to winter they followed the final, disastrous act in the tragedy that was England's troubles. The army, angry at Parliament's endless negotiations with the imprisoned king, seized power and ejected the pro-negotiation members from the House of Commons. The tiny remaining Rump Parliament then voted to put Charles I on trial for treason. International opinion was outraged, but by the evening of January 30, 1649, the king was dead, beheaded in front of huge crowds outside his old banqueting house at Whitehall. Six weeks later Parliament ordered that William and a handful of other leading royalists "be proscribed and banished as enemies and traitors, and die without mercy, wherever they shall be found within the limits of this nation, and their estates be confiscated."[16]

That summer, the Newcastles' health worries reasserted themselves. Still failing in their desire to have children, the couple tried new remedies. For William's impotence there was "Doctor Farrer's Fortification, a great secret"—white crystals extracted from wood ash, which were to be taken in wine for six mornings, and then "expect the effect." Meanwhile Margaret took "Doctor Farrer's Receipt for the Sterility in Women"—a decoction of herbs to be injected into the womb with a syringe morning and night for several days.[17] But their efforts still resulted in failure.

For Margaret it was a matter of considerable guilt. She knew it was "the part of every good wife to desire children to keep alive the memory of their husbands' name." Sterility was commonly blamed on the woman, and Margaret readily accepted that her body was the physical cause. But the moral responsibility, she suggested, lay elsewhere: it was God who "ordered it . . . making me barren."[18] In reality, however, the physiological origin of the couple's childlessness is not so clear. Now in his midfifties and formerly a womanizer, William could have been sterile.[19] And although chronic menstrual problems were common in women due to dietary deficiencies, there is no evidence in the family's medical manuscripts that Margaret had irregular periods. Whatever the cause, the couple eventually had to accept their childlessness, and after 1649 they collected no new remedies for sexual problems.

Melancholy again afflicted the Newcastles. Both were anxious patients, dosing themselves too strongly and with too many different medicines, from which they expected to see instant effects, and Sir Theodore Mayerne's letters were often blunt. "To cure my Lady Marquess your wife," he told William, would be a hard task, "not so much for the nature of the disease, which is rebellious, as for the disposition of the patient, who will not willingly submit to the counsel of her physicians, be they never so good and so skillful." Now suffering from hemorrhoids, Margaret "hath been purged and let blood very much and without doubt too much," he warned, "since it hath been done by her own directions." Instead of treating herself "by piecemeals, according to her custom," it was vital that she follow his prescriptions systematically over a long period, "and if she find not ease immediately, she must not leave all, as I fear she will, but she must be constant, or else she shall not be cured." Mayerne's elaborate recommendations—based as usual on the principle of purging the noxious melancholic humors from the body—would structure Margaret's days throughout the year.

In the autumn, the course of treatment began with a clyster of flowers and herbs injected into the rectum, followed the next morning with a strong purge of rhubarb and spices (after which Margaret had to spend all day in her bedchamber). On the next day, she was bled in the right arm, and then for six days a julep of apples, barley, hartshorn, and ivory shavings in wine was to be drunk at 7 A.M. and 4 P.M. Then, after another day in bed with a strong purge, Margaret could begin to take Mayerne's "steel liquor." This was the principal remedy in which the great physician set his trust—a solution of white mineral crystals (made by standing steel shavings in spirits of wine and oil of brimstone) dissolved in an infusion of apples, fern roots, flowers, "nephritic wood" from a particular Mexican tree, ivory, and spices, heated in a *bain-marie* for a week. This concoction Margaret was to take every morning at six, followed by an hour in bed and two hours of moderate exercise; on every third day the purge was to be strengthened by adding extra rhubarb and senna.

The steel medicine was truly foul—"a drench that would poison a horse," commented another female patient: it "makes me so horridly sick that every day at ten o'clock I am making my will, and taking leave of all my friends . . . 'Tis worse than dying by the half."[20] As with all purges, the patient had to remain at home, within reach of a lavatory, until the medicine had done its work. And all this, in a "rooted and inveterate" case like Margaret's, the doctors recommended should continue "for some years together, in the Spring and Fall."

As the heat of summer approached and the strongest purges were no longer safe, Margaret was to start drinking the mineral waters of Spa—sold in Antwerp in three-pint glass bottles. Each morning she must increase her dose, from one pint on the first day to six pints on the fifth, "and so every day to increase," taking as much as "her stomach can endure," accompanied by aniseed comfits. The entire fizzy dose having been consumed within the space of an hour, she should take some exercise, followed by a period of rest, when she was not allowed to sleep. In the middle of the day, after the waters had done their work, she could eat a dinner of partridges, chicken, or mutton, washed down with Rhenish wine or more Spa water. Then she was to have a lukewarm bath, scented with mallows, violets, and other herbs, and at supper to eat very lightly of either eggs or prunes. If her hemorrhoids still swelled, Mayerne counseled her to apply leeches to them in the afternoons, with a physician present to supervise the quantity of blood removed. She must have a physician in attendance throughout, Mayerne warned, to treat the Spa water's possible side effects of headaches and dizziness. Then, in the autumn, she must return once more to the steel drink, combined with black hellebore. She should be bled too, ideally in her thigh, "but fair ladies who have dainty husbands do not willingly admit of that subjection." Throughout all this, Mayerne advised, his patients must stay cheerful. "The mind hath a great commandment and power of the body, and therefore keep your mind as clear and most pleased as you can."[21]

IN 1648, when Margaret and William arrived in Antwerp, they found a large English mercantile community but almost no "persons of quality" of their own class with whom they might mix socially. Far away also from the political councils of the English court at the Hague, they now had long solitary leisure hours to fill. This was exactly the life William had sought in leaving Rotterdam. He loved to pursue his wide-ranging interests in literature, music, weapons, and horsemanship, and he seized this opportunity to restart his manège, establishing his own private riding house in Antwerp, where he and Captain Mazine began to train the two expensive horses that William had bought in Paris.[22]

But much of his time William spent with Margaret, talking and joking, telling her of his experiences of life "in the great world" and of his own reflections on that world.[23] This was Margaret's ideal of the very "best kind of discourse"—a style of conversation "most various, free and easy," ranging through a huge diversity of topics. From the histories of different countries, with their laws, religions, and wars, William's talk would pass to great generals and their strategies. Famous statesmen too he told of, and the different systems of government, with "the beginning of states, their falls, [and] the causes of their risings and their ruins." From trade and colonization they passed on to architecture and education, to the work of Europe's great philosophers and historians, both ancient and modern, and to assessments of the relative merits of the famous poets. William spoke of the fashions of different nations in sports, dress, diet, and entertainment, and of the tyranny or clemency of kings with their "factions, their splendours, their decays, their pastimes and recreations." He told Margaret too of the sorts of heroines who fired her imagination—of "women famous for beauty and martial exploits."[24]

As before with her childhood family, Margaret found that her passionate devotion kept her a riveted listener, utterly engrossed in what her husband said. "When the nearest and dearest of my friends speak," she noted, "I give such an attention to them as if I had no other thoughts . . . I cannot forget anything they say, such deep impressions their words print in my brain." William's talk especially, with its "lively descriptions," was inspirational. For instance, when he told her of anatomy, with "all the parts of the animal body and how they are formed and composed," then she would "conceive it as perfectly to my understanding as if I had seen it dissected, although I never did."[25]

With his broad gentlemanly learning and long life experience, William could teach her something of everything, and Margaret felt she was gaining a share of the wisdom she so admired in her husband. William had become "my only tutor" and she was his "scholar"—"not so apt a scholar as to improve much in wit," she demurred, "yet I am so industrious a scholar as to remember whatsoever he hath said and discoursed to me." "My Lord was the master and I the prentice," she described their relationship again, and "so I do daily learn knowledge and understanding, wit, and the purity of my language."[26]

This grand new educational endeavor was a business of delight to Margaret. "When my Lord admits me to his company," she enthused, "I dance a measure with the Muses, feast with the sciences, or sit and discourse with the arts."[27] And with the pleasure went a more serious experience—the transition from childhood to an adult comprehension of the world. "From the time of twelve years old, I have studied upon observations and lived upon contemplation, making the world my book," Margaret explained,

> but I found the world too difficult to be understood by my tender years and weak capacity, that till the time I was married I could only read the letters and join the words, but understood nothing of the sense of the world, until my Lord . . . instructed me, reading several lectures thereof to me, and expounding the hard and obscure passages therein.[28]

Margaret also learned from William's scholarly brother. Sir Charles Cavendish was at the cutting edge of modern research in algebra and geometry. He eagerly discussed with Europe's leading mathematicians the latest attempts to square the circle, to calculate tangents to curves, and to find methods for solving quadratic and cubic equations. He was also collecting the unpublished papers of his mathematical friends—the proofs and theorems of Pierre de Fermat, Roberval, Descartes, and others—which he intended eventually to publish. Into so technical a specialism neither Margaret nor William could follow him, but philosophy was a subject of more general interest, and here Sir Charles's notebooks and letters provide informal snapshots of the family's studies.

Atomism was as ever a major preoccupation—and especially its application to understanding the human mind. Emotion, sense perception, and rational thought—developing mechanical models for these processes was an important goal for philosophers like Hobbes, Descartes, and Kenelm Digby, and their results were of vital interest to many exiled royalists. With a science of the human mind, they hoped, it would be possible to understand and thus control human beliefs and behavior, ensuring England a peaceful populace and no further danger of civil war. In 1649 Hobbes's *Humane Nature . . . being a discovery of the faculties, acts and passions of the soul of man, from their original causes* was published, dedicated to William, who had first asked the philosopher to write up his ideas on the subject. In February 1650 the Cavendish family was eagerly discussing the merits of Descartes's rival work, *Passions de l'Ame*, recently published in Amsterdam. Hoping like others for a science of human behavior—one that would take on all the certainty of mathematical proof—Sir Charles Cavendish attempted to formulate a system of equations that would relate the magnitudes of various desires and fears to a final outcome of decision and action.[29]

With these psychological studies went a broader interest in human anatomy and physiology. The structure and operation of the stomach, liver, heart, and brain were all at the forefront of contemporary medical research, and Sir Charles took notes on the revolutionary observations of the sixteenth-century anatomist Vesalius, as well as the more recent work of Descartes and Gassendi. He was especially fascinated by William Harvey's innovative theory of the circulation of the blood, first published with systematic experimental proofs some twenty years before. Overturning the ancient Galenic medical theory—that the blood was fed into and used up by the tissues of the body, so that it must be continuously generated in the liver from food digested in the stomach—Harvey's theory demanded a complete new system of physiology, and Sir Charles listed a whole range of questions that researchers must now answer.

In the family laboratory (where Sir Charles was currently attempting to develop a copying machine), Margaret became involved in many of the experiments that most puzzled and fascinated contemporary philosophers. Here she saw the strange behavior of mercury—a liquid that would readily divide "into little spherical bodies, running about, though it be ne'er so small a quantity"—an effect she would later use as an analogy to explain her theory of the operation of the mind. She became well acquainted with the process of chemical distillation, which "from a gross substance extracts the . . . essence and spirits," producing "several extractions, as it were, out of one and the same thing," and she observed the action of acids, which "cut and divide all that opposeth their way" and which would even "eat into the hardest iron"—providing her with another parallel for the activity of the mind.[30] Her viewing of human organs—"brain . . . heart . . . stomach, liver, lights [lungs], spleen, and the like"—pickled in jars provided her only observations of human anatomy, while her inspection of plant and animal material through her microscope suggested to her that much of the natural world might be made by a process like weaving.[31] In optics, she had seen the dramatic effect produced when a burning glass focused the sun's rays to a point, and she knew the recently discovered and as yet unexplained phenomenon of how the "most various colours in the world" are produced when light passes through a triangular glass prism. She also observed how, when a glass of water was turned upside down on top of another vessel of water, none of the water in the glass flowed out—a strange effect akin to the Torricelli experiment,* which was currently fascinating and puzzling philosophers, and which Sir Charles Cavendish had seen while the family was still in Paris.[32] Then, at night, Margaret could join the two brothers in their telescopic observations. To aid her understanding of these, Sir Charles, in the autumn of 1650, bought from the Amsterdam instrument-maker Willem Blaeu a three-dimensional model of the Copernican planetary system. In this Margaret would be able to see all the complex details of circles and epicycles that astronomers used to model the motions of the planets before Johannes Kepler's elliptical orbits gained widespread acceptance later in the century.[33]

Sir Charles was an avid reader, and the latest philosophical and scientific works poured into the Cavendish household from all over Europe. In June 1650 Gassendi's systematic reworking of the ancient atomist theories of Epicurus arrived, long awaited by Sir Charles and finally published the year before in Lyons. It was an exciting work, a major contribution to contemporary philosophy, but Margaret could not have read the *Animadversiones in Decimum Librum Diogenis Laertii* herself. Like almost all serious works of philosophy, it was in Latin: even books of politics and ethics like Hobbes's *De Cive* were originally written and published in Latin, intended for an international community of scholars rather than a general English reading public. Only recently had philosophical works begun to appear in vernacular languages. In 1650, Margaret

---

*The Torricelli experiment involved a long tube of mercury in place of the glass of water. When inverted over a basin of mercury, the mercury in the tube would drop, but only by a certain amount and no more. It was the space left at the top of the sealed tube that fascinated philosophers: was this evidence for the long-disputed existence of a vacuum?

could read Descartes's newly published *Passions de l'Ame* in English translation, but the majority of texts were inaccessible to her.[34]

In such circumstances Margaret's knowledge of philosophy and the sciences was inevitably dependent on the men in her life—and especially on Sir Charles Cavendish. From him, as from her brother John before, she continued to acquire a basic understanding of the technical terminology of scholars— "the language of the arts and learned professions," of philosophers, theologians, physicians, mathematicians, astronomers "and the rest of the gown-tribe," William later explained. Predestination, free will, transubstantiation, dilation, contraction, *materia prima*, arteries, veins and the ventricles of the heart, choler, phlegm, apoplexies, convulsions, dropsies, the insoluble problem of squaring the circle, meridians, zodiac, ecliptic, tropics, poles— Margaret knew something of them all.[35] And from Sir Charles's conversation, she also learned of the theories of the great philosophers of both the ancient and the modern world. Seneca, Lucretius, Descartes, Gassendi, Hobbes—"I have heard the opinions of most philosophers in general," Margaret wrote, yet "not thoroughly discoursed of." "I have gathered more by piece-meals than from a full relation or a methodical education."[36]

While Sir Charles provided a scholarly input of academic knowledge, William's philosophical teaching of Margaret was more personal, derived from his own "natural inspection and judicious observation of things." As he related such matters as his explosive researches on saltpeter and brimstone, which had revealed to him the true nature of the Sun ("nothing else but a very solid body of salt and sulphur, enflamed by his own violent motion upon his own axis"), Margaret was full of admiration. "Although my Lord has not so much of scholarship and learning as his brother," she admitted, "yet he hath an excellent natural wit and judgement, and dives into the bottom of everything . . . by which he hath found out many truths."[37]

Much of William's talk centered on his political ideas. The exiled royalists were obsessed with questions about what had gone wrong with their old regime and allowed the Civil War to happen. How should a king and his ministers govern? How could royal rule be made strong, ensuring lasting political stability? Even now, in Paris, Hobbes was embarking on his *Leviathan*, aiming at a systematic theory of the ideal monarchical government: Margaret would finally be able to read his political views for herself in 1651, when the *Leviathan* was published and the *De Cive* also appeared in English translation, four years after its original Latin publication.[38] Meanwhile, William told her of his own, rather different views on royalist government. Where Hobbes advocated improving the education of the common people so they would not be deceived into rebellion by the speeches of treacherous demagogues, William thought that the masses were already overeducated. Too much reading and debate in both politics and religion had made them disputative and factious, fomenting sedition and leading to war. And so he proposed a radically reformed royalist state, where priests led common prayers but did not preach thought-provoking sermons or engage in theological disputes; where the common people would be entertained with Sunday sports and holidays, but denied newspapers and grammar school education. The upper classes too would be transformed: no more would effete courtiers gain the king's favor and steal the country's wealth through lucrative monopolies and taxes. Instead the old nobility must be the king's deputies. Content with their own wealth, they would allow England's people to enrich themselves through trade; and by their training in the martial exercises of chivalry, with the control of a powerful army, the nobles could root out any rebellion.

William also read to Margaret, sharing with her his enthusiasm for poetry and plays. He had studied the art of reading aloud with his old friend, the playwright Ben Jonson, and Margaret found him in this, as other things, inspirational. "In truth I never heard any man read well but my husband." "Like skilful masters of music, which can sing and play their parts at the first sight, so my husband at the first reading will so humour the sense and words of the work, as if he himself had made and writ it."[39]

Among the rest, William read the two plays he had written before the Civil War. *The Variety* and *The Country Captain* were racy social comedies that Margaret might well have seen with her sisters when they were performed in London by the King's Men at the Blackfriars playhouse, in 1639 or 1640.[40] Now preparing these two works for publication—they were printed anonymously in London in 1649, advertised as "written by a person of honour"—William found Margaret an appreciative audience. She loved his "wit, humour and satire," as well as the realism by which he "imitates the humours of men so justly as he seems to go even with Nature." "In truth, he is as far beyond Shakespeare for comical humour as Shakespeare beyond an ordinary poet in that way."[41]

In William's plays the "chief design," Margaret saw, was "to divulge and laugh at the follies of mankind; to persecute vice, and to encourage virtue."[42] Moral didacticism was generally thought essential to good literature, and in Paris William Davenant was now writing his epic poem *Gondibert* with just such an aim. In his preface, dedicated to William, the Cavendish household found the ideas of both Davenant and Thomas Hobbes on how literature could best instill morality.[43] These lessons made a deep impression on Margaret, and her own fiction and drama, which she began to write a few years later, would be created with the explicit intention of teaching. However, the examples of behavior she would offer her readers in these strikingly woman-centered works were often radically unconventional.

Margaret was also finding inspiration outside the home. Flemish and Dutch culture actively encouraged the work of intelligent and artistic women. In Utrecht, Anna Maria van Schurmann was probably the most learned woman of her century. A source of Dutch national pride as "the incomparable heroine" and "our famous Sibyl,"* she was also the author of *Amica Dissertatio De Capacitate Ingenii Muliebris ad Scientias*, a powerful argument for the improvement of women's education, which was published in English translation at Leyden in 1639 as *The Learned Maid, Or, Whether a Maid May be a Scholar?* Accomplished poets like Anna Roemers Visscher were admired as "the Tenth Muse," "the Belgian Sappho," "the Minerva of the Netherlands," while the outstanding Antwerpian singer Francisca Duarte achieved renown as "the Nightingale."

The Cavendish family was connected to this wider world through a distant cousin of William's. Utricia Swann, née Ogle (William's mother's maiden name), had grown up in the Netherlands, the daughter and granddaughter of English officers serving in the Dutch army. In 1645 she had married William Swann—a captain in the Dutch forces who would go on to a knighthood and a distinguished diplomatic career. By the time the Cavendishes arrived in Antwerp in 1648 Utricia was known in all the best circles of Dutch society. In Utrecht she discussed the latest books with her friend Anna Maria van Schurmann, while at the Hague she was well connected at the court of the English princess royal, Charles I's daughter, Mary, who had married the stadtholder, William II of Orange. Here she was a close friend of Constantijn Huygens, the stadtholder's secretary, with whom she studied music. Utricia was a talented singer whose beautiful voice and sympathetic interpretation of songs were eagerly sought after by composers like Huygens. In Brussels she was an old friend of the duchess of Lorraine—the two enjoyed making music together—and in Antwerp Utricia could introduce William and Margaret to the wealthy and cultivated Duarte family.

Gaspard Duarte, the father, was a Portuguese merchant and banker now long naturalized in Antwerp. With his two sons, Jacques and Gaspard, he traded in diamonds, pearls, coral, and jewelry, selling to the nobility and royal courts of northern Europe, and investing his vast riches in a lifestyle of great elegance. The family's house on the Meir, Antwerp's grandest street, John Evelyn admired as a "palace . . . furnished like a prince's." Outside was a garden with orange trees, while inside was an outstanding art collection, including Titians, Tintorettos, Bassanos, two Breughels, "an infinity of good Van Dycks,"

---

*The Sibyls were famous wise women of ancient Greece and Rome.

and a Raphael.[44] "The most beautiful house in Antwerp"[45]—and doubtless several times the size of the Newcastles' residence in the Rubens House—the Duartes' residence provided a temporary home for the city's most eminent visitors: the prince of Orange, Constantijn Huygens and the duchess of Lorraine often stayed with the family when they were in Antwerp. An introduction to the household was eagerly sought by every tourist who passed through the city, not only for the sake of its art collection but also for the entertainment provided by this outstandingly musical family. Father, sons, and the four daughters—Leonora, Catharina, Isabella, and Francisca (the famous "Nightingale")—made up a "fine consort" of lutes, viols, virginals, and voices whose "rare music" everyone admired.[46]

Gaspard and his sons traveled often to England in the jewel trade, and the family all spoke English well, enabling Margaret and William to form a close attachment here, sharing their interests in literature and music with the younger generation of Duartes. Jacques, the composer of the family, set William's love poems to music, and his sister Leonora sang them—with such beauty and passion, Margaret thought, as to draw the soul itself up "from all other parts of the body" to sit in the chamber of the ear, where "as in a vaulted room . . . it listens with delight, and is ravished with admiration." Margaret loved the sisters' company. With them she emerged so far from her shyness that on one occasion, when Francisca and Catharina visited her in the Rubens House, "their good company put me into a frolic humour, and . . . I sung to them some pieces of old ballads." When they begged her to sing some of William and Jacques' songs, however, she had to refuse: "I could not sing any of those songs . . . neither having skill nor voice . . . instead of music, I should make a discord, and instead of wit, sing nonsense, knowing not how to humour the words, nor relish the notes."[47]

Margaret and William also got to know Béatrix, duchess of Lorraine, who lived with her sister Mademoiselle de Beauvais, at the castle of Beersel, about five miles south of Brussels. Brussels was the capital of the Spanish Netherlands, about thirty miles from Antwerp—just a day's journey by barge on the canals. Home of the province's governor, the city supported a substantial community of English exiles. Here there were regular Anglican church services, plays every day in the theaters, duels, carriage drives, and frequent balls. The city's pleasure-loving society often drove out to join the entertainments laid on at the duchess of Lorraine's court at Beersel. Each evening there were elaborate "sports of wit"—formalized literary salon games overseen by the duchess from her throne of state on the dais at the head of the room. Sometimes one of the company, as "diviner," offered witty interpretations of the imaginary dreams told by the rest. On other occasions an "oracle" provided clever answers to riddling questions. In the game of "lotteries" they all wrote fortunes for their friends; in that of "wonders" they vied to produce humorous, paradoxical reflections on human society; and in "wishes" friends and lovers asked ingenious favors from each other. Some nights the servants dressed up as gypsies to tell fortunes, and on others there were plays and masques acted by the duchess's courtiers.

In these entertainments the duchess's protégé, Richard Flecknoe, acted as informal master of the revels, composing proverbs for the company to act out in dumb show as well as more elaborate dramatic pieces—a pastoral called "Love in his Infancy," which centered on the duchess's year-old son, and a series of masques that told the duchess's unfortunate life history in allegories.* Flecknoe was an English Catholic lay-priest whose witty company, with his capabilities as poet, playwright, and musician, made him a welcome guest in the aristocratic households where he often lived for months or years at a time. After his religion, the great love of his life was conversation and good company, especially that of the ladies. His attentive courtliness, his care in picking up their dropped fans, gloves, and handkerchiefs or finding their lost lapdogs, won him their friendship; his skill as a lutenist rounded out their musical consorts and accompanied their singing; his conversation on languages, morals, and society, with stories of his travels through Europe to Turkey and then the Cape Verde Islands, Tenerife, and Brazil, entertained their afternoons.

The pastimes of Beersel conformed closely to Margaret's ideal of cultured social life—conversation "most various" mixed with "discourses of mirth, songs, verses, scenes and the like"[48]—and she and William formed a close friendship with Flecknoe. In 1651, after he fell out with the duchess of Lorraine, Flecknoe came to live with them at the Rubens House, where he continued to write the series of "characters" he had begun at Beersel. One of these—titled "Of one that is truly noble, made at Antwerp, Anno 1651," a eulogy of William's virtue, courtesy, liberality, and loyalty to the king—formed part of Flecknoe's repayment for his patrons' hospitality. Other literary payments described William as "the most praiseworthy man alive" with "the most of the nobleman in him, the most of true greatness," one who "in these calamitous times" of exile could "nobly suffer . . . with brave resolve, without a groan." To such flattering verses, William responded in kind.

---

*Béatrix de Cusance was the duke of Lorraine's second wife, whom he married while his first wife was still living. The duke's argument that his first marriage was forced on him by his father and had never been consummated was ignored by the pope, who refused to annul it and excommunicated both the duke and his duchess Béatrix until they finally agreed to separate. Both now lived apart near Brussels where the duke, having been expelled from his duchy, commanded mercenary forces in the service of the Spanish.

Flecknoe, thy verses are too high for me,
Though they but justly fit thy Muse and thee;
Caesars should be thy theme, on them to write,
Though thou'dst express them more than they could fight.

From here, William went on to liken his protégé's work to Homer and Virgil.[49]

Flecknoe and Margaret also became friends. His influence—and that of salon culture more generally—would soon become apparent in her writing.

MARGARET FOUND HER MIND in a ferment, buzzing with ideas "like a swarm of bees." New experiences and information inspired her so irresistibly that "my fancy will build thereupon, and make discourse therefrom." Early in 1650, she began to write about everything that excited her.[50]

She wrote of the whole world of social virtues and vices—of love and hate, honesty, friendship, flattery, envy and revenge, of pride (a good thing in women when it served to distance them from men who wanted to corrupt their chastity), and of fear (a necessity in human society, she thought, making citizens law-abiding and peaceable). She wrote of marriages happy and unhappy, of education, hospitality, and of feasting—an excess that she denounced as immoral "in the unnecessary destruction of so many creatures": overindulgence in food was a "greater fault" than overindulgence in alcohol, she argued, since the second only harmed the individual, while overeating wasted essential resources, causing "famine and plagues . . . which are able to destroy a kingdom."[51]

She discussed her own ideals of feminine behavior and of masculinity—"it is more proper for a gentleman to be active in the use of arms than in the art of dancing"; "he is not worthy the name of gentleman that had rather come sweating from a tennis court than bleeding from a battle," she thought, following the martial ethos of her brothers and husband.[52] She also wrote of books and authors, of languages and translation, and of the true nature of wit: "the purest element and swiftest motion of the brain," "wit is neither to be learnt nor gotten, for it is a free gift of Nature, and disclaims art."[53] Theorizing about the qualities and purposes of good poetry, history, and drama, and warning of the dangers of too much scholarship, she was here establishing the literary principles that would guide much of her future writing.

Margaret set herself many questions to debate. Was Roman Catholic monasticism a good or a bad thing? Was it better in life to be intelligent or rich or beautiful? What was the best way to win fame? Were practices like Hindu suttee, where the wife died with her husband, a product of marital love or of society's "vainglorious customs"?[54] Was the ancient Roman practice of suicide a sign of courage or fear?* She also wrote of the feelings of her own life—of the irresistible allure of fame, of the discomfort caused by shyness, and of the difficulties of a second wife entering her husband's family.

Much of Margaret's writing was influenced by the conversation and literary games of feminine salon culture, with its taste for wit and wordplay. Striking, far-fetched comparisons—as when Margaret likened poetry and history to the dances of the French galliard and the Spanish pavan—were a prominent feature of the style, and many of the pieces she wrote consisted largely or wholly of extended similes. Her essay titled "Of Several Writings," for instance, formed an elaborate analogy between literature and human society, where different kinds of books were revealed as judges, lawyers, hangmen, ambassadors, merchants, conjurers, cut-purses, bawds, jugglers, and mountebanks. Another piece likened different kinds of wit to the various planets and seasons.

In the style of the game of "wonders" played at the duchess of Lorraine's court, Margaret also wrote pieces that created surprising paradoxes in their descriptions of human society. One pair of essays, for instance, set up the dilemma that "those fames that is gotten in the wars sound louder than those that are gotten in peace" yet "it is a better and more certain reputation" to be famous for wisdom in peace than for courage in war: in Margaret's eyes, courage was a less valuable virtue since it "is only exercised in destruction," whereas wisdom "is always exercised in . . . the ways of peace."[55] Other titles, such as "Peace shews the best wits, [but] war the most writers" or "A man that is mad is not out of his wits," set up the strange wonders that their essays would then justify and explain. (Margaret's explanation of these two was that war gave the most subjects for writing but "wit is purest and finest when the mind is most quiet and peaceable"; meanwhile, a madman, though speaking without judgment, might yet say things that were witty.)[56]

In another salon tradition, Margaret created fifty-five short allegories. The mind is a garden, the world is a shop, fortune is a mountebank cozening fools, the head is a parliament of thoughts or a wilderness of wild beasts (while thoughts are pancakes tossed in the pan of the brain), married life is an *olio podrido*—a rich stew—of troubles and vexations. She also composed a hundred and forty-one "short essays," much like the proverbs that Flecknoe had created for the company at Beersel to act out. "It is better to live with liberty than with riches," she wrote; "there is no sight so unpleasant as affectation," "there is none so apt to revenge as those that have been forgiven," "many times

---

*Margaret tended to the second opinion in these last two questions, and she preferred intelligence above wealth, and wealth above beauty, as the best means to happiness.

guiltiness is more confident than innocency," and "it is worthy the observation to regard the odd humours of mankind, how they talk of reason and [yet] follow the way thereof so seldom."[57]

Many of Margaret's predominant subjects for writing—literature, languages, translation, the nature of wit, fame, friendship, conversation, and society—were the core interests of salon culture, all discussed by Flecknoe with the ladies at Beersel. And in the salon tradition of "characters" or "portraits"— a genre of writing especially beloved of Flecknoe—Margaret composed a series of descriptions of the great men and especially women of history. Queen Elizabeth I she portrayed as a powerful and crafty woman who "clothed herself in a sheep's skin, yet she had a lion's paw and a fox's head; she strokes the cheeks of her subjects with flattery while she picks their purses; and though she seemed loth, yet she never failed to crush to death those that disturbed her ways"; she was the "mistress of the sea" who "maintained more foreign wars at one time than any of her predecessors before her." She had made a great monarch, Margaret argued, opposing the common belief that it was Elizabeth's male ministers who deserved the credit for her successes.[58]

Margaret also offered a novel interpretation of Richard III as a good king who made wise laws, criticizing instead his successor Henry VII as a tyrant who demanded heavy taxes from his subjects. She defended the reputation of Cleopatra, traditionally "infamous for a whore." Rather, Margaret argued, Cleopatra had been "constant to those men she had taken"—first Julius Caesar "whilst he lived" and then Mark Anthony. "If the men had more wives than they should have, or put away good wives for her sake, that was their inconstancy and we must not make their faults her crimes." By contrast, she criticized Odysseus's wife, Penelope, normally admired for her resistance to her many suitors: Penelope should have been stronger, Margaret argued; she should never have allowed herself to be courted at all; her tolerance of her suitors showed that "she loved to have her ears filled with her own praises."[59] Like Flecknoe, Margaret also wrote "characters" of personality types as well as of individual people, and one of her longest pieces, called "Of fools," contained portraits of every conceivable variety of this human weakness—the amorous fool, the self-conceited fool, the passionate fool, the luxurious fool, the learned fool, and many others.[60]

Salon culture was stereotypically "feminine"—aristocratic women were the principal participants as well as the main audience and arbiters for "sports of wit" and salon conversation. But, inspired by the talk of William and his brother, Margaret also entered "masculine" domains, normally thought improper for women's discussion. She wrote pieces on politics, setting out her ideal form of monarchical government, describing the virtues required in a prince and his politicians, and advocating the necessity for grand state cere-mony, which "strikes such a reverence and respect in the beholders" as "to make way for command and obedience." She attacked the parliamentarians as "robbers" who stole the population's lives, religion, friends, laws, liberties, and peace; yet she opposed any overly tyrannical autocratic government, since human nature "cannot endure to be bound beyond the strength of moderate liberty."[61] Addressing the question of the cause of the English Civil War, it was "the misplacing of honours that causeth rebellion," Margaret argued, following some of William's views closely: "if honour be placed by favour and not for merit, it brings envy to those which are honoured, and hatred to the Prince" which in turn "brings war and ruin to the kingdom."[62]

From politics Margaret turned to war. Histories that told of 100,000 dying in a single fight were false, she wrote, for William had told her "that thirty thousand on each side is as much as can fight in one battle."[63] She was also relying on her husband's knowledge as she wrote of the economics of sup-porting an army, of strong and weak strategic positions, of rash commanders, and of the ideal tactics for a general, who should not lead his own vanguard in a battle, but should be ready to join the fray and encourage his men when they grew weary (this strategy had brought William his own success at the Battle of Adwalton Moor in 1643).

But if many of Margaret's more "masculine" pieces were influenced by William, there were also others expressing opposition to her husband's politi-cal views. When William told her his belief that Catholic France suffered eco-nomically from her "many thousand clergymen and most of their orders, good for nothing, but bread eaters," bringing "no honey to the hive of the common-wealth," he sparked Margaret off to write one of her longest pieces, weighing up the pros and cons of monasticism. Her final conclusion was diametrically opposed to her husband's: monks' celibacy reduced the population, preventing civil war, she argued, and their sparing diet did not deplete society's precious resources. "Surely monastical lives are very profitable to the commonwealth, whatsoever it be for the soul, for it keeps peace and makes plenty, and begets a habit of sobriety which sets a good example."[64]

In philosophy too—another "masculine" study normally reserved for seri-ous scholars—Margaret was inspired by William and his brother, and she vigor-ously joined in debates and controversies. She refuted the traditional idea that seawater ran underground everywhere "through veins in the earth" and then rose up to cause freshwater springs: surely salt water could not be made fresh in this way, she argued. She cast ridicule upon those philosophers who thought matter was eternal: if so, she reasoned, it would be a deity like God himself, which no one would want to believe. And she rebutted the theory that gold mines were caused by the sun's rays: we see for ourselves, she objected, that the sun cannot pierce far enough even to warm a small underground cellar.[65]

Based on the family's telescopic observations, she proposed her own answer to the current controversy over the nature of the Moon: it could all be water, she suggested, and the mountains revealed by the telescope could be merely reflections of those on the Earth. She also commented on the different appearances of sand and water when seen through a microscope. And she offered possible accounts for a wide range of unexplained natural phenomena—for thunder and lightning, wind and rain, the waves of the sea—and for a host of diseases: apoplexy, fevers, agues, smallpox, and others. She wrote on the importance of a balanced, moderate diet—"nothing preserves health more and lengthens life"—and she commented on the usefulness of various medical treatments.[66]

The question of women and their proper role in society was a recurrent theme. Even a natural philosophical essay could become a discussion of women's issues, as when Margaret used the philosophical commonplace that change is natural in all physical things to argue that "it is natural to be in one mind one minute, and in another the next"—a defense of women's stereotypical fickleness and changeability.[67] Among her many essays on social life and morals, the topics of silence and vanity—two of women's conventional virtues and vices—especially interested Margaret, producing much longer pieces. Silence was only sometimes appropriate, she argued—"in some cases it is better to speak too much than too little"—while vanity resulted from man's natural desire to please himself, a desire that was God-given and which did no one any harm.[68]

Margaret again defended women in "Of Painting"—an elaborate argument in support of women's right to make themselves beautiful with "curling, powdering, pouncing, clothing, and all the varieties of accoutrements." Margaret successively undermined all the accusations of vanity, false appearances, lasciviousness, and sexual enticement that clergymen and moralists used against women, and turned them on their head. Surely the arts of war should be more criticized than such peaceful feminine arts, "for the one destroys mankind, this increaseth it; the one brings love, the other begets hate." And then there were economic arguments, for women's adornments were "the cause of employing the greater part of the commonwealth": "for example, how many trades belong from the silkworm to the lady's gown? and from the golden mine to the [gold] lace that is laid upon [that gown]?" she demanded.[69]

Margaret also joined the *querelle des femmes,* the lively contemporary debate concerning women's reputed inferiority to men. Here she refuted the standard religious arguments that male superiority was proved by Christ taking a man's body, and by Adam being created before Eve. On the first, Margaret objected, the Holy Spirit had taken the shape of a dove, so were doves superior to men? And on the second, the Devil was made before Adam, so who was superior?[70]

Often Margaret showed herself a traditionalist in questions of feminine morality. On the virtue of chastity she was adamant: promiscuous women were "the most foulest and falsest creatures of all Nature's works," while the incorruptible were "angels." Adultery in a woman was much worse than in a man, she thought: while a man dishonored only himself, a woman dishonored her whole family and made people call her husband "a fool, a coward, and all they can think to be bad in a man."[71]

On the relationship of marriage, Margaret's views were complex. On one hand, she seemed to follow convention in accepting the inferiority and subservience of women. The husband's proper role was the same as that of a nurse taking care of children, providing bodily maintenance, protection, and education: "though women be not so innocent [as children], yet they are as powerless," she felt.[72] Yet Margaret saw this role of nurse as involving nurturing more than authority: husbands should "strive to please, and yield to" their wives "in all things but what will do them harm." "A wise man rules his family with gentle, kind and seasonable persuasions." Such a husband would gain his wife's respect, and the willing obedience that came with it. Furthermore, despite what she wrote about women's weakness and ignorance, a wise man should take his wife's advice: Julius Caesar would not have been murdered if he had listened to his wife, Margaret noted, and Mark Anthony leaving his wife for Cleopatra "lost him the third part of the world."[73]

IT WAS EARLY IN 1650, just as Margaret was beginning to write, that William returned to political life.*With an invasion force preparing in Scandinavia, the exiles' hopes were again high, and King Charles II—as Prince Charles had become on his father's execution—now made William a Knight of the Garter and appointed him commander of the risings planned for the North of England. Their greatest expectations lay in Scotland, for the Scots were angry at England's unilateral execution of Charles I—the man who was their king too—and they now recognized Charles II as their rightful monarch. When commissioners came from the Scottish Parliament to negotiate with Charles II and his courtiers on the terms of his restoration to the throne,

---

*The coincidence of these two events is no accident: in childhood too Margaret had turned to writing when she lost the constant companionship of her favorite sister. Catherine Lucas married when Margaret was twelve—the age at which she always stated she had begun to write.

William traveled to join them at Breda, leaving Margaret and Sir Charles Cavendish behind in Antwerp.[74]

Appointed to the king's Privy Council, William joined the majority of courtiers in advising Charles that the best route back to royal government of all his realms was to make an agreement with the Scots. But the Scottish commissioners were demanding huge concessions: their king must adopt the Presbyterian faith and he must sign the Covenant—the Scots' renunciation of the Anglican religion, which had prompted Charles I's wars of 1639 and 1640. William was furious, but when he protested vehemently to the earl of Cassilis, head of the Scottish commission, he gained only a stern Presbyterian rebuke "for his customary swearing."[75] The Scots would make no compromise, so Charles—with little intention of keeping his word—finally agreed to all their terms, and was granted full sovereign power in Scotland. In June he sailed for his new kingdom with a following of courtiers. Among them was William's old friend Lord Widdrington but not William himself, whom the Scots refused to receive.

Instead, William returned to Antwerp, where the household was suffering from ever greater poverty. With English relations like the countess of Devonshire refusing to lend him even "a little money," William felt alone and abandoned. "My acquaintance hides themselves from me, and my friends and kindred stand afar off," he lamented. "Affection [is] fled from the face of the Earth, and friendship buried alive and no faith left in Israel."[76]

His children, however, "did all that lay in their power to support and relieve my Lord . . . in his banishment," Margaret later recalled with gratitude.[77] But in 1650, with William's estates under parliamentary sequestration, their means were limited. Jane, always the family's manager, had successfully petitioned Parliament for a fifth of the income from William's lands—the legal entitlement of the families of all royalist delinquents. As part of this portion, Jane had succeeded in including the family's house at Welbeck, and she and her sister Frances continued to live here, supervising the estate business astutely. Servants were laid off to cut down expenses, and the accounts of the steward, Thomas Bamford, who ran the grange farm—supplying meat, butter, and grain to the Welbeck household—were carefully checked. Money was sent to London, to their brothers Charles and Henry, who still had no lands or income.[78] At Welbeck Jane did what she could for her father, ensuring that the family portraits and tapestries—of huge sentimental value to William—were maintained in good condition, and selling her own jewels to raise money for his maintenance in exile. But when the jewels were gone, the already overstretched estate income could provide little support for the establishment at the Rubens House: any relief that Henry had brought with him to Antwerp, when he left England in April 1650, would soon have been used up.[79]

By December William was begging the king to send him money from Scotland, but Charles too was short of cash and could only offer the hope that he might have spare money in the future, "but what that will be, or how long before it be received, is so uncertain that without doubt your Lordship ought not to rely upon it," the duke of Buckingham advised, from the king's side. But William's credit had finally run out. "None will lend me two shillings here, but fly me," he wrote back to the duke, "as if I was the arrantest knave and rogue in the world; I vow to God the ridiculousness of it makes me laugh heartily." William could make a joke of anything, but the matter was serious—"[I] know not how to put bread into my mouth," he added. Reduced to extremities, William, as before in Paris, fell back on the idea of rich marriages for his sons: less than a year after his arrival, Henry was dispatched by his father, "a lusty bachelor begging homeward for England," William hoped.[80]

Meanwhile in Antwerp the population of impoverished English émigrés was steadily increasing. Sir Edward Hyde, the king's chancellor of the Exchequer, arrived in the summer of 1651 to join his wife and children, who had been in the city since 1649. Hyde had just returned from an embassy to Spain and he brought with him a special privilege: the right to hold Anglican church ceremonies in this otherwise Catholic Spanish province. In his chapel the whole English community gathered regularly, and Sir Charles Cavendish and Hyde became close friends. The two gentlemen-scholars met up every day to talk: Hyde "took most delight in" Sir Charles's conversation, which exhibited "all the knowledge and wisdom that arts and sciences could supply." But even as the English community grew, William continued to spend his time with Margaret—"having married a young lady, [he] confined himself most to her company, and lived as retired as his ruined condition in England obliged him to," as Hyde put it.[81]

Margaret felt that her studies with William gave her a new emotional balance. Before, she had felt unhappy, distracted, powerless. "My own thoughts . . . were like travellers seldom at home, and when they returned [they] brought nothing but vanity and uneasy fashions . . . troubling themselves with trifles, putting my mind in disorder." But now education had enabled her "to settle my mind on the ground of peace." No longer were her emotions at the mercy of events. Under William's teaching, wisdom and reason now made her mind a stronghold, fortified with patience "lest our enemy misfortune should surprise it," and guarded by truth "lest falsehood should undermine it." It was an ethos of self-sufficiency, where true happiness was found in the mind rather than in external things. "Wisdom and wit are to be preferred before riches and beauty," Margaret argued, because "wisdom makes a man happy all his life, in governing his passions [and] in choosing his ways"; "he that hath a true-born wit hath all."[82] This philosophy, perfectly adapted to coping with the troubles of exile, would remain her ideal for the rest of her life. But in 1651 political and then financial crisis would overcome both her and William's capacity for patience in adversity.

Arriving in Scotland in June 1650, Charles II had immediately become involved in war with parliamentarian England, whose invasion force under Oliver Cromwell had crossed the border at the same time as Charles himself arrived by ship from the Netherlands. In September, Cromwell captured Edinburgh; eleven months later he took Perth, cutting the Scottish army's supply lines. Charles's only hope lay in a rapid march into England, to join forces with the risings long prepared there by William and others.

In Antwerp, the exiles watched events, powerless. "Every letter and book of news we gravely deliver our opinions thereof, but first wipe our mouths formally with our handkerchers, spit with a grace, and hem aloud, and then say little to the purpose," William recounted, "then we shake our heads and shrug our shoulders with prudence, saying time will produce more."[83] His own attempts to hire foreign troops for an invasion force—from the elector of Brandenburg, the duke of Lorraine, and the king of Denmark—were proceeding painfully slowly, and his correspondence with England to coordinate royalist uprisings was well known to Cromwell's intelligence network. In April 1651 his sons, Charles and Henry, were suspected of plotting against Parliament and arrested with their brother-in-law, the earl of Bridgewater. Meanwhile parliamentarian spies opened William's letters, broke their codes, or extracted their messages written in invisible ink, and then forwarded on skillfully forged copies, keeping their discoveries secret. Double agents infiltrated the exiled royalist community, and William was in despair. "He doth think you deal with the Devil; that as soon as things be thought of, you know them," one agent told Parliament's spymaster, George Bishop, following a successful information-gathering visit to the Rubens House.[84]

So Charles II, already defeated in Scotland, found almost no one in England prepared to rise in his support. Pursued southwards by Cromwell's superior army, he and his army finally paused to rest and recruit at Worcester on August 22. Six days later Cromwell arrived and laid siege to the city; in his final onslaught, after another six days, the royalists were utterly routed. William's old friend Lord Widdrington was already dead, killed in a minor skirmish in Lancashire, and now no one knew what had become of the king. In Antwerp, Margaret watched horrified as William "fell into so violent a passion, that I verily believed it would have endangered his life." It was two months before the news finally came that Charles, having journeyed for six weeks round England in disguise, had crossed safely to France. William was overjoyed at his old pupil's safety—"never any subject could rejoice more than my Lord did," Margaret thought—but all hopes of returning home to England were now dashed. Impoverished exile stretched ahead, unending.[85]

Everywhere the royalist émigrés were near to destitution. In France Henrietta Maria had gone into a monastery to save expense. In the Low Countries, William joked, the court of James, duke of York, Charles II's younger brother, contained "no more than was in Noah's Ark, eighteen person [sic] with some beasts, and these eighteen persons are in fifteen factions at least."[86] In Antwerp, families like the Hydes faced the real possibility of starvation, and at the Rubens House William's brother, Sir Charles, "would often say that, though he could not truly complain of want, yet his meat never did him good by reason . . . that he was never sure after one meal to have another." "I was never afraid of starving or begging," Margaret insisted, but clearly the possibility had crossed her mind. Tempers frayed under the strain, and Margaret later wrote of the rancorous squabbles she saw erupting between women who had formerly been close friends—"truly, great misfortunes make us apt to quarrel with ourselves," she reflected.[87] But she would never tell her readers of the bitter quarrel that was now dividing the Cavendish family itself—a quarrel over the conflicting demands of money and honor, in which William and Margaret stood on one side against Sir Charles on the other.

Since August 1649, when Sir Charles had paid Parliament the fine of £1,500 due for his Civil War delinquency, he had been receiving the rents from his English estates—moneys that formed a substantial help to the Antwerp household. But early in 1651, the parliamentary Committee for Compounding received reports that Sir Charles was "a very dangerous person" who "adhered to Charles Stuart, the late King's son, and is abroad without leave."[88] Immediately his estates were again placed under sequestration, and this time he could only redeem them by returning to England in person, a thing he dreaded beyond all. He feared imprisonment, "which, he said, his constitution would not bear." But even more, he feared the Engagement—the oath of loyalty that a parliamentary act of January 1650 now required all men to take before they could receive justice from any court of law. To have to swear to "be true and faithful to the Commonwealth of England as it is now established, without a King or House of Lords" was anathema to Sir Charles. And although he was "in very visible want of ordinary conveniences," yet he still "protested that he would rather submit to nakedness, or starving in the street, than subscribe to the Covenant or Engagement, or do anything else that might trench upon his honour or his conscience."[89]

But William and Margaret—"those whom he loved best"—begged him to go and compound for his estates. They argued that he should not value his conscience so highly, that he should not be governed by honor, that it "would expose him to famine, and restrain him from being charitable to his best friends." Sir Charles, normally so gentle and modest, became deeply offended. "He would no more admit any discourse upon the subject," he finally told them indignantly. And so, in desperation, William went to his brother's friend Sir Edward Hyde. Without telling him of Sir Charles's prior refusal and the dishonorable arguments they had already used on him, William asked Hyde to persuade Sir Charles to go.[90]

Hyde, like William, was one of the named traitors whom Parliament had banished on pain of death, and he had already decided not to seek pardon and attempt to compound for his estates: it was better "to starve really and literally," he thought, "than do anything contrary to my duty." But, for William's sake, he did speak to Sir Charles, urging "that the benefits that might result from this journey were great, and very probable . . . and the mischiefs he apprehended were not certain, and possibly might be avoided." Imprisonment was "seldom used but to persons under some notable prejudice" and Sir Charles was "of the few who had many friends and no enemies." The Engagement, though still a legal requirement, was in fact "not pressed but upon such persons against whom they [Parliament] had a particular design"; Sir Charles could always refuse to take it and "return without the full effect of his journey." And to these honorable arguments Sir Charles finally conceded.[91]

As preparations were made for his departure, it was decided that Margaret should accompany him, to attempt to gain some income from William's estates. These, sequestrated long before, had finally been confiscated in July 1651, and were now to be sold to fund Parliament's long-running war in Ireland.[92] William himself, a traitor hated by Parliament and banished on pain of death, could do nothing. But his wife could petition for the one-fifth proportion to which all delinquents' wives—judged by English law to be innocent, politically inactive dependants of their evil-doing husbands—were entitled.

So, early in November, Margaret abandoned the writing that had brought her such pleasure for the past eighteen months. Locking her manuscript away in a chest for safety, she prepared to leave the husband she loved so passionately.

> *Beyond expression's grief when we did part,*
> *My blood went back, and shrunk up was my heart;*
> *My cheeks drowned in a sea of tears, so cried*
> *My heart,*

wrote William, not knowing when he would see his wife again. And Margaret too would tell of the "weeping departures" of royalist wives, forced to travel not for "sport and fashion" but for bare subsistence. "Their minds swim in troubled tears and are blown with sighs . . . whilst they are swimming on the dangerous sea in barks or ships of wood, blown by blustring winds."[93] Setting off on these stormy travels with her brother-in-law and a small group of servants, Margaret feared that they ventured life itself.

Chapter Eight

Poet and Petitioner,
1651–1653

*I*n spite of Margaret's fears, the journey to London brought no dangers— but it was unexpectedly interrupted after the party landed at Southwark. Taking rooms for the night, they found in the morning that they had brought "so small a provision of money" from Antwerp they could not pay their bill. Only when Sir Charles Cavendish pawned his watch could they proceed up the Thames to London, where lodgings had been prepared for them in one of the grand houses of Covent Garden, close to the house of Margaret's favorite sister, Catherine Pye.[1]

Here they made ready to petition the Committee for Compounding. Unlike Sir Charles, Margaret had no fear of having to swear the Engagement. Women had been explicitly excluded after debate in the House of Commons, when an MP mockingly asked if Parliament really intended to force women— who normally played no part in public life—to swear a political oath: the scope of the act was duly amended from "persons" to "men." But paradoxically this very exclusion had brought women out into the arena of public affairs. "Tis observed here that wives have far better success in their solicitations than we men," one royalist wrote home from London. "Do as our sages do," another advised a friend, "instruct your wife and leave her to act it with the committees; their sex entitles them to many privileges."[2]

But Margaret, knowing herself "unpractised in public employments" and "naturally bashful," had no desire to speak at the Committee for Compounding, and she asked her brother John to present her case. John's legal expertise and position as head of the Lucas family made him Margaret's ideal representative and he prepared her formal written petition, asking that she receive one-

fifth of William's estate "according to the ordinances of Parliament, [she] having no other means of livelihood."[3] On December 10, 1651, he and Margaret
and Sir Charles drove into the City, to Goldsmiths' Hall—"that damned
house," as another petitioning royalist called it[4]—in Gresham Street just north
of St. Paul's Cathedral, where the Committee for Compounding regularly sat.
"But when I came there," Margaret recalled,

> I found their hearts as hard as my fortunes, and their natures as cruel as my
> miseries, for they sold all my Lord's estate, which was a very great one, and
> gave me not any part thereof, or any allowance thereout, which few or no
> other was so hardly dealt withal.[5]

The committee denied her petition absolutely, giving two reasons. First,
William as "the greatest traitor to the State" was "an excepted person,"
excluded from Parliament's forgiving laws to old royalists; and then Margaret
had not innocently married him before the war but only "since he became a
delinquent, so that at the time of marriage he had no estate." Margaret, both
too shy to speak and too proud to show her disappointment, "whisperingly
asked my brother to conduct me out of that ungentlemanly place," and she
made no further appeals. Later she felt she ought to have done more, but now,
"despairing . . . and not knowing where the power lay, and being not a good
flatterer, I did not trouble myself or petition my enemies."[6]

Sir Charles, however, was more successful. Appearing in front of the committee on the same day as Margaret, he pleaded "that he was abroad for his
health" and had "not engaged in the least against Parliament" since he compounded for his estates two years before. The committee ordered an inquiry
into whether there was "any other charge against him . . . than his being
beyond seas, which is not prohibited" and, pending their decision, he and Margaret stayed on in Covent Garden.[7]

It was to be a long wait as Sir Charles's business ground slowly through the
various committees. In the meantime the Cavendishes still had "nothing to live
on [and] must of necessity have been starved, had not Sir Charles got some
credit of several persons"—an accomplishment of "great difficulty," Margaret
noted, when "all those that had estates were afraid to come near him, much
less to assist him, until he was sure of his own estate. So much is misery and
poverty shunned!" To add to their worries, Margaret received a letter from
William, telling her he had no money and could get no more credit so that "if
his brother did not presently relieve him, he was forced to starve." Using "his
utmost endeavour," Sir Charles borrowed another £200 to send to Antwerp.
But by the time it arrived William "had been forced to send for all his credi-

tors, and declare to them his great wants and necessities"—a tale of misfortune that "made such an impression in them that . . . instead of urging the payment of his debts, [they] promised him that he should not want anything . . . furnishing him with all manner of provisions and necessaries for his further subsistence; so that my Lord was then in a much better condition amongst strangers, than we in our native country," Margaret recalled.[8]

William's sons were also in London—"no less in want and necessity than we, having nothing but bare credit to live on," Margaret found—and she now met her husband's daughters for the first time. Jane, two years older than Margaret, still remained unmarried, as did her youngest sister, Frances: dependent on the income Parliament allowed them from William's estates, they would have no dowries for marriage unless Sir Charles succeeded in settling the family's finances. Though both still lived at Welbeck, they made occasional visits to London to see their sister, Elizabeth, countess of Bridgewater, who split her time between her husband's country seat in Hertfordshire and Bridgewater House in the capital (where Margaret's old acquaintance Mr. Benoist was employed as tutor to the couple's eldest son). Hers was a close and loving marriage. The earl passionately admired Elizabeth, who brought him "all the happiness that a man could receive in the sweet society of the best of wives . . . who was all his worldly bliss."[9] The only cloud was the children they lost: Henry, Frances, and "my dear girl Kate" all died painfully within days or months of their births. Grief-stricken, Elizabeth wrote epitaphs for them—"she was so good, she never slept nor played at sermon nor prayers," she remembered of the twenty-two-month-old Kate. She prayed to God that she would be able to acquiesce gladly to His will but, pregnant again, "lay not Thy heavy hand of justice and affliction on me, in taking away my children in their youth, as Thou wast pleased to take my last babe Frances," she begged.[10]

Margaret often saw what remained of her childhood family too. Besides Catherine, there were her sisters Anne and Elizabeth, her brother John and his wife (who also stayed in Covent Garden when in London), and her sister-in-law Mary, widow of her brother Thomas, who was living in London with her children. With them Margaret exchanged visits and occasionally went out to "take the air," as they had before the war.[11]

But London and its life were changed from Margaret's childhood memories. The theaters were closed—many, like the Whitehall masquing house, had been demolished—and public practice of the Anglican religion was outlawed. Although Hyde Park remained open and Margaret and her sisters sometimes drove there with the others, the elegance and sparkle were dimmed: there was no royalty now to set the tone, to lead fashion and attract the crowds, only "an assembly of wretched jades and hackney coaches," John Evelyn complained.[12]

The city had a plebeian feel. Margaret, like other royalists, abhorred the new customs and she denounced in particular the (lower-class) women who now acted as "pleaders, attorneys, petitioners and the like, running about with their several causes, complaining of their several grievances, exclaiming against their several enemies . . . trafficking with idle words . . . such as had nothing to lose, but made it their trade to solicit."[13] She wrote too in ridicule of the women preachers in the puritan sects that now proliferated under Parliament's greater religious tolerance.

For the most part, the old royalists lived in retreat, avoiding public notice. Only in a few private homes was the prewar court culture of art, music, drama, and literature kept alive, and one of these was the house of Henry Lawes, where Margaret went with Sir Charles Cavendish "to hear music . . . three or four times."[14] Before the war, Lawes had been a musician in the Chapel Royal and the King's Private Musicke, a composer esteemed by the foremost poets—Davenant, Herrick, Waller, Milton, Suckling, Donne, and others—for his musical settings of their works. Now, like other royal musicians, he made his living by teaching music to the aristocracy and by holding musical meetings for paying guests—the first origins of modern London's concert-going culture. With Margaret and Sir Charles came many of London's old royalists: Sir Edward Dering and his wife (one of Lawes's pupils), John Birkenhead and Sir William Davenant (both of whom Margaret had known in Paris),* and the earl of Bridgewater, whose family were long-standing patrons of Lawes. In July 1652, to celebrate the tenth anniversary of the earl's marriage to William's daughter Elizabeth, Lawes arranged a concert, which Margaret and Sir Charles doubtless attended.

At Lawes's house Margaret found a culture of female aristocratic singers, musicians, poets, and composers that would inspire her emulation. Inspiring too was this circle's culture of royalist polemic: Lawes set to music, performed, and later printed the political poetry of John Birkenhead and many other old cavaliers, including the poem "Love and Loyalty" written by Margaret's dead brother, Charles. Here Margaret could also have met England's foremost female poet. Katherine Philips was the center of an informal society of literary friends, largely women, who took pen names from classical and pastoral tradition—Philips herself was "the Matchless Orinda." Her poetry was already celebrated within this circle and, despite her reluctance to publish, a few verses were now beginning to appear in print. Four of her poems

---

*Davenant had arrived in England in 1650 as a prisoner, captured off the French coast while setting out on a mission from Queen Henrietta Maria to the colony of Virginia. He was released from the Tower of London in 1652.

would be set to music by Lawes and printed in the songbooks he started to publish in 1653.[15]

Meanwhile, Sir Charles Cavendish's financial business was proceeding slowly. On January 15, 1652, the Committee for Compounding allowed him once more to receive the rents from his estates "on security, pending enquiry," providing the family with a real cash income at last. But it was reported that he had been at Breda with William in 1650 and had kissed the king's hands, and if this treason were proved Sir Charles would lose his estates again. Then, in February, Parliament's Treason Trustees began to sell all William's vast estates. Spread through Northumberland, the Midlands and the West Country, manors, parks, meadows, woods, cottages, farms, granges, watermills, coal mines, quarries, lordships, baronies, mansion houses, and castles—the sales would continue steadily through 1652 into the spring of 1653. Sir Charles, still not discharged from sequestration, could do nothing as the family homes at Welbeck Abbey and Bolsover Castle were sold off to old parliamentarian officers.[16]

Sometimes Margaret drove the few streets from Covent Garden to Drury House, just north of the Strand, "to enquire how the land was sold."[17] But her powerlessness in the face of this systematic dispossession could only further lower her spirits, already depressed by her absence from William. Alone in Antwerp, he was again writing poetry for her, full of the agony of separation and protestations of his eternal, undimmed love. The whole world changed when they parted, he told her; night descended, everything stood still; aching, weeping, heavy, he was "cold as congealed ice . . . my tears converted to a shower of hail."

Morbid visions, called up by grief and loneliness, haunted William, waking and sleeping, and his poems told Margaret the horrific tales of his imaginings. A beautiful prince was cruelly murdered; a bloody battle ended in scenes of chaos, with rivers turned to blood and bodies lying disemboweled and headless; and a "tender virgin" was violently raped—she begged her attacker to kill her and he mangled her with his knife and threw her over a cliff; the wild beasts, who came for food, wept and licked her wounds before they buried her.[18]

Deep melancholy settled on Margaret. Fearing for "my Lord and husband, knowing him to be in great wants, and myself in the same condition," she was unable to sleep and soon felt unwell. Sir Theodore Mayerne, now consulted in person, despaired of his refractory patient—"the last time that I spake to my Lady about her health, she did hear patiently [and] resolve to do; but that resolution did quickly pass and she did nothing," he complained to William.[19] But Margaret was also consulting a new doctor, perhaps finding the elderly Mayerne too grandly self-important to talk to. Physicians, like most "wise learned men," she commented, "think it a discredit to discourse learnedly to ignorant women, and many learned men speak most commonly to women, as women do to children, nonsense, as thinking they understand not anything."[20]

Walter Charleton was a different kind of man. About Margaret's age, he was working as Mayerne's assistant and had just started his own fashionable practice in Russell Street in Covent Garden. Oxford educated, where he had been appointed physician to King Charles I during the war, he was cultivated and well connected, a friend of Hobbes and John Evelyn and of William's cousin, the chemist and botanist Henry Pierrepont, marquess of Dorchester. A keen natural philosopher, whose youthful espousal of the ideas of Paracelsus and Van Helmont had recently been replaced with a passion for the sorts of atomist theories the Cavendish family promoted, he doubtless discussed with Margaret the theories and ideas they shared, flattering her too with his talk of "the honour and pleasure of sometimes attending you, and hearing your more than ingenious discourses." Starting out from a relationship of doctor and patient, the two developed an intellectual friendship, which, for all Charleton's flattery of his aristocratic patroness, was also surprisingly honest, the young physician daring to give Margaret not uncritical feedback on her philosophical work.[21]

In spite of her physicians' attentions, Margaret's mood remained heavy. At home, Sir Charles pursued his mathematical and scientific studies, visited regularly by Hobbes, William Petty, and others.* But Margaret could have no place in such scholarly gatherings.[22] Once, running into Hobbes as he was leaving the house, she "told him as truly I was very glad to see him, and asked him if he would please to do me that honour to stay at dinner"—perhaps her longest speech to the philosopher—"but he with great civility refused me, as having some business, which I suppose required his absence."[23] Margaret was left as usual to the solitude and worries that so dominated her time.

Especially at night she was unhappy, kept awake by the "discontented thoughts" that filled her mind. She needed a diversion, a cure for melancholy, she realized, and so she "strove to turn the stream," directing her thoughts deliberately once more to creativity and imagination. Margaret had already written in Antwerp of the restorative power of poetry, which "revives the spirits" and "animates the mind": "it assuageth grief, it easeth pain . . . and sweetens the whole life of man." Thus it was to writing poems that she now turned, finding in her Muse a gentle companion whose "sportings," "visions," and "fairy

---

*Hobbes, whose radical writings were tainted with atheism, had fallen out of Charles II's favor in Paris; he was also a virulent critic of Catholicism, and early in 1652 he returned to England, thinking it safer than France.

dancing" occupied her lonely hours, even "in the dead of night," until finally she felt ready to "rest and sleep out all the night."[24] As the months passed, Margaret would assemble a large volume of verse.

Poetry was the commonest nonreligious genre of writing produced by women of Margaret's class. Poets like Katherine Philips and William's daughters, Jane and Elizabeth, wrote for their family and friends—poems of love and friendship, of praise and congratulation, or of consolation in bereavement, celebrations of marriages, or laments at parting and separation, or, like William's daughter Elizabeth, elegies for dead children. Strengthening the social and family ties of their circle, such writing formed a part of women's domestic role in life, and few strayed beyond. A notable exception was the New England poet Anne Bradstreet, who boldly expanded into a more "masculine" poesy with her philosophical verse dialogues of "The Four Elements" and "The Four Humours in Man's Constitution," her political reflections in a "Dialogue between Old England and New, concerning their present troubles, Anno 1642," and her long verse history of "The Four Monarchies"—Assyrian, Persian, Greek, and Roman. With the title of *The Tenth Muse Lately Sprung up in America*, her poems had recently been printed in England (without her consent), and they perhaps played some part in inspiring the vast range of "masculine" topics on which Margaret now began to write.

Exceptionally for a poet of her class, whether male or female, Margaret produced no love poetry at all. The genre was stale, she thought, "a tree whereon all poets climb" which now

> . . . *is left so bare and poor*
> *That they can hardly gather one plum more.*[25]

Neither did congratulatory and complimentary verses hold any attraction for her, containing "only flattery, rhyme and number." She wanted a grander theme, "such a subject as hath ground and room for wit and fancy to move on."[26] And so, inspired by her studies with William and his brother, she began to create a body of philosophical verse, setting out her own version of atomism.*

---

*The tradition of writing philosophical poetry went back to the earliest Greek philosophers; Lucretius's atomism was the greatest example surviving from antiquity, and although no translation was available yet for Margaret to read, she would have known his work through William and Sir Charles. Many of her contemporaries still produced their philosophy in verse—the Cambridge academic, Henry More, had recently written his own Platonist system in the style of Spenser—and even philosophers writing in prose often had a poetic sensibility: Kepler, publishing his theory of the elliptical orbits of the planets, composed in an inspired, oracular style and quoted poets as his authorities. The Baconian tradition was only gradually establishing the sharp distinction between philosophy and poetry that would become the accepted norm by the early eighteenth century.

There were four principal kinds of atoms, Margaret supposed—earth, air, fire, and water—all made of the same kind of matter, but differing because of their different atomic shapes, which gave them different physical properties. Fire atoms, sharp and pointed, pierced into bodies, dissolving them in flame; air atoms, long hollow cylinders, spread everywhere like the threads of a spider's web; earth atoms, square and flat, were heavy and inert; water atoms, hollow spheres, flowed easily over each other and joined naturally to form spherical drops of liquid. Starting from the motions, combinations, and separations of these basic atoms, Margaret set out, with the grand ambition characteristic of atomists, to explain all the observed phenomena of the natural world. Life and death, health and diseases, the motion of the tides, gravity, thunder, rain, fog, winds, echoes, the roaring of the sea, the heat of the Earth's center—she wrote brief verse theories of them all. She joined the long-running controversy over the existence of vacuum: opposing Descartes's plenism, she argued that there must be empty space,

> And were all matter fluid, as some say,
> It could not move, having no empty way.

She disliked Descartes's theory of vision too, which made light a secondary quality, a mere experience generated in the eye and brain, rather than a real property existing in the outside world. Margaret commented, remembering the poetry she loved:

> If so, poor Donne was out, when he did say,
> If all the world were blind, 'twould still be day.[27]

Combining atomism with the old Aristotelian conception of the four elements, Margaret's was an eclectic theory in the English tradition of Kenelm Digby and Walter Charleton, as opposed to the purely mechanical, clockwork-like systems of the continental philosophers, Descartes and Gassendi. Her atoms had sympathies and antipathies that made them join to form bodies or battle to cause dissolutions; they had natural motions; they acted on each other at a distance. Her theory was rich in allegory and analogy: even a small spark of fire would, like a mouse with cheese, eat through all; a small flame grew as more fire atoms came like crows to join the feast; the Earth's hot center was like a human heart, she wrote. Motion Margaret personified as a wild masculine figure with a "subtle wit," who directed the atoms to become his bawd, procuring new young bodies for him to embrace; the atoms danced to the time of his music.

Inspired, like many other writers, by the exciting revelations of her age's new scientific instruments, Margaret's philosophical poetry imagined the possibility of new worlds, as yet unseen and unvisited. But where John Wilkins and others followed the telescope and journeyed outwards, with imaginary voyages to the Moon, Margaret followed her microscope inwards, speculating on the possibility that there might be tiny worlds within our own—worlds of miniature men and women farming, gardening, living in commonwealths, and fighting wars. There might be layers of worlds within worlds, like a nest of boxes, she suggested, and her poem "A World in an Ear-Ring" conjured up the wonders that might hang from a lady's ear, undetected.[28]

This spirit of speculation and imagination was at the core of Margaret's theorizing. Since observation and knowledge of things so small as atoms was impossible, she thought, philosophy could not be a serious study, but was rather "to be used as a delight and recreation in men's studies, as poetry is." "Nature is too various to be known, and her curiosities too subtle to be understood," she had written in Antwerp, rejecting as impossible the certain knowledge to which philosophers like Descartes aspired. Her own atomism was a "fancy," she now wrote, a "fiction . . . not given for truth, but pastime."[29] Several of her philosophical poems criticized humanity's obsession with seeking for an understanding it could never obtain,

> *Spending that life which nature's God did give*
> *Us to adore Him and His wonders with,*
> *With fruitless, vain, impossible pursuits,*
> *In schools, lectures and quarrelling disputes,*
> *But never give Him thanks that did us make,*
> *Proudly, as petty gods,* * ourselves do take.*[30]

This critique of human arrogance was a frequent theme in the other poetry Margaret now wrote. Her two poems "The Hunting of the Hare" and "The Hunting of the Stag" abandoned the human perspective to tell their stories from the point of view of the quarry—an unconventional move that turned these works into passionate denunciations of human cruelty and pride. When "poor Wat," the hare, is finally killed,

> *Men, hooping loud, such acclamations make,*
> *As if the Devil they did prisoner take,*

---

*I.e. little or minor deities, demigods.

> *When they do but a shiftless creature kill;*
> *To hunt there needs no valiant soldier's skill.*

And Margaret went on to point out mankind's hypocritical dual standards:

> *When they do lions, wolves, bears, tigers see*
> *To kill poor sheep, straight say, "They cruel be,"*

while men themselves

> *. . . for sport or recreation's sake*
> *Destroy those lives that God saw good to make:*
> *Making their stomachs graves, which full they fill*
> *With murthered bodies that in sport they kill.*
> *Yet man doth think himself so gentle, mild,*
> *When he of creatures is most cruel wild.*[31]

"A Dialogue of Birds" developed this theme further. Walking in the fields and woods, Margaret listened as sparrow, magpie, finches, linnets, partridge, woodcock, quail, peewit, snipe, swallow, and parrot each told of mankind's particular cruelties to their kind—hunting them with dogs and hawks, wasting their flesh in gluttonous feasting, shooting them for eating a little fruit, tying them on a leash of string to amuse a child, or caging them and forcing them to learn to sing or talk. Even for an oak tree—"king of all the wood," cut down by his overambitious, ungrateful subjects, mankind—her verses arouse our pity.[32] Margaret was setting herself against the entire Judeo-Christian tradition of man's superiority over the natural world and his God-given right to use it as he wills. For all we know, she argued in yet more poems, beasts, birds, and fishes might have as much intelligence as us, or even more.

These works were not just critiques of society, but also admonishments to Margaret's own pride and ambition, which she expressed in other poems.

> *What creature in the world, besides mankind,*
> *That can such arts and new inventions find?*

she demanded in "A Discourse of Pride."

> *Man can distil and is a chemist rare,*
> *Divides and separates water, fire and air . . .*
> *Makes creatures all submit unto his will,*

> *Makes fame to live, though death his body kill . . .*
> *There's none like man, for like to gods is he:*
> *Then let the world his slave and vassal be.*

Carried away, she continued into her next poem, "Of Ambition":

> *Give me a fame that with the world may last,*
> *Let all tongues tell of my great actions past;*
> *Let every child, when first 'tis taught to speak,*
> *Repeat my name, my memory for to keep.*
> *And then, great Fortune, give to me thy power,*
> *To ruin man, and raise him in an hour.*
> *Let me command the Fates and spin their thread;*
> *And Death to stay his scythe when I forbid . . .*
> *And let me like the Gods on high become,*
> *That nothing can but by my will be done.*

But at once, Margaret rebuked herself with another poem, "Of Humility":

> *When with returning thoughts myself behold,*
> *I find all creatures else made of that mould.*
> *And for the mind, which some say is like the Gods,*
> *I do not find 'twixt man and beast such odds:*
> *Only the shape of men is fit for use,*
> *Which makes him seem much wiser than a goose.*[33]

Margaret's poems played out the unending internal conflict she felt between the (feminine and Christian) virtue of modesty and her own ardent aspirations for achievement and recognition. Was fame just "a word, an empty sound" with "neither soul nor substance," as her poem "Of the Shortness of Man's Life, and his Foolish Ambition" argued? Or was it the quality that made men "like to gods" who "live for ever," as "A Moral Discourse betwixt Man and Beast" concluded?[34]

Moral dialogues and discourses were a common poetical genre, produced by Milton and Marvel [Marvell] among others, and Margaret used the form to discuss a wide variety of ethical questions, with personifications such as Love and Hate, Wit and Beauty, Melancholy and Mirth, Riches and Poverty debating their relative merits. She wrote too a series of "fancies," like the allegories among her Antwerp essays, but now in verse. A body of these, likening the world to the grand establishment of a semidivine aristocratic Nature, expressed Margaret's feminine interests in dress and domesticity. The brain was "Nature's [dressing] cabinet" containing "many a fine knack"—colored ribbons of fancies, fans of opinion, veils of forgetfulness, black patches of ignorance to stick on the faces of fools. The Fates were Nature's servants in "housewifery," spinning her flax to make the "cloth of life." While Nature herself lived in divine happiness, dancing on the Milky Way to the music of the heavenly spheres, humanity's basic condition was unhappiness. In Nature's market they bought pains and illnesses, before Death, as Nature's cook, prepared them for her table, roasting the flesh with fevers, boiling it in dropsies, pickling it in sea-water drownings, or cutting throats to make blood puddings. Death was ever present in these poems: he pulled out the torn, old clothes from Nature's wardrobe; amongst her household officers, he was the "receiver" to whom Life was "to pay and give out all." And in Margaret's creation myth, when Nature called on her female servants Motion, Figure, Matter, and Life to make the universe and mankind, the male figure of Death was the opposing force they feared, who sent "black despair," pains, and diseases to attack humanity.[35]

Many of the poems were sad in tone, reflecting Margaret's dominant mood of dissatisfaction with the injustices and trials of her life. In one dialogue, the Body reproached the Mind with causing all its pains and unhappiness:

> What bodies else but man's did Nature make,
> To join with such a mind no rest can take;
> That ebbs and flows, with full and falling tide,
> As minds dejected fall, or swell with pride?[36]

In another, Man reproached Nature for making him unhappy:

> To give us sense, great pains to feel,
> To make our lives to be Death's wheel;
> To give us sense, and reason too,
> Yet know not what we're made to do . . .
> Reason doth stretch man's mind upon the rack,
> With hopes, with joys pulled up, with fear pulled back . . .
> For Nature, thou mad'st man betwixt extremes,
> Wants* perfect knowledge, yet thereof he dreams . . .
> Man knowledge hath enough for to inquire,
> Ambition great enough for to aspire:
> And knowledge hath that yet he knows not all,
> And that himself he knoweth least of all.[37]

---

*I.e. lacks.

Like many contemporary poets, Margaret preferred a state of solitary, even mourning, melancholy over the "vain and fruitless pleasures," the "light and toyish things," of mirthful society. In the manner of John Milton's recently published poems "L'Allegro" and "Il Penseroso," she composed a verse dialogue between the personified figures of Melancholy and Mirth, where Melancholy was clearly the winner in debate.[38] This melancholic sensibility led her also to idealize the darkness of night over the bright, cheery colors of the day. Her "Dialogue betwixt the Earth and Darkness" had begun with the unhappy Earth's complaint,

> *O horrid Darkness and you powers of Night,*
> *Melancholy shades made by obstructed light;*
> *Why so cruel? What evil have I done,*
> *To part me from my husband, the bright Sun?*

But it ended with Darkness's loving description of the delights he had to offer:

> *I am thy kind, true and constant lover,*
> *I all your faults and imperfections cover.*
> *I take you in my gentle arms of rest;*
> *With cool, fresh dews I bathe your dry, hot breast . . .*
> *Then slight me not, nor do my suit disdain,*
> *But when the Sun is gone, me entertain,*
> *Take me, sweet love, with joy into your bed,*
> *And on your fresh green breast lay my black head.*[39]

This passage provides an example of the explicit sensuality in Margaret's writings that readers for more than two centuries would find coarse and unladylike, contributing to her image as "Mad Madge."

Margaret also wrote verse stories of war and ruin, similar in spirit to the poems William was sending from Antwerp, ending with scenes of horror and carnage and the pathos of the dying left on the battlefield: some prayed to live, some burned for revenge, some smiled or murmured, and some, in pain, longed for death. The tone was one of loss and futility: men's hopes for conquest and glory in war were nothing but vanity, Margaret concluded.

> *Thus various fortune on each side did fall,*
> *And Death was only conqueror of all.*[40]

In sorrowing mood, Margaret wrote a series of laments for her dead family. "An Elegy on a Widow" celebrated Margaret's mother as a "pattern" of virtuous widowhood. "On a Mother that died for grief of her only Daughter" commemorated Margaret's sister Mary as an ideal of parental love. And "On a beautiful young Maid that died" mourned Mary's daughter in terms reminiscent of Donne's *Anniversaries*. These poems did not name their subjects— only those who knew Margaret's family history well would identify her relations here. But "An Elegy on my Brother, killed in these unhappy Wars" was a piece of public poetry, for Sir Charles Lucas was a well-known royalist martyr, his fame celebrated and his death lamented by many poets more established than Margaret. Buried by his enemies in an unmarked grave, Charles had his true tomb in Margaret's memory, she wrote. Daily she visited this shrine to weep:

> *My sorrows incense strew of sighs fetched deep,*
> *My thoughts do watch while thy sweet spirit sleeps.*
> *Dear blessèd soul, though thou art gone, yet lives*
> *Thy fame on earth, and men thee praises give;*
> *But all's too small, for thy heroic mind*
> *Was above all the praises of mankind.*

Here Margaret was entering the territory of royalist polemic, as written by the circle of Henry Lawes. Many of her other poems also had political overtones. "Of a Funeral" told of a burial without mourners, the body borne by enemies amidst universal rejoicing—a story that could apply equally to Margaret's brother or to King Charles I. "Comparing Waves and a Ship to Rebellion" was an allegory of the Civil War, satirizing the "rude multitudes" of parliamentarian rebels as wild stormwaves assaulting the lone, heroic ship of the king.

> *And if their power gets the upper hand,*
> *They'll make him sink, and then in triumph stand*
> *Foaming at mouth, as if great deeds th' had done,*
> *When they were multitudes, and he but one.*[41]

"Of an Island" and "The Ruin of the Island" lamented the wreck of an idyllic England. "Of the Death and Burial of Truth" and "A Battle between Honour and Dishonour" mourned the modern world's moral fall. "The Animal Parliament," composed in prose, told of an ideal royalist commonwealth in the human body, where the rational soul ruled as king over the commoners—the passions and appetites of the body. In a parody of recent political events, the passions in the

House of Commons complained of their grievances—the body's rotted teeth, its nose destroyed by syphilis, its stomach overwhelmed in drink. But departing from real history, Parliament's grievances are cured with medicines in Margaret's story: "God save the King. God save the King," they cry loyally.[42]

Margaret also told her own storm-tossed life history in the sort of biographical allegory that Flecknoe had created for the duchess of Lorraine at Beersel. In "Phantasm's Masque . . . Similizing a young Lady to a Ship," Margaret recreated the sort of courtly dramatic entertainment that was now suppressed in parliamentarian England, with masquers acting out the tale that Fancy narrated—a story of how the young lady (or ship) was driven from the Land of Happiness amidst "storms of war" and "showers of blood."

> *Then fears like to the northern winds blew high,*
> *And stars of hope were clouded in the sky.*
> *The sun went down of all prosperity.*

In Paris the ship finally finds a haven "to mend her tattered and torn barque again." Bought by "a noble lord," she sails on the sea of honor, "balanced . . . with spice of sweet content" until

> *At last a storm of poverty did rise,*
> *And showers of miseries fell from the skies,*
> *And thundering creditors a noise did make*
> *With threatening bills, as if the ship would break.*

"Forced towards the northern pole," she was cast up safely on the coast, but Margaret still worried for the fate of

> *. . . this ship so tattered, torn and rent*
> *That none but gods the ruin could prevent.*[43]

HOWEVER, BY THE SUMMER OF 1652 the Cavendishes' financial affairs were at last improving. Sir Charles's estates were discharged from sequestration in June, some six months after his petition at Goldsmiths' Hall; by the autumn he was settling the family in some security. He leased many of his newly regained estates to trustees, to provide an income for Henry, Jane, and Frances, and he assigned his own country house at Wellingore in Lincolnshire as a residence for Henry. Other lands were leased to provide marriage portions for Jane and Frances, and for Elizabeth, countess of Bridgewater, whose dowry William had still not paid. Meanwhile, William's eldest son, Charles, viscount Mansfield, himself petitioned Parliament and managed to repossess as his own inheritance the substantial estates his mother had brought into the family as her dowry.[44]

The two Charleses, uncle and nephew, now bought back some of William's confiscated lands that had not yet been sold off by Parliament, using trustees to conceal the family's involvement from the public eye. The two men they employed were John Hutton, a lawyer and Midlands landholder, and William Clayton, a prosperous Derbyshire lead merchant, whose father had been a tenant of William's in the 1630s.[45] Clayton's brother Andrew had already entered the Cavendishes' service just before the war, as a receiver of William's tithes and rents; by the early 1650s he was one of the overseers of the grange farm at Welbeck, where he was also in charge of the family's ready money, paying out cash to cover their personal expenditure.[46] Hutton and the Clayton brothers became trusted servants. In 1652, their purchases from the Treason Trustees were vital in preserving William's estates and "particularly his houses, woods and parks from ruin and destruction."[47]

Sir Charles Cavendish also managed to buy back the two family houses at Welbeck and Bolsover for his nephew Charles, viscount Mansfield—but only by paying above the market value and selling some of his own property.[48] Bolsover, however, was no longer habitable. Margaret's poem "A Dialogue between a Bountiful Knight and a Castle ruin'd in War" told of the desolation Sir Charles found when he visited this once beautiful place, whose outworks, garden and courtyard walls, turrets and doors had all been demolished by Parliament's army. "Alas, poor Castle, how thou art changed!" lamented the Knight, and the Castle told its story. Built by "your most valiant father," the Castle had looked out happily over the lush vale below. But now, filled with rubbish heaps, its windows broken, choked and dry with all its water pipes cut off, it begged the Knight to buy back its freedom, which he promised to do, vowing also to "supply thy former spring" with his heart, "from whence the water of fresh tears shall rise."[49]

Margaret and Sir Charles had become close during their time in London. One of her poems tells how, coming into her chamber and finding her writing about the court of the fairies—a kind of verse made fashionable by Shakespeare's *A Midsummer Night's Dream*—

> "I pray," said he, "when Queen Mab you do see,
> Present my service to her Majesty."

Margaret bowed low to the queen, kissed her gown, and, kneeling,

> *In whispers soft I did present,*
> *His humble service, which in mirth was sent.*[50]

She was hugely grateful to this man who was "so nobly generous, carefully kind and respectful to me," only from the affection he bore to his brother, she thought, "for I dare not challenge his favours as to myself, having not merits to deserve them." Sir Charles was "the preserver of my life," she later remembered of this time in London: his "favours and my thankfulness ingratitude shall never disjoin."[51] But even from Sir Charles and William Margaret kept secret the plans she was now forming for her poetry.

By the autumn of 1652, Margaret had completed a large body of verse. "It is not excellent, nor rare, but plain," she thought.

> *I language want to dress my fancies in,*
> *The hair's uncurled, the garments loose and thin;*
> *Had they but silver lace to make them gay,*
> *Would be more courted than in poor array.*

She could offer readers only the simplest hospitality: "I cannot serve you on agate tables and Persian carpets, with golden dishes and crystal glasses, nor feast you with ambrosia and nectar," she apologized. "Yet perchance my rye loaf and new butter may taste more savoury," Margaret hoped, herself preferring a plain, unlearned style.[52]

"What writing soever is darkened or obscured . . . by hard and unusual words, grows troublesome and unpleasant to the readers," Margaret had written in Antwerp. "The best poetry is plain to the understanding, of easy expressions, and full of fresh and new conceits: like a beauty that every time it is looked upon discovers new graces." "Scholars are never good poets," she thought, "for . . . their head is nothing but a lumber stuffed with old commodities."[53] Instead of the literary influences of a wide reading, she aspired to freedom, independence, power, boldness, individuality in her work—the marks of a noble, aristocratic spirit.

> *Give me that wit whose fancy's not confined,*
> *That buildeth on itself, not two brains joined . . .*
> *But like the Sun, that needs no help to rise,*
> *Or like a bird in air, which freely flies.*
> *Give me the free and noble style . . .*
> *Give me a style that Nature frames, not Art,*
> *For Art doth seem to take the pedant's part,*

> *And that seems noble which is easy, free,*
> *Not to be bound with o'er-nice pedantry.* *[54]

Margaret recognized that her poems contained inelegancies of expression and faults in rhyme and meter—the collection had, after all, been written at speed, and much of it at night—but language was not the most important quality in a poet, she thought. It was "wit" and "fancy"—the imagination, ideas, invention, imagery of poetry—which were the vital ingredients, and Margaret criticized contemporary writers for their excessive concern with language,

> *As if fine words were wit, or one should say*
> *A woman's handsome if her clothes be gay . . .*
> *Fancy is the form, flesh, blood, bone, skin;*
> *Words are but shadows, have no substance in.*[55]

Overall Margaret was pleased with her poems

> *Reading my verse, I liked them so well,*
> *Self-love did make my judgement to rebel,*

she told her story in "The Poetress's Hasty Resolution." Her ambitions for achievement and public recognition in life were driving her to think of publishing her work, but for Margaret this was an agonizing decision.

> *Reason observing which way I was bent,*
> *Did stay my hand, and asked me what I meant . . .*
> *"For shame leave off," said she, "the printer spare,*
> *He'll lose by your ill poetry, I fear.*
> *Besides the world hath already such a weight*
> *Of useless books, as it is over-fraught.*
> *Then pity take, do the world a good turn,*
> *And all you write cast in the fire and burn."*
> *Angry I was, and Reason struck away*

---

*Margaret's preference for originality and invention over scholarship in literature was common amongst the seventeenth-century gentry classes (and amongst those writers like Hobbes and Davenant who sought their maintenance in aristocratic or royal households, rather than in the universities). William was a passionate proponent of this ideal: "that which they call learning puts a good wit out of the right way of knowledge with false arts," he would advise King Charles II.

When I did hear what she to me did say.
Then all in haste I to the press it sent,
Fearing persuasion might my book prevent.[56]

Printing her work was doubly taboo for Margaret, forbidden her by the values of both class and gender. The gentlemen-poets of court culture rarely printed their verses: such publication would profane their work, exposing it to the vulgar eyes of all. Instead they made handwritten copies for circulation within the elite circles to which they belonged, thus retaining some control over their readership and keeping up a literary exclusivity that added kudos to their work. On the rare occasions when their poems were printed, they appeared anonymously, billed simply as "written by a person of quality"—or "by a person of honour," as William's book of plays had been described in 1649. For women of this class the dishonor of publishing was further multiplied by moral considerations. Modesty, silence, obedience, self-effacement—the central concepts of female virtue—would all be violated by publication, and women who printed their works risked shame and denunciation. "Your printing of a book, beyond the custom of your sex, doth rankly smell," one man wrote to his sister: "what will you make yourself to be?"[57]

After the paucity of women's publications in the first four decades of the seventeenth century, the rise of puritanism and the relaxation of censorship during the Civil War had created an explosion of religious and political publishing, in which many women joined: during the 1650s almost five times as many books by women were printed as during the 1630s.[58] But these parliamentarians offered no useful precedent for Margaret—Quakers, Baptists, Levelers, they were precisely the "women . . . pleaders, attorneys, petitioners and the like" she so despised. Of literary works by upper-class women, only nine had appeared in print in the last fifty years, all but one of them published without their authors' permission, and the one exception had ended in disaster. Lady Mary Wroth, publishing her romance, *Urania*, in 1621, had met such virulent opposition for her story's perceived similarities to real people and events that she had been forced to discontinue publication and destroy the copies: the work would not be printed again until 1991—and even then only in part. A complete version appeared in 1995.

Margaret knew well of Mary Wroth's fate and she viewed her own plans for publication with great trepidation.

Work, Lady, work; let writing books alone,
For surely wiser women ne'er wrote one,

she expected her male readers to say, as Lord Denny had written to Mary Wroth.* This was a woman's proper sphere—needlework, spinning, baking, cooking—Margaret knew, although she attempted to escape such duties with the excuse that "my Lord's estate being taken away, I had nothing for housewifery or thrifty industry to employ myself in." Her fears at straying beyond this feminine domesticity to publish her book were "as big as the world," she wrote, "yet my hopes fall to a single atom . . . if I am condemned, I shall be annihilated to nothing." But she could not restrain herself from publishing. Her desires for public achievement and some memorial after death were too great, her fears of anonymity and oblivion too consuming. "I am resolved to set it at all hazards," she wrote in the bold language of gamblers, "and if I lose, I lose but the opinion of wit." "Where the gain will be more than the loss, who would not venture?" she argued, "and why should not I venture, when nothing lies at stake but wit? Let it go; I shall nor cannot be much poorer. If Fortune be my friend, then Fame will be my gain, which may build me a pyramid, a praise to my memory."[59]

Margaret prepared for publication, arranging her poems into sections. Her atomist work she dedicated "to natural philosophers"; her allegories "to poets"; her dialogues and discourses "to moral philosophers"; her stories of war "to soldiers." "To all writing ladies" she dedicated her poems of Queen Mab and the fairies—works rich in the creative imagination, or "fancy," which she thought was an especially female attribute.** And, in expectation of the criticism she knew would come, Margaret composed a series of prefaces in self-defense, justifying writing and publishing as a proper occupation for women.

Her poetry did no one any harm, she argued; it lay far from "the muddy and foul ways of vice." "To deny the principles of their religion, to break the laws of a well-governed kingdom, to disturb peace, to be unnatural, to break the union and amity of honest friends, for a man to be a coward, for a woman to be a whore"—these were real (and mostly parliamentarian) vices, and Margaret reminded her readers "that my book is none of them." "Why should I be ashamed or afraid where no evil is, and not please myself in the satisfaction of innocent desires?" she demanded.[60]

Not only was writing harmless, Margaret wanted to persuade her readers: it was actually a proper and virtuous occupation for women, "the harmlessest

---

*Margaret's knowledge of this attack on Wroth probably derived from oral tradition, since Denny's verse was not printed. The two versions of it that now survive in manuscript are both different from the one that Margaret here quotes, perhaps just from memory.

**Pierre Le Moyne's *Gallerie des Femmes Fortes* had also argued that women possessed greater powers of imagination than men.

pastime" for the extended leisure hours, the "waste time," which fashionable ladies might spend much worse. "Sure this work is better than to sit still and censure my neighbours' actions, which nothing concerns me; or to condemn their humours, because they do not sympathise with mine . . . or ridiculously to laugh at my neighbours' clothes, if they are not of the mode colour or cut, or the ribbons tied with a mode knot." "All these follies, and many more may be cut off by such innocent work as this," Margaret argued. To the men who said that writing was improper for women she retorted scornfully with the wish that their own nearest relations, "as wives, sisters and daughters, may employ their time no worse than in honest, innocent and harmless fancies."[61]

To her women readers Margaret had much more to say, with two prefaces dedicated "to all noble and worthy ladies" and "to all writing ladies." She asked them to support her in common cause against her male critics, and addressed to them her revolutionary claim that "poetry, which is built upon fancy, women may claim as a work belonging most properly to themselves." It was women who were truly artistic and imaginative, she argued, "their thoughts . . . employed perpetually with fancies" not only in the "many and singular choices of clothes and ribbons and the like" that were involved in their fashionable dressing, but also in the "mixing of colours . . . and divers sorts of stitches" of their needlework, in their cooking of "all manner of meats," and in their many domestic decorative arts, making "flowers, boxes, baskets with beads, shells, silk, straw, or anything else." They were living in "an age when the effeminate spirits rule . . . in every kingdom," Margaret wrote, thinking of the many women who now wrote books, even if only in private, of the female preachers and prophets of the puritan sects, of the women courtiers who acted in court masques, of the new fashion for actresses on the public stage, which she had seen on the Continent, and of the many female monarchs that this period of history had produced—Mary and Elizabeth I in England, Mary Queen of Scots, Queen Christina of Sweden, and the French queen regents Marie de' Medici and Anne of Austria. In such an age, Margaret exhorted her women readers, "let us make the best of our time" in politics and government, in divinity, in philosophy, or poetry, "or anything that may bring honour to our sex, for they are poor, dejected spirits that are not ambitious of fame."[62]

Margaret was proposing an alternative model of feminine behavior, based on the French fashion for heroic women. For all of humanity, not just men, she claimed, "tis a part of honour to aspire towards a fame. For it cannot be an infamy to seek or run after glory, to love perfection, to desire praise."[63] (This was, of course, precisely the sort of self-publicizing that *was* traditionally regarded as an infamous vice in women.) Margaret wanted to present the publication of her poetry not as a violation of the feminine virtues of modesty, silence, and chastity, but as an honorable act, even a moral or religious duty.

> *To desire fame, it is a noble thought,*
> *Which Nature in the best of minds hath wrought.*

> *Nature a talent gives to every one*
> *As Heaven gives grace to work salvation from . . .*
> *If men be lazy, let this talent lie,*
> *Seek no occasion to improve it by,*
> *Who knows but Nature's punishment may be*
> *To make the mind to grieve eternally?*
> *That when his spirit's fled and body rot*
> *To know himself of friend's and world's forgot.*[64]

However, for all her self-justifications, Margaret had still not dared to tell her relatives of her plans for publication—"I have not asked leave of any friend," she noted, "for the fear of being denied made me silent: and there is an old saying, that it is easier to ask pardon than leave, for a fault will sooner be forgiven than a suit granted."[65] The only person Margaret confided in was her maid, Elizabeth Chaplain—now Mistress Topp, since her marriage to an English merchant in Antwerp. In spite of her marriage, Elizabeth had accompanied her mistress back to England, and she played a crucial role in encouraging and assisting Margaret's first publication. To her Margaret dedicated one of her prefaces, and in reply Elizabeth composed a letter praising both Margaret's poetry and her personal qualities. Printed with Margaret's prefaces, this letter by someone who had "been brought up from my childhood . . . always in your ladyship's company" vouched for Margaret's virtue, shoring up the honor, honesty, and modesty that she put at risk by her act of publication.[66]

It was presumably Elizabeth too who acted as go-between, carrying Margaret's manuscripts and letters to the booksellers in the City who would publish the *Poems and Fancies*, as she now named her volume. The area around St. Paul's Cathedral was the heart of the London book trade. Here the wealthiest booksellers had their shops, producing volumes by the nation's leading authors for sale to the highest class of clientele. In the cathedral churchyard itself, the partnership of John Martin and James Allestrye, at the sign of the Bell, was London's foremost publishing house, and it was here that Margaret sent her book. It was a valuable commodity for a publisher: the rarity and novelty, the social and sexual allure of feminine aristocratic authorship would fascinate England's reading public.

Martin and Allestrye used some of London's best printers, and Thomas Roycroft—whose polyglot Bible was the outstanding English publishing achievement of the century—produced Margaret's poems in a lavish folio volume. With spacious pages of very large print, it matched its author's social status in grandeur. The whole volume Margaret dedicated "to Sir Charles Cavendish, my noble brother-in-law" in gratitude for all he had done for her and William. "Your kindness hath been such as you have neglected yourself, even in ordinary accoutrements, to maintain the distressed," she now publicly acknowledged: "I am your slave, being manacled with chains of obligation." She hoped that "such a patron may gain my book a respect and esteem in the world."[67] And, to balance this dedication on its first page, Margaret ended her book with a poem modestly acknowledging William as the only inspiration for all her poetry.

EVEN BEFORE SHE PUBLISHED her *Poems and Fancies*, Margaret had become a talking point for London society. Her plight as William's wife—penniless and dispossessed, when other royalist wives could claim an income from their husbands' estates—made her remarkable, and rumors told of the petitioning speeches she had made "at this committee and at that committee," and even to Parliament itself. When these stories got back to her, Margaret was hurt, hating that people should think she could so demean herself. "I did not stand as a beggar at the Parliament door," she protested vehemently, "neither did I haunt the committees."[68]

Margaret's individual style of dress had also begun to attract the attention of society gossip. "Report did dress me in a hundred several fashions," she heard, for although she went out only rarely, Margaret always paid careful attention to her appearance, dressing "myself . . . in my best becoming."[69] For what she was actually wearing, we have only one piece of contemporary evidence—a report by the duchess of Lorraine, which reveals that Margaret wore ribbons around her wrists or arms in an unusual way. But the overall effect is clear, for society found Margaret's dress "extravagant"—strange, wild, fantastic, excessive, beyond the bounds of normal propriety.[70] This reputation for eccentricity was only increased when the *Poems and Fancies* appeared at the beginning of 1653.[71]

For so aristocratic a woman to publish her own writing was an unprecedented event, and Margaret's work was instantly in demand. "Let me ask you if you have seen a book of poems newly come out, made by my Lady Newcastle," the young Dorothy Osborne wrote from Bedfordshire to her fiancé, William Temple, in London, fascinated by the stories she had heard.

> For God's sake, if you meet with it, send it me; they say 'tis ten times more extravagant than her dress. Sure, the poor woman is a little distracted, she could never be so ridiculous else as to venture at writing books, and in verse too. If I should not sleep this fortnight, I should not come to that.[72]

Many features of Margaret's writing contributed to this impression of eccentricity. First there was the "masculine" content of her verses. The philosophical theorizing, the political satire, the bloody scenes of war, the moral debates and denunciations of humanity's pride, these were all properly topics for men not women. In addition, Margaret's views were often unusual. Her philosophical poems provided perhaps the first atomic theory of nature to be published in England,* and reeked of the atheism for which the ancient Greek atomists, Democritus and Epicurus, were notorious. Margaret's theory, like theirs, was systematically materialist. Life and death, health and sickness, even human behavior and large-scale social phenomena such as war and peace, "all things are governed by atoms," she proclaimed, leaving no room for human free will or divine providence in a world she described as created by Nature not God.[73] This dangerous free thinking was also seen in Margaret's only religious poem, "The Motion of Thoughts," where the inspiration of a divine vision soon gave way to expressions of her own deeply skeptical attitude to Christian belief.

Dorothy Osborne was shocked when she finally obtained a copy. "You need not send me my Lady Newcastle's book at all," she wrote to William Temple, "for I have seen it, and am satisfied that there are many soberer people in Bedlam. I'll swear her friends are much to blame to let her go abroad."[74] But other readers admired Margaret's poems. Mildmay Fane, earl of Westmorland, a royalist who had printed his own poetry in 1648 (though only for private circulation), composed a laudatory poem, praising Margaret's wit, fancy, and style, and wrote it into the front of his own copy of the *Poems and Fancies*.[75] Meanwhile Edmund Waller, the witty gentleman-poet who had dined at the Newcastles' house in Paris, told his friends that "he would have given all his own poems to have been the author of" Margaret's verse tale "The Hunting of the Stag"; but when accused of insincerity he replied with the witticism "that

---

*Publication of the newly revived theory of atomism had so far centered on France, with the work of Descartes and Gassendi. Margaret's friend Walter Charleton only published his own atomist theory in England the following year, in his *Physiologia Epicuro-Gassendo-Charltoniana*.

he could do no less in gallantry than be willing to devote all his own papers to save the reputation of a lady, and keep her from the disgrace of having written anything so ill."This story, along with the other rumors about Margaret, passed freely round London society.[76]

WHILE HER *Poems and Fancies* was still with the printers, Margaret had already begun to write again—a new philosophical theory, composed mainly in prose, though some parts were again in verse. Her new ideas were no longer based on the four kinds of atoms—earth, air, fire, and water—that the *Poems and Fancies* had put forward as the primary building-blocks of the universe. Instead Margaret posited a single kind of matter, which had different "degrees" of density, hardness, weight, and motion. She rejected her old idea of motion as a separate principle, acting on atoms to cause change in the world. In her new theory, all matter contained innate motion within itself, but in different degrees. The thinner, lighter degrees of matter—the "extracts," "spirits," or "essence" of matter, as Margaret called them, using the terminology of the chemist's laboratory—contained more motion, by which they pierced into and exerted power over the duller, heavier degrees of matter. "They are of an acute quality, being the vitriol, as it were, of nature," Margaret explained. Cutting and carving the heavier matter—"as aqua-fortis will eat into the hardest iron and divide it into small parts"—these spirits directed matter in all its changes and motions, governing the formation and dissolution of all the bodies of the universe, working in the same way as builders, cooks, and weavers to shape the duller matter into ordered forms.[77] The thinner, higher spirits— "agile" and "always in motion"—were actually alive, Margaret thought, "for when matter comes to such a degree it quickens." And living inside them was the thinnest, most active extract of all: "rational spirits." Stronger than the "spirits of life"—just as aqua-fortis is stronger than ordinary vitriol—these were the spirits that produced thought, memory, imagination, and knowledge in the brain, as they formed themselves into different shapes and patterns of motion.[78] But such spirits also existed outside the human brain, she argued. Since everything in the world moves and changes, the whole world—animal, vegetable, and mineral—must be alive and rational. "Whatsoever hath an innate motion hath knowledge," even plants and stones. Each knowledge was different in kind because of the different shapes and material compositions of the bodies it was contained in, "yet it is knowledge."[79]

Margaret worked in haste, hoping to add her new theory to the *Poems and Fancies,* which was already in the press. In the three weeks she allowed herself, she had only time to outline her basic theory and sketch how it might be applied to explain a few phenomena—life and death, rationality and emotion, change, growth and decay, the differences of animals and plants, the nature of light and the motions of the planets and the tides. On the much-debated question of whether a vacuum could exist in nature, she made equal cases both for and against, without making any choice between them—showing her characteristic interest in making arguments rather than reaching resolutions. For the rest, she could only add a six-page list of the phenomena she would have liked to explain and the questions she wished she had answered, as she hurried her manuscript off to the printers. But even so, it arrived a week too late, and the *Philosophical Fancies*, as Margaret named her work, would have to wait some five months before it came out as a separate book—a small octavo volume, published by Martin and Allestrye, again printed by Thomas Roycroft and dedicated to Sir Charles Cavendish.[80]

But all this frenetic literary activity could not keep Margaret from her melancholy. She was still not sleeping, still not well, still missing William desperately. From Antwerp, his poems begged her to return to him, telling how he spent his days in "love dreams," imagining her arrival, hoping for her letters that never seemed to come.

> Then went to bed, and sighed, then dreamed of thee,
> So all the night was in thy company.
> The pillow in my arms I filled with kisses;
> When waked, found that they were but empty blisses,
> And sighed again, and thought thou wert unkind
> And asked what news, and how did stand the wind,
> Asking what ships from England hither came
> And whom by land, what boats from Amsterdam.

"Banished" from Margaret, unable to go to her in England, he felt powerless.

> There's no misfortune, misery can be
> Or torture, like my grief in wanting thee.

What if she abandoned him and stayed on indefinitely with her family in England? He could only hope that "thou'rt constant." But Margaret was just as anxious and unhappy at their separation. When she heard, soon after she sent her *Philosophical Fancies* to the printers, that William was ill—"committed to my chamber there I lie, no breath but sighs," he told her—she could wait no longer.[81]

With the Cavendishes' financial affairs at last reduced to order, Sir Charles resolved to accompany her. However, as they made their preparations, he fell ill with a violent fever that left him too weak to travel. The doctors advised that he should "go into the country for change of air" and so Margaret, impatient to rejoin her husband, decided to leave without him. On Wednesday, February 16, 1653, the Council of State issued a warrant permitting "the Lady Newcastle, with four men-servants and four maid-servants, to pass into Flanders." But the authorities required all travelers leaving the country to take the Engagement—swearing loyalty to the parliamentary government "without a King or House of Lords"—and this she refused to do. The battle of wills that ensued was only brief, for women's political compliance was of little importance compared to men's. On March 2, a new order came from the Council of State: "that the Lady Newcastle with her servants be permitted to pass out of England without having the taking of the Engagement pressed upon them."[82]

Leaving London, Margaret felt that she had begun to achieve something in life. No longer was her time wasted or misspent. Now that she was using "all the life" and "all the wit that Nature to me gave" in writing books, her fear of death, of leaving no memorial behind her, was receding.

> But if the ruins of oblivion come,
> 'Tis not my fault, for what I can is done.

Looking ahead to Antwerp, she thought not only of the husband she so missed, but also of the collection of essays she had left behind there. "I will, if God give me life and health, finish it and send it forth in print," she promised.[83]

Chapter Nine

Writer in Exile,
1653–1655

It was a true lovers' reunion when Margaret and William met after fifteen months apart. William was witless with relief, with joy, with passion—

> *I smile, would speak, would kiss and toy;*
> *My heart so pants, thy hand doth wring;*
> *At nothing laughs and everything . . .*
> *Would kiss, but love amazèd seeks*
> *Whether thy forehead, nose, or cheeks,*
> *Thy pretty chin, neck, or love's nests,*
> *Thy milk-white, panting, twin-like breasts.*
> *I then would bite thine ear, then spy*
> *And long to kiss each loving eye.*

Another poem relived the moment of their meeting—how their eyes first met, then drew them together so their lips joined in numberless kisses, in front of all their attendants. William was now desperate to indulge in all love's pleasures:

> *Sweet, let us love enjoy,*
> *And play and tick and toy,*
> *And all our cares will drown;*
> *Smile, laugh, and sometimes frown . . .*
> *Then whisper in each ear,*
> *Love's pretty tales to hear.*

If wanton, cry "Oh man!"
And strike me with your fan.
If offer thee to dandle,
Then rap me with the handle.
For all this, I'll not miss
Thy lips, but steal a kiss.[1]

Margaret found a husband not only in love but also totally supportive of her writing and publication, for which she was hugely grateful. "Your Lordship is an extraordinary husband," she acknowledged: reading and approving of her works and giving her "leave to publish them" was "a favour few husbands would grant their wives," and she knew that William would be liable to criticism. "Too fond and indulgent . . . just so is a husband condemned if he humours and pleaseth his wife in letting her have her will in honest and not dishonourable recreations." But William paid little attention to society's comments and opinions, its fashions and fads. He did not adopt the latest "mode-phrases" in his talk, nor the newest fashionable foods and drinks—"as chocolata, limonada and the like"—in his diet. Instead he followed his own tastes. He rode and fenced (when "the fashion is for tennis or pall-mall"). He passed his time with reading and writing, rather than the ever-popular cards and dice. He dined at home with Margaret, although fashionable gentlemen commonly went out together to eat in ordinaries and taverns. He was now fifty-nine and identified himself as an older man, too sane and rational, too "experienced and wise," to follow "the mode."[2] But, despite his age, he would still be a good husband, he promised Margaret:

I know I'm old, it is too true,
Yet love, nay, am in love with you.
Do not despise me, or be cruel,
For thus I am love's best of fuel:
No man can love more, or loves higher,
Old and dry wood makes the best fire,
Burns clearest, and is still the same,
Turned all into a living flame.
It lasts not long, is that your doubt,
When am to ashes all burnt out?
A short and lively heat that's pure
Will warm one best, though not endure.

With William's support, Margaret established herself firmly in her literary career. Soon after her return to exile, she and William began sending copies of her books out to friends and acquaintance. To Sir Edward Hyde—now part of Charles II's court in Paris—went the *Poems and Fancies* in May 1653. A month later the *Philosophical Fancies* arrived in Oxford, for the Bodleian Librarian, Thomas Barlow, one of the University's most learned authorities in theology and philosophy. At the Hague, Constantijn Huygens also received Margaret's *Poems*, and later in the year William sent both books to another distinguished scholar. Robert Creighton, a prominent royalist clergyman now subsisting in exile in the Netherlands by working as a private tutor to English gentlemen's sons, was an occasional visitor at the Rubens House when he passed through Antwerp.[3]

Letters of effusive thanks soon returned, acknowledgements for "books rare and transcendent, distilled from the brain of a most noble Minerva, a Lady . . . whom delicacy of education, height of birth and place, might well have exempted from such inferior employments: yet composed with so curious art, quick style, refined airy notions, words so proper, elegant and delightful both in verse and prose, that I must ever admire the harmony of her inspiring soul," as Creighton put it.[4]

But Hyde's letter to William was more worrying. He praised Margaret's poems, but also suggested that a woman, "unskilled in any but our mother tongue," could hardly have written such a book, so full of learning, with "so many terms of art, and such expressions proper to all sciences." The judgment that Margaret's work was too good to have been produced by a mere woman was in a sense a compliment. But it also contained the implication that she had not really written her book—a common response to women's writing of the time, and one which the authors found deeply hurtful. Anne Bradstreet had already written of such responses to her own poems:

> I am obnoxious* to each carping tongue,
> Who says my hand a needle better fits,
> A poet's pen, all scorn, I should thus wrong;
> For such despite they cast on female wits:
> If what I do prove well, it won't advance,
> They'll say it's stol'n, or else, it was by chance.

In the 1680s, Anne Killigrew, maid of honor to the duchess of York, experienced similar disappointment when she began to circulate her unpublished poems amongst her acquaintances:

---

*I.e. vulnerable.

Like Aesop's painted jay I seemed to all,
Adorned in plumes I not my own could call:
Rifled like her, each one my feathers tore,
And, as they thought, unto the owner bore.
My laurels thus another's brow adorned;
My numbers they admired, but me they scorned.[5]

Already, while she was still in London, Margaret had begun to hear "that my first book was thought to be none of my own fancies." The "masculine" content of her verse suggested to many that it was the work of some male relative, concealing his authorship under her name. Margaret had tried to make the best of it. "If any thinks my book so well writ as that I had not the wit to do it, truly I am glad for my wit's sake . . . that is thought so well of." But immediate denial of the rumors was vital if she was to keep possession of her own work and so, just before she left England, Margaret added an extra epilogue to her *Philosophical Fancies*. She assured her readers that she had no friend "so foolish as to be afeared or ashamed to own their own writings." "Truly I am so honest as not to steal another's work and give it my own name."[6]

Soon after her return to Antwerp, Margaret began to prepare her essays for publication. In London, she had already chosen a title for her new book: *The World's Olio*.[7] This referred to the great Spanish stew—known in its native land as an *olla podrida*—which was now becoming fashionable in England for aristocratic entertaining. Composed of the richest ingredients—beef, mutton, chickens, bacon, sausages, all cooked together with expensive foreign spices and onions, garlic, pumpkins, cabbages, and other vegetables, until the meat fell from the bone—the olio symbolized the lavish entertainment that Margaret wanted to offer her readers, and suggested too the huge variety of ingredient essays that this literary dish contained.* It was, as her friend Walter Charleton commented, "an elegant and most accommodate title."[8]

But when Margaret unlocked her essays from their chest and began to read, she was disappointed. In many places her ideas were badly expressed. "A little more care might have placed the words so as the language might have run smoother, which would have given the sense a greater lustre," was Margaret's public comment on what she found, but the problems were not so superficial as this suggests. Some of her thoughts were explained so briefly that they were

---

*Laying on grand hospitality was an important part of an aristocratic woman's domestic duties, and Margaret often described her writing with feminine metaphors of dining, feasting, and cooking. Calling her book an "olio" in 1653, Margaret makes probably the first ever use of the word in English to mean a literary miscellany.

obscure; elsewhere, arguments were so compressed they seemed non sequiturs. Essays were badly organized, going off at a tangent part way through as Margaret was sparked off towards some new direction, so that their titles bore little relation to the main subject discussed. Vital words or phrases were omitted. Chains of thought became so complicated with multiple ramifications that they were never completed; complex sentences were incorrectly formed, changing subject or grammatical construction midway, coming to no clear conclusion.[9]

These were all elementary mistakes, but Margaret had received no formal education in even the most basic writing skills, and these essays were her first return to writing as an adult. Looking back at her work, she could see that revision would be an enormous undertaking—"to me it seemed as if I had built a house and, not liking the form after it was built, must be forced to take it in pieces and rebuild it again, to make it of that fashion I would have it." But such a task was too daunting, too difficult, too disagreeable to be faced. "There is more pleasure and delight in making than in mending," "I have my delight in writing," and "my readers would have found fault with it [even] if I had done it as [best] I could."[10] Margaret tried to reconcile herself to her essays as they stood but, frustrated and dissatisfied, she felt inferior as a writer.

"It cannot be expected I should write so wisely or wittily as men, being of the effeminate sex, whose brains Nature hath mixed with the coldest and softest elements."* Dismissing more "feminist" arguments—that women "were made equal by Nature" but men had "usurped a supremacy to themselves," making women "more and more enslaved . . . which slavery hath so dejected our spirits as we are become so stupid that beasts are but a degree below us"—Margaret asserted a fundamental and innate difference between men and women. Compared to the "masculine" oak, women were like willows, "a yielding vegetable, not fit nor proper to build houses and ships." Or they were like the hen blackbird, which "can never sing with so strong and loud a voice, nor so clear and perfect notes as the cock." Or like the Moon, "pale and wan, cold, moist and slow . . . [with] no light but what it borrows from the Sun." They might exceed men "in tender affections, as love, piety, charity, clemency, patience, humility, and the like." But "women can never have so strong judgement, nor clear understanding, nor so perfect rhetoric," Margaret was sure, and her evidence was copious. "What woman ever made such laws as Moses?" she demanded.

---

*Here she followed the traditional view, derived from Aristotle and Galen, that women's bodies contained more of the colder and moister humors, lacking the heat that made men strong, active, intelligent, and creative.

What woman was ever so wise as Solomon or Aristotle? . . . so eloquent as Tully? so demonstrative as Euclid? so inventive as Seth or Archimedes? . . . It was not a woman that invented perspective glasses to pierce into the Moon; it was not a woman that found out the invention of writing letters and the art of printing . . . of gunpowder, and the art of guns. What women were such soldiers as Hannibal, Caesar, Tamberlain, Alexander, and Scanderbeg? What woman was such a chemist as Paracelsus? such a physician as Hippocrates or Galen? such a poet as Homer? . . . such an architect as Vitruvius? such a musician as Orpheus?

Margaret despaired of her sex: "what did we ever do, but like apes, by imitation?" "Allowed so much idle time 'that we know not how to pass it away," women were as free to study as men, and so their lack of intellectual achievement could only result from the natural weakness of their brains.[11]

But many of the faults in her writing, which Margaret angrily attributed to her own inferiority as a woman, could have been the result of dyslexia. Like many dyslexics, Margaret experienced difficulty putting her ideas into both written and spoken language: "my words run stumbling out of my mouth, and my pen draws roughly on my paper, yet my thoughts move regular in my brain," she said. Though she wrote as fast as she could—in fact "so fast as I stay not so long as to write my letters plain"—her struggling hand often lagged far behind her ideas, so that "many fancies are lost, by reason they oft times outrun the pen."[12] This was what produced the omitted words and phrases in her essays, the sentences that changed direction or were left uncompleted—a common feature of dyslexia and one that would recur in Margaret's later books, especially where her thought was flowing fast and freely, as when writing her autobiography.

Then too there is her illegible handwriting, a "ragged rout" as she described it, the letters so ill formed that "some have taken my handwriting for some strange character."[13] Peppered with smudges and scratches, Margaret's manuscripts were also full of crossings-out, not only of ill-spelt words, which she then corrected, but also of words that she rewrote in identical form—a clear sign of her low confidence with a pen. The love letters she sent to William during their 1645 courtship are an untidy scrawl, in many places scarcely decipherable. "Pray lay the fault of my writing to my pen";* "if you cannot read this letter blame me not, for it was so early I was half asleep"—a self-conscious Margaret hoped these postscripts would excuse her to her lover.[14]

---

*I.e. to a quill that had not been properly cut and prepared for her, and so would not write well.

These twenty-one love letters are almost the only samples of her hand-writing to survive, for after marriage Margaret employed scriveners and sec-retaries even for the personal letters that, according to etiquette, she ought to have written in her own hand. As Margaret explained in the postscript she added to one of her letters to Constantijn Huygens, reproduced here with her original spelling and punctuation: "S[r] I would have writt my leters to you in my own hand but be reson my hand written is not legabell I though you might rather have gest at what I would say then had read what I had writt this is the reson they wer writt by an other hand."[15]

All seventeenth-century spelling shows variation and irregularity, but women had consistently worse spelling, punctuation, and grammar than men—"false English being particularly entailed upon the sex," as one woman writer complained.[16] Well-born ladies like Margaret were commonly less liter-ate than their immediate social inferiors, the daughters of clergymen and oth-ers who might need to write to earn their living as ladies' companions, governesses, or school teachers. So Margaret's failure to punctuate—her love letters are written entirely without punctuation, there are no periods to sepa-rate sentences, nor any capital letters even for proper names, excepting only her signature—was not exceptional. Her many phonetic spellings are also not too unusual in women's manuscripts of the period—words like "humbell," "forst," "reseved," "infinnightly obleged," "shur," "passhonit," "sattisfackshon," with "prays" for praise, "malles" for malice, "angare" for angry, "pollese" for pol-icy. Many spellings reflect Margaret's aristocratic pronunciation: "sarves" and "parson" for service and person, "ded" for did, "gelty" for guilty, "willinly" and "wrightin" for willingly and writing, "pickter" for picture, "intrist" for interest. But other orthography is more erratic, suggesting again the possibility of dyslexia. The word "queen" appears in four different forms, including "Qeene" and "Quine," while "descouersce" (discourse) reveals Margaret's confusion when facing long strings of letters. "Enemies" made another problem, resulting in four very different spellings: "enemenys," Margaret wrote, and "a nemeies" for an enemy's. Letters and syllables were omitted or inverted, another com-mon feature of dyslexia: "hapnes" for happiness, "woring" for warning, "resoveled" for resolved, "unsel" for uncivil. And this occurred even in writing words so familiar as her own name. Usually signing her love letters "Margreat Lucas," she also wrote "Margraet," "Luas" and "Luca." "It is against Nature for a woman to spell right; for my part, I confess I cannot," Margaret fumed.[17]

In spite of the problems she found in her essays, Margaret was still deter-mined to publish *The World's Olio*, hoping that even an inferior work might bring her the renown as an author she so desired. Fame, she thought, could come without rhyme or reason, without worth or virtue, the result merely of fickle Fortune—"a powerful princess; for whatsoever she favours the world admires, whether it be worthy of admiration or no; and whatsoever she frowns on the world runs from, as from a plaguy infection." Despairing of pleasing "the learned," she aimed instead for ordinary readers, hoping to "be praised in this by the most, although not the best. For all I desire is fame, and fame is nothing but a great noise, and noise lives most in a multitude; wherefore I wish my book may set awork every tongue."[18]

Preparing her manuscript for publication, Margaret arranged her essays into three books of three parts each. Book 1 centered on literary, social, and political topics. Book 2 contained her allegories, aphorisms, and characters of great figures of history. Book 3 was devoted to philosophy: moral, natural, and medical. She included her attack on women and their abilities as one of the book's prefaces, hoping thus to excuse her essays' failings and forestall the criticisms she expected from her readers. She also wrote dedications for the book—to Fortune, whose favor she so wanted, and to her husband, who had enabled her to write. "You are my wit's patron," she told William: "if there be any wit, or anything worthy of commendations [in this book], they are the crumbs I gathered from your discourse, which hath fed my fancy." In return, he composed a poem in praise of her rich olio of wit—the first of many laudatory verses he would produce for inclusion at the front of her books. Margaret also wrote a dedication to Sir Charles Cavendish, in gratitude for all he had done for her and William. "Although I'm absented from your person, yet not from your favours," she acknowledged.[19]

THE WORST OF Margaret and William's money troubles were now over. Margaret's return had precipitated their last financial crisis, when "the creditors, supposing I had brought great store of money along with me, came all to my Lord to solicit the payment of their debts." However, William's earnest assurances that he would pay them "so soon as he received any money" immediately obtained him a new line of credit and thereafter, with an income from his family in England, the couple lived in much greater security.[20] By the winter, Margaret was involved in the complexities of choosing herself a string of pearls from Paris. With a careful eye to the family's finances, she took the smaller of the two sizes offered—saving face by saying it was "because they are so clear"—and she paid in ready money, sending £10 to Paris in the expectation that cash would get her a better bargain.[21]

Money was also spent on William's stable of manège horses, which he gradually increased until he owned eight exceptionally fine animals. The fame of one in particular, "a grey leaping horse," reached as far as Paris, where the duc de Guise, "also a great lover of horses," offered 600 *louis d'or*—around

£500—for him. But William would never sell his horses. "Good horses are so rare as not to be valued for money," he said. He loved the Spanish and Barbary breeds best of all, as being the noblest and most intelligent: the Spanish in particular were "strangely wise, beyond any man's imagination," he thought. Margaret observed that "some of them had also a particular love to my Lord." Whinnying and trampling their feet, "they seemed to rejoice whensoever he came into the stables." "They would go much better in the manège when my Lord was by, than when he was absent; and when he rid them himself, they seemed to take much pleasure and pride in it."[22]

William was one of the foremost horsemen in Europe and many visitors came to see him ride. When Don John of Austria, governor of the Spanish Netherlands, was in Antwerp on political business, his entire court drove to the Rubens House.* Margaret counted seventeen coaches parked outside and William more than twenty. William rode three horses for their entertainment and Captain Mazine another five. The marquess of Caracena, Don John's successor as governor, came too. Though he had recently been ill, William rode again, in rapid pirouettes that made him "so dizzy that I could hardly sit in the saddle"; the Spaniards of the court "crossed themselves and cried 'Miraculo.'" The prince de Condé, the landgrave of Hess, the duke of Oldenburg, the prince of East Friesland, the many travelers who passed through Antwerp—Germans, Dutch, Italians, English, French, Spanish, Poles, Swedes—all came to see his manège. Often William found his huge riding house so full of people "that my esquire, Captain Mazine, had hardly room to ride." Although William rode privately every day "for his own exercise and delight," he displayed his skills only to the most important visitors: the rest had to be content with watching Mazine.[23]

As a privy councillor and the most senior English nobleman in Antwerp, William headed the city's émigré population. English residents and travelers alike called to pay their respects, to swap the latest news and share in music, literature, and the wide-ranging conversations William loved. Royalist agents like the marquess of Ormonde—a courtier close to Charles II who often passed through Antwerp on his master's business—were frequent visitors. As the king's representative, William intervened to prevent the émigrés' duels (usually quarrels over gambling). He received information concerning suspected parliamentarian spies and sent it on to the English court. William corresponded regularly with the king and with Sir Edward Hyde, sending them the news from the Netherlands, and receiving in return their information on the broader political picture.[24]

—————————

*Juan-José, alias Don John, was the favorite illegitimate son of King Philip IV of Spain.

By the end of 1653, the royalists' fortunes had sunk to yet another low. In England, Oliver Cromwell was Lord Protector. Grasping firmly the reins of government at home, he was also successful abroad, with a powerful army and navy and a shrewd diplomacy. In April 1654, Cromwell concluded an advantageous treaty ending the two-year-old Anglo-Dutch War: royalist agents were now barred from the Dutch United Provinces. He made treaties of friendship with Sweden, Portugal, and Denmark, and a commercial pact with France. Charles II was no longer welcome to remain in Paris, and in July he departed for Germany, where the many states of the Holy Roman Empire had agreed to offer him a home and an income. In Antwerp, as in all the cities of the Spanish Netherlands he passed through, Charles was received with full royal honors. William waited on his king and former pupil, paying him his "humble duty," and Charles visited the Rubens House to see William ride. Then the court moved on to Spa, where the king spent the summer with his sister, Mary, wife of William II of Orange, before continuing to Cologne.[25]

Margaret had mixed feelings towards the visitors who flocked to the Rubens House. On one hand she expressed distaste for the ordinary chitchat of social callers—"for the most part . . . frivolous, vain, idle, or at least but common and ordinary." She describes herself as often sitting in company dreaming, so wrapped up in her own ideas that she heard nothing of what was going on around her.[26] Yet she clearly enjoyed the visits of friends like the Duarte sisters. With them she shared not only music, but also intellectual discussion: on one occasion she and Leanora "fell into a discourse of the elixir, or philosophers' stone," Leanora maintaining that it might make gold, while Margaret argued the opposite.[27]

She also made at least one close male intellectual friend during these years. Constantijn Huygens, Heer van Zuilichem, was a wealthy aristocrat and distinguished diplomat and statesman, secretary to the prince of Orange at the Hague. He was also one of the most cultivated men of his time—music-lover, performer and composer, classical scholar, theological writer, connoisseur of art and amateur painter, horseman, fencer, and all-round athlete, an able mathematician who applied his skills to code breaking and designing canals and locks, an admired poet who wrote in Latin, French, Italian, and Spanish as well as Dutch. A friend of Descartes, he was an adherent of the new philosophy and an eager experimenter in optics and chemistry—an interest that, with poetry and art, he had shared with his wife, Susanna, until she died in 1637. He spoke English well, for he had three times visited England, where he was knighted by King James I and became a friend and admirer of John Donne, whose poetry he later translated into Dutch. A witty conversationalist, charming, elegant, cosmopolitan—both Francophile and Anglophile—he was also a ladies' man, sharing his interests in learning, literature, and music with a wide circle of female friends, including Anna van Schurmann, Utricia Swann, and the duchess of Lorraine. With these friends he was courtly, flattering, attentive: to the duchess he regularly sent dresses, oriental rarities imported by the Dutch East India Company, and semiprecious stones gathered on his own estates.

In 1653, Huygens was one of the recipients to whom Margaret and William sent the poems she had published in London. "A wonderful book, whose extravagant atoms kept me from sleeping a great part of last night in this my little solitude," he wrote to Utricia Swann from his castle at Hofwijk.[28] Huygens visited Antwerp regularly during the 1650s, often staying at the Duarte family's house and meeting up with the duchess of Lorraine. When he called at the Rubens House, the company's conversations turned to learning, and in particular philosophy. He questioned Margaret closely about her own theory of natural philosophy, drawing out her "solutions . . . upon divers questions moved in a whole afternoon." Probably too he joined her in her laboratory where, he knew, she dirtied many times each week the white petticoats she wore to protect her fine clothes from her experiments. With courtly elegance, Huygens begged to be permitted to be counted as one of Margaret's admirers. He composed English verses in her praise as he drove home to the Hague. And she replied with appropriate modesty, thanking him for his letter and verses, in which he had praised her work more than it deserved.[29]

Just one of their many intellectual discussions still survives in correspondence dating from the spring of 1657, when Huygens wrote from the Hague to ask for Margaret's opinion of one of the strangest experiments of the day. Recently discovered in France, Prince Rupert's drops were small bubbles of glass, round at one end, with a long tail at the other. Huygens sent some to Margaret and told her their mystery. They were all but unbreakable with hammers or great weights, yet if you snapped off even the smallest tip of their tails with a finger, the whole thing would explode into powder with a loud bang. The explosion was not dangerous, he told her, but if she was afraid, then,

> Madam, a servant may hold them close in his fists, and yourself can break the little end of their tail without the least danger. But, as I was bold to tell your Excellency, I should be loth to believe any female fear should reign amongst so much over-masculine wisdom as the world doth admire.

Margaret was overawed by his request for her views. The phenomenon was the most celebrated paradox of its day. Louis XIV had consulted the Académie Française, but so far no one had found an explanation. "It were a presumption to give my opinion after these famous and learned philosophers," she told Huygens. Yet, since he requested it, she did proffer a theory—in terms of the chemical behavior of "oily spirits or essences of sulphur," which acted like gunpowder to cause the explosions. To the question of how these oily spirits had got into the glass, she responded that it would be no more difficult than the making of ladies' earrings, where colored silks were incorporated inside blown glass spheres.

Intrigued by Margaret's theory, Huygens tested it by placing one of the glass drops in a fire and heating it "to the reddest height of heat," expecting that this would cause any "sulphureous liquid gunpowder" such as she postulated to explode. But there was no reaction: only, Huygens found, when the drop cooled, it had lost its power to explode. He reported his results to Margaret, suggesting they might help her to refine her theory. In response, she apologized for her weak judgment, but still maintained her original hypothesis: Huygens's fire had probably evaporated all the sulphurous liquid in the glasses before any explosion could occur, she argued. But, unwilling to be overly dogmatic, she also suggested that if her first idea was wrong, then perhaps the drops' explosions were caused by "pent up air enclosed therein, which, having vent, was the cause of the sound or report which those glasses gave."[30]

Unless she was with such favorite friends, Margaret preferred to spend her time alone with her thoughts and her writing. With her ever-active imagination and her irresistible drive to create, she was never bored or lonely—so long as "I be near my Lord, and know he is well."[31] During 1653 and 1654 she wrote new essays to complete her *World's Olio*; even after her manuscript had gone off to the printers in London in the autumn of 1654, she continued to add more.[32] She wrote of the "corruptions of the air" that caused ill health. She developed at length a model for an ideal royalist state: formal contracts between king and subjects ensured good government, while strict, even harsh, laws ensured political stability.[33] In addition to these essays, she was writing on natural philosophy again. Gradually she expanded the new ideas she had outlined in her *Philosophical Fancies* into an encyclopedic theory of the natural world and all its phenomena—the sort of ambitious system to which philosophers like Descartes, Gassendi, and Hobbes all aspired.

Like many seventeenth-century writers, Margaret thought best on her feet, and she would often walk "a slow pace in my chamber, whilst my thoughts run apace in my brain." Sitting down to write, she sometimes spoke out loud as she worked, finding that it helped her thoughts flow smoothly.[34] She was now producing a few completed sheets each day, and these pages went out daily to the professional copyists who prepared neat transcripts of her works, ready for the printers. In the straitened circumstances of exile, Margaret could not afford a university-educated secretary, such as the nobility commonly employed, but had to rely on scriveners—tradesmen who "only could write a good hand, but neither understood orthography, nor had any learning." Inevitably copyists' errors crept in, and the problem was further exacerbated by Margaret's poor handwriting—"so bad as few can read it so as to write it fair for the press."[35] Margaret was well aware of the trick of the scriveners' trade—to space the lines widely and write the words as large as possible, since they were paid by the page—but she only discovered the errors they had introduced after her books were printed. Preferring the delights of creation to the labors of correction, and fearing that these old ideas might "disturb my following conceptions," Margaret did not check the completed copies before sending them off to Martin and Allestrye in London, who forwarded them on to the printers.[36]

It was during printing that the often highly idiosyncratic spelling and punctuation of seventeenth-century authors' original manuscripts was standardized, as the compositor put the letters of type into the blocks. But further copying errors were also introduced. English printing businesses were small affairs, with just a few workmen employed with one to three printing presses on the ground floor of the printer's house. Their stock of type was soon exhausted in setting a small batch of pages, so each batch was immediately printed off and the type taken back off the blocks to be reused for the next section of the book. Authors who wanted to check their proofs thus had to "attend the press" at least daily, checking each batch of pages as it came ready for its print run. To more eminent authors, printers might send proofs each day, but only if the writer was available in London. For Margaret, on the far side of the Channel, there was no such opportunity. Her first few books appeared completely unrevised, without even the printed list of errata normally included at the end of the text. There were mistakes in spelling and grammar—many doubtless her own, but "the printer should have rectified that" she responded angrily when her readers complained of them. In her *Poems and Fancies* she eventually counted more than 200 printing errors—errors that caused at least a portion of the false rhymes and numbers her readers criticized.* The change of speakers in her verse dialogues was unmarked. Misprinted words altered the meanings of whole passages, both here and in her *World's Olio*, producing misunderstandings or nonsense. "Wanting" appeared as "wanton," "ungraceful" as "ungrateful," "muffler" as "muster." In one poem, "blazing like flaming fire to burn" was altered into "blazing like to a fir'd gun." Singulars became plurals,

---

*Though the *Poems* were printed while Margaret was in London, they were not corrected at the proof stage either. Presumably, as a novice author, she had not known the complex arrangements writers commonly made to ensure their books were well printed.

and vice versa. The last essays she wrote, after her *Olio* was already in the press, were placed in the wrong sections of the book.[37] Though Margaret does not mention it, and perhaps did not notice, there were also gross errors in the punctuation the printers supplied to her originally unpunctuated texts. In her essays, commas and colons often appear instead of periods. The punctuation was misplaced, breaking up the sense where it should have been united, while elsewhere real breaks in meaning went unmarked—presumably all the result of the printer's failure to understand Margaret's overcomplicated thoughts, which thus became in print even harder for the reader to understand.[38] Sometimes the best way to follow a section of her text is to read it as if it had no punctuation, ignoring all the marks put in by printers.

Only one error in her *Poems* did Margaret manage to have corrected—a mistake on the title page itself, where the book's author was billed as "the Right Honourable, the Lady Margaret Countesse of Newcastle." This was a political matter. The English Parliament, not recognizing the validity of King Charles I's rule after the outbreak of war in 1642, had refused to recognize the noble titles he conferred on his followers. In England Margaret's brother was thus still Sir John Lucas; William was only an earl and his wife a mere countess. When Margaret objected, a new sheet was eventually printed, describing her simply as "the Right Honourable the Lady Newcastle." But by then most of the title pages were already printed. Some continued uncorrected, but in others there are handmade corrections in black ink: "Countesse of" has been boldly crossed out; in some, "Marchioness of" has also been written in.[39]

From the printers, Margaret's books returned to Martin and Allestrye's shop in St. Paul's Churchyard, to be sold either bound or unbound.* Some copies the booksellers forwarded to Margaret in Antwerp: when they arrived she burned her original manuscript, which she had kept safely until then in case of disasters.[40] Other copies were sent to the London bookbinder employed by Margaret to prepare the copies she presented to her English friends—Sir Theodore Mayerne, Walter Charleton, Thomas Barlow, and others.[41]

With the improved Cavendish family finances, Margaret also now arranged to have illustrations produced as frontispieces for her books, it "being customary for most writers to set their figures of their persons before the figure of their brain or mind, I thought fit to do the like," she explained.[42] Antwerp was Europe's foremost center of copperplate engraving, producing the finest illustrated books and atlases. Here in the sixteenth century, the virtuoso engraver Hieronymus Cock had developed new techniques for render-

---

*Unbound copies allowed purchasers to choose the binding that best suited their pocket or their existing library of books.

ing the depths of shapes and shadows with lines and hatching. In the early seventeenth century—under the driving impulse of Rubens, who wanted quality reproductions of his images to disseminate through Europe—further improvements brought the art of engraving to a perfection that would not be excelled in the 300 years for which copperplates remained the finest method of printed illustration. Gradually the techniques of the Rubens school spread through Europe, but in England in the 1650s printers could not match them.

To draw up designs for her frontispieces, Margaret chose the local artist Abraham van Diepenbeeck. Diepenbeeck had worked under Rubens, turning the master's ideas for prints into detailed pen and wash sketches from which the engravers then worked. He had painted some commissions for Antwerp's religious buildings but, by the 1650s, his main work was as a designer (or "inventor") of engravings and stained-glass windows. Using a wide range of visual motifs from Rubens and other artists to create images rich in meaning, he was known throughout the Netherlands as a master of the art.

With him Margaret settled on two designs. In one she appears as a classical heroine, draped in loose robes, wearing sandals, and standing in a statue's niche between pillars in the form of busts of Minerva and Apollo—embodiments of knowledge and the arts, who turn their heads in her direction.* Mixed with these classical motifs, there are marks of Margaret's nobility. Her drapes are lined with ermine and edged with rich jewels and embroidery. On her head she wears a coronet topped with fleurs-de-lis, the distinctive mark of a marchioness's rank before the Restoration.[43] Cornucopias of fruit at the picture's edges complete the impression of riches. Margaret's posture, as befits a heroine, is confident and masculine. The hand resting on her hip is a common pose in the portraits of kings, aristocrats, and great men, not normally seen in portraits of women. From her raised niche, she stares confidently out at the reader, an inscrutable, authoritative, perhaps challenging gaze.

The second design that Margaret chose also centers on motifs of her literary and aristocratic identity, but here the grand, mythical style is replaced with more literal and mundane images from real life. She sits facing the reader beside her writing table, where pen, ink, and paper are neatly laid out. On the table there also stands a fine carriage clock, a wealthier version of the hourglass commonly included as a *tempus fugit* motif in the portraits of writers, representing the serious use to which they put their time. Margaret's plain dark dress suggests the simple black commonly worn by scholars and clergymen; her heavy chair with wooden arms is the sort of seat in which such learned men are often depicted. Again she wears a marchioness's coronet. A bell on the

---

*Minerva, goddess of war and learning, was the archetypal heroic woman.

table indicates her ability to ring for her servants. Above her hangs the broad canopy of a cloth of state—a mark of social status allowed only to persons of the rank of viscount and above.[44] On the wall behind her and on the floor beneath her chair are rich carpets, a normal component in noble and royal "states." In front of her, separating her from the viewer, is a low balustrade such as was normally used to divide the monarch or aristocrat on their dais from the rest of the room. Myth enters the picture only in the form of winged putti, who hold olive branches and a laurel wreath over Margaret's head—representations again of her tutelary deities, Minerva and Apollo.

Both images show Margaret in the solitude she so prized—the physical solitude that allowed her to write, as well as the intellectual solitude, the "singularity," she wanted as an original thinker. In both, she is distanced from the viewer, grandly elevated on her dais or in her niche. But where the more mythical image suggests confidence, perhaps even arrogance, in its bold frontal stare, the more "realistic" picture hints at Margaret's shyness and insecurity. Here the tilt of her head and her sideways glance suggest the posture she fell into naturally, with "my head . . . bent downwards through bashfulness," when she was feeling "extremely out of countenance."[45]

Nobody now knows exactly how Margaret used these frontispiece illustrations. They appear in some copies of her books but not in others, without any obvious pattern. Perhaps she sent some to her London bookbinder for inclusion in the copies she gave to her friends.[46] Perhaps they went to Martin and Allestrye for inclusion in luxury copies for customers of greater means.[47] In their shop in St. Paul's Churchyard these pictures were most likely displayed prominently in the window, advertising Margaret's books to passersby and window-shoppers—a normal use of decorative frontispieces. Clearly these illustrations were important to Margaret herself. With their carefully chosen motifs, they displayed the revolutionary female, aristocratic, literary identity she was creating for herself.

Her life of writing had become Margaret's major occupation. Only one regular diversion took her away from it—the drive in her coach "which we here call a 'tour.'"[48] Late in the afternoon each day the coaches of Antwerp's grandees met on the Meir, the widest and wealthiest street, where the Duartes had their palatial residence. From here they drove through the squares and streets and up onto the massive walls that enclosed the city.[49] These sixteenth-century defenses were one of Antwerp's greatest marvels. Earth ramparts clad in stone, with eight towers spaced along their length, the walls were so thick that three broad tree-lined avenues ran along their top. "There was nothing about this city which more ravished me than those delicious shades and walks of stately trees, which render the incomparably fortified works of the town one of the sweetest places in Europe," John Evelyn rhapsodized.[50] Here the coaches drove, with views inwards over roofs and towers and steeples, and outwards over the rich countryside of gardens that supplied the city's fresh produce. Beneath them the moat was 150 feet wide; loaded carts passed constantly into the city over the bridges.

But more important than this geographical view was the social viewing that occurred, for the tour was a gargantuan social ritual of display, "where all the chief of the town go to see and to be seen," as Margaret put it. When she and William first arrived in Antwerp, just four coaches had made the tour—their own, that of the city's Spanish governor, and two others, probably including the Duarte family's. But as the English émigré population increased, the tour too had grown. "All those that had sufficient means, and could go to the price, kept coaches," Margaret observed. Numbers were often swelled by the many travelers who passed through Antwerp, "many times persons of great quality," Margaret noted, "great princes or queens," who joined the throng "to see the customs thereof."[51] Fashions, dresses, equipages, the appearance and behavior of eminent persons all came under scrutiny. The duchess of Lorraine came regularly with her court, and reported to Constantijn Huygens on Margaret's modish appearance, with or without ribbons on her arms.[52] Occasional participants included King Charles II and the many foreign monarchs and nobility whose visits at his manège William and Margaret recorded. All drove out with their entourages of court personnel: sometimes Margaret counted "above a hundred" coaches making the tour together.

For Margaret, participation in the ritual was a vital means of keeping up the grandeur and visibility that were essential to aristocratic status—now especially important in exile, where there were none of the normal ceremonies of English life. Despite her preference for a solitary life of writing, "I would not bury myself quite* from the sight of the world," she explained. Besides, she added, such outings often brought "new materials for my thoughts and fancies to build upon."[53] Personalities, behavior, fashions were all there to be observed. And amongst Antwerp's many eminent visitors, there was one who was especially exciting for Margaret—Queen Christina of Sweden, who stopped in the city in June 1655, on her way to Rome.[54] Given a man's education, as her father had directed, Christina was an athletic horsewoman, an accomplished linguist, a keen scholar—especially in philosophy and theology—and an enthusiastic patron of music and the arts. Crowned king of Sweden, she succeeded her father as head of the Protestant alliance in the Thirty Years War. In 1648 her armies sacked Prague, carrying the city's

---

*I.e. completely.

The gatehouse of St. John's Abbey at Colchester in Essex. This is the only building that still survives from Margaret's childhood home.

Margaret's eldest sister, Mary, c. 1635. Mary Lucas married the courtier Peter Killigrew in 1625, when Margaret was only two, but she continued to see her younger sister frequently, both in London and in Colchester.

William Cavendish in his early fifties, as Margaret first knew him. He wears a buff coat and breastplate, indicating his Civil War service as Lord General of the King's Army in the North.

Margaret, Duchess of Newcastle, school of Samuel Cooper. William and Margaret exchanged such portrait miniatures as love tokens during their courtship in Paris in 1645.

One of the love letters which Margaret sent to William in 1645. "My ordinary handwriting is so bad as few can read it," she commented—a problem which led to many printing errors in her earliest published books.

Margaret's brother, Sir Charles Lucas, painted in Oxford during the Civil War by William Dobson. Charles was one of the royalists' most able cavalry commanders, rising to become Lieutenant-General of the King's Horse in 1645.

King Charles I and Queen Henrietta Maria dining in public, by Gerrit Houckgeest. Such scenes were a regular part of court ceremonial, and as one of the Queen's maids of honour, Margaret would have stood for hours in the semi-circle of courtiers behind the royal couple.

The Rubens House in Antwerp, the Newcastles' home from 1648 until 1660. On the right is Rubens' great studio; on the left, the family's living quarters; beyond the arched screen lie the gardens.

William was famous as one of the foremost horsemen in Europe. Here he directs the training of his manège horses in Antwerp, while his equerry Captain Mazine rides, and his manservant, John Proctor, holds his master's cloak.

William's scholarly younger brother, Sir Charles Cavendish, who lived with the Newcastles in Paris and Antwerp and taught Margaret philosophy.

William's daughter, Jane, by his first marriage. Jane managed the family's estates at Welbeck during her father's absence in the Civil War.

Jane Cavendishe Eldest Daughter to Wm Duke of Newcastle Married to Cha: Cheney of Chesham Boys, Esqr This Lady kept Garrison for her Father at Welbeck, against y^e Parliament ARMY.

William's son, Henry, Second Duke of Newcastle. Relations between Henry and his father and step-mother became very strained during the 1660s.

King Charles II, after Samuel Cooper. The King visited the Newcastles at the Rubens House several times during their exile in Antwerp.

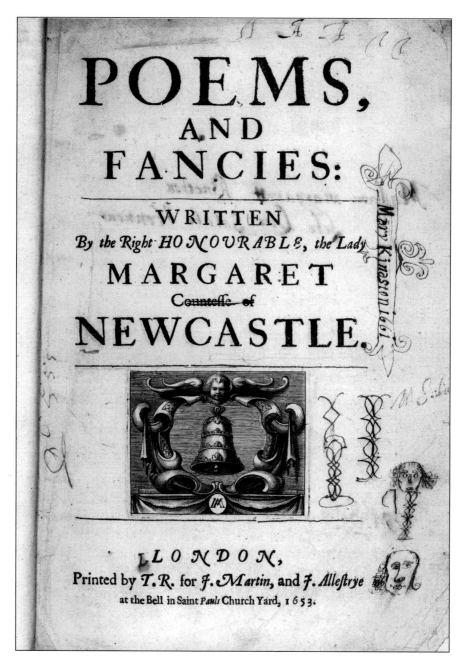

POEMS,
AND
FANCIES:

WRITTEN

By the Right HONOURABLE, the Lady

MARGARET

Countesse of

NEWCASTLE.

Mary Kingston 1661

LONDON,
Printed by *T.R.* for *J. Martin*, and *J. Allestrye*
at the Bell in Saint *Pauls* Church Yard, 1653.

The title-page of Margaret's first book, which she wrote and published while she was in London in the early 1650s. This copy has been embellished by its young female owner with caricatures of the author.

Here on this Figure Cast a Glance,
But so as if it were by Chance,
Your eyes not fixt, they must not stay,
Since this like Shadowes to the Day
It only represent's; for still,
Her Beuty's found beyond the Skill
Of the best Paynter, to Imbrace,
Those lovely Lines within her face,
View her Soul's Picture, Judgment, witt,
Then read those Lines which Shee hath writt,
By Phancy's Pencill drawne alone
Which Peece but Shee, Can justly owne.

One of the three illustrated frontispieces which Margaret created for her books in Antwerp. Here she appears in heroic and classical mode, flanked by Minerva and Apollo, patrons of learning and the arts.

A second frontispiece, showing the author seated at her writing table. Above, winged putti salute her fame with olive branches and a laurel wreath, symbols of her literary accomplishments.

The third frontispiece, created especially for *Natures Pictures*, Margaret's volume of short fiction, in 1656. Here she sits with William and his married children, telling stories by a winter's fire.

'A Ball' by Abraham Bosse, c. 1657. Believed to show the exiled King Charles II dancing at The Hague, this image suggests the scene at the Rubens House when the Newcastles entertained the English court in 1658.

The south front of Welbeck, with its formal gardens. The Smithson wing (left) was remodelled by William's father, while the other buildings reveal the house's origin as a medieval monastery.

Welbeck, seen from the great court, with William's black page displaying one of his horses. On the right is the porter's lodge, leading to the main entrance of the house.

William on horseback, in front of Bolsover Castle. The gallery range (right) was built by William during the 1630s, and he and Margaret created new state rooms here in the 1660s.

Margaret, Duchess of Newcastle, probably painted c. 1665 to celebrate the King's grant of a dukedom to the Newcastles. Margaret appears in her ermine-lined state robes and a "heroic" feathered hat.

William, Duke of Newcastle, as an old man. By the time Margaret was forty, William was almost seventy and beginning to suffer from Parkinson's disease.

Newcastle House in Clerkenwell, where Margaret and William lived during their visit to London in 1667. The house was later given to Margaret as part of her marriage jointure.

The grave monument of the Duke and Duchess of Newcastle in Westminster Abbey. William holds a general's baton and Margaret a book, pencase, and ink, the symbols of their achievements in life.

wealth of art treasures back to Sweden. Christina also headhunted scholars and artists throughout Europe; Descartes joined her court just before his death in 1650. With her masculine identity as king and scholar, Christina adopted male styles of dress—long coats and doublets, men's shoes and stockings, a soldier's periwig and neck-scarf, a black velvet cap, which she doffed in courtesy like a man. "Her voice and actions are altogether masculine," commented a Parisian aristocrat. With a "masculine haughty mien" and "none of that modesty which is so becoming, and indeed necessary, in our sex," Christina behaved like a heroine from romance.[55] As she traveled through Europe, crowds flocked to see her, and she further encouraged their fascination by appearing in theatrical costume as an Amazon warrior. It was a scenario of female power and romance that Margaret herself would act out to the crowds of London in 1667. In 1655, when Christina visited Antwerp, Margaret's thoughts turned to writing stories about women and the ambitious undertakings that might be possible in their lives.

All their rich Antwerp life, William and Margaret knew, they owed entirely to Sir Charles Cavendish—to his submission to the Goldsmiths' Hall Committee and his subsequent settling of the family finances. He was their savior, whom they remembered regularly in their prayers, asking that he would receive "blessings from Heaven."[56] So, in February 1654, they were both devastated when they heard that he had died suddenly in England, unable to recover his strength after his fever a year before. Margaret was tormented by guilt. "Heaven knows I did not think his life was so near to an end, for his doctor had great hopes of his perfect recovery," she wrote, attempting to justify her decision not to accompany Sir Charles into the country, "where I should have been a trouble, rather than any way serviceable, besides more charge* the longer I stayed." She paid impassioned tributes to his virtues—"a person of so great worth, such extraordinary civility, so obliging a nature, so full of generosity, justice and charity, besides all manner of learning . . . that not only his friends but even his enemies did much lament his loss."[57] Sir Charles was one of the people of whom "I shall lament the loss so long as I live." "My mind is benighted in sorrow, insomuch as I have not one lighted thought; they are all put out with the memory of my loss," she wrote, "in too deep a melancholy to be diverted" by a friend's offers of entertainments and balls. In Paris, Sir Edward Hyde paid his own tribute to his old friend, "who cannot be enough lamented as one of the most excellent persons the world had, of the greatest virtue and piety." "The taking away such men . . . is a sad continuance of God's judgement upon us," he thought.[58]

---

*I.e. expense.

William was left in "extreme affliction"—he and his brother had "loved each other entirely." Throughout the spring he suffered agonizing attacks of colic, combined with dizziness and weakness in his limbs. From London, as usual, came the prescriptions of Sir Theodore Mayerne and his apothecary Charles Rust: purges (rhubarb and senna), vomits ("crocus metallorum"), bleeding ("not to exceed 3oz [of blood] at a time"), and a cooling diet (whey, spinach, lettuce, apples). Laudanum "and other opiate medicines" were sometimes prescribed, Mayerne told his patient, "but I give of them as little as I can." Instead he recommended baths to relieve the pain, and regular drinking of cold water, with "good claret wine* at meals, if it be pure." Mayerne cautioned William especially against his "continual use of tobacco"—"a stinking commodity which doth spoil the brain," he told his patient, "but a tobacconist is not easily persuaded against his ill custom, for which I am sorry." As usual, William was collecting receipts from all his friends, a propensity that Mayerne knew well: William should "not harken to so many flying physicians, viz. all the world that speaketh to him, of which every [one] hath a receipt, without ground or reason for the most part, which are not worthy the hearing," Mayerne commented.[59]

Gradually William's health improved, but by then Margaret herself was unwell. There was a "melancholic sourness" in her stomach—probably the acid of indigestion—and she was drinking large quantities of water and passing a great deal of urine, which contained worrying white crystals. When consulted, Mayerne feared she might be developing diabetes and he recommended that she mix her water with "a fourth part of good, mild and comfortable old claret wine." If she did not want to take wine on a regular basis, he prescribed an infusion of roots and herbs. Spa water and steel liquor he recommended as usual, to clean out her system. And he advised a change in lifestyle. "Her ladyship's occupation in writing of books, with a sedentary life, is absolutely bad for health," he warned.[60]

Thus began Margaret's long-running conflict with William over exercise and fresh air. Margaret wanted her now aging husband to conserve his health by indulging less frequently in the exertions of the manège—"it may be feared your violent exercise may have done hurt," Charles Rust had suggested in a recent letter.[61] William, on the other hand, wanted Margaret to get out more "to take the air for my health." When he reproached her, she promised to reform, as she also did when she was ill. But soon she forgot her promise, or else performed the most minimal exercise she could, looking out of her window once or twice, and walking "two or three turns in a day in her chamber."[62]

---

*Claret at this time was either red wine of any kind, or rosé.

More distressing to Margaret than these medical concerns were her readers' continuing attacks on her books. She had not really written them herself, critics still suggested: it would be impossible for an unlearned woman. Her ideas were not original, they added, but "gathered . . . from several philosophers." And her grammar and spelling, and the rhyme and meter in her poetry, were all faulty. Stung by such wide-ranging assaults, Margaret decided to add detailed self-defenses to her soon-to-be-published *World's Olio*: the "Epistles" she composed were inserted into the text, one appearing after each of the three parts of Book 1 of the *Olio*.[63]

Here Margaret swore to her readers "upon the grounds of honour, honesty and religion," "upon my conscience and truth," that her books were "my own." "My head was the forge, my thoughts the anvil to beat them out, and my industry shaped them and sent them forth to the use of the world." She had been able to write them, she explained, because she had lived in the world, with "liberty" to see it and "conversation to hear of it." Especially she had learned from William, and she told her readers of their master-scholar relationship. "If I had never married the person I have, I do believe I should never have writ so as to have adventured to divulge my works," she acknowledged. "I think that not any hath a more abler master to learn from, than I have . . . for I have learned more of the world from my Lord's discourse, since I have been his wife, than I am confident I should have done all my life, should I have lived to an old age."

But, accused of stealing her ideas from other philosophers, Margaret needed to limit the influences she admitted. She had learned from her own family and from no one else, she insisted. How could she have taken her ideas from other philosophers, when "I never conversed in discourse with any an hour at one time in my life"? "I may swear on my conscience, I never had a familiar acquaintance or constant conversation with any professed scholar in my life," she persisted.

However, these defenses were not enough for Margaret. She wanted more: to justify her work—that of an ill-educated woman—as equal in value to the work of men. Women writers, lacking men's formal education, knew they thereby lacked "all advantages, but mere *Nature*," as the playwright Delarivière Manley would complain some forty years later.[64] So it was to "natural capacity" and "natural education" that Margaret now appealed. "In the school of life," she argued, there was a "natural education" available equally to all.* Every

---

*As before when justifying her poetry, Margaret is here again drawing on gentlemanly ideals of natural ability and a broad experience of life as more important than any formal scholastic education. As William put it: "a good memory, a good wit . . . and a good judgement . . . and all those naturally, with education in great cities at home and abroad, in several courts and in several armies, is beyond all the educations in all the universities in the world."

object in the world acted as a "natural tutor," teaching knowledge when humanity's innate capacities for observation, imagination, reason, and understanding applied themselves to it. This process of "natural reason," Margaret argued, was a gift of nature, "general to mankind," male and female, rich and poor alike, and it was sufficient by itself to gain true knowledge of the world "without the help of education."[65] Seeking evidence for her views, Margaret turned, like so many contemporary writers, to the Bible. In the Old Testament she found a time before the existence of schools, when "natural reason was the first educator" and "did first compose commonwealths, [and] invented arts and sciences." Here were many stories of "poor peasants" who, without any education, had yet become great political leaders, poets, prophets, eloquent orators, wise philosophers, and skilled physicians. If nature so generously distributed her gifts to these men whom "fortune hath cast out and education hath neglected," why, Margaret asked, should her readers think that nature would not also give such gifts to her, "who have been honourably born, carefully bred, and nobly married to a wise man"?[66] Margaret's self-confidence as a writer was growing. Before, it was only imagination or "fancy" that she claimed as a feminine quality, enabling women to write poetry as well as men. Now she thought women might lay claim to knowledge and rationality too.

BY THE TIME THE *World's Olio* was published at the end of 1654, Margaret had already completed her new philosophical treatise.[67] Intended as a full, systematic exposition of her own original theory, this was an ambitious project, a total departure from the poems and essays she had written previously, "short works" of the kind that she thought suited to women's "brief wit."[68]

In print the book was 172 folio pages long, divided into five parts. Part 1, setting out Margaret's basic theory of the "degrees" and "spirits" of matter, reprinted her *Philosophical Fancies*. The only substantial change was the omission of two imaginative verse sections—one likening the rational spirits to bees flying out of the body to gather honey for the brain, the other conjuring up different possible worlds, where animals were made of coral or flowers or wood, and flies were made of diamond—which now seemed inconsistent with Margaret's increasingly serious and ambitious aims in philosophy.

Then the rest of the treatise was all newly written. Part 2 continued the basic exposition of Margaret's theory, going over much of the same ground as Part 1, but explaining it more fully or in different ways. She identified six "principal motions," which her active spirits—what she now called "innated matter"—possessed. Every change in the world was produced by combinations of these six—contraction, attraction, retention, dilation, expulsion, and digestion—which all occurred in many different forms. She expanded particularly on her theory's animism. Innated matter could perform infinitely various motions, "making infinite kinds of knowledge." Infinity had no end, so there was no "most or least" in knowledge, and mankind was wrong to think it had "supreme knowledge."

Then Part 3 applied the idea of innated matter and its six kinds of motion to explaining a huge range of phenomena in what would normally be called the inanimate world—though Margaret, of course, considered all of nature to be animate and alive. Her theories here took in the nature of liquids and solids, freezing, thawing and evaporation, metals and magnetism and the action of the compass needle, fire and its physical and chemical effects, heat and cold, the nature of light and the production of colors, the motion of the planets, the rising and falling of the tides, the nature of thunder and lightning. Some of her explanations were distinctively feminine. Light, water, and air, she proposed, were all composed by "spinning motions," by which she meant not the movement of a spinning-top turning on its own axis (such as contemporary male philosophers used in their own theories), but the motion by which a woman spun an even thread out of a ball of wool or flax, at once both pulling and twisting, "equally drawing out long parallel lines, with an extraordinary swiftness, evenness, smallness and straightness."[69]

Parts 4 and 5 of the work turned to a consideration of the human body. First Margaret discussed psychology, applying her idea of innated matter to explain the operation of the five senses and the nature of emotions and thoughts, imagination, memory, understanding, sleep, and dreams—all subjects of central concern to contemporary philosophers. Then, following this treatment of "the orderly course of nature" in a normal, healthy body, she proceeded to "the natural wars in animal figures"—disease.[70]

Medical treatment was a normal part of women's household duties and Margaret, like other girls, would have learned such skills from her mother. She knew Gerard's *Herbal*—the standard domestic medical textbook—"which no question is a very rare book, and certainly describes the tempers of herbs, fruits and drugs very learnedly." But Margaret was more critical of how Gerard used these drugs in treatment, "for I believe where one is rightly applied, forty are falsely applied."[71] Like most lay people, she had her own views on the best remedies for particular diseases. She created her own medical receipts and she commonly treated herself, letting blood and taking vomits, purges and other medicines without consulting a physician. Like others too, she commented and advised on the illnesses of friends and servants.[72] Such lay knowledge was respected by medical practitioners, who often gathered recipes and treatments from friends and patients, and Margaret offered this medical section of her philosophy to the "grave judgements" of professional physicians.[73]

Here she analyzed many different illnesses—nausea, dizziness, fevers, consumptions, apoplexies, convulsions, cramps, colics, colds, and others—in terms of the six kinds of innated motion. She also employed the traditional theory of the four humors—blood, bile, phlegm, and melancholy. But treating illness purely as an imbalance of the bodily humors was not sufficient, she argued: many diseases resulted rather from "disordered motions in the body," which attacked its normal operation.[74] Margaret suggested her own medicines to rectify these disordered motions, and she criticized traditional medical practice. Physicians knew far too little about the body, its diseases, and the drugs they prescribed, "which makes them cure so few." Their remedies were mere "chance-medley," applied "neither . . . knowingly, nor skilfully, but customarily, because they are usually given in such diseases, whereof some do mend, others do die with them."[75]

Expanding her *Philosophical Fancies* almost sevenfold, this new treatise was ambitious not only in scope but also in Margaret's growing independence of thought. The animism of her theory—the idea of a living, feeling, thinking nature—was totally opposed to the strictly mechanical atomism she had learned within the Cavendish circle of philosophers. In spite of the affection she still felt for her own atomist theory, published just two years before in her *Poems and Fancies*, Margaret now attacked the whole notion of atomism as an impossible basis for a theory of nature. "Fleeing about, as dust and ashes that are blown about with [the] wind," atoms could only make "an infinite and eternal disorder" in the world, she argued. The random motions of "such wandering and confused figures" could never produce the ordered structures and intelligent design she so admired in nature, with "such rare compositions . . . such exact rules, such undissolvable laws . . . such order, such method, such life, such sense, such faculties, such reason, such knowledge, such power."[76] The change to an animist theory was important for Margaret. By denying the uniqueness of human rationality and elevating the rest of nature, she was bringing her philosophy into line with her own feelings—her distaste for man's pride and his cruel exploitation of the world around him.

Her philosophy had become Margaret's preferred work—"my best belov'd and greatest favourite."[77] It was an elevated, improving study, she thought, which "pleases the curiosities of men's minds": "it carries their thoughts above vulgar and common objects, it elevates their spirits to an aspiring pitch; it gives room for the untired appetites of man to walk or run in." The philosophical method—reasoning from observed effects to infer the likely internal, hidden mechanisms underlying them—appealed to her penchant for imagination and creativity: "so working a brain I have that many times on small objects or subjects [it] will raise up many several fancies and opinions." And, compared to works of fiction, there was the additional excitement of a sense of discovery, "for next to the finding out of truths, the greatest pleasure in study is to find out probabilities," Margaret commented. All philosophers (with the notable exception of Descartes) agreed that their method of reasoning could only produce probabilities: since the underlying mechanisms in nature were too small to be observed directly, true and certain knowledge of them was impossible, at least for the present. Margaret thus felt quite justified in putting forward her own views: "the study is only conjectural and built upon probabilities, and until probabilities be condemned by absolute and known truth, let them have a place amongst the rest," she urged her readers.[78]

For a long time the title of this new book remained undecided: even as publication approached, Margaret still called it "an additional part, to join with my book of *Philosophical Fancies*." It is likely that the words of her maid, Elizabeth Topp, eventually suggested a name to Margaret: *The Philosophical and Physical Opinions*.[79] The choice reflected her growing seriousness, her increasing investment of effort and emotion in this study. No longer did she dismiss natural philosophy as mere "fiction"—an enjoyable entertainment where neither real truth nor useful practical applications could be discovered. Instead, "there may be many touches* found out by experiences and experiments," she now thought. While the underlying mechanisms of nature "are hid from us . . . being invisible to the sense of man," yet some knowledge of causes was possible—although "we know but parts and pieces."[80] The insights that philosophy gave into "all vegetables, minerals and animals" brought the promise of improvement in every area of human endeavor and especially in medicine, farming, navigation, and the colonization of the New World. "There is no art nor science but is produced thereby," Margaret proclaimed. But she worried that her work would not be appreciated in England, where natural philosophy was as yet but little studied. It was on the Continent—especially in Roman Catholic institutions like Mersenne's Minim friary in Paris and the Jesuit college in Antwerp, where "monastical men . . . live contemplary lives, despising the vanities of the world"—that Margaret saw the study flourishing. With English an unimportant language, hardly known abroad except among merchants in the Netherlands, her great regret was that she could not write in Latin to reach this wider audience.[81]

IN JANUARY 1655, after sending her *Philosophical and Physical Opinions* to the printers, Margaret again heard of readers' attacks on her books. Her informant was Walter Charleton, who wrote with thanks for her gift of a copy

---

*I.e. proofs.

of the *World's Olio,* and with praise for its contents. But he also told Margaret what the London public was now saying.

> Madam, among those who have perused your writings, I meet with a sort of infidels, who refuse to believe that you have always preserved yourself so free from the contagion of books and book-men [as you claim]. And the reason they give me is this; that you frequently use many terms of the schools . . . with sundry feathers taken out of the universities, or nests of divines, philosophers, physicians, geometricians, astronomers, and the rest of the gowned tribe.

For each of these learned professions, Charleton listed the technical terminology Margaret had used. How could she know such language without scholarship, unless "all these scholastical terms and notions may be brought into the world with us" at birth? Charleton asked.[82]

Margaret was deeply hurt. Here she again saw the masculine prejudice that an unlearned woman could not have written her books, and she rushed to refute the charges in a new series of prefaces for the *Philosophical Opinions.* Her tone was angrier, more bitter than before. In "this ill-natured and unbelieving age . . . it were an endless work to answer every idle and impertinent question, or malicious objection." Her critics were rigid, unjust, false, malicious, spiteful, she charged: they even took her own earlier apologies "out of some of my Epistles . . . to throw against me, which is most base and cruel." "Those that have noble and generous souls will believe me," she trusted. For the rest— the "base and mechanic souls"—"I care not what they say."[83]

Of course Margaret cared deeply, but all she could do was repeat and elaborate on arguments she had already used before. She defined what she meant by a "professed scholar" to shore up her claim that she had never conversed with any. She argued that William and her family, though learned, were not professed scholars. She distinguished the "visiting and entertaining discourse" of social conversation—which she had occasionally shared with scholars—from serious, scholarly discourse, which she had never joined. She pointed out that the (supposedly difficult and abstruse) technical terms of the arts and sciences were "customarily taught all children from their nurses' breast, being ordinarily discoursed of in every family that is of quality." "I must have been a natural fool if I had not known and learnt them." And she reasserted her ignorance of the work of other philosophers. "I never spake to Monsieur Descartes in my life, nor ever understood what he said, for he spake no English, and I understand no other language." To Hobbes she had spoken fewer than twenty words. She had read half of Descartes's *Passions de l'Ame* and all of Hobbes's *De Cive*, but nothing more.[84] Attempting to defend herself against her readers' attacks, Margaret was being pushed into an ever more extreme position.

There is a sense of powerlessness—of hopeless, endless repetition—in these new prefaces. If Margaret's readers had not believed her before, why should they now? And their continued distrust, with its implicit accusation that she was lying, was most distressing of all. "Condemned as a dissembler," how could she make people believe her?[85]

It was now that William came to Margaret's aid. As a man his word had more authority than hers, and as a gentleman he could not be contradicted without the risk of a duel—a conflict few would seek with one of the most accomplished swordsmen of his day. In a four-page prefatory epistle—"to justify the Lady Newcastle, and truth against falsehood, laying those false and malicious aspersions of her, that she was not author of her books"—he now answered Charleton's report point by point.[86] Margaret had "never conversed with any professed scholar," he repeated for his wife. "I assure you, her conversation with her brother and brother-in-law were enough, without a miracle or an impossibility, to get the language of the arts and learned professions . . . it is not so difficult a thing." William systematically demystified the universities' supposedly recondite learning. The terms of theology were "not so hard": "every tub-preacher discourses of them, and every sanctified wife gossips them in wafers and hippocras* at every christening." For philosophy, with its language of contractions, dilations, "rarifications," and condensations, "I confess in the Latin it seems very learned, but in the English very vulgar." The terms of medicine "truly a good farmer's wife in the country, by seeing one of her sheep opened, may well understand." The circles, squares, and lines of geometry were understood by "joiners and carpenters, therefore surely this Lady is capable of them." And as for the famously insoluble problem of squaring the circle, "who lives that hath not heard of it?"

Margaret's poems were her own, "all new-born fancies, never touched of heretofore," he assured readers. Of her essays, "not the fortieth part of her book" was derived from things "she hath heard from me." "All the rest are absolutely her own in all kinds: this is an ingenuous truth, therefore believe it." "Then this Lady's philosophy is excellent . . . and the truth is that it was wholly and only wrought out of her own brain." William ended his preface formally: "whatsoever I have writ is absolutely truth, which I here as a man of honour set my hand to." Anyone who now denied Margaret's authorship of her books

---

*Spiced wine.

would be accusing a man of honor of lying: a challenge to a duel would surely follow. William's words accomplished what Margaret's never could have done. These attacks on her were never repeated.[87]

To William, the assaults on Margaret's books seemed incomprehensible—except on one supposition. "Here's the crime," he guessed: "a lady writes them, and to entrench so much upon the male prerogative is not to be forgiven." This sense of male prejudice—of "the careless neglects and despisements of the masculine sex to the effeminate"—was growing on Margaret too. Contempt for women, "thinking it impossible we should have either learning or understanding, wit or judgement, as if we had not rational souls as well as men"—this was why readers had attacked her books. And this masculine contempt really made women inferior, she thought, inculcating "a custom of dejectedness . . . which makes us quit all industry towards profitable knowledge." Occupied "only in low and petty employments," women lost their "higher capacities . . . so as we are become like worms that only live in the dull earth of ignorance." Of course women would have less "understanding and knowledge," less "prudence and invention" than men, "for we are kept like birds in cages to hop up and down in our houses, not suffered to fly abroad to see the several changes of fortune and the various humours ordained and created by nature." "We are shut out of all power and authority, by reason we are never employed either in civil nor martial affairs, our counsels are despised and laughed at, the best of our actions are trodden down with scorn": all through "the overweening conceit men have of themselves and through a despisement of us"—"an opinion which I hope is but an erroneous one."[88]

Less than two years before, confronted with the inadequacies of her essays, Margaret had written that women were naturally inferior to men, their brains composed of softer, colder, moister elements. Now her readers' attacks had prompted her into a complete reversal: women shared men's rational souls, and were inferior only by nurture, not nature.[89]

Margaret dedicated her book with this new "feminist" preface to Oxford and Cambridge Universities, an unusual act for a woman, she knew, but "I hope . . . not unnatural . . . nor impudence."[90] The subject matter suggested such a dedication: natural philosophy was still largely an academic study in England; its rise to fashionable popularity among the genteel classes was only just now beginning. Also, William thought that scholars would be less likely to attack Margaret's work with "false aspersions." "I know gown-men will be more civil to her, because she is of the gown too," he joked, and Margaret accepted his view, hoping "that if a right judgement and a true understanding and a respectful civility live anywhere, it must be in learned universities." So it was to "wise school-men and industrious, laborious students" that she made her case for a reassessment of women's abilities, asking them to receive her *Philosophical Opinions* "without a scorn, for the good encouragment of our sex, lest in time we should grow irrational as idiots." Their notice—even their neglect—would "be honour enough for me," she told them.[91]

Chapter Ten

Satirist and Storyteller,
1655–1658

*M*argaret had scarcely finished her *Philosophical Opinions*, before she
threw herself into a new book, different in kind from any she had
written so far. *Nature's Pictures* was a collection of stories of huge variety and
range, encompassing satires, comedies, tragedies, love stories, animal fables,
dialogues, fairy stories, heroic romances, allegories—even autobiography.
Some stories were very short, others the length of a short novella; some were
written in verse, others in prose. By turns fanciful, reflective, exuberant,
melancholic, funny, bitter, argumentative, and visionary in tone, the collection
displays Margaret's great versatility as a writer.

Although Margaret included some elements of fantasy—especially in
those stories she described as "poetical" and "romancical"—her main aim was
to write realistic fiction: "lively descriptions" or "pictures" of nature, without
the wild fantasies of superhuman heroism, martial exploits, and languishing
lovers that she criticized in both epic poetry and literary romances. "Containing more lies than truth, more impossibilities than probabilities"—("for what
one man can disorder or rout an army with his single strength or courage?")—
such stories could "neither be pleasant nor profitable," she thought. Samson's
biblical feats of strength were true, she granted, but such extraordinary deeds
could occur only by divine miracle and were not proper subjects for fiction.
"Though the ground or subject of an heroical story or poem may be feigning,
yet the several actions should be natural, not beyond the power of men, nor
unusual to their practice."[1]

Margaret wanted her stories to remain close to the real world so as to
offer her readers actual possibilities, ideas for ways of living, talking, acting,

which they could imitate in their own lives. She hoped by this means to fulfil her culture's ideal of didacticism in literature: to "damn vices, kill follies, prevent errors, forewarn youth, and arm the life against misfortunes: likewise to admonish, instruct, direct and persuade to that which is good and best."[2]

Nature's Pictures began with a scene familiar from her own life—a group of men and women gathered around the fire in winter. Amidst the sounds of "rustling, twattling silks . . . creaking chairs and whisperings," with the men spitting and blowing their noses, each of the company took it in turn to tell a story, creating a framed collection of tales in the manner of Chaucer and Boccaccio.[3] These were popular works that Margaret probably knew well, along with more modern collections like Marguerite de Navarre's *Heptameron* and Robert Greene's *Penelope's Web*—the stories told by Odysseus's wife Penelope and her maids while they unpicked her weaving each night.

Like Chaucer, Margaret told this group of framed tales in verse. She dealt with relationships: constancy and inconstancy in love, pregnancies outside wedlock, marital infidelity, abandonment, bereavement, courage, kindness, vanity, deceit, despair, and suicide. Authoritarian parents break their children's love matches. Jealousy makes marriages miserable. A bored husband divorces his wife for another woman and then regrets it. Faithful lovers triumph over adversity. The company beside the fire discuss the outcomes of these tales—praising or criticizing the views they offer of love and marriage and of men and women, playing out the battle between the sexes. Successive narrators, male and female, answer each other with tales in defense of their own sex. Men argue for women's folly and vanity. Women's stories portray men's faithlessness and inconstancy. A bachelor praises the joys of a single life; a woman responds with a story showing the greater unhappiness that marriage brought to wives than to husbands.

Such *questioni d'amore* and debates on the relative merits of men and women formed a common theme of the games of raillery that were central to fashionable, courtly conversation. Margaret herself engaged in such repartee with her husband. Sparring on one occasion on the question of why women talked too much (one of womankind's stereotypical vices), Margaret had said it was because of their sense of inferiority to men, "striving to take off that blemish from their sex of knowing little, by speaking much," while William answered that "women talk because they cannot hold their tongues."[4]

In Margaret's stories the disagreements were often more acrimonious than this. The men cried out against a woman who ended her story "most spitefully." A woman criticized the "rusty tongue" of one of the male narrators. "Such men I hate that wrong their wives," one of the women exclaimed in response to a tale of marital tragedy: "all adulterers I wish might have a violent death, and an untimely grave."[5]

Margaret herself as author offered no definitive resolution to these debates. Rather, *Nature's Pictures* was meant to raise questions for her readers to ponder and discuss. She and William envisaged real-life groups gathering "to waste a tedious winter's night" beside the fire, with sweetmeats and wine. Reading Margaret's stories aloud, such companies would then "gossip" over the issues they raised, just as in the book, until they retired weary to bed, when "sleep seize you with delight."[6]

Towards the end of Margaret's fictional storytelling session, her characters turned to tales of the Civil War. All the narrators were royalists, and all told "melancholy" tales. A rich kingdom was reduced to "martial law," an ancient stone cross was pulled down "in a rage," a church "profaned by sinful men" and left as a stable. One of the women narrators related Margaret's own memories, of a paradise of fertile lands, with barns full and "orchards thick planted" and "crystal brooks" running between every field,

> *Where cowslips growing, which makes butter yellow,*
> *And fatted beasts, two inches thick with tallow,*
> *And many parks for fallow deer to run,*
> *Shadowed with woods.*

The country's natural riches meant that "those that industrious are, can nev'r be poor," until

> *. . . rebellions, like a watery flood,*
> *Overflows all monarchy in royal blood.*

Another woman told, as if it were her own, the story of Margaret's petitioning of Parliament.

> *But when I asked, no pity could I find,*
> *Hard were their hearts, and cruel every mind.*

Another, whose memories made "her heart to ache," told of "my brother . . . murthered in cold blood, encircled round with enemies." It was the story of Margaret's brother Charles, whose courage, burning like the sun, "knew no fear" as he faced the firing squad and "grim Death" himself. Margaret's narrator described the miracle that had followed his martyrdom:

> *Where his blood's spilt, the Earth no grass will bear.*
> *As if for to revenge his death, the Earth*
> *Was cursed with barrenness.*[7]

Margaret, through her storytellers, was publicly defying the parliamentarian regime in a book that was to be published in England. One of her narrators warned the rebels of the torments of a bad conscience:

> *In life no pleasure take, yet fear to die,*
> *No mercy can they hope from Gods on high.*

"Inhereditary* royalty is sacred," another character warned later in the book. "Many times the gods punish with plagues and other miseries those people that make a king of their own choosing, and justly, since kings are God's vicegerents, or deputies on Earth."[8]

This framed collection of short stories filled a quarter of *Nature's Pictures* and formed Book 1 of the work. The succeeding ten books, written almost entirely in prose, contained separate stories, unconnected by any frame of storytellers. In Book 2 the tone lightened, moving from the largely tragic stories of Book 1 to a collection of "comical tales," satirizing the follies and vices of society. In "The School's Quarrels" Margaret ridicules the disputatious nature of academics and clergymen: a scholarly debate degenerates into a slanging match; "heretic, and Beelzebub, and Whore of Babylon," these supposedly dignified men call each other, before resorting to physical violence, with torn books, hair, and academic gowns. "The Observer" lampooned the vices of royal courts—lazy, drunken guards in the guardchamber, amorous adventures and jealous political factions in the presence chamber, while the king and queen talk of nothing but "plays, balls, huntings, progresses and the like."

Margaret used her stories to propose revolutionary modes of life to her readers, and especially to women. In "The Matrimonial Agreement" she imagined a remedy for women's powerlessness in marriage: a young lady who fears unhappiness in a married life refuses to marry unless her lover signs a formal document allowing her to leave him and live with other men, with a generous allowance from his estate, if she even suspects him of being unfaithful. This heroine eventually marries, "considering withal, that marriage gave a respect to women," especially once age had stolen their beauty. But in other stories

---

*I.e. hereditary.

Margaret challenged the conventional view that marriage was the necessary goal of a young lady's life. In "The Discreet Virgin" the heroine refuses to marry, citing men's rudeness, drunkenness, and vanity. "Men in this age are far worse than women, and more ridiculous in their behaviours," she argues. "In their dressings and fashions they are more fantastical, various and unconstant than women are." Another story, "Ambition preferred before Love" presents a young lady who will not marry even a good husband. Men keep their wives "fast locked in their arms, or tie them to household employments," preventing their attempts "to climb to Fame's high tower," she objects.[9]

Book 3 brought a brief interlude of what Margaret called "romancical" or "poetical tales." Her fantasies included a journey to the center of the Earth guided by a witch; two young ladies disappointed in love who find consolation when they are carried off on a voyage of discovery in the chariot of the Muses; and the drunken antics of the ancient poets on Mount Helicon. There were also allegories, telling of the marriage of Life and Death, of the rule of King Reason and Queen Wit over the Land of Plenty, and of a man's visit to the castle of the soul.[10] Book 4 continued with "moral tales," a group of animal fables—"of the ant and the bee," "of the woodcock and the cow," "of a butcher and a fly"—modeled on Aesop.

Book 5 saw a return to realism, with a collection of dialogues. "A great lady and her maid of honour," "a contemplary lady and a poet" and "the wise lady, the learned lady, and the witty lady" all debated how it was best to live. Then Books 6 to 10 contained five much longer stories, one in each book.

"The Contract" told of a young lady whose unusual upbringing—a masculine education in philosophy, history, and poetry—had given her a wisdom beyond both her years and her sex. Yet she falls in love in spite of herself, and with the most unsuitable man—a rake "who loves his luxuries," the same man who was unwillingly betrothed to her when she was a child and who later broke their engagement to marry his mistress. Refusing the rich marriage to a much older man that her guardian attempts to arrange for her, she dares to break the normal codes of feminine morality by declaring her affection to the man she loves.

"The Tale of a Traveller" turned to the quandaries of a male protagonist—a young gentleman whose fashionable education on the grand tour brought him no practical benefits whatever. He finds happiness only when he settles on his own estate, resolving to hold no public offices, even the prestigious and normally coveted post of Justice of the Peace—just as Margaret's father had done when he returned to St. John's from his long, enforced exile abroad.

In "Assaulted and Pursued Chastity" Margaret took up a common theme from contemporary romances with the resourceful, even heroic, Lady Travellia, who saves herself from a dastardly prince, "a grand monopoliser of young virgins," by adopting male dress and fleeing aboard ship, only to face further adventures. Living with cannibals, she is able to learn their language and save herself from the pot by her eloquent public speaking—a true writer's fantasy of the power of words. Later in the story, Travellia becomes an able regent in a foreign land—ruling with such justice and wisdom "as begot such love in every heart that their mouths ran over with praises"—before leading the army to victory against an enemy invader.

Such ambitious views of women's abilities were also central to "The She Anchoret"—Margaret's longest story and one of the two that she considered "most solid and edifying."[11] The heroine, brought up by her widowed father, abandons the world when he dies and, "although she had many rich and honourable and importunate suitors, yet she resolved to live like a kind of an anchoret's life . . . vowing chastity and a single life." Soon her wisdom makes her "as famous as Diogenes in his tub" and "all sorts of people resorted to her, to hear her speak . . . to get knowledge and to learn wisdom," as she conversed with them through a grate in the wall of her hermitage. Philosophers, physicians, theologians, judges, lawyers, and politicians all came to ask her opinions—on the immortality of the soul, the nature of the sun and the planets, on medicines, diseases, love, politics, the existence of evil, and whether man had free will. Tradesmen came for advice on how to grow rich; "housekeepers and masters of families" asked questions on etiquette and hospitality; married men asked "what was the best course to keep their wives honest," while their wives wanted to know "what they should do if their husbands' whores did enslave them." Lovers came to find out "what made love so painful"; old people asked "what made man afraid to die." But this unconventional life story ends in tragedy. When a neighboring king falls in love with the anchoret and insists on marrying her, she is forced to commit suicide to protect her own country from war and remain true to her vows of chastity. "Honour, prudence, love and justice bids me die," she says as the poison does its work.

At the end of these ten books of fiction, Margaret added one nonfictional tale: "A True Relation of my Birth, Breeding and Life." This autobiography was both a loving tribute to the two royalist families to which she belonged and a careful construction of her identity as a woman author. Its story offered readers further suggestions for lives and mores, both male and female, conventional and unconventional.

Margaret began her story with her father. His "heroic spirit," his idealism, justice, and honor, his natural nobility—these were all important to her view of herself, since exceptional women were commonly seen as inheriting their more masculine virtues from their heroic fathers.[12]

Her mother, brothers, and sisters also received admiring, affectionate portraits. But Margaret's passionate devotion to her family, and her resentment at the suffering that war had brought them, resulted in selective and idealized reminiscences. The autobiography makes no mention of the Lucases' long-running, acrimonious disputes with Colchester's townspeople. "I observed that my mother nor brothers, before these wars, had never any lawsuits but what an attorney despatched in a [legal] term with small cost," Margaret stated confidently, before admitting that "if they had, it was more than I knew of." The family's hardheaded exploitation of their estates, their insistence on their rights however small, and the financial acumen that their neighbors condemned as greed are all omitted. The only hint is in Margaret's admiration of her mother as "very skilful in leases . . . of lands, and court keeping, ordering of stewards, and the like affairs." Margaret portrayed her mother as a recluse, conforming to the conventional ideal of virtuous widowhood. "She made her house her cloister, enclosing herself, as it were, therein, for she seldom went abroad, unless to church."[13] The truth was rather different: Elizabeth managed the Lucases' lands, engaged in lawsuits and went up to London for the season with the rest of the family. Margaret also omitted to mention the involvement of her brother John and her brother-in-law Sir Peter Killigrew in the widely hated court regime of Charles I, so that her account of the misfortunes brought by the Civil War—destruction, dispossession, death—comes as a tale of persecuted innocence, with the Lucases appearing as blameless victims of the pride and violence of the lower classes, suffering merely because of their loyalty to the king.

Margaret told of her exile and the finding of true love—"not amorous" but "honest and honourable"—of the closeness of the marriage that followed, and the courage and hope in adversity that she and her husband shared. The "True Relation" was a tale as heroic and romantic as any of her fiction. Then, at the end of her narration, Margaret drew an extended portrait of her own character—of her unresting imagination, her "addiction" to a life of "contemplation" as both child and adult, of her love of solitude, her passion for "singularity," her writing, her ambition, and her "melancholy."

Melancholy was always an important part of Margaret's self-definition. In Galenic medical theory, melancholy (or black bile) was one of the four humors responsible for health and illness, and its imbalance in the body caused not only physical symptoms but also psychological and personality traits. Melancholics lived solitary and spoke little; in company, they were often shy, fearing to disgrace themselves. Fearful, physically inactive, predominantly sad in mood, strong-willed and hot-tempered when roused, prone to hypochondria and insomnia—all these were stereotypical characteristics of the melancholic which Margaret recognized in herself. Other standard traits were less appealing. Greedy, miserly, selfish, proud, jealous, hostile, misanthropic, rude—her enemies would later accuse Margaret of all these melancholic attributes,* but in her autobiography she carefully distanced her personality from them. She was "not crabbed or peevishly melancholy," she told her readers. Rather, hers was "soft, melting, solitary, and contemplating melancholy."[14]

Here Margaret was referring to a more positive, even heroic, notion of melancholy, derived from Aristotelian rather than Galenic thought. According to this tradition, which had become hugely fashionable in the Renaissance, melancholy was the source of all human greatness and creative genius, giving the finest scholars, writers, artists, orators, and statesmen their insight, intelligence, and imagination. "Melancholy men of all others are most witty," explained the Oxford scholar Robert Burton in his immensely popular and often reprinted work, *The Anatomy of Melancholy*. Their melancholy "causeth many times divine ravishment, and a kind of enthusiasmus . . . which stirreth them up to be excellent philosophers, poets, prophets, etc." Or, as Margaret herself put it:

> Those that be naturally melancholy have the soundest judgements, the clearest understanding, the subtlest observation and curiousest inventions, the most conceptions, the finest fancies and the readiest wits; likewise the strongest passions and most constant resolution.[15]

Her own creative experience—of thoughts so prolific that there was scarcely time to speak or write them before they were crowded out by the rush of new ideas—was typical of the divine inspiration of the melancholic.

All through Europe, but especially in England, writers great and small eagerly identified themselves as melancholics—loners whose lives of contemplary solitude and sweet sadness inspired their work.** For Margaret, as a relatively uneducated woman writer who aimed for originality of thought rather than polish in language, the notion was especially inspirational, supporting her own view that a writer's ability derived from innate natural genius rather than any formal training. To her, melancholy was more than a source of creativity. It was a moral ideal of how to live:

---

*Even more severe traits of melancholy, although Margaret was never accused of them, included kleptomania, hallucinations, phobias, obsessions, paranoid delusions of grandeur, and even werewolfism.

**Some of the greater exponents included Milton, Donne, Francis Bacon, Edmund Spenser, and Philip Sidney.

True melancholy is a serious consideration; it examines the worth and nature of everything; it seeks after knowledge, and desires understanding; it observes strictly, and most commonly distinguisheth judiciously, applyeth aptly, acteth with ingenuosity, useth time wisely, lives honestly, dies contentedly, and leaves a fame behind it.[16]

Melancholy was, by ancient tradition,[17] a "disease of heroes,"* and Margaret often described her own aspirations in heroic terms, aligning herself with the current continental fashion for heroic women. "I confess my ambition is restless, and not ordinary," she told her readers.

Though I wish none worse than they are, yet it is lawful for me to wish myself the best, and to do my honest endeavour thereunto. For I think it no crime to wish myself the exactest of Nature's works, my thread of life the longest, my chain of destiny the strongest, my mind the peaceablest, my life the pleasantest, my death the easiest, and to be the greatest saint in heaven; also to do my endeavour, so far as honour and honesty doth allow of, to be the highest on Fortune's wheel and to hold the wheel from turning, if I can.

This superhuman aspiration for personal excellence and achievement—this "noble ambition," as Margaret called it—was the sort of knightly, courtly quest for honor and greatness by which the heroic women of literary romances might live. But it was hardly appropriate for ordinary life, conforming to neither conventional Christian morality nor the requirements of feminine modesty. So Margaret endeavored in her autobiography to justify such unconventional mores: "if it be commendable to wish another's good, it were a sin not to wish my own," she wrote, appealing more to pagan Greek and Roman standards of virtue than to Christian. "But I fear my ambition inclines to vainglory," she apologized, "for I am very ambitious; yet 'tis neither for beauty, wit, titles, wealth, or power, but as they are steps to raise me to Fame's tower, which is to live by remembrance in after-ages."[18]

Beauty, wealth, titles—these were conventional paths to fame for royal and aristocratic women, yet Margaret increasingly eschewed them. "Though I am ambitious, yet it is not for such trifles."

I should weep myself into water if I could have no other fame than rich coaches, lackeys and what state and ceremony could produce, for my ambition flies higher, as to worth and merit, not state and vanity; I would be

---

*Hercules, Ajax, and Bellerophon had all suffered melancholic madnesses.

known to the world by my wit, not by my folly, and I would have my actions
so wise and just as I might neither be ashamed nor afraid to hear of myself.

For such achievements, "my endeavours shall never be wanting as long as my
life doth last."[19]

Yet as a woman Margaret knew she could not follow the military, diplomatic, political, or legal careers by which men commonly earned their fame.
"All heroic actions, public employments, powerful governments and eloquent
pleadings are denied our sex in this age, or at least would be condemned for
want of custom," she regretted. "Reading history," she admitted, "I find in
myself an envy, or rather an emulation towards men."

> And of all the men I read of, I emulate Julius Caesar most, because he was a
> man that had all these excellencies, as courage, prudence, wit, and elo-
> quence, in great perfection, insomuch as when I read of Julius Caesar, I can-
> not but wish that Nature and Fate had made me such a one as he was; and
> sometimes I have that courage, as to think I should not be afraid of his des-
> tiny, so I might have as great a fame.[20]

"Tis true, death is terrible to think of," she wrote, yet "I could willingly part
with my present life to have it redoubled in after memory."[21] This desperate
aspiration, for which she could find no other outlet, Margaret explained to her
readers, "is the cause I write so much, for my ambition being restless . . . hath
made that little wit I have to run upon every subject I can think of, or is fit for
me to write on."[22]

BY THE LATE SUMMER OF 1656, Margaret had completed *Nature's Pictures*
and sent it off to her London publishers.[23] As usual, her book was exceptional.
Mary Wroth was the only woman to have published a work of original English
fiction before Margaret, with disastrous results, and no woman had ever published—or probably even written—an autobiography like Margaret's.
Couched purely in secular terms, with none of the religious reflection that was
a normal preoccupation of women who kept diaries or wrote accounts of their
lives, the "True Relation" presented an unorthodox, individualistic woman
who was not afraid to admit to her unfeminine, perhaps even unchristian,
ambitions.*

---

*Margaret's autobiography freely admitted her delight in dressing and fashions—the vanity of
women that seventeenth-century moralists so eagerly denounced. By contrast, the countess of Warwick,
Lady Anne Fanshawe, and many other women who looked back on their lives, rejected their earlier interests in fashions, regretting the frivolity of their youth with a more mature religious sense.

Margaret knew she was breaking with convention. "Why hath this lady writ her own life, since none cares to know whose daughter she was or whose wife she is, or how she was bred, or what fortunes she had, or how she lived?" she wrote, voicing the criticisms she expected from her readers. But this story was written not for them, she answered, but for the future—"to tell the truth, lest after-ages should mistake."[24]

For her new book Margaret again commissioned Abraham van Diepenbeeck to design an illustrated frontispiece, even though she had experienced some dissatisfaction at his earlier results. Diepenbeeck, like his master Rubens before him, had a tendency to produce overly rounded, foreshortened faces in his portraits, and Margaret thought that none of the frontispieces he produced for her was "done truly to life." Each face was slightly different, and though not entirely without resemblance to her, yet "those lines that do resemble are buried amongst those that do not resemble, so as the whole picture is unlike," she noted.[25]

Whereas its two predecessors could be used in any of Margaret's books, Diepenbeeck's new illustration was intended specifically for *Nature's Pictures*, showing Margaret and William presiding over the sort of winter's fireside storytelling that the book itself contained. As before, considerable thought had gone into the design. The original idea of seating the couple beneath a cloth-of-state, shown in Diepenbeeck's preparatory sketch, was abandoned in favor of a more informal, everyday image, a quality emphasized by the presence of servants, attending to the company's needs. John Proctor stands behind the Newcastles, holding William's hat, while another servant opens a window to let out the strand of smoke which can be seen escaping from the fireplace.

However, as in Margaret's other frontispieces, there is also an element of heroic classicism. She and William both wear laurel wreaths, representing their poetic identity as writers. This feature was added after Diepenbeeck's preliminary sketch, and in turn necessitated another departure from the original plan: in accordance with etiquette, the other men's hats were all removed from their heads in the finished frontispiece, since William—the most eminent man in the gathering—was now himself hatless.* Margaret's posture was also altered. Where the sketch had shown her with her hand raised as if telling a story, the final printed image shows her in passive repose—perhaps a gesture towards conventional ideals of feminine modesty.[26]

---

*Unlike their nineteenth- and twentieth-century successors, seventeenth-century men normally wore their hats indoors, even when seated at table, except when etiquette demanded otherwise, as a mark of respect to social superiors.

The frontispiece advertised Margaret's book as a contribution to the homemade entertainment that was a normal part of aristocratic life. But it also contained a message at once more personal and more political. The company around the table with William and Margaret consists of William's five children—Jane, Elizabeth, Charles, Henry, and Frances—and their spouses. William's hand points easily towards them, in portraiture's conventional symbol of paternity.

> *My Lord and I here in two chairs are set,*
> *And all his children, wives and husbands, met,*
> *To hear me tell them tales . . .*

Margaret's verse explains.[27] With William's coat of arms carved prominently over the room's fireplace, indicating the location as one of his houses, Welbeck or Bolsover, the whole image forms a wistful imagining of exile ended, of restoration and family reunion—a hoped-for political future that still seemed impossibly distant.*

In England, William's children were now all married. May 1653 had seen Henry's marriage to his cousin Frances, eldest daughter of William Pierrepont, a wealthy Nottinghamshire landowner and younger brother of the marquess of Dorchester. It was a rich match, bringing Henry a dowry of £5,000 in addition to various estates.[28] It also brought him connections high up in England's parliamentarian regime. Nicknamed "Wise William," Henry's new father-in-law was a shrewd and respected politician who had served as a member of Parliament throughout the Civil War and was now one of Oliver Cromwell's most trusted advisers. By 1657, Henry was a privileged visitor to the Lord Protector's court at Whitehall, dining with Cromwell and his inmost circle.[29]

In 1654 the remaining siblings also married. Frances wedded Oliver St. John, earl of Bolingbroke, while Jane married Charles Cheyne, a Buckinghamshire gentleman of royalist sympathies who had, like many young men, spent the Civil War years on the Continent, performing the grand tour. Jane was apprehensive of marriage and sorry to leave Welbeck, but she was lucky enough to find a husband who loved her and treated her as if "he was still a wooer." "You told me it would be always so, being the nature of the person," she gratefully acknowledged to her brother Charles, viscount Mansfield.[30]

---

*The five figures seated on the opposite side of the table, facing the reader and clearly illuminated, are probably William's children, while their spouses sit with their backs to the reader. But the long-imagined family reunion depicted in the frontispiece would in fact never take place, since Charles, viscount Mansfield, died a year before the Restoration.

Charles himself married the Dorset heiress Elizabeth Rogers. The match, arranged by Sir Charles Cavendish and her relatives some three years before, was a shrewd exchange of money (hers) for social honors (his),[31] but the couple seemed happy together, living at Welbeck with occasional visits to London. Charles remained emotionally close to his sisters, advising on their health during pregnancies, and anxiously awaiting the outcome of difficult childbirths. With Jane in particular he maintained a weekly correspondence, full of wit and affection. She was now living in Chelsea, her house continually filled with friends and society, "Chelsea being as pleasant a place for inviting of company as any I know, and being not far from Hyde Park," though "I like much better the solitary walks of Welbeck than the crowd and dust of that park," Jane told her brother. She often saw her sisters, Frances and Elizabeth, when they were in town, but Henry remained a more distant figure, unmentioned in his sisters' letters. He was sometimes a dinner guest at Welbeck, but his notes to his brother are formal in tone, filled with business rather than affection.[32]

Like Henry, Charles was actively accommodating himself to England's new political establishment, with the parliamentarian general John Lambert, now a member of Cromwell's Council of State, as his patron. Through Lambert, Charles was finally successful in his petition to be included in the Act of Oblivion, by which Parliament had pardoned almost all royalist delinquents for their actions in the war.* With further influential connections in the North of England, he also managed to avoid the crippling taxes that local government imposed on delinquents.[33]

At Welbeck, Charles assumed all the manifold responsibilities of the head of the family. Through a network of agents and bailiffs, he managed the family's still-substantial estates, centered around Welbeck and extending into Northumberland, Kent, and the West Country. John Hutton and William Clayton were his closest counselors, carefully guiding the young man through all the complexities of his new business.

Life at Welbeck retained much of its aristocratic grandeur, with elegant gardens, riding, hawking, bowling, dinner entertainments, and fashionable clothes from London tailors. Charles consulted London's leading physicians; he appointed clergymen to the family's parishes; he was a patron of musicians.[34] But his finances were tight and large sums were hard to find. He was still struggling to pay his sister Jane's dowry some two years after her mar-

---

*Like his father and others of the most prominent royalists, Charles had been excluded by name when the act was originally passed. He was now allowed the benefit of the act on the grounds that he had been a minor, forced to accompany his father against his will, and had taken no active part in the war, "being weak of body and constitution."

riage, and the major rebuilding needed at Bolsover Castle remained undone, though minor repairs were carried out. There were also his father's prewar debts to be repaid, and William and Margaret's Antwerp household was almost entirely dependent on him for funding.[35]

With all these demands, Charles had resorted to selling lands as soon as he arrived at Welbeck—sales that continued for years, as William and Margaret remained in financial need. By legal deeds, William had surrendered all control of his estates, "the better to enable his support abroad in his exile and the better to provide for his children at home."[36] Although he corresponded regularly with his sons—using pseudonyms like John Forrest and Robert Deane, in hopes of escaping parliamentarian detection—he had little close knowledge of the business being done in England. Some estates were mortgaged; on others, long leases were set to bring in large sums immediately. But mainly it was sales—houses, farms, woods, fields, entire manors, even a barony and a tower.[37]

In Antwerp, William and Margaret's exile dragged on. Publicly they maintained a resolute, even defiant, front. "Patience hath armed us, and misery hath tried us and finds us fortune-proof," Margaret proclaimed in her autobiography.[38] But in private she told William of her fears—that the king would never be restored, that they would never return home. Her husband rebuked her gently, telling her she "could never be happy if I . . . entertained nothing but doubts and fears." "My Lord was never without hopes," Margaret wrote. But to others, William did occasionally admit his despondency, wishing that he might find reason for even false "flattering hopes," which at least "would somewhat qualify our miserable condition."[39] He kept up his correspondence with the English court, but there was little for him to do. Cromwell's intelligence network quickly uncovered plans for an uprising in England in the summer of 1655, and the plotters—including Margaret's brother John—were all arrested. With the rest of the prisoners, John became the subject for a satirical verse, probably written by his friend Sir John Denham:

> *Lord Lucas is fast, and will be the last**
> *Because he's so learned a peer.*
> *His law will not do 't, nor his logic to boot,*
> *Though he make the cause never so clear.*[40]

William spent most of his time in the diversions of cultivated leisure. After his daily exercise in riding and fencing he loved, like Margaret, to write. With

---

*The last to be released.

an easy creativity, he composed a plethora of poems, ranging from love poetry for Margaret to long verse tales like "The Beggars' Marriage" and "The Philosopher's Complaint." For lyric poetry he had an especial taste. "He is the best lyric poet in this age, nay in my judgement, in any," Margaret thought, "for I have seen him make twenty songs upon one theme or subject, as music, and not one song like another."[41] His songs were often set to music—by their Antwerp neighbor, Jacques Duarte, and by the former court musician Nicholas Lanier, now an art dealer living on the Continent and trading into England.

William was also writing plays, reading them aloud to Margaret, although he kept them back from publication in hopes of the English theaters opening once again for performances.[42] *A Pleasant and Merry Humour of a Rogue* was a burlesque of comic lowlife, a form William especially enjoyed and which he wrote well. Various fragments of William's dramas from this period survive among his manuscripts, and it was perhaps now that he wrote *The Exile* and *The Heiress,* comedies attributed to him that no longer survive.[43] William also wrote shorter dramatic pieces for current performance. His pastorals and masques in the style of prewar court culture—now surviving only in fragments—were intended as after-dinner entertainments for guests at the Rubens House.[44]

But William's real labor of love was his book on horsemanship. Containing his own techniques of riding and training horses for the manège (as well as a range of advice on topics such as buying and breeding horses, medicines, and the design of harnesses), *La Méthode Nouvelle et Invention Extraordinaire de Dresser les Chevaux* would become a classic work, consulted by readers throughout Europe for the next hundred and fifty years and more. William had written it—in English—during Margaret's stay in London, but its production in print would take another five years. First a reliable translator was needed, for William wanted to publish in French to reach a continental audience. William worked closely with his translator, checking everything himself.[45] Then more than forty illustrations were designed. Like Margaret, William turned to Abraham van Diepenbeeck, who produced not only practical images—of horses undergoing training, of saddles, bridles, spurs, and bits—but also nostalgic depictions of William and his horses at home in England, in front of the buildings that he and his father had put up at Welbeck and Bolsover. Finally Diepenbeeck's designs went out to various Antwerp engravers.

"I am so tormented about my book of horsemanship as you cannot believe, with a hundred several trades, I think, and the printing will cost above £1,300," William told a friend in 1657. The book, with its lavish double-folio sized copperplate prints, was a luxury item that William himself could not afford to produce, but he had found financial backers in two court agents, Sir

Henry Cartwright and William Loving. "I hope they shall lose nothing by it, and I am sure they hope the like," William added.[46]

Unlike his plays, which appeared anonymously, William intended to publish this more aristocratic work under his own name. Wanting a title page at once impressive and socially correct, he consulted the most senior English herald, Sir Edward Walker, the Garter King-of-Arms, still with Charles II's court in exile. Walker confirmed that there were precedents that entitled William, as a marquess and a Knight of the Garter, to take the courtesy title of prince.[47] Accordingly, when his book finally came out in 1658—dedicated to King Charles II, whom he had first taught to ride—William would style himself "le très noble, haut et très puissant Prince, Guillaume, Marquis et Comte de Newcastle," listing too all his prewar court offices.

But by then, Margaret had already begun to use the princely title herself. *Nature's Pictures*, in 1656, had billed its author as "the thrice noble, illustrious and excellent Princess, the Lady Marchioness of Newcastle."* High social status was especially important to Margaret as a woman writer, giving her an authority and right to speak beyond the norms that applied to most of her sex. It also gave her some protection from the criticism that her unusual mode of life was liable to bring. "If you were not a great lady," Margaret told herself, "you would never pass in the world for a wise lady, for the world would say your singularities are vanities."[48] The grand style of "Princess" would appear on the title pages of all her subsequent books.

Nature's Pictures had marked a new development in William and Margaret's relationship. Here three of William's own verse tales of comic lowlife appeared, mixed with Margaret's poems in Book 1, and William also composed the wedding and mourning songs for three of Margaret's stories—a striking role-reversal: women rarely published books of their own but might have short pieces of their work included in books by male relatives or friends.[49] No longer did Margaret see her relation to her husband in terms of "master" and "scholar." Rather, she now wrote, "our wits join as in matrimony, my Lord's the masculine, mine the feminine wit." "We are married, souls, bodies and brains, which is a treble marriage, united in one love, which I hope is not in the power of death to dissolve." And the couple's new literary collaboration would continue just as closely in Margaret's next book, which was already well advanced by the time *Nature's Pictures* was published.[50]

---

*"Thrice" here translates the French "très," meaning very, highly. Whether in response to Margaret's continued insistence, or to the Cromwellian regime's relaxation of restrictions on old royalists, the title page of the *Philosophical Opinions* in 1655 had already given Margaret her title of "the Lady Marchioness of Newcastle," omitted from her first books.

The idea of writing plays had first occurred to Margaret as she listened to William reading her his own,[51] but the work she now began was quite different from her husband's drama, or anyone else's. The three unities—of place, time, and action—that governed the construction of classical drama (written by Ben Jonson and his followers in England), she rejected as artificial and unrealistic. "Plays are to present the natural dispositions and practices of mankind," Margaret argued, so why should the action be confined to a single place and a single day? And why should comedies end with all the characters brought together on stage in the final scene, "which in my opinion shows neither usual, probable, nor natural"?

> I think it as well, if not better, if a play ends but with two persons, or one person upon the stage; besides, I would have my plays to be like the natural course of all things in the world, as some die sooner, some live longer, and some are newly born when some are newly dead, and not all to continue to the last day of judgement.

With the English theaters closed by Parliament, Margaret wrote her plays for reading rather than performance, and this liberated her work from the practical constraints imposed by the stage. Like many other royalists who now published their drama—often as an explicit act of resistance to England's parliamentarian government—Margaret felt free to depart from recent prewar stage convention and write longer plays, often divided into two five-act parts. Great length "might tire" theatergoers, "who are forced or bound by the rules of civility to sit out a play, if they be not sick," Margaret explained, "but for readers the length of the plays can be no trouble nor inconveniency, because they may read as short or as long a time as they please."

But Margaret went beyond her royalist contemporaries to innovate much more radically. With rapidly changing, short scenes, she advanced several separate strands of plot all in parallel—a technique for heightening suspense that is now common in television drama, especially soap operas, but would be impractical on the stage. And, rejecting the convention of unity of action that is still basic to drama and fiction alike, she saw no reason why the characters of these various plot strands should have any connection to one another, either by blood or acquaintance. "The world is wide and populated," Margaret argued: "plays are to present the general follies, vanities, vices, humours . . . passions . . . manners and practices of the whole world of mankind." And with "all these varieties" as their subject matter, why should plays "force them together . . . making the persons of each humour, good fortunes, misfortunes, nations and ages to have relations to each other"?[52]

Margaret had decided not to write the "ridiculous jest" nor the "wanton love" that were common features of contemporary comedies.* Also, her plays would have "no plots, nor designs, nor subtle contrivances and the like." This rejection of devious characters who hatched cunning plans—a common story line that provided contemporary comedies and tragedies with much of their excitement—was also a feature of the plays written by William's daughters during the war, a feature that they saw as distinctively feminine:

> 'Tis woman all the way,
> For you'll not see a plot in any act.

Margaret feared her readers would object "that my plays are too serious," too "dull and flat."[53] But, like William's daughters, she was more interested in creating a drama of ideas, centering on characters facing important life choices who discuss and decide what they should do and how they should live.

Just as with *Nature's Pictures*, Margaret envisaged groups of people gathering to read her plays aloud and discuss the choices and actions and the moral and intellectual issues presented. For this purpose, her revolutionary plot construction—with each play containing several parallel, often unconnected, story lines—was ideal. Margaret wrote her story lines separately then interwove them, "ordering and joining" the scenes with "great pains" to make a complete play.[54] In the finished product, the alternating scenes from the different story lines, with their diverse lives and characters, reflected on and contrasted with each other, enabling Margaret to raise questions and suggest meanings for her readers that would never arise from each story told in isolation.

Many of Margaret's plays dealt with women discussing their hopes and fears as they faced courtship and marriage. How should they choose their partners? Was romantic love desirable? What would their marriages bring? Should they even marry at all?

To choose a good husband would be impossible, fears Mademoiselle Solid in the comedy *The Several Wits*: "I may be betrayed by flattery, outward garb, insinuations or falsehood." "That little reason I have tells me, to be a wife is to be unhappy, for content seldom in marriage dwells, disturbance keeps possession." She prefers a solitary life over the folly and gossip of society.

Meanwhile Mademoiselle Volante spends her time tricking all the men she meets into thinking she is in love with them.

---

*William wrote for her the most "wanton" scenes in the book, where three gentlemen vie to corrupt a country wench in her play *The Lady Contemplation*.

"But where is the pleasure, Lady?" an older matron asks her.

"Why, in seeing their fantastical garbs, their strutting postures, their smiling faces . . . and then I laugh in my mind to think what fools they are." She, like Solid, resolves never to marry.

Juxtaposed with both of them is the beautiful Mademoiselle Caprisia, whose "tongue is as sharp as a serpent's sting."

"You are the rarest beauty and the greatest wit in the world," Monsieur Importunate courts her, but when he insists on stealing a kiss, she curses him.

"Hell take you, or Earth devour you like a beast, never to rise* . . . May you be blown up with pride, until you burst into madness."

In the play *Wit's Cabal,* the young women again discuss the troubles of marriage. Mademoiselle Faction and Mademoiselle Ambition would like to find good husbands but agree that they may exist only "in our thoughts, but not actually in the world."

"I wonder our sex should desire to marry," Superbe reflects. "When we are unmarried we are sued and sought to, and not only mistress of ourselves but our suitors: But when we are married, we are so far from being mistresses, as we become slaves."

"There is no act . . . proves us to be so much fools as we are as in marrying," agrees Mademoiselle Pleasure.

As the courtships of the play advance, the tension builds, with the women facing unpromising suitors like Monsieur Satyrical, Monsieur Sensuality, and Monsieur Vain-glorious.

"All the ladies in the city are in love with me," boasts the last of these, "but I mean to marry none but Mademoiselle Ambition . . . for she is rich." "I will only keep her for breed[ing], and [will] entertain myself and lead my life with Mademoiselle Pleasure, and she shall share the riches that Mademoiselle Ambition brings."

"What greater slavery is there than to be tied to one woman?" demands Monsieur Sensuality. He hates the European system of monogamy where the wife, "being sole mistress" in the house, "grows proud, imperious, insults and domineers, and disputes with her husband for preheminency." Instead he advocates the Turkish harem, "where men have many wives, concubines and slaves" and "the women are humbled into a submission, each woman striving which can be most serviceable, and who can get most love and favour."

Despite their protestations, most of the women do finally marry, but the various relationships have been so questioned—their incompatibilities and battles of wills so clearly displayed—that the reader is left wondering how these

---

*I.e. in resurrection after death.

marriages can possibly turn out well. It is the same paradox as is posed by the apparent "happy ending" of marriage in Charlotte Brontë's *Jane Eyre:* can Jane really be happy with a man like Mr. Rochester?

In *Love's Adventures,* Margaret brought such questions to the fore by contrasting romantic young lovers with already married couples. The story of young Lady Orphant—who disguises herself as a boy so that she can follow the man she loves to the wars—is played out against the plot of Lady Ignorant, who is unhappy because her scholarly husband neglects her and spends all his time alone with his books. When Ignorant finally persuades Sir Peaceable Studious to go out into society, she becomes more unhappy than ever. Studious—wise in his books, but foolish in the ways of the world—becomes an obsessive gambler, loses all his money at cards, flirts with his wife's friends, and makes love to her maid.

Similarly in *The Matrimonial Trouble,* young Mistress Forsaken journeys overseas, hoping to win back her lover, while parallel plots question the desirability and happiness of marriage. Some of the nine unhappily married couples portrayed eventually resolve their problems, but other marriages end in divorce or murder.

Arranged marriages were a particular target of Margaret's satire. "Pray, sir, do not force me to marry a child, before you know whether she will prove virtuous or discreet," Lord Singularity begs his father, in the opening speech of *Love's Adventures.*

"Come, come, she is rich, she is rich," his father argues. "For shame! Take courage, and be not afraid of a woman," he adds when his son fears to end up a cuckold.

Lord Singularity escapes by fleeing abroad, but in *The Religious* Lady Perfection and Lord Melancholy marry in compliance with their parents' wishes. Their union is never consummated, however, for both take religious vows and enter monasteries. In a parallel plot, Mistress Odd-Humour refuses the suitor her father has chosen, complaining that he negotiates like "a merchant's trafficking . . . to make a bargain, not to woo a mistress"; he would be but "a husband bought."[55] At the play's close, she is still unmarried—an ending seldom seen in contemporary comedies, but one that Margaret used fairly often.

Margaret's plays were also exceptional in their concentration on women. She had a higher proportion of female characters than other playwrights, and she gave them more lines to speak, often including scenes of entirely female dialogue.*[56] Her play *The Female Academy,* for instance, centered on a school

---

*While women characters, on average, speak only a quarter of the lines in the plays written by seventeenth-century men (and only just over a third of lines in plays written by women), they speak two-thirds of Margaret's lines, and they frequently make the opening and closing speeches of her plays.

where young women engaged in public speaking on a range of topics, thus learning "to speak wittily and rationally, and to behave themselves handsomely." In *The Unnatural Tragedy* the Sociable Virgins meet regularly for intellectual and moral discussion. They "rail against men"; they advocate women's involvement in government; they criticize the work of the greatest (male) historians and poets, and lament the lack of heroes like Caesar and Alexander among the men of the modern world. However, their "feminist" critique is undercut by two older matrons who rebuke them for talking "like young ladies, you know not what"—a further spur for the readers' discussions that Margaret hoped her plays would inspire.

In several plays, Margaret told the stories of exceptional women who entered the traditional male domains of war, politics, and academia, where they displayed a "masculine" courage and ability, fulfilling Margaret's own frustrated ambitions for a "heroic" life. In *Love's Adventures,* Lady Orphant fights with courage in foreign wars, makes public speeches to admiring audiences and even defeats Rome's cardinals in theological debate, finally winning the love of the man she seeks. Another martial woman appears in *Bell in Campo,* where Lady Vittoria accompanies her husband to the wars and ends up saving her country by leading an army of women against the enemy. Their grateful king rewards these "heroickesses" with honors and grants a range of domestic privileges to all the women in his kingdom. "They shall sit at the upper end of the table above their husbands . . . they shall keep the purse . . . they shall go abroad when they will, without control, or giving any account thereof." However, Margaret's heroic women did not always end so happily: in *Youth's Glory and Death's Banquet,* Lady Sanspareille becomes a great philosopher but dies young. In Margaret's common fashion, all these plays also included contrasting parallel plot lines, telling of nonheroic women who live by society's normal mores—again providing readers with opportunities for comparison and debate.

As William and Margaret's literary collaboration continued, Margaret's plays included many sections written by her husband. He contributed several of the prologues and epilogues that introduced and wrapped up the plays. He wrote the speeches of admiration with which male audiences greeted Lady Sanspareille's lectures in *Youth's Glory and Death's Banquet*. And for *The Lady Contemplation* he composed a series of "wanton" scenes that culminate in Sir Golden Riches's successful seduction of the country wench, Mall Mean-bred. William portrayed this sort of comic lowlife especially well, and Margaret was keen to use what she thought were her husband's best talents—his "masculine wit," as she called it. In consequence, William wrote all of the songs included in her plays, "for I being no lyric poet, my Lord supplied that defect of my brain with the superfluity of his own." Each of these contributions from her husband Margaret carefully labeled with its true authorship—"writ by the Lord Marquess of Newcastle"—so "that my readers may know which are his, as not to cozen them, in thinking they are mine."[57]

Margaret wrote quickly, and her huge dramatic output (fourteen plays, with five of them in two parts of five acts each) was finished all too soon.

> *My poor plays, like to a common rout,*
> *Gathers in throngs, and heedlessly runs out . . .*
> *So quickly writ that I did almost cry*
> *For want of work, my time for to employ.*

Idleness horrified Margaret. It was, she thought, the greatest evil of her class, especially its female part.

> The truth is, our sex hath so much waste time, having but little employments, which makes our thoughts run wildly about, having nothing to fix them upon, which wild thoughts do not only produce unprofitable but indiscreet actions, winding up the thread of our lives in snarls on unsound bottoms.*

Margaret hated the "foolish extravagancies, debauched luxuries and base vices" of the rich, "which idleness and vacant time produceth." For herself, she was desperate to keep working,

> *Like as poor labourers, all they desire*
> *Is to have so much work it might them tire.*[58]

Feeling a moral imperative to be always "employed to some good use"—"for the riches of the mind must do as other riches, which is to disperse about, not to lie unprofitably hid and hoarded up"—her one fear was "lest my brain should grow barren, or that the root of my fancies should become insipid, withering into a dull stupidity for want of maturing subjects to write on."[59]

After completing her plays, Margaret had just one more idea for a book to write. A biography of William, she thought, was a work "very fit for me to do," and she was probably inspired in particular by the publication in 1658 of Sir William Sanderson's *Compleat History of the Life and Raigne of King Charles*—an account of recent English history that was heavily biased towards the parlia-

---

*In this mixed metaphor, the limited thread of a lifetime becomes an anchor cable, wasted in tangles on the treacherous seabed of "indiscreet actions."

mentarian view. Compiled largely from the weekly published gazettes of news, Sanderson's book contained "more falsehoods than truth," Margaret wrote, and she was especially angry at the mistakes it made in recounting both William's prewar entertainments of the king and queen at Welbeck and his part in the Civil War.[60]

Margaret knew well that her husband had many enemies—not only parliamentarians, but also rivals in the royalist camp. Commentators on both sides had criticized William's military career, especially his flight from England after the Battle of Marston Moor, and many of Charles II's current advisers judged him unfit for political responsibility. "You will find the Marquess of Newcastle a very lamentable man," Edward Hyde had cautioned his old friend, Secretary of State Sir Edward Nicholas, during the royalists' negotiations with the Scots at Breda in 1650: "God help us, when Hamilton, Mr. Long, Newcastle and Buckingham rule in Council!"[61]

Since those days William's political influence had declined dramatically. Hyde was now the king's chief counselor, appointed lord chancellor in 1657. Margaret was furious, "much grieved that my Lord, for his loyalty and honest service, had so many enemies." Her new book was her chance to disprove them all. Detailing her husband's many abilities, his wisdom, foresight, successes, his great deeds both military and political, it would, she promised William, "set forth and declare to after ages, the truth of your loyal actions and endeavours, for the service of your King and country."[62]

It was an ambitious task, Margaret knew. She had no experience or training in writing history, and so, fearing that she would commit many faults "for want of learning," she asked William "to let me have some elegant and learned historian to assist me." It was an unprecedented request from a writer determined always to be original and individual, and William refused it. He and his secretary would help her, but only by supplying information about William's career before he had met her. Thereafter she must rely on her own memory. When Margaret objected "that without a learned assistant, the history would be defective," William only replied "that truth could not be defective." So, "forced by his . . . commands," Margaret would "write this history in my own plain style . . . relying entirely upon truth."[63]

She started at once, writing to William's secretary in England to ask for the information she needed. John Rolleston had accompanied his master throughout the Civil War, and then remained in the family's employ at Welbeck when William himself fled abroad after Marston Moor. But Margaret waited in vain for his reply. Unable to proceed with her only idea—and refusing to write again the same kinds of books as she had already written, "which would be as tedious as endless"—Margaret was finally "forced to sit idle, as having no work to do, which troubled me much, not knowing what to write of."[64]

Eventually a new idea came. She would write a series of "sociable letters," as she called them—a correspondence with an imaginary female friend.

> Since we cannot converse personally [Margaret wrote, setting out her project], we should converse by letters, so as if we were speaking to each other, discoursing our opinions, discovering our designs, asking and giving each other advice, also telling the several accidents and several employments of our home-affairs, and . . . what discourses we have in our gossiping-meetings, and what reports we hear of public affairs and of particular persons.[65]

Letters had a long tradition as a literary form. In the ancient world, Cicero, Seneca, Pliny the Younger, St. Augustine and St. Paul had used them as a vehicle for expressing their moral, philosophical, or religious views. More recently, James Howell's *Epistolae Ho-elianae* (published in London in four volumes between 1645 and 1655) was a work closer to Margaret's in its conception of "familiar letters"—intimate, chatty letters written to friends, full of observations and reflections on society and its manners. But Margaret's immediate inspiration may have come rather from her old associate of exile, the poet Richard Flecknoe. Flecknoe had returned to England in 1653, but he still maintained close ties with the Newcastles. Around 1656 he dedicated to William his latest book—*A Relation of Ten Years' Travel in Europe, Asia, Affrique and America*, told entirely "by way of letters occasionally written to divers noble personages, from place to place." Flecknoe's letters, like Howell's, were written to real people, but in other respects they resembled Margaret's closely. Telling stories of everyday life with humor and satirical insight, putting forward opinions on a range of social, moral, and literary topics, and expressing the warmth of their feelings, all three authors cemented close bonds of friendship with their (real or imaginary) correspondents.[66]

Like her plays, Margaret intended her letters "to express the humours of mankind, and the actions of man's life." "The truth is, they are rather scenes than letters," Margaret admitted, but she nonetheless decided to put her new ideas into epistolary rather than dramatic form. "I saw that variety of forms did please the readers best," she explained (variety was one of the chief principles of seventeenth-century aesthetics). Another consideration was "the brevity of letters" compared to "the formality of . . . plays, whose parts and plots cannot be understood till the whole play be read over, whereas a short letter will give a full satisfaction" on its subject at once.[67]

Margaret's letters portrayed many contrasting character types. There was a gentleman who married his kitchen maid, a woman who beat her unresisting husband in public, a lord "totally governed" by one of his servants, and a woman—"the Lady P. Y."—who "spends most of her time in prayer."[68] Then there was "Mrs. P. I.," an old friend transformed by religious conversion. "She hath left curling her hair, black patches are become abominable to her, laced shoes and galoshes are steps to pride, to go bare-necked she accounts worse than adultery; fans, ribbons, pendants, neck-cloths and the like are the temptations of Satan and the signs of damnation." "She is become an altered woman," Margaret reported. "You would not know her if you saw her."[69]

One letter told of three young ladies who "are resolved never to marry." A second described an older woman "grieving for the loss of her beauty," while another lady said she preferred rather to "die before her beauty than that her beauty should die before her." Another letter recounted the story of a mercenary man who agreed to marry a ten-year-old girl for her money. Yet another told of a wife who "hath a conversible and ingenious wit, yet not being very handsome, her husband hath got him a mistress, who is very beautiful." Yet the wife was untroubled, expecting her husband to "be more delighted with her wit than with his mistress' beauty." "Besides," added the wife, "I am so delighted and wedded to my own wit that I regard not my husband's amours."[70]

Many of the letters told stories from Margaret's own life. "Full of fear," she wrote of a political crisis in Antwerp. Angry mobs had plundered a magistrate's house and now thronged the city's streets. Women wept, trumpets sounded, and drums beat. The city's Spanish garrison was arming, "and to make it the more fearful, the great bell, which is only rung in time of danger, either in cases of fire, or war, or mutinies or the like, sounds dolefully." Margaret's maids, as frightened as she, relayed the latest rumors to her—"some, that the army is coming to destroy the city, and others, that the soldiers have liberty to abuse all the women, others, that all in the city shall be put to the sword."[71]

Other letters told of Antwerp's many entertainments. Rope-dancers, tumblers, jugglers, and actors could all "be seen for money . . . at several times of the year." Trained animals—"acting baboons and apes"—were exhibited, as also were strange exotica—dromedaries, camels, and lions. Among the many "monsters" on public show, a woman was brought to Margaret "who was like a shag-dog, not in shape but hair, as grown all over her body, which sight . . . troubled my mind a long time." More enjoyable for Margaret was a mountebank who set up a stage and actors in order to sell his quack medicines. Fascinated by the skill of the actor who played the fool, and by this man's wife—"the best female actor that ever I saw," utterly convincing whether she appeared in her petticoats or dressed as a man in doublet and breeches—Margaret hired a room overlooking the stage and went every day to watch their performances, though "I did not understand their language." Then there was Antwerp's Shrovetide carnival, "the most pleasant and merry time in all the year in this city, for feasting, sporting and masquerading." Men dressed as women, and women as men, and masked devils ran through the streets. The next morning, Ash Wednesday, the whole population, men, women, and children appeared "marked . . . with a black mourning cross on their foreheads" to attend church.[72]

A series of letters told of Antwerp's severe winter weather when, in spite of the furs they donned, the fires they built, and the hearty fare at dinner—beef, cabbage, sausages, carrots, marrowbones, pork, mutton, veal, poultry, with a "sea of wine, beer, and ale"—"yet for all this," Margaret reported, "we are beaten into the chimney-corner, and there we sit shaking and trembling like a company of cowards, that dare not stir from their shelter." At night, the snow-covered streets filled with courting couples ("dressed anticly . . . with feathers and rich clothes") driving past in their sleds, the men whipping up their horses to a gallop, "whilst footmen run with torches" beside them. By day, skaters gathered on the frozen moat outside the city walls and, despite Margaret's reluctance to leave the fireside, William one day persuaded her to drive out in her coach to watch. Sitting "warm enclosed in a mantle," she began to wish she could join the skaters—but only "as one of the skilfullest and most practised, and with security the ice was so firm as not to break." Returning home, Margaret's fancy conjured up a "moat frozen in my brain into a smooth, glassy ice, whereupon divers of my thoughts were sliding, of which, some slid fearfully, others as if they had been drunk . . . and some slid quite off their feet, and fell on the cold hard ice . . . yet most of my thoughts slid with a good grace and agility."[73]

Many letters told of Margaret's internal life—her imaginations, her ambitions, her fears, her affections, the happiness of her contemplative solitude, the torment of her shyness. Others recounted comic stories of her social gaffs and domestic inadequacies. Two letters described how, joining the philosophical and theological discussions of William and his friends, Margaret made them all laugh with her simplicity and innocence. Another told of an all-female "gossiping-meeting" to celebrate a child's christening. Here, having rebuked the other women for complaining of their husbands' faults, Margaret was scolded so violently that she fled speechless. "It hath so frighted me as I shall not hastily go to a gossiping-meeting again," she added. "As those that become cowards at the roaring noise of cannons, so I at the scolding voices of women." In two further letters Margaret laughed at her own childhood writings, her sixteen "baby books," which now seemed to her merely "a frippery or broker's-shop, wherein is nothing but remnants, bits and ends of several things, or like tailors' shreds, that are not fit for any use." Denouncing their "mist of nonsense, and clouds of ignorance," she mentioned the idea of burning them and these books do not now survive.[74]

Material for another tale of self-ridicule was provided by the complaints of Margaret's neighbors—that "my waiting-maids were spoiled with idleness, having nothing to do but to dress, curl and adorn themselves." When Margaret confronted her maids they laid all the blame on her, saying "that I did not set them to any employment . . . and that the truth was, they oftener heard of their lady, than heard or saw her themselves, I living so studious a life as they did not see me above once a week, nay, many times, not once in a fortnight." Resolving to reform and assume her proper domestic duties, Margaret summoned "the governess of my house"—the woman, probably her old maid Elizabeth Topp, to whom she entrusted all her day-to-day household affairs—and she "bid her give order to have flax and wheels bought, for I with my maids would sit and spin." But the governess only smiled "to think what uneven threads I would spin." "You will spoil more flax than get cloth by your spinning, as being an art that requires practice to learn it," she told her mistress, who was now "very much troubled . . . for I thought spinning had been easy." Margaret's high hopes for self-sufficiency in household linen—table cloths, napkins, sheets, underwear—were dashed, but she would not give up.

Knowing she had no skill in needlework—"for which I did inwardly complain of my education, that my mother did not force me to learn to work with a needle"—she then remembered watching her sisters make silk flowers. Again Margaret summoned her governess, "and told her that I would have her buy several coloured silks, for I was resolved to employ my time in making silk-flowers." But "madam, neither you nor any that serves you can do them so well as those who make it their trade," the governess objected, "wherefore you had better buy those toys, if you desire them."

Then Margaret decided "I would preserve, for it was summertime, and the fruit fresh and ripe upon the trees." But the governess only asked "for whom I would preserve, for I seldom did eat sweet-meats myself, nor made banquets for strangers." Besides, the governess added, think of the cost of the sugar and coal, "which go to the preserving only of a few sweet-meats that are good for nothing but to breed obstructions and rot the teeth." Far better, she argued, for Margaret's maids to be employed reading books, which "will enrich their understandings, and increase their knowledges, and quicken their wit, all which may make their life happy." "They cannot employ their time better than to read, nor your Ladyship better than to write." Though thinking that her writing was of little real use, Margaret yet decided to return to it, "not knowing what else to do." "I am fit for no other employment but to scratch paper," she concluded.[75]

These apparently autobiographical letters pose a puzzle to Margaret's readers. How far are they true descriptions of real events, how far embroidered or even invented to make a good story? They are narrated in the first person, but can this "I" who writes the letters be identified precisely with Margaret herself, or is she partly a fictional construction, created for this book? Did Margaret really have this discussion with her governess, or is this letter a comic fiction that also serves to justify Margaret's unconventional literary life to her contemporaries? Certainly, Margaret was not as domestically feckless as she here suggests. She was a shrewd money manager and, while in Antwerp, she collected a variety of culinary recipes from friends and relations—recipes for "almond butter," "barley cream," "white sugar candy," mead, metheglin,* for boiling and saucing or stewing a carp, and a method of fattening chickens.[76] Similarly, Margaret's comic letters portray her as socially distanced, both from gossiping women and from the debates of learned men, yet she had close friendships with women like the Duarte sisters and with philosophical men like Constantijn Huygens and Walter Charleton. Emphasizing, even exaggerating, her solitude and social isolation, both here and in her autobiography, had a double function for Margaret. Reinforcing her identity as a melancholic genius, this self-portrayal also defended her against the charges of immodesty and immorality that she feared her public profile as a woman writer would bring.

Margaret's letters tease her readers with the half-concealed identities of the many people who appear named only with initials. Various characters— "Lord W.N." (for William Newcastle), "Lord N. W.," "Lord N.N.," and "M.N." (for the marquess of Newcastle)—all seem to be modeled, at least to some extent, on her husband, while a musical lady called Mrs. D.U. is clearly one of the Duarte sisters.[77] Lord L.U.—who "studies, reads, writes, travels, inquires and searches for right and truth, because he is a wise man"—must represent Margaret's brother John, Lord Lucas. But are Mrs. P.I. and Lady P.Y., criticized in the letters for their excessive religious devotion, really intended to represent Margaret's sister, Lady Catherine Pye, whose daily prayers we know Margaret had found tedious as a child?[78] Again, Lord C.R. represents King Charles II ("Carolus Rex") in a letter that describes events similar to what really happened when the king visited the Newcastles in Antwerp.[79] But should we also

---

*A spiced form of mead, often used medicinally.

recognize the king in the Lord C.R. of a second letter—"an effeminate man" who spends his time "dancing, fiddling, visiting, junketting, attiring"?[80]

Like her plays, Margaret intended her letters "for profitable use," suggesting examples for her readers to imitate or shun. But where the plays' dialogue form had restricted Margaret to simply reporting her characters' actions and speeches—leaving her readers to resolve all the moral issues for themselves, with little authorial guidance—in her letters Margaret was free to pass comment on the events she described. Taking on the confident, authoritative voice of the social satirist, she reflected not only on her characters and their lives but also on the fashions and mores of her society—questioning, condemning, approving, laughing, moralizing, issuing judgments on etiquette and taste.

Her view of human nature was often pessimistic. Ignorance, envy, excessive emotion ungoverned by reason, vanity, pride, selfishness, disloyalty, sexual promiscuity, boasting, gambling, spiteful gossip—she ridiculed or denounced them all. "Constancy is as rarely seen as a blazing star,"* she wrote. "There are more cowards than valiant men." Seven-eighths of mankind "are ignorant dolts." "I do not wonder that there are pimps or bawds, for base vices and wicked baseness are too frequent in this age to be wondered at." "Surely the world was never so filled with fools."[81]

Male or female, old or young, scholarly or ignorant, aristocratic or plebeian, Anglican or puritan, no one escaped Margaret's satire. But especially she attacked the vices of her own class—the privileged and idle rich. Fashionable society was obsessively competitive, containing "more vainglory than pleasure, more pride than mirth, and more vanity than true content." "Everyone is against all, and all against everyone," she wrote in a reversal of the famous cry of the Three Musketeers. She mocked society's affected manners as "antic follies." She denounced its mindless following of fashion, making nothing but "mode-minds, mode-bodies, mode-appetites, mode-behaviours, mode-clothes, mode-pastimes or vices, mode-speeches and conversations." Its "malignant contagion of gossiping" she particularly disliked.[82]

As a moralist Margaret was conservative, supporting many of her society's traditional values, in spite of her own unconventional ambitions. She praised men for their valor and wisdom, women for their modesty, chastity, kindness, and good sense. The good wife "is patient with her husband's anger . . . obedient to her husband's honest commands, and had rather die or endure torment than to part or be divorced from him." "Those women who strike or cuckold their husbands are matrimonial traitors, for which they ought to be highly punished . . . for adultery they ought to suffer death."[83]

---

*I.e. a comet.

She also accepted many of her society's negative stereotypes of women—their endless talkativeness, their vanity, folly, and ignorance, their lack of self-control. And in her attacks she did not spare herself. She too spoke "foolishly," she thought, being just as subject as other women to "the nature of our sex (which is that we cannot refrain our tongues from speaking, although it be on such themes as we understand not)." Her overindulgence in fresh fruit, eating "so much as to make myself sick," proved her just as intemperate as other women, whose "appetites govern and rule the whole course of their lives." Luxury, Margaret wrote, was one of women's greatest pleasures, "in so much as they are for the most part eating."[84]

Margaret's satiric voice is often caustic, her anger scathing, and she feared her readers would criticize this too outspoken wit, "like meat that's too much brined and over-salt." She herself disliked the cruelty and abuse meted out by "satirical speakers" as she called them—people like pedantic scholars, alehouse pot companions, and scolding women whose talk was filled with "bitter reproofs . . . censuring and backbiting," "speaking ill of particular persons." But "satirical writers" were different, she argued. They attacked only "the general vices, follies and errors of mankind, pointing at no particular," and their aim was essentially constructive.* She summed up her intention:[85]

> *My wit indites for profitable use,*
> *That men may see their follies and their crimes,*
> *Their errors, vanities and idle times,*
> *Not that I think they do not know them well,*
> *But lest they should forget, I'm bold to tell.*

At first Margaret wrote quickly—more than sixty letters in only a fortnight, she later said. She had originally planned to publish the letters as an appendix to her volume of plays, now ready to be sent to the printers in England. But seeing how her new work had grown, and "fearing I should surfeit my readers with too great a volume," she changed her mind. Packing off her plays, she retained her letters, intending to make them up to a round hundred and then publish them as a separate volume. But exhausted by the rapid procession of her books—natural philosophy, then stories and plays, all written in the space of about four years—Margaret was finally forced to a halt, "finding my spirits of fancy grow weak and dull." "Having lately writ twenty-one plays,

---

*Of course Margaret's naming of her characters with initials did tend to point at real people, despite what she said here in self-defense.

with twelve [prefatory] epistles and one introduction, besides prologues and epilogues . . . my wit is drawn dry."[86]

Further discouragement soon followed, when news came that the ship carrying her plays to England had sunk and her work was "drowned . . . in the salt sea." Though somewhat consoled by the safety of her original manuscript—which she had as usual kept with her to be destroyed only when she saw her work in print—Margaret was nonetheless "extremely troubled."[87] She would send no more manuscripts to England. Publication of both her letters and her plays would now have to wait until she herself returned home.

Chapter Eleven

Restoration, 1658–1662

*I*n 1656 King Charles II had left Germany for Flanders, where the Spanish government, at war with both France and Cromwellian England, offered him an invasion force of 6,000 troops, fully paid and equipped, if the royalists could only secure an English port for landing them. Funded by a monthly pension from the Spanish, Charles and his court settled first at Bruges and then in Brussels, where they worked (often hard but always ineffectively) to raise rebellion in England. Meanwhile the king's military followers formed into regiments, Irish, Scots, and English. With Charles's brother James, duke of York, as commander in chief, they joined the Spanish defense against a combined French and English attack.

Since the negotiations with the Scots at Breda in 1650, William and Margaret had seen the king only once, when he passed through Antwerp on his way from France to Germany. But now, with Charles just thirty miles away, they could rejoin English court life. There were visits to Brussels, ostensibly "to take the air" as a spy reported to Cromwell, but doubtless also for William to share the king's political councils. Here too Margaret would have seen her old philosophical friend Walter Charleton, who joined the court in the spring of 1656. Though rumored to be a Cromwellian spy, "for which he is well rewarded," Charleton was nevertheless appointed royal physician to Charles II.[1]

King and court were also occasional visitors at the Rubens House. With William, they repaired to the riding house where, on one occasion, Charles himself rode. William, who had first taught the young prince to ride some twenty years before, was overjoyed to see "that His Majesty made my horses go better than any Italian or French riders (who had often rid them) could do." On another occasion, the two men competed at the archery butts where Charles, the loser, jokingly accused William of being a sharp gambler—

"although their stakes were not considerable, but only for pastime," Margaret noted. The king's wit was always ready for pleasantries. Passing through Antwerp one time, he dined privately with William; seeing Margaret afterwards, "he did merrily and in jest tell me that he perceived my Lord's credit could procure better meat than his own."[2]

In many ways, the Newcastles really were better off than their monarch. Charles II—a political embarrassment to the Spanish, who hoped to make peace with Cromwellian England—had as yet received no official recognition from the government, whereas William, like other royalist exiles, had been exempted from paying all taxes and excise.[3] With Spanish funds depleted by the loss of two American treasure fleets, captured by Cromwell's navy, Charles's government pension was paid only irregularly. Meanwhile William received £500 every quarter from his sons in England, and a further £100 from his daughter Jane. It was not a great deal—only a little more than the income William had provided as his youngest son's inheritance before the war. But with strict economy, and with the credit extended by the Antwerp tradesmen who supplied the household's daily needs, it was possible to live "nobly, plentifully and pleasantly," Margaret found.[4]

During 1658 the Newcastles' finances improved further, when William's son Charles, viscount Mansfield, sold off a substantial family estate near Welbeck. Much of the £2,730 raised went straight to the Rubens House, where William spread it among his many creditors. At the same time he consolidated the household's debts, taking out loans from two of Antwerp's wealthiest English merchants and using them to pay off "such scores as were most pressing, contracted from the poorer sort of tradesmen." Margaret, with her faith in the buying power of cash, was probably the moving force behind a further measure, as the household began to "send ready money to market"—"to avoid cozenage," Margaret explained, "for small scores run up most unreasonably, especially if no strict accounts be kept and the rate [of interest] be left to the creditor's pleasure." By these means, "there was in a short time so much saved as it could not have been imagined."[5]

In February 1658 much of British émigré society descended on Antwerp, where Charles II met his brothers James, duke of York, and Henry, duke of Gloucester, and his sister Mary, princess of Orange for a few days. Courtiers filled the city with their fashionable occupations—gambling, quarrels, duels, gossip, political news and speculation. On Tuesday, February 16, the ceremonies of the Order of the Garter, normally held at Windsor Castle and rarely performed in exile, were briefly revived. William and the earl of Bristol together presented the Flemish nobleman, Jean Ferdinand de Marsin, comte de Graville (appointed lieutenant general of the British army in Flanders the year before) to the king, who knighted him and bestowed the insignia of George and Garter. Then the Newcastle household spent the next day, Wednesday the 17th, preparing for what Margaret modestly called "a small entertainment" for "all the royal race."[6]

That evening high society thronged to the Rubens House. As well as the four British royals for whom the event had been arranged, the invited guests included the earl of Bristol and his grown-up children, the duchess of Lorraine with her son and daughter, and Jacques Duarte and his sisters. Behind them came a crowd of courtiers and onlookers, all struggling at the doors for admission to the splendors within. "Loud music"—perhaps a fanfare of trumpets and drums—welcomed the king's entry. Then, when everyone was placed, the proceedings opened with a speech delivered by Michael Mohun. Believed by many of his contemporaries to be "the best actor in the world," Mohun had acted leading roles in the prewar London theaters, and then joined the royalist army, where he still served as a major.[7] Tonight, though, he resumed theatrical costume, appearing in a black satin robe, with a garland of gilded bay leaves on his head, to recite the verses William had written for the occasion—a panegyric of Charles II, "wherein as much was said of compliment to his Majesty as the highest hyperboles could possibly express," one observer thought.

After two hours of dancing—French dances, elegant and courtly—the Newcastles' black page boy entered, and sang a song, with words written by William and music composed by the former court musician, Nicholas Lanier. Black servants were still rare in Europe, so the page's prominent role in entertaining the king was a mark both of the Newcastles' high aristocratic status, and of the honor they desired to show their monarch. "Dressed all up in feathers" (in a manner perhaps intended to echo the costume of American Indians), he also provided an element of the exotic. Next came "a great banquet," borne in on eight vast platters by sixteen gentlemen of the king's court, and served with "wine and other drinks . . . to all the company." Then "they danced again for two hours more"—boisterous English country dances now that the evening was wearing on.

The occasion was a social gem in miniature. In the elegant but constricted space of the Rubens House, guests admired their hosts' arrangement of "all circumstances of greatness in a little volume," and conflicting rumors circulated over who was the true author of their entertainment: some thought that Margaret not William had written the verses they heard. Meanwhile, the ladies took note of Margaret's latest mode of dress: "The Marchioness of Newcastle wears no ribbons," the duchess of Lorraine observed with interest.[8] At last the entertainment closed with an epilogue, again spoken by Major Mohun, prophesying the restoration of Charles II to his throne.

The next day, all was quiet in Antwerp. Society rested. The only event of any import was the sudden appearance of the lord chancellor, Sir Edward Hyde, who had absented himself from the Newcastles' festivities. "The Lord Chancellor is strangely recovered of his gout," one courtier commented wryly, while another speculated that Hyde had hidden himself away until now for fear that "the ladies might have taken him out to dance." Then on Friday the post filled with letters as the courtiers informed their less fortunate friends of how "we spend our time merrily here."[9]

However, with so many courtiers gathered together, such merriment could not last. "I fear faction . . . [will] speedily ensue," William's old friend Sir Edward Walker predicted on Friday, February 19, and within just a few days William and Margaret were thoroughly embroiled. In spite of their grand hospitality and their friendly relations with the king, the Newcastles were political outsiders who had been told nothing of the latest plan to restore Charles II to his throne. William was judged unfit to receive "so important a secret"—"it might as well be proclaimed at the cross," one of Hyde's agents commented. But rival courtiers, jealous of Hyde's influence with the king and eager to stir up trouble, now leaked the great secret: the marquess of Ormonde, his identity concealed beneath a wig, was already in London, conducting secret negotiations with royalist agents in hopes of raising a rebellion against Cromwell. Furious at his exclusion from the plot, William spoke freely, telling all who came to the Rubens House that Ormonde could never succeed. When Hyde's agents tried to persuade him that Ormonde was still in Germany, William only replied that his sources were impeccable and then continued to rant.

Margaret was even angrier, convinced that the husband she so admired deserved a leading role in political life. She "hath the vanity to swear (God damn her) the affair cannot, nor shall not, be effected without her husband," an agent reported to Secretary of State Sir Edward Nicholas. It was she who had stirred up William to be so angry, the same observer thought. Lacking all prudence, the couple continued to talk of the matter until their words reached Hyde himself, who reported them to the king. Charles was "much offended" but, feeling "real kindness" for his old tutor, he blamed the affair rather on "the malice of those who informed him." His reproofs to William were gentle, and when the court left Antwerp a few days later the two parted friends.[10]

Margaret, however, remained sore at the criticism she had received. Anxious to justify her behavior, she added an account of the incident to her "sociable letters." "Truly those words I spoke were not through an evil design or malicious nature," she explained. She had acted only with "good intention" towards the king and Ormonde, and "out of a deep consideration of the evil that was likely to ensue both to their honour and disadvantage of their affairs." Declaring her doubts, she hoped, would "make them circumspect and cautious in their adventures, as to consider their own weakness and their enemies' power, and not rashly to venture hand over head." "Neither were these words spoken in a public assembly, but in my private house," she added, "and every-one's house is, or should be, a privileged place, out of which informers ought to be banished, rather than the owners condemned."[11]

Meanwhile Ormonde's mission, like all its predecessors, came to nothing. Chased round London by Cromwell's spies, while the rain washed the color out of his wig, the marquess soon returned to the king, reporting that no rebellion was possible. Only in September 1658, when Oliver Cromwell died, did the royalists' fortunes begin to change. Richard Cromwell succeeded his father as Lord Protector, but in April 1659 the army seized power. Always politically radical and long dissatisfied with the Protectorate, they reestab-lished the same revolutionary Parliament that had executed King Charles I in 1649. Against so unpopular a regime there was finally the real possibility of raising a royalist rebellion.

In Antwerp hopes were high at this "most excellent news." Eagerly, William gathered the latest information from English merchants and travelers. "Great confusions and alterations is daily looked for, and I hope in God it will produce excellent things for the King," he wrote, but "we have so many lies here at Antwerp that we know not what to believe."[12] That summer there were scattered royalist rebellions, all easily crushed by the army. But as the political divisions among England's governors grew and the army first dismissed their Parliament and then recalled it, the exiles were not discouraged. By December 1659, William was confident that Charles II could expect "a speedy restora-tion."[13]

As his long-cherished hopes for this "happy restoration" gradually turned into "firm belief," William began to compose a "little book" of political advice for the benefit of his royal master.[14] The work was in a long tradition of advice books written for monarchs by their subjects—a tradition that included both Machiavelli's *Il Principe* (written for Lorenzo de' Medici) and Thomas More's *Utopia* (for Henry VIII).

William's book was a thorough guide to how a restored English monarchy should be governed. Starting with the army and militia—the force on which he believed a king's power must rest—William proceeded to the navy and the merchant shipping. Then came religion and the church: Anglicanism must be reestablished, William argued, because of the power it gave the king, making him "not only an absolute king, but pope within your dominions." To prevent a return of civil war, religious debate must be prevented and orthodoxy enforced, "for controversy is a civil war with the pen, which pulls out the sword soon afterwards." As for the law, the abuses of the most notorious courts—like the Court of Wards, where young people were "bought and sold like horses"—must be reformed, and the "most horrid corruption" that William had seen amongst judges before the war must be prevented. Merchants and manufacturing industries must be encouraged as the true basis of the country's wealth, while monopolies—"the most destructive thing to the Commonwealth in the world"—must be abolished. Various features that William admired in the Netherlands were also recommended—draining lands and planting acorns were important agricultural measures, he suggested, while two forts like those at Antwerp should provide military dominance over London, "that great leviathan, that monster . . . that rebellious city" that had headed the opposition to the king during the Civil War.

As for the king himself, William advised the necessity of keeping up the grandest ceremonial both "in your own person and court." In public appearances, the king must "show yourself gloriously to your people, like a god . . . and when the people sees you thus, they will down of their knees, which is worship, and pray for you with trembling fear and love, as they did to Queen Elizabeth"—who was so admired, William recalled, that "of a Sunday when she opened the window, the people would cry, 'oh Lord, I saw her hand, I saw her hand'." William also cautioned Charles II against the many errors that had been committed by his father and grandfather in failing to follow this great queen's example: the Stuarts' worst fault, he thought, was their immoderate spending, which had subjected them to Parliament's power. Last of all, William gave brief advice on governing Scotland and Ireland, and on foreign relations.

The work was the summation of William's long political experience, systematizing the maxims and opinions that he had been telling Margaret for years.[15] In his pragmatism, his secularism, his advocacy of the strong rule of an absolute monarch, William reveals his close affinity with authoritarian political theorists like Machiavelli and Hobbes. His aim, he told the king, was "to present your Majesty with truths, which great monarchs seldom hear," truths that were "not only the honestest, but so the wisest, that a dutiful servant can offer." And with this very private concern, William had no intention of printing his "little book." Instead he copied it out neatly in his own hand—a mark of respect to its royal recipient. His manuscript copy was then finely bound—in white vellum, lettered in gold, and tied with blue silk ribbon—before being sent to the king.

In June, amidst all the Newcastles' hopes and plans, had come devastating news from England. William's eldest son, Charles, viscount Mansfield, had died of a "dead palsy"—a stroke—although he was only in his thirties.[16] "He was a matchless son, a truly noble and virtuous person," Sir Edward Nicholas attempted to console William. "It has pleased God to take him to Himself as too good for this wicked world; it must be a great comfort that he is translated to a better place."[17]

The loss of their favorite brother fell heavily on William's daughters, who also grieved that Charles had left no children. Even "a girl of his would have been some comfort," Elizabeth wrote to her sister Jane, but Charles's only daughter had died in infancy. For some months there were hopes that his widow might yet be pregnant, but by September the prospect of an heir was fading. Charles's younger brother Henry now assumed the title of viscount Mansfield—with unseemly haste, his sisters thought, for if Charles's widow should yet produce a son, Henry would have to give up the title, which "will be much to his dishonour." "Tis happy we have a brother to hold up the family," Elizabeth tried to persuade herself, but Henry's coldness and pride offered his sisters little compensation for the loss of the witty, warm-hearted Charles.[18]

On William—desperate for male heirs "to inherit his estate and to keep up his family"—the pain of Charles's loss fell especially heavily. Now there remained only Henry, who himself had just one surviving child, his four-year-old daughter Elizabeth—"pretty Betty" or "the little lady" as the family called her.[19] Guilt again haunted Margaret. In one of her "sociable letters" she tried to answer her conscience, arguing that a woman whose husband already had sons by his first marriage had no need to regret her own childlessness. But in reality William needed a grandson before Margaret could absolve herself from blame. For Henry and his wife to have "many sons" would be "the greatest blessing" she could have, Margaret told her husband. Daily she hoped and prayed "for that comfort to us all."[20]

Financial worries also followed on Charles's death. Henry, as the new viscount Mansfield, inherited the house at Welbeck and the majority of his brother's estates, but many lands also went to Charles's widow, according to the couple's marriage treaty of 1654. William urged his younger son to reach an agreement with the widow and take the lands from her on a long lease, thus keeping them in the family's control.[21]

Much more important to William were the household contents, which were now forfeit to pay off the debts Charles had left on his death. There were family portraits by Steenwijk and Van Dyck "which are most rare," as well as rich wall hangings and upholstery—always among the most valuable of seventeenth-century house contents. One state bed alone was upholstered in purple velvet, with gold lace and embroidery worth at least £300. William was tormented that these family heirlooms, "so long gathering by your ancestors, should be destroyed in a moment." "As you love me and yourself, save the best of the goods," he begged Henry. Everything should be valued—"and goods are never appraised at a third part of their value," William advised—and then Henry should buy the most precious items, even if it meant selling land to raise the money. "The land may easily be recovered but these things never."[22]

But distrust was growing between father and son. William begged Henry not to believe the "parasitical, sycophantical rascals, fools and knaves" who warned him that his father would shortchange him in financial matters.

> If ever I see you [in England], I will give you the money and the goods to boot, so that all my intention is but to save them for you. For I protest that is all the design my wife and I have in that business, for believe me she is as kind to you as she was to your brother, and so good a wife as she [is] all for my family, which she expresses is only you.

"I pray you, as you love me, take them and save them for yourself," William wrote, as his letters went unanswered. "I am in great pain until I hear you do so."[23]

His desperation was compounded by financial necessity: he had not yet received his quarterly allowance—£500 from Henry and a further £100 from Jane. "I am daily and infinitely tortured with my creditors," he told his son. Only in mid-November did relief finally come, when William heard that Henry had bought back the family heirlooms, and that his own income would arrive in Antwerp shortly. Just one worry remained: Henry wanted to begin major building alterations at Welbeck. "Let it alone for a while," William begged, "for truly if, please God, I ever see you, I will make Welbeck a very fine place for you."[24]

Then, early in 1660, the government of England changed again. Amid growing political disorder, Parliament requested protection from George Monck, the general commanding the English army in Scotland. On February 3 Monck and his soldiers entered London; a few weeks later he dissolved Parliament and ordered new elections. Soon Monck and other of England's most powerful men were negotiating secretly with the exiled king.

Charles's own inclinations were always for an absolutist monarchy. By the end of his reign he would achieve many of the authoritarian measures that William had recently proposed in his little book of political advice—notably a royal financial supply independent of Parliament and a standing army under the king's direct command, permanently ready to crush rebellion. But now he was in no position to make demands, and along with his three closest advisers—Edward Hyde, Edward Nicholas, and the marquess of Ormonde—he produced a masterpiece of compromise. The Declaration of Breda, issued on

April 4, promised pardon for all parliamentarians, except the few regicides responsible for the execution of Charles I. Almost all matters of church and state were referred to the decision of future parliaments.

This was the sort of restoration of royal rule that William had most feared. The king needed to take "a good army," either French or Spanish, he had advised Edward Nicholas just five weeks earlier, "for you know what this Parliament did heretofore."[25] However, the new Parliament that met on April 25 was fervently pro-royal. In spite of the law forbidding their election, many old royalists won seats. William's son, Henry, was elected as an MP for Derbyshire—aided by "a trick of returning the writs," and accompanied by a troop of cavalry to quell the Anabaptists who, "believing his passion to serve the King, threatened to take him dead or alive."[26] Elsewhere, Henry's father-in-law "Wise William" Pierrepont was also elected, as was Jane's husband, Charles Cheyne. Just six days after convening, the new Parliament received the Declaration of Breda and voted unanimously to restore the king. Two weeks later, Charles moved to the Hague, where Dutch and British joined in a week of celebrations, with banquets, balls, speeches, fireworks, and gun salutes.

Leaving Margaret in charge of the house in Antwerp, William rushed to join the king. Rewards—in the form of noble titles and government offices—were beginning to be distributed, and William was concerned to secure both his own position and that of his son, Henry. In particular he hoped to be made master of the horse, governing the royal stables and orchestrating all the king's journeys and processions. Like William's earlier job as governor of the Prince of Wales, it was a post of grandeur and honor, without the arduous paperwork and interpersonal machinations involved in real political office. The appointment would also acknowledge his position as one of Europe's leading equestrians.

However, at the Hague, the king told William that the post was already promised to George Monck. Duke of Albemarle, Knight of the Garter, commander in chief of the army, privy councillor—Monck was showered in honors and powerful positions as a reward for his role in engineering the Restoration. Many of the exiled courtiers were also rewarded. Edward Hyde was confirmed in his offices, while Henrietta Maria's agent Lord Jermyn was made earl of St. Albans. But William received nothing. Charles was friendly and the duke of York offered him the use of one of the British ships waiting to transport the court to England. But William declined. Ordering his servants to hire him his own ship, he took leave of the king and set out for Rotterdam with a large group of friends and followers. However, seeing the "old rotten frigate" that William's servants had hired, most of the company turned back, saying they "would not endanger their lives in it." Only young Lord Widdrington, the son of William's Civil War friend, remained, being "resolved not to forsake my Lord," Margaret recorded.

William embarked at once, "so transported with the joy of returning into his native country, that he regarded not the vessel" (which did indeed sink on its next voyage). However, he and Widdrington were soon becalmed in the North Sea. Six days and six nights passed before William saw the smoke of London on the skyline, as if in a dream. "'Surely,' said he, 'I have been sixteen years asleep and am not thoroughly awake yet.'" That night he slept at Greenwich, "where his supper seemed more savory to him than any meat he had hitherto tasted, and the noise of some scraping fiddlers he thought the pleasantest harmony that ever he had heard." There he was finally reunited with Henry, who had almost given up his father for lost when he found that William was not among the king's party, which had already landed at Dover. "With what joy they embraced and saluted each other, my pen is too weak to express," Margaret wrote.[27]

She herself was still in Antwerp, "left alone there with some of my servants." From the Hague, William had written to tell her of his intention to return to England, at the same time "commanding" her to stay behind "as a pawn for his debts, until he could compass money to discharge them." Her wait now stretched into months for, although "my Lord's affection to me was such that it made him very industrious," yet "it being uncertain . . . whether he should have anything of his estate, made it a difficult business for him to borrow money."[28]

In London king and court were once again established at Whitehall, while a busy Parliament forged the details of the Restoration settlement, addressing such vexed questions as the punishment of the regicides and the restoration of the Crown and church lands that had been confiscated and sold off to private individuals during the Interregnum. William, still one of the king's privy councillors, returned regularly to his seat in the House of Lords. Here, although no general law had been passed for restoring their confiscated possessions to the king's followers, eleven named lords were given permission to present private bills to the House "for reparation of their losses." On August 7, William combined with the duke of Buckingham and the earl of Bristol to bring in the first such bill.[29] As it passed through the Lords and then received royal assent, William could at last borrow the money he needed to release his wife from pawn.

But when Margaret began to pay off their Antwerp debts, she found that the money sent by William was some £400 short of what she needed, "what with the expense I had made in the meanwhile, and what was required for my transporting into England, besides the debts formerly contracted." Margaret knew she could, just "upon my own word," have borrowed much more than this from Antwerp's citizens, "yet I was unwilling to leave an engagement amongst strangers." So she sent for one of Antwerp's wealthiest English merchants, John Shaw, and asked him for the loan she needed.[30]

To arrange the details of the business, Margaret relied on Francis Topp, the husband of her waiting-maid Elizabeth (née Chaplain). Little evidence now remains to tell us about this obscure Antwerp merchant. Genealogists suggest a possible link to the Topp family of Stockton in Wiltshire, and Francis was perhaps the Mr. Topp, also called Mr. Hartopp, who lent money to several royalist exiles in Antwerp during the late 1650s.[31] Certainly Francis Topp had become very useful to the Newcastles. In 1658, he was one of the two merchants who lent William the money he needed to consolidate all his smaller debts to tradesmen. Thereafter, Topp rendered further service, gathering English political news and regularly advancing credit to the Newcastles a couple of months before the arrival of William's quarterly income from England.[32] Now, in September 1660, Topp presented Mr. Shaw with the Newcastles' outstanding bills for payment—£200 owed in rent for the Rubens House, £90 owed to the coachmaker, £170 owed for silks and velvets, plus a further £190 for beer. The final grand total was £676 3s.[33]

Meanwhile there was a house full of possessions, the accumulation of fifteen years of exile, to be packed up. There was doubtless a profusion of the fine furniture, glassware, and tapestries for which Antwerp was widely famed. One set of tapestries in particular, representing the four Evangelists, was so fine that tourists seeing it in England readily believed reports that it had cost William £2,000. Then too there was Margaret's microscope and all the lenses and tubes for the telescopes that the family had acquired in Paris. A weighty collection of copperplates—forty-odd from William's book of horsemanship—was also carried to England, as probably were the three plates Margaret used as frontispieces to her books.[34]

As her departure approached, Margaret received a formal visit from Antwerp's city government. Through Jacques Duarte as interpreter, the magistrates said polite farewells to one of their city's most eminent residents, telling her how they "rejoiced at our happy returning into our native country, and wished me soon and well to the place where I most desired to be." William had already asked Margaret to excuse his hasty departure from the city and she rose to the occasion, offering the magistrates "mine and my Lord's hearty thanks for their great civilities, declaring how sorry I was that it lay not in my power to make an acknowledgement answerable to them." After the magistrates had left, their servants returned "(as the custom there is) with a present of wine," which Margaret received "with all respect and thankfulness."

The formalities over, Margaret and her servants left with their baggage train for Flushing, some fifty miles away, where they hoped to find safe passage on an English man-of-war. Finding no suitable ships in port, they waited, for Margaret was "loath to trust myself with a less vessel." At last she heard there was a Dutch man-of-war waiting to accompany a convoy of merchants to England. Sending for the captain, Margaret asked if she could travel aboard his ship, and he willingly obtained his government's permission. Margaret and her "chief servants" embarked on the Dutch naval vessel, while the rest sailed with the household goods, aboard "another good strong vessel, hired for that purpose."[35]

ENGLAND WAS IN EUPHORIA at the Restoration. The king's entry into London in May had been a thing of wonder,

> with a triumph of above 20,000 horse and foot, brandishing their swords and shouting with inexpressible joy: the ways strewed with flowers, the bells ringing, the streets hung with tapestry, fountains running with wine . . . the windows and balconies all set with ladies, trumpets, music and [myriads] of people flocking the streets.

"I stood in the Strand and beheld it and blessed God," John Evelyn recalled. To him, as to many others, it seemed a divine miracle that, "after a most bloody and unreasonable rebellion of near twenty years," the king should finally be reinstated "without one drop of blood, and by that very army which rebelled against him." "Such a restoration was never seen in the mention of any history, ancient or modern, since the return of the Babylonian captivity," Evelyn exclaimed. "Praised be forever the Lord of Heaven, who only does wondrous things."[36]

For Margaret there was huge relief at surviving the poverty of exile. "Certainly, it was a work of Divine Providence," a "blessing of the eternal and merciful God, in whose power are all things." The future, however, she regarded with caution. "Princes forget to reward when they have power, although they never forget to promise rewards when they have no power," she had already predicted: "we shall only find ruins, meet with opposers and have debts attend upon us."[37]

Nonetheless, Margaret was furious when she confronted the reality. In London she found William, not in his grand town house at Clerkenwell, but living in lodgings—"I cannot call them unhandsome; but yet they were not fit for a person of his rank and quality, nor of the capacity to contain all his family. Neither did I find my Lord's condition such as I expected."[38] All William's services and sufferings for the royalist cause still remained unrewarded. He had no place in the Committee for Foreign Affairs—the inner circle of the king's advisers, which included William's old rivals Edward Hyde and the marquess of Ormonde, along with former Cromwellians like George Monck. Hyde had now emerged as the king's principal minister, a position he would hold for seven years.

"Out of some passion," Margaret demanded that they leave town and retire to live on William's country estates, but her husband only "reproved me for my rashness and impatience." William still had business to complete in London. Although the estates confiscated by the Interregnum government had now been restored to him by private Act of Parliament, many possessions still remained in a legal limbo. Lands which he or his sons had themselves sold during the Interregnum were not covered by the act. To recover such property, which included his Clerkenwell town house, William would have to go to law—a complicated, expensive, and time-consuming affair.[39] Then too there were the lands that had been bought by regicides. These, by Act of Parliament, were now all given to the king, who passed them on to his brother James. Only by the duke of York's special dispensation would these estates return to William's hands.

Most other royalists, without the private Act of Parliament allowed to William, were even worse off. Margaret's brother John would have to recover all his own confiscated estates through the law courts. For destruction of property, for household contents confiscated, for the financial difficulties suffered while paying off the Interregnum government's crippling fines on delinquents, there was no redress whatever. John took what revenge he could, prosecuting his old Colchester enemies for misappropriating charitable funds.[40] But the family's home at St. John's, twice ruined because of their loyalty to the king, would never be restored. By the eighteenth century the area within the old abbey walls had become a garden, and only the great gatehouse and the garden mount remained from the Lucases' occupation, as they still do today.[41] John's bitterness was further compounded by the loss of his wife. Lady Anne Lucas died on August 22, 1660, the eighteenth anniversary of the looting of St. John's, leaving a single daughter, Mary, who would inherit all her father's lands.[42]

Soon after Margaret's arrival in London, William managed to move the household into grander accommodation. Dorset House, situated on Salisbury Court, just south of Fleet Street, was the town house of the earls of Dorset. However, Margaret was still unhappy, "we having but a part of the said house in possession." Furthermore, the move suggested that William had no plans for the swift departure from London that she so desired.[43]

The elegance of London life resumed. King and court drove once again in Hyde Park, with "abundance of gallantry."[44] Anglican ceremonies returned to the churches. Public theaters reopened. The reception rooms of Whitehall thronged with high society, decked out in its finest. Foreign ambassadors and English country gentry alike paid their respectful addresses to the new monarch. Royal processions passed through the streets, where old friends met once again after long separation.

Charles II and his brothers passed their evenings as the supper guests of the numerous aristocrats now gathered in the city, and it was probably for such an occasion at Dorset House that William composed a new royal entertainment, celebrating the king's restoration. In more humorous vein than the Antwerp entertainment of 1658, the piece included a comic Welshman and a sick poet, who faints away when he finds himself tongue-tied in the presence of the monarch. Dances and five songs—requiring three singers and a band of instruments—completed the spectacle.[45]

Many old friends from exile doubtless visited the Newcastles at Dorset House, and among the rest came Richard Flecknoe. Flecknoe now praised William lavishly as a "god of hospitality," and for Margaret he composed a lengthy poem, "The Portrait of William, Marquis of Newcastle." Eulogizing her husband's many virtues—his "piercing wit," his "quickness, energy and force," his Civil War generalship, his aristocratic largesse, his literary production—the poem ended with a joyful prophecy of the couple's imminent return to the Midlands when, amidst the dancing of "the nymphs and swains of Sherwood,"

> Welbeck and Bolsol* shall behold again
> Their noble lord as flourishing, and more,
> Than e'er in better times he was before.

Flecknoe had the verse printed in a three-page pamphlet especially for Margaret, and he also included it in the volume of *Heroick Portraits*, which he published in 1660 in praise of Charles II and other desirable royal and aristocratic patrons.**

William's children were in London too, with the grandchildren whom he had never seen. Frances would remain childless, but Jane had a son and two daughters, while Elizabeth, pregnant almost every year, bore nine children—of whom five sons and one daughter survived. In 1660 a second daughter was

---

*I.e. Bolsover Castle.
**Flecknoe had recently been writing verses in praise of Cromwell but now he, like many other English poets, did a rapid U-turn.

born to Henry, named Frances after her mother, but there was still no male heir for William.

Margaret returned from exile full of gratitude to her stepchildren "who did all that lay in their power to support and relieve my Lord their father* in his banishment." They were "dutiful and obedient children, free from vices, noble and generous both in their natures and actions," she added.[46] Yet the relationship was not as straightforward as her published writing suggests. Henry's suspicions of his father and stepmother's financial plans had already surfaced in 1659. With William's daughters there was a further source of friction. Although Jane and Elizabeth were keen writers (like Margaret herself), they conformed to their culture's ideal of feminine modesty, shunning publication and writing only for their inmost family circle.[47] Elizabeth encouraged her own daughter (also named Elizabeth) to write, and the female family's attitude to Margaret's public literary career is clearly apparent in a poem the young Elizabeth wrote for her mother.

> *Madam, I dedicate these lines to you,*
> *To whom, I do confess, volumes are due,*
> *Hoping your wonted goodness will excuse*
> *The errors of an infant, female muse.*
> *'Mongst ladies, let Newcastle wear the bays,*
> *I only sue for pardon, not for praise.*[48]

Eventually William received some reward for his long loyalty to the king when, on September 21, 1660, he attended the court at Whitehall to be sworn in as a gentleman of the bedchamber. This was one of the highest court appointments: the gentlemen attended on the king through the day in the most private spaces of the court—the privy chamber, withdrawing chamber, and the bedchamber. But for William the post was a sinecure—at once symbolizing the king's favor and bringing a salary of £1,000 per annum.[49] A job of more real power came his way on October 1, when Charles II made him lord lieutenant of Nottinghamshire—an appointment he had held for some eighteen years before the Civil War. William would return home to Welbeck as the most important man in his county, the king's immediate deputy in the administration of both the law and the armed forces.

Soon after this (and not very long after Margaret's arrival in London) William told her that "he had dispatched his business and was now resolved to remove into the country." The wagons to transport their goods were already

---

*And thus Margaret herself, of course.

ordered—"no unpleasant news to me, who had a great desire for a country life." As etiquette demanded, William went to Whitehall to request the king's permission to depart from the court, so "that he might retire into the country to reduce and settle, if possible, his confused, entangled and almost ruined estate."

> "Sir," said he to his Majesty, "I am not ignorant that many believe I am discontented; but I take God to witness that I am in no kind or ways displeased; for I am so joyed at your Majesty's happy restoration that I cannot be sad or troubled for any concern to my own particular."

The next day he and Margaret left London for the Midlands.[50]

THE JOURNEY NORTH took up to a week. One hundred and twenty miles from London, the travelers crossed the River Trent and entered Nottingham, "one of the most pleasant and beautiful towns in England." Beneath the now-ruinous castle where Charles I had raised his standard eighteen years before, the town looked out over a lushly meadowed vale. Long wide streets ("much like London") divided houses "lofty and well built." In the "incomparable fine marketplace" was "a vast plenty of provisions and those of the best sort"—fish from the Trent, local meat, corn, liquorice, livestock, and firewood, cheeses from Warwickshire, and foreign imports brought by water from Hull, as well as the products of the town's own industries: earthenware, glass, knitted stockings, and some "excellent" strong pale ale. Nottingham was not just the county town but also "the most considerable [town] in all that part of England."

Next day came the final leg of the journey. Just outside Nottingham, the travelers entered Sherwood Forest, whose ancient stories told of Robin Hood and "trees so entangled in one another, that a single person could hardly walk in the paths of it." The woods were now much thinner—intensively managed to provide timber for the local charcoal industry, or kept as hunting parks for the aristocracy—but they still covered most of the western part of the county, crossed by streams flowing east to the Trent, and interspersed with villages and farmland. This was William's homeland, populated with his friends and relations, his tenants and his servants. To the west, as the ground climbed towards the wild moors of the Derbyshire Peak District, lay the houses of Hardwick and Chatsworth, built by William's grandmother, Bess of Hardwick, and now owned by his cousins, the earls of Devonshire. To the east, in Lincolnshire's rich lowland of meadows, orchards, and cornfields, William's son, Henry, lived at his house of Glentworth. To the north, William's estates extended into Yorkshire. Then, a hundred miles further north, he was one of largest landowners in Northumberland, related through his mother to many of the county's leading families.

Some twenty miles from Nottingham, in a valley surrounded by woods, the travelers finally reached Welbeck itself, "noble, large and magnificent."[51] The house spread wide and low, its three wings forming a T shape. The main approach—through an archway in the fanciful stable-block that William had built in the 1620s—brought one into the great court. On the left lay the riding house, also built in the 1620s, where William trained his horses. Ahead, beyond the double gates by the porter's lodge, was the west front of the main house, with stairs running up to a grand porch. Inside was fine living accommodation and the medieval great hall, decorated with painted carving.

This wing formed the stem of the T that made the house. The T's top—looking out southwards over formal gardens, with a canal and a pair of water houses—was in two parts. The eastern end still retained the irregular facade and gothic arched windows of the old monastery on which the house was based. But the western end had been remodeled by William's father, working with the architect Robert Smithson, to create a masterpiece of Jacobean formality, with regular ranks of square-topped mullioned windows beneath twin towers and a central cupola. The whole formed a curious mixture of ancient and modern—there were even some half-timbered buildings on the east front—but everyone agreed that it was "a noble edifice," a "palace . . . handsome and stately," where

> . . . the rooms be vast and everything
> Seems made for entertainment of a king.[52]

However, the Newcastles' arrival in the autumn of 1660 was not so grand. They found the house "much out of repair," and all the furniture that William remembered in his old home—"very noble and rich"—was gone. Silver plate worth £3,800, with "several curiosities of cabinets, cups and other things," had been taken by Welbeck's royalist garrison: William had been paid only £1,100 for it, "which money was sent him beyond the seas."[53] Of all the gleaming golden lamps, the precious tapestries shining with scarlet and gold, the carpets and thrones and purple pillows that had greeted King Charles I at Welbeck in 1634, little remained. There survived only "some few hangings and pictures"—the tapestries and family portraits by Steenwijk and Van Dyck that William had especially asked Henry to save. Of the 150 suites of hangings that had embellished the rooms of William's various houses "there were not above ten or twelve saved." All the sets of fine table linen—including one bought especially for the entertainment of Charles I and Henrietta Maria, at a cost of

£160—were gone. Even William's most basic "household stuff"—the bedding and linen, and the kitchen equipment of pewter and brass—was lost, all except "some few old featherbeds, and those all spoiled, and fit for no use."[54]

The effect was devastating. However, the house was not completely empty. Henry's wife, Frances, had kindly left some of her own furniture behind for her in-laws, "the Marquesses," when she and her husband vacated the house early in October. Six bedsteads, thirteen tables, two screens, four sets of chairs and stools, six gilt candlesticks, two red leather carpets and two suits of armor, with four iron grates and various pots and pans and other kitchen equipment—for all these items William would reimburse his son the following summer.[55]

From Welbeck, the Newcastles soon drove out to inspect William's more extended possessions. At Bolsover Castle, his second grand house, just over the border into Derbyshire, they found even worse. Not only were the rich furnishings and paintings gone, but the building itself was "half pulled down."[56] Occupied by parliamentarian troops until 1649, the castle had then been made "untenable as a garrison" by the destruction of its outer walls and other defenses. In 1652 its purchaser had begun further demolition, planning to sell off the valuable building materials. Although the castle was soon repurchased by Sir Charles Cavendish, there had been no money for major restoration, and William found his riding house and other buildings roofless and semiruinous.[57]

Elsewhere the story of devastation continued. Vast swathes of woodland had been felled by their parliamentarian purchasers—Margaret later put a value of £45,000 on the timber thus lost—and of eight hunting parks, only that at Welbeck itself remained untouched, saved by Sir Charles Cavendish. William found the others "totally defaced and destroyed," their trees cut down, their fences demolished, and their deer gone. At Clipstone, seven miles south of Welbeck, he was especially distressed. This had been his favorite park, two miles across, "containing the greatest and tallest timber-trees of all the woods he had." Here he had left "a pleasant river . . . full of fish and otters" and grounds "well-stocked with deer, full of hares . . . partridges, poots, pheasants, etc., besides all sorts of waterfowl; so that this park afforded all manner of sports, for hunting, hawking, coursing, fishing." Now it had all disappeared. A parliamentarian soldier had bought the park, set up a forge, and felled the trees to make the charcoal he needed for smelting. Timber worth £20,000 had gone. Throughout their time together, Margaret had always found her husband's patience so great "that I never perceived him sad or discontented for his own losses and misfortunes." But finally, at Clipstone, she saw him troubled, "though he did little express it, only saying he had been in hopes it would not have been so much defaced as he found it, there being not one timber-tree in it left for shelter."[58]

In the face of such losses, William doubted whether he would have any-thing left "for himself" at all. After his sons' many land sales and leases, it was unclear what properties he still owned. He would have to examine the legal status of every one of his prewar possessions, consulting with the Welbeck estate staff who best knew what had been done in his absence—principally John Hutton and the Clayton brothers. In the law courts he would achieve only limited success. Some properties he would never recover. Others he regained only for his own lifetime: on his death, Henry would not inherit them.[59]

In January 1661 more loans, totaling £9,000, were taken out to cover the family's short-term need. Land sales also began, necessary for repaying William's many debts—including the dowries of his daughters Jane and Frances, still not settled in full. Selling rights to mine coal and fell woods for charcoal brought in further cash.[60]

Another priority was the grange farm, which supplied the Welbeck house-hold's basic necessities. Here William had lost everything he had left behind in 1642—not only corn and cattle, but his fine stud of breeding horses, in addi-tion to farm horses, coach horses, hackney horses, and his beloved manège horses. Some basic supplies had been left behind by Henry in 1660—eleven cows and a bull, three asses, four carts, eight wains, twelve plough heads, plus a store of corn in the barn, sixty loads of coal and some fields sowed with oats—but early in 1661, William ordered a plan drawn up for the major restocking that was necessary. That year sixty bullocks, twelve cows, six teams of oxen, six horses and hundreds of sheep and pigs would be bought at a cost of over £700. Pastures were assigned to all of them, while other fields were sown with oats and barley. William also bought "the best mares he could get for money" and reestablished his breeding stud.[61]

Deeply occupied in these affairs, William took no part in Charles II's coro-nation in London in April 1661. Henry, now master of the robes to the king, represented the family there. He also attended the Garter ceremonies at Windsor Castle as his father's proxy: William was thus officially installed in the order to which he had been appointed in Breda in 1650.[62] William and Mar-garet were still at Welbeck on the great day of May 29—both the king's birth-day and the first anniversary of his return to England ("the happiest day which this poor kingdom hath in many years beheld")—which was celebrated with a special service of thanksgiving in the family chapel.[63] It is thus unlikely that they attended the reburial of Margaret's brother Charles four days later in Colchester. To be interred with his ancestors in the family vault at St. Giles's had been Sir Charles Lucas's last request, which his brother John now fulfilled. Beneath the family's funeral pall of purple velvet, embroidered by his mother or one of his sisters in 1628, Charles was borne in state on June 2, 1661, to the new grave he would share with his comrade in arms and in death, Sir George Lisle. A plain black marble slab marks the tomb, commemorating these "two most valiant captains . . . by the command of Sir Thomas Fairfax, then general of the Parliament army, in cold blood barbarously murdered."[64]

For the rest of their lives William and Margaret would leave Welbeck only rarely and for short periods. William was glad to be spending "his old age in a private life in his country." "I have often heard your Excellency," Welbeck's chaplain noted, "discoursing of . . . that sweet privacy and retirement his Majesty is pleased to grant your Lordship here in the country, where you live free from the noise and cumbrance of court and city . . . I know you think it greater happiness . . . than all the offices and honours which your exemplary loyalty has merited."[65]

This idealizing of a country life was typical of disappointed courtiers, offering them some consolation for their failure, and Margaret frequently wrote on the topic in her "sociable letters," which she continued to augment with new work after the Restoration. She had no desire "to live in a metropolitan city, spread broad with vanity, and almost smothered with crowds of creditors for debts."

> For my pleasure and delight, my ease and peace, I live a retired life . . .
> [which] is so pleasing to me as I would not change it for all the pleasures of
> the public world, nay, not to be mistress of the world, for I should not desire
> to be mistress of that which is too big to be commanded, too self-willed to
> be ruled, too factious to be governed, too turbulent to live in peace, and
> wars would fright, at least grieve me, that mankind should be so ill-natured
> and cruel to destroy each other.

"In short," Margaret concluded, "there is so much difference in each sort of life as the one is like Heaven, full of peace and blessedness, the other full of trouble and vice."[66]

By the autumn of 1661 William had a fair idea of his financial position. It was not the ruin he had feared, but there were still huge outstanding debts to be repaid, in addition to the current expenses of running the household at Welbeck. The income from his land rents would never suffice and so, unable to sell many of his lands because they were protected for his heirs by legal entails, William resorted to a massive program of leasing, settling long-term tenants on his estates in return for an immediate large down payment or "fine." In the West Country, where William had inherited vast estates from his grandmother, Bess of Hardwick, this program was managed by Francis Topp, who had accompanied Margaret home from Antwerp.[67]

Like other important estate personnel, Francis and Elizabeth Topp had their own room in the house at Welbeck, with board and lodging provided also for their servants and horses.[68] But much of their time was spent in the West Country, where William wanted to raise £15,000 from leases. While Francis sought out new tenants or conducted delicate negotiations with existing ones, and then waited for them to raise the necessary cash, the couple lived at Tormarton in Gloucestershire, where they leased the manor house from William, setting themselves up as minor country gentry. Here Elizabeth carried out Margaret's commissions—in November 1661 she was recruiting dairy maids for Welbeck—while Francis wrote regularly, telling William how his business was progressing. From the merchants of nearby Bristol he also sourced fine cheeses, Spanish tobacco, and sweet wine from the Canary Islands, all packed onto carts for Welbeck. Then the couple moved on to London, carrying William's newly raised money, ready to "pay all that your Excellence have commanded." From here, in January 1662, Francis dispatched New Year's gifts for all the household: "two boxes directed to my Lady"* (contents unspecified), and nine barrels of oysters—three for William, two for Welbeck's chaplain Mr. Ellis, and one each for four other prominent servants, Mr. Clayton, Mr. Proctor, Mrs. Evans, and Mrs. Perkins. Gradually Francis would become indispensable.[69]

While Topp handled the West Country estates, Andrew Clayton managed much of the remaining business. He traveled regularly into Northumberland to collect the rents and other sums raised by William's bailiffs and receivers. At Welbeck, he took in the moneys from William's Midlands estates and chased up the many late payments. Part of this income he sent down to London "for his Lordship's occasions"—doubtless paying old debts as well as settling new bills for fine clothes and other London luxuries. The rest Clayton sealed up in bags and deposited at Evidence House, William's treasury, where all his cash and legal deeds were kept by John Proctor, who had the only key.[70]

Consulting frequently with William, Clayton also made all the detailed arrangements for northern leases and sales of lands and woods. His influence with his master was well known and many came to him with requests that he favor their affairs "amongst those persons of quality with whom you daily converse." Prospective tenants and purchasers made their offers through him. Existing tenants with grievances, clergymen dissatisfied with their small vicarages and poor parishes, servants seeking employment at Welbeck—all approached Clayton with their petitions, and in return for his good offices he was well rewarded. "My care shall be that you shall not repent your so doing,"

---

*I.e. to Margaret.

as one clergyman put it. "The marking money [will be] to yourself, or a good gelding to the value of it," a hopeful tenant offered more bluntly. Some petitions William referred to Clayton, who was trusted to decide himself what was "equal and just."[71]

Clayton's multifarious duties also included much of the day-to-day running of Welbeck itself, where he was always available to receive William's "and his Lady's . . . commands."[72] He paid the taxes and tithes, the London lawyers' fees, and Captain Mazine's expenses in William's reestablished manège. He purchased wine and corn, fat oxen and sheep, as well as necessary "household stuff"—kitchenware, blankets, and rugs. He bought presents for William's children and sent Henry his quarterly allowance of £500. He supervised and paid the builders repairing Welbeck and Bolsover, and early in 1662 he arranged the wagons needed to carry deer to Clipstone Park, now newly fenced. Clayton handled much of the household's ready money, sometimes withdrawing as much as £3,000 in three months from John Proctor at Evidence House.[73]

By the winter of 1661/62, Welbeck was restored to something like normality. Within the house, kitchen boys and scullery maids, housemaids, tailor, William's barber "and his man," cook, caterer, butler, and usher of the hall served the needs of family, guests, and servants. Entertainment came from the viol player, Mr. Young, and religion from the household's chaplain, Clement Ellis. Under Margaret's authority, the female side of the house was headed by Mistress Perkins, probably employed as Margaret's housekeeper or "governess" now that Elizabeth Topp was often away from Welbeck. Margaret herself was not closely involved. "Though my husband is pleased to make me mistress of his house and household-servants," she explained, "I have an under-officer . . . which is the governess of my house, and she receives my general orders, and executes the particular household affairs." Under Mistress Perkins worked Mistress Remington and Mistress Evans. The latter, probably serving as Margaret's chief waiting-maid in Elizabeth Topp's place, was entrusted with Margaret's most delicate and confidential business. Then, beneath these, were more inferior servants, including Elizabeth Topp's nurse and "Dutch Jane," who had presumably accompanied the household from Antwerp. Outdoors, the Welbeck staff included four grooms, a footboy, a coachman, a postilion, and the blacksmith "and his man" employed in the stables block under Captain Mazine. The baker, brewer, cooper, granary man, gardener, laundress and washmaids, porter, gamekeeper, falconer, and goatherd worked in the house's surrounding offices and grounds.[74]

The whole busy community was kept largely self-sufficient in basic necessities by Welbeck's grange farm, another of Andrew Clayton's responsibilities.[75]

Here a staff of eleven or more worked full time in a mixture of arable, dairy, and livestock farming. Oats formed by far the largest arable crop, delivered weekly to Welbeck's stables, where the diet of William's manège horses was supplemented with a small amount of peas, also supplied by the grange. The grange's other arable crops were carried to Welbeck's granary, where the granary man oversaw their storage and distribution. To the brewhouse went barley and malt to make the household's ale, stored in casks made by Welbeck's own cooper, while wheat and rye went to the bakehouse. Here the baker used the best wheat flour to make pastry and fine white manchet bread, while the coarser siftings mixed with rye flour went to make the grayish cheat bread eaten by the lower servants.

A herd of twenty-four cows supplied up to ten gallons of milk and cream to Welbeck each week. The remainder was made into butter and cheese at the grange—an operation of real mass production: more than forty cheeses stood aging on the dairy shelves at a time, while around 750 pounds of butter was used at Welbeck in a three-month period. In the grange's poultry house some forty hens supplied the household with up to six dozen eggs every week, while "Alice the crammer of pullen" force-fed chickens, turkeys, geese, and ducks for the Welbeck tables. Beef, mutton, lamb, pork, bacon, veal, goatmeat—all were supplied from the grange, while hides, sheepskins, and wool, along with other excess production, were sold for cash. Each week seventy pounds of tallow from the animal carcasses was sent to the local chandler, offsetting most of his bill for the 1,500 candles supplied to Welbeck each year. Wagons and men from the grange carried wood from William's forests to bakehouse and brewhouse, while the coal used in the house—600 loads in a year—probably also came from William's own mines. Only a few imports were needed. The fruit from Welbeck's orchard was supplemented with exotics, like melons and oranges, sent up from London. Wine and tobacco also came from London or Bristol, while other groceries—barrels of herring and salt-fish, vinegar, salt, pepper, sugar, and spices (principally cinnamon, cloves, mace, and nutmeg)— were bought locally.[76]

The senior servants in this elaborate organization, all receiving salaries of £50 per year, were gentlemen with their own small country houses in addition to their Welbeck lodgings. Andrew Clayton and his brother leased William's manor house at Whitwell, three miles west of Welbeck. Captain Mazine lived four miles in the opposite direction, at the manor house he had built on William's lands in Carburton, while John Rolleston lived five miles to the south of Welbeck, at William's manor of Sookholme. As William's secretary, Rolleston kept all the Welbeck estate accounts and wrote up the neat copies of his master's literary works. Along with Clayton and others, he was also frequently employed as witness and trustee in William's never-ending legal business, which was overseen by John Hutton, the household's lawyer.[77]

In the autumn of 1662, one such piece of business was Margaret's jointure. Normally when an aristocratic couple married, a formal legal settlement was made whereby, in return for the wife's dowry, the husband made over certain estates, which she would inherit after he died—her jointure. The system gave the widow financial independence and a dower house of her own, while leaving the bulk of the family's estates and houses to be inherited by the male heir. However, when the Newcastles married in 1645, William owned no estates and Margaret had no dowry. Only now, with William's lands restored, could the matter be concluded.

In London, John Hutton approached the attorney general "for his advice what way to proceed." Next the papers were drafted, submitted to the attorney general for alteration, and then "engrossed"—copied in large legal characters onto parchment—before being signed, witnessed, and sealed. Margaret's property, if she survived William, would be vast. In the Midlands she would have three manors—Chesterfield, Woodthorpe, and Bolsover—with all their lands, and Bolsover Castle as her grand dower house. In Northumberland seven more manors, including Bothal, Ogle, and Hepple, plus some other lands, gave Margaret a further 16,000 acres, intended to bring her a yearly income of £1,025.[78]

Margaret admired the energy and dedication with which William—already approaching his sixty-seventh birthday when the couple first reached Welbeck—abandoned his literary pursuits and threw himself into the "many troubles [and] great cares" of restoring "his torn and ruined estate." Knowing the huge debts her husband still owed, she felt that she too should do her part and "serve your Lordship in such employments which belong to a wife, as household affairs." With Edward Denny's verse against Mary Wroth returning to her mind—"Work, lady, work, let writing books alone"—Margaret "resolved to employ all my thoughts and industry in good housewifery." To do otherwise would be "sordidly base, which is a vice your Lordship hates."[79]

Though she had no skills in feminine domestic accomplishments—in sewing, spinning, or cookery—yet "I am not a dunce in all employments," Margaret told her husband. From her mother she had learned to "understand the keeping of sheep and ordering of a grange indifferently well," aptitudes that could now increase the household's income. Yet, with her aspirations for achievement and recognition, Margaret found her good intentions came to nothing. "My scribbling takes away the most part of my time," she apologized to William. "I cannot for my life be so good a housewife as to quit writing." "The truth is I have somewhat erred from good housewifery to write."[80]

In these circumstances, Margaret was hugely grateful for William's continued support. "Your lordship never bid me to work, nor leave writing, except when you should persuade me to spare so much time from my study as to take the air for my health," she acknowledged. In the face of continued outside criticism, it was a consolation that William at least liked her books. It was his "approvement" that made her "confident and resolute to put them to the press and so to the public view, in despite of these critical times and censorious age."[81]

Margaret's first publication after her return to Welbeck was the book of plays she had completed several years before in Antwerp. Now newly copied from her original manuscript, *Plays Written by the Thrice Noble, Illustrious and Excellent Princess, the Lady Marchioness of Newcastle* came out at the beginning of 1662, complete with its original prefaces, which Margaret had prepared in exile.[82] Like all its predecessors, this book was again published by Martin and Allestrye, but it was the last of her books they would handle.

In 1655 Margaret had begun to take more care about producing accurate books, including an errata list for the first time in her *Philosophical Opinions*, after she found her text disfigured by wrongly placed punctuation and multiple misprints—including "infinite" for "finite," "exterior" for "interior," and "reins" for "veins." However, printing faults continued so frequent in Margaret's subsequent books that her errata lists could correct only "the most considerable errors of the press, which make any alteration in the sense, or may occasion a mistake in the readers; many others of less note . . . as mis-spellings, omissions, misplacing of letters, syllables, and sometimes words . . . are too numerous to set down." Margaret was frustrated and upset, and she placed the blame firmly on the printers, rather than on her Antwerp copyists or on her own poor spelling and handwriting. "I confess I cannot spell right," but "I suppose it belongs more to the corrector of the press to spell right than to the writer," she argued. "Before the printer spoiled my book . . . it was good."[83]

Now returned to England, Margaret took steps to improve the accuracy of her books. At Welbeck she had her own learned secretary, who made the fair copies of her works and then carried his transcripts down to London. After publishing her *Plays*, Margaret no longer used a large firm of booksellers. Instead she went direct to small London printers, financing their work herself and spending "great sums of money" in the process, according to Walter Charleton. The arrangement gave her much greater control over production and resulted in more careful printing, without the numerous errors of her earlier works. By 1663 she had formed a settled relationship with the printer William Wilson, whose shop was at the sign of the three foxes in Long Lane, on the northern edge of the city's main publishing district around St. Paul's

Cathedral. Here Margaret's secretary attended the press daily, correcting the proofs as each batch of pages came ready for printing.[84]

The first book to be published under this new arrangement was Margaret's *Orations of Divers Sorts, Accommodated to Divers Places*, which came out in the autumn of 1662.[85] Margaret had long envied men their training in classical rhetoric, which gave them the ability "to speak rationally, movingly, timely and properly."

> There is a strange hidden mystery in eloquence [she wrote], it hath a magical power over mankind, for it charms the senses and enchants the mind, and . . . forces the will to command the actions of the body and soul to do, or to suffer, beyond their natural abilities . . . it can civilise the life by virtue, and inspire the soul with devotion . . . it can enrage the thoughts to madness, and cause the soul to despair . . . it can make men like gods or devils.[86]

When Margaret had first thought of producing a book of speeches, she had rejected the idea. "How should I write orations, who know no rules in rhetoric, nor never went to school, but only learned to read and write at home?" "I want* wit, eloquence and learning for such a work." Besides, she would never find enough topics to fill a book, "for orations for the most part are concerning war, peace, and matters of state and business in the commonwealth, all which I am not capable of, as being a woman, who hath neither knowledge, ability, nor capacity in state affairs." However, as she experimented at writing "as many as I can find subjects to make orations of," a whole book did develop, one quite different from any written by her predecessors.**[87]

Margaret's principal innovation was the storytelling format she adopted, setting her collection of speeches in an imaginary country, which yet resembled England in many ways. The book began in the capital city, in "the chief marketplace" ("as the most populous place, where usually orations are spoken"), where the people had assembled to decide whether they should go to war. Here a warmonger debated with pacifists on the morality of war in general, reflecting Margaret's interest in using her orations to explore important moral and social issues and the arguments that could be made both "*pro and con*."[88] Then other speakers turned to considering the particular wars they might face—wars "with their neighbour-nation" as well as civil war. Further

---

*I.e. lack.

**Cicero's legal and political speeches were the great classical precedent, but orations were also found scattered through the works of ancient historians, who reported (or fabricated) the great words spoken by generals and politicians at crucial moments in their stories.

speeches proposed political measures that Margaret thought essential to England's well-being: the founding of colonies, the maintenance of a strong navy (without which an island nation "can have no safety"), and the need for the people "to pay contribution-money towards the maintenance of the army"—one of William's current preoccupations as lord lieutenant of Nottinghamshire.

Imagining that the people in her marketplace were "more apt to make war than to keep peace," Margaret next conducted her readers "into the field of war," where generals made various speeches—consoling an army for losing a battle, maintaining morale in the face of hunger and sickness, encouraging fearful soldiers, and reproaching those who had fled from the enemy. Less conventionally, Margaret also wrote speeches for the common soldiers, who argued over whether to accept a city's surrender and whether to mutiny against their commanders. Here her book departed from the traditional aim of orations—to provide model speeches for the ruling class to use in public life. Instead, Margaret's work would portray different classes and character types, who were all allowed a voice.

From the battlefield, Margaret returned to her city, now "burnt to the ground in the war." Here political leaders make speeches, inciting the population to action and resolve. As the city is rebuilt, debates take place on press censorship and on religious toleration—both very live issues in Restoration England—and speakers present Margaret's own views (unopposed by any debate) on the uselessness of the grand tour and the importance of well-written plays in the education of young gentlemen. An oration "against those that lay an aspersion upon the retirement of a nobleman" defended those (like William) who retired to the country in "just discontent" when they went unrewarded after long loyalty, dispossession, and exile during a civil war.

With the city rebuilt, Margaret took her readers to the law courts, to hear "several causes pleaded." In this section, she produced some of her most revolutionary arguments—questioning the very moral foundations of her society—as lawyers defended clients who had been charged with the capital crimes of adultery and theft. "The desire of procreation is born and bred in all nature's animal creatures," the lawyer argues in the first case. "It may more justly be pardoned than gluttony, which was the cause of man's fall, witness Eve and the forbidden fruit." "Since it is a natural effect for males and females to be adulterers, at least lovers, you may as soon destroy all animal creatures as [destroy] this sin, if it be one."

Meanwhile, on the charge of theft, the defense lawyer argued that the accused was a "poor man" who had "nothing of his own to live on," so that he had been "necessitated to take from other men." Appealing to the idea of natural law, the lawyer went on to make a kind of proto-Marxist argument that all property is theft. Nature, he claimed, "made all things in common, she made not some men to be rich and other men poor, some to surfeit with overmuch plenty and others to be starved for want." It was the makers of laws and the founders of political states who were the "grand and original thieves and robbers," "for they robbed the rest of mankind of their natural liberties and inheritances, which is to be equal possessors of the world."[89]

In both these cases, the prosecution lawyer had the last word, expressing his and conventional society's repulsion at the wickedness of the defense's arguments. From the literary convention that the last speaker in a debate is taken to be the winner, it was thus implied that Margaret did not really advocate this free-thinking morality herself. But she had given the longest, most impassioned, most persuasive speeches to the defendants, and her readers were shocked by these sections of her book. She was "speaking too freely and patronising vice too much," they charged.[90]

From the law courts, Margaret next took her readers to the royal court, "to wait upon the King's Majesty" and to eavesdrop on the business of the Privy Council, where the same grievances that the prewar Parliament had brought to Charles I were raised and debated. Unlike real events, however, Margaret's king's speeches "to his rebellious rout" were effective and his subjects repented their misdeeds. Then Margaret took her readers "to visit the sick" and hear a series of deathbed speeches. Accounts of virtuous deaths were often published as models for readers, and Margaret's writing here was largely conventional, as was the series of laudatory funeral orations that followed after "death has released those sick persons of their pains."[91] Continuing in church, readers were presented with a series of sermons and marriage orations, before returning to the marketplace for further social and political debate. Here one of the orators spoke "against the liberty of women." His argument—that women should be kept at home and not allowed to meet together to "corrupt and spoil each other, with their vanities, paintings and gossipings"—so angered the female part of his audience that, after the men had gone, they met secretly in a "private conventicle" to discuss how they could "unite in prudent counsels, to make ourselves as free, happy and famous as men."

However, such a union proved impossible, since the women could not even agree on whether they really were oppressed. "We have no reason to speak against men, who are our admirers and lovers; they are our protectors, defenders and maintainers . . . we complain of men as if they were our enemies, whenas we could not possibly live without them," one of the speakers maintained. Even those who believed that women were unhappy could not agree on what to do about it. One despaired: "we may complain, and bewail our condition, yet that will not free us; we may murmur and rail against men, yet they regard not what we say . . . our power is so inconsiderable as men laugh at our weakness." Another suggested that women should imitate men to prove they were not inferior: "let us hawk, hunt, race and do the like exercises as men have, and let us converse in camps, courts and cities, in schools, colleges and courts of judicature, in taverns, brothels and gaming houses, all which will make our strength and wit known, both to men and to our own selves . . . so will our bodies and minds appear more masculine, and our power will increase by our actions." But the next speaker denounced this as "a strange and unwise persuasion . . . for we cannot make ourselves men." Rather women should be "modest, chaste, temperate, humble, patient and pious," ensuring they were "acceptable and pleasing to God and men." "Why should we desire to be masculine, since our own sex and condition is far the better?" the last speaker argued. The women's debate raised many of the issues from the contemporary *querelle des femmes*, but Margaret and her women characters could decide on no solution to the quandary they faced.

For readers "who regard not what women say," Margaret next proceeded to a country market town, where a group of gentlemen at an inn discussed the delights and the difficulties of their rural life, before settling down to make themselves "dead drunk." Then, out in the fields "under a spreading tree . . . the country clowns or peasants speak, concerning their own affairs and course of life."

After this "field of peace" came a visit to "a disordered and unsettled state or government," where the story mirrored the real events of the English Civil War. First there were speeches against taxes and tax collectors, government ministers and magistrates. Then other orators spoke "to hinder a rebellion," but without success. The victorious army refused to be disbanded, and took on itself the authority to decide its country's new form of government. The result resembled Cromwell's Protectorate, and included a speech refusing the absolute power and title of king, as Cromwell himself had done. The book ended on a lighter tone, with "scholastical orations," where Margaret ridiculed the follies of university scholars—their lazy, sleepy natures, their pointless, nonsensical debates, involving nothing more important than logic-chopping, their conceited belief in "their own wit and judgement."

As she finished writing, Margaret still worried that her book would not match up to her readers' expectations. In particular, she thought her speeches were too long and loosely written: "had I been a learned scholar, I might have written my orations more short . . . and more compendiously." Fearing that her work was too artless, she consulted the Newcastles' old servant, Mark Anthony Benoist, now employed in London as tutor to the sons of William's daughter, Elizabeth, countess of Bridgewater. Benoist liked her manuscript: the best oratory was natural, he replied. And so Margaret, consoling herself with the thought that the length of her speeches might at least make the book an easier, pleasanter read (since very condensed writing was difficult to follow, requiring "some study to conceive and understand . . . the author's meaning"), proceeded with her plans for publication. Offering the work to her readers, she hoped "that every several oration may be acceptable to your minds, profitable to your lives, and delightful to your hearing."[92]

Chapter Twelve

Revisions and Controversies, 1663–1667

*M*argaret's *Philosophical and Physical Opinions* remained "the darling of my affection"—"for though it hath put me to more study and harder labor than my other works, yet being of a more ingenious nature, I love it best." Since its publication in 1655 she had maintained an abiding interest in philosophy, continuing to write occasional pieces on the subject, which she included in *Nature's Pictures* and the *Plays*, and in her as yet unpublished collection of "sociable letters."[1] In Antwerp she had performed experiments in her laboratory and debated with Constantijn Huygens and others, and at Welbeck she and William continued their earlier study of astronomy. In February 1662 the "famous and long tube perspective glasses" owned by William's cousin, the earl of Devonshire, were sent over from Hardwick. A workman was also offered, to make "fit tubes and frames" and a sighting device, since the earl, with Thomas Hobbes as his expert technician, had so far utterly failed to see "anything to any purpose" with his giant lenses improperly mounted. But with proper equipment, the Welbeck astronomers were expected to be able "to see the admirable forms of Saturn and Jupiter (much mentioned of late)."[2]

When she had first begun to write on philosophy ten years before, Margaret had "never read, nor heard of, any English book to instruct me."[3] But by the early 1660s natural philosophy, with all its attendant paraphernalia of telescopes and experiments, had become a fashionable gentlemanly pursuit in England, sponsored by the Royal Society, which was established in London in 1660 under the king's patronage. A wide range of philosophical books were now available for English readers. Some were translations from Latin but many were original works by English philosophers—both academics like Henry

More and Royal Society gentlemen like Robert Boyle—who now chose to publish in their native tongue for this growing home market.

At Welbeck, Margaret began to read a wide range of this new literature— no simple undertaking, even though these philosophical books were in English. The complex, technical terminology of the discipline was generally used without definition, even by popularizing authors like Boyle. Frequently Latinate in origin, it would be readily understood by readers with a university background, but Margaret was often in difficulties. In spite of the earlier grounding she had received from her brother John and from Sir Charles Cavendish, she still found at first that these "words of art . . . were so hard to me, that I could not understand them, but was fain to guess at the sense of them by the whole context."[4]

Margaret's new reading program resulted from a significant shift in her attitude to her own work and its relation to that of other scholars. When she first began to write on philosophy, she had seen no point in reading, even "had I understood several languages, as I do not." She was already working at the limit of her capacity, with "my head . . . so full of my own natural fancies as it had not room for strangers to board therein."

> Besides, I have heard that learning spoils the natural wit, and the fancies of others drive the fancies out of our own brains, as . . . troublesome guests that fill up all the rooms of the house.

To become truly learned seemed an impossible task, utterly alien to her own feminine nature, "for learning requires close studies, long time and labour."

> Our sex takes so much delight in dressing and adorning themselves as we for the most part make our gowns our books, our laces our lines, our embroideries our letters, and our dressings are the time of our study; and instead of turning over solid leaves, we turn our hair into curls.[5]

Dyslexia may have contributed to her preference for oral learning, but Margaret dismissed herself as "like a poor, lazy beggar, that had rather feed on scraps than work or be industrious to get wealth." Preferring rather to "write by guess than take the pains to learn every nice distinction," she had accepted the resultant inadequacies in her work—that she might "be deceived in my understanding" or even "be absurd and err grossly." But by the 1660s, although still believing herself "uncapable of learning," Margaret was determined to understand the "scholastical expressions" used by other writers, and she kept up a serious course of reading.[6] A single bill for books bought for her in London by Mark Anthony Benoist in July 1664 came to £39 14s.—for which she would have received around one to two hundred volumes.[7]

As she read, Margaret grew dissatisfied with her *Philosophical Opinions*. Although she had written it "as plain as I could," yet she now realized that "for want of scholarship, I could not express myself so well as otherwise I might have done."[8] Standard philosophical terms were misapplied in her text. For instance, she used the word "form" to mean basic inanimate matter, in direct opposition to the term's established usage in Aristotelian philosophy. For the concept of an essence or definition of a thing—what the Aristotelians meant by "form"—Margaret used her own term, "interior or intellect nature." Elsewhere "transmigration" appeared where "transmutation" was meant (whether by Margaret's own misunderstanding or by her printer's mistake) and the error was uncorrected in the errata list.[9]

In many places Margaret had invented her own philosophical terminology, often without any explicit definition of its meaning. "Innated matter," "only matter," and "incipit matter" were neologisms whose meanings could only be extracted from her text with difficulty. "Incipit matter" was particularly challenging to readers, probably being transcribed letter-for-letter from Margaret's ill-spelt manuscript by printers who never guessed that she might mean "insipid matter."[10] Further confusion resulted because Margaret's own philosophical language had evolved and changed as she wrote, making her terminology unsystematic. Having defined "form" as "dull matter" or "matter moved," she later abandoned the usage, preferring instead to say "the dull part of matter." "Form" she then applied in its everyday sense, meaning the shape of a body. Meanwhile, "mind" or "matter moving" at the beginning of her book soon became "the spirits, or innate matter," then "spirits of sense" or "sensitive spirits." Later still these "sensitive spirits" were distinguished from the "rational spirits" that made up the mind.[11] Every philosopher's terminology is somewhat individual, requiring careful study to understand precisely what is meant, but Margaret's is often bewildering, especially when combined with her text's confusingly formed sentences and misplaced punctuation. The problem had only been exacerbated by her decision to incorporate the text of her *Philosophical Fancies*, written in a hurried two weeks in 1653 and almost entirely unrevised, as the first part of her *Philosophical Opinions*. No wonder that readers complained that her theory was "too obscure, and not plain enough for their understanding."[12]

Margaret now regretted that she had published her *Philosophical Opinions* "too soon to have them artificial and methodical," and she was angry with her younger self's naive ambition and enthusiasm.

> Self-conceit, which is natural to mankind, especially to our sex, did flatter
> and secretly persuade me that my writings had sense and reason, wit and
> variety; but judgement being not called to counsel, I yielded to self-conceit's
> flattery, and so put out my writings to be printed as fast as I could, without
> being reviewed or corrected: neither did I fear any censure, for self-conceit
> had persuaded me I should be highly applauded.

However, she was still committed to her philosophical ideas. "Although they may
be defective for want of terms of art and artificial expressions," she admitted,
"yet I am sure they are not defective for want of sense and reason." Determined
to get her theories accepted, she began to revise her *Philosophical Opinions* for a
second edition, aiming "to make it more intelligible for my readers."[13]

Margaret substantially rewrote Part 1 of her book, which in the first edition had consisted of an almost exact reprint of her *Philosophical Fancies*.[14] All
verses and fanciful similes were now omitted, to make a serious philosophical
work in prose. And from the very beginning Margaret introduced and defined
a clear, systematic terminology, abandoning all her varied vocabulary of
"mind," "matter moving," "sensitive spirits," and "innated matter," and adopting
in its place the more conventional "animate matter" divided into two kinds—
"sensitive matter" and "rational matter." She went carefully over her material,
explaining, arguing, even repeating herself in different places, in an attempt to
make her theory both clear and convincing. The result was a general exposition
of her basic philosophical tenets—of the nature of only matter, its degrees,
motions, and activities—set out in logical order, starting from first principles.

After this introductory Part 1, Margaret made radical alterations to the
arrangement of the rest of her treatise. In the original edition she had proceeded to further general explanation of her theory, then to the phenomena of
inanimate nature, ending with a discussion of humanity and diseases. This represented the conventional ordering of Creation, proceeding from its lowest to
its highest forms. But now Margaret decided to proceed straight to a discussion of mankind in a newly written Part 2, dramatically representing in the
book's very organization her belief that "that animal named man" was not some
superior overlord of nature, "the supreme creature of all creatures" as he arro-
gantly claimed, but merely one of the parts of "infinite matter."[15] This arrangement perhaps also had an epistemological point—that we, humanity, are a part
of nature, studying nature in philosophy, so we must understand ourselves
before we can understand what we experience of the rest of the world.

Margaret's account of mankind proceeded in orderly fashion from a general account of how animate matter composed the human body, to the shape
and motions of the body, then to the mind and the thoughts, and a theory of

how the mind and body interacted. Then, in Part 3 (also newly written), she went on to a detailed examination of psychology, with discussions of imagination, thought, knowledge, and faith—including a careful consideration of whether religious faith could produce effects in the outside world. "It is probable that if there be a sympathy between the outward object and the inward thoughts, it may work some effect, but not so much as to remove mountains," Margaret concluded.[16] This part ended with a series of refutations of the psychological views of other philosophers, inspired by her program of reading.

Then, in Parts 4 to 7, Margaret returned to the material of Parts 2 to 5 of the original edition. First was a general treatment of motion and animate matter and their effects and activities in the world (now Part 4, formerly Part 2). Then came a discussion of the four elements—earth, air, fire, and water—with all the phenomena they produced, including the weather, tides, magnetism, colors, and the motion of the planets (Part 5/Part 3). Then Part 6 reprinted most of Margaret's original material on mankind—on the passions, the brain, thoughts, sleep, dreams, the five senses—going over some of the same ground as her new Part 2. The book ended, like its predecessor, with a discussion of diseases.

In these last four parts, some sections of the original edition were reproduced verbatim, but many sections Margaret rewrote entirely, often changing the ordering of her discussions as well.[17] In places she actually changed her views. For instance, she had originally thought color to be "nothing else but the lines of light broken by several forms and figures," but now she proposed a more complex theory, involving natural, accidental, and artificial colors. "Natural colours" were actually inherent in things, she argued: grass is green even if there is no light to see it by.[18] She also expanded these four parts with much new material. Even before she had first published her *Philosophical Opinions* in 1655, Margaret was already dissatisfied with the last part, on diseases, thinking that it could have been enlarged "much to the advantage," and so Part 7 of her new book was especially increased in size.[19] Plague, smallpox, measles, agues, coughs, gangrenes, gout, wens, the different methods of letting blood—these were just some of Margaret's new topics. Kidney and bladder stones were inoperable (unlike stones in the ureter), she advised, but they could all be prevented by avoiding "violent exercises" and "fiery meats."[20] Striving for a complete exposition of her philosophy, Margaret also added material that she had previously included in her *World's Olio*.[21]

Margaret worked hard and with care, and where she did include her original discussions from the first edition, they were often significantly edited. Rewordings and expansions clarified her ideas; new arguments gave them extra support.[22] Anthropomorphic similes—for instance, likening the motions of heat and cold to the armies of the Goths overrunning Europe, or to a gardener pushing a garden roller—were now removed by an author who felt capable of explaining her ideas in literal, philosophical language.[23] Errors in the original—whether produced by Margaret or her printers—were now corrected. "Transmigrations" was altered to "transmutations" and, in the brain, the "dia mater" became the "dura mater."[24] Mistakes in punctuation—some of them as serious as sentences broken by misplaced periods—were also amended, and complicated sentences that had been incorrectly formed were now grammatically correct.[25]

The resultant book was vastly expanded—172 pages of the original became 458 of the new edition—but there were still mistakes. Margaret wrote "sufficient cause" where she meant necessary cause, she invented words like "exteriously" and "interiously," and she freely admitted her continuing lack of philosophical knowledge. Especially she apologized for her inadequate understanding of human anatomy, derived only from conversation—gathering "here a bit, and there a crumb of knowledge"—and from the human organs she had seen pickled in jars. Beyond these, she had seen "the entrails of beasts"—but only in the kitchen, dressed for cooking, or else in the butchers' shambles, where they "cut the throat of a beast, or rip up the body, where the guts and garbage would burst out, but that gave me not much more knowledge, not seeing how they lay in their bodies." In these circumstances, it would be "a wonder [if] I should not err," not only in the "names and terms" of the anatomists, but also in mistaking or misplacing the parts of the body,

> for truly I never read of anatomy, nor never saw any man opened, much less dissected, which for my better understanding I would have done; but I found that neither the courage of nature, nor the modesty of my sex would permit me.[26]

Preparing her new edition for publication, Margaret still feared it would be unclear to readers and she added a number of prefaces "to hinder objections which might be made, by explaining some terms which I use in this work": dozens of definitions and fine distinctions followed.[27] Her prefaces also apologized for the book's repetitions—which "I could not well avoid"—and for any disorganization readers might find: "the variety of several discourses in every several chapter did so employ my brain as it had neither room nor time for such inferior considerations, so that both words and chapters take their places according as I writ them, without any mending or correcting." "The truth is my work goes out into the world like an unpolished stone." Margaret could only hope that "it will meet with such understanding readers as will not undervalue the inward worth, through a dislike to the outward form." She had one consolation in a book so "plain and vulgarly expressed": at least it might be readily understandable, "having not so much learning as to puzzle the reader with logistical, metaphysical, mathematical, or the like terms."Thus "the truth, or at least the probability thereof, might not be lost in the labyrinth of sophistry, produced from the corruption of logic and the mixture of several languages." "The best natural philosophers are those that have the clearest natural observation and the least artificial learning," she still believed.[28]

Nonetheless, despite this implied distrust of university scholarship, when her book was printed late in the spring of 1663, Margaret sent many copies to her connections at Oxford and Cambridge universities. She also sent copies of her *Orations*, newly reprinted that spring, perhaps because her first print run had been too small for demand.[29] The approval of so learned a readership— which soon reached Margaret in the form of letters of thanks for her gifts— brought her reassurance. She was also keen to have their assistance in finding translators. Margaret had long wished to have her philosophy appear in Latin, to reach the continental audience who, she thought, would appreciate it more than English readers. Otherwise, "I fear me my book will be lost in oblivion."[30] Now she approached two Oxford dons with her request, sending them copies of her latest books.

Jasper Mayne had been William's chaplain at Welbeck before the war. A fashionable playwright and prolific poet as well as a scholar and clergyman, he had begun at Welbeck to translate Lucian's *Dialogues* into English for his patron's "private entertainment." At Oxford he was now a canon of Christ Church (in addition to his other prominent church posts as archdeacon of Chichester and a chaplain in ordinary to King Charles II), and he soon found a translator for Margaret—"an ingenious person of this College"—who would "undertake the work whenever you shall be pleased to assign his task."

Meanwhile, Margaret's second request went to Thomas Tully, the principal of St. Edmund Hall, another chaplain in ordinary to the king. "The books you condescended to bestow upon me have turned a sorry study into a rich library," he thanked Margaret in June 1663. On the flyleaf of his copy of the *Philosophical Opinions* he noted names of possible translators for all the books she had so far published, and by the spring of 1664 the project was well under way. Mayne had passed *Nature's Pictures* "into the hand of [as] fit a person to translate them into Latin as I think either University can afford," while Dr. John Harmar, selected by Tully, put at least one of Margaret's plays into Latin, "for which he was well rewarded" (although the result was never published). Mayne had also commissioned a young student, recently arrived in Oxford from Eton, to translate Margaret's poems. Reading through the sample of translation that resulted, "in some parts," Mayne reported to Margaret, "I find him happy enough. But there were problems with her atomist verses, in particular, where "your excellent fancy expressing itself sometimes in terms of art, and words only known to philosophy, he tells me the hardest part of his task will be how to find out current Roman words to match them." Mayne had instructed his acolyte to read Lucretius, who could provide a model of atomic philosophy written in Latin verse. But this translation, like all the others, came to nothing. At Christ Church, James Bristow, commissioned to Latinize Margaret's philosophy, abandoned the project "finding great difficulties therein, through the confusedness of the matter."[31] Margaret herself perhaps stopped others, for she refused to accept inferior translations "disfigured with mistakes." "I had rather my book should die in oblivion, than to be divulged to disadvantage."[32]

Margaret attempted to present a careless front to her readers. She wrote and published books, she told them, "only for my own pleasure, and not to please others: being very indifferent whether anybody reads them or not; or being read, how they are esteemed." But in reality Margaret knew she depended on the approval of others to achieve her literary ambitions, and so, in 1663, she turned her attention to her *Poems and Fancies,* long criticized for errors of rhyme and meter.[33]

No longer satisfied with rhyming "weight" with "fraught," "coil" with "child," or "like" with "right," Margaret replaced these and many like them, altering whole couplets where necessary to work in her new and perfect rhymes.[34] She changed yet more verses to make her meaning clearer. In her atomist poems, especially, sections of verse that were incomprehensible in the original edition (in some places because of printers' errors, in others because of Margaret's own difficulty in first writing them) now became clear and well expressed.[35] Everywhere, new punctuation made her meaning clearer. Awkward phrases were replaced with language that flowed; reexpression of her ideas made the words fit the meter. The improvements were dramatic and extensive; scarcely a poem was left unchanged. But occasionally, as Margaret corrected a rhyme or regularized the language, there is a sense of losing her original directness, the force and vitality of her own, individual voice.[36]

The new edition of the *Poems and Fancies* came out early in 1664,[37] and in the same year Margaret finally published her *CCXI Sociable Letters,* now grown far beyond her original plan for one hundred letters.* The result had also transcended her original idea of recounting a life of feminine visits, entertainments, "gossiping-meetings," and household employments. In addition to new

---

*The book contained 201 letters written to Margaret's imaginary female friend, plus a further ten at the end, written to real people, including Leanora Duarte and Margaret's sisters Catherine and Anne.

letters telling of her life in England—of her pleasure in a country retirement and of the possibilities this opened up for "recreation, pastime and harmless sports"[38]—the completed book contained many extended, essay-like pieces on a wide range of intellectual and literary subjects. In theology, she argued for the superiority of practical religion over a life of prayer and contemplation: "one good deed is better than a thousand good words . . . one act of upright justice, or pure charity, is better than a book full of prayers." In politics, she criticized the democratic government of the Dutch United Provinces, and advocated monarchy as "certainly the best and happiest government." In astrology, she dismissed the view that the planets influenced the course of our lives, but supported the idea that they affected our health.[39] She attacked literary romances for their obsession with "amorous love," leading their women readers to "fall in love with the feigned heroes and carpet-knights, with whom their thoughts secretly commit adultery."[40] She assessed the lives and characters of great figures from history—Julius Caesar, Pericles, Cato, and Lucretia (the wife of the Roman king Tarquinius Collatinus, who committed suicide after she was raped).[41]

Such subjects were "not fit nor proper for a woman to discourse or write of," Margaret felt—and these letters often ended with apologies and disclaimers. "Madam, these causes are not for our sex to discourse of," she concluded, after criticizing the Church of England for allowing laymen to read the Bible. "I'll leave off judging of such master-poets as my pupil-aged wit cannot understand," she ended a letter of literary criticism. "Should I live to Methusalem's age, my wit would be but a novice, my judgement an ignorant fool, and my opinions erroneous, for women are neither fit to be judges, tutors, nor disputers."[42]

Yet in spite of such modest professions, Margaret wrote on a great number of "masculine" topics, always expressing her opinions confidently until the letters ended. Literary topics in particular inspired some of the book's longest letters. In an examination of epic poetry, Margaret criticized Homer for filling his verses with "more lies than truth, more impossibilities than probabilities" and for the "clownish and rude expressions" of his language—though here she could only judge the translation. Preferring Sir William Davenant's *Gondibert*, "as being most and nearest to the natures, humours, actions . . . and abilities of men," she yet disliked Davenant's overly precious language, his "extraordinary choice phrases." Virgil she disliked both as a man (for his "insinuating craft" and gross flattery of the emperor), and as a poet (for the imitative quality of his work). By contrast, she thought, "sweet Ovid" was "open and free"; his poetry was "full of fancy"; his *Metamorphoses* contained "hundreds of stories," unlike Virgil's *Aeneid*, which had just one, and a "tedious" one at that. Ovid and Shakespeare were Margaret's favorite authors (after her husband, of course). Shake-speare she especially admired for his lifelike character portrayals, "witty, wise, judicious, ingenious and observing." Exceptionally among writers, he was able to portray every kind of person, "of what quality, profession, degree, breeding, or birth soever."

> Nor did he want wit to express the divers and different humours, or natures, or several passions in mankind; and so well he hath expressed in his plays all sorts of persons, as one would think he had been transformed into every one of those persons he hath described . . . nay, one would think that he had been metamorphosed from a man to a woman, for who could describe Cleopatra better than he hath done, and many other females of his own creating?[43]

Margaret saw Shakespeare as a writer who relied, as she did, on natural wit rather than an extensive classical education. His work proved the truth of her literary theory—that it was wit not scholarship that made the good writer—and this discussion in the *Sociable Letters* is now thought to be the first general prose assessment of Shakespeare's drama ever written.[44]

As she wrote on such topics, Margaret saw the potential the letter form offered for intellectual debate, and she decided to produce a new, more specialized volume of correspondence: *Philosophical Letters: or, Modest Reflections upon some Opinions in Natural Philosophy, Maintained by Several Famous and Learned Authors of this Age*. Already in 1663, when she published the second edition of her *Philosophical Opinions,* Margaret had recognized that this work would not be enough. New theories were always slow to find acceptance, their unfamiliarity making them "no more understood at first than if they had [been] written or spoken in unknown languages." But all other philosophers had an advantage over her in this lengthy and difficult process: "being men, . . . they had liberty not only to write their opinions, but to preach, teach, and instruct others to understand them." Oral teaching and dialogue were the key to successful persuasion, yet they were denied to Margaret, "for it is not proper for my sex to be a public orator, to declare or explain my opinions in schools, and if it were, yet I have neither confidence nor learning to speak to an assembly, nor in such forms or phrases as masters of learning use." In her play *Youth's Glory and Death's Banquet*, she had imagined her philosopher-heroine, Lady Sanspareille, pursuing a public career lecturing to male audiences. But in the real world, this option was not open to Margaret, "wherefore I fear the right understanding of my philosophical opinions are likely to be lost, for want of a right explanation."[45]

However, it was possible to create written dialogue at least in letters, she realized, and so she now imagined the same female correspondent from the *Sociable Letters* writing to "propound several philosophical questions to me to resolve." Since Margaret believed that the best way to explain her own ideas was "by arguing, and comparing other men's opinions with them," her book would consist of "answers" to sections of the works of "several famous and learned authors," sent by her imaginary correspondent for comment. After setting out each rival opinion she wished to discuss, she proceeded to criticism—arguing that it was incoherent, inconsistent with nature, or logically impossible—before expounding her own views on the same subject. In addition to explaining her ideas and arguing for their truth, this construction allowed her to position herself with respect to other major philosophers, demonstrating her difference and thus originality.[46]

Margaret selected "four famous philosophers of our age" as her main opponents, beginning with Hobbes and Descartes, whose ideas she had been accused of stealing, back in the 1650s. Their mechanical systems had inspired the atomism of her *Poems and Fancies* in 1653, and she still agreed with their most basic tenet: "that all bodies of this universe are of one and the same matter, really divided into many parts, and that these parts are diversely moved."[47] However, the animism of her subsequent theory—her belief that motion was innate to matter, rather than a separate external principle acting on it—was directly opposed to their mechanism. Accordingly she concentrated her attacks on those areas of her opponents' philosophies where this disagreement was most marked—their theories of motion and collisions, of perception, psychology, and the relation between mind and body. Hobbes's theories on these subjects Margaret had read for herself, in the first part of the *Leviathan* and in his *Elements of Philosophy*.* But Descartes's philosophy was unavailable in English, and the sections of his *Principia Philosophiae, Discours de la Méthode,* and *Meteorology* on which Margaret commented were all specially translated for her, perhaps by her secretary.**

From these mechanical philosophers, Margaret proceeded to two philosophers who shared her basic belief in animism, although the details of their theories were utterly different. Henry More, "that learned philosopher and divine," was a fellow of Christ's College, Cambridge, where he was one of the founders of a revived and Christianized Platonic philosophy. Unlike Mar-

---

*Published in English in 1651 and 1656, respectively.

**The *Discourse on Method* had appeared in translation in England in 1649 but was probably unavailable by the time Margaret returned home at the Restoration.

garet, More adhered to the mechanists' view that matter was inert and inactive. His animism lay in an immaterial "hylarchic spirit," which pervaded all of nature: active and intelligent, this spirit directed all the motions and changes of passive matter, causing order in the universe and carrying out God's will. Margaret objected to this idea—how could something immaterial act on something material? she demanded—and she responded at length to More's many arguments against the idea of self-moving matter, which was basic to her own philosophy. More claimed that such a belief was "atheistical," denying divine activity in the world, but Margaret turned the charge of atheism back on More himself. It was "irreligious" to invoke "immaterial spirits, like so many several deities, to rule and govern nature": "I fear the opinion . . . will at last bring in again the heathen religion, and make us believe a god Pan, Bacchus, Ceres, Venus and the like."[48] More's whole philosophical project, intended to support Christian religion by demonstrating the activity of divine providence in nature, in fact had the reverse effect, she argued. His attempts to prove the existence of God only called into question a belief that no one would otherwise have doubted: "it [is] impossible, almost, that any atheist should be found in the world: for what man would be so senseless as to deny a God?" More's arguments for the immortality of the human soul were equally redundant, for this too was an obvious truth, believed by Muslims and Jews as well as Christians. When More described his philosophy as "the key that unlocks the Divine providence," Margaret was outraged. "Surely God, who is infinitely wise, would never entrust so frail and foolish a creature as man . . . as to let him know his secret counsels . . . I am in a maze when I hear of such men, which pretend to know so much, as if they had plundered the celestial cabinet of the omnipotent God."[49]

From More, Margaret moved on to "that famous physician and chymist," Jean Baptiste Van Helmont, whose *Oriatrike or Physick Refined* had become available in English in 1662.[50] A Belgian who had died twenty years before, Van Helmont was a follower of the Paracelsian philosophy and a proponent of chemical medicine against established Galenic practice. In his sensibility to nature, he was the closest of these philosophers to Margaret, denying human superiority over the rest of Creation and sharing her idea that natural objects taught you as masters. Like Margaret (and contrary to More and most other philosophers), Van Helmont believed that matter had innate activity within it, but his account of this active matter, deriving from the arcane mysteries of alchemy, was completely alien to Margaret's background in mechanical philosophy. "Ideas, Archeus, Gas, Blas, Ferment, and the like"—Van Helmont's basic tenets were "so strange . . . so obscure, intricate and perplex, as is almost impossible exactly to conceive them; whenas principles ought to be easy, plain and without any difficulty to be understood." From philosophy, Margaret proceeded to attack Van Helmont's medical theories, including his arrogant belief that a single chemical medicine could cure all fevers. Instead she defended the traditional practices of bloodletting, purging, "issues, cauteries, clysters and the like" as "very necessary and profitable for the prolonging of life, and taking away of diseases." In general, she disliked his "too great presumption," displayed in the "spiteful reproaches and bitter taunts" that he cast on traditional physicians: "there is hardly a chapter in all his works which has not some accusations of blind errors, sloth and sluggishness, ignorance, covetousness, cruelty and the like."[51]

The final section of Margaret's book contained brief discussions of various other philosophers: William Harvey, Galileo, her old friend Walter Charleton, Robert Boyle, and several others who went unnamed even by initials. She ended with explanations of various sections of her *Philosophical Opinions* which, even in the second edition, still presented "some obscurity and difficulty of being understood."[52]

As before, so in this new "book of controversies," Margaret was exceeding the bounds of femininity, for "women are neither fit to be judges, tutors, nor disputers."[53] But more worrying was her break with the conventions of her class. Virulent book wars were common amongst scholars, vying with each other to establish their own opinions and reputations, but polite society took no part in them. Gentlemen did not contradict each other, unless they wished to fight a duel, and William, like the rest of his class, despised scholarly disputations as "a pedantical kind of quarrelling, not becoming noble persons."*

"Although you have always encouraged me in my harmless pastime of writing, yet was I afraid that your Lordship would be angry with me for writing and publishing this book," Margaret wrote to her husband. But she had no choice if she was to make her new theories "more known, easy and intelligible." "I have not contradicted those authors in anything but what concerns and is opposite to my opinions; neither do I anything but what they have done themselves, as being common amongst them to contradict each other," she excused herself.

> There is nobody that doth esteem, respect and honour learned and ingenious persons more than I do: wherefore judge me neither to be of a contradicting humour, nor a vain-glorious mind for dissenting from other men's opinions,

---

*The very word "quarrel" had different meanings for these different classes: amongst scholars a quarrel was a verbal dispute, written or spoken, but for gentlemen it was a duel.

but rather that it is done out of love to truth and to make my own opinions the more intelligible.[54]

Margaret carefully defined the style and boundaries of her disputes. Sharing the common belief that political and religious controversies had been prime causes of the Civil War, she avoided matters "of either Church or State," at least "as much as I can."[55] She also argued with her opponents as politely as possible. She would not claim truth, "infallible and undeniable," for her ideas, accusing "all others of ignorance," as Van Helmont did. Rather, "I am as willing to have my opinions contradicted, as I do contradict others." "If anyone can bring more sense and reason to disprove these my opinions, I shall . . . either acknowledge my error, if I find myself in any, or defend them as rationally as I can."[56]

Eager for a response, Margaret dedicated her book to Cambridge University, and she sent presentation copies to the university, to St. John's (William's old college), and to Henry More at Christ's.[57]

WITH MANY OF THEIR DEBTS still unpaid, financial worries remained a preoccupation for the Newcastles. Late in 1662 William had asked the king for repayment of the money he had lent to Charles I during the Scots War of 1639. Of the £10,000 principal, only £3,500 still remained unpaid, but William also charged interest for twenty-three years, bringing the total back to £9,240. This the king categorically refused to pay, and an impasse resulted since William, having himself borrowed the money in 1639 and paid interest "ever since the debt was contracted," equally refused to accept the principal money alone. Only in the summer of 1664 was the matter finally resolved, through the intervention of his son, Henry, now serving as a gentleman of the bedchamber at court. William, it was agreed, would give up all claim to the debt in return for the gift of a dukedom, for which the king's normal charge was £10,000. William still had to pay some £887—in customary fees to the heralds, courtiers, and civil servants involved, and there was a nine-month delay, which the king required in order "to accommodate it to some other ends of mine." But on March 16, 1665, the letters patent were passed, making William and Margaret duke and duchess of Newcastle, and raising Henry from viscount Mansfield to earl of Ogle.[58]

In May the Newcastles, now amongst the highest aristocrats in the country, traveled down to London in true grandeur. Outside the capital they were met by "many of the nobility"—William's friends and relations—who joined the couple's "princely train," and accompanied them into the city. The next day they went to court "in great state," and William thanked the king for his new honor. Charles, still fond of his old tutor, responded with noted warmth.[59]

Doubtless during this time in London Margaret also saw the remaining members of her childhood family, with whom she and William maintained close ties. After the Restoration, Margaret's brother John and her brother-in-law Sir Edmund Pye had joined the political axis of the Newcastle clan in Parliament. They also acted as trustees for Margaret's marriage settlement in 1662, and in 1663 the tie was further cemented when John's only daughter and heiress, Mary Lucas, married William's cousin, the earl of Kent. However, evidence of Margaret's more personal connections with her brother and sisters is almost entirely lacking, since hardly any of her correspondence now survives: a single, undated letter from her sister Anne, still unmarried and living with their brother John, is the only indication of how the family kept in touch.[60]

The Newcastles' stay in the capital was lavishly expensive. Debts exceeding £700 were run up with one silk merchant alone,[61] and it was probably now that Margaret had her portrait painted by Peter Lely, the leading portraitist of Restoration society. The picture is atypical of Lely's work, which usually represented female subjects in informal (even flirtatious) pose, wearing simple, loose (and often revealing) drapes, rather than the stiff and elaborate costumes of aristocratic real life. Instead Margaret stands straight, full length, staring out at the viewer, with the fingertips of her outstretched right hand resting lightly on the carpet-covered table beside her—a stance of authority adopted in the portraits of such powerful women as Henrietta Maria and Lady Anne Clifford. She is wearing formal court dress, with a tightly boned, long-waisted bodice and a long overskirt, broadly slit up the front to reveal the underskirt—all richly decorated with patterned brocade, as had become fashionable since the Restoration. From her shoulders hangs her red velvet peeress's robe, whose ermine lining Margaret's left hand proudly displays to the viewer. These robes, given to peers at their investiture, were afterwards worn only on the most ceremonious royal occasions—principally coronations. With part of a great classical column dimly visible in the background, this was an image of grandeur, rank, authority, and wealth, created to celebrate the Newcastles' recent rise to the top of the ladder of aristocratic status. Margaret's apparel departed from court dress in only one respect. Instead of a peeress's coronet such as she had worn in two of her frontispiece portraits by Van Diepenbeeck, she now wore a black velvet cap topped with feathers. Often adopted as an element of classical, heroic dress in portraits (as opposed to real life), this added a suggestion of Margaret's "masculine," "heroic" identity as an author to an otherwise feminine, aristocratic portrayal.*[62]

---

*This portrait, like Van Diepenbeeck's, shows features typical of its painter—a long face and long, heavily lidded eyes, in Lely's case—and so again may not be a good likeness of Margaret.

The Newcastles did not remain long in London—perhaps because William's town house at Clerkenwell had still not been restored to him. They had probably left before the end of June, by which time the capital was in the grip of the plague. Charles II, his court and Parliament moved to Oxford, and a month later the king's brother James, duke of York, traveled north with his wife and court to spend the late summer in York. All along their route, the gentry and nobility came out to pay their respects. Margaret's brother John was among those who met the royal couple near Woburn; in Nottinghamshire, William's son, Henry, headed the eminent society who welcomed them to the county. As lord lieutenant, William had organized seven companies of cavalry to parade, and two of these escorted the procession north to the Yorkshire border. Not far from Welbeck, William and Margaret greeted the duke and duchess in state and then accompanied them for some miles on the road. Margaret, wearing a riding dress with a knee-length waistcoat like a man's, attracted people's notice not so much by the masculinity of her costume—following the Restoration, the waistcoat or "vest" was commonly worn by court ladies for riding, though some male observers disapproved—as by the behavior she combined with it. In place of a lady's curtseys, she honored the company by making formal "legs and bows to the ground with her hand and head." Perhaps she was adopting a masculine manner that she felt suited her "heroic" identity as an author. But, whatever her own rationale, Margaret caused both amusement and astonishment by this "behaviour [which] was very pleasant, but rather to be seen than told."[63]

That summer Richard Flecknoe came to Welbeck, also fleeing the plague. Since the Restoration, he had carefully maintained his connection with the Newcastles, reprinting the poems he had written for them in Antwerp, and dedicating his play, *Love's Kingdom*, to William in 1664. The poems he now wrote at Welbeck—as thanks for his patrons' extended hospitality—provide brief sketches of the household's life. Margaret's closet, where she sat and wrote, provoked the poet's wonder:

> *What place is this? Looks like some sacred cell*
> *Where ancient hermits formerly did dwell . . .*
> *Is this a lady's closet? 't cannot be,*
> *For nothing here of vanity we see,*
> *Nothing of curiosity, nor pride,*
> *As all your ladies closets have beside.**

---

*The closet, a small room opening out of the bedchamber, was commonly used as a dressing room where intimate friends could also be received.

> Scarcely a glass or mirror in 't you find
> Excepting books, the mirrors of the mind . . .
> Here she's in rapture, here in ecstasy,
> With studying high and deep philosophy.

William appears as Flecknoe's ideal aristocratic patron,

> Who does not proudly look that you should doff
> Your hat, and make a reverence twelve score off, *
> Nor take exceptions if at every word
> You call him not "your Grace," or else "my Lord";
> But does appear a hundred times more great
> By leaving it, than by keeping state. [64]

The house itself was "builded great":

> No petty garnishments that look so spruce,
> As they were more for ornament than use . . .
> But all large and capacious you find,
> Justly proportioned to the owner's mind,
> All great and solid, as in ancient times,
> Before our modern buildings were our crimes.

Flecknoe published these verses the following year, along with poems for other royal and aristocratic patrons which he wrote during his stay at Welbeck. His book, *A Farrago of Several Pieces Newly Written*, he dedicated to Margaret, "in sign of gratitude" for the hospitality he had received "under your Grace's roof":

> If I appear too presumptuous to dedicate so little and worthless a work as this to your Grace, who writes so great and worthy ones, I hope in your goodness, Madam, you will pardon me; for to whom should the little fly for protection, but to the great? And the worthless, but to the worthy? [65]

Flecknoe stayed at Welbeck through Christmas and into the new year, lapping up the rich goodies that this "royal place" had to offer—not only food and drink but a variety of "recreation, pastime and harmless sports." [66] Breakfast

---

*I.e. from a great distance.

was light: William consumed "a glass of sack* . . . with a morsel of bread." Then, about 10 A.M., the whole household, including the upper servants like Andrew Clayton, gathered to watch William's horses in the manège, either in Welbeck's riding house or outdoors in Great Court if the weather was fine.[67] William, in his early seventies, still exercised his fencing skills regularly. But he no longer rode every day, having at last been persuaded by Margaret's constant worry "that when he had overheated himself, he would be apt to take cold." He had also begun to suffer the first symptoms of Parkinson's disease—a condition which degenerated rapidly between 1665 and 1667, by which time his hands shook constantly. During these years, he brought builders to Welbeck to add a balcony at one end of the riding house. From here, he and the rest of the company watched the horses below, ridden by William's grooms "whom he instructs in that art for his own pleasure."** While Margaret reflected on the intelligence the animals displayed, which proved her philosophical theory that "reason is in those creatures which have not speech," Flecknoe admired the building's "vast extent," seeing a "mighty temple" inhabited by equine demigods. In the neighboring stables, rich with decorative gables, domed pavilions, stone-vaulted roofs, and pedimented windows reminiscent of the banqueting house at Whitehall, Flecknoe found a "princely palace,"

> And 'twas but fit they should be so, where all
> The horses you of princely race might call.[68]

By 1668, the building's residents included thirteen manège horses, fourteen colts, six foals, and six mares to draw the family's coach, in addition to the horses belonging to Welbeck's upper servants. Margaret had her own horse here—a bay nag, light and small, doubtless trained in the manège as William recommended for "every horse that wears a bit," making them "firm on the hand, both for readiness and safety." Riding out to take the air for her health, as William wished, Margaret would sometimes have been accompanied by her husband on one of the three pad-nags he kept for gentle riding, and sometimes by Elizabeth Topp, whose own nag and mare were stabled with her mistress's.[69] It was doubtless on such rides that Flecknoe admired Margaret's goodness of heart: "when she sees one in misery, how tender and compassionate she is, even like that noble tree, ready to wound herself to afford balm and cure for

---

*Dry white wine from Spain or the Canary Islands.

**Captain Mazine, appointed an equerry of the royal stables, was now "constantly in London."

others' wounds."* Margaret held to an essentially practical religion—"one act of upright justice or pure charity is better than a book full of prayers"—and she had strong views on the best means of aiding those suffering from poverty:

> [Benefactors] ought to distribute their gifts themselves, and to be industri-
> ous to know and find out those that do truly and not feignedly want; neither
> must their gifts make the poor idle, but [they must] set the idle awork; and as
> for those that cannot work . . . as the old, sick, decrepit and children, they
> must be maintained by those that have means and strength.

When Margaret found such a deserving case herself, she acted on her beliefs: during 1667 Andrew Clayton's accounts record that "the poor woman of Lang-with" was being supported with regular payments of a shilling, "allowed by her Grace."[70]

The mornings at Welbeck were also a preferred time for literary work—before the thoughts became "mixed with the species and distractions of the day," Flecknoe commented.[71] By the mid-1660s, William had returned to his writing, creating short entertainments like "A Debauched Gallant" and "The Lottery" for his Welbeck guests, as well as composing a full-length play, *The Humorous Lovers*, for the London stage. Another play, *Sir Martin Mar-all*, he wrote only in draft form: after its completion by the popular dramatist and future poet laureate, John Dryden, this would become a hugely successful play, revived repeatedly in London playhouses until the 1690s. In addition to these plays, William also now completed the new book on horsemanship that he had begun while still in Antwerp. *A New Method and Extraordinary Invention to Dress Horses and Work them according to Nature* recorded William's "thoughts and . . . new experiments about that art" since the publication of *La Méthode Nouvelle* in 1658. A smaller volume than its predecessor, without engraved plates, it was published in London in 1667 and dedicated again to Charles II.[72]

Dinner, in the early afternoon, was the main meal of the day. Before the war, William's love of medieval tradition had kept the whole household dining together in Welbeck's hall, but after the Restoration he and Margaret probably ate privately with their guests in the parlor. Prewar records show William's table loaded with meat, both boiled and roasted. Three joints of beef, two of mutton with porridge, two of veal, with a goose or a young pig, and some-times a capon, made up the first course, accompanied by "salads and other

---

*True balsam, or balm of Gilead, was a resin extracted from the tree *Balsamodendrum gileadense*, used as an antiseptic on wounds.

small boiled meat to furnish the table, as neat tongue etc." Then the second course comprised a joint of lamb with two rabbits, two chickens, and four pigeons, "or some other fowl after the same proportion." Venison, ducks, turkeys, partridges, pheasants, quails, gulls, pewits, plovers, and larks were all consumed on festive occasions, while salmon, trout, carp, lobsters, crabs, flatfish, eels, and lampreys supplied the great table on days when the lower household ate salt-fish and herrings. Despite this largesse, William ate moderately, "so as to satisfy only his natural appetite," drinking a glass of small beer to quench his thirst at the beginning and end of the meal, with a glass of sack in the middle. Margaret was even more "sparing." Fearing the consequences "if I should eat much and exercise little," she would often fast, "though I have an indifferent good appetite." Her preferred food was "a little boiled chicken* or the like, my drink most commonly water." She also drank "clarified whey," but she avoided cream, "by reason the nature of cream is hot, and my diet is for the most part cooling."[73]

Outdoors, Welbeck offered a variety of pastimes. For the men, the bowling alley lay on the eastern edge of the grounds: for the ladies, there were walks in the water gardens to the east and south of the house, where ornamental canals ran beneath little stone garden houses, designed by the Smithsons for William's father. Beyond Welbeck's castlelike turreted gatehouse, the park seemed an Arcadia, Flecknoe thought, with

> . . . trees so thick and fair they seem th'abodes
> Not only of rural birds, but rural gods.**

Here there were deer hunts—with gentlemen on horseback and huntsmen afoot following the hounds—while hawking parties of ladies and gentlemen met in more open country. William also rode regularly through the park to visit his breeding stud of horses, grazing on the grange lands beyond. These rural pursuits were "far nobler pastimes than carding, dicing and tennis-playing," Margaret commented.[74]

One of the Newcastles' great enthusiasms was architecture, and Margaret took an especially close interest in the major building work now going on at her dower house at Bolsover, which she loved to speak of as "her own . . . stately buildings."[75] Bolsover Castle stood some six miles from Welbeck, high on a ridge overlooking the lush Vale of Scarsdale. Here lay William's lands, which Margaret would inherit if she survived her husband—the castle's deer

---

*A luxury in the days before battery farming.
**These trees remained a marvel to eighteenth- and nineteenth-century visitors.

park, and meadows rich as gardens, where sheep and cows grew fat on "fresh green grass and yellow cowslips."[76] Hills closed the view to the west. To the south, atop the same ridge as Bolsover, could be seen the two halls at Hardwick, built by William's grandmother, Bess of Hardwick.

The twelfth century castle at Bolsover was ruinous when William's father bought the site in 1608; four years later, he cleared the ground and began to build. The so-called Little Castle that he and the architect Robert Smithson designed was a romantic recreation of a medieval castle keep. Tall and square, surmounted by turrets and battlements, with windows kept to a minimum and arrowslits added to increase the military effect, it was a product of the chivalric culture then fashionable at Prince Henry's court, which had molded William's character. After Sir Charles's death in 1617, William completed the project, in collaboration with Smithson's son John, and the resulting interiors display their owner's fanciful wit and sense of humor, his eclecticism, love of grandeur, expensive taste, and his wide knowledge of contemporary art and architecture.

In the basement kitchens and the first-floor reception rooms elaborate vaulted stone ceilings continued the gothic style of the exterior, but fancifully mixed with classical columns and wall paintings derived from classical mythology. In the large hall, where the whole household dined, wall paintings depicting the labors of Hercules continued the heroic theme begun by the figure of Hercules carved in stone over the castle's main entrance. Together they stated William's own identity and ideals. Hercules was the "active friend of Virtue," supporting her through his "mighty labour" and "godlike travail," winning himself immortal fame[77]—just as William himself aspired to serve the Stuart monarchy through his aristocratic strength and virtue.

Beyond the hall, a smaller dining room was intended only for family and friends. Gilded wooden paneling lined the walls, and paintings of the five senses conjured an appropriate tone of fleshly delights. This, as almost all the rooms, contained a large, hooded fireplace, carved in local "marbles"—pink, white, black, and speckled—in a whimsical blend of gothic and classical style. Though probably inspired by the designs of the Italian architect, Serlio, the fireplaces were developed in prolific variety, each one unique.

On the floor above, the Star Chamber continued the imaginative and opulent tone, its blue ceiling scattered with gilded stars, its walls paneled and painted with biblical figures. Next door, the Marble Closet provided a more intimate space for the reception of privileged guests, with luxurious hangings, expensively glazed walls, and paintings of the Virtues; its large window opened onto a balcony, in the Italian style newly fashionable in London. Nearby, William's bedchamber had two closets, for the reception of the very greatest guests. In the Heaven Closet, the walls were decorated with one of the earliest examples of English chinoiserie, the design picked out in shell gold—four hundred times more expensive than gold leaf. Its ceiling-painting depicted Christ's Ascension, celebrated by cherubs playing every imaginable instrument—embodying William's passion for music. Manuscript sheets held by the cherubs contain a ballad of Robin Hood, William's Sherwood Forest hero. In the Elysium Closet, the ceiling was a witty mirroring of this Christian scene. In a scene copied from the Palace of Fontainebleau, Jove replaces Christ in the ceiling's illuminated center, while the other pagan gods disport themselves around the edges.

Outdoors, William constructed a garden to the east and south of the Little Castle enclosed by a high wall on whose top ran a broad walk. The centerpiece was a fountain, decorated with urinating cupids beneath a statue of Venus—modeled on an original in Florence, and symbolizing William's taste for physical love. Surrounding this, below ground level, stone beasts and satyrs and the heads of the Roman emperors were visible from the wall-top walk but not from the surrounding gardens. A sequence of garden rooms, built within the wall's thickness, offered spaces for solitary contemplation or companionable entertainment.

The Little Castle, its rooms splendid but relatively small in size and number, made an aristocratic lodge for occasional retreat rather than a full-size residence. So, when William was appointed lord lieutenant of Derbyshire in 1628, further building had begun. The new wing, extending southwards along the edge of the ridge, provided a gallery 140 feet long, well lit by large windows with views over the vale below—a place for exercise, conversation, and entertainment. Behind this, a series of grand state rooms provided a luxurious, up-to-date living space, where Charles I and Henrietta Maria were probably entertained in 1634. These rooms looked out eastwards over the castle's great court, on the south side of which William also added a new equestrian wing more than ninety yards long, with smithy, stables, and a large riding house for the manège.

But in October 1662, when all this was settled on Margaret, only the Little Castle remained structurally intact, and even this was uninhabited and unfurnished. Repairs had begun on the riding house earlier in the year, but the wall-top garden walk was in ruins, and the gallery wing remained roofless and at least partly derelict. In May 1663, building work began in earnest, continuing for more than five years. Under the supervision of the architect Samuel Marsh, the gallery was remodeled and the neighboring state rooms completely rebuilt in enlarged form. With a spacious dining room at the north end, nearest the Little Castle, followed by a great chamber, a withdrawing room, and then a bedchamber—a grand room intended for the reception of guests as much as for sleeping—the suite conformed to the most up-to-date ideas of aristocratic ceremony. Arranged in a long line, with the central doors all aligned, the rooms formed a series of ever more private and privileged spaces, through which guests would proceed only as far as their social status permitted: only the most eminent would reach the bedchamber at the farthest end.

By 1666 the basic shell was finished, with a grand new entrance from the castle's great court, flanked by a pair of monolith columns and topped with William's coat of arms carved in stone. Above, stone crenellations and chimneys were now being added, while below windows and doors and fine marble fireplaces were going in. The bathing house was already complete, and beyond the bedchamber a dressing room and a "closestool room" were under construction—both comfortable rooms, with fireplaces for heating. A warren of vaulted rooms in the basement provided such necessary services as kitchens, sculleries, and cellars. When finally complete, the new building would offer William and Margaret a second home that combined comfort with aristocratic magnificence. In the riding house, there was a new viewing gallery like that at Welbeck. Outside, the battlements of the wall-top walk around the fountain garden were being rebuilt; the garden itself had been returfed and a roller was purchased to maintain the lawn. But for the moment there was still only "a naked house . . . unclothed of all furniture."[78]

Despite their continuing debts, the Newcastles spent lavishly on this building work—at least £1,700 in the first two years alone—and money was also liberally consumed at Welbeck, where William maintained "the magnificence and grandeur of our ancient nobility," keeping up an aristocratic establishment that was more medieval than modern in its extravagant scale.[79]

William had resumed his prewar status as the leading nobleman of the North of England, beloved by the gentry for his "liberal hospitality and constant residence in his country," and Welbeck was often full of visitors. Throughout the spring and summer, county society flocked to the monthly horse races William had established in 1662 "for the pleasure of the gentry . . . [and] his Lordship's own contentment." Ladies dressed in their finest sat in their coaches, while many of the gentlemen galloped beside the race, which tested endurance as much as speed, with three consecutive runs over a five-mile course determining the overall winner.[80] Hunting and hawking brought further guests, and Christmas in particular was a time of open house, with food and entertainment available for all comers, both rich and poor. Any thought that "our recreations . . . may be sociable, but they are very chargeable"* would have been ignoble.[81]

---

*I.e. expensive.

William was famed for the lavish entertainments he had provided for the king and queen before the war, and his greatest piece of hospitality after the Restoration was probably that arranged in September 1665, when the duke and duchess of York were invited to stay at Welbeck on their return south from York. The duke himself was kept away by political business, but the duchess came. William and Margaret had known her in Antwerp as plain Anne Hyde, the teenage daughter of the lord chancellor, before she got pregnant and rushed into a widely unpopular marriage with the king's younger brother. But despite her lowly origins, the duchess "was splendidly entertained" with her court and other great society, including the duke of Buckingham and William's son, Henry, who quarreled and almost fought a duel.[82]

Welbeck was a hub not only of social, sporting, and cultural life but also of political power. As duke of Newcastle, William was the first-ranking nobleman of northern England. Through his mother, the heiress of the barony of Ogle, he was related "to most of the most ancient families in Northumberland, and other the northern parts," while his father's family brought similar connections in the Midlands. At the head of a complex network of affiliations—ties not only of blood and marriage, but also of friendship and hospitality, of military camaraderie from the Civil War, of mutual favors and services, and of shared political and financial interests—William was a man to be reckoned with. A local clergyman who displeased him (by marrying some of William's servants against his wishes) was investigated by the church authorities and faced excommunication if he could not gain William's forgiveness. Even the law was not above him: witnesses were well paid for their court appearances in his behalf, while juries in the local assizes at Nottingham and Derby were "spoken to."[83]

Appointed chief justice in Eyre by the king in July 1661, William presided over England's forests north of the River Trent. He appointed the forest officials, issued licenses for felling, ordered the arrest of deer-stealers, and decided which encroachments on the forests were to be punished and which ignored. At the forest court, held by his deputies at the Swan Inn in Mansfield, his protégés were favored when they claimed lucrative rights such as assart, purpresture,* and common over areas of woodland.[84]

Meanwhile, as lord lieutenant of Nottinghamshire, William took supreme command (under the king) of the county's legal administration and militia forces. He recommended gentlemen for appointment as justices of the peace and had the power to judge any law cases brought directly to him. He set local

---

*The former allowing them to grub up trees to create arable land, and the latter allowing them to enclose land and build on it, after payment of rent.

taxes to pay for the militia, and used his influence with county society to raise the loans needed to pay for Charles II's Dutch wars. His deputy lieutenants—themselves powerful local gentlemen—and all the officers in the militia were appointed by William. As head of local security, William received intelligence information from around the country and arranged for the surveillance of "powerful factions" disaffected with the government—"the fanatics . . . the Romanists and Presbyterians." In times of political crisis, like the Yorkshire Plot of 1663, he called out the militia and arrested suspected plotters. However, during the court's harsh crackdown after this plot, he provoked the government's anger by failing to prosecute his prisoners.[85]

Although William remained retired from London, he had considerable influence at court and in Parliament through his son. Occupying prominent positions close to the king, first as master of the robes until 1662, and then as a gentleman of the bedchamber, Henry also received particular favor from the king's brother, James, duke of York, who promised him equal advancement with the duke of Buckingham. In the House of Commons—where he sat first as MP for Derbyshire in 1660, and then as MP for Northumberland from 1661 until William's death—he was a loyal supporter of Crown policies, voting in the informal block controlled by the courtier Lord Wharton, which also included Margaret's brothers-in-law Peter Killigrew and Edmund Pye.* He associated closely with two rising northern politicians of his own generation—Sir George Savile (later first marquess of Halifax) and Sir Thomas Osborne (later first earl of Danby and then duke of Leeds). Though he served on few parliamentary committees and made few speeches in the Commons, he was a powerful broker behind the scenes, whose presence was seen as "absolutely necessary" for the passing of disputed measures.[86]

Business kept Henry in London much of the time, where he acted as William's agent, carrying his father's requests or excuses to courtiers and king, and relaying their instructions on Midlands affairs. He sent the latest news to Welbeck and told his father of his own political business, seeking his approval. For advice, however, he went to his friends—to Sir George Savile, Sir Thomas Osborne, and the young Lord Widdrington—and the relationship with his father was often strained. Henry's letters went unanswered for weeks when William disapproved of his decisions, but if he failed to tell his father everything, then William reproached him, saying that "he took it unkindly I would not acquaint him," provoking passionate self-justifications in return. Visits to Welbeck were infrequent and performed more for duty than pleasure.[87]

---

*There were as yet no formal political parties: the Whigs and Tories began to form during the Exclusion Crisis of 1679–1681.

Much of the friction was financial. Before the Restoration Henry had been owner and manager of Welbeck and all its estates, but now he was reduced to living on an allowance of £500 per quarter, subject to his father's continuing good will. Living in London in the fashionable splendor expected of courtiers, he found his income completely inadequate and ran up debts of £6,000 in just three years including £700 spent on two coaches and eight Flanders mares, £1,000 on furnishing his London house, and £2,000 on fine clothes. Called to account, he had to tell his father every detail of his expenditure and explain the £2,000 debts he had already contracted in the Interregnum—even though he had now repaid all but £400 of the total. Explaining also how he had spent more than £7,000 raised from sales of lands during the Interregnum—on buying back William's confiscated estates, on paying off his brother's debts, on election expenses at Derby in 1660, plus £1,000 "spent in living better . . . than my revenue allowed, your Lordship being pleased to command me to go . . . to live at Welbeck"—Henry concluded his letter with an abject apology. "I humbly beg your Lordship's pardon I have been no better manager."[88]

"I hope my father loves me": Henry was plagued by "melancholy splenetic apprehensions." He fretted constantly over William's disapproval, recounting their latest differences blow-by-blow to his friends.[89] By 1665 his fears had crystallized on the issue of the fate of his children. After a third daughter, named Margaret in honor of her step-grandmother, Henry and Frances had finally had a son in 1663: Henry, or "sweet Harry," as William called him.[90] But Henry senior, watching as his father continued selling estates to pay off his never-ending debts, worried that there would be little left for him and young Harry to inherit. Drawing up detailed inventories of his father's possessions, he calculated that William had had an annual income of over £19,000 before the Civil War, but now land sales had reduced this figure to £14,000. Of this, Henry himself received an allowance of only £2,000 to support his growing family. And William's sales "in reversion" were a further grievance. Estates sold this way remained in William's possession, bringing him in their rents while he lived, but they passed to their purchasers as soon as he died. Henry's income when he inherited would thus be further reduced by almost £3,500 per year.[91]

Uncertain of what he would eventually inherit from William, Henry was unable to make any formal financial provision for his children. He apologized desperately to his wife, calling down on himself "all the punishments this life can afford and, in the next world, eternal damnation" if he failed to make such provision after his father's death. But in the meantime he bitterly regretted his generosity three years before, when he had allowed William to break the entail on the lands needed for Margaret's marriage jointure without making any provision for their return to the male line of the family after her death. Amidst rumors of "unjust, subtle designs" at Welbeck, Henry wanted a formal legal settlement drawn up to ensure that these and all William's other remaining lands would eventually pass to him and his family. Not daring to approach his father in person, he sent John Hutton to Welbeck.

William was furious, and swore that the land was "as sure to you as all the settlements in the world could make it," Hutton reported. "He wondered his son should trouble himself with nothing—for that it was not imaginable that he should dispose of it from him and his." Henry, however, was not reassured, and on March 19, 1666, he and his wife sent a pair of letters to Welbeck, setting out their concerns. Horrified by their hints and innuendoes, William replied to each of them separately. "Honesty is my mistress, which I will ever serve faithfully," he assured Frances. And to Henry there was more.

> We are all honest folks here . . . and I am confident you never had an ill opinion either of my love to you and yours, or that I was a fool, or that any had taken a lease of governing me . . . though I am very old, I do not yet dote, thank God.[92]

Although William vigorously asserted his independence from any sinister influence, Henry had grounds for suspicion. In Margaret's writings there were clear descriptions of how women, despite their exclusion from public life and all "matter of governments," could yet "govern the world" by "an insensible power."[93]

> We women are much more favoured by Nature than men, in giving us such beauties, features, shapes, graceful demeanour, and such insinuating and enticing attractives, as men are forced to admire us, love us, and be desirous of us, in so much as, rather than not have and enjoy us, they will deliver to our disposals their power, persons, and lives, enslaving themselves to our will and pleasures.[94]

Margaret also wrote of how wives deceived and directed their husbands to gain their own way, either by anger—"the Furies are no more turbulent, nor worse natured" than some women—or by "insinuating and flattering." "Gentle persuasions, meek submissions and subtle insinuations" were more effective than "railing and exclamations," she believed, but she could easily be suspected of practicing both techniques of persuasion. While her dedicatory epistles lauded William to the skies, her autobiographical writings revealed her capacity for passionate anger. Talking to William one time, "I told him that I did speak sharpest to those I loved best. To which he jestingly answered, that if so, then he would not have me love him best."[95]

Henry's suspicion also fell on Francis Topp, Margaret's natural ally, as husband to her lifelong friend, Elizabeth. By the mid-1660s, Topp had taken over Andrew Clayton's role as Welbeck's factotum. He now purchased the household's necessaries; he paid the servants, the lawyers, the builders at Bolsover. He sent Henry his quarterly allowance and ordered William's and Margaret's medicines from their London apothecary. He received the money and accounts from Welbeck's grange farm, and he was taking an increasing role in managing William's northern as well as western estates.[96]

On his return to Welbeck in 1660, William had instituted a program of vigorous management policies on his estates, designed to maximize the family's income. Enclosing commons, draining marshes, and clearing woods to create new ploughland were all measures on which he was enthusiastic.[97] In many places he abandoned the traditional system of small copyholds and tenancies in favor of letting large blocks of land to a single wealthy tenant—a modern practice that brought in larger rents and simplified the collection process, but necessitated the eviction of all the existing occupants. Surveys were also undertaken, enabling lands to be revalued and higher rents to be set; tenants who refused to pay the new rate were removed.[98]

Under such rack-renting, many tenants found that, far from making a profit, they were losing money each year. Bringing formal petitions to William, they requested new surveys and rent reductions; when this failed, they vacated lands they could not afford to farm.[99] Those who remained often found it impossible to pay their rents, especially in periods of agricultural recession. The luckier ones had their possessions confiscated to pay their debts, but many tenants were evicted.[100] Although Margaret claimed that her husband was all "noble bounty and generosity," having "no self-designs or self-interest," the surviving estate papers suggest rather that William insisted strictly on his rights, however small. Tenants were charged higher rents for lands they themselves had paid to improve; disputes with the townspeople of Chesterfield were energetically prosecuted; profits were boosted by requiring tenants to grind their corn only in William's mills; neighbors' farm animals who broke down fences and strayed onto Welbeck lands were impounded and only returned when their owners paid for their "trespass."[101]

William's estate commissioners often had great difficulty carrying out his instructions. Reliable new tenants could not always be found and evicted tenants sometimes refused to leave, especially during harsh winter weather. Heavy Northumberland snows regularly prevented collection of the December rents; only in May, when local beast markets recommenced and the tenants could again sell their goods, was cash available to be sent to Welbeck. Political crises like the abortive Yorkshire Plot of 1663 also prevented markets and made tenants unwilling to buy the new leases William wanted to sell. The commissioners, forced to bring their master the bad news, often experienced William's "high displeasure," as he went into "a great passion both with us and the tenants."[102] The tenants "are rebellious subjects, not paying us our rents duly and truly; besides they are apt to murmur at the least increase of our farms [in rent] . . . the tenants and servants grow rich, but their masters and landlords become poor"—Margaret was perhaps thinking of some of her husband's outbursts when she wrote this speech for one of the country gentlemen in her *Orations*.[103]

But the tenants themselves, unaware of such rages, continued to think "honourably" of their noble landlord. William's everyday charm confirmed the belief that he was not really responsible for their hardships, and Andrew Clayton too preserved the tenants' good will, being always "very civil" to them, even though he was often enforcing William's rack-renting policies. It was Francis Topp who took the blame. By 1667 he was reckoned to be the chief manager of William's business affairs. Energetic and capable, determined to get his master what he wanted, Topp was uncompromising in his approach. Suspicions of bribery and dishonest accounting were vigorously investigated. The maximum possible rent was demanded for every piece of land. And Topp's blustering, bullying manner towards the poorer tenants—threatening to punish those who were in arrears by exacting the rent with "treble damages" ("that will make them examples, when it hath cost them three times more")—only caused further alienation. It was "the crossness . . . of Mr Topp" that caused their sufferings, the tenants believed.[104]

Topp had become William's most trusted adviser. In sharp contrast with his treatment of the tenants, he was all flattery, eagerness, and exaggerated self-abasement when dealing with his social superiors, deluging them with "your Excellencies" and "your Honours" and professions of his "duty and all faithfulness."[105] His ability to manage his master's moods and time his approaches well was widely acknowledged, and his assistance was eagerly sought by those who had business with William—even by the distrustful Henry.[106] Having managed to persuade his father to make the "grand settlement" he desired—establishing a new entail on all William's lands, so that they could be passed only to his male heirs—Henry approached Topp in April 1666 to make sure that the legal papers were drawn up quickly and signed. Topp, hoping to "remove all doubts in the family" of his own intentions, promised that the business would be done at once, assuring Henry at the same time that it was even "more my lord duke's and my lady duchess's desires than it can be your honour's." However, it was not until October 13, 1666, that William finally signed the large parchment sheet of the indenture, restricting himself to a mere life interest in all the estates he had previously owned outright. No longer would he be able to sell lands to raise the money he needed to pay off his debts. And he would be equally unable, should he desire it, to give any of these estates to Margaret, as an increase in her marriage jointure. Henry's inheritance was now secure, and in the following year he made formal financial provision for his own children.[107]

DESPITE WELBECK'S MANY DISTRACTIONS, William and Margaret still spent much of their time together. It was not the modern fashion—Restoration ladies increasingly led separate lives, going about with their women friends and maids to visits and public entertainments, rather than spending their time in their husbands' company—but Margaret defended her practice as "a loving and agreeable course of life."

> Better keep to an old fashion, which is becoming, easy and commodious, than follow a new, vain and mis-becoming fashion . . . 'tis more seemly, graceful and becoming for a wife to have her husband always with her.[108]

The couple's talk ranged widely—through taxation, education, religion, censorship, legal and political abuses and reforms, the faults of human nature, observations on history, politics, and economics, and their personal experiences of war, exile, and restoration. Margaret was no longer just a listener. She often directed the conversation, telling William of her philosophical reading, or presenting her own observations and ideas for his comment. Sometimes she rallied her husband, challenging his views, but William always had the last word in this repartee, whether because of his quicker wit or Margaret's willingness to be beaten.[109] Nonetheless, their discussions and debates were a vital inspiration for her writing—"like as a pair of bellows to a spark of fire in a chimney . . . so his discourse doth set the hearer's brain on a light flame, which heats the wit, and enlightens the understanding." Just as skilled fencers or tennis players required "a skilful opposite," so even "the greatest wits that are, or ever were, cannot discourse wittily unless they either imagine or else have a real witty opposite to discourse wittily to."[110] Material from William's talk— his theories of human nature, his view of whether man would ever fly— entered Margaret's books, and she continued to include occasional sections of his writing.[111] Always, when she finished a book, she submitted it to him, seeking his "approvement" and "leave to publish."[112]

Margaret had become a more serious, committed writer than her husband. She abandoned her genteel, amateurish negligence and feminine modesty to engage in scholarly controversy. She worked hard at revising her books herself,[113] where aristocrats normally preferred to have their work polished by a professional writer—as William had employed the playwright James Shirley to complete his comedy, *The Country Captain*, before the war. But far from disapproving of her break with convention, William admired his wife, preferring her work above his own. Her writing's power—either "to fetch a tear or make a smile"—made Margaret an "empress in sovereign power" over her readers' emotions: "I saw your poems, and then wished them mine."[114] Compared to his own still pond, her inspiration was an "eternal spring and running stream,"

> *So clear and fresh, with wit and fancy store,*
> *As then despair did bid me write no more.*
>
> *'Tis supernatural, nay, 'tis divine,*
> *To write whole volumes, ere I can a line.*

Reversing the normal relation of the sexes, William predicted it would be his wife, not he, who would gain "eternal fame" as a writer:

> *You conquer death, in a perpetual life;*
> *And make me famous too in such a wife.*[115]

During the winter of 1665 to 1666, when Flecknoe found her "studying high and deep philosophy" in her closet, Margaret was working on a second volume of philosophical controversies, intended to supplement her *Philosophical Letters* with discussions of a new group of opponents. In her previous book, Margaret's aristocratic standards of politeness and open-mindedness in dispute had led her to approve wholeheartedly of the work of Robert Boyle, "that learned and ingenious writer." Creating a philosophy intended for the gentlemen of the Royal Society, Boyle shared her concern to establish good manners in philosophy. "He is a very civil, eloquent and rational writer; the truth is, his style is a gentleman's style," she enthused.[116]

But as she read more of the new "experimental philosophy" produced by the Royal Society, Margaret found it less appealing, and she was especially provoked by the book published in 1665 by Robert Hooke, Boyle's assistant, now employed as the society's "curator of experiments." *Micrographia, or some Physiological Descriptions of Minute Bodies* described the microscopical researches that Hooke had undertaken for the society in 1663, including observations of the seeds of plants and of insects and their parts—the stings of bees, the complex eyes and feet of flies. With lavish engraved illustrations paid for by the society, the book was the first detailed account of microscopical observations ever published. But the *Micrographia* was more than a mere research report: it was also a manifesto, advertising the society's program, its aspirations and achievements. Hooke claimed that experiments were the only true foundation for a philosophy of nature, that the society's experimental results were certain, incontrovertible truth, and that their discoveries would bring practical benefits as great as the inventions of printing and gunpowder, producing revolutions in the arts of navigation and agriculture, and restoring mankind to its pristine knowledge and happiness before the Fall.

These claims were what really offended Margaret, and through detailed examination of Hooke's observations, she systematically undermined them.

Microscopes and other experimental apparatus produced "fallacies, rather than discoveries of truth," distorting the very phenomena they were intended to reveal, she argued. As the magnification of a lens became greater, so did the distortion; minute flaws in the glass produced more distortions or multiple images of a single object. How was it possible to know whether what you saw through the microscope was a true representation, when even Hooke himself admitted that, with the light coming from different angles, the same object appeared to have very different shapes? Philosophy could not be based on such "deluding arts." Reason, not observation, was "the best informer": even experimental philosophers, who claimed to rely only on observation, must use reason first of all, in order to choose and design their experiments. Her own philosophical method—a balanced combination of the reason and observation that were the two faculties inherent in all natural bodies, in their "rational matter" and "sensitive matter"—was the best, as being the most natural and so least likely to be distorted.[117]

Furthermore, Margaret argued, even if Hooke's microscopical observations were accurate, they were nothing more than "superficial wonders." Displaying only the surface appearance of bodies, not their "interior forms and motions," they told us nothing of the underlying causes in nature and so had no philosophical use. And they were just as useless for any practical improvements:

> The inspection of the exterior parts of vegetables doth not give us any knowledge how to sow, set, plant and graft; so that a gardener or husbandman will gain no advantage at all by this art: the inspection of a bee through a microscope will bring him no more honey, nor the inspection of a grain more corn.

Margaret hated the experimenters' arrogance in thinking that mankind was somehow outside and above nature, capable of "power over natural causes and effects," when in fact humanity was merely a small part of nature and experimental researches were nothing more than "useless sports," fit only for boys not men.[118]

Margaret was not alone. The experimenters' grandiose utopian promises of almost limitless human improvement—which smacked of the Interregnum parliamentarian reformers who had indeed inspired many of them, including Robert Boyle—offended other old royalists, who were also angered by the Royal Society's success in gaining royal patronage, and the rapid career advancement achieved by its members in both church and state. All the attacks on the society in its early years came from this political background. Thomas Hobbes had been first, with his *Dialogus Physicus* of 1661—a personal attack on Robert Boyle and his air-pump experiments performed at the society. Margaret's *Observations upon Experimental Philosophy*, published in 1666, was the second work from within this group. She was followed in 1670 by the most vitriolic anti-experimentalist of all: Henry Stubbe produced a series of books, encouraged by John Fell, a former royalist officer, now dean of Christ Church in Oxford, and a correspondent of Margaret's and William's. Finally, the most entertaining of these attacks came in 1676, in *The Virtuoso*, a comedy by the playwright Thomas Shadwell, a literary protégé of the Newcastles. All these critics shared the same basic viewpoint—that the society's lengthy researches produced no useful result, either in philosophical understanding or practical applications.

From Hooke's *Micrographia*, Margaret extended into a broad critique of experimental philosophy, attacking Robert Boyle's studies of heat and cold as well as other researches promoted by the Royal Society. She also took this opportunity to discuss the theories of the ancient philosophers, as described in Thomas Stanley's *The History of Philosophy*. Previously she had been highly critical of these philosophers, and especially of Aristotle, whose views unjustly dominated intellectual life in the universities, she felt. But now, in response to the experimental philosophers' own merciless attacks on Aristotle, she expressed a more positive view. All men, both ancient and modern, were equally "subject to errors," she pointed out. And at least the ancients were original, unlike their modern successors. Patching together their philosophy with "parcels taken from the ancient," the experimental philosophers were not only thieves but dangerous rebels, she charged, "like those unconscionable men in civil wars, which endeavour to pull down the hereditary mansions of noblemen and gentlemen, to build a cottage of their own."[119]

As before in the *Philosophical Letters*, Margaret expounded her own views for comparison with those of the philosophers she discussed. She also added a final section to her book, more than twenty pages long, containing explanations of "obscure and doubtful passages" in the latest edition of her *Philosophical Opinions*. It was a long and difficult labor, and as she worked Margaret found light relief in writing a new work of fiction "to divert my studious thoughts."[120] Partly inspired by her studies of experimental philosophy, *The Description of a New World, Called the Blazing World* was a work of varied and surprising imagination, combining elements of fantasy, science fiction, romance, utopian political theory, and philosophical and theological debate—the longest piece of fiction Margaret wrote.

The story began in "romancical" style, with a young lady carried off against her will by a man who has fallen in love with her. But when his ship is driven by storms into the frozen northern seas, all the men die of cold, and the young lady alone is carried into another world, joined to her own at the North Pole. Stories of voyages to the strange world of the Moon had become fashionable, inspired by the discoveries of the telescope. Margaret knew of the ancient work of Lucian and the modern story by Cyrano de Bergerac, as well as John Wilkins's book of lighthearted lunar speculations, *The Discovery of a New World in the Moon*. But her own work was different, entering a whole new world "of my own creating," and so giving her imagination completely free rein.[121]

The Blazing World—named for the extraordinary brightness of its comet-like stars, which made its nights "as light as days"—was inhabited by strange races of men: some stood upright, but were shaped like animals, birds, and fishes, while others, of human form, were not white and black but all colors, blue, green, purple, red, and orange. It was a place of untold wealth, with gold and jewels in abundance, and whole cities built of agate, amber, and coral, as well as marble. The world had never known war, since all its inhabitants spoke a single language and were ruled over by one emperor, who lived at Paradise, a city built all of gold. Here the young lady arrived after a long voyage, and the emperor fell in love and married her. Retiring from public life, he "gave her an absolute power to rule and govern all that world as she pleased."[122]

First the empress called together the world's statesmen and priests so as to learn of their wise government and laws—an interlude in the style of Thomas More's *Utopia* and its many successors. Then the story entered its "philosophical" phase, which occupied over a quarter of the whole. The empress founded schools and learned societies for her "ingenious and witty" subjects, each of whom was assigned to the "profession . . . most proper for the nature of their species." "The bear-men were to be her experimental philosophers, the bird-men her astronomers, the fly-, worm- and fish-men her natural philosophers, the ape-men her chemists, the satyrs her Galenic physicians, the fox-men her politicians, the spider- and lice- men her mathematicians, the jackdaw-, magpie- and parrot-men her orators and logicians, the giants her architects, etc."[123] As the empress summoned each kind in turn to tell her of their discoveries, Margaret promulgated her own views on the world of learning. She satirized scholars in general: for their quarrelsome natures, their interminable, pointless wrangling over intellectual questions they can never resolve, their ignorance of practical, useful knowledge, and their use of obscure technical terminology, which even they could not explain. The parrot-orators break off mid-speech, confused by the complexities of their own artful rhetoric; the bird-logicians, displaying their (and Margaret's own) knowledge of all the complex modes and figures of the Aristotelian syllogism, also show how ridiculous and useless are these "formal argumentations." Especially she attacked experimental philosophers: the bear-men quarrel endlessly over what they can see through their telescopes; the empress demonstrates the "insufficiency" of their microscopes with the same arguments Margaret had already employed against Hooke; when the empress requires them to break their glasses, they are reduced to humiliation, begging to be allowed to keep them, for "we take more delight in artificial delusions, than in natural truths." Meanwhile, the fish-men and the satyrs reveal that the anatomical researches undertaken at the Royal Society are "useless inspections." It is the worm-men, the lowliest and least promising of creatures, who bring "the most rational" opinions to the empress, presenting arguments from Margaret's own philosophy.[124]

Next the empress turns to religion, converting her subjects to her own, true faith. In a newly built chapel, lined with the mysterious firestone her worm-men have fetched for her from a volcano, she preaches "sermons of terror to the wicked," threatening them with everlasting fire, while secret pipes and taps supply water to the firestone around them, making it burn bright and hot.* Then the empress expands her researches into theology, questioning the immaterial spirits her fly-men had summoned for her. Fascinated by the illumination promised by the Jewish cabala—a mystical method of interpreting the Old Testament—and by its modern successors, like John Dee's number mysticism, she finally resolves to compose her own version, with the spirits' assistance. Needing a scribe, she rejects all the ancient philosophers—too "wedded to their own opinions"—and all the moderns—"so self-conceited that they would scorn to be scribes to a woman." The duchess of Newcastle is eventually selected, on the spirits' advice: "although she is not one of the most learned, eloquent, witty and ingenious, yet is she a plain and rational writer . . . and she will without question be ready to do you all the service she can." Thus Margaret enters her own story (a feature not uncommon in utopias and accounts

---

*Margaret's invention of this mineral was perhaps inspired by the fantastic story, printed in John Lyly's *Euphues: The Anatomy of Wit*, of a firestone in Liguria that was quenched by milk and reignited by water.

of imaginary voyages), but only her soul, without her body, can travel to the Blazing World. There she and the empress enter "according to Plato's doctrine" into "a conversation of souls," developing "such an intimate friendship between them, that they became platonic lovers, although they were both females."[125]

Together, they invent imaginary worlds, advised by the spirits that this will make them happier than the military conquest of any real worlds. Using her own philosophical principles "of sensitive and rational self-moving matter," the duchess creates a world "so curious and full of variety, so well ordered and wisely goverened, that it cannot possibly be expressed by words."[126] When the empress becomes bored, the duchess conducts her soul on a tour of her own world, ending with a visit to Welbeck, where the duke entertains them in his mind, with "scenes, songs, music, witty discourses, pleasant recreations and all kinds of harmless sports." Back in the Blazing World, the duchess advises the empress on political reforms, especially on the disbandment of all her newly founded learned societies, whose "perpetual disputes and quarrels" the empress now fears may cause Civil War.[127] Then, when the empress hears that her old home country is threatened with war, the duchess becomes her military strategist, discovering a way to transport the empress, with her fish-men and a large supply of firestones, from the Blazing World into her own old world. Here they wreak such destruction on her country's enemies that they all submit and her native country becomes "the absolute monarchy of all that world."[128]

This last, utterly "fantastical" section of the work displayed Margaret's passion for power, her ambition so great that "no creature in the world was able to know either the height, depth or breadth of" it. "As ambitious as ever any of my sex was, is, or can be," she wanted to "be a great princess . . . an Empress of a world, and I shall never be quiet until I be one."[129] But she was happy to center these aspirations only on her writing and imagination, she explained. Her interior, imaginary world she could make and change however she pleased, "without control or opposition," gaining "as much pleasure and delight as a world can afford," without the "disturbances and . . . deaths" caused by empire builders in "this terrestrial world." And so she resolved to "reject and despise all the worlds without*me, and create a world of my own."[130]

> Though I cannot be Henry the Fifth, or Charles the Second, yet I endeavour
> to be Margaret the First; and although I have neither power, time nor occa-
> sion to conquer the world as Alexander and Caesar did; yet, rather than not

---

*I.e. outside.

be mistress of one, . . . I have made a world of my own: for which nobody, I hope, will blame me, since it is in everyone's power to do the like.

No longer did she envy the great figures of antiquity—the courage of Hector and Achilles, the wisdom of Nestor, the eloquence of Ulysses, the beauty of Helen. Finding all the "delight and glory" she desired in her imaginative life, she was content with "the figure of honest Margaret Newcastle, which now I would not change for all the world."[131]

Margaret published her *Blazing World* in 1666, "as an appendix" to her *Observations upon Experimental Philosophy*—"to delight the reader with variety, which is always pleasing," just as Kepler had added a romance of a voyage to the moon to his own philosophical work. But she also issued her story as a separate volume, for the benefit of those, "especially ladies," who would never open a work of "serious philosophical contemplations."[132] Thus her self-portrait of heroic ambition would reach the widest possible audience, while the book's long philosophical middle section presented a large body of Margaret's arguments and ideas in a palatable fictional setting for these general readers.

By the time her *Observations* and *Blazing World* were printed, Margaret had several other books well advanced, "which shall, if God grant me life and health, be published ere long." There was a new collection of plays and a revised edition of *The World's Olio* in preparation, but the first to be printed was the biography of William that she had begun and then abandoned some eight years before.[133] With a large body of literature to her name, Margaret's own ambitions were increasingly satisfied, and she felt free to return to this work, dedicated to her husband's fame more than her own. This was an important project for her—a tribute of affection to the man she loved, a payment of thanks for his constant love and support—but it was also "so hard a task" that only her "love to his person and to truth" had encouraged her through to completion.[134]

Margaret portrayed herself as "an impartial historian," writing "truly, honestly and uprightly, without any aggravation, or feigned illustration."[135] But in fact she had a definite agenda—to disprove William's enemies by demonstrating his loyalty, wisdom, and multifarious abilities—and throughout the work her evidence was carefully selected and directed towards this end, romanticizing and idealizing her hero-husband. It was especially important to answer the many critics of his Civil War career. So, after only the briefest account of William's ancestry and upbringing, his first marriage and his early political career, almost a quarter of the book was taken up with just two years of his life. Vaunting her husband's skill as a general and his army's successes, Margaret here passed in silence over the failures others criticized—his delight in artistic distractions and his unwillingness to commit his forces to the large engagements that many royalists had desired.[136]

This account, ending with a careful justification of William's controversial decision to flee into exile after the Battle of Marston Moor, formed Book 1 of Margaret's work and was based largely on the information of her husband's secretary, John Rolleston.[137] Then Book 2, recounting the couple's long exile and eventual return to England at the Restoration, was based on Margaret's own memories. Its dominant theme was of hardships and disappointments bravely and uncomplainingly endured, and its story ended in a detailed calculation of William's vast financial losses caused by the Civil War—clear, quantitative proof both of William's supreme "loyalty to his King and country" and of the injustice he had suffered in receiving so little reward at the Restoration. Throughout the work Margaret repeatedly asserted her husband's love for the king and his readiness to make any self-sacrifice—even "his life and all he had left him"—in the royal service. Dedicating the completed book to King Charles II, she ensured that her reproach reached the right man.[138]

Within this life story, Margaret incorporated many named acknowledgments, scrupulously repaying the debts of gratitude she and William felt to have amassed, especially during their exile—to Edward Hyde for persuading William's brother to compound for his estates in 1651, to Sir Charles himself for saving the family estates, to William's children for their financial support, to the Duartes "for their great civilities," to the people of Antwerp and especially William's creditors there for their "charity and compassion." Angry at her husband's sufferings, Margaret also wanted to settle old scores by naming and shaming his enemies—necessary, she thought, to present his actions in the best possible light. But here William intervened, forbidding her "to mention any thing or passage to the prejudice or disgrace of any family or particular person (although they might be of great truth)." Though she felt her story "much darkened" by this restriction, Margaret promised her dutiful "submission" to William's more generous nature. Apart from obscure hints—"of the treacherous cowardice, envy, and malice of some persons, my Lord's enemies, and of the ingratitude of some of his seeming friends," of his "great private enemies," of the "juggling, treachery and falsehood in his own army, and amongst some of his own officers"—she obeyed her husband's "commands to conceal those things" almost to the letter.[139] Just two passages in her completed work—describing Charles I's failure to pay the troops William had raised for his war against the Scots, and identifying Lord Goring and Sir Francis Mackworth as guilty of "invigilancy and carelessness"—were too pointed for William, and in almost every copy of the book these were inked out by hand. However, in some copies the print could still be read through the ink; in others, fascinated readers tried to remove the ink, or wrote the words (probably derived from other, less darkly obliterated copies) back in by hand themselves.[140] In these two cases, at least, Margaret had successfully circumvented her husband's censorship.

The calculation of William's financial losses at the end of Book 2 brought Margaret's chronological story to an end. Then Books 3 and 4, forming almost half of the whole work, dealt with more general topics: William's character, his education, his power and noble honors, his conversation and opinions. Here her book clearly showed its inspiration in the passionate love and loyalty Margaret felt towards her husband. Twenty years of attentive watching and listening resulted in a mass of closely observed, intimate details. William's home life and recreations, his conversation, jokes and mottoes, his appearance, dress and diet—Margaret's affection recorded all these everyday minutiae which, though commonly ignored as trivia by biographers before Boswell's *Life of Johnson*, are in fact essential to the conjuring of a real, living portrait.[141] Her book—*The Life of the Thrice Noble, High and Puissant Prince, William Cavendish, Duke, Marquess and Earl of Newcastle*—was the first biography of a husband published by a wife, and it struck a chord with other women, who perhaps read this more than any other work of Margaret's.[142] At least two—Lucy Hutchinson from the parliamentarian camp, and Anne Fanshawe from the royalists—were inspired to imitation. Their biographies, written soon after Margaret's was published, follow her lead in recording intimate, domestic portraits, and vindicating their husbands' careers and reputations.[143]

Chapter Thirteen

The Talk of the Town, 1667

William's London town house, known as Newcastle House, stood half a mile north of the City in the fashionable village of Clerkenwell, where many aristocrats and wealthy merchants had their London residences. Built by William around 1630 on the ruins of the nunnery of St. Mary, the great house—two stories plus cellars and attics, with at least thirty-five rooms heated by fireplaces—was in the formal Palladian style, then newly introduced from the Continent by Charles I and his courtiers. At ground level a completely windowless wall faced out to the road, from which a coach gateway led into an enclosed courtyard. Ahead lay the house's main entrance, leading to a two-story hall, which gave access to a pair of grand reception rooms facing out to the gardens behind, one on each floor: "the great dining room" and "the red chamber."[1] On either side of the courtyard, two symmetrical wings displayed externally the new internal regularity that the Palladian style had introduced to England: from the main central reception rooms, equal paired suites of rooms opened on both sides, one each for husband and wife, consisting of withdrawing chamber, bedchamber, and closets—spaces not only for solitude but for private, separate entertaining. Behind the house extended two acres of grounds, with stables and coach house, an orchard, and a garden, along one side of which ran the old nunnery cloister, its stone-vaulted roof decorated with carved flowers.[2]

It was a perfect nobleman's town house, but in 1654, with William's permission, his son Charles had sold it to pay off one of his father's prewar debts. Since the Restoration, all William's attempts to regain the house by process of law resulted in failure. So, early in 1666, he finally agreed to repurchase it, raising the money he needed by selling one of his Midlands estates for £2,400.[3] At last, he and Margaret would be able to join London society in proper style.

In July 1666, Francis Topp and a party of servants were dispatched to prepare the house "for the reception of his Grace and family," and late in March 1667 the Newcastles began to prepare for departure. The servants who remained behind at Welbeck were put on board wages, the bailiff at the grange farm was directed to sell its excess produce, no longer needed in the house, and Andrew Clayton was put in charge of all the estate's affairs, being ordered to pay the bills, receive the rents, and forward moneys to London as necessary. On April 1 William with "his duchess, family and retinue" passed out of Welbeck's gates, where Clayton disbursed eight shillings and tuppence in customary charity to the assembled poor, "by their Graces' command."[4]

About a week later they arrived in London, and Newcastle House filled with visitors, calling to pay their respects to these aristocratic grandees "newly come out of the North." Amongst the first, as gossip eagerly reported, was the king himself, who came to visit Margaret—a great mark of honor. Then a host of others followed: northern relatives and friends like the marquess of Dorchester and Jocelyn Lord Percy, soon to be earl of Northumberland; old learned associates like Walter Charleton; former companions of exile like the Evelyns and George Morley (Edward Hyde's chaplain in Antwerp, now bishop of Winchester); and newer aristocratic acquaintances like Lord George Berkeley and his wife. Invited guests came to midday dinner, sat on into the long afternoon visiting hours, then departed as new social callers joined the company—only to be displaced in their turn by yet newer arrivals.

Some of these visitors William and Margaret entertained jointly in the central public reception rooms of Newcastle House. Others Margaret received alone in her private apartments, where they "sate discoursing" with her, often in her bedchamber. This, in the fashion of the day, would have been richly furnished for such occasions, with a vastly expensive damask or velvet state bed, a suite of finely upholstered chairs and stools, an assortment of tapestries, candelabra, silver and porcelain vases, and various furniture—cabinets and chests, tea tables, screens, and looking glasses, either richly japanned or made of exotic woods and precious metals.* Here Margaret regularly held court to large audiences who were fascinated by this "person who has not her equal possibly in the world, so extraordinary a woman she is in all things." John Evelyn alone, "much pleased with the extraordinary fanciful habit, garb, and discourse of the Duchess," visited at least four times in three weeks, twice by himself and twice accompanied by his wife, Mary.

---

*During the previous nine months, Francis Topp had spent £1,045 in London, much of it probably on furnishing the house. A further £1,700 was consumed during the Newcastles' three-month stay.

Even now, in her midforties and famous as an author, Margaret was still plagued by shyness, especially when facing strangers or large groups. Being "surprised with a visit" that she did not expect could be devastating, throwing her thoughts into "a confused disorder," leaving her speechless, or stammering out "pieces of words, or pieces of the letters of words." Turning pale as death, or blushing red "as if . . . drunk," shaking all over, "I have been often so out of countenance, as I have not only pitied myself, but others have pitied me, which is a condition I would not be in." The humiliating memories of such occasions were for Margaret "as great an affliction as the mind can have," but although she "strived and reasoned" with herself, she could not be rid of this "natural," "inbred" bashfulness. It was not any feeling of shame of herself, "of my mind or body, my birth or breeding, my actions or fortunes," she thought. Rather it was "a fear of others," of their rudeness, criticism, or ridicule (which her own unconventional identity and behavior might well be expected to provoke). As such, she judged her shyness was incurable, since human nature could never be reformed. But there was one consolation: "most commonly it soon vanisheth away, and many times before it can be perceived."[5]

Even so, Margaret's manner remained awkward and constrained, as she labored to entertain her guests "handsomely, civilly, courteously." Thinking "it is a less fault to err with too much civility than with too much neglect," she fell over herself to be friendly and welcoming.[6] Greeting visitors "in a kind of transport," she treated them "with extraordinary kindness," before accompanying departing guests right through the house and out into the courtyard—an elaborate mark of respect, far beyond the requirements of etiquette. John Evelyn was flattered by these attentions, but his wife took offence at Margaret's nervous mannerisms. "Her gracious bows, seasonable nods, courteous stretching out of her hands, twinkling of her eyes, and various gestures of approbation"—all these Mary Evelyn judged excessive, beyond even "the imagination of poets, or the descriptions of a romance heroine's greatness." And Margaret's careful politeness—"her way of address to people more than necessarily submissive; a certain general form to all, obliging, by repeating affected, generous, kind expressions; endeavouring to show humility by calling back things past"—was seen as officious and condescending, a form of false modesty, designed only to magnify and "improve her present greatness." Margaret gushed nervously, calling Mary "daughter" in gratitude for the many kindnesses that Mary's mother, Lady Browne, had shown her during her difficult days of courtship in Paris. But Mary's resentment only grew as she recalled how Margaret had promised her £1,000 at her own wedding in Paris—a promise now long forgotten by Margaret.

Nerves could make Margaret endlessly talkative. "My tongue runs fast and foolish," speaking "so much, and fast, as none can understand."[7] She knew that her talk was sometimes "extravagant" and "unnatural"—a product of thrusting a normally solitary, "contemplative person" suddenly into society—and she worried that in her "superfluity" of "idle, vain discourse," spoken "without thinking," she would "rather discover my imperfections . . . than gain applause by my wit."[8] Nonetheless, she felt compelled to talk. People expected special behavior from a writer, she thought: they wanted to see an author's literary invention and style displayed in his everyday conversation. Scholars and poets appearing in public were commonly despised "if their conversations be as other mens." "Lord! Is this the learned man that is so famous, that writ such and such books? how simply he looks! . . . how sneakingly he appears! . . . I heard no wit from him, but he spoke as other men ordinarily do," she had heard society, and especially women, say (even though these same people would laugh at authors "or account them mad, if they should speak otherwise," she thought).[9]

In 1655 or 1656 Margaret had also heard that people doubted she had written her books, because she never spoke of them or quoted from them when entertaining visitors. Cicero, Homer, Virgil, Ovid, Euclid, Aristotle: none of these great authors could repeat their works by heart, she was sure. And William told her that, after completing his own poems, "he doth so little remember any part in them, that when they have been a short time by, and then read them over, they are new to him." Furthermore, "it would seem self-conceitedness" and "an indiscretion" to talk of herself and her works in ordinary social mixing. She would offend against conventional morality by speaking too much, "for the truth is, women should never speak more than to ask rational questions, or to give a discreet answer to a question asked them . . . they ought to be sparing of speech, especially in company of men." But, wanting to keep possession of her works, Margaret had felt "forced" to change her manner, and so she began to talk of her books "more . . . than otherwise I should have done."[10]

Social callers at Newcastle House in 1667 found their hostess determined to prove herself an author. Having carefully memorized sections of her works—able even to cite references "line and page"—Margaret talked at length of her philosophical and theological views and the adventures of the characters in her fiction. Having just finished her biography of William, which would come out that summer, she spoke much of their past exile and present change of fortune, emphasizing her husband's "prodigious losses in the war, his power, valour, wit, learning and industry."

At the same time, she felt guilty at thus engrossing all the conversation.

> Truly I condemn myself; for it is an indiscretion . . . and I repent it both for
> the disfiguring of my works, by pulling out a piece here and a piece there,
> according as my memory could catch hold; also for troubling, or rather vex-
> ing, the hearers with such discourses as they delight not in.

She tried to mollify the effect by adapting herself to her guests, altering topics
to discuss "poetry, or natural philosophy, or moral philosophy," according to
where she thought their interests lay.[11] To Walter Charleton she talked at length
of her philosophy and of her frustration at not getting others to accept it.
Complaining especially of the prejudice of the universities, which continued to
study only Aristotle,* she mentioned also her great desire to have her works
translated into Latin, to reach a continental audience that might be more
receptive. Then, when new guests entered, she moved on to new subjects—
"an account of her religion" for George Morley, bishop of Winchester, followed
by stories "of some of her nymphs" for the aristocrats in the company.

Margaret's conversation, at once intellectual, authoritative, and freely
wide-ranging in topic, was distinctly "masculine" by the standards of the time.
She knew well the attendant perils:

> A woman . . . striving to make her wit known by much discourse loses her
> reputation, for wit is copious and busies itself in all things and humours and
> accidents, wherein sometimes it is satirical and sometimes amorous and
> sometimes wanton, which in all these women should shun.[12]

In particular, she risked alienating her female guests, who—unable or unwilling to join these unfeminine discussions, and wanting only to engage in their
normal social gossip and chat—would soon feel neglected and become "spiteful or angry."[13] But it was her male visitors that Margaret was most concerned
to impress. Only men were writers, critics, and university scholars: they were
the arbiters of taste, the makers or breakers of literary and intellectual reputations. And with visitors like John Evelyn and Walter Charleton she achieved
great success. Fascinated by this "very singular" person, they were happy to sit
"discoursing" at length on philosophy and the sciences, listening, arguing, and
complimenting by turns. But Evelyn's wife, Mary, left on the sidelines, was
furious: "my part was not yet to speak, but admire; especially hearing her go

---

*The traditional curriculum was criticized by many contemporary philosophers, who sought to
replace Aristotle.

on magnifying her own generous actions, stately buildings, noble fortune, her lord's prodigious losses . . . what did she not mention to his or her own advantage? . . . Never did I see a woman so full of herself, so amazingly vain and ambitious."

Mary Evelyn was herself a cultured, well-read woman, who took great pleasure in her correspondence with the Oxford don, Ralph Bohun. But she felt no sympathy for Margaret's intellectual aspirations.

> Women were not born to read authors and censure the learned . . . to give rules of morality and sacrifice to the Muses. We are willing to acknowledge all time borrowed from family duties is misspent; the care of children's education, observing a husband's commands, assisting the sick, relieving the poor and being serviceable to our friends are of sufficient weight to employ the most improved capacities amongst us . . . Raillery may make me go beyond my bounds, but when serious, I esteem myself capable of very little,

she told Bohun.[14] Deeply shocked by Margaret's confident, masculine talk—"which is as airy, empty, whimsical and rambling as her books, aiming at science, difficulties, high notions, terminating commonly in nonsense, oaths and obscenity"—she rushed, like Dorothy Osborne fifteen years before, to suggest insanity.

> I acknowledge, though I remember her some years since and have not been a stranger to her fame, I was surprised to find so much extravagancy and vanity in any person not confined within four walls.

And, again like Dorothy Osborne, Mary Evelyn was not only offended: she also felt decidedly threatened. Somehow Margaret raised the horrifying suggestion in these more conventional women's minds that they might become like her. So, likening her hostess to a chimera—a grotesque, terrifying, fire-breathing hybrid monster of ancient myth—Mary Evelyn hastened to depart, "for fear of infection." Appalled that much of society approved of Margaret—and especially angry that even "men who are esteemed wise and learned" preferred Margaret's poetry above that of the modest, retiring Katherine Philips (whose work had just been published posthumously, although she never permitted it to be printed during her lifetime)*—Mary Evelyn had just one comforting thought. "I hope, as she is an original, she may never have a copy."

---

*Katherine Philips had died of smallpox in 1664.

For these entertainments Margaret dressed with "infinite care." She wore no makeup apart from powder, not only because it was dangerous—"for most paintings are mixed with mercury"—but also because she found the preparative masks and ointments disgusting: "horrid to look upon," smelly, "wet and greasy and very unsavoury." But she paid great attention to the curls of hair which, in contemporary style, she combed down individually onto her forehead. And she adopted with enthusiasm the fashion for black velvet or silk patches "curiously cut and stuck upon the face."* "Like wise sentences in a speech, they give grace and lustre," she thought: artfully positioned, they also hid the pimples which had been bothering her since the previous summer.[15] Mary Evelyn was critical of the result—"her face discovers the facility of the sex, in being yet persuaded it deserves the esteem years forbid"—but Samuel Pepys thought Margaret, now aged forty-four, "a very comely woman."

Taking "more pleasure to devise a fashion than to follow it," Margaret still designed her own dresses, aiming to display her "fancies," "judgement and wit."[16] She knew that the result—"extravagant, and beyond what was usual and ordinary"—would lay her open to accusations of folly and vanity, but she nonetheless felt driven to this expression of her individuality.

> "I endeavour," said she, "to be as singular as I can; for it argues but a mean nature to imitate others . . . I had rather appear worse in singularity, than better in the mode."[17]

Guests at Newcastle House certainly noticed their hostess's clothes. "Extraordinary, fanciful . . . extravagant . . . very singular," "particular, fantastical," they called them—although "not unbecoming a good shape, which she may truly boast of," Mary Evelyn admitted. And when Margaret went out in public, into London's streets and theaters, her appearance caused a sensation.

Almost immediately on their arrival in town, the Newcastles had gone to the theater in Lincoln's Inn Fields, where William's newly finished comedy of fashionable London life, *The Humorous Lovers*, had opened at the end of March, produced by the Duke's Company under the management of Sir William Davenant. For the occasion Margaret donned a special outfit of her own designing—"an antique dress" in classical style, which bared her breasts, revealing "scarlet trimmed nipples." Intended to suggest the heroic women of antiquity and contemporary romances, this costume displayed Margaret's chosen identity as a woman author—masterful, heroic, romantic—and it would not have

---

*Stars, hearts, half-moons, and lozenges were popular shapes, and fashionable ladies sometimes wore as many as fifteen at once.

been out of place in the semiprivate, aristocratic contexts of court masques or portrait painting, where loose classical drapes and naked breasts (complete with nipples reddened with cochineal and veins painted blue, to emphasize the whiteness of the flesh) were not uncommon, though frequently denounced by moralists. But in a public playhouse Margaret's breasts, "all laid out to view," called to mind not so much ancient heroism as the licentious dress of contemporary actresses and prostitutes, and London's gossip filled at once with stories of the occasion. "The Duchess of Newcastle is all the pageant now discoursed on." "All the town-talk is nowadays of her extravagancies." With *The Humorous Lovers* appearing anonymously, everyone believed that Margaret, not her husband, had written the piece, and the reports of her behavior at the theater only encouraged this view.* "Mightily pleased" with the performance, she had publicly thanked the actors from her box at the end of the play, one story reported. "A triumphal chariot with twelve horses and another with eight white bulls was prepared" for her entry to the theater but was never used, because she appeared "incognito,"** another told, rather less believably.[18]

Samuel Pepys, a rising clerk at the Navy Office, avidly lapped it all up, fascinated by the extraordinary literary and social phenomenon that Margaret had become. "The whole story of this lady is a romance, and all she doth is romantic," he recorded in his diary on April 11, as he embarked on a quest for his own sighting of Margaret—a hunt which would affect his movements for the next seven weeks. Already on March 30, before Margaret's arrival in town, he had been to see "the silly play of my Lady Newcastle's called *The Humorous Lovers*"—"the most silly thing that ever came upon a stage; I was sick to see it, but yet would not but have seen it, that I might the better understand her."† Then, on the evening of April 11, having heard the stories of Margaret's appearance at the theater and the king's subsequent call at Newcastle House, he went to Whitehall, where Margaret was expected "to make a visit to the Queen." The court was crowded with hopeful viewers, "as if it were the Queen of Sweden" herself who was to come, Pepys noted.‡ But he, with the others, "lost my labour, for she did not come this night." The cause of Margaret's absence lay in the livery she had chosen for her footmen. Instead of the customary dark wool, these were dressed all in velvet—a vastly expensive osten-

---

*It was not until ten years later, when the play was printed, that William would be identified as the author.

**Perhaps wearing a mask, as ladies sometimes did at the theater.

†Pepys's judgment of the play should not be taken too seriously: he also thought Shakespeare's *A Midsummer Night's Dream* was "the most insipid ridiculous play that ever I saw in my life."

‡Christina, whom Margaret had seen in Antwerp, was now traveling through Germany, attracting huge crowds.

tation on Margaret's part, since silk velvet was the most costly material after only cloth of gold or silver—and they were already talked of everywhere. Their "affected velvet caps," in imitation of the king's own servants, had been forbidden at court by the lord chamberlain, gossip now reported.[19]

Only ten days later did Margaret finally return Charles II's social call and make her first appearance at court. She entered Whitehall with a procession of three coaches: the first, drawn by two horses, contained her gentlemen attendants; the second, with six horses, carried Margaret herself; in the last, four horses drew her waiting-women. For so great an occasion Margaret would be wearing what she called "fashions of grandeur, which are more for grace and becoming than for ease or use." "Gowns with long trains, straight bodies, heavy embroideries and laces, jewels in the ears . . . high-heeled shoes . . . feathers": all these were "fit only for courts, at masques, plays, balls and triumphant shows." Margaret called first on the king, who then "sent the Lord Chamberlain to conduct her to the Queen." Here, with her gown's train carried by a young lady dressed in white satin, Margaret violated court etiquette: since the rules of precedence allowed only the woman of highest status in a company to have a female train-bearer, Margaret should have carried her own train, or given it to one of her gentlemen attendants. Also unusual was the behavior of the king, who came to visit Margaret in the queen's apartments, whether as a mark of respect to her and William, or out of a sense of fun, or fascination for Margaret's unusual dress and behavior, no one said. The spectacle was impressive, and the visit was "thought extraordinary."[20] Margaret's fanciful costumes were a byword of the court. When a cruel practical joke led an aristocratic lady to appear at the gates of Whitehall dressed as a Babylonian princess, with "at least sixty ells of gauze and silver tissue about her, not to mention a sort of pyramid about her head, adorned with a hundred thousand baubles," Charles II reflected for some minutes, and then said: "I bet it is the Duchess of Newcastle."[21]

However Pepys, unwarned of Margaret's coming, had missed her visit to court. After a long Sunday—spent in planning to buy himself a coach and build a coach house, to accord with his ever-increasing wealth and status, and an afternoon visit to the church in Hackney, where he admired the newly introduced church organ and the pretty pupils of the local girls' schools—he passed the evening at home, reading Paul Rycaut's *Present State of the Ottoman Empire*, which he had bought recently, it being "much cried up."[22]

During the next two days he was also absent from the annual celebrations of the Order of the Garter—banquets, church ceremonies, and processions in which William participated as one of the knights, and which Margaret perhaps also attended. Traditionally held at Windsor Castle, these had been relocated to London this year, "to show some jollity" and "make the best countenance we can" in the face of the current war with the Dutch. It was especially important to impress the Swedish ambassadors who were acting as mediators, attempting to negotiate a peace that the English, unprepared for war, desperately hoped for.[23] On the following evening Margaret paid a long overdue social call to the duchess of York, whom she and William had entertained at Welbeck eighteen months before. Margaret appeared "in the same equipage in which she visited the Queen," but Pepys, occupied in his Navy Office business, again missed her.[24]

Only on April 26 did Pepys finally see Margaret for the first time. Driving from Whitehall towards the City with Sir William Batten, one of his Navy Office superiors, he saw the procession of her coaches and velvet-clad footmen coming the opposite way. Eagerly he peered into the passing vehicles and registered "my Lady Newcastle . . . as I have heard her often described . . . with her velvet-cap, her hair about her ears, many black patches because of pimples about her mouth, naked necked, without anything about it, and a black juste-au-corps." Margaret was again wearing a hybrid male-female outfit. Her patches and low neckline were fashionable female dress, and this femininity was further emphasized by her failure to wear any form of lace collar or gauze scarf over her exposed shoulders and neck, as was customary for women when out of doors. But her juste-au-corps was the knee-length coat now fashionable for men: though sometimes worn by ladies for riding and traveling, it had definitely masculine connotations in a London social setting. Margaret's velvet cap was probably also a masculine item, perhaps in the style of a doctor's bonnet, as worn in the universities, or a physician's cap. It may also have been inspired by the man's fur-lined black velvet cap that Queen Christina of Sweden sometimes wore, and doffed in masculine manner.[25] On this occasion, Pepys gained only a brief glimpse of Margaret: "I hope to see more of her on May Day," he consoled himself.

But on May 1, when fashionable society traditionally gathered to drive in Hyde Park, Pepys and Sir William Penn, another of his Navy Office bosses, found only "a horrid dust and number of coaches, without pleasure or order." The park was busy far beyond normal, with people all hoping "to see my Lady Newcastle." And so Pepys was again disappointed, "she being followed and crowded upon by coaches all the way she went, [so] that nobody could come near her." He noted her large black coach, decorated with silver instead of the customary gold, "and so with the curtains and everything black and white"—a color scheme that Margaret had doubtless selected not only from love of singularity but also to go with the silver and black of the Cavendish family arms blazoned on its sides. Within, Pepys could just make out that she was wearing her velvet cap. But after half an hour in the park, he and Penn decided to leave, "weary of the dust and despairing of my Lady Newcastle." They drove east and north towards Clerkenwell, hoping to catch Margaret as she returned to New-castle House, "but we staying by the way to drink, she got home a little before us, so we lost our labours."

On Monday, May 6, William and Margaret again attended the theater in Lincoln's Inn Fields for a special performance of *The Humorous Lovers* attended by "the King and the grandees of the court."[26] Pepys, however, was busy in his office all afternoon. Only on the 10th did he get another chance to see Mar-garet when, on his way to the Navy Office, he sighted her coach ahead of him, "with 100 boys and girls running looking upon her." Hoping to overtake her, "he drove hard towards Clerkenwell . . . but . . . she got home before I could come up to her." He remained undaunted—"I will get a time to see her"—but had to wait another twenty days before he finally achieved his ambition.

Margaret, having "a great desire" while she was still in London to visit the Royal Society and "see some of their experiments," had talked of the matter to some of her philosophical friends, and at the society's meeting on May 23, Lord George Berkeley raised her request, announcing that she especially "desired to be invited." The proposal was highly controversial, for the young society had many enemies—political, intellectual, and religious, in the univer-sities, the church, and the College of Physicians, and amongst the aristocracy and gentry—and was fearfully protective of its reputation. In her *Observations upon Experimental Philosophy*, published only a year before, Margaret herself had attacked two of its leading lights, Robert Boyle and Robert Hooke, as well as its whole program of research. With London's gossip now full of her unusual behavior, many fellows feared that the society would lay itself open to ridicule, especially in the form of humorous verse ballads. However, two more of Mar-garet's friends—Walter Charleton and the earl of Carlisle—seconded Lord Berkeley's proposal, "pressing that it might be put to the vote." The fellows finally voted in favor, and Charleton and Lord Berkeley were dispatched to inform Margaret that she would "be entertained with some experiments at the next meeting."

The occasion was universally recognized as "extraordinary." Though for-eign ambassadors and visiting royalty had been received by the society before, this would be "the first time" the fellows had "beheld a lady" in their midst, and expectation was high of what "ingenious remarks" this philosophical prodigy might make on the "curious experiments" selected for her "entertainment." For Pepys and many fellows like him, who lacked the social status and connec-tions to call at Newcastle House, this was a unique opportunity to see and hear

Margaret at close quarters. And so, on the afternoon of Thursday, May 30, the "stately room" in Arundel House—the town house of the earls of Arundel at the western end of the Strand, where the society had met since their original meeting place in Gresham College in the City was destroyed in the Fire of London the year before—was crowded with "much company, indeed very much company, in expectation of the Duchess."

The meeting had already begun with ordinary business—the reading of the society's latest philosophical correspondence—when news came of Margaret's arrival at the gate, "with glorious train and gilded coach, and horse with many a tassle." In grand, aristocratic manner, she was wearing a gown with an especially long train—eight feet of it, borne "in great pomp," by the six waiting-women who attended on her. But other features of her outfit, which probably included a wide-brimmed cavalier hat and her usual knee-length juste-au-corps, were so masculine that John Evelyn took her for "a cavalier, but that she had no beard."

From the courtyard, Margaret was ushered into Arundel House by a delegation of aristocratic fellows, including Lord Berkeley, the earl of Carlisle, and the duke of Somerset. Then, in a ceremony that the society's governing council had devised especially for the occasion, she was greeted at the door of the meeting room itself by the president, Lord Brouncker, with the society's large golden mace, given them by the king, borne before him.

Amidst the hurry and din of the eager spectators, Brouncker conducted Margaret to the place of honor, a seat at his right hand, at the long table where the experiments were to be performed. Behind her stood the chief of her waiting-women, named Ferrabosco, a member of a celebrated family of Italian musicians, who was said to sing "most admirably."[27] Rumor reported that she was a great beauty and that Margaret expected her to "kill the gallants" if she but showed her face. So it was on her, as well as Margaret, that the assembled "philosophers did peer" from all around the table.

The society's council had chosen a range of experiments for the occasion, many of them having a clear philosophical purpose but all ending in some dramatic effect, surprising and wonderful, such as the society thought most suitable for entertaining visiting grandees. Robert Boyle's air pump, first invented some nine years before—the society's most valued possession, at once expensive, rare, and productive of an endless variety of experiments—was always favored for such entertainments, and Margaret was shown a range of phenomena in it.[28] First the instrument's glass globe, nine gallons and three pints in volume, was evacuated using the pumping mechanism—a piston attached to a rack and pinion device, moved by turning a hand crank—which had been built by Robert Hooke. The globe, sealed and detached, was placed on a scale and weighed. Then it was opened to allow the air back in. The increase demonstrated the "weight of the air" the globe contained. In two further experiments, Margaret saw how water began to bubble away as the air was pumped out, and how an apparently empty bladder, pressed flat and sealed, swelled up inside the emptying globe.

Mixed with these were various other showy demonstrations. A small globe-shaped magnet moved a scattering of iron filings, demonstrating the Earth's magnetic field. A louse was placed under Robert Hooke's microscope for Margaret to inspect—one of the experiments that she had attacked in her *Observations* the year before. "Several experiments of mixing colours," devised by Boyle, were followed by the surprising spectacle of "two cold liquors by mixture made hot."* The wonder of cohesion was displayed using two highly polished marble discs that could not be separated as increasingly heavy weights were hung from the lower one: a total of forty-seven pounds was required to pull them apart. Pepys was most impressed by a piece of roasted mutton that, immersed in "a certain liquor of Mr. Boyle's suggesting" ("oil of vitriol"), turned in a moment "into pure blood," as he and Evelyn and probably everyone else thought. Evelyn recognized that this experiment was designed to show the working of digestion in the stomach, but Pepys just found it "very rare."

Margaret, the honored audience for all this show, was overcome. Surrounded by a crowd of learned men, most of them complete strangers, "with never a woman but myself," she had no idea "how to behave myself" and was "extremely out of countenance."[29] The presence of philosophers whom she had herself attacked in print—Robert Boyle, Robert Hooke (the society's curator of experiments, who actually performed the experiments she watched), and Henry More (who was visiting from Cambridge)—only increased her awkwardness. All that she could say in response to the rapid succession of experiments was that "she was full of admiration, all admiration," and her eagerly expectant viewers were horribly disappointed. "The Duchess hath been a good comely woman; but her dress so antic and her deportment so unordinary, that I do not like her at all, nor did I hear her say anything that was worth hearing," Pepys noted in his diary. "After they had shown her many experiments, and she cried still she was 'full of admiration,' she departed," escorted out to her coach by the same aristocratic delegation that had brought her in.

Margaret had become a celebrity, drawing huge crowds wherever she went. Her determined individuality and her universal fame left contempo-

---

*As the chemical reaction between the liquids generated heat.

raries with few comparisons—romance heroines came to mind, as did the queen of Sheba[30] and Christina, queen of Sweden—but her literary career was without any parallel at all, and added considerably to the fascination she exerted over London society. Her name as a female philosopher gained her a mention in one of Andrew Marvell's poems, written this year.[31] Her dress, her words, her carriages and servants, her presence or absence here or there— these had filled the capital's gossip for seven weeks and more. And as London residents kept their country correspondents abreast of all the latest news, reports reached even as far as Cumberland.[32]

But then, on June 11, the English world changed, when news came that the Dutch fleet had entered the Thames. That night the Dutch burned the English warships still lying in the navy docks at Chatham, unprepared for sea. Londoners, "in a panic fear and consternation . . . flying none knew why or whither," expected any day to see the enemy ships sailing up the river. Many fled the town; others, like Pepys and Evelyn, rushed to send away their valuables, fearing English looters as much as foreign invaders. But the Newcastles stayed on at Clerkenwell. To leave now would smack of cowardice and desertion, and William briefly involved in the court's military plans. He and Margaret, however, now ceased to feature in London's gossip, which was obsessed only with the war and "the evils of our time." At court, the politicians bandied recriminations. In the streets, the crowds talked of treason in high places, blaming "the Papists," those ever convenient English scapegoats. Dinner conversations filled with gloom as guests predicted "that this nation will be undone," or reported the prophecies of one Tom of the Wood—a hermit living near Woolwich, who had foretold the Fire of London the year before and "now says that a greater desolation is at hand." Pepys, having made his will and sent his father and wife and all his worldly wealth into the country, was fully occupied in his office, unwilling even to appear "with a woman in a coach" for fear of accusations of idleness. Meanwhile John Evelyn busied himself in military affairs, inspecting the new defenses being hurriedly built by the river. The comic ballad he had begun to write, telling of Margaret's visit to the Royal Society, was abandoned uncompleted.[33]

Margaret's activities during the crisis passed unremarked by diarists or letter writers. Early in July, soon after the Dutch retreated from the Thames, the Newcastles' departure went equally unnoticed, but at Welbeck they were received in grand manner. The rooms and offices were all newly cleaned; the baker fired up the ovens and prepared fresh manchet bread; for their celebratory dinner Andrew Clayton bought six dozen crayfish and a dozen bream.[34] No expense had been spared on the couple's excursion into London society, and Margaret—despite her fears and her frequent previous statements of her preference for a life of country retirement over the vanities of a metropolitan city—had enjoyed herself. Hoping for many such visits in the future, she persuaded William to add the Clerkenwell town house—which had not been included in Henry's "grand settlement" of 1666—to her marriage jointure. If she survived her husband, as seemed likely given their relative ages, Margaret would inherit the Newcastles' palatial London residence, as well as Bolsover Castle.[35]

Chapter Fourteen

Queen of Philosophers, 1667–1673

*I*n 1666, after her previous printer went out of business, perhaps killed in the Great Plague, Margaret had again changed her publishing arrangements. Her new printer, Anne Maxwell, was a widow who had taken over her husband's business after his death in 1665. At her house in Thames Street, on the southern edge of the publishing district around St. Paul's Cathedral, she now employed three compositors and three pressmen, working on two presses. In the summer of 1667, soon after Margaret's return to Welbeck, Maxwell produced the *Life of William Newcastle*,[1] and in the following year she printed a further six books for Margaret. Four were new editions of previously published works—*Observations upon Experimental Philosophy*, *The Blazing World*, *Poems and Fancies*, and *Orations*—reissued almost unaltered from their latest impressions, but there were also two new books.

Plays Never Before Printed contained four new comedies, most or all of them written since the Restoration.* *The Sociable Companions, or the Female Wits* was a farce on the plight of the impoverished royalists who returned from exile at the Restoration. While the men, despairing of ever regaining their fortunes, spend their time drinking and joking in taverns, their sisters also lament their fate—wondering "why those women that was neither factions, ambitious, covetous, malicious, nor cruel, should suffer in the wars with the men"—but they resolve to win themselves wealthy husbands by their wits. Of necessity, the

---

*As in her earlier volume of plays, the songs were largely written by William—contributions acknowledged by printed slips that were pasted into the book.

three women choose a usurer, a lawyer, and a physician, for the Civil War has left only men of these professions rich, "like as vultures after a battle, that feed on the dead or dying." The rest of the play, deriving most of its humor and excitement from the ingenious plans used by the "female wits" to trick their victims into marriage, departed radically from Margaret's earlier drama, where she had rejected the use of such "plots . . . designs . . . [and] subtle contrivances." In this respect, and in its recognizably real English setting, *The Sociable Companions* lay much closer to the conventions of Restoration comedy than her previous work.

Margaret continued her satirical attack on the present state of England "since the wars" in *The Bridals*—a comedy denouncing the falsehood, hypocrisy, greed, sexual libertinage, tavern life, and overblown "court-talk" of fashionable society, whose dissolute lifestyle turned "day into night, and night into day." Portraying bawdy wedding celebrations and the jokes and tricks of Mimick the Fool, the play again came closer to contemporary comic conventions than Margaret's earlier work, where she had avoided both "ridiculous jest" and "wanton love." Its principal resemblance to the plays written in exile lay in the debate between Mimick and Lady Vertue on the subject of women.

The Presence was another detailed satire on real life, but this time drawn from Margaret's much earlier experiences. Its story of Mademoiselle Bashful—the new maid of honor, unhappy at court—was very closely autobiographical, and provided plenty of opportunities for portraying the scandalous immorality of courtiers like Monsieur Mode (a pleasure-seeking, conscienceless atheist, who advises the other men on how to court twenty women at once and sleep with all of them), and Monsieur Spend-all (a compulsive gambler who, in search of riches, cynically marries a woman he hates). Meanwhile, the story of the princess who falls in love "with an Idea she met with in a dream" ridicules the fashion for platonic love that was popular at Henrietta Maria's court during Margaret's residence. A third plotline, denouncing the notorious injustices of the Court of Wards, was omitted when Margaret decided it would make her play too long. Perhaps she also thought it was no longer so important, after the court was abolished at the Restoration, but she still printed it, along with extra scenes from Bashful's story, at the end of *The Presence*.

The last complete play in the volume, *The Convent of Pleasure,* was more similar to Margaret's earlier drama. Avoiding a specific setting derived from her life experience, it returned to her former themes of how women should live, and especially whether they should marry. Lady Happy, left a rich heiress on her father's death, refuses all her suitors and turns her house into an all-female monastic institution, dedicated to the worship of the goddess Nature and the enjoyment of "the variety of pleasures" she offers. Even the delights of courtship are possible, when some of the women dress as men and woo the others in manner of a "loving servant." Dramatic entertainments are put on, plays within the play, in which Margaret again portrays the troubles of a married life—violent, drunken, spendthrift, faithless husbands; women's sickness in pregnancy; the pains of childbirth, with the attendant risk of death; grief at children's deaths; mothers' dissatisfaction when grown-up offspring disappointed their high hopes—confirming the convent's women in their rejection of a traditional life of marriage. But life is disrupted when a great foreign princess—"a princely brave woman truly, of a masculine presence"—arrives to join the convent, and Lady Happy is horrified to find herself falling in love. Despite her arguments—"why may not I love a woman with the same affection I could a man?"—she fears that the goddess Nature will punish her for this unnatural love. The couple kiss and acknowledge their love, but Lady Happy has lost her characteristic cheerfulness and become lean and pale. Eventually the "princess" is revealed as a man in disguise—a prince who rules a rich and powerful neighboring country—and the couple marry. But, as with many of Margaret's earlier plays, the question of whether they will be happy together remains unresolved. There are some good signs: the prince has been shown to be capable of sympathy with women and joining closely in their lives, and Margaret regarded her own marriage to a supportive husband as the happiest form of life. But her suggestion in the play is perhaps that Lady Happy will regret her choice. The plays within the play clearly have this implication, and the ending—where the prince is easily persuaded to give away Lady Happy's house, which as her husband he now owns—has clear references to Margaret's earlier writings on how foolish it is for a woman who has her own property to marry and lose it all to her husband. Like her earlier plays, this was a more serious, thought-provoking work than most contemporary comedies. It also broke with convention in its use of cross-dressing. While women characters in plays commonly adopted male disguise, the reverse was unusual. The result in *The Convent of Pleasure* was exceptionally dramatic and risqué, since Margaret left not only the characters but also her readers equally ignorant of the true, male identity of the princess, allowing real tension to develop as Lady Happy and "she" fall in love.

At the end of her volume, Margaret's compulsion to publish everything she wrote led her to include the beginning of a play that she had originally intended to publish with her *Blazing World* but had abandoned uncompleted. "A Piece of a Play" was clearly going to be another vicious satire on Restoration society—this time on its obsession with fleeting and foolish fashions, both in clothes and in wit. Written as the Newcastles prepared for their London visit of 1667, its first scene also included a fictionalization of Margaret herself as the singular Lady Phoenix, who is reported to be "coming to town in such splendour as the world never saw the like." Wild rumors of her dress, her equipage, her pride, her vanity, her feeding "only upon thoughts": these fill the town's talk, but no one really knows her; it is all just gossip. What will happen when she arrives? Will her singularity, her grandeur, and her "studious nature" bring triumph or humiliation? Perhaps it was Margaret's inability to resolve this question about her own identity and her impact on the world that made her unable to finish this play.

The second of the new books that Margaret published in 1668 was the *Grounds of Natural Philosophy*, which she described as a new edition of her *Philosophical Opinions*, although it was in fact an almost total rewrite. Its title, "grounds," was an indication of Margaret's aim—to expound the basic first principles, the bare essentials, of her philosophy as clearly as possible.[2] Her style was terse: in simple, short, direct statements she set out her long-developed theory, with little of the argument, explanation, and illustration by specific examples that she had used to support her views in the *Philosophical Opinions*. The 450 pages of her 1663 work were now pared down to 230 pages plus appendices.

With the benefit of a wide philosophical reading, she now knew exactly where her views departed from those of other philosophers and how to state her own ideas on these points clearly, persuasively, and succinctly.[3] There were also new opinions in the book, where Margaret's thinking had changed over time. For instance, her earlier works had reached no conclusion on the much-disputed contemporary question of whether a vacuum could exist in nature, but she had now decided a vacuum was impossible, since it would destroy nature's unity and create disorder, whereas we plainly see order in the world.[4] She had also reversed her former views on predestination and free will. In place of the strict determinism of her atomism—and the authoritarian model that had followed in the first edition of her *Philosophical Opinions*, where rational spirits were presented as controlling and ordering the rest of matter—Margaret now insisted that all parts of nature "have free will to move after what manner they please." Now she understood the world's workings in terms of the mutual "consent of associating parts," of cooperations produced by "general agreement." One body could not act on another, forcing it to move or change: the most it could do was to "occasion" another body to choose, out of its own free will, to change or move itself.[5] Where, five years before, she had described the rational spirits as forcing the rest of the body to work to satisfy the mind's ambitions, now she saw the rational and sensitive spirits as sharing their ambition, and working "in one society" to achieve fame.[6] As Margaret's own ambitions were increasingly satisfied and the deprivations of exile receded into memories, she saw the world around her in terms of greater freedom and empowerment, removing the compulsion and powerlessness that had originally been central to her philosophy.

As in her *Philosophical Opinions*, so too in the *Grounds of Natural Philosophy*, Margaret proceeded from the general first principles of her philosophy to a discussion of the more specific workings of nature—to medicine and diseases, the elements, metals, magnetism, and a range of other phenomena. Compared to her earlier work, her tone was now more cautious. Building her lifelong admiration for the richness and variety of nature into her new system, she now stressed the complexity and diversity of natural phenomena, the many different forms in which they could exist, the many different causes they might have. Knowledge of this infinity, she emphasized throughout, could only ever be partial and imperfect. In her discussion of medicine, especially, she was determined not to theorize without good grounds, and so she restricted herself to the description and classification of diseases, without any of the suggestions for remedies that her earlier work had contained. The change perhaps owed something to the influence of the Royal Society, whose much-vaunted Baconian research program demanded a complete collection and classification of the observed facts, before any attempt at theorizing. But Margaret's new approach was also a direct result of her long-held skepticism on the possibility of human knowledge. She was in fact a far more thoroughgoing skeptic than the philosophers of the Royal Society. Robert Boyle and others modestly professed that their knowledge of nature was imperfect and their theories could not be proved to be true, but they still believed that one day, in the future, truth could be attained, and this was what they worked towards. Margaret, however, believed that such perfect knowledge was in principle impossible, even in the future, simply because of the infinity of nature and the finiteness of humanity. On the much disputed topic of gravity, for instance, she thought it would be impossible to understand why different bodies rise or fall in different ways, since the causes involved are "so many . . . as they are neither known, or can be conceived by one finite creature."[7] When she refused to rush into recommending remedies for diseases, she was also bringing her medical discussion into line with her previous statements on the inadequacy of contemporary medicine, and the necessity for physicians to improve their knowledge of drugs, illnesses, and the body before undertaking treatments.

Margaret dedicated her book "to all the universities in Europe."[8] With its new simplicity of structure and terseness of style, she was clearly hoping that her philosophy would now reach the continental readership she had so long desired, and in this same year she also finally achieved her great ambition to have some of her work translated into Latin. Seeking a suitable translator for her *Life of William*, she had again approached her connections in the English universities, but the twenty-page sample that returned to Welbeck for her approval was judged inferior, perhaps by Margaret's secretary since she could not herself read Latin. Rendering the English too literally, its language was awkward, its style unclassical. Margaret rejected it, but soon found a more able translator in her old friend Walter Charleton, with whom she had already discussed her desire to put her works into Latin when she was last in London. Well read in the classical historians and philosophers, Charleton published his own medical researches in Latin, and he now produced a much freer, more polished translation than that from the universities.[9] Adding copious details and embellishments, he turned Margaret's work into the sort of elegant Latin prose—full of nested clauses, rounded periods, and balanced oppositions—beloved of classical stylists. For this new book, Margaret abandoned her usual printer—perhaps because Anne Maxwell could not offer a compositor fluent in Latin. Instead, *De Vita et Rebus Gestis Nobilissimi Illustrissimique Principis Gulielmi Ducis Novo-Castrensis Commentarii* was issued in 1668 by Thomas Milbourne, who had recently printed William's latest book on horsemanship.

Margaret eagerly sent copies of this new book, with a selection of her latest English works, to her old acquaintances on the Continent—to the French nobleman d'Auissone, to the Duarte family, and to Samuel Sorbière, the fashionable Parisian physician, philosopher, and savant whom the Newcastles had probably met at the Hague in the late 1640s. Here she found an appreciative audience. While d'Auissone and Jacques Duarte picked out her philosophy in particular for praise, Sorbière wrote back with the news that he was proposing her example as a model for all the ladies he met in Parisian salons.[10]

Since the Restoration, Margaret had also enlarged the circle of correspondents in England to whom she presented copies of her books. Thomas Hobbes, Walter Charleton, Henry More, and John Fell, dean of Christ Church: some of the country's foremost scholars were among those who gratefully acknowledged these literary gifts, often expressing their surprise at having received such "extraordinary favour"—too great an honor for "a poor impertinent thing in black," one academic told her. In her eagerness for recognition as a writer, Margaret was reversing the normal social roles: as Hobbes pointed out to her, it was properly the scholars, the social inferiors, who should eagerly give their books to her, seeking notice from the great aristocratic patron, not vice versa. Yet Margaret knew that scholars were the most appropriate readers for her more learned works, especially her philosophy, and she regarded it as vital for writers to ensure that their books reached those who were "known to delight in such subjects their books treat of."[11] Of all the recipients of her books, Henry More was the most surprised. He had never met Margaret or William, and the parcel of books he received included her *Philosophical Letters*, where he found "a confutation of sundry passages in my writings." With no wish to become embroiled in a philosophical quarrel with one of England's greatest aristocratic ladies, More composed a brief letter of thanks, with no detailed intellectual content.[12]

Margaret stayed closer to social norms when she gave books to members of her own class. To relatives like the earl of Devonshire and the husbands of William's daughters went copies of her *Plays* and *Orations* in 1662—appropriate works for a gentlemanly class whose business lives centered on public speaking and who often passed much of their leisure in London's theaters.[13] Margaret also gave books to friends like Lord Berkeley and the Essex gentleman Samuel Tuke, who had fought alongside her brother, Charles, at Colchester in 1648 and then got to know Margaret in exile. To the gentleman scholar John Evelyn she sent a wider range of work, including "all the profound as well as politer subjects." A prolific author himself, Evelyn replied to these gifts in kind. In 1665 he sent Margaret his new translation of a French work on architecture. In 1670, after long sufferings of guilt at the pile of her books in his study still unacknowledged, he sent her the new edition of his *Sylva*—a proposal for how the vast deforestation of England during the Interregnum could be remedied.[14]

Especially important to Margaret were the universities, those "stars of the first magnitude, whose influence governs the world of learning."[15] In Antwerp she had asked Constantijn Huygens to present all her books so far printed to Leyden University, and in November 1658 he had taken to the university's rector both the books and a Latin index of their contents, which Margaret had had specially printed.[16] While in exile she had also sent a small number of her books to the librarians of the two English universities: Thomas Barlow at Oxford and William Moore in Cambridge. The librarian always received a copy of his own, plus one or two extra, which Margaret asked him to present to the library itself and perhaps the university's vice chancellor and a few others.[17] With her increased wealth after the Restoration, she expanded the system dramatically, donating books to most of the separate colleges in Oxford and Cambridge as well as to the universities themselves. Her philosophical work in particular she wanted appreciated here, where the subject was studied professionally, but she also sent copies of her other books. It was now a servant—probably her secretary—who distributed the books through the universities, and Margaret also employed her secretary to write the corrections from the errata lists by hand into these presentation copies—a vast task that was not always completed before the books were delivered to their recipients. Until 1667 the work was neatly done, so as to resemble print; then a new, less painstaking hand appears, after Margaret's first secretary died while attending the press during the printing of her *Life of William*.[18]

Although Margaret now arranged and financed her own printing, without the services of a large firm of booksellers, her works were readily available for sale and achieved a wide readership. Even as far afield as the remote village of Rydal in the Lake District, the landed gentleman Sir Daniel Fleming could easily order her *Life of William* through his agent in Kendal—at a cost of 4s. 6d. including delivery. In London this same work circulated round female society. Betty Turner, the wife of one of Samuel Pepys's colleagues in the Navy Office, lent her copy to Pepys's wife, from whom Pepys himself borrowed it in March 1668 when, suffering from sore eyes but knowing "not how in the world to abstain from reading," he wanted a book that was "a fair print." Pepys was an unfaithful and authoritarian (though also often affectionate) husband, who quarreled bitterly with his wife when she wanted to wear clothes he did not approve of, and he soon found the book's admiring, affectionate tone and its revelations of the Newcastles' most intimate life deeply offensive. To him Margaret's biography seemed "a ridiculous history . . . which shows her to be a mad, conceited, ridiculous woman," while William was "an ass to suffer her to write what she writes to him and of him."[19]

Others, however, were enthusiastic about the *Life of William*. The senate of Cambridge University admired the "loftiness of the argument, and elegancy and spruceness of the style." Of all her works, this was their favorite. Flecknoe composed a poem specially:

> *Ne'er was life more worthy to be writ,*
> *Nor pen more worthy of the writing it . . .*
> *Betwixt you both your fame will never die,*
> *But one give t' other immortality.*

"Your Grace hath done right to one of the most illustrious heroes of our age . . . [and] hath sweetly and wonderfully twisted the faithfulness of an historian with the affections of a wife," one correspondent wrote, praising Margaret as "an heroine whose pen is as glorious as his sword."[20]

Margaret's aspiration to be appreciated as a heroic woman was widely successful. John Evelyn likened her to a vast range of learned ladies, including Zenobia, queen of Palmyra (who had led her armies against the Roman Empire), Isabella the warrior queen of Castille, Katherine of Aragon, Elizabeth I, Christina of Sweden, Anna van Schurmann, and Katherine Philips. But in the variety of her literary achievements Margaret excelled them all, he decided: "all these, I say, summed together, possess but that divided which your Grace retains in one [person]." Walter Charleton similarly placed her "alone, and at the upper end in the Gallery of Heroic Women, and upon a pedestal more advanced than the rest"—a reference to Le Moyne's book *The Gallery of Heroick Women*, which had come out in English translation in 1652. "You exceed all of your delicate sex, not only in this age, but in all ages past," he told Margaret: "you are the first great lady that ever wrote so much, and so much of your own: and, for ought we can divine, you will also be the last." Margaret had "convinced the world, by her own heroic example, that no studies are too hard for her softer sex, and that ladies are capable of our admiration as well for their science as for their beauty," he told the Royal Society. Others, with the traditional *querelle des femmes* in mind, saw Margaret as the example that proved that women were equal, or even superior, to men. "Your Grace hath convinced the world, by a great instance, that women may be philosophers, and, to a degree fit for the ambitious emulation of the most improved masculine spirits," as one correspondent put it. "There is no sex in the mind," Margaret's writings showed.[21]

> Madam, you have scaled the walls of Fame,
> And made a breach where never female came . . .
> Majestic Quill! that keeps our minds in awe,
> For Reason's kingdom knows no Salic law* . . .
> The court, the city, schools and camp agree,
> Welbeck to make an university
> Of wit and honour, . . .
> A lady whose immortal pen transfers
> To our sex shame and envy, fame to hers.[22]

However, the fashion for heroic women was never as widely established in England as in France, and more conventional women often found Margaret's "masculine" behavior a threat. Mary Evelyn and Dorothy Osborne—who were both highly literate, but preferred to exercise their intelligence and creativity only within the private, domestic, "feminine" sphere—were among her sharpest critics. A heroine, Mary Evelyn thought, might arouse the world's wonder, but would gain "little of esteem . . . the influence of a blazing star** is not more dangerous or more avoided." But a few women who shared Margaret's unusual literary aspirations approved wholeheartedly. In 1658 the astrologer Sarah Jinner—perhaps the first woman to make a financial income

---

*The Salic law excluded women from taking the throne of France.

**I.e. a comet, often believed to be an evil omen.

from her writing—issued the first of her annual almanacs, praising learned female authors, of whom Margaret was the outstanding example of the time.[23] Fifteen years later Margaret was again publicly honored by a woman, when the exceptionally learned Bathsua Makin published her *Essay to Revive the Antient Education of Gentlewomen*, proposing the reform of feminine education to include more masculine, learned studies as well as the domestic skills of housewifery. Makin devoted about a third of her book to proving that women were capable of intellectual accomplishments, principally by citing examples from history and the present day. Among many others appeared "the present Duchess of Newcastle [who], by her own genius rather than any timely instruction, over-tops many grave gownmen."*[24]

Margaret received much praise from her correspondents. Her poetry was commended for its "life and spirit," "equally free, and copious upon all occasions." She proved the truth of Plato's doctrine—"that poesy is not a faculty proceeding from judgement or acquired by labour and industry; but a certain divine fury, or enthusiasm, which scorning the control of reason, transports the spirit in raptures."[25] Her prose works—essays, stories, plays, and letters— were admired for the commentary they offered on human society in "those many . . . satirical remarks upon the manners of men and women which you have frequently interspersed." The role of moralist and social commentator was conventionally well suited to Margaret's status. Great ladies, like the duchess of Lorraine, were accorded respect and authority as they presided over the society in their salons, supervising the behavior of the company, directing and if necessary disciplining their debates, acting as arbiters of taste and manners, issuing reflections and judgments on matters social, moral, religious, and intellectual. Accordingly, Margaret's work as a satirist was well appreciated. Walter Charleton praised her *World's Olio* for its "smart invectives" and "solid arguments" against the common vices of the age. "What sex, age, constitution, condition is there, whose most secret ulcers the sharpness of your wit and pen hath not lanced open to the bottom?" Her book proved that "the delights of a soul well ordered according to the rules of virtue and honour are infinitely more charming and desirable than the most magnified pleasures of the body," even including "that rank appetite of the flesh, commonly called lust." Meanwhile Thomas Hobbes, the philosopher who believed in the power of drama to teach proper morals, admired Margaret's plays, "filled throughout with more and truer ideas of virtue and honour than any book of morality I have read."[26]

---

*I.e. university academics.

The universities too were fulsome in their praise—especially of her philosophy. In 1658 Leyden echoed classical writers' comments on Virgil, Homer, and Socrates when they hailed Margaret as "Princeps ingenii"—the prince of all wit*—and after the Restoration the two English universities also gave her books "a very honourable and public reception." At Cambridge in particular her works were praised as "sublime and excellent things" and their author was addressed in a style reminiscent of the ancient Roman emperors: "Margareta I, Philosophorum Princeps"—Margaret the First, Prince of Philosophers, who had conquered and pacified the commonwealth of learning.[27]

Historians have often dismissed the praise that Margaret's writings received as mere flattery—the purely formulaic payment due to a noblewoman who distributed free copies of her books—and to modern eyes the compliments paid her can easily seem overblown and extravagant. But we must remember that this was an age with a taste for hyperbole, and that the aim of this standard rhetorical technique was to use exaggerated expressions (which were not meant to be taken literally) not to lie or to ridicule but to express a genuine strong feeling.[28] The detailed content of the praises that Margaret received from many different people was highly consistent: she was repeatedly celebrated as a satirist, as a writer of free and natural style, as a heroic woman—which argues that she was being genuinely appreciated in these modes by many of her contemporaries. The sincerity of these praises is further confirmed by the fact that some correspondents at least mixed praises for some parts of Margaret's work with criticisms of others. Despite Margaret's high social status, Walter Charleton was not afraid to tell her that he disagreed with her natural philosophy and that her poems contained errors of rhyme and meter. Similarly, an anonymous poet writing on Margaret's achievements concluded his verse with criticism of her "ambition above mortal state," arguing that her lifelong pursuit of fame was irreligious and futile.[29]

Some of those who praised Margaret clearly had private interests to serve—hopes of financial reward could easily be motivating the comments made by writers seeking literary patronage, or by William's old Cambridge college, asking for funding for a building project they could not afford to complete—but many of her admirers had no obvious advantage to gain. Constantijn Huygens, who admired Margaret's "masculine" wisdom and courage and spent time with her discussing philosophy, certainly had no need to flatter an impoverished English exile, when he was himself a nobleman who occupied

---

*The term "prince" was especially appropriate, since it applied equally to male and female rulers: it had been adopted in the sixteenth century as the official title of the first English queens regnant, Mary and Elizabeth.

one of the most influential posts at the court of William of Orange. Sarah Jinner and Bathsua Makin could have no material hopes from their praises, since they remained unacquainted with Margaret.

Many admirers also made their comments where Margaret would never hear them. Mary Evelyn's indignation at the "wise and learned" men who preferred Margaret's poetry to that of Katherine Philips reveals the nature of the discussions of her work that went on in Margaret's absence. Similarly, John Evelyn's comment—that Margaret was foremost among those learned Englishwomen who deserved to have medals struck in their honor—was not printed until twenty-four years after her death.[30]

The comments written inside copies of her books by their owners are especially revealing. The poet Edmund Waller continued to ridicule her.

> New Castles in the air this lady builds,
> While nonsense with philosophy she gilds,

he wrote on the flyleaf of his copy of the 1663 edition of her *Philosophical Opinions*. But other readers responded differently:

> All the Graces here are met
> To make a pearl* of Margaret,

Mildmay Fane, earl of Westmorland, wrote into his own copy of Margaret's *Poems and Fancies*.[31]

And in Oxford University's copy of the *Philosophical Opinions*, the Bodleian librarian, Thomas Barlow added the note: "ex dono illustrissimae Heroinae Margaretae Novo-Castrensis Marchionessae Authoris." His praise of Margaret as "a most illustrious heroine" continued in his own copy of the *Philosophical Fancies*, on whose title page he also wrote the motto, αἰὲ ἀριστεύειν, a quote from Homer's *Iliad*, where a father advises his son, departing to die in the Trojan war, "always to be the best and excel over others"—a truly heroic rendering of Margaret's own lifelong quest for excellence.[32] Barlow, an outstandingly learned man who was also noted for his generous patronage of other, less fortunate scholars, was genuinely sympathetic to Margaret's work and aspirations. Corresponding with her while she was in exile, he had encouraged her with news of a manuscript in the Bodleian Library that argued for the superiority of women over men. Her writing proved its truth, he told her.[33]

---

*A pun on Margaret's name, which means "pearl."

Margaret's philosophical work, in particular, was taken far more seriously than historians have tended to think. Nehemiah Grew—the son of a schoolmaster who would later pioneer the study of plant anatomy and become secretary of the Royal Society—studied the first edition of her *Philosophical Opinions* closely, probably while he was a student at Cambridge. Intending to familiarize himself with a broad range of contemporary arts and sciences, he undertook a course of private reading and assembled a mass of notes in his commonplace book, including a detailed, eight-page summary of Margaret's book.[34] And philosophical friends—Constantijn Huygens, Walter Charleton, and John Evelyn—all engaged in lengthy discussions with her, either face to face, or by correspondence.

Margaret was very keen to engage in philosophical debate, even beyond the circles of her immediate acquaintance. Publishing her two books of controversies, the *Philosophical Letters* and *Observations upon Experimental Philosophy*, she likened herself to her swordsman husband. Just as a duelist would fight only the most honorable and valiant opponents, so she was "resolved to argue with none but those which have the renown of being famous and subtle philosophers."[35] But she feared that, despite her public challenge issued in print to named opponents, no one would answer her. "I cannot conceive why it should be a disgrace to any man to maintain his own or others' opinions against a woman, so it be done with respect and civility," Margaret wrote, but she knew that philosophers were likely to think her "an inconsiderable opposite, because I am not of their sex."

> I have been informed that if I should be answered in my writings, it would be done rather under the name and cover of a woman than of a man; the reason is, because no man dare or will set his name to the contradiction of a lady.[36]

And to some extent her expectations were correct. When Henry Stubbe attacked the Royal Society in 1670 using arguments similar to those employed in Margaret's *Observations upon Experimental Philosophy*, his pamphlets caused a crisis of confidence in the society and resulted in a virulent book war, whereas Margaret's *Observations* stirred up no printed response at all. Similarly Henry More, to whom she sent her *Philosophical Letters* soon after its publication, disdained to answer her arguments against him. "I believe she may be secure from anyone giving her the trouble of a reply," he told his philosophical friend Lady Anne Conway—although he did suggest at the same time that she might herself consider "answering this great philosopher."[37] But Anne Conway—an animist whose views on the identity of matter and spirit, combined with an interest in the cabala, placed her closer intellectually to Margaret than to Henry More—never answered Margaret's book either.

Only once was Margaret opposed by name in print—in a small book entitled *Du Verger's Humble Reflections upon some Passages of the Right Honourable the Lady Marchioness of Newcastle's Olio*, published in London in 1658. The author— seemingly a Catholic Englishwoman, incredibly well read in theology—told how she had first taken great delight in Margaret's book, especially seeing in it a support to "the honour of our nation and sex, wherein we have had but few arguments of such ability." But when she reached Margaret's essay called "A Monastical Life" she was appalled, finding her intellectual diet transformed from "dainties so delicately dressed" to "morsels so wallowish and unsound (that I may not say wholly corrupted) that my stomach began to rise." Citing a huge range of authorities at length—from the Bible through the church fathers to modern Jesuit writers—Du Verger set out to prove that Margaret's information and arguments were all "stale, unsound, corrupted." Her work was in part an angry attack on the secular tone of Margaret's essay—which examined monasticism purely in terms of its effects on human society, presenting all religious ceremonies merely as ways to amuse and occupy the populace—and it was in part Catholic polemic against the Protestant religion. Margaret, however, declined to reply. Although the book had appeared "under the name of a woman," its true author was a man, she believed: "it will easily be known; for a philosopher or philosopheress is not produced on a sudden." Such "a hermaphroditical book," written "with fraud and deceit," she judged "not worthy taking notice of."*[38]

Although Margaret's philosophical work provoked no explicit printed responses, she did not go unanswered, despite Henry More's prediction. Joseph Glanvill, rector of the Abbey Church in the increasingly fashionable spa resort of Bath, was an enthusiastic disciple of More's Platonic philosophy, who attempted to write to Margaret in reply to her *Philosophical Letters* as soon as it came out. However, when his letter "miscarried in the way" he waited until she was in London in 1667 before writing again. Introducing himself as "an admirer" of her "most ingenious writings," he also enclosed a copy of his latest book, as some excuse for his possible "indecorum in the boldness of [making] such unknown addresses."[39]

Glanvill's disagreement with Margaret centered on the animist materialism of her natural philosophy—her belief that matter was innately active and intelligent, and that there were no immaterial spirits in nature. Like almost all

---

*In fact the author may have been a real woman—Susan Du Verger, who had translated selections of the writings of a French bishop into English during the 1630s.

other English philosophers of the period (including both Robert Boyle and Isaac Newton), Glanvill believed that it was essential to find evidence of immaterial forces working in nature, thus providing proof of God's existence and involvement in the world, and building the sort of Christianized philosophy they all desired. In this context, Margaret's views—that nature was eternal, infinite, and entirely material, existing largely independent of God and acting of its own free will—seemed dangerously irreligious, as she well knew.[40] When other philosophers wanted to use the argument from design as proof of the Christian religion, Margaret's opinion that the order and beauty of the world, and the origin of all the species, derived not from God's "divine counsel and prudence" but from "the wisdom of nature or infinite matter" could only be seen as an encouragement to atheism.[41] And this appearance of atheism was only confirmed by her nonphilosophical writings, where she freely admitted her fear of death and doubt of an afterlife, her inability to find reasons for Christian belief (which thus could only be based on blind faith), and her preference for an atheist's "humanity and civility towards man" over any form of religious fanaticism, which "begets cruelty to all things."[42] Margaret's emphasis on the importance of finding happiness in life smacked of the Epicurean pursuit of pleasure—a philosophical system notorious for its atheism. Still further evidence of her startling free thought appeared in her defense of women's dressing (commonly seen as irreligious worldly vanity), in her willingness to argue in support of immorality (as when she defended stealing and adultery in her *Orations*), and in her expressions of moral relativism (as when she wrote that "it is time and occasion that makes most things good or bad . . . custom and the law make the same thing civil or pious, just or unjust").[43]

Margaret was a practicing Anglican who frequently asserted her unquestioning belief in that faith, but her true religious feelings were open to question. She had married a man who, though also a conforming Anglican, was widely reported to have no serious religious faith, "neither feared God nor the Devil, believed Heaven or Hell,"[44] and Margaret herself clearly lacked the profound Christian sense that informed the lives and occasional writings of many more devout women. If she had any strong religious feeling, it was towards the natural world and its manifold wonders, rather than towards a distant, invisible God. At a time when Christian religion was seen as the only incentive towards morality and thus vital for supporting the whole fabric of society, many of her views were alarming.

In 1667 Glanvill opened up all these religious questions through the subject of witchcraft. Both he and Henry More believed it was essential to establish the true occurrence of witches and other supernatural phenomena, since this would prove the real existence of an immaterial realm, thus supporting the truth of Christian religion against atheism. The two men were dedicated to collecting case histories of witchcraft and demonic possessions, and sightings of ghosts and fairies. But Margaret in her *Philosophical Letters* had attacked More's belief in witches.

> Though I believe that there is a Devil, as the Word of God and the Church inform me, yet I am not of the opinion that God should suffer him to . . . make such contracts with man as to empower him to do mischief and hurt to others.

She granted that More's "many discourses and stories" of "strange effects" were very probably true, but argued that it was "a great folly" to ascribe them to immaterial spirits: "the nearest way is to ascribe such unusual effects or apparitions as happen sometimes rather to matter that is already corporeal, and not to go so far as to draw immaterial spirits to natural actions." There were many strange operations in nature—"sympathy, antipathy, magnetism and the like"—which we, "not knowing their causes . . . do stand amazed at."

> And by reason we cannot assign any natural cause for them [we] are apt to ascribe their effects to the Devil; but that there should be any such devilish witchcraft which is made by a covenant and agreement with the devil . . . I cannot readily believe. Certainly, I dare say, that many a good old honest woman hath been condemned innocently, and suffered death wrongfully, by the sentence of some foolish and cruel judges.[45]

Now Glanvill invited Margaret to further debate on the subject by sending her his newly published book, *Philosophical Considerations touching Witches and Witchcraft*.

Margaret eagerly seized this opening. Sending Glanvill in return some of her own books, she also wrote a long letter attacking the arguments of his book and setting out her own theory. As the two exchanged letters over the next couple of years, a detailed philosophical and theological controversy was played out. Glanvill endeavored to reveal inconsistencies in Margaret's view of matter as innately active, supporting instead More's Platonic idea of a "soul of the world" or "plastic nature" as a necessary and immaterial organizing force in the world. He tried to persuade her to believe in the orthodox story of God's creation of the world ex nihilo. Margaret offered to send him her *Observations upon Experimental Philosophy* and he in return promised to seek out a copy of his now out of print *Lux Orientalis*, where he defended More's Platonic doctrine of the preexistence of souls before birth. On this subject, Margaret posed a dilemma—if souls were eternal then they were gods, but if they were created then God must also have created sin—which Glanvill then strove to overturn. As she continued her vigorous attacks on the More-Glanvill doctrine on witches, he sent her the expanded new edition of his book—now entitled *A Blow at Modern Sadducism* in some Philosophical Considerations about Witchcraft*—as soon as the first copies were available in December 1667. "I have in it answered some of your Grace's objections," he told her. The following year he also sent his *Plus Ultra, or the Progress and Advancement of Knowledge since the Days of Aristotle*—a defense of the experimental research program of the Royal Society that Margaret had attacked in her *Observations*, prompting a new epistemological debate in their correspondence.[46] Both of Glanvill's books were clearly replies to Margaret's views, but neither mentioned her by name. Margaret went similarly unnamed by Glanvill's fellow Platonist, Ralph Cudworth, a colleague of Henry More's at Cambridge, who attacked her view that matter had free will as the most dangerous form of atheism in his *True Intellectual System of the Universe*, published in 1678.[47]

Despite Glanvill's many objections, Margaret remained confident in her own theory. Publishing her *Grounds of Natural Philosophy* in 1668, she reaffirmed her animist materialism and her belief in nature's free will. She also added an appendix more than seventy pages long, in response to the theological questions raised in her debate with Glanvill. Part 1 of the appendix restated her basic philosophico-religious beliefs in opposition to Glanvill—including her rejection of the existence of immaterial substances and her belief in the eternity of the natural world. She also extended the scope of her materialism, now arguing that Christ and Heaven and Hell (and probably the angels and devils) were all material, not spiritual.

Part 2 moved on to a topic that was preoccupying the Cambridge Platonists: the question of what physical means God would use to accomplish his plan for the world. Thomas Burnet, a disciple of Henry More's at Cambridge, was now working on his own *Sacred Theory of the Earth*, discussing the state of the world in the time of Adam, the processes by which God had produced Noah's Flood and the effects it had had, how America had first been populated, and how, at the end of time, God would dissolve the present world in fire, before making new heavens and a new earth where, in "a blessed age," man would live without evil and sin.

It was the last of these topics that interested Margaret. She discussed the dissolution of the world, and she speculated on the possibility of a perfect world, where matter worked entirely regularly, producing only happiness, while in

---

*One of the three Jewish sects of the New Testament, the Sadducees denied the resurrection of the dead, and the existence of angels and spirits.

another, purely irregular world, there would be only pain and misery. She went on to the resurrection of humanity, and the character of the (purely material) newly made Heaven and Hell (created by Nature, working on God's orders) to which they would be sent. Then in Parts 3 and 4 she returned to a detailed discussion of her regular and irregular worlds. Concerned to avoid any appearance of heresy or irreligion, she issued a careful disclaimer to her readers: "pray mistake not these arguments; they are not arguments of such worlds as are for the reception of the blessed and cursed humans, after their resurrections." Yet, given the religious content of Part 2, this was clearly what she had in mind as she wrote. And Margaret's concern with understanding the nature of the afterlife promised by Christianity is confirmed by the final section of the appendix, Part 5. Here she discussed the "restoring-beds, or wombs" by which Nature would be able to restore the decayed bodies of humanity, ready for resurrection. Perhaps thinking of the desecrated bodies of her relations in the Lucas family vault in Colchester, Margaret worried that incomplete bodies might be unsuitable for resurrection, before reassuring herself with the idea that the restoring-beds might be able to work with just the basic carcass of bones. A resurrected humanity, she hoped, would return to the peak of their youth and strength, combined with their more mature wisdom.

By now Margaret had achieved a prominent place in English intellectual life. No longer did anyone suggest that she might not have written her books. In fact it was William whose reputation now suffered, as many believed that Margaret had written his entertainment for the royal court in Antwerp, and all of London in 1667 attributed his play *The Humorous Lovers* to her. With William, Margaret had also attained celebrity as an aristocratic patron of letters. Flecknoe dedicated his new play *The Damoiselles à la Mode* to the couple in 1667, and continued to publish verses in their praise in the volumes of epigrams that he issued annually. New protégés included the successful dramatists John Dryden (soon to be poet laureate) and Thomas Shadwell, who both acknowledged their "great obligations" for the "so many and extraordinary favours" they had received. Dedicating their plays to the Newcastles, they celebrated Welbeck as a sanctuary to which "all poets . . . fly for protection"—"indeed the only place where the best poets can find a good reception." Shadwell was especially grateful. Having neither government nor church sinecure nor "the fortune of a gentleman" to supplement his inadequate royalties from the London theaters, he was often forced to leave his plays for "other business of advantage." The Newcastles' financial generosity bought him time for writing, and Welbeck offered the ideal retreat. Here he joined the family's "public and private conversation" and spent some time each day alone with William, discussing work in progress. He also had literary discussions with Margaret,

> *She to each skilful man of art*
> *Her conversation freely doth impart,*

he recorded gratefully. Shadwell dedicated two of his first five published plays to William and one to Margaret, who, in return, sent him her most recently printed books. Margaret was known for her "great mercy" and generosity towards even "the meanest *devotos*," and at least one other writer besides Glanvill took the "boldness" of introducing himself by sending her one of his books during these years.[48] Margaret, widely hailed as "the Queen of Sciences," the "height of National honour," "the unequalled daughter of the muses," receiving "a tribute of applause from the persons of most fame this age affords," could feel that much of her literary ambition was now fulfilled.[49] With most of her books currently available in print, she turned her energies towards other areas.

EVEN SEVEN YEARS AFTER the Restoration, the Newcastles' finances remained in a desperate state. Despite having sold lands worth £56,000 to pay off debts, "a great many" loans were still outstanding. The portion of his income that William had set aside for repaying his debts was utterly inadequate, and his payments often did little more than keep up with the interest that was continually accruing. Some creditors, still owed money from before the Restoration, were threatening William with legal action, or the dishonor of having his bonds sold to professional moneylenders. New mortgages were still being taken out on various Welbeck properties, and lawsuits over disputed landownership continued well into the 1670s.[50]

The couple's growing disappointment and cynicism was exacerbated by Margaret's *Life of William*, published in 1667. Here, based on the extensive legal and financial records kept in Evidence House by John Proctor, Margaret had set out detailed calculations of the vast losses her husband had suffered for his loyalty to the king. After totaling the annual income from every estate, and multiplying by the eighteen years of William's absence from Welbeck, her result was truly shocking. More than £400,000 had been lost in income alone. Compounding this figure with interest at the normal commercial rate of 6 percent, and adding the values of woods felled (£45,000) and of lands lost through various causes related to the war (a further £138,000), she reached the astronomical total of £941,303.[51]

Margaret knew that she was open to criticism for exaggeration, especially for her decision to add interest into her calculation and for the high values she had put on William's estates.* Yet she reckoned that she had, if anything, underestimated her husband's overall losses, having included in her calculation only those figures "that are certainly known" from the estate records.** Other losses to which she could not put precise figures—buildings and their contents destroyed, farm stock and horses lost, and the cost of repairing and replacing all these—would more than compensate for any overvaluations in her calculation, she was sure.[52]

William now complained openly of how he had been "damnified" in the wars. The idealistic loyalty to the king that had governed his life for so long was visibly fading. Determined to recoup whatever money he could, he had begun to pursue financial policies of dubious legality, bringing himself into "evil fame in court and country." By May 1667 the news had reached "even so high as the King's ears" that William was felling the royal woods in Sherwood Forest for his own profit. And, despite Margaret's claim that her husband had loyally paid all his taxes since the Restoration, he was now noted at court for nonpayment of his "creation moneys"—sums due annually to the king from recently created lords. At the same time, John Hutton's legal researcher was hunting the state records in London for ancient rights, long disused, that William could claim as his due from the Crown. And in the following year, William demanded from the king the salary owed to him as a gentleman of the bedchamber, which, in a noble spirit, he had never claimed since his appointment eight years before. In November 1668 he received the full outstanding arrears—£8,083 6s. 8d.—plus the promise of future annual payments of £1,000.[53]

Margaret herself, observing that William's estate was "so much ruined by the late Civil Wars, that neither himself nor his posterity will be able so soon to recover it," now began to take a close interest in her husband's business concerns.[54] From her mother, Margaret had imbibed the vital importance of supervising the estate personnel closely. Clamping down on dishonesty was the key to profits, she believed, "for there is an old true saying, 'the master's eye makes the horse fat.'" Even a gentleman of small fortune could live well if he only took the trouble "to look into his own estate industriously, to know

---

*By using the maximum possible figure for each estate, she had arrived at a figure for her husband's prewar annual income that was some £3,000 higher than the figure of £19,257 Henry calculated independently at about the same time.

**Margaret's result, though huge, was not inconsistent with the calculations made by other dissatisfied royalists after the Restoration. The marquess of Worcester put his own losses as high as £700,000, and Lady Ann Fanshawe would produce a similarly large figure in her biography of her husband, written about ten years after Margaret's work.

and understand the value of his lands justly, to endeavour to have his rents paid duly,* and not suffer his servants to cozen him either by flattery or excess."[55]

This ideal of close scrutiny would be central to Margaret's program of estate management.** From 1667 more detailed accounts were demanded from Edward Bilbie, the steward of Welbeck's grange farm, and in the following year these were explicitly addressed to Margaret as well as William. By June 1669 it was being generally reported that Margaret "hath all the power given to her to manage his Grace's estate for seven years"; new tenants were now unwilling to commence farming until they had received her approval for their leases. On untenanted lands in Nottinghamshire Margaret also kept cattle herself, until new occupants could be found. Over the next year she inspected the estate affairs increasingly diligently, checking a wider range of accounts, and to facilitate this work she instructed John Rolleston in 1670 to draw up a new more accurate rent-roll, detailing all the income due from the Welbeck estates.[56]

Under Margaret's growing authority Francis Topp retained his influential position. Although William ultimately signed all the legal papers, it was often Topp and Margaret who chose new tenants and replaced unreliable estate commissioners, aiming to improve the collection of the rents. Topp was also often in London, where his mercantile connections and persuasive business manner won the Newcastles such financial advantages as reductions in the interest due on their debts. Here he also performed a variety of other business for the couple, buying them oranges and other luxuries, and distributing Margaret's books to her London acquaintance.[57]

For his services, Topp was rewarded far beyond his basic annual salary of £50. At Welbeck he and his wife made free use of the facilities, even leaving their children in the nursery at William's expense when they went to London. Topp's medicines, sent from the Newcastles' London physician, were charged to William's bill. In 1662 he and Andrew Clayton, exploiting their influence with William, had formed a business partnership to mine lead and coal on the Welbeck estates, and in later years William's favor brought Topp further success in his private business dealings in the Midlands.[58] The patronage that the Newcastles bestowed on him was exceptional: through William's intervention at court, Topp even achieved the high honor of a baronetcy, normally reserved for

---

*I.e. the full amount at the correct time.

**Margaret's involvement in her husband's estates was not unparalleled. Her contemporary, Elizabeth Walker—posthumously celebrated as a model wife and "landlady" in the biography written by her clergyman husband, Anthony—had been given £19 of her husband's annual rents to manage herself. Margaret's own mother had managed her sons' estates in Colchester.

the heads of leading county families. Given by the king in 1667, the honor was regranted in 1668, this time with the provision that Topp was to be exempted from the fee of £1,095 that was "usually paid for that dignity."[59] William's children were outraged. Jane and Henry's wife, Frances, shared bitter witticisms about the couple they continued to call merely "Mr. Topp and his wife," although their proper mode of address was now "Sir Francis and Lady Topp." "Vanity hath got the better of covetousness," the two sisters-in-law agreed, after the Topps began driving in their carriage with fashionable London society in Hyde Park: "I believe he could have wished I had not seen him there," Jane reported. Both blamed Topp for the coldness of their relations with William, especially after Topp had told Jane that the £1,000 her father had promised her was "not yet due." "Truly, I expect nothing he can keep from me," Jane told Frances. "I am of your opinion, he intends none of my Lord's children any good, and am very sorry he should so much waste the estate as you mention. Methinks there might be some means contrived to hinder him. I would assist in anything I could."[60]

Despite the "grand settlement" that William had signed in October 1666, entailing his estates to his male heirs, Henry and Frances continued to worry about their financial future. As William grew older, Henry took an ever-increasing role in northern politics, performing many of his father's duties as lord lieutenant of Nottinghamshire and chief justice in Eyre. In 1670 he and William were jointly appointed lords lieutenant of Northumberland, but it was Henry who did all the work, commanding the northern militia forces and using his influence as governor of Newcastle-upon-Tyne to ensure the town's compliance with the king's policies. Still serving as a gentleman of the bedchamber to Charles II, in addition to his appointment as one of the king's privy councillors in 1670, Henry was living as a great aristocratic grandee—with all the attendant political power, and the vast expenses to match—but he was still only receiving an income of £2,000 per year from his father, which was sometimes paid late. Inevitably, he was heavily in debt, and he was now also having to stand as joint security for his aging father's loans. William was taking the money for current use, but it was Henry who would have to repay these debts if his father died leaving them still outstanding.[61]

Margaret got on well with Henry's children—Elizabeth, Frances, Margaret, and Katherine, and especially his son, young Henry, viscount Mansfield, who reached his seventh birthday in 1670. "Harry loves my wife better than anybody, and she him, I think," William reported from Welbeck when all his grandchildren came to stay without their parents that January. After young Henry returned home, Margaret maintained the connection with private letters and messages through his father. "I am . . . glad my Lord Mansfield did kindly accept of my letter, but sorry he hath got a knock upon his forehead," she wrote to Henry, adding a rather ribald joke about cuckolds' horns: "pray tell his Lordship from me, if he were a married man it would be a dangerous bump."[62] But despite Margaret's obvious affection for Henry junior, Henry senior remained suspicious of his stepmother's intentions, and he watched Margaret's and Topp's work in the Welbeck estates with anxiety.

By 1668 Margaret was taking specified profits from Welbeck's grange farm for her own use. In June she received a slightly larger payment than her husband from this source—£103 9s. 6d., principally for sales of wool, sheepskins, hides, and tallow. The £3 9s. 6d. she gave back to Edward Bilbie as a gratuity, and he forwarded the remaining £100 to Mark Anthony Benoist in London to fund his purchases of books, fruit, and medicines on her behalf. In December William ordered a further £100 to be withdrawn from Evidence House for his wife's use. The following year, unwilling to withdraw more money from his treasury, William ordered Andrew Clayton to chase up various arrears of rents and to pay the moneys direct to Margaret—amounting to some £105 throughout the year. Again a fair proportion of the money went to Benoist in London; the remainder Margaret kept in her own hands.[63]

These were relatively small sums, but Margaret's plans for felling large areas of woodland on the Welbeck estates were much more worrying for Henry. By the terms of the "grand settlement" of 1666, William was not allowed to sell his estates, but he was entitled to fell the trees that stood on the land: this would raise vast immediate sums, but would also drastically reduce Henry's inheritance. In 1668 Margaret had begun to press for large-scale felling in Sherwood Forest. Two woods were sold that year, but William was unwilling to fell the £16,000 worth of timber that she advocated. Perhaps it was the interests of his son that held him back: in May, Henry had protested at the "great waste" he found in some of the family's woods in Yorkshire, begging that no more trees be cut down.[64] But there was also the question of whether William really had the legal right to fell the Sherwood timber, which had first been claimed by his ancestors on possibly dubious grounds. Since the Restoration William had used his position as chief justice in Eyre over all the northern forests to validate his own claim to these rights, concealing the maneuver by temporarily selling the lands in question for peppercorn sums to Andrew Clayton and John Rolleston, and then buying them back. However, he was perhaps still afraid that felling these woods might rouse the king into investigating his activities. In any event, in the autumn of 1670, two years after Margaret's first suggestion, the £16,000 worth of timber remained standing. But Margaret was still urging that it be felled, and Henry's anxiety continued.[65]

A further cause of resentment lay in the Newcastles' extravagant spending on Bolsover Castle. Through 1667 into 1668 building work continued here, as stone masons, bricklayers, carpenters, glaziers, plasterers, a wood carver, and a locksmith brought the new gallery range to completion, under the supervision of the architect Samuel Marsh. By the summer of 1668 a housekeeper had been installed, and the rooms of the Little Castle, at least, were ready. A roughly contemporary inventory suggests the incredible richness of their contents: chairs upholstered in cloth of silver in the dining room, Spanish tables in the passageway outside, gilt leather chairs in the Star Chamber above, and featherbeds with fine silk quilts in chambers hung with tapestry. Adjoining the Star Chamber, the marble closet had become an intimate reception room: with crimson silk hangings, couches covered in matching silk quilts, chairs, a table, and a looking glass, it was at once snug, opulent, and feminine.[66] The castle would become Margaret's home if she survived her husband. Its lavish renovation was unlikely to be of any benefit to Henry, a mere seven years younger than his stepmother. It was Welbeck, his future home as head of the family, that he wanted improved. Before the Restoration, William had promised his son that he would, on his return to England, "make Welbeck a very fine place for you," but in fact the extensive program of improvements desired by Henry would have to wait until after his father's death.[67]

In the meantime, Henry's anxieties about his future were aggravated by the report that Margaret had begun to examine the precise terms of his "grand settlement" in order to discover possessions of William's that had not been included. Henry had already lost the inheritance of the family's grand town house at Clerkenwell, which William had given to his wife in January 1668 "for the increase of her jointure." And on January 22, 1670, a new indenture, signed by William, granted all his "waste grounds* . . . within the Forest of Sherwood . . . or elsewhere within the realm of England" to Margaret, "for the better increase of her jointure, and for other good causes and considerations." Even after this, there were still estates worth some £2,000 per year in income "left out of the grand settlement" that Margaret was hoping to secure for herself. On October 29, 1670, she achieved part of her aim, when William again added to her jointure: this time it was the manors of Sibthorpe and Clipstone, with his favorite Clipstone Park, providing an annual income of £800. Henry was watching his inheritance draining away while Margaret, perhaps feeling some guilt at her own self-interest, reminded herself that William's grandmother—the founder of his family's fortunes, Bess of Harwick, or more properly Elizabeth, countess of Shrewsbury—had only done the same, enriching herself through the generous jointures she received from each of her four hus-

---

*Uncultivated lands, especially commons, "not . . . let to any tenant or farmer."

bands before spending her widowed old age in grand building projects at nearby Hardwick.[68]

Among the Welbeck servants it was now being said that Margaret's "whole care and study was nothing more than to enrich herself for a second husband," as Bess had done.[69] But Margaret's own writings—on the impropriety of remarriage for widows, and on the folly of those women who gave up their independence and possessions to a second husband—suggest that she was thinking rather of a single life. Widowhood could be a period of great independence and power for aristocratic women with generous marriage jointures. Mary, countess of Pembroke, for instance, had occupied her widowhood in writing, literary patronage, building, administering her own and her son's estates, and governing the city of Cardiff. And Lady Anne Clifford, after two unhappy marriages, spent her old age managing the beloved northern estates that had been her father's. Here she rebuilt six of the Clifford family's castles and several local churches, wrote an autobiography and a family history, and commemorated herself and her family in the "Great Picture" that she had painted.[70]

By the autumn of 1670, Margaret's involvement in the Welbeck estates was causing resentment among the estate personnel as well as with Henry. Andrew Clayton was especially angry. Margaret's close inspection of the estate accounts made his normal operations impossible, preventing him from taking the bribes and cuts from tenants with which, until now, he had supplemented his basic salary.[71] Clayton told friends how "he was weary of his employment and would gladly be gone," but William, trusting his old servant, "would not permit him to leave him." And Clayton feared that, even if he did leave, Margaret's suspicions would prevent him from getting his "general release"—the document of indemnity he needed from William, acknowledging that all his accounts balanced, and discharging him from any further financial liability. Unwillingly Clayton stayed on, but his resentment grew—especially after he missed a rich match with a local widow, "who would very gladly have intermarried with him," bringing him "a fortune of £4000," if he had left Welbeck. He could only look to the future for relief. William, approaching his seventy-seventh birthday and aging fast under the effects Parkinson's disease, "could not live long," Clayton believed. By allying himself with Henry's interests in the estates, he could ensure that he succeeded Francis Topp as the most favored and trusted employee when the new heir inherited.

And so Clayton began, "ever underhand," to oppose Margaret's plans. Her desired sale of the £16,000 worth of timber in Sherwood he had so far "by one shift or other prevented . . . and when no other means would serve, he underhand kept off the chapmen that should buy it." Her new jointure that was in preparation in October 1670 he promised "he would prevent if by any means he could." But Margaret, increasingly aware of his secret opposition, now "hated him perfectly for it," and the jointure was signed by William without Clayton's knowledge.[72]

Desperate to "put a check to her Grace's proceedings," Clayton "had studied all ways in the world how to give her Grace a dead blow, and to divert his Grace's affections from her." It was probably his influence that stirred up the "sharp and passionate quarrels" between Margaret and William, which Clayton reported himself "often involved in." The quarrels raised Clayton's hopes. If the accusations he had prepared against Margaret could only be brought to William's attention, he believed they would cause the couple to separate. His only problem was that "he could not find out any person living that would or durst tell his Grace such things as he had to say."[73]

Then, at the end of October 1670, two of Clayton's Northumberland friends arrived at Welbeck. John Booth was a clergyman who had been installed as tenant of William's castle and lands at Bothal by Margaret and Topp in 1668, against the wishes of his Northumberland neighbors. Since then Booth had risen to become one of Welbeck's receivers of rents, and had joined in Clayton's dishonest transactions with the tenants. The second man was Francis Liddell. A horse breeder who had occasional dealings with the Welbeck stables, he was also tenant of William's estates at Ogle. Here Liddell's proper annual rent was £180, but in the mid-1660s Clayton had illicitly reduced these payments by £10 per year; and in the autumn of 1668, before Margaret had begun to examine the accounts closely, he had promised a further reduction of £20. In return, Liddell had given Clayton a young gelding, valued at £80, and a brood mare worth a further £20; he had also promised the best colt bred from his black Barbary stallion that year.[74]

But on Thursday, October 29, 1670, when Liddell asked Clayton to fulfil his part of the bargain, he was disappointed. "The Duchess did so narrowly of late inspect his Grace's affairs, as that he could make no alteration of the rental without being discovered," Clayton had to explain. To the further request that he persuade William to repay a longstanding debt to Liddell, Clayton also replied in the negative, saying that Margaret "positively obstructed his Grace from paying of that £500." As Liddell—in great need of money to fund the coal mine he was just opening up—nonetheless continued to press hard for "the performance of [these] two things," Clayton began to unburden all his grievances to his two friends, demonizing Margaret as a selfish, greedy, angry monster whose "delight [was] to ruin all persons that she had to do with"—just as "the old Countess of Shrewsbury," William's grandmother, Bess of Hardwick had done. "He had heard her Grace say [that]

. . . she was a Duchess, and consequently a greater person than a Countess, and would out-do her in that kind," Clayton reported, and "he much feared, if her Grace were not some way prevented, she would engross the whole [estate] revenue into her hands, and confound all retainers to the family." Already she had ordered Rolleston "to draw up new and perfect rentals," which would remove all opportunities for graft, and Clayton further believed that "it was her Grace's design to let the whole estate" to a single tenant. "There were propositions passed to that purpose between his Grace, Mr. Ashton of Middleton, and himself; and he said if that took effect, her Grace would break up the family and go to rant* at London."[75]

As Clayton talked, Booth and Liddell grew fearful for their own fates. Under a new management regime—whether Margaret's or some new super-tenant's—they might well both face eviction from their farms, while Booth could lose his employment as a receiver. Booth's fears were especially stirred by Clayton's report that Margaret "had a pique" against him in particular. Distrusting his accounts, she had issued a "special caution" that they "should neither be signed nor any discharge given him, but [only] a bare receipt for so much money paid in." Having "already threatened . . . to call him to a grand account whenever she pleased, and [that she] would certainly ruin him," she had now ordered her lawyer to draw up a full list of charges against him, Clayton reported.

On Friday, October 30, the three men met again. All morning and into the afternoon, they "discoursed these things over and over again, with many other aggravating circumstances," until finally Clayton suggested a remedy. In an anonymous letter, written "in an unknown hand" and sent from some distant posthouse, they could safely present his accusations against Margaret to William. Once William and his wife had separated, as Clayton was sure they would, then Clayton, "paramount in his Grace's whole concerns," would be able to serve his friends "according to their merit and desire." Liddell was at once enthusiastic on "the joint advantages that it might produce to us all." While Liddell would get his £500 and his rent reduction, Booth would be able to hold his post as accountant and receiver "without danger," his rent could be reduced by £5 per year by Clayton, and Clayton would also ensure that he obtained a formal lease for a twenty-one year term, which William had already promised him but which, "as Clayton pretended, her Grace obstructed."

Next morning, Saturday the 31st, the three men reconvened in Clayton's chamber at Welbeck, where pen, ink, and paper were ready. Liddell preached

---

*With the word "rant," Clayton was dismissing Margaret's intellectual talk as extravagant, unintelligible bombast, just as Mary Evelyn had done three years before.

again—this time on the opportunity here "delivered into our hands to do ourselves good and serve the family of Newcastle" at the same time. Then, with "the doors locked upon us," the three sealed their agreement with "damned reciprocal vows of secrecy." Booth, chosen as writer, took notes while Clayton dictated a plan for the letter: first William would be reminded "of that great honour and esteem the world had for him before the late Rebellion," and then informed that "now he went much less in the opinions of all, the cause whereof, right or wrong, we were to cast upon her Grace." By three in the afternoon, this outline had been put "into wicked and unhappy words," but Clayton remained dissatisfied. The letter's accusations—that Margaret had brought her husband into dishonorable repute "both in the court and country"—were too general, he thought. Clayton wanted to add a specific charge against Francis Topp and so the letter ended with "that damned scandal"— almost certainly an allegation of sexual misconduct between Topp and Margaret. After Booth had made a neat copy and Liddell had sealed it, the three conspirators knelt on the floor. "With our right hands all closed together and the letter in the middle, we bound ourselves under a curse of damnation and destruction to our posterities for ever, if ever that letter or the contents thereof was by any of us discovered to our prejudices."

On the following morning, Sunday, November 1, Booth's servant boy was dispatched on horseback. Riding along tracks in Sherwood Forest to bypass the local posthouse at Tuxford, and then on back streets through Newark to avoid the notice of William's lawyer Richard Mason, who lived there, he eventually delivered the letter late in the evening at the postmaster's house in Grantham, before lodging for the night "at some obscure inn at the end of the town," as he had been instructed. It would take him all the next day to ride back to Welbeck, but the letter itself had by then already arrived, reaching the house about midmorning with the rest of the post from Tuxford.[76]

Clayton and Booth were absent: fearing that their faces would betray their guilt, they spent the day in riding over to Sookholme, to take Booth's Northumberland estate accounts to John Rolleston for approval. Liddell alone stayed behind. That evening, concealing himself in the darkness of the woods just outside Welbeck's great gate, he met his two returning friends to tell them "with much joy" that he had seen their letter delivered into William's hands by John Proctor.

Booth and Clayton went in to supper as usual, but before they were half done Clayton was summoned to William. The letter itself was not produced—William had no desire to spread the slanders it contained—but he told Clayton that he had received "a libel" and that he had shown it to Margaret, who "was somewhat suspicious" that Clayton or Gilbert Eagle, her principal opponents in the estate business, "had a hand in it." William how-ever, incapable of doubting such long-trusted employees, "had satisfied her of their innocence." He rather "suspected that acute rascal the parson of Mans-field"—a neighboring town that represented one of the greatest local chal-lenges to William's authority. Clayton had plainly misjudged the strength of the Newcastles' relationship, in spite of any quarrels they may have had. Unquestioningly loyal to Margaret, William was furious at this libel, which "abused Peg, as he pleased to call her Grace, abominably." "If he could find out the author, he would have his ears," he swore—no empty threat when the legal punishment for libel "against a magistrate or public person" was to have one's ears cut off, as had happened to William Prynne for his abuse of Queen Henrietta Maria before the Civil War. Yet Clayton retained some optimism. Arriving in Booth's chamber after an hour closeted with his master, he reported that "his Grace did not resent it so highly as he hoped he would have done; yet none knew what effects it might have afterwards." The three con-spirators agreed "to be secret and to wait the event."

Meanwhile investigations were set in motion. The local postmasters were summoned and questioned, who all agreed the letter must have come "from the North." It was probably in consequence of this lead that "all the Northum-berland men" at Welbeck "were called before their Graces in the Gallery" for examination. But Margaret still suspected conspiracy closer to home, and she sent her maid Mistress Evans to Tuxford "in her Grace's coach" to make further inquiries. Clayton, beginning to fear discovery, pulled the original draft of the letter out from its concealment in his stocking and burned it.

But it was not until June the following year that real discoveries began, when Booth, back in Northumberland, wrote an ill-advised letter to Liddell and neglected to send it through private channels. When Liddell opened the letter in public company at Welbeck, its incriminating contents were soon dis-covered and he was prevented from answering it himself. The reply that Booth received, sent in Liddell's name but in fact written by someone else at Wel-beck, alerted him to his danger and he left home at once. Clayton and Liddell, fearing that he would confess all, sent messengers to find him. He must call at Clayton's house at Whitwell, they said, and approach William through Clayton as intermediary, who promised he "would pawn his life to bring me off." But Booth no longer trusted Clayton. Instead, "resolved to cast myself upon their Graces' mercy," he sent his own petition directly to William. As a result, Booth was invited to draw up a full confession "of that horrid conspiracy against her Grace." He signed this on July 1, promising that he would testify to its contents "upon my oath in any court or before any judicature" when called upon. In return he was allowed to go free, although dismissed from his post as receiver and accountant. Two days later, Liddell signed the same document, acknowledging "all and every matter and thing therein contained . . . really true," and echoing Booth's readiness to testify in court. It was Andrew Clayton, by now a fugitive in hiding, for whom William's vengeance was reserved.[77]

In preparation for legal proceedings a second copy of the confession was drawn up, with Booth and Liddell's signatures now formally witnessed by three of William's most trusted servants. On July 14 Booth and these witnesses appeared before a local justice of the peace—a confidential agent also employed by William in his (sometimes questionably legal) forest business— and Booth swore to the truth of his confession.[78] In the meantime, William approached legal counsel and was advised on how to ensure Clayton's conviction—both by using "the fittest" justices and jury, drawn from William's own Midlands territories, where he had greatest influence, and by making Booth and Liddell king's witnesses, which would render Clayton unable to call either counsel or witnesses to speak against them. Since it was clear "that the libellous matter doth concern a public person of honour and that the design was wicked, to work dissolution between a great peer of the realm and his wife," the full punishment would indeed be "by fine, imprisonment and loss of ears," the lawyer confirmed.[79]

But William never took this course against Clayton, being unwilling to damage Margaret's reputation by bringing the letter's scandalous accusations into the public domain, even to the limited extent that this process of law in "private sessions" would require. Instead, he sought to achieve his revenge by charging Clayton with massive embezzlements, which he had in fact never committed. The evidence, however, lay ready in the Newcastles' hands, created by Clayton's own sloppy record keeping. Clayton had handled vast sums on the Newcastles' behalf, and while he had dutifully signed receipts for the cash he took from John Proctor at Evidence House and for the rents he received from the estate bailiffs, he had often failed to demand receipts from those to whom he paid money out, leaving it open for the Newcastles to claim that he had stolen it. The Welbeck accounts were now carefully examined to prepare a prosecution, and showed that Clayton owed William at least £10,000. Orders were sent out for his arrest, with the further direction that he was to be released on bail only if he provided security of at least £20,000—a sum he would never be able to find.

Facing the certainty of imprisonment until he could clear himself, which he might never manage given his inadequate records, Clayton realized that he was "in great danger to be ruined and destroyed," and he remained in hiding from the law. At the same time, he carefully prepared to make a countersuit against the Newcastles, hoping in this way to escape their prosecution. In a petition direct to the lord keeper of the great seal, he set out his case—that it was really William who owed him money, not vice versa—providing detailed accounts of the "very many great sums" that he had spent on the Newcastles' behalf, which had been offset only partially by the moneys he received back from the estates. William and Margaret both knew well that he had paid the full amounts according to their orders, he asserted, but even so it would be "very difficult, if possible" at all, to prove his case. Many of the records he had kept were still in his chamber at Welbeck, which had been locked against him: his servants were permitted to remove the trunks of Clayton's clothing, but they could take no papers whatsoever. And there were few witnesses for him to call in his support: William and Margaret had given him many of their orders in private, and many witnesses of other transactions were dead, or aged and infirm, or so disposed in William's favor that Clayton would not receive "the benefit of their testimony at any trial"—all matters "well known to the aforesaid Duke and Duchess." In these circumstances, Clayton asked that the case be heard in the lord keeper's court, where he could call witnesses who now lived overseas, and he requested the lord keeper to summon both William and Margaret to appear in person to answer all these countercharges against them.[80]

Clayton's stratagem appears to have succeeded: the Newcastles do not seem to have prosecuted their own suit against him any further. Although deprived of his employment, he was otherwise unscathed and continued as a tenant of the Welbeck lands and manors to which he already held leases. But Clayton was nonetheless determined to exact his own revenge on the informer, John Booth. In conjunction with other enemies, "many, rich and maliciously bent," that Booth had made in Northumberland, Clayton bribed former servants of Booth's to bring charges against him for coin clipping, a crime punishable by death.* They made their accusation at the York assizes early in 1672, but the trial fell through when the original witnesses refused to testify. However, at the Newcastle assizes in the summer of 1673, a new witness made further accusations. In spite of William's representations—producing evidence that Booth had not clipped the coin of the Welbeck rents, as this witness alleged, and informing the judge that Booth was being maliciously prosecuted by old servants who had been dismissed from their employment as a result of his revelations of their "diverse great enormities and most vile and wicked practices"—this time Booth was convicted. He was saved from "a most ignominious death" only when, with William's support, he petitioned the king directly for pardon.[81]

---

*Cutting the edges off gold and silver coins to gain the value of the precious metal removed was counted as treason, since it defaced the king's image on the coins and threatened the monetary stability of the nation.

Francis Topp also suffered in the aftermath of the conspiracy. When the anonymous letter arrived at Welbeck in November 1670, Topp had been away on William's business—probably in London, where he regularly resided at Newcastle House for long periods.[82] After the accusations he may never have returned to Welbeck, but his wife, Elizabeth, and their daughter, Frances, seem to have stayed on with Margaret into 1671. However that July they left suddenly, apparently in disgrace. Perhaps this was a result of Booth's confession that same month. Or perhaps it had to do with the discovery, in June, that Topp had embezzled £300, which he was supposed to have used to pay off some of William's debts. Topp had absconded very thoroughly with the money: having first told the principal creditor that he had no need to pay because of privilege of Parliament (to which he was not at all entitled, since he was not a member of Parliament), he then gave out rumors of his own death to escape payment. Instead it was William who finally paid the money to his creditors in July 1672.[83]

Whatever the precipitating cause, Margaret had finally lost her lifelong female companion and friend, and Henry's family were jubilant. In London his wife's family relayed the news to each other, feeling great "satisfaction that the Lady Topp and her daughter is gone from Welbeck, I hope never to return thither any more."[84] There is no evidence that any of the Topp family ever did return to Welbeck. Francis died in 1676, leaving the baronetcy and the Gloucestershire manor that he had acquired from William to his son John. Elizabeth survived her husband, living on the jointure of £200 per annum he had provided for her, until she died at a ripe old age in 1703.

But any hopes that Henry and his family had of benefiting from the Topps' departure went unfulfilled, as Margaret, freed from Clayton's opposition, only intensified the estate policies William's children objected to. In the month following Booth's confession, she revived William's long unexercised right to confiscate unbranded cattle from common lands in Sherwood Forest: amidst the political unrest of 1671, her action caused widespread panic as malcontents spread rumors that the king was going to "seize on all the unbranded cattle throughout the nation." Margaret's long-advocated policy of mass forest fellings was also now put into effect, and negotiations with merchants quickly proceeded into a series of large sales of William's timber in Sherwood.[85]

Henry noticed the change of atmosphere within weeks of Booth's confession, and reported himself "very melancholy, finding my father more persuaded by his wife than I could think it possible . . . I thank God my little family are in health: the joy I take in it cannot be taken away from me by the unkindness to us at Welbeck."[86] Perhaps William and Margaret suspected that Henry's influence lay behind the conspiracy, and the possibility of his involvement is certainly suggested by the feeling of "kindness" he still professed for

Andrew Clayton many years afterwards. Only in the late 1680s did the two fall out, after Henry realized that Clayton had been cheating him for years by paying the rents for the Welbeck lands where he was a tenant at a reduced rate, which he had arranged while still serving as William's estate steward. Despite Henry's attempt to prosecute him in 1687, Clayton would return to the family's service in the 1690s, when he became again a trusted estate manager, this time for Henry's favorite daughter, Margaret, and her husband, who inherited all the Welbeck property on Henry's death in 1691.

AT WELBECK THE NEWCASTLES' grand round of aristocratic entertaining and political business went on unchanged. William's manège remained one of the principal sights of the Midlands. The "stables, riding-houses and horses . . . are more extraordinary than are to be seen in Europe, if the curiosity and excellency of their manège discipline and methods be considered," reported the gentleman-philosopher, Thomas Povey, during his tour through the Midlands in 1668. Looking forward eagerly to his visit, Povey hoped to see not only Welbeck's equestrian paraphernalia but also its famed inhabitants—"the Queen of Sheba and her more considerable Prince," he joked.[87]

William had become a legend in his own lifetime, renowned for the vast expense of his prewar royal entertainments, for his Civil War generalship, his long loyal exile, and his vast financial losses. Although he had passed much of his political business into Henry's hands, he was still revered as the head of northern and Midlands society, a grand old man who had known some gentry families for as many as five generations. The Yorkshire gentleman Sir John Reresby proudly recorded his own family's long association with the elderly duke, naming his firstborn son William in honor of the great man, who stood godfather to the boy. William's exceptional old age had become part of his myth: even when he was only approaching his seventy-fifth birthday, he was already rumored to be "near eighty years of age." Although deteriorating physically, he was still intellectually sharp—"very ingenious and present to himself," as Reresby noted, while John Dryden also commented on his patron's "vigour of . . . mind."[88]

By the time he was seventy-six, William had seen three of his adult children die before him. Next after his eldest son, Charles, had been Elizabeth, countess of Bridgewater, who died aged thirty-seven in June 1663 after she went into premature labor during her husband's imprisonment for dueling. In October 1669 Elizabeth's elder sister, Jane, followed her, at the age of forty-eight. Flecknoe and at least one other poet wrote funeral elegies for the family's consolation, commemorating Jane's charity to the poor and her many other virtues, including her writing of poetry:

An art she knew and practisèd so well
Her modesty alone could it excel
Which, by concealing, doubles her esteem.[89]

The contrast with Margaret's public writing career, whether or not intended, was certainly obvious.

Within two years of Jane's passing, William had begun to make preparations for his own death. Early in 1671 he approached the king to ask for the privilege of being buried in Westminster Abbey, along with monarchs and other great figures—a request that was readily granted. By July 1672 the vault in the Abbey's north transept where he and Margaret would be buried had been completed under the supervision of Mark Anthony Benoist, who had taken over Francis Topp's role as the Newcastles' principal London business agent.[90]

During his final years, William continued his literary pursuits as keenly as ever. After arranging in 1671 for the translation of his latest book on horsemanship into French, he moved on to prepare a new comedy for the London stage, based on the short entertainment, *A Pleasant and Merry Humour of a Rogue,* which he had written in Antwerp. Adding extensive new material, some of it derived from the royal entertainment he had written for Charles II just after the Restoration, William created *The Triumphant Widow*—the story of a wealthy widow, Lady Haughty, who is courted by a multitude of suitors, eager to acquire her riches. The central theme—of a woman's predicament as she faces choosing a (probably unsatisfactory) husband—was clearly influenced by Margaret's earlier plays, as also was the ending where, extremely unusually in contemporary drama, the principal female character remains happy and unmarried, "triumphant" over men. William passed his draft to Thomas Shadwell for completion and, with some substantial additions of Shadwell's, the play was performed under the direction of Sir William Davenant at the playhouse in Dorset Gardens in 1674.[91]

By 1671 Margaret had also returned to her writing. In that year she published new editions of two early works, *The World's Olio* and *Nature's Pictures*. To both she made for the most part only minor changes of wording, making her language simpler and more direct—especially necessary in *The World's Olio*, the first book she had written as an adult. Here essays whose original titles had been unclear or misleading were given new headings, and a fair proportion of the overcomplicated and grammatically incorrect sentences were restructured. Longer essays were now broken into paragraphs, and some signposting of changes of topic was added, making her train of thought easier to follow. Errors in the arrangement of the shorter essays and allegories of

Book 2, probably introduced into the original edition by the printers, were also corrected, but in neither *The World's Olio* nor *Nature's Pictures* was there any major new writing.

The most significant changes were the omissions. From the historical section of *The World's Olio*, two of the original essays—criticisms of King James I and King Henry VII—were now left out: perhaps it was no longer tactful after the Restoration to disparage monarchs, especially when one of them was the present king's grandfather. Later in the book, Margaret also omitted an essay "Of Revenge for Ill Words"—perhaps too sensitive a topic after Clayton's libel. And in *Nature's Pictures*, a story of a young lady's visit to Elysium, where she met famous lovers of the past, was altered so that it no longer contained the original biblical references. Julius Caesar's involvement with a Vestal Virgin, and Nero's amour with his mother remained in the revised text, but Solomon's "seraglio of mistresses" and Lot's incestuous relationship with his daughters were both excised, perhaps because Margaret had no desire to undermine the restored Anglican church.[92]

In both books Margaret took the opportunity to update her prefatory addresses to her readers, making them more appropriate to her identity as an established literary figure. From *Nature's Pictures* she omitted the most acutely apologetic of her original prefaces, and she rewrote the others into a single preface, much less self-critical in tone than its predecessors. In *The World's Olio* she left the prefaces at the front of the book largely unaltered, but she removed all the later epistles to the reader that she had interspersed through the original edition. These had been written in 1655 in response to readers' attacks on her first published books—the *Poems and Fancies* and *Philosophical Fancies*—but by 1671 they were no longer necessary. Margaret's authorship of her books was now undisputed, and the errors of meter and rhyme that readers had criticized in her poems had largely been corrected in the later editions. Her former expectation that "I cannot hope to have any acceptance among the learned" was long disproved, and the story the epistles told about Margaret as an author—emphasizing her lack of reading and education, and her reliance on natural ability and a purely oral education from William—was no longer an accurate description of a mature writer who had by now read widely, as Benoist's sizeable purchases of books on her behalf indicate.[93] This same change of literary identity no doubt underlay Margaret's decision to omit from her new edition of *Nature's Pictures* the autobiography with which she had originally ended the book. Fifteen years on, and after some twenty-six years of marriage and more than twenty years of writing, its story of her early formation as an author, from childhood through her time at court and into the first years of marriage, now lay far in the past.

Margaret had now issued revised editions of all but one of the books she had originally written before the Restoration, and by 1672 she had moved on to new research in philosophy. In August she was absorbed in magnetic experiments involving "filings of the loadstone." These she sent to Benoist in London, who promised to show them "to several persons" there to find out whether her results "be right or no." Perhaps Margaret was hoping to develop a theory of the loadstone, a topic into which she had previously not dared to venture, since it had already puzzled "so many learned men" and she had not herself "had much experience of it."[94] Certainly she was again reading widely, and embarking on new writing—a box of books and Dutch quills had arrived from Benoist in July, and by June of the following year she owed him £20 for such items. She may have been working on a completely new book of poetry during these years, and she was perhaps also preparing a second edition of her first volume of plays—her only book written in exile that still remained unrevised.[95] But none of these projects reached publication, for on December 15, 1673, Margaret died at Welbeck at the age of fifty.[96]

No evidence remains of her last days, but the very lack of any doctors' consultations suggests that she died suddenly, perhaps from a heart attack or stroke, rather than after a long illness or decline. Margaret had never expected to live to a great old age, regarding herself as "tender and weak" and "not . . . so healthful as I wish I were."[97] Her overenthusiastic use of purging, vomiting, and bleeding to combat her medical complaints during the years in Antwerp would have done nothing to strengthen her constitution. After the Restoration her new London doctor, Matthew Boucheret, repeated Sir Theodore Mayerne's earlier advice against her self-prescription of strong drugs, but Boucheret's own recommendations seem just as punishing to modern eyes. In August 1666, when Margaret was suffering from stomach troubles and "blemishes in her face," he told her to "take a vomit, or else one of the doses of purging powder I sent in May." Two years later he sent her thirteen pounds of "plaster for fontanelles"—a paste to be spread on the skin, causing open ulcers through which, it was thought, the harmful humors of the body would be evacuated.[98]

Margaret knew that her constant, sedentary occupation in writing, "living too much . . . retired" with little exercise or fresh air, was bad for her health. "Certainly an over-studious mind doth waste the body," she commented. But she was not prepared to compromise her chosen "course of life."[99] People who lived only with an eye to maintaining their health spoiled the very life they were trying to preserve, she thought, making their time "troublesome and full of vexation, with barring themselves of those things that otherwise they would enjoy." Death was inevitable, however much one tried to avoid it, and human life was always short: even if she could "live out the course of nature, or could live so long as Methusalem," still "when the time were past, it would seem as nothing, and perchance I should be as unwilling to die then as if I died in my youth, so that a long and a short time of life is as one and the same." And what was there really to fear in death? It was life, not death, that brought pains and troubles, "for the mind in life is fearful, and the body is seldom at ease." The grave would bring only peace:

> *Without disturbing dreams they lie asleep.*
> *No rambling thoughts to vex their restless brains,*
> *Nor labour hard to scorch and dry their veins.*
> *No care to search for that they cannot find,*
> *Which is an appetite to every mind.*[100]

She was not afraid of "the strokes of death, nor the pains," which would in any case soon be over. It was only death's "black oblivion" that she feared. And so she had made her choice: she would prefer "a short but profitable life" rather than "a long and idle" one, "for 'tis better through industry to leave a little to after age[s], than die so poor as to leave nothing . . . and be quite forgotten." With this ideal, she had worked single-mindedly: even when she was unwell, her "great desire" for "studying and writing" had still driven her on, "even to the prejudice of my own health." She would "willingly quit" her present life, she repeatedly wrote, if she could only achieve her desire to "leave some mark" and "live in a general remembrance" after her death. This survival in her books and in human memory was the only kind of afterlife that seemed real to her. The spiritual immortality promised by Christianity was too different from her present life, too unknown and unimaginable, to offer Margaret much consolation in the face of death. And so she hoped that even in a Christian resurrection she might still be glad of her life's literary achievements:

> *Who knows but that man's soul in fame delights*
> *After the body and it disunites?*
> *If we allow the soul shall live not die,*
> *Although the body in the grave doth lie . . .*
> *Why may not then some love of fame remain?*[101]

Writing the first volume of her plays back in Antwerp in the 1650s, Margaret had created the character of the ambitious and intelligent young Lady Sanspareille in her own image. Like Margaret, Sanspareille had become a philosopher and gained the applause of the male world of learning. Striving always "to get the highest place in Fame's high tower," Sanspareille had shared her creator's heroic but also self-destructive ideals, preferring that she should "rather fall in the adventure, than never try to climb." And like Margaret, she had died suddenly and young, of unknown causes, but with the clear suggestion that she had somehow destroyed herself with work. Both women also left behind much older male relatives, devoted to ensuring their continued earthly fame. In Sanspareille's case it is her father who speaks the laudatory oration at her funeral. For Margaret it was William, now just past his eightieth birthday, who arranged for the full honors of a heraldic funeral, which he knew his wife would have wanted.

At Welbeck, now hung with black velvet and baize, Margaret's body would have been embalmed and laid out in state to be viewed by the mourners. Then, towards the end of December, her final journey to London began, accompanied by a large procession of the family servants. At Newcastle House in Clerkenwell, where they arrived on January 3, 1674, Margaret's body again rested amidst the black hangings of mourning until the day of the funeral. On the evening of Wednesday, January 7, the funeral procession departed for Westminster Abbey, lit through the dusk by the torches they bore. At its head were the servants of the earl marshal, the ceremonial head of the College of Heralds, followed by a large body of the Newcastles' servants, all wearing the customary long black cloaks and mounted on horseback. Then came the Welbeck chaplain, Clement Ellis, and four of the heralds, one of them bearing Margaret's duchess's coronet in state on a black velvet cushion. In the otherwise black-clad procession, the heralds' tabards provided a dramatic splash of color, with the red, yellow, and blue of the royal coat of arms. The only other brightness was on the hearse that followed, where Margaret's own coat of arms—consisting of the Lucas family arms, impaled with the seven different devices that formed William's full personal arms—stood out prominently against the black velvet pall that covered her coffin, and on the long black coats covering the six horses who drew the hearse. Behind came the black-draped coaches of the mourners, first "many of the near relations of the Duke and Duchess" and then the coaches of the rest of the nobility. Southwards they proceeded through Smithfield into the heart of the City, and then turned westwards along Fleet Street and the Strand to Westminster.

At the west door of Westminster Abbey, the procession was met by William's old friend John Rosen, bishop of Rochester and dean of Westminster, with the prebends and choir. Margaret's coffin now led the long walk up the Abbey's nave, carried by four of her most socially eminent male relatives, including William's grandson viscount Brackley (the eldest son of Elizabeth, countess of Bridgewater) and Margaret's own nephew Charles, Lord Lucas (the eldest son of her brother Thomas), who had succeeded to the title after her brother John died in 1671. Margaret had remained close to her childhood family, and by William's "express desire and direction" the chief mourners who followed immediately behind the clergy and the four heralds were her favorite sister, Catherine, and her sister Anne. After them, also according to William's wishes, came the other principal female mourners—Catherine's three daughters, Henry's wife, Frances, William's only surviving daughter, also named Frances, "and several other ladies"—followed by the men, Henry with the earl marshal of England, and then "many of the nobility and persons of quality." In the vault William had built beneath the Abbey's north transept the mourners parted from Margaret, after the final words spoken by one of the heralds,

> Thus it hath pleased Almighty God to take out of this transitory life to his Divine mercy the most high, mighty and most noble Princess, Margaret Duchess of Newcastle, late wife of the most high, mighty and most noble prince, William Duke of Newcastle now living.[102]

But William himself was not present. Too old and ill to make the weeklong journey, he had put all the arrangements in London into Benoist's hands. He perhaps found some consolation during the months that followed in the poems that arrived from Cambridge dons, and from Clement Ellis, Thomas Shadwell, and others, celebrating Margaret for her "perfections . . . numberless"—her books, her learning and the "powerful reason" of "her mighty mind," as well as her beauty and her virtues (principally generosity, civility, and her absolute loyalty to her husband).

> *In wit and sense she did excel all men,*
> *And all her sex in virtue did outgo,*

Shadwell proclaimed; "she was the best of women, best of wives."

> *So vast a knowledge ne'er was yet confined*
> *Within one single woman's mind.*
> *Her fancy it was strong, so great her wit,*
> *That nothing but her judgement equalled it,*

added another, now anonymous, poet. But it was Welbeck's chaplain, Clement Ellis, who, having lived closest of all these writers to Margaret, now best caught the unresting energy of her spirit, consoling William with the thought that "great wits can never die":

Her sprightly soul, full of etherial fires,
Up far above our regions now aspires
To seek new game, since all things here below
Grew stale, and nothing left she did not know . . .
She soon too active for her body grew. [103]

Committed to preserving his wife's memory as a writer, William arranged for these poems to be published, along with a selection of the letters of praise Margaret had received during the past twenty years. *Letters and Poems in Honour of the Incomparable Princess, Margaret, Duchess of Newcastle*, which finally came out in 1676, drew together correspondence from three of Europe's foremost universities, as well as from a host of eminent individuals. Including letters from English, French, and Dutch aristocrats, from distinguished scholars and academics, from philosophers, savants and gentleman-intellectuals, playwrights and poets, bishops and other leading clergy, librarians and fashionable physicians, the book demonstrated Margaret's widespread connection and high reputation throughout the seventeenth-century intellectual world. [104]

William, left alone at Welbeck with only his servants, had begun to attract scandal within only a few months of Margaret's death. Henry and Frances were alarmed by the widespread rumors that some of the younger maidservants, "being presumptuously and extravagantly ambitious," had designs of becoming William's third wife. Concerned to stave off this new blow to their family's prospects, they sent a carefully worded letter to William, asking that they and their children might be allowed to come to live at Welbeck, both "for your Grace's ease . . . and the continuance and increase of your Grace's immortal honour." They would be no trouble, they promised. They would pay for their own wine, sugar, soap, and other groceries, and William would be welcome to reduce their allowance. None of their friends would disturb Welbeck "at meals or night time"; callers would "only come to see your horses" in the morning, or else during the afternoon visiting hours. And by entertaining all the family's guests at their own house at Worksop, they would relieve William of his onerous social duties. "We will be as obedient and observant of your Grace . . . as your son was formerly at ten years of age." [105] In July 1674 Henry and Frances and their daughters moved into their new home, accompanied by the congratulations of Frances's aunt, Lady Armyne, who wished her niece "all the satisfaction and contentment which your ladyship expected in so splendid and magnificent place." [106]

Meanwhile the couple's son, Henry, viscount Mansfield, now aged eleven, was continuing his aristocratic education in Paris, under the supervision of Mark Anthony Benoist. At the court of Louis XIV, young Henry was "much admired" for his directness, vivacity, and self-confidence, and William himself was still remembered "with great respect" by "many persons of the first quality."[107] William had great hopes for his grandson and was already beginning marriage negotiations on his behalf. The match he so desired—to Elizabeth Percy, the sole heiress of the eleventh and last earl of Northumberland— would be a grand union of the two foremost aristocratic dynasties of the North, and of their vast material wealth. But with the seven-year-old girl's grandmother, the dowager countess of Northumberland, deciding that the matter must rest until her granddaughter was old enough to make her own choice, William would not live to see the result. It was left to Henry and Frances to continue the delicate negotiations, which finally resulted in the long-desired wedding in 1679. However, Henry junior died of a fever only eighteen months after the marriage, leaving his parents to pay his large debts, of which they had known nothing. His father ended up bitterly regretting the match, which he now thought had "destroyed" both his son and himself.[108] Having no male heir, Henry would eventually bequeath Welbeck, Bolsover, and most of his family's wealth to his favorite daughter, Margaret, and her husband, John Holles, earl of Clare, for whom the title of duke of Newcastle was re-created in 1694.

In the meantime, William was also looking to his family's future with the new building project which he began late in 1674. He had bought the site of Nottingham Castle back in 1663, but his long-cherished plans for it had so far gone unrealized, perhaps because of lack of funds while Margaret's new building at Bolsover Castle was underway. Now, however, he cleared the remains of the old Norman castle and began to build a grand country house. The vast square pile, inspired by the Capitoline Palace in Rome and by illustrations in Rubens's *Palazzi di Genova*, was in the very newest style, predating the similar and now much more famous house that William's cousin the duke of Devonshire would begin some ten years later at nearby Chatsworth. In part it was a monument to William's father, who had himself long admired the potential of the site, with its commanding views over the countryside for some twenty miles around. But the house, dominating the county town of Nottingham from its clifftop location, was also an apt statement of the family's current social and political preeminence in the Midlands, and of William's aspirations for his descendants.[109]

In these last years, William continued his patronage of Thomas Shadwell, who still brought his work in progress to Welbeck. Shadwell dedicated two more comedies, *The Virtuoso* and *The Libertine*, to him: *The Virtuoso* was especially appropriate, since it ridiculed the same fellows of the Royal Society whom Margaret had herself attacked in her *Observations upon Experimental Philosophy.*[*][110]

In the autumn of 1675 William himself returned to writing. Love poetry and drinking songs—his favorite genres—came numerously from his pen, mixed with pastoral dialogues of shepherds and shepherdesses, and comic verses on the power of money and on the ridiculous state of an aged lover. Three were visions of Margaret, enthroned in light, surrounded by cherubim and seraphim whose heavenly music made William "wish himself dissolved for to be there." With his mind traveling back to the distant past, William also wrote poems on crossing the Thames by boat from Blackfriar's stairs, and on the departure of Henrietta Maria and her army for their march south to Oxford during the Civil War. The effects of Parkinson's disease had by now rendered his handwriting almost completely illegible, and under each poem John Rolleston wrote out a neat copy. But William's inspiration flowed as freely as ever, and he composed verses steadily for a year, sometimes as many as nine in a month. Only in September 1676, as his health deteriorated, did the stream begin to dry: his last dated poem, a cheerful drinking song, was written on October 27.[111]

That month he wrote his will. Henry's inheritance was already secured by earlier legal settlements, and William's only concern now was to ensure that his building project at Nottingham Castle would be completed after his death "in the same manner as he intended to have done if he had lived." Strict stipulations required Henry to spend £2,000 per year on the work until it was finished. The result, as William had desired, was an exceptionally fast build: by the summer of 1678, Benoist reported that "this great house, so lately begun, and all of free-stone" was ready for its roof; the whole was expected to be completed during the next year, when William's statue "on horseback, of stone, will also be set up."[112] The building—with its array of vast state rooms, lined with paneling and expensive tapestries, its long gallery hung with family portraits, and its opulent state bedchamber, with the bed railed off from the rest of the room in the old manner—would attract the admiration of visitors for decades.

In December 1676 William's final illness came on suddenly, almost exactly three years after Margaret's death. Henry, caught unawares in London, rushed

---

*After William's death in 1676, Shadwell also took on the duties of literary executor, arranging for William's last two plays, *The Humorous Lovers* and *The Triumphant Widow* to be printed in 1677, thus finally correcting the previously widespread misattribution of the first of these to Margaret.

back to Welbeck, managing to make the journey in just four days, but his arrival early in January was too late. His father had already died on Christmas Day, just past his eighty-third birthday.[113] Again Newcastle House in Clerkenwell was draped in black for the reception of the body. But William had asked for a private funeral, without all the heraldic pomp he had arranged for Margaret three years before, and so the procession that set out for Westminster Abbey on Monday, January 22, 1677, was small. Henry remained at Welbeck, leaving Captain Mazine, now living in London as equerry to the king, to make all the arrangements. Behind the hearse, Jane's husband, Charles Cheyne, followed as chief mourner, accompanied by just three or four coaches, containing only William's closest relations. Through the darkness of night, chosen as the best time to ensure "all the privateness possible," they followed an unfrequented route through outlying fields and past garden walls, skirting the City itself. Finally, as he had wished, William was laid "privately . . . without any funeral solemnity" beside "my late dear wife Margaret."[114]

Above them, in the Abbey's north transept, there still stands the monument William created before he died. Now it is tucked away among a profusion of eighteenth- and nineteenth-century tombs and statues that create an impression closer to an overstocked antique shop than a church. But when it was put up it would have dominated the space, standing centrally in the transept, while the older Tudor aristocrats' tombs (including that of William's grandmother, Bess of Hardwick) were set back against the walls. On the tomb's front are two inscriptions. The lower one, in Latin, commemorating William's many court and government offices and especially his services to the royal cause in the Civil War, was composed after his death by the herald, Sir William Dugdale. But the lines above it, in English, dedicated to Margaret's memory, were almost certainly written by William himself, as a tribute to the wife he had so loved and admired.

> Here lies the loyal Duke of Newcastle and his Duchess, his second wife, by whom he had no issue: her name was Margaret Lucas, youngest sister to the Lord Lucas of Colchester, a noble family: for all the brothers were valiant, and all the sisters virtuous. This Duchess was a wise, witty and learned lady, which her many books do well testify; she was a most virtuous and a loving and careful wife, and was with her Lord all the time of his banishment and miseries, and when he came home never parted from him in his solitary retirements.

Above these words at head-height, two lifesize figures carved in white marble lie side by side on the flat tabletop of the tomb, dressed in their long, ermine-lined state robes and ducal coronets, each bearing the symbols of their life's great achievements. William, clad in armor and lying on a rush mat such as was used by soldiers during campaigns, grasps his general's baton in his right hand, while his left hand holds the medallion of St. George that formed part of the insignia of the Knights of the Garter. Beside him lies Margaret, her left hand resting lightly on a book, with pen and ink ready for use.[115]

Epilogue

B y the end of her life, Margaret had become a prominent figure of the Restoration world and, like all celebrities, she had attracted ridicule and criticism as well as admiration. While other women poets like Katherine Philips, who modestly kept their work within the private sphere of friends and family, were never openly attacked, Margaret became the subject of at least three verse satires. At about the same time as John Evelyn wrote his comic ballad, telling the story of her visit to the Royal Society in mock-heroic style, another, anonymous, poet composed a ballad called "The Session of the Poets," designed to be sung to the popular tune of "Cock Laurel." The verse ridiculed every major poet of the day, describing how they each came in turn to the court of Apollo, seeking the god's approval for their work, only to be denounced for their "abuses of wit" and sent away in disgrace. Davenant, Flecknoe, Waller, Denham, Dryden, and Abraham Cowley were all included, and Margaret's appearance is a clear indication of her significance in the English literary scene.

The ballad laughed at William as well, mocking his long support of his wife's career by showing him appearing before Apollo astride one of his horses, with Margaret's literary work stuffed into his breeches. To the god's horror, William unbuttons his fly and pulls out "his wife's poems, plays, essays and speeches."

> "Whoop," quoth Apollo, "what a Devil have we here,
> Put up thy wife's trumpery, good noble marquis,
> And home again, home again take thy career,
> To provide her fresh straw and a chamber that dark is."*[1]

---

*The standard accommodation for madmen, as provided for Malvolio in Shakespeare's *Twelfth Night*.

In the context of the poem's other literary victims, this attack on the New-castles was not especially cruel. Far more vitriolic and more personal was the last of the satiric verses written on Margaret—a mock-epitaph composed after her death, perhaps in response to the many laudatory verse epitaphs that William collected and published in her honor in 1676. The poem was recorded by John Stainsby, a London legal clerk who had been born in Derbyshire and who traveled north in the vacations, gathering local antiquarian information for his friend, the herald and scholar-collector Elias Ashmole. Perhaps Stainsby himself composed the epitaph, but more probably he collected it during his travels.[2] Whoever wrote it, however, the epitaph's detailed knowledge of Margaret's life at Welbeck (especially in her estate management) and its strength of feeling on the subject make it quite different from the two other verse satires, and suggest that its author had personal connections in the Midlands.

The epitaph begins innocuously enough, with conventional praise of the virtues of the deceased. But then the author describes how his writing was interrupted by the Devil, who insisted on completing the verse himself:

> *"Here lies wise, chaste, hospitable, humble—"*
> *I had gone on, but Nick began to grumble:*
> *"Write, write," says he, "upon her tomb of marble*
> *These words, which out I and my friends will warble:*
> *'Shame of her sex, Welbeck's illustrious whore,*
> *The true man's hate and grief, plague of the poor,*
> *The great atheistical philosophraster,*
> *That owns no God, no devil, lord nor master;*
> *Vice's epitome and virtue's foe,*
> *Here lies her body, but her soul's below.*'"*

The charge that Margaret was a whore, seen here but nowhere else in contemporary sources, suggests the possibility that the contents of Clayton's libelous letter against Margaret had leaked out into local society, despite William's attempts to conceal them.[3]

However these satirical caricatures had little effect on the image of Margaret that survived into the next century. The Stainsby epitaph, preserved only in two manuscripts belonging to Elias Ashmole, was not rediscovered until the mid-twentieth century, while Evelyn's comic ballad also remained in manuscript and has never been printed in its entirety. "The Session of the Poets" was printed in 1697, in a collection of verse satires on prominent public figures,

---

*I.e. in Hell.

but it was not published again until the 1960s. In the eighteenth century, Margaret's reputation was based on the largely favorable account of her work provided by the literary critic, Gerard Langbaine.

Langbaine's *Account of the English Dramatick Poets,* published in 1691, presented Margaret as a *laudabilis heroina,* a praiseworthy heroine, and "a lady worthy the . . . esteem of all lovers of poetry and learning." To playwriting in particular "she had a more than ordinary propensity," he added. And, while admitting that her plays had been criticized by some, he suggested that "if it be considered that both the language and plots of them are all her own, I think she ought with justice to be preferred to others of her sex, which have built their fame on other people's foundations." The *Life of William* he praised as "the crown of her labours." Langbaine's opinion was hugely influential. His comments were paraphrased closely by Giles Jacob, in his *Lives and Characters of all the English Poets* of 1719, which added only one piece of new information— that Margaret was "the most voluminous dramatic writer of our female poets." And Jacob's account would be quoted almost verbatim by the mid-eighteenth century literary historians George Ballard and Theophilus Cibber.[4]

While Langbaine and Jacob had concentrated on Margaret's writings, Ballard and Cibber were more interested in her life. Both presented her marriage as exemplifying the eighteenth-century ideal of feminine domesticity and sentimental matrimonial attachment. "During the gloomy period of exile," they recorded, she had been "a most agreeable companion" for William, enlivening his "melancholy" retirement. In consequence of this vision, both Ballard and Cibber portrayed Margaret's serious dedication to writing as beginning only after the Restoration, when her duties of cheering and consoling her husband were no longer necessary. Margaret had become the model wife, "her person . . . very graceful; her temper naturally reserved and shy . . . truly pious, charitable and generous . . . an excellent [domestic] economist, very kind to her servants; and a perfect pattern of conjugal love and duty." But she had one important failing, according to Cibber: "her Grace's conceptions . . . were frequent, but all of the poetical or philosophical kind, for though she was very beautiful, she died without issue"—a serious moral flaw that, Cibber suggested, had made her "very reserved and peevish . . . having never been honoured with the name of mother."

Ballard and Cibber provided a variety of information on Margaret's life, much of it unreliable. Ballard's *Memoirs of Several Ladies of Great Britain who have been Celebrated for their Writings,* appearing in 1752, contained the false information that Margaret had been "the youngest daughter of Sir Charles Lucas," and that she had returned to Antwerp from England in 1653, bearing "a considerable sum" of money for her husband's relief. These two "facts" were reproduced uncritically in Cibber's *Lives of the Poets of Great Britain and Ireland,* published the following year.[5]

Various apocryphal stories about Margaret began to circulate in the second half of the eighteenth century. Cibber was the first to report that Margaret "kept a great many young ladies about her person, who . . . slept in a room contiguous to that in which her Grace lay, and were ready, at the call of her bell, to rise any hour of the night to write down her conceptions, lest they should escape her memory"—a story clearly false, since Margaret states that she wrote in her own hand and that she sometimes went for days without seeing her waiting-maids.[6] Nonetheless this tale was often repeated, becoming modified in the retelling, until Michael Lort, D.D., F.R.S., antiquary, and Regius Professor of Greek at Cambridge University, recorded he had "heard or read somewhere" that John Rolleston had slept in a closet opening out of Margaret's bedchamber, so that he could rush out, pen at the ready, in answer to her calls of "John, I conceive."[7]

According to another anecdote, William had been congratulated by a friend on having such a wise woman for his wife, and had replied "Sir, a very wise woman is a very foolish thing."* In another, Margaret demanded of Bishop John Wilkins, who had published a treatise on the Moon and its possible inhabitants, "how she should get up to the world in the Moon which he had discovered." "Oh, Madam," Wilkins was supposed to have replied, "your Grace has built so many castles in the air, that you cannot want a place to bait at." The ingredients for this story were clearly provided by Margaret's and Wilkins's writings. Wilkins had discussed in his treatise the need for some "castle in the air" to stay in on the way to the Moon, and Margaret's *Sociable Letters* had imagined another lady attacking her for her contemplative life, "employing my time only in building castles in the air." In her *Observations upon Experimental Philosophy,* she had also attacked the Fellows of the Royal Society, of whom John Wilkins was one, for busying themselves "more with other worlds than this they live in"—a useless waste of time, "unless they could find out some art that would carry them into those celestial worlds, which I doubt will never be."[8] But, despite its dubious authenticity, the tale of the duchess and the bishop was repeated through the nineteenth century.

By the mid-eighteenth century most of Margaret's writings had disappeared from view. None of her books had been reprinted since the second edition of her *Life of William,* issued in 1675, and her original volumes had become so rare and expensive that George Ballard, while researching his *Memoirs of Several Ladies of Great Britain,* had only been able to consult a selection of them. In

---

*A story perhaps inspired by the saying of Erasmus that "a wise woman is twice a fool."

1755 a few of her poems became available to readers once again, printed in a two-volume collection of *Poems by Eminent Ladies*, edited by George Colman and Bonnell Thornton. Many similar anthologies of women's poetry followed, to feed the demands of an ever-increasing female readership, and their professed aims were high—to show "that great abilities are not confined to the men, and that genius often glows with equal warmth, and perhaps with more delicacy, in the breast of a female," as Colman and Thornton put it. But they all included only a very skewed selection of Margaret's work, creating a distorted image of her as an author to satisfy later standards of taste and femininity.

Seventeenth-century readers had appreciated Margaret as a heroic woman, rivaling men in her "wit and sense," and the "strong reason" of "her mighty mind."[9] But by the mid-eighteenth century, female authors were no longer supposed to write like men. Instead, their works were supposed to display all the "feminine virtues." Delicacy, tenderness, refinement, purity, beauty, grace—these formed "the peculiar province of the gentle powers of woman," while the "masculine" qualities of vigor, wit, and wisdom lay outside her proper sphere. Incapable of "the grander inspirations of the Muse," female poets could write neither of Homeric battles, nor of Milton's Heaven and Hell. Their special talent lay in "what is light and elegant . . . and all the gentle feelings of the heart." And their proper role in literature was as "the mothers of England," nurturing the minds of British children and supporting, "under the most pleasing forms, the value and beauty of industry, patience and docility— of every virtue, in fact, which all must desire to see practised by youth and respected by manhood."[10]

To fit Margaret into this mold, eighteenth- and nineteenth-century editors were extremely selective in forming their anthologies. They gave no place to the atomist poems that had occupied about a fifth of her *Poems and Fancies*. Her questioning attitude to traditional Christian faith, her denunciations of human arrogance and cruelty, her poems of war and her political and social satires went unnoticed. But all the anthologies included her poem "The Pastime and Recreation of the Queen of the Fairies," with its pretty imagery of "fairy fry" dancing on molehills, and of gnats singing for the entertainment of the queen, who drives out after dinner in a nutshell coach drawn by crickets. Its "delicate and ingenious" fancies were worthy of Shakespeare's *Midsummer Night's Dream*, critics wrote. And equally admired was her "Dialogue between Melancholy and Mirth," whose sentimental conjuring of the delights of lonely retreat and contemplation was admired as "true poetry," "so extremely picturesque." It had inspired Milton's great pair of poems, *L'Allegro* and *Il Penseroso*, many critics thought, although Milton's verses had in fact been published before Margaret's, so that the influence, if any, must have worked the other way.[11]

But even these two most favored poems of Margaret's were almost always printed incomplete, omitting those sections that offended against the editors' sense of decency. Colman and Thornton's original anthology of 1755 had begun the trend. With no comment whatsoever to tell the reader what they had done, the two editors cut out the grotesquerie of Margaret's description of the fairies' diet—including ants' eggs, flies, and dormouse milk—and of the mischief they practiced on humans, holding up hens' rumps to prevent them from laying, and lying concealed as a piece of fat in a pudding to choke the eater and cause wind in the stomach. Similarly earthy or physical sections were also excised from the "Dialogue between Melancholy and Mirth," creating an impression of a much prettier, quainter verse than Margaret had actually written. Only two nineteenth-century editors were scrupulous enough to print these poems complete, but both felt driven to add derogatory notes warning the reader of the bad taste they displayed. "It seems a little wonderful that a lady of so high rank, and mind so cultivated, could use language so coarse and disgusting as is here seen," was the comment on one of the offending sections of "Melancholy and Mirth" provided by Sir Samuel Egerton Brydges in the edition of *Select Poems of Margaret Cavendish,* which he published at his private press at Lee Priory in Kent in 1813—the first volume devoted entirely to Margaret's writing to be published since 1675. And on the subject of Margaret's fairy poetry, "perhaps it would be difficult to point out a composition which contains a more extraordinary mixture of imagination and coarse absurdity," added Alexander Dyce in his anthology, *Specimens of British Poetesses,* published in London in 1827.

For most nineteenth-century critics, Katherine Philips was the foremost female poet of the seventeenth century—a place she achieved "not exactly by merit," they admitted, "for Aphra Behn surpassed her in genius, Margaret, Duchess of Newcastle in versatility, and Catherine Trotter in professional zeal; but by the moral eminence she attained through her elevated public career and which she sealed by her tragical death." It was Katherine Philips's feminine modesty and the sentimental personality she constructed in her verses that so appealed to this later period, making her shine out as "a sweet woman in a corrupt society."[12]

Of Margaret's many prose writings, only her two biographical works received much in the way of praise during the nineteenth century. Her autobiography had fewer of the "great absurdities" that marred her other writings, noted Sir Samuel Egerton Brydges, when he published an edition of this work in 1814. The *True Relation* would both "entertain and instruct" its readers, he thought: in the "simplicity" and "exquisite naïveté" with which Margaret told her story, there lay both "charm" and "amusement."[13] And in the early 1820s the essayist Charles Lamb wrote enthusiastically of Margaret's *Life of William,* a book "at once both good and rare," deserving only of the finest bindings: "no casket is rich enough, no casing sufficiently durable, to honour and keep safe such a jewel." With his self-professed taste for "the oddities of authorship," "out-of-the-way humours and opinions," and "heads with some diverting twist in them," Lamb was a great admirer of Margaret's, and he mentioned her four times in his hugely popular *Essays of Elia.** To him she was "that princely woman," "a dear favourite of mine, of the last century but one—the thrice noble, chaste and virtuous, but again somewhat fantastical and original brained, generous Margaret Newcastle."[14] "Madge Newcastle," he named her affectionately, or "dear Margaret Newcastle." And when he and the essayist William Hazlitt discussed who, of all the figures of history, they would most like to have to dinner, "Lamb declared for the Duchess."[15]

But Margaret's nonbiographical prose had fallen into disfavor. Her essays and letters went unnoticed, except for the briefest mention by Lamb. Her fiction was forgotten, apart from two stories from *Nature's Pictures,* which had been reprinted in Alexander Nicol's *Poems on Several Subjects, both Comical and Serious,* published at Edinburgh in 1766. Her philosophy was regarded with distaste—"her worst foible," part of the "chaos" and "sad heaps of rubbish" that critics now saw her writings as largely consisting in.[16] And her plays were utterly repugnant to an age that regarded itself as more "delicate" and "refined" (we might say more prudish) than its predecessors. Margaret's often caustic voice as a social satirist now seemed grossly unfeminine. And her forthright treatment of such topics as sexual desire, marital infidelity, and incest continued to shock readers well into the twentieth century. Her earthy humor—as when a jester and a cook-maid joke that the fleas in their clothes will "commit fornication"—was judged "unspeakably low." How this "noble and virtuous," this "chaste and highborn" lady could have tolerated let alone written such "indecency and obscenity" was incomprehensible.[17]

As nineteenth-century critics grew increasingly aware of Margaret's deviations from contemporary taste, she came to be seen as a woman of bizarre character—a baffling mixture of the most "eminent . . . feminine virtue" with "a mind of considerable power and activity . . . but not one particle of judgement or taste."[18] She had had ability, even "genius," many admitted, but her writings were "ruined by deficient culture [and] by literary dissipation." "We are too frequently shocked by expressions and images of extraordinary

---

*One of the features that Lamb admired in Margaret's work was her colorful and inventive use of language. The word "romancical," coined by Margaret in *Nature's Pictures* and reused in her *Life of William,* did not reappear in the English language until Lamb deliberately revived it from her work in 1822.

coarseness." "She pours forth everything with an undistinguishing hand, and mixes the serious, the colloquial, and even the vulgar, in a manner which cannot be defended."[19] Margaret had become an inspired, but utterly fantastic, figure, the possessor of "a wild native genius" who, in her flights of fancy, rode the poets' winged horse Pegasus at a gallop, "giving an entire loose to the reins" of judgment.[20] The "heroic" side of her character also came to be criticized. Louisa Costello's *Memoirs of Eminent Englishwomen* charged Margaret with self-sufficiency, presumption, and arrogance. She was "a kind of overgrown, spoilt girl," added Eric Robertson.[21]

In 1840 Margaret was being noted as "the most astounding person that flourished during the Stuart dynasty," and by 1850 she had become "the eccentric Duchess."[22] No enormity was thought too great to attribute to this excessive individualist: the antiquarian James Crossley, who now owned the manuscript of the love poems that William had written for Margaret in the 1640s, had even persuaded himself that Margaret had herself made corrections to her husband's work (although the handwriting is clearly William's, not Margaret's). And in 1872 a new story about Margaret emerged, recorded by the antiquarian Mark Anthony Lower, as he published the first new edition of the *Life of William* to appear in almost 200 years. "I feel certain," Lower noted in his preface, "that no modern reader, on a candid perusal of her writings, will concur in attributing to her the nickname which her jealous (female?) contemporaries gave her—'*Mad Madge of Newcastle!*'"[23]

Lower, as so often with historians in this period, gave no source for his claim, and scholars have sought in vain for any earlier reference to the nickname. When I first encountered the story I assumed, as others had done, that he must have had access to some historical record that no one else has seen. But as I pursued further research on Margaret, it began to seem unlikely that the nickname had been widespread among her contemporaries, as Lower claimed. It appears nowhere in the many contemporary accounts of her that we do have—neither in John Evelyn's diary, nor in the letters of Dorothy Osborne, Mary Evelyn, and Constantijn Huygens, nor in the various newsletters that record her activities in London in 1667. Samuel Pepys, especially, was keen to record every item of gossip he could gather about Margaret in his diary: if he had known her as Mad Madge, it would hardly have taken him seven weeks of following her around London in 1667, followed by a careful consideration of her *Life of William* some ten months later, to reach his conclusion that she was "a mad, conceited, ridiculous woman."[24] Pepys's comment was clearly a personal judgment formed as a result of his own studies, rather than in response to some widespread nickname. Furthermore, there is no evidence that any contemporary ever named Margaret "Madge": "Peg" was the familiar name used by William for his wife. It was her early nineteenth-century admirer, the essayist Charles Lamb, who seems first to have named her "Madge Newcastle," as a mark of his affection.[25]

And so I came to accept that there might well be no seventeenth-century source for the Mad Madge nickname. Given all the other apocryphal stories about Margaret, which even professors at Cambridge University were happy to record on the basis of "I have heard or read somewhere . . . ,"[26] perhaps it was more likely that Mark Anthony Lower had constructed his story of "Mad Madge of Newcastle" out of a combination of misremembered details. Lamb's nickname could have provided the "Madge Newcastle" part, while the "madness" part could have arisen not only from the growing nineteenth-century view of Margaret as wild, bizarre, and eccentric, but also from the rediscovery of a couple of seventeenth-century texts. John Evelyn's diary and correspondence, first printed from the original manuscripts in 1818, contained Mary Evelyn's letter describing Margaret as a person of "so much extravagancy and vanity" that she ought to be "confined within four walls."[27] In 1825 Pepys's comments on Margaret also appeared, when his shorthand diary was deciphered and published for the first time. After a period of some 150 years, during which no suggestions of madness had been made, these two allegations were again revived. And this view of Margaret was further popularized by Sir Walter Scott, who gave her a cameo appearance in his historical novel, *Peveril of the Peak.* Here "that old madwoman the Duchess of Newcastle," the writer of nothing but "trash," "an entire raree-show in her own person. . . indeed a sort of private Bedlam-hospital,* her whole ideas being like so many patients crazed upon the subjects of love and literature" comes to visit the court of Charles II, where her last visit is laughingly remembered for her appearance in a train as long as a comet's tail.[28]

The Mad Madge nickname was readily accepted by Lower's contemporaries and successors, to whom it would have seemed an apt summary of their own view of Margaret, and the story that she had been widely judged mad by her jealous contemporaries became established as historical "truth." In the late nineteenth century, the *Dictionary of National Biography* recorded that Margaret's "appearance in theatrical costume, and her reputation for purity of life, together with her vanity and affectation, contributed to gain her a reputation for madness." "Styled by her contemporaries 'Mad Madge of Newcastle,'" she had been "regarded . . . merely as a harebrained eccentric," Cokayne's *Complete Peerage* stated in the early twentieth century.[29]

---

*I.e. lunatic asylum

Backed by the authority of the Mad Madge nickname, some twentieth-century writers went further, suggesting that Margaret had been not just an eccentric with a reputation for madness, but had actually been mad. The unusual story line of Margaret's *Blazing World* was sure proof "that its creator was, on one occasion at least, dangerously far from sanity," wrote Henry Ten Eyck Perry in his study of *The First Duchess of Newcastle and her Husband as Figures in Literary History,* published in 1918—only the second book-length work on William and Margaret ever published. Although he intended to "rationalise the eccentric figure which tradition has built up, and to substitute for it a more human personage," Perry in fact described Margaret as a "warped and lopsided" personality, the victim of her own "overactive, unrestrained imagination." Her books were "for the most part extremely tedious," "verbose and tiresome," "undramatic" and "monotonous." Her authoritative writing persona he found utterly repellent: "in the fifteen years following 1645 Margaret Cavendish changed from a sweet, attractive, if unusual, girl to a self-absorbed, self-satisfied, and eccentric woman."[30]

The early twentieth century represented the nadir of Margaret's reputation, both as a person and as a writer. And the most influential figure in her demolition was the essayist, novelist, and literary critic, Virginia Woolf. Looking back into history for female literary forebears, Woolf was disappointed to find no one with whom she could identify: there had been no role for "middle-class women with nothing but brains and character at their command." Believing that literature could be produced only by the middle classes working for money within a busy, urban setting, Woolf thought it impossible that Margaret—"the lonely aristocrat shut up in her country house among her folios and her flatterers," writing "without audience or criticism"—could have been a real writer.[31]

Woolf's portrait of the Newcastles, living "together in the depths of the country in the greatest seclusion . . . scribbling plays, poems, philosophies, greeting each other's works with raptures of delight," echoed the words of Horace Walpole, who had been the sole voice of criticism during the eighteenth century, portraying William and Margaret as "a picture of foolish nobility . . . retired to their own little domain, and intoxicating one another with circumstantial flattery on what was of consequence to no mortal but themselves." Nineteenth-century commentators, even those expressing criticism of parts of Margaret's writings, had dismissed Walpole's words as mere spite, "full of ill-nature and deficient in truth," coming from a man who was both "inclined to sarcasm, and . . . infected with an artificial taste." But by the early twentieth century, with the justifying myth of Mad Madge, Walpole's view began to seem realistic.[32]

Other parts of Woolf's discussion were also based heavily on later tradi-tions rather than on primary historical sources. Her character portrait of Mar-garet—"hare-brained, fantastical," "noble and Quixotic and high-spirited, as well as crack-brained and bird-witted"—owed much both to Charles Lamb and the subsequent tradition of Mad Madge. And Woolf painted her picture of Margaret's mental world with considerable color and power. "What a vision of loneliness and riot the thought of Margaret Cavendish brings to mind! as if some giant cucumber had spread itself over all the roses and carnations in the garden and choked them to death."[33]

> Order, continuity, the logical development of her argument are all unknown to her . . . She has the irresponsibility of a child and the arrogance of a Duchess. The wildest fancies come to her, and she canters away on their backs. We seem to hear her, as the thoughts boil and bubble, calling to John . . . "John, John, I conceive!" And down it goes—whatever it may be; sense or nonsense . . . On and on, from subject to subject she flies, never stopping to correct.

> What could bind, tame or civilise for human use that wild, generous, untutored intelligence? It poured itself out, higgledy-piggledy, in torrents of rhyme and prose . . . She should have had a microscope put in her hand. She should have been taught to . . . reason scientifically. Her wits were turned with solitude and freedom. No one checked her. No one taught her. . . . She shut herself up at Welbeck alone . . . scribbling nonsense and plunging ever deeper into obscurity and folly till the people crowded round her coach when she issued out. Evi-dently the crazy Duchess became a bogey to frighten clever girls with.[34]

Woolf's view of Margaret, though heavily based on her own overimagina-tive reconstruction of history, as well as on centuries of often apocryphal tradi-tion, remained influential through much of the twentieth century. In 1957, Douglas Grant's biography, *Margaret the First,* was the first study of her to be meticulously researched from the original sources, both printed and manu-script. Significantly more sympathetic than Woolf's account, Grant's book yet followed many of Woolf's judgments, presenting Margaret as a detached, overly flattered aristocrat, and criticizing her writing as confused, rambling, silly, and tedious. Margaret remained for him, as for Woolf, a figure incapable of rigorous and connected thought, a wild escapist, happiest in the realms of "extreme . . . ridiculous fantasy." And Grant's belief in this image was so great that he denied the evidence uncovered by his own research. Despite his quota-tion of letters from Constantijn Huygens and Mark Anthony Benoist that proved the opposite, Grant continued to repeat Woolf's unfounded assertion that Margaret had never performed any experiments on which to base her philosophy. Her theories, he wrote, had been the product of her "fancy" alone. And despite Margaret's statement that she could not bear to entrust the revision of her philosophy to any other person, "but would obstinately suckle it myself and bring it up alone, without the help of any scholar," Grant found it "impossible to believe" that Margaret herself could have revised her books for their second and third editions—"a task so absolutely at variance with her impatient and wandering temperament." The work "must have been entrusted to her secretary or to the household chaplain or to one of her dependent men of letters," he concluded.[35]

During the 1980s, as interest in women's history grew, Margaret and her books began to receive greater attention. However, she was still seen as a maverick figure, too much of an individualist to be taken entirely seriously. Feminists found her unsatisfactory as a forebear, her advocacy of women's rights and abilities in some parts of her writings marred by her outspoken criticism of their stereotypical failings and vices in other parts. Many of the old myths were repeated unchallenged: that she was completely untrained and had never read books, that she had not revised her works herself, that she was solitary and isolated, protected from all criticism by her high social status, that she was too outrageously idiosyncratic to have had any literary influence on other women. Her plays and philosophy, which Virginia Woolf had singled out as "intolerable" and "futile," were especially condemned: the plays were too wordy, too undramatic to be performable, while the philosophy was "obscure and contradictory." One study even saw The Blazing World as a display of paranoid schizophrenia.[36]

Amidst such disparagement it is hardly surprising that the core of the Mad Madge myth—that Margaret had been an eccentric who received only ridicule and criticism during her lifetime—was still accepted. Commentators readily dismissed the many praises she had received as mere flattery, while taking seriously all the criticisms and satires as representative of a consensus of opinion.* Her own readiness to laugh at herself, the many apologies contained in her prefaces, and her obvious expectation that her writing would be attacked all

---

*The dangers of taking satire too seriously are apparent in the case of John Evelyn, author of the comic ballad on Margaret's visit to the Royal Society, who must also have sincerely admired Margaret: in his Numismata, a treatise "of medals ancient and modern," published twenty-four years after her death, Evelyn proposed Margaret as the first of those members of the "learned, virtuous and fair sex" who deserved to have medals struck in their honor.

went to confirm the view that she had been a figure of fun, disliked by her contemporaries.

Only during the last decade or so has Margaret's achievement received greater appreciation. A broad range of recent studies—of her philosophy, plays, poems, essays, orations, and fiction—have related her work to that of her contemporaries, showing that she was not a disconnected eccentric, but was an active participant in seventeenth-century intellectual life. Margaret is emerging as a writer of impressive energy and range, capable of sharp commentary and observation on the world around her, of detailed philosophical argument and analysis, and of creating fiction containing strong characters, lively dialogue, and original social vision. From being dismissed as undramatic, her plays have become some of her most admired works, fascinating readers with their powerfully expressed debates and their imaginative portrayal of the possibilities of women's lives: they are at last beginning to be publicly staged.[37] *The Blazing World* has also become a particular focus for study, appreciated as "a pioneering female, and perhaps even feminist, Utopia."[38] The Margaret Cavendish Society, founded in 1997, has played a significant role in fostering this growing enthusiasm, and an increasing quantity of Margaret's work—spanning fiction, plays, philosophy, poetry, and letters—is now available to readers in modern editions.

The figure of Margaret herself is also surfacing, shedding the accumulated myths and traditions of three centuries. Modern readers see in her neither the eighteenth century's ideal of retiring feminine virtue, nor the late nineteenth and early twentieth century's wild and unstable eccentric. Instead they find a woman at once sophisticated and multifaceted, "canny and audacious," the possessor of both "considerable intellect and intrepid originality." The reference books are being rewritten, with Margaret now billed as "one of the most interesting and versatile writers of poetry, prose and drama of her day."[39]

'List of Abbreviations

SL　　　*CCXI Sociable Letters* (London, 1664)

TR　　　*A True Relation of my Birth, Breeding and Life*, as printed in LWN, 151–178

WO　　　*The World's Olio* (London, 1655)

WO2　　*The World's Olio*, 2nd ed. (London, 1671)

OTHER ABBREVIATIONS

BL　　　British Library

CSPD　　*Calendar of State Papers, Domestic*

DNB　　*Dictionary of National Biography*

HL　　　Huntington Library

HMC　　Historical Manuscripts Commission

LP　　　*Letters and Poems in Honour of the Incomparable Princess, Margaret, Dutchess of Newcastle* (1676)

NA　　　Nottinghamshire Archives

NUL MS　University of Nottingham, Department of Manuscripts and Special Collections, Portland Manuscript

OED　　*Oxford English Dictionary*

PRO　　Public Record Office

SP　　　State Papers

VCHE　　*Victoria History of the County of Essex*

Notes and Sources

PROLOGUE

1. PaF A3r–v. Figures on women's publishing come from Crawford, "Women's Published Writings," 265, 269.

2. PaF A4r–v.

CHAPTER 1:
THE LUCASES OF ST. JOHN'S

The description of Margaret's appearance is based on surviving portraits of her, her sister Mary and her brother Charles, and on Margaret's TR, SL 266–9, and LWN xxxvi.

The account of Essex and Colchester is based on:
Norden, *Speculi Britanniae Pars*
Defoe, *Tour*
Fiennes, *Journeys*
Camden, *Britannia*
Schellinks, *Journal*
Hunt, *The Puritan Moment*
Holmes, *The Eastern Association*
Morant, *History and Antiquities of Colchester*
VCHE, vols. II and IX
Edwards, *History of Essex*.
Additional information on St. John's comes from:
John Speed's map of Colchester, in his *Theatre of the Empire of Great Britaine*
James Deane's map of Colchester in 1748, in Morant, *History and Antiquities of Colchester*
de la Serre, *Histoire de l'entrée de la reine mère*
Wills of John Lucas and Sir Thomas Lucas: PRO PROB 11/38 and PROB 11/118
Letter of Sir John Lucas: PRO SP 16/449.

1. Fuller, *Worthies*, 320. In the quotations throughout this book, I have changed the original spellings (and capitalization) to modern British standards. I have also altered punctuation, where it helps to make the texts flow more easily for modern readers, and I have tacitly corrected errors such as occasional omitted letters in the original sources.

2. Norden, *Speculi Britanniae Pars*, 7.

3. Walter, *Understanding Popular Violence*, 105.

4. Only 15 percent of the prominent families of Essex had acquired their estates before 1485, compared to around 75 percent of families in the more traditional county of Kent: Hunt, *The Puritan Moment*, 15–16.

5. In addition to Grant, *Margaret the First,* and Appleby, *Our Fall*, information on Thomas Lucas can be found in Cooper and Cooper, *Athenae Cantabrigienses*, I: *1500–1585*; *Rolls of Parliament 1278–1503*, VI, 536; and Thomas Lucas's will, PRO PROB 11/24.

6. Emmison, ed., *Feet of Fines*, V: *1547–1580,* 9.

7. *CSPD 1547–1623*, item 812; Hoak, *The King's Council*, 220–222.

8. Information on John Lucas comes from Appleby, *Our Fall*; Grant, *Margaret the First*; Morant, *History and Antiquities of Colchester*; Rickwood, "Members of Parliament"; Walter, *Understanding Popular Violence*.

9. Emmison, ed., *Feet of Fines*, V, 11 and passim.

10. *VCHE*, IX, 303–304; wills of John and Sir Thomas Lucas, PRO PROB 11/38 and 11/118.

11. For Thomas Lucas, the main sources are Appleby, *Our Fall*, and Grant, *Margaret the First*, supplemented by Venn, *Alumni*; Rickwood, "Members of Parliament"; Fuller, *Worthies*, 345; Walter, *Understanding Popular Violence*, 86–89;

VCHE, IX, 260–261; and Thomas's will, PRO PROB 11/118.

12. Morant, *History and Antiquities of Essex*, passim; Emmison, ed., *Feet of Fines*, V, VI passim; and PRO SP 14/79 (Inquisition postmortem) suggest the size of Lucas landholdings. *CSPD 1625–1649, Addendum*, 468, and *A True Relation, or, Catalogue of the Gentry*, 6, provide indications of annual income.

13. Appleby, *Our Fall*, 13–14; Walter, *Understanding Popular Violence*, 85–89, 100; *VCHE*, IX, 100, 110.

14. He would always consider himself a bad penman: PRO SP 16/521/42.

15. TR 155.

16. Sources for Thomas Lucas: TR; Venn, *Alumni*; Appleby, *Our Fall*; Grant, *Margaret the First*. HMC, *11th Report*, Appendix VII, 134, and PRO SO 3/2/62 suggest the identification of Sir William Brooke as the younger brother of the courtier Lord Cobham, and brother-in-law to the secretary of state Sir Robert Cecil.

17. *CSPD 1601–1603*, 98, 111; HMC, *Salisbury Manuscripts*, Appendix XII, 450–451; Appleby, *Our Fall*.

18. PRO SO 3/2/62; HMC, *11th Report*, Appendix VII, 134.

19. Cokayne, *Complete Peerage*; Grant, *Margaret the First*; Appleby, *Our Fall*; PRO SP 14/9, f. 16; PRO PROB 11/118.

20. TR 156.

21. TR 155. Contrary to some historians' claims, Thomas Lucas was never knighted: TR 155; College of Arms MS I.31.

22. TR 155.

23. TR 156–157, 165; Appleby, *Our Fall*, 18–19, 22–26; *CSPD 1627–1628*, 497; PRO SP 16/6/105. On Mr. and Mrs. Eyres: Walter, *Understanding Popular Violence*, 169, and sources cited there.

24. BL Harleian MS 1542, ff. 58v–59r. Margaret's funeral certificate, College of Arms MS I.31, f. 64, conclusively establishes her date of birth as 1623. For other evidence for this, see: Perry, *The First Duchess of Newcastle*, 46–47; Battigelli, *Margaret Cavendish*, 117–118. The rival tradition, a date of 1617, probably derives from BL Addit. MS 12514, f. 297, where Margaret's death

in 1673 "aetatis suae 51mo" could be misread as "57mo." Infant mortality figures from Thomas, *Religion and the Decline of Magic*, 5.

25. TR 158; Chester and Armytage, *Allegations for Marriage Licences*, II, 195; Appleby, *Our Fall*, 19, 23, 28.

26. TR 159.

27. TR 158.

28. Appleby, *Our Fall*, 23–28.

29. PRO SP 16/7/27.

30. Scudéry, *Artamenes*, dedication to Lady Anne Lucas. See also Firth, ed., "Verses on the Cavaliers Imprisoned in 1655."

31. TR 159.

32. PNBP, *The Presence*, 93–96, 99–102, 121–123.

33. PRO SP 16/7/27, SP 16/6/105. For Harsnet's long-standing connection with the Lucas family: Walter, *Understanding Popular Violence*, 167.

34. *CSPD 1625–1626*, 117. Also 102, 111, 152, 165; *CSPD 1627–1628*, 497; Henning, *History of Parliament*, 679–680.

35. SL b1v; TR 165, 156; PRO PROB 11/147.

36. TR 160.

37. Grant, *Margaret the First*, 40; Walter, *Understanding Popular Violence*, 94; Appleby, *Our Fall*, 24; *CSPD 1640*, 62; Clarendon, *History*, II, 318.

38. TR 165. Also 156.

Chapter 2:
Childhood Ambitions,
1623–1642

Information on children's literacy learning and normal reading matter comes from:

Avery, "The Beginnings of Children's Reading".

For comparison and supplementary information on the education and cultural life of girls of Margaret's class, I have used memoirs of her female contemporaries, especially

Fanshawe, *Memoirs*

Rich, *Autobiography of Mary, Countess of Warwick*

Williamson, *Lady Anne Clifford*.

Important previous accounts of Margaret's childhood, on which I have drawn, are:

Grant, *Margaret the First*

Mendelson, *Mental World of Stuart Women*.

1. TR 164, 156, 157, 156. See also TR 165; SL 317–318.

2. TR 157; WO 79.

3. PaF A4r–5v. See also LWN (1667), 56. Elizabeth was probably a poor relation of the Lucases or the daughter of a family servant: Fraser, *The Weaker Vessel*, 311–319, 346, for waiting-women and their duties.

4. Makin, *An Essay*, 3.

5. As quoted in Gilbert and Gubar, *The Madwoman in the Attic*, 55.

6. TR 156; SL 367.

7. TR 157–158.

8. SL 50, 156.

9. SL 22–23, 156.

10. LWN xxxvi; WO H3r–v.

11. TR 172–175; SL 355, 138.

12. TR 172, 174, 172; LWN xxxvi; SL 267.

13. SL 273.

14. SL 268, 427–429; TR 172–174; PL b2r.

15. SL b1r–v.

16. TR 175.

17. See Grant, *Margaret the First*, 113–114; Cocking, "Originality and Influence," 46–64.

18. Margaret quotes Donne in PaF 39; PW 396; she quotes Marlowe in PNBP *The Presence*, 11. Her elegy on her niece's death, PaF "194–195," is strongly reminiscent of sections of Donne's *Anniversaries*. Her skepticism towards the new experimental philosophy, her fear of its dangers, and her general feeling of the unimportance and unreliability of all human studies—central ideas to the philosophy she wrote in later life— are all sentiments found powerfully expressed in Donne's poems.

19. WO 12, 13; PPO a2r.

20. SL 259; WO 17.

21. LWN xxxvi–xxxvii.

22. SL 338, 244–248; also SL 51–53. For teenage girls discussing their lovers, see Houlbrooke, *English Family Life*, 27–28. A similar range of girlhood reading is seen in the books in the "Great Picture" of Lady Anne Clifford: see

Williamson, *Lady Anne Clifford.* For women's reading, see also Fraser, *The Weaker Vessel*, 120, 123; Hull, *Chaste, Silent, and Obedient*.

23. TR 159–160. For women's excursions to garden and countryside, see Fraser, *The Weaker Vessel*, 36; Lanyer, "The Description of Cookham."

24. Scudéry, *Artamenes*, dedication to Lady Anne Lucas; SL 423.

25. SL 427–429. For the traditional lore preserved by women, see Mendelson and Crawford, *Women in Early Modern England*.

26. TR 175.

27. PPO A4r–v. Also B1r–2r; TR 174; WO E2r.

28. TR 175.

29. TR 175.

30. WO 87; PaF A3r. Margaret has written "cloaths," which could indicate cloths or clothes.

31. TR 175.

32. TR 174.

33. TR 163, 155, 157.

34. TR 174; SL 166, C2r, 56, 388.

35. Shakespeare, *King Richard III*, III, 1, 87–88.

36. Thucydides, *The Peloponnesian War*, 151.

37. SL 178; WO 50, 1. See also WO 58; Gagen, "Honor and Fame."

38. PPO B3r; WO 2.

39. PW 609; PaF Aa1v.

40. Crawford, "Women's Published Writings," 265, 269.

41. PW 182–183, 220–222.

42. TR 161. Also, TR 168–169.

43. TR 159, 158, 155, 163–164.

44. SL 422–424. Also, TR 162, 164.

45. TR 176.

46. SL 423.

47. TR 177; PaF "167."

48. PPO2 [250]; TR 175.

49. TR 175.

50. NUL MS PwV90, ff. 25r–v.

51. Henning, *History of Parliament*, 305.

52. TR 160, 166.

53. TR 156, 160; Job 1:4.

54. TR 160.

55. For London playhouses and plays of the 1630s: Harbage, *Annals of Drama*; idem, *Cavalier*

Drama; Hotson, *The Commonwealth and Restoration Stage*.

56. TR 160, supplemented with Chancellor, *Pleasure Haunts of London*; Brett-James, *Growth of Stuart London*; Evelyn, *Diary*; Williams, *Royal Parks*; Ralph, *Sir Humphrey Mildmay*.

57. Poem attributed to Sir John Denham, in Firth, ed., "Verses on the Cavaliers Imprisoned in 1655."

58. Scudéry, *Artamenes*, dedication to Lady Anne Lucas; Johns, *Nature of the Book*, 66–68.

59. PNBP, *The Presence*, 33.

60. Henning, *History of Parliament*, Foster, *Alumni Oxonienses*.

61. NP 190, 188.

62. NP 188. For Stuart masques: Strong, *Art and Power*.

63. WO 17, H3r.

64. TR 160.

CHAPTER 3:
THE COMING OF WAR, 1642

Background sources for national politics and the war:

Kenyon, *The Civil Wars*
Wedgwood, *The King's Peace*
idem, *The King's War*.

Sources for events and politics in Essex:

Hunt, *The Puritan Moment*
Holmes, *The Eastern Association*.

Principal sources for the Lucases' involvement in the outbreak of the war:

Walter, *Understanding Popular Violence*
Appleby, *Our Fall*
CSPD

Sources for the riot in August 1642:

Mayor Thomas Wade's report to Parliament (House of Lords, Braye-Teeling MS. no. 11)

Ryves, *Mercurius Rusticus*

Walter, *Understanding Popular Violence*

Parliamentarian newsletters (*Thomason Tracts*, E 114 (34) and E 114 (36); Clarendon, *History*, II, 318–9).

1. PRO SP 16/451/25.

2. As quoted in Walter, *Understanding Popular Violence*, 97. Walter provides a very full discussion

of the Lucases' long-running disputes with their neighbors.

3. Clarendon, *History*, II, 318.

4. De la Serre, *Histoire de l'entrée de la reine mère*, 11–19.

5. As quoted in Walter, *Understanding Popular Violence*, 166. See also 147, 167.

6. PRO SP 16/449/25, 16/451/25.

7. As quoted in Wedgwood, *The King's Peace*, 316.

8. As quoted in Hunt, *Puritan Moment*, 287.

9. As quoted in Hunt, *Puritan Moment*, 289.

10. As quoted in Walter, *Understanding Popular Violence*, 101.

11. As quoted in Holmes, *Eastern Association*, 38, 35.

12. For the riots: Walter, *Understanding Popular Violence*; Appleby, *Our Fall*; Ryves, *Mercurius Rusticus*; House of Lords, Braye-Teeling MS 11; *Thomason Tracts*, E 114 (30), E114 (34), E114 (36), and E 202 (42); BL Harleian MS 163, ff. 107v–108.

13. House of Lords, Braye-Teeling MS 11. Walter, *Understanding Popular Violence*, 36, assesses the probable scale of destruction.

14. HMC, *5th Report*, 46; Walter, *Understanding Popular Violence*, 152–153.

15. TR 163.

16. Walter, *Understanding Popular Violence*, 140, 155; BL Harleian MS 163, ff. 107v–108; Holmes, *Eastern Association*, 41–44.

17. For the Killigrews and Elizabeth Lucas, see Henning, *History of Parliament*; Green, ed., *Calendar of the Committee for Advance of Money*, 192, 416; idem, ed., *Calendar of the Committee for Compounding*, 799; Wood, *Life and Times*, I, 85.

18. As quoted in Strickland, *Lives of the Queens of England*, IV, 225.

19. TR 161. For her admiration of Henrietta Maria as a heroic woman, see also LWN 18.

20. PNBP, *The Presence*, 98; TR 162.

21. TR 161.

22. *A True Relation, or, Catalogue of the Gentry*; Green, ed., *Calendar of the Committee for Advance of Money*, 188. For Pye's arrival in Oxford, see idem, ed., *Calendar of the Committee for Compounding*, 1443. John Lucas did not leave for Oxford immediately on his release from prison (Lloyd,

Memories, 474), but he had arrived for the Battle of Newbury in September 1643.

23. Margaret's statement that she was at court for "almost two years" (TR 162) would suggest that she only went to Oxford after December 1643. But her autobiography is often very unreliable in its estimates of dates and periods of time—putting her brothers' deaths in the wrong order, for instance (TR 165), and stating that she and her husband were in Rotterdam "some six months" (TR 166) when in fact it was no more than three (see BL Addit. MS 4278, ff. 273, 278). She must never have kept a diary to which she could refer when she came to write her own life, and so I have assumed that she traveled to Oxford soon after the queen arrived there, when she would have had her siblings' assistance and protection for what was in effect an illegal journey through enemy territory.

24. Green, ed., *Calendar of the Committee for Advance of Money*, 192, 416; idem, ed., *Calendar of the Committee for Compounding*, 1439. Margaret mistakenly asserts that her mother had her estates sequestered: TR 162.

CHAPTER 4:
A LADY AT COURT, 1643–1645

The account of Civil War Oxford is based on
Wood, *Life and Times*, I, 67–110.
Dugdale, *Life, Diary and Correspondence*
Roy and Reinhart, "Oxford and the Civil Wars"
Roy, "The City of Oxford"
Varley, *The Siege of Oxford*.
Information on the queen's court and its routine comes from:
Society of Antiquaries, *Collection of Ordinances*, 340–51.
Somerset, *Ladies-in-Waiting*
Hibbard, "The Role of a Queen Consort."
Accounts of the Civil War are based on:
Kenyon, *The Civil Wars*
Wedgwood, *The King's War*.
For Margaret's brothers' involvement in the war:
Appleby, *Our Fall*.

Information on Henrietta Maria, her flight to France, and her court in Paris comes from:
Strickland, *Lives of the Queens of England*, IV
Hamilton, *Henrietta Maria*.
For Paris and the Louvre:
Ranum, *Paris in the Age of Absolutism*
Hautecoeur, *Paris*
Evelyn, *Diary*, II.

1. As quoted in Roy and Reinhart, "Oxford and the Civil Wars," 701.
2. Fanshawe, *Memoirs*, 111; TR 162.
3. Aubrey, *Brief Lives*, 186.
4. SL 326–328.
5. Henrietta Maria, *Letters*, 144, 87, 118–119.
6. LWN 94.
7. *Thomason Tracts*, E 53 (21). On Oxford's artistic culture: Rogers, *William Dobson*; Hamilton, *Henrietta Maria*; DNB; Hotson, *Commonwealth and Restoration Stage*, 6–22.
8. Society of Antiquaries, *Collection of Ordinances*, 341.
9. PNBP, *The Presence*, 17.
10. Hibbard, "The Role of a Queen Consort," 403–409.
11. Clarendon, *Four Portraits*, 125–127.
12. Smuts, *The Culture of Absolutism*, 145–149, 287–318, and passim.
13. SL 38; TR 173. Also SL 200–202.
14. PNBP, *The Presence*, 16.
15. SL 345; PW 202. Margaret's account of her time at court is TR 161–162.
16. TR 161, 162; Cavendish, *Phanseys*, 101.
17. TR 161; PNBP, *The Presence*, 112, 36, 37.
18. TR 162.
19. WO 32, 48.
20. PPO B1r; PaF "167." See also TR 161.
21. SL 386–387.
22. Appleby, *Our Fall*, 72–86, 163–164.
23. As quoted in Hamilton, *Henrietta Maria*, 204.
24. *Mercurius Aulicus*, March 30, 1644.
25. TR 177.
26. BL Addit. MS 12184, f. 314; PaF 156.
27. Evelyn, *Diary*, II, 149.
28. Evelyn, *Diary*, II, 155.

29. D'Ormesson, *Journal*, I, 224–225; BL Addit. MS 12184, f. 329; Strickland, *Lives of the Queens of England*, IV; Hamilton, *Henrietta Maria*.

30. PaF 156.

31. Appleby, *Our Fall*, 106–116.

32. PPO2 391–392.

Chapter 5: The Marquess and the Queen, 1645

Principal sources for William's family and the events of his life:

LWN

Trease, *Portrait of a Cavalier*

Turberville, *History of Welbeck Abbey*.

Supplementary sources for William's cultural and intellectual life during the 1630s:

Perry, *The First Duchess of Newcastle*

Articles by Brown, Raylor and Bryce, Rowe, Hulse, and Clucas in *The Seventeenth Century*, 9 (1994).

Jacquot, "Sir Charles Cavendish and his Learned Friends", part I

PPO2, p. 463.

Girouard, *Robert Smythson*

Faulkner, *Bolsover Castle*

Worsley, *Bolsover Castle*.

For his Civil War career, Margaret's LWN is supplemented by:

Clarendon, *History*

Kenyon, *The Civil Wars*

Trease, *Portrait of a Cavalier*.

William's love poems and Margaret's letters in reply are printed (from BL Addit. MSS 32497 and 70499) in Cavendish, *Phanseys*. The poem and letter numbers cited in the notes refer to this edition: the poem numbers are the same in the original manuscript. Margaret's letters are also printed (with the same numbering) in Goulding, *Letters from the Originals at Welbeck* and in Battigelli, *Margaret Cavendish*, Appendix B.

Important previous accounts of William and Margaret's courtship:

Grant, *Margaret the First*

Mendelson, *The Mental World of Stuart Women*.

Sources for St. Germain:

Evelyn, *Diary*, II, 110–12

Heylyn, *France Painted to the Life*

Houdard, *Les Châteaux de Saint-Germain-en-Laye*, II, 115–87.

1. LWN 45; Society of Antiquaries, *Collection of Ordinances*, 348–349. LWN 111 and various portraits for William's appearance.

2. The *DNB* erroneously dates William's birth to 1592. For the correct date, see: Perry, *The First Duchess of Newcastle*, 7; Trease, *Portrait of a Cavalier*, 17–18, and sources cited there.

3. William was the couple's second son, born late in 1593 (Cokayne, *Complete Peerage*). The first son, Charles, had died in infancy. He should not be confused with William's younger brother, also named Charles: see Parry, "Cavendish Memorials."

4. Trease, *Portrait of a Cavalier*, 21–28; Rowe, "My Best Patron," 203–204.

5. BL Addit. MS 70499, ff. 196–200. See also LWN 101 for William and his wife's affection for each other, and Bodleian MS Rawlinson Poet. 16, p. 31 for children who died young.

6. Hutchinson, *Memoirs of Colonel Hutchinson*, 117. Other important sources: Cust, *The Forced Loan*, 24–25, 118–119, 197–198, 250, 290; Brown, "Courtesies of Place," 150.

7. *Hartlib Papers*, 30/4/2A (*Ephemerides 1639*).

8. As quoted in Brown, "Courtesies of Place," 166–167.

9. BL Harleian MS 6988, ff. 111–112.

10. Clarendon, *History*, I, 164.

11. Clarendon, *History*, I, 164.

12. Clarendon, *History*, III, 382, 392–393; LWN 95. See also LWN 110.

13. LWN 41, 99; Clarendon, *History*, III, 382.

14. LWN 39.

15. LWN 41.

16. *CSPD 1644*, 378, 379.

17. Clarendon, *History*, III, 380–383; Warwick, *Memoires*, 257.

18. As quoted in Warburton, *Memoirs of Prince Rupert*, II, 126, n. 2.

19. LWN 98. Also 41, 43, 92, 93, 97.

20. LWN 43–45; Henrietta Maria, *Letters*, 261.

21. *CSPD 1644–1645*, 464–466, 623.

22. Henrietta Maria, *Letters*, 305; *Thomason Tracts*, E262 (23).

23. LWN 45.

24. Cavendish, *Phanseys*, poems no. 33, 8.

25. Cavendish, *Phanseys*, poems no. 5, 8. Poems 1, 6, 8, 50, 55 also describe Margaret's beauty.

26. Cavendish, *Phanseys*, poem no. 21. Praise of Margaret's personal qualities appears also in poems 33, 50, 51. For William's admiration of her intelligence and wit, see poems 21, 33, 50, 51; PNBP, *The Presence*, 106.

27. TR 162. See also PNBP, *The Presence*, 106.

28. PNBP, *The Presence*, 110–111. This conversation and Margaret's responses to William in her letters conform closely to the ideals of courtship presented in etiquette manuals such as T. Harper, *The Mirror of Compliments* (London, 1634).

29. Evelyn, *Diary*, III, 77.

30. PNBP, *The Presence*, 36, 42.

31. LWN 45.

32. Henrietta Maria, *Letters*, 305 ff. provides dates of residence.

33. Cavendish, *Phanseys*, poem no. 4 can be dated to late August by its reference to the siege of Bristol. The couple were married before 20 December: BL Addit. MS 70499, f. 299.

34. Cavendish, *Phanseys*, poems no. 13, 61, 26.

35. Cavendish, *Phanseys*, poems no. 4, 5. See also poem 7.

36. TR 162.

37. Eph. 5:22–23, quoted in Gouge, *Of Domestical Duties*, 157.

38. Brathwaite, *The English Gentlewoman*, "To the Gentlewoman Reader."

39. Starr, *"The Concealed Fansyes,"* passim. The marriage themes of the play are discussed in Ezell, "To Be Your Daughter in Your Pen," 289–290. For the presence of all three sisters at Welbeck at this time, see Jane and Frances's letter to Lord Fairfax, printed in Starr, *"The Concealed Fansyes,"* 804.

40. WO 85; SL 184.

41. SL 184–185, 425, 124, 425. See also 350.

42. TR 162; SL b1v. See also TR 162; LWN 109–111.

43. Cavendish, *Phanseys*, poem no. 29.

44. Warwick, *Memoires*, 257; Pepys, *Diary*, VIII, 163.

45. LWN 95, 96; SL 338.

46. TR 162; SL 175; PW 212. See also SL 116, 161, 350; TR 162.

47. Cavendish, *Phanseys*, letter no. 2.

48. Cavendish, *Phanseys*, letters no. 3, 2, 3.

49. Cavendish, *Phanseys*, letters no. 9, 10, 12.

50. PNBP, *The Presence*, 119–120. For the real occurrence of this fictional event, see Cavendish, *Phanseys*, letter no. 12.

51. Cavendish, *Phanseys*, letters no. 1, 4, 10. Also letter no. 8.

52. Cavendish, *Phanseys*, letters no. 10, 18. Letter no. 2 mentions another offer of renunciation.

53. Cavendish, *Phanseys*, letters no. 12, 16.

54. Cavendish, *Phanseys*, letter no. 1. Also letter no. 2.

55. PNBP, *The Presence*, 51, 37.

56. Cavendish, *Phanseys*, letters no. 10, 18.

57. Cavendish, *Phanseys*, poem no. 47; PNBP, *The Presence*, 119.

58. Cavendish, *Phanseys*, poem no. 47.

59. Cavendish, *Phanseys*, poem no. 53.

60. Cavendish, *Phanseys*, letter no. 13.

61. Cavendish, *Phanseys*, poems no. 31, 34.

62. Cavendish, *Phanseys*, poem no. 29.

63. Cavendish, *Phanseys*, letter no. 14.

64. Cavendish, *Phanseys*, letters no. 1, 2. See also letter no. 5.

65. Cavendish, *Phanseys*, letter no. 16.

66. Cavendish, *Phanseys*, letter no. 18. For the marriage arrangements, see also Evelyn, *Diary*, III, 480–481.

67. Cavendish, *Phanseys*, letter no. 19. See also poem no. 67; letters no. 15, 18.

68. Cavendish, *Phanseys*, letters no. 20, 21.

69. Cavendish, *Phanseys*, letter no. 21. Also letter no. 20.

CHAPTER 6:
PARISIAN WIFE, 1646–1648

LWN 45–7 is Margaret's own account of this period.

The main sources for Paris and its English émigré life are:

Ranum, *Paris in the Age of Absolutism*

Faugère, *Journal*

Evelyn, *Diary*, II and III, passim.

Sources for the Cavendishes' learned friends:

Martinich, *Hobbes*

Hobbes, *The Correspondence*

Petty, *A Discourse*, the dedication to William Cavendish

Edmond, *Rare Sir William Davenant*

Gabrieli, *Sir Kenelm Digby*

Petersson, *Sir Kenelm Digby*

Bligh, *Sir Kenelm Digby.*

The main sources for Parisian atomism are:

Clucas, "The Atomism of the Cavendish Circle"

Kargon, *Atomism in England*, chs. 6 and 7.

Discussion of Sir Charles Cavendish's intellectual life in this and subsequent chapters is based on:

Jacquot, "Sir Charles Cavendish and his Learned Friends", part II

Hervey, "Hobbes and Descartes"

Sir Charles' correspondence with John Pell (BL Addit. MSS 4278 and 4280), much of which is printed in Halliwell, *A Collection of Letters*, and Vaughan, *The Protectorate of Oliver Cromwell*, II, Appendix.

For the Civil War and the Lucases' part in it:

Kenyon, *The Civil Wars*

Appleby, *Our Fall.*

Background information on telescopes and microscopes comes from:

Daumas, *Scientific Instruments*

Background sources on health used in this and subsequent chapters:

Babb, *The Elizabethan Malady*

Klibansky et al., *Saturn and Melancholy*

Eccles, *Obstetrics and Gynaecology*

Beier, *Sufferers and Healers.*

1. Goulding, *Catalogue of Pictures*, no. 362.

2. Aubrey, *Brief Lives*, 58; Clarendon, *Life*, I, 126–128; idem, *History*, III, 375.

3. Jane was born c. 1621, Elizabeth in 1625–1626, Charles in 1626–1627, Henry in June 1630, and Frances probably after that: Faulkner, *Historical Description of Chelsea*, I, 224; Ballard, *Memoirs of Several Ladies*, 285; NUL MS Pw1 644; Henning, *History of Parliament*, 33.

4. Bodleian MS Rawlinson Poet. 16, pp. 1, 3, 4, 5, 7, 8, 10, 12, 15, 20, 21, 29, 35, 38, 39, 42, 43. The poems may have been written largely or entirely by Jane, since there are poems dedicated to Elizabeth and Frances and Lord Brackley (pp. 11, 19, 22, 28), but none written to Jane. Only the pastoral and the play in the same volume are definitely attributable to both sisters working together.

5. Both play and pastoral survive in William's copy, Bodleian MS Rawlinson Poet. 16. The play has been printed in Starr, "*The Concealed Fancies*" and in Cerasano and Wynne-Davies, *Renaissance Drama by Women*, 127–154. Its date is revealed by its prologue's reference to the authors' ages as eighteen and twenty-two. The pastoral refers to William being in France (p. 83 of MS), but was written before Elizabeth left Welbeck late in 1645 (p. 73 of MS).

6. Starr, "*The Concealed Fansyes*," 803–804; *CSPD 1644*, 131; HMC, *Hastings Manuscripts*, II, 125–129; *Mercurius Belgicus*, E3r.

7. Elizabeth was still present at Welbeck in April 1645 (see the letter printed in Starr, "*The Concealed Fansyes*," 804), but she had left by November (NA MS DD 421/1). She gave birth to her first child at Ashridge a year later (HL Ellesmere MS 8348).

8. Bodleian MS Rawlinson Poet. 16, p. 84. Also pp. 49, 50, 157.

9. Starr, "*The Concealed Fansyes*," 815–823.

10. Ezell, "To Be Your Daughter in Your Pen," 290–293.

11. Bodleian MS Rawlinson Poet. 16, p. 2.

12. NUL MS Pw1 146. See also NUL MSS Pw1 83–89, 118–122; Bodleian MS Rawlinson Poet. 16, p. 2.

13. NUL MS Pw1 644; NA MS DDHo 18/4; Newman, *Royalist Officers*.

14. BL Addit. MS 6032, f. 127v.

15. Cavendish, *New Method*, 5; LWN 9, 40.

16. Hobbes, *The Correspondence*, 525.

17. Cavendish, *La Méthode Nouvelle* (1658), plate 19; PRO SP 29/398/196; Bodleian MS Rawlinson Poet. 16, p. 24; NUL MS Pw1 316; NA MSS DD2P/24/73, p. 3, DD2P/27/59, DD4P/22/194, DDP6/1/27/19; BL Addit. MS 70500, f. 37.

18. WO 81.

19. TR 177.

20. NUL MS Pw1 316.

21. BL Addit. MS 32497.

22. LWN 109–110; SL b1v; SL 168. See also TR 171.

23. TR 170; PL a1v.

24. TR 162; Cavendish, *Phanseys*, letters no. 15, 13, 17.

25. WO 77, 80, 77; SL 124.

26. *The Kingdomes Weekly Intelligencer,* 23 Feb to 2 March 1646/7: Thomason Tracts, E378 (18).

27. Evelyn, *Diary*, III, 77.

28. Evelyn, *Diary*, II, 536; III, 480; BL Addit. MS 32497, f. 145v.

29. PNBP, *The Presence,* 58.

30. *The Kingdomes Weekly Intelligencer*, 23 February to 2 March 1647; Hotson, *Commonwealth and Restoration Stage*, 22–23.

31. NUL MS Pw1 173. See also BL Addit. MS 4278, f. 259.

32. PW 671. Also Tomlinson, "My Brain the Stage."

33. For the Cavendish circle's interest in opera, see Jacob and Raylor, "Opera and Obedience."

34. Cavendish, *New Method*, 55.

35. Maclean, *Woman Triumphant*, chs. 3 and 7.

36. Clarendon, *History*, V, 185; LWN 43; Newman, *Royalist Officers*.

37. LWN 111; Shadwell, *The Libertine*, dedication to William Cavendish.

38. WO E4r, E2r.

39. Aubrey, *Brief Lives*, 309; Dryden, as quoted in Edmond, *Rare Sir William Davenant*.

40. PPO B3v; Aubrey, *Brief Lives*, 152–154.

41. LWN 106–108, 121–141.

42. Vaughan, *Protectorate of Oliver Cromwell*, 366, 368; Aubrey, *Brief Lives*, 237.

43. Aubrey, *Brief Lives*, 97–99.

44. Evelyn, *Diary*, III, 48. See also 550; Bligh, *Sir Kenelm Digby*, 260. For William's earlier admiration of Digby, see NUL MS PwV 25, ff. 9r, 10r.

45. Aubrey, *Brief Lives*, 309; Petty, *A Discourse Made Before the Royal Society*, A8v–9r; Sir Charles Cavendish's correspondence, BL Addit. MS 4278, f. 213 and passim; PPO B3r; Letter from Mersenne to Comenius, Nov. 22, 1640, *Hartlib Papers*, 18/2/40A; Hobbes, *The Correspondence*.

46. BL Addit. MS 70499, ff. 210–211.

47. PPO B3v.

48. Aubrey, *Brief Lives*, 23.

49. *Nicholas Papers*, I, 72, 70–71; Aubrey, *Brief Lives*, 237.

50. *Mercurius Candidus*, 11–20 Nov. 1646: Thomason Tracts, E 362 (21).

51. Montpensier, *Mémoires*, as quoted in Strickland, *Lives of the Queens of England*, 240. Also, *The Kingdomes Weekly Intelligencer*, 23 Feb. to 2 March 1646/7, Thomason Tracts, E 378 (18).

52. BL Addit. MS 70499, f. 299; Cokayne, *Complete Peerage*; Clarendon, *Life*, I, 95; Bodleian MS Ashmole 832, ff. 217–218; Appleby, *Our Fall*, 116.

53. LWN 45.

54. *The Kingdomes Weekly Intelligencer*, 23 Feb. to 2 March 1646/7, Thomason Tracts, E378 (18).

55. LWN 64; SL 168, 424.

56. As quoted in Appleby, *Our Fall*, 124.

57. Green, ed., *Calendar of the Committee for Compounding*.

58. TR 164, 165.

59. NUL MS PwV 90, ff. 7–7v.

60. NUL MS PwV 90, ff. 1–24, 37–70v are the receipts collected in Paris.

61. LWN 45–46.

62. LWN 46; Green, ed., *Calendar of the Committee for Compounding*, 1799.

63. LWN 47, 46.

64. BL Addit. MS 4278, ff. 271–272; NUL MS Pw1 668.

65. *Hartlib Papers*, 31/22/23A (*Ephemerides 1648*); NUL MS Pw1 668.

66. NUL MS PwV 90, ff. 14–19v.

67. NUL MS PwV 90, ff. 8v–13, 20v–23.

68. LWN 45.

69. NUL MS PwV 90, ff. 19v–20.

70. NUL MS PwV 90, ff. 47v–52r; *Hartlib Papers*, 29/4/21A (*Ephemerides 1654*).

71. NUL MS PwV 90, ff. 65–66.

72. PRO SP 21/9, pp. 148, 151.

73. Lloyd, *Memories*, 476.

74. BL Addit. MS 23206, f. 24.

75. NUL MS Pw1 406. This was perhaps Rhieta's instrument, which is not included in the list of telescopes in NUL MS Pw1 668.

76. LWN 47; Evelyn, *Diary and Correspondence*, IV, 347–348.

Chapter 7:
Dutch Scholar, 1648–1651

LWN 48–56 and TR 166 contain Margaret's account of this period.

Sources for Rotterdam, Antwerp, and Brussels:

Evelyn, *Diary*, II
Verney, *Memoirs of the Verney Family*, III, 46–55
Ray, *Observations Topographical*
Brown, *Account of Several Travels*
Monconys, *Journal des Voyages*, II, 101–8.
Gölnitz, *Ulysses Belgico-Gallicus.*

The account of the Rubens House is based on my own visit there and on:

Depauw, *Rubens House.*

For Sir Charles Cavendish's intellectual interests in Antwerp, the primary sources are:

BL Harleian MSS 6002 and 6083 passim
BL Addit. MSS 4278, ff. 278–321; 4280, ff. 133–8.

For William's political views, the main sources are LWN (especially Book IV) and his book of advice to Charles II, as printed in Slaughter, ed., *Ideology and Politics.* The text is also available in Anzilotti, *An English Prince.*

Sources for the Cavendishes' acquaintance in the Low Countries:

Huygens, *De Briefwisseling*, V, passim
Huygens, *Correspondance et Oeuvres Musicales*
Pohl, *Die Portuguiesen in Antwerpen*
Flecknoe, *A Relation of Ten Years Travell*
Flecknoe, *A Treatise of the Sports of Wit*
Doney, *The Life and Works of Richard Flecknoe*

For discussions of the Worlds Olio, see Donawerth, "Conversation and the Boundaries of Public Discourse"; Suzuki, "The Essay Form as Critique."

For historical background during the Interregnum in this and subsequent chapters:

Hutton, *Charles the Second*
Ollard, *Clarendon and his Friends*
Underdown, *Royalist Conspiracy in England.*

1. LWN 48.
2. LWN 48–49.
3. HMC, *12th Report,* Appendix, IX, 27–28.
4. Clarendon, *History*, IV, 386.
5. Carter, *A True Relation.*
6. Evelyn, *Diary*, III, 177.

7. LWN 49; TR 158, 165. For Thomas Lucas's death: *DNB* and PRO PROB 11/213.
8. SL 177–178.
9. SL 238–239; PW A7c. For Margaret's paraphrase of Horace, see SL 226–229.
10. LWN 50; TR 166. For William's finances, see LWN 50 and HMC, *Pepys Manuscripts*, 228.
11. Verney, *Memoirs of the Verney Family*, III, 50.
12. LWN 50.
13. LWN 50.
14. LWN 50–51.
15. BL Addit. MS 4278, f. 278.
16. *CSPD 1649–1650*, 39.
17. NUL MS PwV 90, ff. 81v–82v.
18. SL 183.
19. Margaret Cavendish, *The Convent of Pleasure and Other Plays*, ed. Shaver, 4.
20. Osborne, *Letters* 56 (letter 10).
21. NUL MS PwV 90, ff. 3–5, 18v, 25–32, 96, 117.
22. LWN 51. For William's riding house, see Cavendish, *New Method,* b1v, c2v.
23. PPO A3r.
24. WO 16; PPO A4r. See also LWN, Book IV, for the range of the couple's later conversations.
25. PPO B1r.
26. LWN xxxvi; WO E3v; WO E2r.; PPO A4v.
27. PPO A4r.
28. WO H3r. See also LWN xxxvi.
29. BL Addit. MSS 4278, f. 293; 6083, ff. 168–169, 177–178.
30. PhF 12; PPO, "A Condemning Treatise of Atoms"; PhF 10, 18. See also PhF 15, 30, 38, 69. See BL Addit. MS 4280 f. 135 for Sir Charles's copying machine.
31. PPO 100–101; PhF 28.
32. PaF 22–23; PPO 81; PaF 20–21. For Sir Charles and the Torricelli experiment, see *Hartlib Papers*, 8/29/1A–2B.
33. BL Addit. MSS 4278, f. 304; 4280, f. 138.
34. PPO B3v.
35. PPO A1v–A2v.
36. PPO B3v, B1r.
37. LWN xxxvi, 97–98; PPO2 463; LWN 106.
38. Margaret notes reading the *De Cive* in PPO B3v.
39. SL 362–363.

40. Harbage, *Annals of Drama*.

41. LWN 109; SL 338.

42. LWN 109.

43. BL Addit. MS 4278, f. 295.

44. Evelyn, *Diary*, II, 67; Monconys, *Journal des Voyages*, II, 101–102.

45. Huygens, *Briefwisseling*, V, 250.

46. Huygens, *Correspondance et Oeuvres Musicales*, ccl; Evelyn, *Diary*, II, 67.

47. SL 427–429.

48. WO 16.

49. Flecknoe, *Aenigmatical Characters* (1665), 77–78; idem, *Miscellania*, 71–72; idem, *A Relation of Ten Years Travel*, "To the Lord Marquess of Newcastle." For Flecknoe's residence in Antwerp, see also Flecknoe, *Aenigmatical Characters*, 62, 69; idem, *Miscellania*, 49.

50. PPO B1v, B1r. WO A3v and PhF 90 date the beginning of Margaret's writing.

51. WO 33, 34.

52. WO 110.

53. WO 5, 11.

54. For the possibility that Margaret's "Of Women Dying with their Husbands" was a response to Montaigne's essay "De Trois Bonnes Femmes," see Suzuki, "The Essay Form," 4.

55. WO 2, 3.

56. WO 11, 23.

57. WO 110–121.

58. WO 126. William too was unconventional in seeing Elizabeth I as an ideal ruler: Slaughter, ed., *Ideology and Politics*, 45 and passim.

59. WO 127–128, 131, 133.

60. WO 68–71.

61. WO 51, 42, 57.

62. WO 50.

63. WO 54.

64. Slaughter, ed., *Ideology and Politics*, 15; WO 29–30.

65. WO 169–171, 117, 171.

66. WO 181.

67. WO 162.

68. WO 18–19, 36–38.

69. WO 84–87.

70. WO 83–84.

71. WO 74, 75.

72. WO 81. Also 46, 71, 77–78.

73. WO 71, 83. On obedience and the relationship of marriage, see also WO 27, 80–81, 155.

74. BL Addit. MS 37998, f. 68; BL Harleian MS 6852, ff. 335–350; BL Addit. MS 4278, f. 298.

75. Clarendon, *Calendar of State Papers*, II, 53–54.

76. William to an unnamed Scottish or Irish nobleman, October 30, 1649, NUL MS Pw1 537.

77. LWN 101.

78. Green, ed., *Calendar of the Committee for Compounding*, 1732; Bodleian MS Rawlinson Poet. 16, p. 23; NA MS DD4P 58/25 (Bamford's accounts, August 1654).

79. LWN 69–70; PRO SP 25/64, p. 244.

80. BL Addit. MS 70499, f. 317; letter from William [to the Duke of Buckingham], February 8, 1651, printed in Firth, ed., "Letters of the Duke of Newcastle and Colonel Hutchinson" and in LWN 204–205.

81. Clarendon, *Life*, I, 126.

82. WO H3r–v, 90, 119. See also 20, 27, 40, 41, 65.

83. William's letter of February 1651, LWN 204–205.

84. Nickolls, ed., *Original Letters*, 77. See also 50; *CSPD 1651*, 155, 162, 527; *CSPD 1651–1652*, 13. For William's negotiations for troops see Nickolls, *Original Letters*, 77; Clarendon, *Calendar of State Papers*, II, 105–107.

85. LWN 55. For the Antwerp news concerning Charles, see Clarendon, *Calendar of State Papers*, II, 568–581.

86. William's letter of February 1651, LWN 204–205.

87. LWN 64; SL 242.

88. Green, ed., *Calendar of the Committee for Compounding*, 2022. See also 2021; Clarendon, *State Papers*, III, 34, 223.

89. Clarendon, *Life*, I, 127; Kenyon, ed., *The Stuart Constitution*, 307–308.

90. Clarendon, *Life*, I, 126–127.

91. Clarendon, *State Papers*, III, 23–24; Clarendon, *Life*, I, 127–128.

92. Firth and Rait, eds., *Acts and Ordinances*, II, 520–548.

93. BL Addit. MS 32497, f. 71; SL 197. For details of the departure, see Clarendon, *State Papers*, III, 34; WO A3v.

CHAPTER 8:
POET AND PETITIONER,
1651–1653

Margaret's own description of this period of her life is in TR 166–71; LWN 56–8.

Sources consulted for life in Interregnum London include:

Higgins, "Women in the English Civil War"

Spink, *Henry Lawes*

Evans, *Henry Lawes*

Philips, *The Collected Works*, 1

Lawes, *Ayres and Dialogues*

Lawes, *The Second Book of Ayres*

Chalmers, "Dismantling the Myth"

Sharp, "Walter Charleton's Early Life".

On women's poetry and publishing, I have consulted:

Ezell, "To be your daughter in your pen"

Greer et al., eds., *Kissing the Rod*

Crawford, "Women's Published Writings 1600–1700"

Woudhuysen, *Sir Philip Sidney and the Circulation of Manuscripts.*

For Margaret's poetry, I have consulted:

Battigelli, *Margaret Cavendish*

Walker, "Longing for Ambrosia"

Cocking, "Originality and Influence"

Grant, *Margaret the First*

Rees, "Sweet Honey of the Muses".

On Margaret's philosophy in this and later chapters, I have referred to:

Battigelli, *Margaret Cavendish*

Blaydes, "Nature is a Woman"

Clucas, "The Atomism of the Cavendish Circle"

Hutton, "Anne Conway, Margaret Cavendish and Seventeenth Century Scientific Thought"

Hutton, "In Dialogue with Thomas Hobbes"

Sarasohn, "Science Turned Upside Down"

Price, "Feminine Modes of Knowing"

On the London publishing world, I have used

Plomer, *A Dictionary of the Booksellers and Printers*

Johns, *The Nature of the Book.*

1. LWN 56.

2. Schofield, ed., *The Knyvett Letters*, 151; Verney, *Memoirs of the Verney Family*, II, 240.

3. TR 168; Green, ed., *Calendar of the Committee for Compounding*, 1733–1734.

4. As quoted in Ralph, *Sir Humphrey Mildmay*, 193.

5. TR 166–167.

6. TR 167; Green, ed., *Calendar of the Committee for Compounding*, 1734; TR 167, 168.

7. Green, ed., *Calendar of the Committee for Compounding*, 2022.

8. LWN 56–57.

9. Elizabeth's epitaph, as quoted in Ballard, *Memoirs of Several Ladies*, 285–286. For Jane and Frances visiting London: NA MS DD4P/58/25.

10. BL Egerton MS 607, ff. 120, 23. Beier, *Sufferers and Healers*, 104, contains the physician's account of Henry's death.

11. TR 170. For Margaret's family in London: Green, ed., *Calendar of the Committee for Advance of Money*, 642; Sheppard, ed., *Survey of London*, XXXVI, 8; L. Huygens, *The English Journal*, 107.

12. Evelyn, *A Character of England*, 60.

13. TR 168.

14. TR 169–170.

15. If Margaret did know Katherine Philips, she did not join closely in her society of friendship. Evidence previously thought to prove Margaret's membership of this circle is now known to refer to Mary Cavendish, wife of the earl of Devonshire: Philips, *Collected Works*, I, 213–214, 382.

16. Green, ed., *Calendar of the Committee for Compounding*, 1734–1737.

17. TR 167.

18. BL Addit. MS 32497, ff. 72–87.

19. PaF A7r; NUL MS PwV 90, f. 115r.

20. PPO B4r.

21. LP 145.

22. Vaughan, *Protectorate*, II, 383–384.

23. PPO B3v.

24. PaF A7r; WO 6, 65; PhF 91. Also PaF 122.

25. PaF "141".

26. SL 151.

27. PaF 20–21, 39.

28. PaF 43–46.

29. WO [160], 116; PaF 31; PaF A6r.

30. PaF 18–19. See also 35–36, 39, 40–42, 48.

31. PaF 110–113.

32. PaF 66–75.

33. PaF 93–95.

34. PaF 97–98, 103.

35. PaF 126–136, 1–5.

36. PaF 60–61. The sentiment of this poem is similar to Marvel's "A Dialogue between the Soul and the Body."

37. PaF 58–59.

38. PaF 76–80, 107–108.

39. PaF 64–66.

40. PaF "171".

41. PaF 147–148.

42. PaF "211".

43. PaF 155–157.

44. NA MSS DDP/29/11–13, DDP6/1/3/8, DD4P/35/16, DDP/50/83, DDP6/1/16/54–55; NUL MSS Pw1 629, 644.

45. Green, ed., *Calendar of the Committee for Compounding*, 1735–1737; NA MSS DD/12/1, DDP/42/64, DDP/50/83, DDP/114/92, DD4P/22/146, DD4P/22/164.

46. NA MSS DDP/42/34, DDP/70/41, DD4P/58/25.

47. NA MS DD4P/22/164, p. 8.

48. LWN 58.

49. PaF 89–90. See also *CSPD 1649–1650*, 217–218.

50. PaF "213–214".

51. TR 166, 165.

52. PaF A7v, 232, A6v.

53. WO 9, 10, 5.

54. PaF 154, 110.

55. PaF 125. See also PaF "212".

56. PaF A8r. This verse's reference to the printer's risk of financial loss confirms that it was the booksellers and not Margaret herself who paid for publishing this book.

57. Parker, *The Copy of a Letter*, 13, 5.

58. Figures come from Crawford, "Women's Published Writings."

59. PaF A3v, A6r, A7v. See Wroth, *Poems*, 32–33, for surviving manuscript versions of Denny's poem.

60. PaF A7v, A4v.

61. PaF A5r, A3v.

62. PaF A3r, Aa1v.

63. PaF A4r: this is the text as corrected in the Bodleian Library's copy, P.1.22 Jus Seld.

64. PaF 53, 54.

65. PaF A4v.

66. PaF A5v. For a similarly intellectual relationship between Lady Anne Conway and her gentlewoman, who acted as her "library keeper," see Fraser, *The Weaker Vessel*, 346.

67. PaF A2r–v; PhF B4r–v; PaF A2r.

68. TR 167–168.

69. TR 170.

70. Huygens, *Briefwisseling*, V, 186; Osborne, *Letters*, 81–82 (letter 18).

71. Publication can be dated by *CSPD 1652–1653*, 467, 469; PhF B6r–v, 85; HMC *10th Report*, Appendix, IV, 47.

72. Osborne, *Letters*, 81–82 (letter 18).

73. PaF 16, 1–4.

74. Osborne, *Letters*, 100 (letter 24).

75. HMC, *10th Report*, Appendix, IV, 47; Grant, *Margaret the First*, 129–130.

76. Philips, *Collected Works*, II, 205.

77. PhF 18.

78. PhF 15, 30–31.

79. PhF 52–56.

80. PhF B6r is Margaret's account of writing the book. Handwritten notes on the copies in the British Library's Thomason Tracts and in the Bodleian Library suggest publication was in May 1653.

81. BL Addit. MS 32497, ff. 87r–v, 90r. See also TR 170–171, LWN 58.

82. PRO SP 25/39/64, SP 25/40/35.

83. PhF 78, 90.

CHAPTER 9:
WRITER IN EXILE, 1653–1655

Margaret's own account of this period of her life:

LWN 51–3, 58–62; TR 170–2

Information on seventeenth-century spelling and the preparation of books for printing comes from

Sönmez, "English Spelling in the Seventeenth Century"

Greer et al. eds., *Kissing the Rod*

Johns, *The Nature of the Book*.

Sources for Constantijn Huygens:

Van der Aa, *Biographisch Woordenboek*, III, 467–70

Huygens, *Correspondance et Oeuvres Musicales*

idem, *Briefwisseling*

idem, *Mijn Jeugd*
idem, *Dagboek.*
Roth, ed., *Correspondence of Descartes and Constantijn Huygens.*
For Antwerp engraving, van Diepenbeeck and the production and meaning of Margaret's frontispieces I have consulted:
Riggs and Silver, eds., *Graven Images*
Filipczak, *Picturing Art in Antwerp*
Turner, ed., *The Dictionary of Art*
Fitzmaurice, "Fancy and the Family".

1. BL Addit. MS 32497, ff. 88r, 90v, 96v. The love poems of this period are ff. 88–89, 90v–112.
2. PPO2 "To his Excellencie"; WO 82; SL 131–134.
3. Bodleian MS Clarendon 45, f. 409; Barlow's copy of *The Philosophical Fancies*, now in the Bodleian Library; Huygens, *Briefwisseling*, V, 186–187; LP 88–90.
4. LP 88–90.
5. Bradstreet, *The Tenth Muse*, 4; Killigrew, *Poems*, 45–46.
6. PhF 85.
7. PhF 90.
8. LP 142. For the history of the olio, see *OED* and the sources cited there.
9. For some examples of these problems, see WO 5, where "the water in a cup" simile is obscure (but presumably refers to something like the famous Torricelli experiment, usually done with mercury); WO 6, where the sentence is ill formed and the words "makes men" have presumably been omitted before the phrase "witty in reading"; WO 31–32 and 36–38, where the essays lack coherent structure; and WO 78–79 and 82–83 where the titles bear little relation to the main content of their essays. WO 213 has a complex twenty-four-line sentence that is never completed.
10. WO A3v.
11. WO A4r–A5v.
12. TR 154, 172.
13. TR 172.
14. Cavendish, *Phanseys*, letters nos. 1, 4.
15. Letter from Margaret to Constantijn Huygens, Antwerp, March 30, 1657, BL Addit. MS. 28558, f. 65. The love letters are BL Addit. MS 70499, ff. 259–297.

16. Anonymous, *Six Familiar Essays*, the introductory epistle.
17. WO 93.
18. WO A1r; PaF A3r.
19. WO A1r, A2r, A3r.
20. LWN 59.
21. Bodleian MS Clarendon 47, ff. 84, 146, 374.
22. LWN 51–53; Cavendish, *A New Method*, 49.
23. Cavendish, *A New Method*, b1v–c2v; LWN 60–62.
24. *Nicholas Papers*, II, 56–58; BL Addit. MS 70499, ff. 327–329; LWN 62; Clarendon, *Calendar*, II, passim.
25. LWN 60.
26. PPO A4v, B1r.
27. SL 436–442.
28. Huygens, *Briefwisseling*, V, 186.
29. Huygens, *Dagboek*, 57; Huygens, *Briefwisseling*, V, 284; VI, 293.
30. Huygens, *Briefwisseling*, V, 284–287. For other seventeeth century theories of the drops, and for a modern explanation of the phenomenon, see Brodsley, Frank, and Steeds, "Prince Rupert's Drops."
31. TR 173–174.
32. PPO A3v–A4r.
33. WO 163–164, 205–216.
34. TR 173. Also 172 for her writing practices.
35. LWN xxxvii; TR 172. See also PPO A2v.
36. SL 274; LWN xxxvii.
37. WO 93; PPO A3v–4r. Some other examples of misprints are "clearing" for "clearly," "as if" for "and if," "naturally" for "natural": WO 11, 37, 8.
38. For examples, see WO 31–32, 36–38, 41–42.
39. Based on two copies of the *Poems and Fancies* in the Bodleian Library, one at the University of Leeds, the copy reproduced on Wing microfilm, and copies in the British Library and Cambridge University Library.
40. SL 295–296.
41. NUL MS PwV 90, f. 116r. Also f. 113v.
42. NP [Alv?]. This preface, entitled "Most Noble Readers or Spectators," does not appear in all copies of NP: it is present in the copy in Cambridge University Library.

43. Guillim, *A Display of Heraldrie*, 276.

44. BL Addit. MS 6032. For the "melancholic" content of this frontispiece, see Fitzmaurice, "Fancy and the Family."

45. SL 417.

46. There are frontispieces in a copy of the *World's Olio* that belonged to the Bridgewaters, Margaret's stepdaughter's family, as also in the Newcastles' own copy of the 1668 edition of her *Poems and Fancies*, both now in the British Library. Yet the copy of her *Philosophical Opinions* (1655) that Margaret presented to the Bodleian Library contains no frontispiece.

47. There are certainly many copies containing frontispieces that show no sign of having been presentation copies.

48. TR 173. The *OED* cites Margaret's explanation here as the first occurrence of the word in English.

49. Brown, *An Account of Several Travels*, 31–32.

50. Evelyn, *Diary*, II, 67. The avenues are described in Monconys, *Journal des Voyages*, 105; Ray, *Observations Topographical*, 20.

51. TR 173; LWN 51; TR 173.

52. Huygens, *Briefwisseling*, V, 186–187, 302.

53. TR 173. Chalmers, "Dismantling the Myth" discusses the social functions of Margaret's appearances in the tour.

54. Huygens, *Dagboek*, 57n.

55. Motteville, *Memoirs*, IV, 329, 339, 344. Whitelock, *A Journal*, I, 231–232 provides another description of Christina's dress. I owe these references to Tomlinson, "My Brain the Stage."

56. WO A3r.

57. TR 171; LWN 58. Also Clarendon, *Calendar*, II, 317, 320; TR 166.

58. TR 165; SL 10–11; Clarendon, *State Papers*, III, 223.

59. NUL MS PwV 90, ff. 106v–114, 115v. Idem, ff. 100–106 contain other people's receipts for colic, which William collected.

60. NUL MS PwV 90, ff. 113r, 114v–115v.

61. NUL MS PwV 90, f. 107r.

62. SL b1r, 265–266. This description of "Lady V.R." corresponds closely to Mayerne's description of Margaret's inconstancy in following medical advice: NUL PwV 90, f. 115r.

63. WO E2r–E4r, H3r–v, 93–94. That these epistles were composed at a late stage, after printing had already begun, is indicated by the lack of page numbers for the first two. Three further apologetic epistles were also included later in the book: WO [135–136], [157–159], 178. See also LWN xxxv–xxxvi.

64. Manley, *The Lost Lover*, the preface.

65. WO E2r–3r.

66. PPO B2r, A4v.

67. The title page of the *World's Olio* is dated 1655, but Walter Charleton had already read his copy on 1 January 1654/5: LP 142, 149. The *Philosophical Opinions* must already have been with the printers before this, since a poem Margaret intended for it was mistakenly printed in the *World's Olio*: PPO A3v–4r.

68. SL 226.

69. PPO 77, 86.

70. PPO 104, 127.

71. PPO B4r.

72. NUL MS PwV 90, f. 63r and passim; PPO2 351–352; SL 269–271, 278–280, 288–289, 290–291, 309–310, 322–324, 326–328, 444–448. Many of the medicines that William collected (NUL MS PwV 90) came from lay people, like his cousins the countesses of Arundel and Kent, as well as from professional medical men.

73. WO 200. Also PPO 99.

74. PPO 170.

75. PPO 103–104, 134, 169–170.

76. PPO, "A Condemning Treatise of Atoms."

77. WO [219]; PPO A3v.

78. PPO a1r, 27. Hobbes stated this epistemological position in a letter to William: see BL Addit. MS 70499, f. 210. PPO 26 contains Margaret's account of her philosophical method.

79. WO 200, 180. Elizabeth had referred to Margaret's earlier atomic theory as her "philosophical opinions": PaF A5v.

80. WO [160], 161; PPO 27, 51–52, 67.

81. PPO a1, 51, a2.

82. LP 146–147.

83. PPO A4r, A4v, B1v. Margaret's denial that she had her knowledge "before I was born" and that she "had taken feathers out of the universities" (A4v) show that this preface was composed in response to Charleton's letter.

84. PPO A4r–v, B3v.

85. NP c6r.

86. PPO A1v–A3r. Also LWN xxxv–xxxvi.

87. See LWN xxxv.

88. PPO B2v.

89. The dedication to Sir Charles Cavendish (WO A3r), who died in February 1654, implies that Margaret wrote the WO prefaces at least a year before she composed the last epistles for her PPO, in response to Walter Charleton's letter of January 1654/5 (see note 83 above). However, the opposition of these views—published in the WO and the PPO within a few months of each other in 1655—would later come to reinforce Margaret's reputation for inconsistency, even madness.

90. PPO B3r.

91. PPO A3r, B2v-3r.

CHAPTER 10:
SATIRIST AND STORYTELLER,
1655–1658

Principal works consulted on *Nature's Pictures*:

Hackett, " 'Yet tell me some such Fiction' "

Hackett, *Women and Romance Fiction*

Fitzmaurice, "Front Matter"

Battigelli, *Margaret Cavendish*

Salzman, *English Prose Fiction*.

Principal works consulted on Margaret's autobiography:

Hobby, *Virtue of Necessity*

Findley and Hobby, "Seventeenth Century Women's Autobiography"

Graham, et al. eds., *Her Own Life*

Mason, "The Other Voice."

For Margaret's plays, both here and in chapter 14:

Battigelli, *Margaret Cavendish*

Payne, "Dramatic Dreamscape"

Pearson, *Prostituted Muse*

Pearson, " 'Women May Discourse . . . as Well as Men' "

Rosenthal, *Playwrights and Plagiarists*

Straznicky, "Reading the Stage"

Cavendish, *The Convent of Pleasure*, ed. Shaver

Suzuki, "Margaret Cavendish"

Wiseman, "Gender and Status".

On the *Sociable Letters*:

Cavendish, *Margaret Cavendish: Sociable Letters*, ed. Fitzmaurice.

On melancholy I have used:

Babb, *The Elizabethan Malady*

Klibansky, et al., *Saturn and Melancholy*

In addition to manuscript sources cited, biographical information on William's family both here and in other chapters comes from:

DNB

Cokayne, *Complete Peerage*

Henning, *The History of Parliament*

LWN 116–17

Faulkner, *Historical Description of Chelsea*

Ballard, *Memoirs of Several Ladies of Great Britain*, 283–6.

1. NP c4r–v, title page; SL 257–258, 160–161.

2. NP c2v–3r.

3. NP 49, 1.

4. WO 18.

5. NP 6, 37, 47, 87, 59–60.

6. NP b1r–v.

7. NP 88–93.

8. NP 89, 114.

9. NP 121, 110–113, 120.

10. The last of these allegories is reminiscent of Spenser's castle of the soul in *The Faery Queen*, book 2, canto 9. In addition to Book 3 of NP, pp. 67–70 also contain an allegorical or "poetical" tale, in verse.

11. NP c4v.

12. Margaret would herself portray Henrietta Maria in this light: LWN 18.

13. TR 165, 163.

14. TR 175.

15. Burton, *Anatomy*, I, 461; PPO 128.

16. WO 118.

17. Gellius, *Noctes*, XVIII, 7, 4.

18. NP c1r; TR 176–177.

19. SL 348, 167, 348.

20. NP c1r; SL 51–52.

21. SL 238, 177.

22. NP c1r–v.

23. LP 70–71.

24. TR 178.

25. NP [Alv?]: "Most Noble Readers or Spectators."

26. Diepenbeeck's pen-and-wash sketch is in the British Museum, Department of Prints and Drawings, register number 1858–4–171629.

27. NP A3v. Note that this poem is not included in the copy of NP reproduced on UMI microfilm.

28. The marriage agreements are NA MSS DDP/8/131, DDP6/1/12/1–2.

29. NUL MSS Pw1 377–379.

30. NUL MS Pw1 88.

31. NA MS DD4P/35/12. NUL MSS Pw1 228, 395 date the marriage to 1654.

32. NUL MS Pw1 89. See also Pw1 83–88, 118–122; BL Addit. MS 70499, ff. 337, 341–342. Henry's coldness to his sisters is revealed also in Elizabeth's letter to Jane, September 18, 1659: HL Ellesmere MS 8048.

33. NUL MS Pw1 228 and BL Addit. MS 70499, f. 343 for Lord Lambert. NA MS DDP6/1/31/18–19; NUL MSS Pw1 644, 163–164; BL Addit. MS 70499, f. 339 for Charles's legal and fiscal business.

34. NA MS DD4P/58/25; BL Addit. MS 70499, ff. 333–335, 341–342; NUL MSS Pw1 159, 395; Gamble, *Ayres and Dialogues. The Second Book*, the dedication.

35. LWN 69–70. For financial details: NUL MSS Pw1 89, 130, 152; NA MSS DDP/29/13, DDP/85/39, DD2P/21/1, DD4P/22/146, DD4P/22/186.

36. NA MS DD4P/22/146, pp. 11–12. NA MSS DDP/29/9, DDP/29/10, DDP/114/74, DDP6/1/16/51, DDP6/1/18/21 for other surrenders.

37. NUL MSS Pw1 151, 597; NA MSS DDP/7/9, DDP/17/136, DDP/29/15, DDP/43/36, DDP/70/43–44, DDP/88/8–14, DD2P/21/1, DD2P/24/14, DD4P/22/187, DD4P/75/81, DDP6/1/16/57 and passim. BL Addit. MS 70499, f. 351 and NA MS DD4P/22/146, p. 12 for William's pseudonyms.

38. TR 171. Also SL 197, 349.

39. LWN 59; Bodleian MS Clarendon 47, f. 374.

40. Poem attributed to Sir John Denham, in Firth, ed., "Verses on the Cavaliers Imprisoned in 1655"; Thurloe, *A Collection of State Papers*, III, 574, 593.

41. SL 338.

42. PW A3a.

43. Perry, *The First Duchess of Newcastle*, 145; Van Lennep, ed., *The London Stage*, 154–155.

44. William's surviving literary production from his exile is in BL Addit. MS 32497; NP 20–21, 25, 64–67, 79–82, 97–102, 271; NUL MS PwV 24 passim. Selections from this last are printed in Cavendish, *Dramatic Works*; idem, "A Pleasante & Merrye Humor"; Strong, *Catalogue of Letters*, 57–60.

45. Bodleian MS Clarendon 45, f. 508. See Perry, *The First Duchess of Newcastle*, 139–140, 317–318 for the various editions of William's equestrian works.

46. PRO SP 77/31, f. 441, printed in LWN 206.

47. BL Addit. MSS 37998, f. 82; 70499, f. 347. Walker had first advised William on this subject c. 1653. This is an early use of this courtesy title in English etiquette: *OED* cites 1707 as the first use.

48. BW, "The Second Part," 25–26.

49. NP 20–21, 25, 64–67, 79–82, 97–102, 271 for William's contributions.

50. PW A6a; NP b2r.

51. PW A3a.

52. PW A3d–A4b.

53. PW A5c, A5a; Starr, "The Concealed Fansyes," 806.

54. PNBP, "To the Readers"; PW A5d. *The Presence* in PNBP shows this process of construction uncompleted, with one of the story lines left unincorporated into the rest. For Margaret's instructions on the tones of voice that should be used in reading her plays aloud, see PW A6b.

55. PW 535.

56. Statistics here come from Pearson, *The Prostituted Muse*, 63–65, 127.

57. PW A6a.

58. PW A7a; PaF A5r; PW A4c, A7a. Also SL 3–4, 8, 70–72, 112.

59. PW A5c; SL 14; TR 172. Also SL 382.

60. PW A3c; SL 340. See also LWN xlii. For the identification of Sir William Sanderson, see Margaret Cavendish, *Margaret Cavendish: Sociable Letters*, ed. Fitzmaurice, letter 164.

61. Clarendon, *State Papers*, III, 20; *Nicholas Papers*, I, 173.

62. LWN 138, xxxv.

63. LWN xlv, xxxix.

64. PW A3c; NP c1v; PW [680–681]. For Rolleston see NA MS DD4P/58/25; Hulse, "The King's Entertainment."

65. SL c2r–v, 1. Various commentators have tried to identify Margaret's correspondent with a real person—especially her maid, Elizabeth Topp—but Margaret states that she wrote "only to herself" (SL d1r), and the two correspondents clearly embody different aspects of her own personality. The form of words with which the letters end, "your faithful friend and servant," also indicate that Margaret was writing to a social equal, not a servant.

66. For one of the close parallels between Flecknoe's and Margaret's books, cf. Flecknoe, *A Relation of Ten Years Travell*, 125, 134, with SL 177–179. For some of Flecknoe's views on literary topics, very similar to those expressed by Margaret in SL, see Doney, "Life and Works of Richard Flecknoe," 423–424, 450, 453, and passim. For Flecknoe's continuing connection with the Newcastles, see Flecknoe, *Enigmaticall Characters* (1658), A4r–v, 103–104.

67. SL c2r–v.

68. SL 87, 48, 175, 229, 120–123.

69. SL 103.

70. SL 5–6, 2–3, 366, 72–74.

71. SL 359–360.

72. SL 402–408.

73. SL 396–401. For discussion of these letters, see Fitzmaurice, "Margaret Cavendish in Antwerp."

74. SL 153–155, 223–225, 207–208, 266–269.

75. SL 311–315. Also SL 378 for Margaret's governess.

76. NUL MS PwV 90, ff. 83v–85v, 88–90, 91v, 97r, 196r.

77. SL 23–26, 69, 169, 223, 233, 409, 234.

78. SL 69, 103–105, 120–123, 422–424.

79. SL 409; LWN 63.

80. SL 69.

81. SL 237, 192, 218, 105, 9.

82. SL 113, 61, 97, 131, 180.

83. SL 326, 48–49.

84. SL 208, 212, 40.

85. SL d2r; PW A5a; PNBP, *The Presence*, 3.

86. PW, [681].

87. SL 295–296.

CHAPTER 11:
RESTORATION, 1658–1662

The presentation copy of William's advice to Charles II is Bodleian MS Clarendon 109. There are three published editions of the work:

Strong, *Catalogue*

Slaughter, ed., *Ideology and Politics*

Anzilotti, ed., *An English Prince*

The account of the journey to Welbeck derives from:

BL Harleian MS 4955, ff. 61r–68r

Camden, *Britannia*, 482–4

Defoe, *Tour*, II, 141–6, 155

Fiennes, *Journeys*, 71–4

Percival, *The English Travels*, 96–9.

The description of the house at Welbeck is based on these sources and on:

Girouard, *Robert Smythson*

William Senior's survey map of 1629, held at Welbeck (NA MS DDP/Newcastle Maps for reproductions)

Two drawings by Samuel Hieronymus Grimm (BL Addit. MS 15545, ff. 64–9)

Illustrations in Cavendish, *Méthode et Invention Nouvelle*

Raylor and Bryce, "A Manuscript Poem on the Royal Progress of 1634"

Flecknoe, *Farrago*, 10–12.

1. *CSPD 1656–1657*, 11; Clarendon, *Calendar*, III, 120.

2. Cavendish, *A New Method*, c2r; LWN 62–63.

3. LWN 61; Clarendon, *Calendar*, III, 154.

4. BL Addit. MS 70499, ff. 351v, 353, 357; LWN 65; NA MS DDP/29/5; SL 409; LWN 61.

5. NA MS DD4P/22/146, pp. 11–12, 15–16; LWN 64–65. For Margaret's financial acumen, see Bodleian MS Clarendon 47, f. 146.

6. LWN 63.

7. Highfill, Burnim, and Langhams, *A Biographical Dictionary of Actors*.

8. Huygens, *Briefwisseling*, V, 302.

9. PRO SP 77/32, ff. 29, 30, 32. *CSPD* prints only two of these three letters and mistranscribes "my Lady Marques['s] moor" and "my lord[']s moor" as "my Lady Marchioness Moore" and "Lady Moore" (*CSPD 1657–1658*, 296–297,

311). The "moor" is clearly referred to as "him" however (PRO SP 77/32, f. 30, transcribed in *CSPD 1657–1658*, 311).

10. PRO SP 77/32, f. 29; *CSPD 1657–1658*, 300, 311; PRO SP 77/32, f. 47.

11. SL 369–372. The identities of the king and Lord Ormonde are suggested here by Margaret's use of the initials G.K. and L.O.

12. *Nicholas Papers*, IV, 110–111, 124–125 (also printed in LWN 208–209).

13. Bodleian MS Clarendon 67, f. 150.

14. LWN 65, 100. For dating William's composition of this advice, see Condren, "Casuistry to Newcastle," 165, 173. A date of late 1659 or early 1660 is confirmed by the text's reference to William having "been very sickly of late" (Slaughter, ed., *Ideology and Politics*, 71): cf. William's letter of December 8, 1659, to Edward Hyde, saying "I have been very sick of late, but I thank God I begin now to be restored." Bodleian MS Clarendon 67, f. 150.

15. Cf. LWN Book IV.

16. Trease, *Portrait of a Cavalier*, 178.

17. *CSPD 1658–1659*, 374.

18. HL Ellesmere MS 8048.

19. NUL MS Pw1 371–382; BL Addit. MS 70499, f. 351v.

20. SL 183–187; NUL MS Pw1 78.

21. BL Addit. MS 70499, f. 355.

22. LWN 70; BL Addit. MS 70499, ff. 351–355.

23. NUL MS Pw1 78; BL Addit. MS 70499, ff. 351–355.

24. BL Addit. MS 70499, ff. 351–355.

25. *CSPD 1659–1660*, 378.

26. Clarendon, *Calendar*, V, 1.

27. LWN 65–66.

28. LWN 66–67.

29. Journals of the House of Lords: 1660–1666, passim; HMC, *5th Report*, 155a, 177b.

30. LWN 67; NUL MSS Pw1 407, 408. For Shaw, see Ollard, *Clarendon*, 145.

31. Burke and Burke, *The Extinct and Dormant Baronetcies of England*; Clarendon, *Calendar*, IV, passim. Brown, *An Account of Several Travels*, 31, however, suggests this Mr. Hartopp may have been a relative, rather than Francis himself.

32. LWN 65; *Nicholas Papers*, IV, 110–111; BL Addit. MS 70499, f. 357.

33. NUL MSS Pw1 407, 408.

34. For items carried back to Welbeck, see Percival, *The English Travels*, 98; NUL MS Pw1 668 (in Rolleston's hand); Cavendish, *Méthode et Invention Nouvelle* (1737), "Avertissement sur Cette Seconde Edition," A1v.

35. LWN 66–68.

36. Evelyn, *Diary*, 111, 246.

37. LWN 59; NP 126; SL 343.

38. LWN 68.

39. HMC, *7th Report*, I, 135a; NA MS DD4P/78/4.

40. Walter, *Understanding Popular Violence*, 332–333.

41. James Deane's 1748 map of Colchester, printed in Morant, *History and Antiquities of Colchester*.

42. Cokayne, *Complete Peerage*.

43. LWN 68.

44. Evelyn, *Diary*, 111, 248

45. Hulse, "The King's Entertainment."

46. LWN 101.

47. NUL MS PwV 19, p. 3; Ballard, *Memoirs of Several Ladies*, 284–285.

48. HL Ellesmere MS 8367.

49. *CSPD 1667–1668*, 570, 607.

50. LWN 68–69.

51. Defoe, *Tour*, II, 155.

52. Flecknoe, *Farrago*, 10–11; Evelyn, *Diary*, 111, 126–127.

53. LWN 70, 80.

54. Raylor and Bryce, "A Manuscript Poem"; LWN 70, 80.

55. NA MSS DD4P/63/5, DD4P/58/33–35.

56. LWN 70.

57. *CSPD 1648–1649*, 268–269, 272; *CSPD 1649–1650*, 204, 217; LWN 58; NA MS DD4P/70/1.

58. LWN 79, 70–71; NA MS DDP/27/23.

59. LWN 69, 70, 75, 79.

60. NUL MSS Pw1 601, 602; NA MSS DD4P/35/18–19, DDP/42/65, DD4P/22/188, DDP6/1/17/49.

61. LWN 80–81; NA MSS DD4P/58/33, 34, 36, 38; LWN 81.

62. Bodleian MS Ashmole 1110, f. 171.

63. Ellis, *A Sermon Preached*, A2r–v.

64. Appleby, *Our Fall*, 158–163.

65. Bodleian MS Ashmole 1110, f. 171; Ellis, *A Sermon Preached*, A4r–v. William at least traveled

south briefly in July 1661: Kennett, *Register*, 494. Thereafter the Newcastles seem only to have visited London in 1665 and 1667.

66. SL 167, 56–62, 168. SL 9–10, 169, 206, 226–229, 331–332, 449–452 continue the theme.

67. LWN 70; NUL MSS Pw1 388–391; NA MS DD4P/63/3.

68. NA MS DD2P/24/73, pp. 3–4.

69. BL Addit. MS 70500, ff. 3, 5; NUL MSS Pw1 392, 502; NA MSS DDP/121/7–8, DD4P/63/40.

70. NA MS DD2P/24/73. See also NUL MSS Pw1 592, 449.

71. NUL MSS Pw1 434, 468; NA MS DDP/53/14. Also NUL MSS Pw1 446, 448, 451, 480, 486, 500, and passim.

72. NA MS DD2P/24/73, p. 3.

73. Information derived from NUL MSS Pw1 425–427, 450, 485, 487, 592; NA MSS DD4P/54/54–61, DD4P/63/4, DD4P/70/1; Strong, *Catalogue of Letters*, 56.

74. SL 377–378; NUL MSS Pw1 595, 670. Also NUL MSS Pw1 316, 327, 502–503, 506–507 and NA MSS DD4P/58/68/6, DD4P/58/69/4, DD4P/58/70/3 for Mrs. Perkins and Mrs. Evans.

75. NA MSS DD4P/58/37, DD4P/58/69/2. Clayton was replaced as steward of the grange farm by Edward Bilbie in 1663.

76. Information derived from NUL MSS Pw1 16, 18, 19, 507, 670–671; NA MSS DD4P/58/37–39, DD4P/58/50–65, DD4P/58/68–70; Strong, *Catalogue of Letters*, 56–57; BL Addit. MS 70499, ff. 3–5.

77. For Rolleston, see NUL MSS Pw1 487, 592; Hulse, "The King's Entertainment"; Cavendish, *Dramatic Works*, xxi.

78. NA MSS DD4P/78/4, DD4P/35/21–23, DDP6/1/16/67–69.

79. PPO2 "To his Excellencie"; LWN 100; SL b1r.

80. SL b1v; PPO2 "To his Excellencie."

81. SL b1r; Or a1r–v.

82. LP 67–68, 82–83; PW A3a, A3d.

83. PW [683]; NP 399–402.

84. LWN xliv; LP 108; Plomer, *Dictionary of Booksellers and Printers*, I, 196.

85. LP 77–82.

86. SL 52–54.

87. SL 367–368; Or a3r. See also Sutherland, "Aspiring to the Rhetorical Tradition."

88. Or a3v; SL c2r.

89. Or 81–88.

90. SL c1v–c2r.

91. Or A4r.

92. LP 80–82; Or a2v, B1v.

CHAPTER 12:
REVISIONS AND CONTROVERSIES,
1663–1667

For works consulted on Margaret's philosophy, see notes to chapter 8.

Information on the buildings and grounds of Welbeck and Bolsover comes from:

Girouard, *Robert Smythson*

Worsley, *Bolsover Castle*

Raylor, " 'Pleasure Reconciled to Virtue' "

Illustrations in Cavendish, *Méthode et Invention Nouvelle*

William Senior's plans (NA MS DDP/Newcastle Maps)

Hulse, "Apollo's Whirligig"

Brown, "Courtesies of Place"

College of Arms MS, Francis Bassano's Derbyshire Church Notes, f. 37.

The account of the 1660s building work is based on the first two of the above and on:

NA MSS DD2P/24/73, DD4P/70/1

NUL MSS Pw1 487, 592, 595, 624, 669

Strong, *Catalogue*, 56–57 (This letter can be dated by comparison with NUL MSS Pw1 501, 669).

Principal works consulted on *The Blazing World*:

Kegl, " 'The world I have made' "

Lilley, "Blazing Worlds".

1. NP 399–400. For her philosophical writings, see NP, 287–317, 393; PW, "Youth's Glory and Death's Banquet"; SL 329, 333–334 and passim.

2. NUL MS Pw1 484.

3. PaF A6r.

4. LWN xxxvi.

5. PPO B2r, B4v.

6. PPO 169, B1r; PaF A6r; PL b2r; LWN xxxvi.

7. NUL MS Pw1 592/2. See also NUL MSS Pw1 16, 20, for other sizeable purchases by Benoist for Margaret. The common price range for "genteel" reading (as opposed to ballads and chapbooks) was 3 to 8 shillings for a bound book. Margaret's LWN cost 4s. 6d. in 1667, including carriage to Cumbria (HMC, *12th Report,* Appendix, VII, 377). Occasional luxury volumes could cost significantly more: Speed's *Theatre of Great Britain,* illustrated with maps, cost 40 shillings in 1627. See Johnson, "Notes on English Retail Book-Prices." Margaret's breadth of reading is also suggested by the early eighteenth century sale catalogue of books from the Welbeck library (Holles, *Bibliotheca Nobilissimi Principis Johannis Ducis de Novo-Castro*). This includes (pp. 34, 40) books that were almost certainly Margaret's: she had commented on Havers's translation of *A General Collection of Discourses of the Virtuosi of France* and on works by Henry More and Robert Hooke in her philosophical writings, and she had received John Evelyn's *Sylva* as a gift from the author. Many of the other English books listed in the catalogue had probably also belonged to her.

8. SL c1v; LWN xxxvi.

9. PPO 1–2, 47–49.

10. PPO 96.

11. PPO 1–2, 6, 11, 12–13.

12. SL c1v. For examples of misplaced punctuation destroying her meaning, see PPO 33, 42, 105.

13. PL b1v–b2r, c1r, c1v.

14. A few surviving sections are PPO2 1–2, 5–6, 12.

15. PPO2 27.

16. PPO2 71–72.

17. For instance, chapters 2 to 7 of Part 5 covered the topics of chapters 137, 107, 108, 126, and 87 of Part 3 of the original edition.

18. PPO 81–83; PPO2 215–217. Other changes of opinion appear in PPO2 151–152, 154.

19. PPO 174.

20. PPO2 374.

21. PPO2 203–204, 236, 239–241.

22. For example, PPO2 1–2, 154.

23. Cf. PPO 74, 75 with PPO2 153, 155.

24. PPO2 136–137, 284–287, 396–397.

25. Cf. PPO 33, 42, 155–156, with corrections, PPO2 100, 113, 410–412.

26. PPO2 73, 123–124, 249–251: the latter is reprinted from PPO 99–101.

27. PPO2 Nnn1r–v, d2v.

28. PPO2 b3v–4v, d2v.

29. LP 6–7, 12–14, 68–69, 93–95, 133–135.

30. SL 161–162; PPO a2.

31. Mayne, *Part of Lucian,* A2r; LP 93–97; Tully's copy of PPO2, now in the British Library, classmark 8407.h.9; Wood, *Athenae Oxonienses*; III, 920 for Harmer; idem, *Fasti,* II, 281 for Bristow.

32. PPO a2.

33. PNBP, "To the Readers"; SL c1r.

34. PaF A8r, A8v, 7.

35. For example, cf. PaF 6, 8, 20 with PaF2 6, 11, 27.

36. For example, cf. PaF2 c4r, d4v with PaF A8r, v.

37. LP 10–12.

38. SL 169.

39. SL 120, 136–137, 274–276, 283–288.

40. SL 51–53, 62–64, 108–111, 389–391.

41. SL 39–40, 160–161.

42. SL 145, 173, 259.

43. SL 257–260, 301–305, 338, 244–248.

44. *The Riverside Shakespeare,* 1847.

45. SL 297–298. See also PPO2 b1v; PL a1r.

46. SL 452; PL b1r–v.

47. PL 411, 107.

48. PL 164, 145.

49. PL 220, 230–231.

50. PL 1.

51. PL 239–242, 375, 351.

52. PL 529.

53. SL 259.

54. PL a1r–v, b1v.

55. PL b1v. See also WO 15, 20; SL 84, 172.

56. PL 245, b1r, c1r. See also PL 17.

57. LP 3–5, 17–20, 90–91; Nicolson, ed., *The Conway Letters,* 233–234, 237.

58. *CSPD 1661–1662,* 569, 586; BL Addit. MS 70500, ff. 7, 15, 20; NUL MSS Pw1 329–330; NA MS DDP6/1/27/18.

59. HMC, *Hastings Manuscripts,* II, 152; HMC, *Heathcote Manuscripts,* 191.

60. See *CSPD 1666–1667,* 305, 365; Henning, *History of Parliament*; Cokayne, *Complete Peerage*; NA MS DD4P/35/21; NUL MS Pw1 174.

61. NA MS DD4P/35/29, pp. 1–2.

62. This portrait has been variously attributed to Lely and to van Diepenbeeck (see Margaret Cavendish, *Lives*, ed. Lower, x), but Margaret's appearance in formal court dress in the fashion of the 1660s argues that it was painted in England after the Restoration, rather than in Antwerp. For Lely's portraiture see Millar, *Sir Peter Lely*. The vase in the portrait contains orange tree branches, bearing both flowers and fruit: Goulding, *Margaret (Lucas) Duchess of Newcastle*, 40.

63. *CSPD 1664–1665*, 497, 503; *Hatton Correspondence*, 47. For ladies' riding dress, see Pepys, *Diary*, VI, 172 and n.4; VII, 162; Wood, *Life and Times*, for 1665.

64. Flecknoe, *Farrago*, 13, 11; *Epigrams of All Sorts*, 40.

65. Flecknoe, *Farrago*, 10, *2a–b.

66. Flecknoe, *Epigrams of all Sorts*, 41; SL 169.

67. LWN 112; NUL MS Pw1 316, p. 5; BW 110.

68. LWN 112; PL 41; Flecknoe, *Farrago*, 10–11. For William's development of Parkinson's Disease's characteristic handwriting—shaking, cramped, with the lines rising to the right—see NUL MSS Pw1 391, 528; BL Althorp MS C1 (currently unfoliated).

69. NA MS DD4P/58/70/3; Cavendish, *A New Method*, 10–11.

70. Flecknoe, *Farrago*, 28; SL 121–122; NA MS DD2P/24/73, pp. 35ff.

71. Flecknoe, *Heroick Portraits*, "The Portrait of the Author."

72. Cavendish, *Dramatic Works*; Hulse, "The King's Entertainment"; NUL MS PwV 23, ff. 13–15v; Dryden, *Works*, ed. Loftis, IX, 352–364; Cavendish, *A New Method*, (b)1r; Sönmez, "English Spelling in the Seventeenth Century," I, 88–90.

73. NUL MSS Pw1 671–672; LWN 112; TR 173; SL 309, 323.

74. Flecknoe, *Farrago*, 11; Or 234.

75. LWN 113; Evelyn, *Diary and Correspondence*, IV, 8.

76. PaF 89–90.

77. Ben Jonson's masque of *Pleasure Reconciled to Virtue*. This was performed at court in 1618, the same year that William visited London to purchase paintings and carvings for Bolsover (NUL MS Pw1 553).

78. BW 110.

79. Shadwell, *Epsom Wells*, the dedication.

80. Hutchinson, *Memoirs of Colonel Hutchinson*, 116–117. LWN 218–219. Cf. Defoe, *Tour*, I, 148.

81. Or 234–235.

82. BL Althorp MS C13; BL Addit. MS 70500, f. 25; *CSPD 1664–1665*, 558; Reresby, *Memoirs*, 55–56.

83. LWN 83; NUL MSS Pw1 171, 9, 442.

84. CSPD *1661–1662*, 35; *CSPD 1663–1664*, 421; NA MSS DDP/17/137, DDP/27/29, DD2P/27/2, DD4P/75/11, DD4P/75/42, DD4P/75/48, DDSK/229/1; NUL MSS Pw1 283, 328.

85. BL Althorp MS C13: letter of August 10, 1665. Information also derived from BL Addit. MS 70500, ff. 9–10, 17, 39, 40; CSPD *1663–1664*; CSPD *1665–1666*.

86. NUL MS Pw1 254. Information also derived from *CSPD 1661–1662*; *CSPD 1663–1664*; Henning, *History of Parliament*; BL Althorp MS C1 (items currently unnumbered). For Henry's influence in court and Parliament, see also NUL MSS Pw1 52, 111–112, 190, 191/1.

87. BL Althorp MS C1: Henry's letters to George Savile, dated April 22, September 1, 1665, and May 26, [1665–1667].

88. BL Addit. MS 70500, f. 13.

89. BL Althorp MS C1, letter dated September 1, 1665; BL Addit. 70500, ff. 30–31.

90. BL Addit. MS 70500, f. 17.

91. NA MSS DD4P/54/66, DDP6/4/1/3.

92. BL Addit. MS 70500, ff. 26, 33, 35, 37.

93. SL 27–28.

94. Or 232.

95. SL 17, 216; LWN 141.

96. NUL MSS Pw1 592, 31; NA MSS DD2P/24/73, DD4P/58/68/6.

97. Slaughter, ed., *Ideology and Politics*, 42–44; LWN 121; NA MSS DDP/92/7, DD4P/52/181, DD4P/63/38, DD4P/79/104; NUL MS Pw1 630b.

98. For example, NUL MSS Pw1 428, 473, 630b; NA MS DD4P/63/39.

99. NA MSS DDP/53/16, DD4P/52/167, DD4P/52/288; NUL MSS Pw1 480, 495, 496, 630.

100. NUL MSS Pw1 167, 428, 446, 669; NA MS DD4P/63/23.

101. LWN 111; NA MSS DDP/53/16, DD4P/79/10, DD4P/63/9, DD4P/58/68/6, DD4P/58/69/4; NUL MSS Pw1 470, 520.

102. NUL MSS Pw1 513, 475. Also NUL MSS Pw1 428–429, 454, 473–474, 476, 504, 514; NA MSS DD4P/52/288, DD4P/63/20.

103. Or 234–235.

104. NUL MSS Pw1 520, 505–506, 520. Also NUL MSS Pw1 515–517.

105. BL Addit. MS 70500, ff. 3–6; NUL MSS Pw1 255–256.

106. NUL MSS Pw1 25, 165–166, 265.

107. The grand settlement and related papers are NA MSS DDP/29/21, DD4P/29/23, DDP6/1/12/4, DDP6/1/16/70; NUL MSS Pw1 47, 256. Papers relating to Henry's settlements on his children are NA MS DDP6/1/12/5; NUL MSS Pw1 44, 70.

108. SL 220–221.

109. LWN 108, 121–141.

110. SL 233–234.

111. SL 383–386; OEP 30–32; PPO2 459–464.

112. Or a1r; PPO2 "To his Excellencie."

113. GNP A2v.

114. PW A6c; PaF2 A2r.

115. PL, "To her Excellency"; OEP, "To her Grace the Duchess of Newcastle.

116. PL 495–496.

117. OEP d1r, 1–9.

118. OEP c2v, 10–12, d1r, 10–11.

119. OEP, "Further Observations," 1–2; OEP c2r.

120. BW b*1v.

121. OEP b1v; BW b*2r.

122. BW, "The Second Part," 32; BW 13.

123. BW 17.

124. BW 28, 53, 43.

125. BW 89–90, 92.

126. BW 101.

127. BW 111, 122–123.

128. BW "The Second Part," 20.

129. BW b*2r, 93–94.

130. BW 98; BW, "The Second Part," 121; BW 98.

131. BW b*2r; BW, "The Second Part," 121–122.

132. BW b*2r, b*1r; BW (issued separately from the OEP), "The Preface."

133. OEP q2v.

134. LWN xli.

135. LWN 1; SL 342. See also LWN xxxix–xliii.

136. For some other examples of Margaret's biased reporting, see Perry, *The First Duchess of Newcastle*, 12–14, 81.

137. LWN xliii, xlvii–xlviii for Rolleston's involvement.

138. LWN 79, 93, xxxiv. See also LWN 64, 92, 94, 98, 135.

139. LWN xxxv, xli, 94, 91.

140. Fitzmaurice, "Margaret Cavendish on her own Writing," 302–304.

141. For contemporary patterns of biography, see Wendorf, *Elements of Life*.

142. Pepys, *Diary*, IX, 123.

143. MacCarthy, *Women Writers*, 94–102.

CHAPTER 13:
THE TALK OF THE TOWN, 1667

Unless otherwise stated in the following notes, all information and quotes relative to the Newcastles' visit to London in 1667 are derived from:

Evelyn, *Diary*, III, 478–83

Pepys, *Diary*, VIII, 137, 163–4, 186–7, 196–7, 209, 242–4

Letter from Mary Evelyn to Ralph Bohun, printed in Evelyn, *Diary and Correspondence*, IV, 8–9

John Evelyn's letter to Margaret, printed ibid., IV, 244–6

Letters from Walter Charleton and Lord Berkeley, LP 108–118, 120–2.

For Margaret's visit to the Royal Society:

Pepys, *Diary*, VIII 242–3

Evelyn, *Diary*, III, 482–3

Birch, *History of the Royal Society*, II, 175–8

Minutes of the meeting of the Society's Council on May 23, 1667, as printed in Nicolson, *Pepys' Diary and the New Science*

Walter Charleton's "A Short Harangue Designed to be made to the President of the Royal Society", Bodleian MS Smith 13, pp. 21–3.

John Evelyn's comic ballad, PRO SP 29/450/102.

For the interpretation of Margaret's costumes and behavior in this and the previous chapter, I am most grateful for the generously given comments of Susan North at the Victoria and Albert Museum and Joanna Marschner at Kensington Palace. I have also consulted the following:

Campbell, *Robes of the Realm*

Mansfield, *Ceremonial Costume*

Ribeiro, *Dress and Morality*

Waugh, *The Cut of Women's Clothes*

Cunnington and Cunnington, *Handbook of English Costume in the Seventeenth Century*

Wildeblood and Brinson, *The Polite World*.

1. BL Addit. MS 37998, f. 241.

2. Pinks, *History of Clerkenwell*; Trease, *Portrait of a Cavalier*, 62; NA MSS DDP6/1/27/16–17. Newcastle House was demolished c. 1793: its internal layout is reconstructed here from the standard floor-plan of English Palladian houses.

3. HMC, *7th Report*, Appendix, I, 135a; NA MSS DD4P/78/4, DD4P/54/66, DD2P/10/1.

4. NA MS DD2P/24/73, pp. 3–9, 36, DD4P/58/68/6.

5. SL 280–283; TR 168–169. See also WO 87–88.

6. SL 90; WO 18–19.

7. WO E4r; SL 281, 442.

8. PW 565; SL 450, 348.

9. PW A5a; SL 255–256.

10. TR 151–152; SL 443.

11. TR 152.

12. WO 23.

13. SL 243.

14. Evelyn, *Diary and Correspondence*, IV, 31–32. For the relationship of Margaret and Mary Evelyn, see Harris, "Living in the Neighbourhood of Science."

15. WO 86; PNBP, *The Presence*, 39–40; NUL MS Pw1 31.

16. SL 261; WO 87; PW 90.

17. BW, "The Second Part," 25–26.

18. Pepys, *Diary*; Bodleian MS North, c. 4, f. 146; Van Lennep, ed., *The London Stage*, 108.

19. Bodleian MS North, c. 4, f. 146.

20. HMC, *12th Report*, Appendix, VII, 47; SL 261–262.

21. Hamilton, *Memoirs*, I, 171–172.

22. Pepys, *Diary*, VIII, 173–175; VII, 326.

23. Evelyn, *Diary*, III, 479–480; Pepys, *Diary*, VIII, 177.

24. HMC, *12th Report*, Appendix, VII, 47.

25. Whitelocke, *Journal*, I, 232.

26. HL, Hastings MS 7657, as quoted in Van Lennep, ed., *The London Stage*, 108.

27. Pepys, *Diary*, V, 262.

28. Cf. the plans for entertaining Charles II at the Society: Shapin and Schaffer, *Leviathan and the Air Pump*, 30–32.

29. SL 417.

30. *CSPD 1667–1668*, 602.

31. Marvell, "The Last Instructions to a Painter about the Dutch Wars, 1667," l. 50.

32. HMC, *12th Report*, Appendix, VII, 47, 49; Bodleian MS North, c. 4, f. 146; HL Hastings MS 7657.

33. Evelyn, *Diary*, III, 484–485; Pepys, *Diary*, VIII, 260–274; NUL MS Pw1 12.

34. NUL MS Pw1 12; NA MS DD2P/24/73, pp. 9, 82.

35. NA MSS DDP6/1/27/16–17, dated January 15, 1668.

Chapter 14: Queen of Philosophers, 1667–1673

For Margaret's philosophy see works cited in previous chapters, and:

Rogers, *The Matter of Revolution*.

Information on Margaret's printers comes from:

Plomer, *Dictionary of Booksellers and Printers*

Morrison, *Index of Printers, Publishers and Booksellers*.

Works consulted on Margaret's plays are listed in the notes to chapter 10.

1. LP 25–27, 23–25, 104–105.

2. See PL a1r and PPO2 b1v for "grounds."

3. For example, GNP 1, 2, 4, 7, 8.

4. GNP 4.

5. GNP 6, 17, 61, 222.

6. PPO2 276; GNP 75–76.

7. GNP 226. See also 25, 55, 174.

8. GNP A2r. This dedication is discussed in Sarasohn, "Margaret Cavendish and Patronage."

9. LP 23–25, 110; NUL MS Pw1 609; PPO a2; Wood, *Athenae Oxonienses*, IV, 755; LP 110. See BL Sloane MS 3413 for Charleton's wide reading.

10. LP 75–77, 131–132.

11. LP 67–68, 66; SL 162. Also LP 143.

12. LP 90–91; Nicolson, ed., *The Conway Letters*, 237.

13. LP 67–68, 77–79, 131. Duplicate copies of Margaret's books from the earl of Bridgewater's library are now in the British Library.

14. LP 100–101, 120–122; Evelyn, *Diary and Correspondence*, IV, 244–246 (this letter is wrongly dated 1674).

15. GNP A2r–v.

16. LP 1; Huygens, *Briefwisseling*, V, 312; Grant, *Margaret the First*, 218.

17. LP 66, 67, 70–71.

18. LP 90–91, 93–94; LWN xliv. Fitzmaurice, "Margaret Cavendish on her own Writing," details the distribution of Margaret's books in Oxford and Cambridge libraries and the extent and nature of handmade corrections. For Margaret's own handmade additions to a much earlier volume, see BL copy of PaF: classmark C39h27.

19. HMC, *12th Report,* Appendix, VII, 377; Pepys, *Diary*, IX, 123–124.

20. LP 23–25; Flecknoe, *Euterpe Revived*, 13; LP 104.

21. Evelyn, *Diary and Correspondence*, IV, 244–245; LP 117–118; Bodleian MS Smith 13, pp. 21–23; LP 136; Lloyd, *Memories*, 474. For other similar expressions, see LP 19–20, 26–28, 70–71, 80–82, 101, 103.

22. LP 162–163; BL Addit. MS 34217, f. 17. For biographical information, see *DNB*; Newman, *Royalist Officers*.

23. Evelyn, *Diary and Correspondence*, IV, 32. For Jinner, see Mendelson, *Mental World*, 60.

24. Makin, *Essay*, 10.

25. LP 19–20, 115.

26. LP 147–149, 67–68. See also LP 113–115.

27. LP 2, 93, 4, 34, 152. For "princeps," see Glare, ed., *Oxford Latin Dictionary*, 1458.

28. *OED*.

29. LP 111–112, 115, 165.

30. Evelyn, *Diary and Correspondence,* IV, 9; idem, *Numismata*, 265.

31. As quoted in Perry, *The First Duchess of Newcastle,* 179; Grant, *Margaret the First*, 129–130. Both copies were viewed in the Huntington Library.

32. Barlow's copy of the PhF (Bodleian Library, classmark Art 8° n.2). Thomas Tully's copy of PPO2 (British Library, classmark 8407.h.9) contains a similar note: "ex dono nobilissimae heroinae autoris."

33. LP 70–71. Biographical information from *DNB*.

34. BL Sloane MS 1950, ff. 35–38v. Grew copied in its entirety the poem with which Margaret closed her book. For Robert Hooke's interest in Margaret's philosophy, see Rostenberg, *The Library of Robert Hooke,* 185.

35. PL c1r; OEP d1r–v.

36. PL c1v; OEP d1v; PL c1r.

37. Nicolson, ed., *The Conway Letters*, 237.

38. Du Verger, *Du Verger's Humble Reflections,* the epistle; PL c1r–v.

39. LP 135–136.

40. See PL 8–11, 13–17, 95–96, 141–142, 164.

41. PL 195, 160–161; Ray, *The Wisdom of God*.

42. WO 46.

43. WO 81. See also PNBP, *The Sociable Companions*, 5.

44. BL Addit. MS 70499, f. 198v. See also Hulse, "Apollo's Whirligig," 223–225; *Hartlib Papers, 30/4/2A (Ephemerides 1639)*.

45. PL 227; 298.

46. Glanvill's letters (in probable chronological order): LP 135–136, 137–142, 104–105, 123–127, 102–103, 85, 98–100. Other letters of Glanvill's have been lost (see LP 85), as has Margaret's side of the correspondence.

47. See Rogers, *The Matter of Revolution,* 194–195 and passim; Clucas, "The Duchess and the Viscountess". Margaret's influence on contemporary philosphers and theologians may have been considerable: other, similarly unnamed, references to her theories quite possibly remain to be discussed.

48. The dedications of Dryden's *An Evening's Love* and Shadwell's *The Sullen Lovers, The Humourists, Epsom Wells, The Virtuoso, The Libertine;*

LP 127–130, 135–136, 122–123, 167. For a poem dedicated to Margaret before 1665 by William Sampson, see BL Harleian MS 6947, ff. 318–336.

49. LP 78–79, 29–31, 122–123, 78–79.

50. LWN 75, 79; NA MSS DDP/15/53, DDP/29/24, DD2P/24/63–71, DD4P/22/195, DD4P/35/25, DD4P/63/33; NUL MSS Pw1 19, 260–262, 407–408.

51. LWN 75–79.

52. Henry's calculation is NA MS DD4P/54/66. Margaret's calculation is not as significantly inflated as previous historians have argued on the basis of NUL MS Pw1 331. This, naming John Smithson as one of William's bailiffs, must date from well before the Civil War and so cannot be directly compared with Margaret's figures.

53. LWN 81; NA MS DD2P/27/61; CSPD *1667–1668*, 570, 607; *CSPD 1668–1669*, 83.

54. LWN 104.

55. SL 125; Or 235. See also SL 377; TR 165.

56. Bilbie's accounts are NA MSS DD4P/58/68–70. Other MSS: NA MS DD4P/63/31; NUL MSS Pw1 494, 316, p. 1. The only evidence of Margaret's involvement in the estates before 1667–1668 shows her in dispute with the parson at Bothal (part of her jointure estates) over who had the right to collect the tithes: NUL MS Pw1 512, dated April 1663.

57. NUL MS Pw1 25, 428–429, 432, 515, 516, for replacing tenants and commissioners. NUL MS Pw1 407–408, 507–508; NA MS DD2P/24/73; Evelyn, *Diary and Correspondence*, IV, 246, for London business. Topp's London connections had also perhaps achieved better deals when William wanted to sell lands: cf. NA MS DD2P/10/1 with NUL MS Pw1 463 for sale of the Sutton estate.

58. NUL MSS Pw1 327, 506, 503, 256; NA MS DDP6/1/16/65.

59. *CSPD 1666–1667*, 220; *CSPD 1667*, 235, 348; *CSPD 1667–1668*, 467, 514.

60. NUL MS Pw1 90. See also BL Addit. MS 70500, f. 51.

61. For Henry's political business: NA MSS DDP6/1/1/75, DDP6/1/21/8; NUL MSS Pw1 11, 109, 115, 191; *CSPD 1665–1666*, 475–476; *CSPD 1666–1667*, 384, 412; *CSPD 1670*, 253, 276, 357; *CSPD 1671*, 297; *CSPD 1673–1675*,

222, 312; Newman, *Royalist Officers*; Cokayne, *Complete Peerage*; Henning, *History of Parliament*. For his finances: NUL MSS Pw1 27, 28, 103–105, 168, 326; NA MSS DDP/1/8, DDP/7/14, DDP/83/13, DD4P/41/21, DDP6/1/13/2, DDP6/1/8/2.

62. BL Addit. MS 70500, ff. 53, 85.

63. NA MSS DD4P/58/69/1, DD2P/24/73, pp. 16–21. Benoist's purchases for Margaret: NUL MSS Pw1 16–21.

64. NUL MS Pw1 316, p. 2; NUL MS Pw1 73. The grand settlement is NA MS DDP6/1/12/4. Woods sold in 1668: DD2P/28/43, DD4P /63 /26.

65. NUL MS Pw1 316, p. 2; NA MS DD4P/75/51, pp. 1–5 (whose accusations against William are supported by NA MSS DDP/ 17/137–8, DDP/29/14–16, DDP/29/18–20, DDP/29/25–26, DD2P/22/4, DD4P/75/48).

66. DD2P/24/73, p. 103 and passim; BL Addit. MS 70500, f. 110.

67. BL Addit. MS 70499, f. 355. Henry could afford to begin building work at Welbeck only after he had largely fulfilled the requirements of his father's will regarding building at Nottingham Castle: NA MS DDP6/7/2/238.

68. NA MSS DD2P/27/59, DD4P/35/24, DDP6/1/27/16–17, DDP6/1/27/19, DDP6/ 1/27/21–22 for Margaret's jointures. The opposition of William's family to these settlements can be gauged from the fact that they were no longer appointed trustees, as they had been for Margaret's first jointure in 1662. Some of the later jointures were semisecret, witnessed only by loyal servants like Topp and Proctor, who also acted as the trustees.

69. NUL MS Pw1 316, p. 2.

70. See Hannay, "O Daughter Heare."

71. For Clayton's former graft, see NUL MSS Pw1 26, 434, 439, 468, 480, 492.

72. NUL MS Pw1 316, pp. 1–2.

73. NUL MS Pw1 316, pp. 2–3.

74. NUL MSS Pw1 430, 461, 316, p. 1 for Liddell's history. MSS Pw1 25, 26, 432 for Booth.

75. NUL MS Pw1 316, pp. 1–2. Clayton's likening of Margaret to Bess of Hardwick would ring real alarm bells for his friends. Bess had become notorious in the Midlands for her ruthless estate management, enclosing common land

and thereby leaving local villagers to go hungry; see Durant, *Bess of Hardwick*, 16, 108.

76. NUL MS Pw1 316, pp. 3–5.

77. NUL MS Pw1 316, pp. 4–6. Much of the content of Booth's confession can be confirmed both from other surviving estate manuscripts (which substantiate at least part of what he reports Clayton as saying about Margaret's involvement in the estates) and from internal evidence in the confession (for instance, as cosignatory Liddell corroborates Booth's accusations against himself). For Clayton's flight: NA MS DD2P/24/73, pp. 23, 27.

78. NUL MS Pw1 15; BL Addit. MS 70500, f. 59. For the JP, James Chadwick, see NA MS DD4P/75/51, p. 5 and passim.

79. NUL MS Pw1 317.

80. NA MS DD2P/24/73 is Clayton's petition to the lord keeper. Other evidence in support of Clayton's claims is contained in NUL MS Pw1 621 (a particular of books and papers found in Andrew Clayton's chamber at Welbeck, December 1671), NUL MS Pw1 592 (a particular of moneys paid to Clayton, totaling £8,209, extracted from Rolleston's estate accounts), and NA MS DD4P/54/61 (a particular of moneys Clayton received from Evidence House, "as appears under his hand," for the period 1661–1668, totaling £14,952).

81. PRO SP 29/335/216, 29/337/159, 29/293/64. These manuscripts are partially printed in *CSPD 1671*, 508 (this letter is misdated 1671); *CSPD 1673*, 288; *CSPD 1673–1675*, 4–5. For Northumberland enemies of Booth's, see also NUL MSS Pw1 25, 26, 432, 516.

82. NUL MS Pw1 316, p. 5.

83. NA MSS DD4P/35/29, DD3P/1/1.

84. BL Addit. MS 70500, f. 51. This letter must date from 1670 or after, since it refers to hopes of Henry and Frances's eldest daughter Elizabeth, duchess of Albemarle being pregnant, and she did not marry until December 1669. The continued presence of Elizabeth and Frances Topp at Welbeck until 1671 is argued by Frances's ownership of a copy of Margaret's NP2, published in 1671 (this copy is now in the Brotherton Library at the University of Leeds). See NA MSS DD4P/35/29, DD3P/1/1 for Topp's embezzlement and William's final payment of the debt himself. For the Topps' subsequent history: will

of Sir Francis Topp, PRO PROB 11/351; will of Dame Elizabeth Topp, PRO PROB 11/472, sig. 176.

85. *CSPD 1671*, 426. NA MSS DDP/15/55, DD2P/28/46, DD3P/7/2–3, DDP/15/56, DDP6/1/16/73 for the spate of wood sales in the period September 1671 to July 1672.

86. NUL MS Pw1 538. NA MS DD4P/22/201 for Henry's kindness to Clayton; DD4P/68/2–8 for their dispute in 1687; DDP/114/81–82, DDP/42/68 for Clayton's later employment at Welbeck. Clayton died in 1703 (International Genealogical Index).

87. PRO SP 29/246/145 (partially printed in *CSPD 1667–1668*, 602). See *CSPD 1670*, 522 for another, later visitor.

88. Reresby, *Memoirs*, 75; Dryden, *An Evening's Love*, the dedication. See also, Reresby, *Memoirs*, 55–56, 92.

89. Thomas Lawrence, "An Elegy on the death of . . . Lady Jane," NUL MS PwV 19, p. 3. See also, Flecknoe, *A Collection of the Choicest Epigrams*, 13; HL Ellesmere MS 8348.

90. HMC, *12th Report*, Appendix, VII, 78; LP 107–108; NUL MS Pw1 16. For Benoist's work for William and Henry in London, see NUL MSS Pw1 15–22; *CSPD 1671*, 377.

91. For the play's basis in William's earlier work, and for Shadwell's contributions, see Cavendish, "A Pleasante & Merrye Humor," ed. Needham; Hulse, "The King's Entertainment," 375–383.

92. These omitted sections are WO 125, 127–128, 148; NP 148–149. NP2 also omits the partial prose version of her PaF atomism that Margaret had printed in NP 157–158.

93. WO [136]. Evidence of Benoist's purchases for Margaret: NUL MSS Pw1 16, 20, 592. For further discussion of the differences between the first and second editions of these books, see Hobby, "'Delight in a Singularity'".

94. NUL MS Pw1 17; GNP 225.

95. NUL MSS Pw1 16, 20 for Benoist's purchases. For Margaret's possible revision of her plays, see Fitzmaurice, "Margaret Cavendish on her own Writing," 298–299. Margaret's composition of new poems is suggested by eighteenth-century reports that three folio volumes of her manuscript verses then survived (see Perry, *The First Duchess of Newcastle*, 171, 287; Fitzmaurice,

"Some Problems," 254–255). These volumes have all since been lost. However, given the rarity of Margaret's published volumes by the mid–eighteenth century, they could have been handwritten copies of her PaF made after her death, rather than original manuscripts of works newly written at the end of her life.

96. College of Arms MS I.31, f. 66.

97. SL 327–328, 449. See also SL 215; PhF A4r.

98. NUL MSS Pw1 31, 327.

99. SL 266, 237, 226. Also Mayerne's advice: NUL PwV 90, f. 115r.

100. WO 202; SL 237–238; PaF 108. Also SL 80–82, 178.

101. SL 177–178, 237–238; OEP, "Observations upon the Opinions of Some Ancient Philosophers," 1; GNP 75–76; PPO 53; PaF 53. For similar sentiments see also SL 104, 228, 296, 299, 348, 429; PW A7c; PPO B3r.

102. College of Arms MS I.31, ff. 64–66; BL Addit. MS 12514, ff. 290, 297.

103. LP 165–180. The original presentation manuscript of Clement Ellis's epitaph is BL Egerton MS 2603, f. 68.

104. The volume probably preserves only a small portion of Margaret's correspondence. For some surviving letters that were not included see: Bodleian MS Clarendon 45, f. 409; Evelyn, *Diary and Correspondence*, IV, 244–246 (letter probably dated 1670); Huygens, *Briefwisseling*, V, 286–287; VI, 293; NUL MS Pw1 481. The fact that Margaret distributed her books very widely round Oxford and Cambridge colleges after the Restoration (see Fitzmaurice, "Margaret Cavendish on her own Writing," 300, for details) suggests that she would have received many more letters of thanks from learned institutions than were included in the book. In 1675 a new edition of Margaret's *Life of William*—one of her most admired books—was also published, almost certainly by William's arrangement.

105. NUL MS Pw1 74.

106. BL Addit. MS 70500, f. 69. See also NUL MS Pw1 36.

107. NUL MSS Pw1 172–173. For young Henry's time in France see also NUL MS Pw1 108; BL Addit. MS 70500, f. 69; *CSPD 1673–1675*, 262, 239.

108. NUL MSS Pw1 543–544. For the match, see also BL Addit. MS 70500, f. 57 (probably dating from 1674 not 1671: cf. NUL MS Pw1 192); NUL MSS Pw1 192–207, 410, 623. For Elizabeth Percy's history, see Fraser, *The Weaker Vessel*, 280–282.

109. For William's purchase of the site: NUL MS Pw1 441; NA MSS DD4P 60/16–17; LWN 70–72. For the building itself: Percival, *The English Travels*, 97–98; Fiennes, *Journeys*, 72–73; Defoe, *Tour*, I, 144; Camden, *Britannia*, 487; Dugdale, *Life, Diary and Correspondence*, 418–419; Vertue, *Notebooks*, II, 33.

110. The plays were licensed for publication in February 1677: Arber, ed., *The Term Catalogue*, I, 267. In March 1677 Henry paid Shadwell £22 for this printing: NA MS DDP6/7/2/238. Another dedication to William in these last years was from William Petty: Petty, *A Discourse Made Before the Royal Society*, A3r–12v; BL Addit. MS 72850, ff. 140, 216.

111. William's dated poems are NUL PwV 25, ff. 84r–130r: of these ff. 90r–92r contain the visions of Margaret.

112. Dugdale, *Life, Diary and Correspondence*, 418–419. See also BL Egerton MS 3330, f. 57. William's will is preserved in NA MS DDP6/1/19/30 and PRO PROB 11/353.

113. BL Egerton MS 3330, f. 57; *CSPD 1677–1678*, 545; BL Addit. MS 12514, f. 100.

114. PRO PROB 11/353; BL Addit. MS 37998 f. 241. Also, for the funeral: BL Addit. 12514, ff. 98, 100–101.

115. For the monument, see Parry, "Cavendish Memorials." BL Addit. MS 12514, f. 100 establishes that it was erected by William before he died.

Epilogue

Imortant discussions of Margaret's place in historical tradition, which I have consulted:

Ezell, *Writing Women's Literary History*

Perry, *The First Duchess of Newcastle*

Cavendish, *The Convent of Pleasure*, ed. Shaver, the introduction.

1. *Poems on Affairs of State* (1697), 220–221. For critical commentary on the verse, see Lord,

ed., *Poems on Affairs of State*, I, 327.

2. As he certainly did another epitaph (copied from All Hallows Church, Derby) that is preserved in the same volume of his manuscripts.

3. The poem survives in Bodleian MS Ashmole 36, f. 186v, and MS Ashmole 1463, f. 62b. This second volume, in John Stainsby's hand, also includes epitaphs on Sir Kenelm Digby and William Prynne, and a verse satire "Upon Clarendon House." For information on Stainsby, see Black, *Catalogue of the Manuscripts bequeathed . . . by Elias Ashmole* and the MSS cited there. For Margaret's otherwise unspotted reputation for chastity, see BW, "The Second Part," 26; LP 115.

4. Langbaine, *An Account of the English Dramatic Poets*, 390–391, 394; Jacob, *The Poetical Register*, I, 190–192; Ballard, *Memoirs*, 301; Cibber, *Lives*, II, 165.

5. Ballard, *Memoirs*, 299–301; Cibber, *Lives*, II, 162–165. The incorrect identification of Margaret's father, often repeated by later historians, derived from Joducus Crull's *Antiquities of St Peter's, or the Abbey-Church of Westminster*.

6. Cibber, *Lives*, II, 163–164.

7. For the origins of these stories, see Perry, *The First Duchess of Newcastle*, 74–75, 286–287, 306–307. The story of Rolleston is clearly apocryphal: he was William's secretary, not Margaret's, and he lived five miles away from Welbeck at Sookholme.

8. SL 226; OEP b1v; Wilkins, *The Discovery of a New World in the Moon*, 209–210.

9. LP 165–170.

10. Stodart, *Female Writers*; Dyce, ed., *Specimens of British Poetesses*, iii–iv; Halsted, *The Obligations of Literature*, 96–97.

11. Jenkins, ed., *The Cavalier and His Lady*, 26; Margaret Cavendish, *Select Poems*, ed. Brydges; Town, "A Vision of Female Poets." For the tradition that Margaret's poem had influenced Milton, see Perry, *The First of Duchess of Newcastle*, 177–178. For further discussion of biographies and anthologies of women writers produced during the eighteenth and nineteenth centuries, see Ezell, *Writing Women's Literary History*.

12. Gosse, *Seventeenth Century Studies*; Robertson, *English Poetesses*. See also MacCarthy, *Women Writers*, 29–30; Naess, "Mad Madge and other 'Lost' Women," 198.

13. Brydges's preface to Margaret's autobiography, as reprinted in Margaret Cavendish, *Lives*, ed. Lower, 256, 263, 255, 259, 258, 257.

14. Lamb, *Essays of Elia*, 224, 105–106, 37 ("Detached Thoughts on Books and Reading," "Mackery End, in Hertfordshire," "The Two Races of Men"). Also ibid., 160 ("A Complaint of the Decay of Beggars").

15. Lamb, *Letters*, II, 138; idem, *Essays of Elia*, 160; Lucas, *The Life of Charles Lamb*, 531, as quoted in Margaret Cavendish, *The Convent of Pleasure and Other Plays*, ed. Shaver, 16, n. 21.

16. Jenkins, ed., *The Cavalier and His Lady*, 24, 8, 5.

17. Perry, *The First Duchess of Newcastle*, 230; note by James Crossley in BL Addit. MS 32497, f. 1; Longueville, *The First Duke and Duchess of Newcastle*, as quoted in Margaret Cavendish, *The Convent of Pleasure and Other Plays*, ed. Shaver, 8. For similar comments, see also Ward, *A History of English Dramatic Literature*.

18. Halsted, *The Obligations of Literature*, 114; Dyce, ed., *Specimens of British Poetesses*, 88.

19. Jenkins, ed., *The Cavalier and His Lady*, 8; Margaret Cavendish, *Select Poems*, ed. Brydges; Sir Samuel Egerton Brydges's preface to Margaret's autobiography, as reprinted in Margaret Cavendish, *Lives*, ed. Lower, 256, 263.

20. Colman and Thornton, eds., *Poems by Eminent Ladies*, 198; Town, "A Vision of Female Poets."

21. Costello, *Memoirs of Eminent Englishwomen*; Robertson, *English Poetesses*, 15.

22. Halsted, *The Obligations of Literature*, 114; Crossley's note, dated November 13, 1850, in BL Addit. MS 32497, f. 1.

23. Margaret Cavendish, *Lives*, ed. Lower, ix.

24. Pepys, *Diary*, IX, 123.

25. NUL MS Pw1 316, p. 5; Lamb, *Letters*, II, 138.

26. Walpole, *A Catalogue of the Royal and Noble Authors* (1806), III, 190, n.

27. Evelyn, *Diary and Correspondence*, IV, 8. Dorothy Osborne's comment on Margaret— "there are many soberer persons in Bedlam"— was not published until much later in the nineteenth century.

28. Scott, *Peveril of the Peak*, 182, 569.

29. Cokayne, *Complete Peerage*, IX, 525, n.

30. Perry, *The First Duchess of Newcastle*, 265, 4 (bis), 262–263, 3, 1, 237 (bis), 288.

31. Woolf, *A Room of One's Own*, 39, 54.

32. Walpole, *Catalogue* (1759), II, 13–14; Jenkins, *The Cavalier and his Lady*, 20; Brydges's preface to TR, as printed in Margaret Cavendish, *Lives*, ed. Lower, 255. See also Dyce, ed., *Specimens of British Poetesses*, 89.

33. Woolf, *The Common Reader*, 81; idem, *A Room of One's Own*, 51; idem, *The Common Reader*, 86; idem, *A Room of One's Own*, 52.

34. Woolf, *The Common Reader*, 82; *A Room of One's Own*, 51–52.

35. Grant, *Margaret the First*, 206–208, 195; GNP A2v; Grant, *Margaret the First*, 227. For some similar views, see also MacCarthy, *Women Writers*, 81–82, 123–124, 130–131; Nicolson, "'Mad Madge' and the Wits" in idem, *Pepys' Diary and the New Science*.

36. Woolf, *The Common Reader*, 85–86; Mendelson, *Mental World*, 43; Manuel and Manuel, *Utopian Thought in the Western World*, 7.

37. See Findlay, Williams, and Hodgson-Wright, "'The Play is Ready to be Acted.'"

38. Salzman, ed., *An Anthology of Seventeenth-Century Fiction*.

39. Rees, "Introduction," 321; Gardiner and Wenborn, eds., *The History Today Companion to British History*, 485.

Bibliography

1. Manuscript Sources

The Bodleian Library, Oxford

MSS Ashmole 36, 832, 1110. Manuscripts collected by Elias Ashmole.

MS Ashmole 1463. Papers of John Stainsby.

MSS Clarendon 39, 43, 45, 46, 47, 50, 67, 72. State papers collected by Edward Hyde, earl of Clarendon.

MS Clarendon 109. Presentation copy of the book of advice given to Charles II by William Cavendish, marquess of Newcastle.

MS North c. 4, f. 146. Letter from Charles North to his father, April 13, 1667.

MS Rawlinson Poet. 16. Literary works of Jane Cavendish and her sister, Elizabeth Egerton.

MS Smith 13. Papers of Walter Charleton.

The British Library, London

Additional MSS 4278, 4280. Letters and papers of Dr. John Pell, including his correspondence with Sir Charles Cavendish.

Additional MS 6032, ff. 127–129. Seventeenth century rules of precedence and etiquette.

Additional MS 12184. Dispatches of Sir Richard Browne, 1641–1644.

Additional MSS 12514, 37998. Papers of Sir Edward Walker, Garter King-of-Arms.

Additional MS 15545. Topographical drawings of S. H. Grimm

Additional MS 23206, f. 24. Latin bond for debts of William Cavendish, marquess of Newcastle.

Additional MS 28558, f. 65. Letter from Margaret Cavendish to Constantijn Huygens.

Additional MS 32497. "The Phanseys" of William Cavendish, marquess of Newcastle.

Additional MS 34217, ff. 16v-17. Poem addressed to Margaret Cavendish, Duchess of Newcastle, signed F.F. [Francis Fane].

Additional MSS 70499, 70500. Cavendish family papers (formerly classed as Portland Loan).

Additional MS 72850. Papers of Sir William Petty.

Althorp MSS C1. Correspondence of George, first marquess of Halifax (currently unfolioed).

Althorp MSS C13. Papers of Sir William Coventry (currently unfolioed).

Egerton MS 607. Loose papers left by Elizabeth Egerton, countess of Bridgewater.

Egerton MS 2603, f. 68. Epitaph for Margaret Cavendish, duchess of Newcastle, written by Clement Ellis.

Egerton MSS 3328, 3329, 3330. Correspondence of Thomas Osborne, earl of Danby.

Harleian MS 163. Sir Symonds D'Ewes's journal of the House of Commons.

Harleian MS 1542, ff. 58v–59r. Lucas family pedigree and arms.

Harleian MS 4955. Containing poems by Lancelot Andrews.

Harleian MSS 6002 and 6083. Mathematical papers, including many in the hand of Sir Charles Cavendish.

Harleian MS 6852, ff. 335–350. Royal commission appointing William, marquess of Newcastle as commander of planned risings in the North of England, 1650.

Harleian MS 6947, ff. 318–336. Poem by William Sampson, dedicated to Margaret Cavendish, marchioness of Newcastle.

Harleian MS 6988. Containing correspondence between William Cavendish, earl of Newcastle and Charles, Prince of Wales.

Sloane MS 1950. Miscellaneous tracts in the handwriting of Nehemiah Grew.

Sloane MS 3413. Commonplace book of Walter Charleton.

College of Arms, London

Bassano MS. Francis Bassano's Derbyshire Church Notes.

MS I.31, ff. 64–66. Funeral certificate of Margaret Cavendish, duchess of Newcastle.

Essex Record Office, Colchester

MSS D/Y 2/2–10. Containing various papers concerning the Lucas family.

MS D/ACW6/40. Will of Margaret's grandmother, Mary Lucas.

House of Lords, London

Braye-Teeling MS 11. Mayor Thomas Wade's letter to Harbottle Grimston, August 22, 1642.

Huntington Library, California

Ellesmere MS 8048. Letter from Elizabeth, Countess of Bridgewater to her sister, Lady Jane Cheyne, September 18 1659.

Ellesmere MS 8348. Funeral certificate of Elizabeth, countess of Bridgewater.

Ellesmere MS 8367. Poem by Elizabeth Egerton, written to her mother Elizabeth, countess of Bridgewater.

Ellesmere MS 11143. Account book of Lady Jane Cheyne.

Nottinghamshire Archives, Nottingham

MS DDHo 18/4. Parliamentary election returns at East Retford, November 1640.

MSS classed under DDP/Newcastle Maps. Maps of the Welbeck estates.

MSS classed under DD, DDP, DD2P, DD4P, DDP6. Correspondence and other papers, mainly relating to the Cavendish family's legal, political, financial, and estate business.

MS DDSK 229/1. Sherwood Forest Book: Pleas of the Forest, 1662-1676.

University of Nottingham, Department of Manuscripts and Special Collections

Portland MSS Pw1. Cavendish family letters and papers.

Portland MS PwV 19. Poems of Thomas Lawrence, containing his elegy on the death of William's daughter, Jane.

Portland MSS PwV 21, 22. William's draft of his manual on horsemanship.

Portland MSS PwV 23–6. Poems and dramatic works, mainly by William Cavendish, duke of Newcastle.

Portland MS PwV 90. "A book wherein is contained rare mineral receipts collected at Paris," in the hands of Thomas Farr and William Cavendish, duke of Newcastle.

The Public Record Office, London

PROB 11. Sixteenth- and seventeenth-century wills.

SO 3/2/62. Pardon granted to Margaret's father, 1603.

SP. State papers (domestic).

2 . WORKS BY MARGARET CAVENDISH, DUCHESS OF NEWCASTLE

The Blazing World and Other Writings. Ed. Kate Lilley. London, 1994.

CCXI Sociable Letters. London, 1664.

The Convent of Pleasure and Other Plays. Ed. Anne Shaver. Baltimore, 1999.

The Convent of Pleasure. Ed. Jennifer Rowsell. Oxford, 1995.

De Vita et Rebus Gestis Nobilissimi Illustrissimique Principis, Gulielmi Ducis Novo-Castrensis, Commentarii. London, 1668.

The Description of a New World, Called the Blazing World. London, 1666; 2nd ed. 1668.

Grounds of Natural Philosophy. London, 1668.

Grounds of Natural Philosophy. Ed. Collette V. Michael. West Cornwall, Conn., 1996.

The Life of the Thrice Noble, High and Puissant Prince, William Cavendishe, Duke, Marquess and Earl of Newcastle. London, 1667; 2nd ed. 1675.

The Life of the (1ˢᵗ) Duke of Newcastle and Other Writings. New York, 1916.

The Life of William Cavendish, Duke of Newcastle: To Which is Added the True Relation of my Birth, Breeding and Life by Margaret, Duchess of Newcastle, 2nd ed. Revised with additional notes. Ed. C. H. Firth. London, [1886?].

The Lives of William Cavendishe, Duke of Newcastle, and of his Wife, Margaret Duchess of Newcastle. Ed. Mark Anthony Lower. London, 1872.

Margaret Cavendish: Sociable Letters. Ed. James Fitzmaurice. New York, 1997.

Natures Pictures, Drawn by Fancy's Pencil to the Life. London, 1656; 2nd ed. 1671.

Observations upon Experimental Philosophy. Ed. Eileen O'Neill. Cambridge, 2001.

Observations upon Experimental Philosophy. To Which is Added, the Description of a New Blazing World. London, 1666; 2nd ed. 1668.

Orations of Divers Sorts, Accommodated to divers Places. London, 1662; Reprinted 1663; 2nd ed. 1668.

Paper Bodies: A Margaret Cavendish Reader. Ed. Sylvia Bowerbank and Sara Mendelson. Peterborough Ontario, 1999.

The Philosophical and Physical Opinions. London, 1655; 2nd ed. 1663.

Philosophical Fancies. London, 1653.

Philosophical Letters: or, Modest Reflections upon some Opinions in Natural Philosophy, Maintained by Several Famous and Learned Authors of this Age, Expressed by Way of Letters. London, 1664.

Plays Never Before Printed. London, 1668.

Plays Written. London, 1662.

Poems, and Fancies. London, 1653.

Poems and Phancies, 2nd ed. London, 1664.

Poems, or Several Fancies in Verse: with the Animal Parliament, in Prose, 3rd ed. London, 1668.

The Select Poems of Margaret Cavendish. Ed. Sir Samuel Egerton Brydges. Lee Priory, Kent, 1813.

The Sociable Companions; or, The Female Wits: A Comedy. Ed. Amanda Holton. Oxford, 1996.

A True Relation of the Birth, Breeding, and Life of Margaret Cavendish, Duchess of Newcastle by Herself. Ed. Sir Samuel Egerton Brydges. Lee Priory, Kent, 1814.

The Worlds Olio. London, 1655; 2nd ed. 1671.

3. OTHER WORKS

Anonymous. *Six Familiar Essays.* London, 1696.

Anzilotti, Gloria Italiano, ed. *An English Prince: Newcastle's Machiavellian Political Guide to Charles II.* Pisa, [1988].

Appleby, David. *Our Fall our Fame: The Life and Times of Sir Charles Lucas (1613–1648).* Newtown, 1996.

Arber, Edward, ed. *The Term Catalogues, 1668–1709,* 3 vols. London, 1903–1906.

Aubrey, John. *Brief Lives.* Ed. Oliver Lawson Dick. London, 1958.

Avery, Gillian. "The Beginnings of Children's Reading to c. 1700." In *Children's Literature: An Illustrated History,* ed. Peter Hunt. Oxford, 1995.

Babb, Lawrence. *The Elizabethan Malady: A Study of Melancholia in English Literature from 1580 to 1642.* East Lansing, Michigan, 1951.

Ballard, George. *Memoirs of Several Ladies of Great Britain who have been Celebrated for their Writings or Skill in the Learned Languages, Arts and Sciences.* Oxford, 1752.

Barley, M. W. "John Mazine and Manor Farm, Carburton." *Transactions of the Thoroton Society* 92 (1988), 51–58.

Battigelli, Anna. *Margaret Cavendish and the Exiles of the Mind.* Lexington, Kentucky, 1998.

Bedini, Silvio A. *Science and Instruments in Seventeenth Century Italy.* Aldershot, 1994.

———. *Patrons, Artisans and Instruments of Science 1600–1750.* Aldershot, 1999.

Beier, Lucinda McCray. *Sufferers and Healers: the Experience of Illness in Seventeenth Century England.* London, 1987.

Birch, Thomas. *The History of the Royal Society of London*, 4 vols. London, 1756–1757.

Black, William Henry. *Catalogue of the Manuscripts bequeathed . . . by Elias Ashmole*. Oxford, 1845.

Blaydes, Sophia B. "Nature is a Woman: The Duchess of Newcastle and Seventeenth-Century Philosophy." In *Man, God and Nature in the Enlightenment*, ed. Donald C. Mell, Jr., Theodore E. D. Braun, and Lucia M. Palmer, 51–64. East Lansing, Michigan, 1988.

Bligh, E. W. *Sir Kenelm Digby and his Venetia*. London, 1932.

Bowerbank, Sylvia. "The Spider's Delight: Margaret Cavendish and the 'Female' Imagination." *English Literary Renaissance* 14 (1984), 392–408.

Bradstreet, Anne. *The Tenth Muse*. London, 1650.

Brathwaite, Richard. *The English Gentlewoman*. London, 1641.

Brett-James, Norman George. *The Growth of Stuart London*. London, 1935.

Brodsley, Laurel, Sir Charles Frank, and J. W. Steeds. 'Prince Rupert's Drops.' *Notes and Records of the Royal Society* 41 (1986), 1–26.

Brown, Cedric C. "Courtesies of Place and Arts of Diplomacy in Ben Jonson's Last Two Entertainments for Royalty." *The Seventeenth Century* 9 (1994), 147–171.

Brown, Edward. *An Account of Several Travels Through a Great Part of Germany*. London, 1677.

Burke, John, and John Bernard Burke. *The Extinct and Dormant Baronetcies of England*. London, 1838.

Burton, Robert. *The Anatomy of Melancholy, 3 vols.*, Ed. A. R. Shilleto. London, 1926-1927.

Camden, William. *Camden's Britannia*. Ed. Edmund Gibson. London, 1695.

Campbell, Una. *Robes of the Realm: 300 Years of Ceremonial Dress*. London, 1989.

Carter, Matthew. *A True Relation of that Honourable though Unfortunate Expedition of Kent, Essex and Colchester in 1648*, 2nd ed. Colchester, 1789.

Cavendish, William, duke of Newcastle. *The Country Captaine, and the Varietie, Two Comedies, Written by a Person of Honor. Lately Pre-sented by His Majesty's Servants at the Black-Fryers*. London, 1649.

_____. *Dramatic Works by William Cavendish*. Ed. Lynn Hulse. Malone Society Reprints 158 (1996).

_____. *The Humorous Lovers*. London, 1667.

_____. *La Méthode Nouvelle et Invention Extraordinaire de Dresser les Chevaux*. Antwerp, 1658.

_____. *Méthode et Invention Nouvelle de Dresser les Chevaux*, 2nd ed. London, 1737.

_____. *A New Method and Extraordinary Invention, to Dress Horses*. London, 1667.

_____. *The Phanseys of William Cavendish, Marquis of Newcastle Addressed to Margaret Lucas and her Letters in Reply*. Ed. Douglas Grant. London, 1956.

_____. *A Pleasante & Merrye Humor off A Roge*. Ed. Francis Needham. Welbeck Miscellany 1 (1933).

Cerasano, S. P., and Marion Wynne-Davies, eds. *Renaissance Drama by Women: Texts and Documents*. London, 1996.

Chalmers, Hero. "Dismantling the Myth of 'Mad Madge': The Cultural Context of Margaret Cavendish's Authorial Self-presentation." *Women's Writing* 4 (1997), 323–339.

Chancellor, E. Beresford. *The Pleasure Haunts of London during Four Centuries*. London, 1925.

Charleton, Walter. *Physiologia Epicuro-Gassendo-Charltoniana. Or a Fabric of Natural Science Erected upon the Most Antient Hypothesis of Atoms*. London, 1654.

Chester, J. L., and George J. Armytage. *Allegations for Marriage Licences Issued by the Bishop of London, II: 1611–1828*. Harleian Society 26 (1887).

Cibber, Theophilus. *The Lives of the Poets of Great Britain and Ireland*, 5 vols. London, 1753.

Clarendon, Edward Hyde, earl of. *Calendar of the Clarendon State Papers Preserved in the Bodleian Library*, 5 vols. Ed. W. Dunn Macray et al. Oxford, 1869–1970.

_____. *Clarendon's Four Portraits*. Ed. Richard Ollard. London, 1989.

_____. *The History of the Rebellion and Civil Wars in England Begun in the Year 1641*, 6 vols. Ed. W. Dunn Macray. Oxford, 1888.

_____. *The Life of Edward, Earl of Clarendon*. Oxford, 1759.

_____. *State Papers Collected by Edward, Earl of Clarendon*, 3 vols. Oxford, 1767–1786.

Clucas, Stephen. "The Atomism of the Cavendish Circle: A Reappraisal." *The Seventeenth Century* 9 (1994), 247–273.

_____. "The Duchess and the Viscountess: Negotiations Between Mechanism and Vitalism in the Natural Philosophies of Margaret Cavendish and Anne Conway." *In-between: Essays and Studies in Literary Criticism* 9 (2000), 125–136.

Cocking, Helen Muriel. "Originality and Influence in the Work of Margaret Cavendish, First Duchess of Newcastle." M.Phil. thes., University of Reading, 1972.

Cokayne, G. E. *The Complete Peerage of England, Scotland, Ireland, Great Britain and the United Kingdom.* Revised ed. by Vicary Gibbs et al., 14 vols. London, 1910–1998.

A Collection of Letters and Poems: Written by Several Persons of Honour and Learning, Upon Divers Important Subjects, to the late Duke and Duchess of Newcastle. London, 1678.

Colman, George, Jr., and Bonnell Thornton, eds. *Poems by Eminent Ladies*, 2 vols. London, 1755.

Condren, Conal. "Casuistry to Newcastle: The *Prince* in the World of the Book." In *Political Discourse in Early Modern Britain,* ed. Nicholas Phillipson and Quentin Skinner, 164–186. Cambridge 1993.

Cooper, C. H., and T. Cooper. *Athenae Cantabrigienses*, 3 vols. Cambridge, 1858–1913.

Costello, Louisa Stuart. *Memoirs of Eminent Englishwomen.* London, 1844.

Crawford, Patricia. "Women's Published Writings 1600–1700." In *Women in English Society 1500–1800*, ed. Mary Prior, 211–282. London, 1985.

Cunnington, C. Willett, and Phillis Cunnington. *Handbook of English Costume in the Seventeenth Century*, 2nd ed. London, 1966.

Cust, Richard. *The Forced Loan and English Politics 1626–1628.* Oxford, 1987.

Daumas, Maurice. *Scientific Instruments of the 17th and 18th Centuries and their Makers.* Trans. Mary Holbrook. London, 1989.

Davies, Kathleen M. "Continuity and Change in Literary Advice on Marriage." In *Marriage and Society: Studies in the Social History of Marriage*, ed. R. B. Outhwaite, 58–80. London, 1981.

De la Serre, Puget. *Histoire de l'entrée de la reine mère dans la Grande-Bretagne.* Ed. Richard Gough. London, 1775.

Defoe, Daniel. *A Tour through the Whole Island of Great Britain*, 2 vols. London, 1974.

Depauw, Carl. *Rubens House, Antwerp.* Gent, n.d.

Dictionary of National Biography, ed. L Stephen and S. Lee. London, 1885–1912.

Donawerth, Jane. "Conversation and the Boundaries of Public Discourse in Rhetorical Theory by Renaissance Women." *Rhetorica* 16 (1998), 181–199.

Doney, Paul Herbert. "The Life and Works of Richard Flecknoe." Ph.D. diss., Harvard University, 1928.

D'Ormesson, Olivier Lefèvre. *Journal d'Olivier Lefèvre d'Ormesson.* Ed. M Chéruel. Paris, 1860.

Dryden, John. *An Evening's Love.* London, 1671.

_____. *The Works of John Dryden*, IX: *Sir Martin Mar-all.* Ed. John Loftis. Berkeley, 1966.

Du Bosc, Jacques. *La Femme heroïque, ou les heroïnes comparées avec les heros en toute sorte de vertus.* Paris, 1645.

Du Verger. *Du Verger's Humble Reflections upon some Passages of the Right Honourable the Lady Marchioness of Newcastle's Olio.* London, 1658.

Dugdale, William. *The Life, Diary and Correspondence of Sir William Dugdale.* Ed. W. Hamper. London, 1827.

Durant, David N. *Bess of Hardwick: Portrait of an Elizabethan Dynast.* London, 1988.

Dyce, Alexander, ed. *Specimens of British Poetesses.* London, 1827.

Eccles, Audrey. *Obstetrics and Gynaecology in Tudor and Stuart England.* Kent, Ohio, 1983.

Edmond, Mary. *Rare Sir William Davenant.* Manchester, 1987.

Edwards, A. C. *A History of Essex.* London, 1978.

Ellis, Clement. *A Sermon Preached on the 29th of May 1661.* Oxford, 1661.

Emmison, Frederick George, et al., eds. *Feet of Fines for Essex*, 6 vols. Oxford, 1899–1993.

Evans, Willa McClung. *Henry Lawes: Musician and Friend of Poets.* Modern Language Association of America Revolving Fund Series 11 New York, 1941.

Evelyn, John. *A Character of England*. London, 1659.

_____. *Diary and Correspondence of John Evelyn*, 4 vols. Ed. William Bray. London, 1854.

_____. *The Diary of John Evelyn*, 6 vols. Ed. E. S. De Beer. Oxford, 1955.

_____. *Numismata: A Discourse of Medals, Ancient and Modern*. London, 1697.

_____. *Sylva, or, A Discourse of Forest Trees and the Propagation of Timber in His Majesty's Dominions*, 2nd ed. London, 1670.

Ezell, Margaret J. M. "'To Be Your Daughter in Your Pen': The Social Functions of Literature in the Writings of Lady Elizabeth Brackley and Lady Jane Cavendish." *Huntington Library Quarterly* 51 (1988), 281–296.

_____. *Writing Women's Literary History*. Baltimore, 1996.

Fanshawe, Ann. *The Memoirs of Anne, Lady Halkett and Ann, Lady Fanshawe*. Ed. John Loftis. Oxford, 1979.

Faugère, A. P. *Journal d'un Voyage à Paris en 1657–1658*. Paris, 1862.

Faulkner, Patrick Arthur. *Bolsover Castle, Derbyshire*. London, 1972.

Faulkner, Thomas. *An Historical and Topographical Description of Chelsea*, 2 vols. Chelsea, 1829.

Fiennes, Celia. *The Journeys of Celia Fiennes*. Ed. Christopher Morris. London, 1947.

Filipczak, Zirka Zaremba. *Picturing Art in Antwerp 1550–1700*. Princeton, 1987.

Findlay, Alison, Gweno Williams, and Stephanie J. Hodgson-Wright. "'The Play is Ready to be Acted': Women and Dramatic Production, 1570–1670." *Women's Writing* 6 (1999), 29–48.

Findley, Sandra, and Elaine Hobby. "Seventeenth Century Women's Autobiography." In *1642: Literature and Power in the Seventeenth Century*, ed. Francis Barker et al., 11–36. Colchester, 1981.

Firth, Charles Harding, ed. "Letters of the Duke of Newcastle and Colonel Hutchison." *Notes and Queries* 7th Series, 8 (1889). 422–423.

_____, ed. "Verses on the Cavaliers Imprisoned in 1655 (by Sir John Denham?)." *Notes and Queries*, 7th Series, 10 (1890), 41–42.

Firth, Charles Harding, and Robert Sangster Rait, eds. *Acts and Ordinances of the Interregnum 1642–1660*, 3 vols. London, 1911.

Fitzmaurice, James, "Fancy and the Family: Self-characterizations of Margaret Cavendish." *Huntington Library Quarterly* 53 (1990), 199–209.

_____. "Margaret Cavendish on her own Writing: Evidence from Revision and Handmade Correction." *Papers of the Bibliographical Society of America* 85 (1991), 297–307.

_____. "Margaret Cavendish in Antwerp: the Actual and the Imaginary." *In-between: Essays and Studies in Literary Criticism* 9 (2000), 29–39.

_____. "Some Problems in Editing Margaret Cavendish" In *New Ways of looking at Old Texts: Papers of the Renaissance English Text Society, 1985–1991*, ed. W. Speed Hill, 253–261. Binghamton, NY, 1993.

_____. "Front Matter and the Physical Make-up of *Natures Pictures*." *Women's Writing* 4 (1997), 353–367.

Flecknoe, Richard. *Aenigmatical Characters. Being Rather a New Work than New Impression of the Old*. London, 1665.

_____. *A Collection of the Choicest Epigrams and Characters*. London, 1673.

_____. *The Damoiselles a la Mode. A Comedy*. London, 1667.

_____. *Enigmaticall Characters, All Taken to the Life*. London, 1658.

_____. *Epigrams of All Sorts: I Book*. London, 1669.

_____. *Epigrams of All Sorts, Made at Divers Times on Several Occasions, Being Rather a New Work than a New Impression of the Old*. London, 1671.

_____. *Euterpe Revived*. London, 1675.

_____. *A Farrago of Several Pieces, Newly Written*. London, 1666.

_____. *Heroick Portraits with other Miscellany Pieces, Made and Dedicate to his Majesty*. London, 1660.

_____. *Loves Kingdom. A Pastoral Trage-Comedy . . . With a Short Treatise of the English Stage*. London, 1664.

_____. *Miscellania, Or Poems of All Sorts, with Divers other Pieces*. London, 1653.

_____. *The Portrait of William Marquis of Newcastle. To his Lady, the Lady Marchionesse*. London, 1660.

_____. *A Relation of Ten Years Travell in Europe, Asia, Affrique, and America, All by Way of Letters*. London, [1656?].

_____. *A Treatise of the Sports of Wit*. London, 1675.

Foster, Joseph. *Alumni Oxonienses: The Members of the University of Oxford, 1500–1714*, 4 vols. Oxford, 1891–1892.

Fraser, Antonia. *The Weaker Vessel: Woman's Lot in Seventeenth-Century England*. London, 1984.

Fuller, Thomas. *The History of the Worthies of England*. London, 1662.

Gabrieli, Vittorio. *Sir Kenelm Digby*. Rome, 1957.

Gagen, Jean. "Honor and Fame in the Works of the Duchess of Newcastle." *Studies in Philology* 56 (1959), 519–538.

Gamble, John. *Ayres and Dialogues for One, Two and Three Voices. The Second Book*. London, 1659.

Gardiner, Juliet, and Neil Wenborn, eds. *The History Today Companion to British History*. London, 1995.

Gellius, Aulus. *Noctes Atticae*. Ed. Martin Hertz. Leipzig, 1871.

Gilbert, Sandra M., and Susan Gubar. *The Madwoman in the Attic: The Woman Writer and the Nineteenth-Century Literary Imagination*. New Haven, 1980.

Girouard, Mark. *Robert Smythson and the Elizabethan Country House*. London, 1983.

Glare, P. G. W., ed. *Oxford Latin Dictionary*. Oxford, 1982.

Gölnitz, Abraham. *Ulysses Belgico-Gallicus*. Amsterdam, 1655.

Gosse, Sir Edmund. *Seventeenth Century Studies: A Contribution to the History of English Poetry*, 2nd ed. London, 1885.

Gouge, William. *Of Domestical Duties, Eight Treatises*. London, 1626.

Goulding, Richard W. *Catalogue of Pictures Belonging to the Duke of Portland, K.G.* Cambridge, 1936.

_____. *Letters from the Originals at Welbeck Abbey*. London, 1909.

_____. *Margaret (Lucas) Duchess of Newcastle*. Lincoln, 1925.

_____. *The Welbeck Abbey Miniatures belonging to His Grace the Duke of Portland K.G., G.C.V.O: A Catalogue Raisonné*. The Walpole Society 4 (1916).

Graham, Elspeth, Hilary Hinds, Elaine Hobby, and Helen Wilcox, eds. *Her Own Life: Autobiographical Writings by Seventeenth Century Englishwomen*. London, 1989.

Grant, Douglas. *Margaret the First: A Biography of Margaret Cavendish Duchess of Newcastle 1623–1673*. London, 1957.

Green, Mary Anne Everett, ed. *Calendar of the Proceedings of the Committee for Advance of Money*. London, 1888.

_____, ed. *Calendar of the Proceedings of the Committee for Compounding*, 3 vols. London, 1889–1892.

Greer, Germaine, et al., eds. *Kissing the Rod: An Anthology of Seventeenth-Century Women's Verse*. London, 1988.

Guillim, John. *A Display of Heraldrie*. London, 1611.

Hackett, Helen. *Women and Romance Fiction in the English Renaissance*. Cambridge, 2000.

_____. "'Yet tell me some such Fiction': Lady Mary Wroth's Urania and the 'Femininity' of Romance." In *Women, Texts and Histories 1575–1760*, ed. Clare Brant and Diane Purkiss, 39–68. London, 1992.

Halliwell, James Orchard. *A Collection of Letters Illustrative of Science in England*. London, 1841.

Halsted, Caroline A. *The Obligations of Literature to the Mothers of England*. London, 1840.

Hamilton, Count Anthony. *Memoirs of the Count de Gramont*, 2 vols. Ed. Henry Vizetelly. London, 1889.

Hamilton, Elizabeth. *Henrietta Maria*. London, 1976.

Hannay, Margaret P. "'O Daughter Heare': Reconstructing the lives of Aristocratic Englishwomen." In *Attending to Women in Early Modern England*, ed. Betty S. Travitsky and Adele F. Seeff. Newark, DE 1994.

Harbage, Alfred. *Annals of English Drama 975–1700: An Analytical Record of all Plays, Extant or Lost, Chronologically Arranged and Indexed*. Revised ed. by S. Schoenbaum. London, 1964.

_____. *Cavalier Drama: An Historical and Critical Supplement to the Study of the Elizabethan and Restoration Stage*. London, 1936.

Harris, Frances. "Living in the Neighbourhood of Science: Mary Evelyn, Margaret Cavendish and the Greshamites." In *Women, Science and Medicine, 1500–1700: Mothers and Sisters of the Royal Society,* ed. Lynette Hunter and Sarah Hutton. Stroud, 1997.

The Hartlib Papers: A Complete Text and Image Database of the Papers of Samuel Hartlib (c.1600–1662). Ann Arbor, Mich., 1995.

Hatton Correspondence: Correspondence of the Family of Hatton. Ed. Edward Maunde Thompson. Camden Society, new series 22 (1878).

Hautecoeur, Louis. *Paris,* 2 vols. Paris, 1972.

Havers, G., trans., *A General Collection of Discourses of the Vituosi of France, Upon Questions of All Sorts of Philosophy, and Other Natural Knowledge.* London, 1664.

Henning, Basil Duke. *The History of Parliament: The House of Commons, 1660–1690,* 3 vols. London, 1983.

Henrietta Maria. *Letters of Queen Henrietta Maria.* Ed. Mary Anne Everett Green. London, 1857.

Hervey, Helen. "Hobbes and Descartes in the Light of some Unpublished Letters of the Correspondence between Sir Charles Cavendish and Dr. John Pell," *Osiris* 10, (1952), 67–90.

Heylyn, Peter. *France Painted to the Life.* London, 1656.

Hibbard, Caroline M. "The Role of a Queen Consort: the Household and Court of Henrietta Maria, 1625–1642." In *Princes, Patronage and the Nobility: The court at the beginning of the modern age c. 1450–1650,* ed. Ronald G. Asch and Adolf M. Birke, 393–414. Oxford, 1991.

Higgins, Patricia Mary, "Women in the English Civil War," MA thesis. University of Manchester, 1965.

Highfill, Philip H. Jr., Kalman A. Burnim, and Edward A. Langhams. *A Biographical Dictionary of Actors, Actresses . . . and other Stage Personnel in London, 1660–1800.* Carbondale, Ill., 1973–1993.

Historical Manuscripts Commission, *5th Report.* 1876.

———. *7th Report,* Appendix, Part I. 1879.

———. *10th Report,* Appendix, Part IV: *Manuscripts of the Earl of Westmorland.* 1885.

———. *10th Report,* Appendix, Part VI: *Braye Manuscripts.* 1887.

———. *11th Report,* Appendix, Part VII: *Manuscripts of the Duke of Leeds etc.* 1888.

———. *12th Report,* Appendix, Part VII: *Le Fleming Manuscripts. 1890.*

———. *12th Report,* Appendix, Part IX: *Manuscripts of the Duke of Beaufort.* 1891.

———. *13th Report,* Appendix, Part II: *Portland Manuscripts.* 1893.

———. *Heathcote Manuscripts, 1899.*

———. *Salisbury Manuscripts,* Part XII. 1910.

———. *Pepys Manuscripts.* 1911.

———. *Hastings Manuscripts,* Part II. 1930.

Hoak, D. E. *The King's Council in the Reign of Edward VI.* Cambridge, 1976.

Hobbes, Thomas. *Thomas Hobbes: The Correspondence,* 2 vols. Ed. Noel Malcolm. Oxford, 1994.

Hobby, Elaine. " 'Delight in a Singularity': Margaret Cavendish, Duchess of Newcastle, in 1671," *In-between: Essays and Studies in Literary Criticism.* (2000), 42-62.

———. *Virtue of Necessity: English Women's Writing 1646–1688.* London, 1988.

Hoff, Ursula. *European Paintings before 1800 in the National Gallery of Victoria.* Melbourne, c. 1995.

Holles, John, duke of Newcastle. *Bibliotheca Nobilissimi Principis Johannis Ducis de Novo-Castro etc., Being a Large Collection of Books, Contain'd in the Libraries of the Most Noble William.* William and Henry Cavendish, and John Hollis, Late Dukes of Newcastle. N.p., 1719.

Holmes, Clive. *The Eastern Association in the English Civil War.* Cambridge, 1974.

Hotson, Leslie. *The Commonwealth and Restoration Stage.* Cambridge, Mass., 1928.

Houdard, Georges. *Les Châteaux de Saint-Germain-en-Laye,* 2 vols. Saint Germain, 1910–1911.

Houlbrooke, Ralph. *English Family Life, 1576–1716: An Anthology from Diaries.* Oxford, 1988.

Hull, Suzanne W. *Chaste, Silent and Obedient: English Books for Women 1475–1640.* San Marino, Calif., 1982.

Hulse, Lynn. "Apollo's Whirligig: William Cavendish, Duke of Newcastle, and his Music Collection." *The Seventeenth Century* 9 (1994), 213–246.

———. "'The King's Entertainment' by the Duke of Newcastle." *Viator: Medieval and Renaissance Studies* 26 (1995), 355–405.

Hunt, William. *The Puritan Moment: the Coming of Revolution in an English County*. Harvard Historical Studies 102. Cambridge, Mass., 1983.

Hutchinson, Lucy. *Memoirs of the Life of Colonel Hutchinson*. Ed. Julius Hutchinson. London, 1899.

Hutton, Ronald. *Charles the Second*. Oxford, 1989.

Hutton, Sarah. "Anne Conway, Margaret Cavendish and Seventeenth Century Scientific Thought." In *Women, Science and Medicine 1500–1700: Mothers and Sisters of the Royal Society*, ed. Lynette Hunter and Sarah Hutton, 218–234. Stroud, 1997.

———. "In Dialogue with Thomas Hobbes: Margaret Cavendish's Natural Philosophy." *Women's Writing* 4 (1997), 421–432.

Huygens, Constantijn. *Correspondance et Oeuvres Musicales de Constantin Huygens*. Ed. W.J.A. Jonckbloet and J.P.N. Land. Leyden, 1882.

———. *Dagboek van Constantyn Huygens*. Ed. J.H.W. Unger. Amsterdam Oud-Holland Bijlage 3 (1885).

———. *De Briefwisseling van Constantijn Huygens (1608–1687)*, 6 vols. Ed. J. A. Worp. Rijks Geschiedkundige Publicatiën 15, 19, 21, 24, 28, 32. The Hague, 1911–1917.

———. *Mijn Jeugd*. Ed. C. L. Heesakkers. Amsterdam, 1987.

Huygens, Lodewijck. *The English Journal 1651–1652*. Ed. and trans. A.G.H. Bachrach and R. G. Collmer. Leyden, 1982.

Ingram, Randall. "First Words and Second Thoughts: Margaret Cavendish, Humphrey Moseley, and 'the Book'." *Journal of Medieval and Early Modern Studies* 30 (2000), 101–124.

Jacob, Giles. *The Poetical Register: Or the Lives and Characters of all the English Poets*, 2 vols. London, 1723.

Jacob, James R., and Timothy Raylor. "Opera and Obedience: Thomas Hobbes and 'A Proposition for Advancement of Moralitie' by Sir William Davenant." *The Seventeenth Century* 6 (1991), 205–250.

Jacquot, Jean. "Sir Charles Cavendish and his Learned Friends": I, "Before the Civil War"; II, "The Years of Exile." *Annals of Science 8* (1952), 13–27, 175–191.

Jenkins, Edward, ed. *The Cavalier and His Lady: Selections from the Works of the First Duke and Duchess of Newcastle*. London, 1872.

Johns, Adrian. *The Nature of the Book: Print and Knowledge in the Making*. Chicago, 1998.

Johnson, Francis R. "Notes on English Retail Book-Prices, 1550–1640." *The Library*, 5th series, 5 (1950), 83–112.

Jones, Kathleen. *A Glorious Fame: the Life of Margaret Cavendish, Duchess of Newcastle*. London, 1988.

The Journals of the House of Lords, 226 vols. London, 1509–1992/3.

Kargon, Robert Hugh. *Atomism in England from Hariot to Newton*. Oxford, 1966.

Kegl, Rosemary. "'The world I have made': Margaret Cavendish, Feminism, and the Blazing-World." In *Feminist Readings of Early Modern Culture*, ed. Valerie Traub, M. Lindsay Kaplan, and Dympna Callaghan, 119–141. Cambridge, 1996.

Kennett, White. *A Register and Chronicle Ecclesiastical and Civil*. London, 1728.

Kenyon, John P., ed. *The Civil Wars of England*. London, 1996.

———. *The Stuart Constitution, 1603–1688*, 2nd ed. Cambridge, 1989.

Killigrew, Anne. *Poems*. London, 1686.

The Kingdomes Weekly Intelligencer, 23 February to 2 March, 1646/7. *Thomason Tracts*, E378 (18).

The Kingdoms Intelligencer of the Affairs Now in Agitation in England, Scotland, and Ireland, Together with Foraign Intelligence. London, 1662.

Klibansky, Raymond, Erwin Panofsky, and Fritz Saxl. *Saturn and Melancholy: Studies in the History of Natural Philosophy, Religion, and Art*. London, 1964.

Kramer, Annette. "'Thus by the Musick of a Ladyes Tongue': Margaret Cavendish's Dramatic Innovations in Women's Education." *Women's History Review* 2 (1993), 57–79.

Lamb, Charles. *The Essays of Elia*. London, 1901.

_____. *The Letters of Charles Lamb: Newly Arranged, with Additions*, 2 vols. Ed. Alfred Ainger. London, 1888.

Langbaine, Gerard. *An Account of the English Dramatic Poets*. Oxford, 1691.

Lanyer, Aemilia. "The Description of Cookham." In *Early Modern Women's Writing: An Anthology, 1560–1700,* ed. Paul Salzman, 56–62. Oxford, 2000.

Lawes, Henry. *Ayres and Dialogues, for One, Two, and Three Voices . . . The First Book*. London, 1653.

_____. *The Second Book of Ayres, and Dialogues* London, 1655.

LeMoyne, Pierre. *La Gallerie des Femmes Fortes*. Paris, 1647.

Leters and Poems in Honour of the Incomparable Princess, Margaret, Dutchess of Newcastle. London, 1676.

Lilley, Kate. "Blazing Worlds: Seventeenth Century Women's Utopian Writing." In *Women, Texts and Histories 1575–1760*, ed. Clare Brant and Diane Purkiss, 102–133. London, 1992.

Lloyd, David. *Memories of the Lives of those that Suffered for their Sovereign*. London, 1668.

Longueville, Thomas. *The First Duke and Duchess of Newcastle-upon-Tyne*. London, 1910.

Lord, George DeF. et al., eds. *Poems on Affairs of State: Augustan Satirical Verse, 1660–1714*, I: *1660–1678*. Ed. George DeF. Lord. New Haven, Conn., 1963.

Lyly, John. *Euphues: The Anatomy of Wit*. London, 1578.

MacCarthy, B. G. *Women Writers: Their Contribution to the English Novel 1621–1744*. Cork, 1944.

Maclean, Ian. *Woman Triumphant: Feminism in French Literature 1610–1652*. Oxford, 1977.

Makin, Bathsua. *An Essay to Revive the Antient Education of Gentlewomen*. London, 1673.

Manley, Delarivière. *The Lost Lover*. London, 1696.

Mansfield, Alan. *Ceremonial Costume: Court, civil and civic costume from 1660 to the present day*. London, 1980.

Manuel, Frank, and Fritzie Manuel. *Utopian Thought in the Western World*. Cambridge, Mass., 1979.

Martinich, A. P. *Hobbes: A Biography*. Cambridge, 1999.

Marvell, Andrew, "The Last Instructions to a Painter About the Dutch Wars, 1667," In *The Works of Andrew Marvell,* ed. Andrew Crozier. Ware, Hertfordshire, 1995. 131–153.

Mason, Mary G. "The Other Voice: Autobiographies of Women Writers." In *Autobiography: Essays Theoretical and Critical,* ed. James Olney, 207–235. Princeton, 1980.

Mayne, Jasper. *Part of Lucian made English from the Original, in the year 1638*. Oxford, 1664.

Mendelson, Sara Heller. *The Mental World of Stuart Women: Three Studies*. Brighton, 1987.

Mendelson, Sara Heller, and Patricia Crawford. *Women in Early Modern England, 1550–1720*. Oxford, 1998.

Mercurius Aulicus, Communicating the Intelligence and Affairs of the Court to the Rest of the Kingdom. Oxford, 1643–1645.

Mercurius Belgicus: Or, a Brief Chronologie . . . from the Beginning of this Rebellion, to the 25 of March 1646. N.p., 1646.

Mercurius Candidus, Communicating the Weekly News to the Kingdom of England. London, 1646–1647.

Millar, Oliver. *Sir Peter Lely, 1618–1680: Exhibition at 15 Carlton House Terrace, London SW1*. London, 1978.

Monconys, Balthasar de. *Journal des Voyages de Monsieur de Monconys*, 3 vols. Lyons, 1666.

Montpensier, Anne Marie Louise d'Orléans, duchesse de. *Mémoires*, 4 vols. Ed. A. Chéruel. Paris, n.d.

Morant, Philip. *The History and Antiquities of the County of Essex*, 2 vols. London, 1768.

_____. *The History and Antiquities of the Most Ancient Town and Borough of Colchester*. Colchester, 1768. [The 1789 edition of this work omits much of the Lucas family history included in the first edition.]

Morrison, Paul G. *Index of Printers, Publishers and Booksellers in Donald Wing's Short-Title Catalogue*. Charlottesville, Va., 1955.

de Motteville, Françoise Langlois. *Memoirs for the History of Anne of Austria*, 5 vols. London, 1726.

Naess, Eli Lindtner. "Mad Madge and other 'Lost' Women: The Situation of the Woman Writer in Seventeenth Century England." *EDDA* 4 (1979), 197–209.

Newman, P. R. *Royalist Officers in England and Wales, 1642–1660: A Biographical Dictionary*. New York, 1981.

The Nicholas Papers: Correspondence of Sir Edward Nicholas, Secretary of State, 4 vols. Ed. G. F. Warner. Camden Society, new series 40, 50, 57, 3rd series 31 (1886–1920).

Nickolls, John, ed. *Original Letters and Papers of State, Addressed to Oliver Cromwell*. London, 1743.

Nicol, Alexander, ed. *Poems on Several Subjects, both Comical and Serious*. Edinburgh, 1766.

Nicolson, Marjorie Hope, ed. *The Conway Letters: The Correspondence of Anne, Viscountess Conway, Henry More and their Friends 1642–1684*. Revised ed. by Sarah Hutton. Oxford, 1992.

Nicolson, Marjorie Hope. *Pepys' Diary and the New Science*. Charlottesville, Va., 1965.

Norden, John. *Speculi Britanniae Pars: An Historical and Chorographical Description of the County of Essex . . . 1594*. Camden Society, 1st series 9 (1840).

Ollard, Richard. *Clarendon and his Friends*. Oxford, 1988.

Osborne, Dorothy. *Letters from Dorothy Osborne to Sir William Temple*. Ed. Edward Abbott Parry. London, 1903.

Parker, Thomas. *The Copy of a Letter Wrtiten by Mr. Thomas Parker, Pastor of the Church of Newbury in New England, to his Sister Mrs. Elizabeth Avery, Touching Sundry Opinions by her Professed and Maintained*. London, 1650.

Parry, Graham. "Cavendish Memorials." *The Seventeenth Century* 9 (1994), 275–287.

Payne, Linda R. "Dramatic Dreamscape: Women's Dreams and Utopian Vision in the Works of Margaret Cavendish, Duchess of Newcastle." In *Curtain Calls: British and American Women and the Theater, 1660–1820*, ed. Mary Anne Schofield and Cecilia Macheski, 18–33. Athens, Oh., 1991.

Pearson, Jacqueline. *The Prostituted Muse: Images of Women and Women Dramatists, 1642–1737*. Hemel Hempstead, 1988.

———. "'Women May Discourse . . . as Well as Men': Speaking and Silent Women in the Plays of Margaret Cavendish, Duchess of Newcastle." *Tulsa Studies in Women's Literature* 4 (1985), 33–45.

Pepys, Samuel. *The Diary of Samuel Pepys: A New and Complete Transcript*, 11 vols. Ed. Robert Latham and William Matthews. London, 1995.

Percival, Sir John. *The English Travels of Sir John Percival and William Byrd II*. Ed. Mark R. Wenger. Columbia, MO, 1989.

Perry, Henry Ten Eyck. *The First Duchess of Newcastle and her Husband as Figures in Literary History*. Harvard Studies in English 4. Boston, 1918.

Petersson, R. T. *Sir Kenelm Digby*. London, 1956.

Petty, William. *A Discourse made before the Royal Society The 26 November 1674. Concerning the Use of Duplicate Proportion in Sundry Important Particulars*. London, 1674.

Philips, Katherine. *The Collected Works of Katherine Philips, the Matchless Orinda*, 3 vols. I: *The Poems*; II: *The Letters*. Ed. Patrick Thomas. Stump Cross, 1990–1993.

Pinks, William J. *The History of Clerkenwell*. London, 1865.

Plomer, Henry R. *A Dictionary of Booksellers and Printers who were at Work in England, Scotland and Ireland*, I: *1641 to 1667*. London, 1907.

Poems on Affairs of State: From the Time of Oliver Cromwell to the Abdication of K. James the Second. Written by the Greatest Wits of the Age. London, 1697.

Pohl, Hans. *Die Portuguiesen in Antwerpen (1567–1648)*. Wiesbaden, 1977.

Price, Bronwen, "Feminine modes of knowing and scientific enquiry: Margaret Cavendish's poetry as case study," In *Women and Literature in Britain, 1500–1700*, ed. Helen Wilcox. Cambridge, 1996. 117–139.

Ralph, Philip Lee. *Sir Humphrey Mildmay: Royalist Gentleman: Glimpses of the English Scene 1633–1652*. New Brunswick, NJ, 1947.

Ranum, Orest. *Paris in the Age of Absolutism*. London, 1979.

Ray, John. *Observations Topographical, Moral and Physiological; Made in a Journey through Part of the Low-Countries, Germany, Italy and France*. London, 1673.

———. *The Wisdom of God Manifested in the Works of the Creation*. London, 1691.

Raylor, Timothy. "'Pleasure Reconciled to Virtue': William Cavendish, Ben Jonson and the Decorative Scheme of Bolsover

Castle." *Renaissance Quarterly* 52 (1999), 402–439.

Raylor, Timothy, and Jackson Bryce. "A Manuscript Poem on the Royal Progress of 1634: An Edition and Translation of John Westwood's 'Carmen Basileuporion'." *The Seventeenth Century* 9 (1994), 173–195.

Rees, Emma L. E. "Introduction." *Women's Writing* 4 (1997), 319–321.

———. " 'Sweet Honey of the Muses': Lucretian Resonance in *Poems, and Fancies*." *Inbetween: Essays and Studies in Literary Criticism* 9 (2000) 3–16.

Reresby, Sir John. *Memoirs of Sir John Reresby*. Ed. Andrew Browning. Glasgow, 1936.

Ribeiro, Aileen. *Dress and Morality*. London, 1986.

Rich, Mary, countess of Warwick. *Autobiography of Mary, Countess of Warwick*. Ed. T. C. Croker. London, 1848.

Rickwood, George. "Members of Parliament for Colchester, 1547–1558." *Essex Review* 4 (1895), 110–122.

Riggs, Timothy, and Larry Silver, eds. *Graven Images: The Rise of Professional Printmakers in Antwerp and Haarlem, 1540–1640*. Evanston, Ill., 1993.

The Riverside Shakespeare. Ed. Gwynne Blakemore Evans. London, 1974.

Robertson, Eric Sutherland. *English Poetesses: A Series of Critical Biographies with Illustrative Extracts*. London, 1883.

Rogers, John. *The Matter of Revolution: Science, Poetry and Politics in the Age of Milton*. London, 1996.

Rogers, Malcolm. *William Dobson 1611–1646*. London, 1983.

Rosenthal, Laura J. *Playwrights and Plagiarists in Early Modern England: Gender, Authorship, Literary Property*. London, 1996.

Rostenberg, Leona. *The Library of Robert Hooke: The Scientific Book Trade of Restoration England*. Santa Monica, CA, 1989.

Roth, Leon, ed. *Correspondence of Descartes and Constantijn Huygens, 1635–1647*. Oxford, 1926.

Rowe, Nick. "'My Best Patron': William Cavendish and Jonson's Caroline Drama." *The Seventeenth Century* 9 (1994), 197–212.

Roy, Ian. "The City of Oxford, 1640–1660." In *Town and Countryside in the English Revolution,* ed. R. C. Richardson, 130–168. Manchester, 1992.

Roy, Ian, and Dietrich Reinhart. "Oxford and the Civil Wars." In *The History of the University of Oxford*: IV: *Seventeenth-Century Oxford*, ed. Nicholas Tyacke, 687–731. Oxford 1997.

Ryves, Bruno. *Mercurius Rusticus or, The Country's Complaint of the Barbarous Outrages Committed by the Sectaries of this Late Flourishing Kingdom*. Oxford, 1646.

Salzman, Paul, ed. *An Anthology of Seventeenth-Century Fiction*. Oxford, 1991.

Salzman, Paul. *English Prose Fiction 1558–1700: A Critical History*. Oxford, 1985.

Sarasohn, Lisa T. "Margaret Cavendish and Patronage." *Endeavour* 23 (1999), 130–132.

———. "A Science Turned Upside Down: Feminism and the Natural Philosophy of Margaret Cavendish." *Huntington Library Quarterly* 47 (1984), 289–307.

Schellinks, William. *The Journal of William Schellinks in England*. Trans. Maurice Exwood and H. L. Lehmann. Camden Society, 5th series 1 (1993).

Schofield, Bertram, ed. *The Knyvett Letters, 1620–1644*. London, 1949.

Scott, Sir Walter. *Peveril of the Peak*. Oxford, 1911.

Scudéry, Madeleine de. *Artamenes, or The Grand Cyrus*. London, 1653.

Shadwell, Thomas. *Epsom Wells*. London, 1673.

———. *The Humorists*. London, 1671.

———. *The Libertine*. London, 1676.

———. *The Sullen Lovers*. London, 1668.

———. *The Virtuoso*. London, 1676.

Shapin, Steven, and Simon Schaffer. *Leviathan and the Air Pump: Hobbes, Boyle and the Experimental Life*. Princeton, 1985.

Sharp, Lindsay. "Walter Charleton's Early Life, 1620–1659." *Annals of Science* 30 (1973). 311–340.

Sheppard, F.H.W., ed. *Survey of London*, XXXVI: *The Parish of St. Paul, Covent Garden*. London, 1970.

Slaughter, Thomas P., ed. *Ideology and Politics on the Eve of Restoration: Newcastle's Advice to Charles II*. American Philosophical Society Memoirs 159 (1984).

Smith, Hilda, "'A General Law Amongst the Men . . . but None Amongst the Women': Political Differences between Margaret and William Cavendish," In *Politics and the Political Imagination in Later Stuart Britain: Essays Presented to Lois Green Schwoerer*, ed. Howard Nenner. Rochester, 1997.

Smuts, R. M. *The Culture of Absolutism at the Court of Charles I*. Ann Arbor, Mich., 1980.

Society of Antiquaries. *A Collection of Ordinances and Regulations for the Government of the Royal Household . . . from King Edward III to King William and Queen Mary*. London, 1790.

Somerset, Anne. *Ladies-in-Waiting from the Tudors to the Present Day*. London, 1984.

Sönmez, Margaret J-M. "English Spelling in the Seventeenth Century: A Study of the Nature of Standardisation as Seen through the Manuscript and Printed Versions of the Duke of Newcastle's 'A New Method.' " Ph.D. diss., 2 vols., Durham University, 1993.

Speed, John. *Theatre of the Empire of Great Britaine*. London, 1611.

Spink, Ian. *Henry Lawes: Cavalier Songwriter* Oxford, 2000.

Starr, Nathan Comfort, ed. "*The Concealed Fansyes*: A Play by Lady Jane Cavendish and Lady Elizabeth Brackley." *Publications of the Modern Language Association of America* 46 (1931), 802–838.

Stodart, M. A. *Female Writers: Thoughts on their Proper Sphere and on their Powers of Usefulness*. London, 1842.

Straznicky, Marta. "Reading the Stage: Margaret Cavendish and Commonwealth Closet Drama." *Criticism* 37 (1995), 355–390.

Strickland, Agnes. *Lives of the Queens of England from the Norman Conquest*, 6 vols. Revised ed. London, 1901.

Strong, Roy. *Art and Power: Renaissance Festivals 1450–1650*. Woodbridge, 1973.

Strong, S. Arthur, ed. *A Catalogue of Letters and other Historical Documents exhibited in the Library at Welbeck*. London, 1903.

Sutherland, Christine Mason. "Aspiring to the Rhetorical Tradition: A Study of Margaret Cavendish." In *Listening to their Voices: The Rhetorical Activities of Historical Women*. Ed.

Molly Meijer Wertheimer. Columbia, S.C., 1997. 255–271.

Suzuki, Mihoko. "The Essay Form as Critique: Reading Cavendish's *The World's Olio* through Montaigne and Bacon (and Adorno)." *Prose Studies: History, Theory, Criticism* 22, 3 (1999), 1–16.

————. "Margaret Cavendish and the Female Satirist." *Studies in English Literature 1500–1900* 37 (1997), 483–500.

Thomas, Keith. *Religion and the Decline of Magic: Studies in Popular Beliefs in Sixteenth and Seventeenth Century England*. London, 1997.

The Thomason Tracts, 1640–1661. Ann Arbor, Mich., 1981.

Thucydides. *The Peloponnesian War*. Trans. Rex Warner. Harmondsworth, 1978.

Thurloe, John. *A Collection of the State Papers of John Thurloe Esq.*, 7 vols. Ed. Thomas Birch. London, 1742.

Tomlinson, Sophie. "'My Brain the Stage': Margaret Cavendish and the Fantasy of Female Performance." In *Women, Texts and Histories 1575–1760*, ed. Clare Brant and Diane Purkiss, 134–163. London, 1992.

Town, Mr. "A Vision of Female Poets." *The Connoisseur* 69 (May 22, 1775).

Trease, Geoffrey. *Portrait of a Cavalier*. London, 1979.

A True Relation, or, Catalogue of the Gentry and Persons of Estate in the County of Essex that are Malignants. London, 1643.

Turberville, Arthur Stanley. *A History of Welbeck Abbey and its Owners*, 2 vols. London, 1938–1939.

Turner, Jane, ed. *The Dictionary of Art*. London, 1996.

Underdown, David. *Royalist Conspiracy in England 1649–1660*. New Haven, Conn., 1960.

Van der Aa, A. J. *Biographisch Woordenboek der Nederlanden*, 7 vols. Ed. K.J.R. van Harderwijk and G.D.J. Schotel. Amsterdam, 1969.

Van Lennep, William, ed. *The London Stage 1660–1800: A Calendar of Plays, Entertainments and Afterpieces*, I: *1660–1700*. Carbondale, Ill., 1965.

Varley, Frederick John. *The Siege of Oxford: An Account of Oxford during the Civil War, 1642–1646*. Oxford, 1932.

Vaughan, Robert. *The Protectorate of Oliver Cromwell*, 2 vols. London, 1838.

Venn, John, and John Archibald Venn. *Alumni Cantabrigienses: A Biographical List of All Known Students, Graduates, and Holders of Offices at the University of Cambridge*. Part I: *From the Earliest Times to 1751*, 4 vols. Cambridge, 1922–1927.

Verney, Frances Parthenope, and Margaret M. Verney. *Memoirs of the Verney Family*, 4 vols. London, 1892.

Vertue, George. *The Notebooks*, 5 vols., II. The Walpole Society 20 (1932).

The Victoria History of the County of Essex, II: ed. William Page and J. Horace Round. London, 1907. IX: *The Borough of Colchester*. Ed. Janet Cooper. London, 1994.

Walker, Elaine, "Longing for Ambrosia: Margaret Cavendish and the Torment of a Restless Mind in *Poems, and Fancies* (1653)." *Women's Writing* 4 (1997), 341–351.

Walpole, Horace. *A Catalogue of the Royal and Noble Authors of England*, 2 vols. London, 1759.

———. *A Catalogue of the Royal and Noble Authors of England*, 5 vols. Ed. T. Park. London, 1806.

Walter, John. *Understanding Popular Violence in the English Revolution: The Colchester Plunderers*. Cambridge, 1999.

Warburton, Eliot. *Memoirs of Prince Rupert and the Cavaliers*, 3 vols. London, 1849.

Ward, Sir Adolphus William. *A History of English Dramatic Literature to the Death of Queen Anne*, 2 vols. London, 1875.

Warwick, Sir Philip. *Memoires of the Reign of King Charles I*. London, 1702.

Waugh, Norah. *The Cut of Women's Clothes, 1600–1930*. London, 1968.

Wedgwood, C. V. *The King's Peace, 1637–1641*. London, 1966.

———. *The King's War, 1641–1647*. London, 1958.

Wendorf, Richard. *The Elements of Life: Biography and Portrait-Painting in Stuart and Georgian England*. Oxford, 1990.

Whitelocke, Bulstrode. *A Journal of the Swedish Embassy in the Years 1653 and 1654*, 2 vols. London, 1855.

Wildeblood, Joan, and Peter Brinson. *The Polite World: A Guide to English Manners and Deportment from the Thirteenth to the Nineteenth Century*. London, 1965.

Wilkins, John. *The Discovery of a New World in the Moon*. London, 1638.

Williams, Guy. *The Royal Parks of London*. London, 1978.

Williamson, George C. *Lady Anne Clifford, Countess of Dorset, Pembroke and Montgomery, 1590–1676*. Kendal, 1922.

Wilson, Michael I. *Nicholas Lanier, Master of the King's Musick*. Aldershot, 1994.

Wiseman, Susan. "Gender and Status in Dramatic Discourse: Margaret Cavendish, Duchess of Newcastle." In *Women, Writing, History, 1640–1740*, ed. Isobel Grundy and Susan Wiseman, 159–177. London, 1992.

Wood, Anthony à. *Athenae Oxonienses: An Exact History of all the Writers and Bishops who have had their Education in the University of Oxford; To Which are Added the Fasti, or Annals of the Said University*, 4 vols. Ed. Philip Bliss. London, 1813–1820.

———. *The Life and Times of Anthony Wood: Antiquary, of Oxford, 1632–1695*, 5 vols. Ed. Andrew Clark. Oxford, 1891–1900.

Woolf, Virginia. *The Common Reader*. Harmondsworth, 1938.

———. *A Room of One's Own*. Harmondsworth, 1945.

Worsley, Lucy. *Bolsover Castle*. N.p., 2000.

Woudhuysen, H. R. *Sir Philip Sidney and the Circulation of Manuscripts, 1558–1640*. Oxford, 1996.

Wroth, Mary. *The Poems of Lady Mary Wroth*. Ed. Josephine A. Roberts. Baton Rouge, La., 1983.

Index